$3

W9-CKJ-370

5.3. Russian nationalism in international youth movement

Pattern for Soviet Youth

STUDIES OF THE RUSSIAN INSTITUTE
OF COLUMBIA UNIVERSITY

Pattern
for Soviet Youth

A STUDY OF THE CONGRESSES

OF THE KOMSOMOL, 1918-1954

Ralph Talcott Fisher, Jr.

COLUMBIA UNIVERSITY PRESS

NEW YORK 1959

Fisher, Ralph Talcott.
    Pattern for Soviet youth; a study of the congresses of the
Komsomol, 1918–1954. New York, Columbia University
Press, 1959.

    452 p. 28 cm. (Studies of the Russian Institute of Columbia Uni-
versity)

    Includes bibliography.

    1. Youth—Russia. 2. Vsesoiuznyĭ leninskiĭ kommunisticheskiĭ soiuz
molodezhi.   1. Title.

HQ799.R9F55   301.431   59–5107 ‡
Library of Congress

The transliteration system used in this series is based on
the Library of Congress system with some modifications

Library of Congress Catalog Card Number: 59-5107

Published in Great Britain, Canada, India, and Pakistan
by the Oxford University Press
London, Toronto, Bombay, and Karachi

Manufactured in the United States of America

The Russian Institute
of Columbia University

THE Russian Institute was established by Columbia University in 1946 to serve two major objectives: the training of a limited number of well-qualified Americans for scholarly and professional careers in the field of Russian studies, and the development of research in the social sciences and the humanities as they relate to Russia and the Soviet Union. The research program of the Russian Institute is conducted through the efforts of its faculty members, of scholars invited to participate as Senior Fellows in its program, and of candidates for the Certificate of the Institute and for the degree of Doctor of Philosophy. Some of the results of the research program are presented in the Studies of the Russian Institute of Columbia University. The faculty of the Institute, without necessarily agreeing with the conclusions reached in the Studies, believe that their publication advances the difficult task of promoting systematic research on Russia and the Soviet Union and public understanding of the problems involved.

The faculty of the Russian Institute are grateful to the Rockefeller Foundation for the financial assistance which it has given to the program of research and publication.

Studies of the Russian Institute
Columbia University

TO MY MOTHER

AND THE

MEMORY OF MY FATHER

Preface

THE rulers of the Soviet Union, in striving to strengthen and perpetuate their regime, have placed much emphasis on training the young. For youths aged fourteen through twenty-five and often older still, the chief instrument of indoctrination and control is the All-Union Leninist Communist League of Youth, called "Komsomol" from the initial syllables of the Russian words for "Communist League of Youth." (Throughout this study, the noun and adjective "Komsomol" designates the organization, while "Komsomolite" designates the male or female member of the League.) The present work, using mainly the official reports of the congresses or nation-wide conventions of the Komsomol, studies the development of the Komsomol during the period 1918–54, with particular emphasis on the pattern of attitudes and behavior which the regime, in and through the Komsomol, sought to impose upon Soviet youth.

This pattern represents an important part of the program and goals of the Soviet hierarchy. The Komsomol was designed to embrace the leading elements among Soviet youth, and "youth" as defined for Komsomol purposes has constituted a large segment of the working population. It is important to know in what ways the Soviet regime has tried to use the enthusiasm and initiative of youth; to know how the Party has guided the Komsomol; to know in what respects the regime's policies toward youth have remained constant and in what respects they have changed; to know the functions of the Komsomol in the school, the Army, the factory, and the fields. The activities of the Komsomol since 1918 have touched almost all aspects of Soviet life, and the demands upon Komsomolites have significance for other broad categories of the Soviet population. Thus careful study of these demands should help Westerners better to understand the development, the workings, and the future objectives of the Soviet system.

The selection of the present subject involved difficult problems of focus and definition. The source material is voluminous: the presses of the Komsomol and the Party have issued countless newspapers, magazines, pamphlets, and books, relating as a whole or in part to the Komsomol and its members. On the other hand, the monographic foundations essential to a solid study of the Komsomol have been lacking: none of the Soviet publications provides an objective and systematic analysis of the Komsomol, and non-Soviet scholars have given the Komsomol only brief treatment in books on larger subjects (see the Bibliography). These circumstances forced the present writer to restrict the scope and the central focus of this study, in respect to the subject to be treated and the sources to be used. The topical and the documentary limitations adopted were interdependent.

As to the subject, the focus is on the "Komsomol pattern"—the chronological and topical pattern of demands made upon Komsomolites by the Soviet authorities: the Party, the government, and the Komsomol itself. Included are demands made upon the individual Komsomolite, demands made upon various categories of Komsomolites, and demands made upon Komsomolites in general, or upon the organization that embraces them. The demands range from those for abstract qualities of individual character to those for specific performance in almost any field of Soviet life. The demands vary greatly in intensity and persistence, from a suggestion of the moment to a thundering and sustained command backed by the coercive instruments of the Soviet state. The demands are not always explicit. For example, the Komsomol Regulations prescribed that Komsomol officials be "elected." But the true nature of that demand was revealed less by the formal language of the Regulations than by the elective process actually reported in the proceedings of the congresses. Although it is sometimes convenient to speak of an imaginary "ideal Komsomolite" or "good Komsomolite," who meets all the demands of the regime at a given time, that concept of the abstract ideal is not explicit in the Soviet materials but only inferred from them, and it is used in this work only where it will not obscure the precise designation of the group toward which any particular demand is directed.

As to its documentary base, this study concentrates on the official (usually "stenographic") reports of the twelve Komsomol congresses that were held during the years 1918–54. Several factors dictated concentration upon this source. The writer desired to select, from the mass of literature on the Komsomol, a major sample that was intended primarily for study by Komsomol members themselves; that was authoritative in character; that was comprehensive both chronologically and topically; that was homogeneous enough to permit comparison of period with period and to reveal changes from one period to the next; and that was sufficiently limited in bulk to be explored thoroughly in the present volume. General Party literature does not meet the first requirement; hence the field was narrowed to Komsomol publications. Among the newspapers, *Komsomol'skaia pravda* (Komsomol Truth) is the best single source, but it did not begin publication until 1925, and substantially complete files of this newspaper in the United States date only from 1928. If one were to supplement with other newspapers and with magazines, one would encounter problems of excessive bulk and heterogeneity. Among the magazines for youth, *Iunyi kommunist* (Young Communist), *Komsomol'skaia nedelia* (Komsomol Week), *Molodoi bol'shevik* (Young Bolshevik), and *Molodoi kommunist* (Young Communist) are authoritative, and in combination they would cover the whole time span, but American holdings of these journals are far from complete except for the 1940s and 1950s. To supplement those journals with other publications would have made the bulk unmanageable for the purposes of the present study. Soviet pamphlets and books relating to the Komsomol exist by the hundreds, but they are so heterogeneous and their chronological and topical distribution is so uneven, particularly for the Stalinist period, that they can be used most effectively after a general framework has been established on the basis of a more systematic source. In contrast to the other sources considered, the proceedings of the Komsomol congresses do meet the stated requirements in regard to purpose, authoritativeness, comprehensiveness, homogeneity, and bulk. This does not mean that the proceedings of the congresses are a complete source for the Soviet pattern for youth. Some of the valuable attributes of the proceedings—that they recorded important formal meetings, that they were published for the guidance of Komsomol leaders, and that they were prominently used in part as newspaper propaganda for Soviet youth—also constitute limitations to their usefulness. The proceedings are not a comprehensive source concerning, for example, elements of dissension among Soviet youth. Yet they are vitally important, they are virtually untapped by previous research, and they can be used to survey the subject of the Komsomol for scholars who may wish to explore further the vast and varied literature on Soviet youth and its organization.

In certain respects the topical and documentary concentrations outlined above have been broadened. As to the sources, only the proceedings of the congresses have been examined intensively, but some other materials have been used to a limited extent, especially for the period before 1918, for which it was necessary to use several books and booklets, and for the long period between the Congress of 1936 and the Congress of 1949, for which the newspaper *Komsomol'skaia pravda* was employed to provide continuity. As to the subject, a considerable amount of information has been included on the development, the organization, and the achievements of the Komsomol. Much of that information either supplies general background (since there is no full history of the League to which the reader may be referred), or furthers a proper understanding of the demands upon Komsomolites. (For instance, the statistics on the proportion of women in the League are important to an understanding of the demand to enroll more women as members.) Those items that will be useful principally to future researchers studying the history of Soviet youth have often been relegated to the footnotes in order to preserve, in the body of the text, a rather sharp focus on the pattern of demands.

Only to a limited extent can this volume estimate how far the demands upon Komsomolites were realized in practice. As is shown by the excellent exploratory work of Professor Merle Fainsod (see the Bibliography), a comprehensive estimate of this sort will call for a wide range of material, including particularly autobiographical accounts by former Soviet citizens and extensive interviews. The completion of such larger projects, whether by this writer or by others, awaits the future. Meanwhile this work may help to chart the terrain.

I am glad to be able to express here, albeit inadequately, my gratitude to those who have most generously assisted me in preparing this work. Geroid Tanquary Robinson of Columbia University has helped me from beginning to end with a paternal and self-sacrificing blend of exhortation, encouragement, and unsparing criticism. My first explorations of the topic were facilitated by Margaret Mead, who invited me to interview Soviet refugees and in other ways to learn about the Komsomol while participating in her research project, Studies in Soviet Culture. The Social Science Research Council awarded me the fellowship under which I completed most of my preliminary research. The Russian Research Center of Harvard University, and particularly Raymond A. Bauer and Alex Inkeles, permitted me to broaden my knowledge of the Komsomol through the reading of interview materials. The Library of Yale University, and especially Donald G. Wing, acquired materials important for my research. The anonymous donor of the Blanche Elizabeth MacLeish Billings Memorial Award, at Yale University, enabled me to acquire useful background information through the interviewing of former Komsomol members in Munich in the summer of 1955. Penetrating criticisms on the major portion of the manuscript were offered by Frederick C. Barghoorn, Merle Fainsod, John N. Hazard, Philip E. Mosely, and Sidney I. Ploss. Other especially valuable help, including suggestions on parts of the manuscript, was rendered at various stages by A. Dwight Culler, William H. Dunham, Jr., Barbara Farrell, Mary Q. Fisher, Beatrice Goff, Lawrence A. Harper, Nelly S. Hoyt, Christine Johnson, Ernest Kolowrat, the late George V. Lantzeff, Frederic G. Ludwig, Garrett Mattingly, R. Glynn Mays, W. Kenneth Medlin, Emma R. Poulsen, Sergei G. Pushkarev, Ernest J. Simmons, Timothy N. Sosnovy, Virginia Whitfield, Rena Wilmot, and John H. Wuorinen. William F. Bernhardt of the Columbia University Press gave valuable editorial assistance. It is no mere form to add that at all stages I have relied heavily upon the encouragement and assistance of my wife, Ruth Meads Fisher.

RALPH TALCOTT FISHER, JR.

University of Illinois
September, 1958

Contents

Pattern for Soviet Youth

I. Prerevolutionary Origins
of the Komsomol Pattern

IN the years before the Russian Revolution, the Bolsheviks had no youth auxiliary, but they had many youthful members. Lenin was young when he became a Marxist, and as he maneuvered his Bolshevik faction through its prerevolutionary skirmishes, he could not forget the importance of young people as a source of support for his utopian creed. Someone once complained to Lenin that the Russian Social Democrats were largely youths; that family men were few and were leaving the Party. Lenin retorted by quoting Engels:

Is it not really natural that youth should predominate in our revolutionary Party? We are the Party of the future, and the future belongs to youth. We are the Party of innovators, and innovators are always followed more willingly by youth. We are the Party of selfless struggle against time-worn decay, and into a selfless struggle the first to go is always youth.

And Lenin continued:

We had better leave it to the Cadets [Constitutional Democrats] to collect "worn-out" thirty-year-old ancients, revolutionaries "grown wise," and Social Democratic renegades. We always will remain the Party of the youth of the most advanced class [the proletariat].[1]

Prominent as the young were in the Bolshevik faction, there was no formal distinction drawn between them and the older members, and thus no well-defined pattern for young people or young adults as such. The origins of the Komsomol pattern must therefore be sought among Bolshevik ideas respecting the traits of any good Party member, among Bolshevik views on the relations of the Party to Russian youth in general, and in Bolshevik policies concerning the organizing of youth.[2]

THE GOOD BOLSHEVIK IN LENIN'S WRITINGS

Lenin was more influential than any other individual in determining who could, and who could not, be a member of the RSDLP(B) (the Bolshevik faction of the Russian Social Democratic Labor Party): hence his writings may justifiably be used to construct an image of the prerevolutionary good Bolshevik. That image is epitomized in the word "Partyness": the good Bolshevik was completely loyal to the Party (that is, to Lenin's faction of it) and to Lenin personally; he observed strict discipline in carrying out the policies decided upon by Lenin and his immediate colleagues; he was ready to use any means, irrespective of conventional morality, to advance the Party's ends; he had no close personal relationships except those based on common loyalty to Lenin's Party; and he was an actual or potential leader of the non-Party masses, willing to devote his life to the Party's cause. The virtues of the good Bolshevik were those appropriate to a militant and uncompromising struggle.[3]

LENIN AND RUSSIAN YOUTH

Lenin was eager to recruit youths for his Party and also to influence non-Party youth. As early as 1902, he included in the Party program demands (for such things as free education and state financial aid) that were calculated to appeal to youth. He prized the radicalism of students, and he placed special hope in the turbulence and daring of young factory workers. Beyond the confines of the Party itself, he tried to prod radical youth into revolutionary action against the tsarist regime; his writings reveal a belief that young people, ideologically untrained as they were, were suited to the hazardous role of advance guards or skirmishers who could engage in battle without committing the main body, which was the Party.[4]

THE BOLSHEVIKS AND THE ORGANIZING OF YOUTH
BEFORE THE NOVEMBER REVOLUTION OF 1917

The organizational problem was not readily solved.[5] Before 1905 radical youth organizations were active primarily among students, rather than among worker or peasant youth.[6] The Second Congress of the RSDLP, in 1903, passed the first formal Party resolution on student organizations.[7]

The Second Congress of the Russian Social Democratic Labor Party hails the quickening of independent revolutionary activity among students; proposes that all Party organizations render every possible assistance to these youths in their efforts to organize themselves; and recommends to all student groups and circles: first, that they place in the forefront of their activity the working out among their members of a complete and consistent socialist world outlook, a serious acquaintance with Marxism on the one hand, and, on the other, with Russian populism and Western European opportunism, as the main currents among the foremost contemporaneous rival tendencies; second, that they try, when turning to practical activity, to establish contact beforehand with Social Democratic organizations, in order to utilize their instructions and to avoid in so far as possible any grievous errors at the very beginning of the work.[8]

This resolution was scarcely a blueprint for the Komsomol; it was rather a recognition that most members of the early student groups and circles were *not* Social Democratic.[9]

One group constituted a significant exception. This was the "South Russian Group," born in 1902 at Rostov-on-Don.[10] It was formed by several secondary-school students, newly recruited into the Party, who wished to influence their non-Party schoolmates. Political education became the Group's chief activity. Hectographed leaflets were distributed in Rostov and nearby towns. At its peak the South Russian Group boasted around five hundred members and had contacts as far away as Voronezh and even Baku. It was loosely organized and acted largely on its own initiative. The RSDLP was at this early date too weak to exert any strict control, although *Iskra,* the Social Democratic organ, greeted the South Russian Group in 1903 and urged it to maintain the closest and most conspiratorial ties with the RSDLP.[11] The Group was dissolved in 1904, when its leaders either moved away from Rostov or became absorbed in Party work.[12] This South Russian Group, despite its limitations, may well deserve the distinction of being the earliest recognizable prototype of the Komsomol.[13]

The Revolution of 1905 saw an upsurge of radical activity among Russian youth.[14] Working-class youths of Social Democratic leanings continued to join the Party itself in preference to separate youth organizations.[15] Students, however, formed several avowedly Social Democratic organizations, especially in St. Petersburg, Moscow, and Riga.[16] These student groups were not united nationally. The Bolshevik policy of 1905 respecting youth groups seems to have been to draw as many young radicals as possible directly into the Party, to spur non-Party groups to rebellious actions, and to encourage Social Democratic student organizations, but not to try to unite them into any all-Russian Social Democratic youth movement or formal Party subsidiary.[17]

After 1905 isolated Social Democratic youth groups struggled on.[18] One was the "Student Organization of the PC [St. Petersburg Committee] of the RSDLP." It began in 1905, and by the addition in 1907 of several circles of working youth, became the "Organization of Student and Worker Youth of the PC of the RSDLP." It had a peak membership of about 250 and survived until 1909. As the first Social Democratic youth organization to bring sizable numbers of students and young workers together, it represents another stage in the evolution of the Komsomol.[19] Meanwhile in Moscow a youth organization led by two Bolsheviks, Nikolai I. Bukharin and Grigorii Ia. Sokol'nikov, convoked in 1907 an all-Russian congress of Social Democratic students. The congress, apparently dominated by its Moscow hosts, decided to establish an all-Russian student organization which would follow the Bolshevik wing of the Social Democrats. A Central Committee was set up, but the organization collapsed the next year (1908).[20]

During World War I there arose in Switzerland a "Youth International" whose stand on war coincided with Lenin's. He advocated that it be organizationally independent, while the Bolsheviks should try to steer it along the correct path. One must not, he contended, expect ideological maturity from these "turbulent" youngsters. Against his adult left-wing rivals he demanded a "ruthless struggle." But, said he,

It is another matter with youth organizations which openly declare that they are still learning. . . . Such people we must help in every way, being as patient as possible toward their mistakes, trying to steer them gradually, and primarily through *persuasion,* rather than fighting.[21]

Under the Provisional Government in 1917, radical youth groups blossomed forth.[22] Economic conditions were bad for working youth, and the Bolsheviks hammered away at the Provisional Government's failure to bring immediate improvement. Not being burdened with governmental responsibilities, the Bolsheviks could put forward demands most appealing to youth, such as the six-hour workday for minors, free education, and paid vacations. The Provisional Government proposed to give the vote to those aged twenty and up, but the Bolsheviks —who earlier had been content to ask for twenty-one as the lower limit—kept out in front by demanding the vote for eighteen-year-olds.[23] Favored by their position at the revolutionary extreme, as well as by their conspiratorial tactics, the Bolsheviks extended their influence over larger and larger numbers of Russian youth.

Petrograd was one center of youth activity. There, in May, 1917, arose an organization of factory youth called "Labor and Light." [24] It included Mensheviks, Socialist Revolutionaries, anarchists, and others as well as Bolsheviks. Under the leadership of P. Shevtsov,[25] "Labor and Light" attempted a broad cultural program which would minimize political differences within the group. Such tolerance was poison to the Bolsheviks, and they strove to undermine the group from within.[26] Meanwhile, as early as June, the Bolsheviks set up a rival city-wide youth group under the name "Socialist League of Working Youth," led by a young Bolshevik, Vasilii Alekseev.[27] The Bolsheviks then worked both from within and from without to destroy Shevtsov's group. They soon succeeded. On August 20 (new style dates are used here as elsewhere) an all-city conference of working youth dissolved "Labor and Light" and endorsed Alekseev's "Socialist League of Working Youth of Petrograd." [28] In its new swollen state this organization was no longer strictly Bolshevik in nature, but the Party was evidently able to direct it. By November this body appears to have reached a strength of about fifteen thousand.[29]

In Moscow, Bolshevik efforts met similar fortune. A distinctly Bolshevik youth group was set up in June, 1917, under the name "Youth League of the MC [Moscow Committee] of the RSDLP (Bolsheviks)." It combined students with young proletarians. Most of its members were also members of the Party. It was a rather small, selective organization, numbering not more than two or three hundred.[30] In order to reach broader masses of youth, the Bolsheviks soon began to infiltrate the "Third International," an organization of factory youths which sprang up in July and embraced about one thousand youths before the end of the month.[31] In October the Bolsheviks' small Youth League of the MC of the RSDLP affiliated itself with the larger Third International, which grew into a city-wide organization boasting four or five thousand adherents. The Third International followed the Bolshevik line in urging young people "to prepare themselves actively for armed struggle for Soviet power," although the organization itself did not come under Bolshevik control until after the November coup.[32]

Meanwhile the Bolsheviks had formally examined the advisability of setting up a youth subsidiary of the Party. In the Party Conference of July, 1917, in Petrograd, three possibilities were discussed. One delegate (Rakh'ia) advocated a youth organization directly under the Party. Another (Kharitonov) urged an "independent" organization, implicitly controlled by the Bolsheviks. Krupskaia, Lenin's wife, favored a mass proletarian organization really run by the young people themselves, even if this meant some political "errors." She declared that "friendly relations with young people are essential, otherwise youth will move away from us. Considering the level of knowledge and comprehension among our youth, we cannot insist on Partyness for the Youth Leagues." Basing her conclusion on her study of youth in other countries, she argued that those organizations that were directed by adults remained relatively small, and only those that were independent became mass organizations.[33] In the following month (August), at the Sixth Congress of the RSDLP(B), the issue was debated again, and a considerable range of opinion was expressed.[34] The result was a Party resolution "On Youth Leagues." It declared that "the Party of the proletariat . . . realizes the tremendous significance which working youth has for the working-class movement as a whole. The Congress therefore considers it essential that Party organizations in the provinces give the most serious attention to the matter of the organizing of youth." The resolution said that in Western Europe those youth groups that were most likely to be pro-Bolshevik were those not officially connected with any political party. Hence, the Bolshevik Party must "strive to see that working youth create self-standing organizations, not organizationally subordinated, but only spiritually linked, to the Party." ("Self-standing" [samostoiatel'nyi] must be used in order to indicate that a distinction is made in Russian between being merely "self-standing" and being fully "independent.") The remainder of the resolution made it clear that the Bolsheviks wanted the "spiritual link" between the youth groups and the Party to be a close one. But the resolution shied away from proposing an official youth auxiliary for the Party.[35] The same was true of another resolution of the Congress, which called upon the Party's Central Committee "to set up courses for instructors in the organizing and leading of [local] leagues of socialist youth," but said nothing about combining those leagues into a larger organization.[36]

Thus, even in the Revolutionary year, the Bolshevik view on youth organizations diverged only slightly from its pre-1917 lines. The Bolsheviks wanted to influence youth groups and were ready to organize working-class youth into groups the Party could informally control; but the Bolsheviks still avoided erecting any interclass country-wide youth body formally affiliated with the Party.

The Komsomol pattern was, then, still in its embryonic stage at the time of the Bolshevik Revolution. For its further development it required the stimulus of the practical problems met by the Bolsheviks in their new position of authority.

II. The Establishment of the Komsomol

THE KOMSOMOL CONGRESSES OF 1918,

1919, AND 1920

THE Communist Party established the Komsomol in 1918. The years 1918–20—represented by the first three congresses or general conventions of the Komsomol—constituted the formative period of the new organization. In those years its basic pattern of demands was laid down.

The Party faced two constant and difficult problems in its policies toward youth. One problem was that of inculcating discipline without eliminating initiative. The Bolsheviks believed that a conscious discipline, self-imposed by each in the interests of all, would bring unity of action and purpose and would at the same time foster initiative in the desired directions. But how was this to be achieved? How much external discipline would be needed to form proper habits in the young? How much independence could youth be allowed? How narrowly must initiative be restricted in order to ensure the desired discipline? An excess of dictation from above might reduce the Komsomol's appeal to youth. But too much liberty would run counter to the already-ingrained Bolshevik conviction of the need for unity and control. The problem was somehow to rear young people who possessed both discipline and initiative; to appeal to young people, as well as to command them.

The second problem concerned the roles the Komsomol would perform in the various spheres of Soviet life. How important would the organization be? How large? How selective in its membership? How much responsibility would be delegated to it in the educational sphere? In the economic sphere?

In the military sphere? Would the ideal Komsomolite keep his nose in a book, or would he help actively to run the state? Here, too, the problem of discipline and initiative was involved, for the way in which they were combined would do much to determine the character and range of burdens the League might shoulder in building the socialist state.

To see how these and other problems were handled in the first period of the Soviet regime, one needs to examine first the process by which the Party established the Komsomol. For it was Party policy that determined the relationship between the Party and the League and fixed the shape of the pattern from which Komsomolites would be cut.

THE PARTY AND THE ESTABLISHMENT OF THE KOMSOMOL

Although the idea of a congress to unify the youth leagues had been broached before the Bolsheviks seized power,[1] almost a year of Soviet rule went by before the founding of the Komsomol. The delay is not to be attributed to neglect, for the Bolsheviks in their early decrees took note of the needs of youth.[2] But to organize youth in Bolshevik style was another matter. Bolshevik rule was by no means assured in the country at large. The membership in youth leagues temporarily declined.[3] It might have been risky to establish an all-Russian youth organization before the Bolsheviks could be sure of controlling it. Instead, with what energy they could spare in that first hectic year, the Bolsheviks concentrated on gaining ascendancy within the existing scattered groups of radical youth and establishing loyal youth units in the various regions under their control.[4] In the spring and summer of 1918, provincial conferences of youth leagues were held in several key towns. Then, in the fall of 1918, the Petrograd and Moscow youth bodies formed an organizational bureau which published the call for an all-Russian congress of youth and the eventual establishment of a Red International of youth.[5]

Representatives of various "worker" and "peasant" youth groups met in Moscow from October 29 to November 4, 1918, in what came to be called the First Congress of the Komsomol.

One hundred ninety-four delegates participated (175 or 176 with voting rights, and the rest with "advisory voice," that is, the right to speak but not to vote). They represented 120 youth groups claiming a total of about 22,100 members. Of those delegates whose political affiliation was given, half (88) were Communist Party members, while another 38 were Communist sympathizers, and 45 were non-Party people. There were also three "Social Democratic Internationalists," one "Left Socialist Revolutionary," and one "Anarcho-individualist." [6] While ostensibly the Congress was called to decide whether or not to establish an all-Russian youth organization, the conduct of the first session made it clear that that question had already been decided in the affirmative and that it was the business of the Congress to carry out the decision.[7] From the start, Party members were at the helm. The six individuals who presided successively over the sessions were all Party members, all elected "by list" (i.e., as a group)—in the very first moments of the opening session—to the Presidium which guided the work of the Congress, and all later elected (at the final session) to the Central Committee of the new League.[8]

On the crucial question of the relationship between the Party and the League-to-be, the delegates agreed virtually unanimously that, first, "The League is solidary with the Russian Communist Party (of Bolsheviks)" and, second, "The League is an independent organization." [9] But a hot dispute broke out over whether the new League was to be called "Communist" or not. This was not mere quibbling over a technicality. Nor was it a battle between pro-Communists and anti-Communists, for all arguments, both for and against, were couched in terms of advancing the cause of Communism. It was, instead, one early aspect of the disputes over how much influence the Komsomol would be permitted and how inclusive its membership would be.

Lazar' Shatskin, one of the presiding officers, stated the leadership's case. There were three possible platforms: (1) the "socialist," which would admit into the League socialists of all varieties; (2) the "Third International," which would partially conceal the League's Communist nature; and (3) the Communist platform. The "socialist" platform was ruled out on the ground that other socialists were "rightist elements." [10] The second possibility Shatskin styled as "outdated." It had been proper for an earlier period, when "we were afraid to call our organization Communist, for fear of frightening youth." But, he said, "Now outside of Communism there is no worker movement. All the other movements in the working class have been tossed overboard by the Revolution. Now the Communist Party guides everything, and already no one fears the word 'Communist.'" Thus Shatskin arrived at the name "Communist League of Youth" (Kommunisticheskii soiuz molodezhi), the first syllables of which in Russian went to form the word Komsomol. This name did not mean, he cautioned, that the League would limit its membership to Communists. It would not be a "League of *Communist* Youth." It must admit "the broad masses of still uncommitted worker and peasant youth." [11]

It was for the sake of attracting those very same masses of politically undecided youth that some delegates objected to using "Communist" in the title of the new League. These dissenting delegates proclaimed their loyalty to Communism but said that it was something that "each of us must carry in his heart." There was applause for the delegate who advocated using the name "Third International." But the supporters of the leadership answered in biting tones. The dissenters were accused of displaying "conciliation and class prejudice" and of not being in favor of Communism [12]—a charge which, in that company, was extremely serious.

While subduing these dissenters of the "Right," Shatskin also opposed the "Left." One delegate argued that since the League was subordinate to the Party, it should be made a part of the Party. Shatskin objected that this would impair the "principle of the spontaneous activity of youth" and would "undoubtedly harm the work among the Russian worker and peasant youth." [13] The majority of the delegates followed Shatskin's lead and approved the name "Russian Communist League of Youth." [14] The term translated here as "Russian" referred not to the Great Russian ethnic group alone but rather to the broader area of the former Russian Empire.

The First Congress also established the formal administrative skeleton of the new organization. The All-Russian Congress was made the supreme authority. It was to meet at least once each year.[15] To handle the League's day-to-day affairs until the next meeting of the Congress, a Central Committee was elected, composed of fifteen members and seven "candidate-members," or alternates who could replace regular members. All of those chosen were already in the Party, except one of the candidate-members.[16] The immediate financial needs of the League were apparently provided for by Lenin in an informal order to Sverdlov, chairman of the Central Executive Committee, during the course of an interview Lenin held with the Presidium of the Congress.[17] The League's first set of Regulations was drawn up by the new Central Committee.[18]

The newly born Komsomol received the official blessing of the Bolshevik Party at the Eighth Party Congress, held March 18–23, 1919. A resolution of the Congress (acting on a report by Shatskin) reiterated that Communist activity among youth could best be conducted through "self-standing" Komsomol groups, which would permit the "maximum of spontaneous activity." [19]

Following the Party's Eighth Congress, there occurred a significant redefinition of the Komsomol-Party relationship. A Plenum, or plenary session, of the Komsomol's Central Committee was held April 26–28, 1919. This group of official Komsomol spokesmen (including heads of guberniia—that is, provincial—Komsomol bodies), who can be assumed to have been almost all Party members subject to Party discipline, made a "suggestion" and a "request" that the Komsomol be brought more closely under the direction of the Party.[20] This action was followed, on August 8, 1919, by an authoritative joint resolution of the Central Committees of both the Party and the Komsomol.[21] This directive was more specific than the statements at the First Congress in regard to the manner in which the Party would exercise its guidance of the League. At the top: "The

Central Committee of the RCLY [Komsomol] is directly subordinated to the Central Committee of the RCP [Party]." As to the rest: "The local organizations of the RCLY work under the control of the local committees of the RCP." Thus the Party established two parallel chains of command leading from the Central Committee of the Party to the local Komsomol group. One chain led through the Party pyramid, and the other led through the Komsomol pyramid. To provide another means of control, the resolution directed that all Party members under twenty years of age were to serve also as members of the Komsomol. Using these young Party members, and such other Party members as were necessary, each local Party organization was instructed to set up a Komsomol unit in its locality, if one did not already exist. Still further to ensure Party control, the resolution specifically provided that the Party could send its own organizers into the League to "help" the League (supposedly "with the consent of the latter") and that the Party could establish "fractions" in Komsomol units.[22] Yet in spite of all these provisions for control, the resolution termed the League "autonomous" and solemnly declared:

The spontaneity of the Russian Communist League of Youth is a foundation of its work and an indispensable condition of its existence. Therefore the Party's control over the League must not bear a character of guardianship, or of trifling interference in the organizational, agitational, cultural-educational, and other work of the League, and must be conducted only within the framework of the Regulations of the League and the instructions of the Central Committee of the RCLY [the League]. . . . All misunderstandings between local organizations of the Party and the League are submitted for settlement to higher echelons of the Party and the League.[23]

Meanwhile, dating apparently from the April Plenum of the Komsomol's Central Committee,[24] the official description of the Komsomol's relationship to the Party was changed. Formerly the Komsomol had been called "self-standing" and "independent." But now "independent" was no longer employed; it was replaced, in effect, by "autonomous" (except in the original Program of the League).[25] This change was not commented upon in the proceedings of the next congress, but it seems significant and must have been noticed immediately by all Party members.

From October 5 to 8, 1919, the Komsomol held its brief Second Congress. The number of delegates was given as 429 (of whom 348 had voting rights, while the rest could participate, but without vote). Of the total, 286 (or 66.6 percent) were listed as Party members, 103 as Party sympathizers, and 58 as non-Party people. The League claimed an enrollment of 96,096, but it was subsequently admitted that no accurate count of the members was available.[26]

The Second Komsomol Congress was asked to confirm the August pronouncement of the Party and Komsomol Central Committees. Oskar Ryvkin (reporting on behalf of the Komsomol Central Committee) undertook to justify this joint directive. Whether or not he welcomed this chore, he succeeded in talking about both "autonomy" and "control" in the same paragraph without implying that there might be any contradiction between them. He took special care to explain why it had been necessary to state that the Central Committee of the Komsomol was "directly subordinated" to the Central Committee of the Party. "Why," he asked, "did we not protest against this?" Because "our movement is a part of the whole Communist movement. The responsibility for the whole Communist movement of the whole worker class rests with the Party." Therefore, he went on, "It is natural that the Central Committee of our League must be subordinated to the Central Committee of the Party. . . . Not a single worker of the League can protest against this." While Ryvkin assured his hearers that the Party Central Committee would "treat the wishes of the League with respect," he showed where the authority rested:

Perhaps there will be . . . certain moments when the Central Committee of our League will not agree with the policies of the CC [Central Committee] of the Party. But we must say that since our Program is the Party's program, and our tactics are the Party's tactics, then politically, also, our CC must be subordinate to the CC of the Party.[27]

Behind those official formulas, at the Second Congress it became clearer than before that the members of the Komsomol Central Committee were not only collectively but also individually subject to Party control. Two members of the first CC, it was revealed, had been removed from the CC simply by virtue of the Party's having given them a new assignment.[28] Thus the high Komsomol body (the First Congress) that formally elected them did not possess the authority to see that they actually served on the CC. On the new Central Committee elected by the Second Congress, all of the members and candidate-members were Party people.[29] In this connection (and since the Party affiliation was not always specifically mentioned in regard to the members of later CC's) an incident in the deliberations is significant. A delegate proposed that all nominees for the CC must be Party members. The chairman spoke contemptuously of this suggestion as coming from a person "who apparently does not know the first thing about the youth movement." He added: "We, of course, are all following the Communist Party. If by chance non-Party members should get on the CC, then they would sign up [i.e., join the Party]. I propose to remove this question from discussion." The majority sustained the chair.[30]

The Party made its authority felt in the way in which it prematurely closed the Second Congress. The announcement that the Congress must end abruptly, on account of the military situation, was first made (on October 7) without being labeled as a Party command, but the source of this command was later made known by V. Nevskii, a spokesman of the Party's Central Committee.[31]

Following the Second Komsomol Congress the membership rose rapidly, reflecting the Bolshevik fortunes in the Civil War. Starting from perhaps about 96,000 in early October (and 101,-000 in mid-December of 1919), the League reportedly grew to 319,000 members by May, 1920,[32] and to 400,000 (almost half of whom were also in the Party) [33] by October, 1920.[34] Many of the newcomers were said to be peasant youths and students.[35]

The influx of unindoctrinated youths hampered the leaders in their progress toward a tighter discipline. The economic crisis was severe. One symptom of discontent was the continuing dispute over "the forms of the youth movement," discussed in the next section. In September, 1920, the Party intervened to remove Dunaevskii and the other prominent nonconformists from their work in the Komsomol. The Party directive announcing their removal stressed that the Komsomol was subsidiary to the Party, and instructed all guberniia committees (*gubkoms*) of the Party to "help" the "healthy elements of the youth movement" to correct any similar instances of poor discipline on the lower echelons.[36]

The Third Congress was held from October 2 to 10, 1920. In addition to hearing Lenin's famous address on youth, the Third Congress enacted a new Program and set of Regulations for the League. The old Program, issued just after the First Congress in 1918, possessed the defect of calling the League a "fully independent organization" and declaring that it was based on "the principle of complete freedom of action." [37] The word "independent," withdrawn from use in 1919, was now repudiated explicitly by Shatskin and Ryvkin, who were the two most prominent Komsomolites at the Third Congress. Shatskin, while insisting on the need for "spontaneous activity," said that to characterize the League as "independent" was an error committed by Western European youth.[38] Ryvkin declared that the erroneous term was used by the "counterrevolution of the Left," which "says that our organization must be politically self-standing—must itself, even if working under general directives, bring to light its own attitudes concerning general political questions; and that in this respect our organization must be independent from head to foot." In rejecting that view, Ryvkin added that "as soon as there is a conflict among us, we will hand it [the conflict] over to the CC of the Party." [39] The approved formulation concerning the League's relationship to the Party was stated in the new Program as follows:

The RCLY [Komsomol] acknowledges the program and tactics of the RCP [Party]; in considering general questions of the life of the Soviet Republic, it [the RCLY] subordinates itself to its [the Party's] political directives and, working under its [the Party's] control, is an autonomous organization. The CC of the RCLY is directly subordinate to the CC of the RCP.[40]

It would seem that although ostensibly the League was to preserve autonomy and spontaneity, in practice any suggestion of decentralization coming from the Komsomol was likely to be regarded by the Party leaders as a threat to Party control and hence an anti-Party action.

THE GENERAL ROLE OF THE KOMSOMOL

Meanwhile the Party's concept of the general role of the League was evolving. In broad terms, that role was to train young people for service in the Party and to assist the Party in current tasks. The Eighth Party Congress (March, 1919) termed the Komsomol a source of "trained reserves" for the Party and said the League's chief tasks were to organize and rear youth in a Communist manner, to build Communist society, and to defend the Soviet Republic.[41] Party spokesmen at the Second and Third congresses of the Komsomol reiterated those concepts.[42]

It was not uncommon, in those early days, to characterize the League even as a sort of leading element of the whole working class. The first Program of the Komsomol, in language reminiscent of Lenin's prerevolutionary writings, said that "youth, as the most active and revolutionary part of the working class, moves in the front ranks of the proletarian revolution." The Komsomol, it declared, had been created in order to unify worker youth, whom it called the "foremost element" of the working class.[43] Similar notions were expressed elsewhere at the first three congresses, by such figures as Trotsky, Bukharin, and Ryvkin.[44] In later days, however, as the Party's control over the League was extended, this "vanguard" concept disappeared from the official lexicon, and Trotsky's use of it in 1919 became one of the "proofs" that he had tried to curry favor with the League and pit the League against his rivals in the Party.[45]

The Komsomol early assumed the role of spokesman for Soviet youth. Already at the Second Congress, when the League boasted a mere 96,000 members, Oskar Ryvkin declared that it was a "mass organization" and that "now we have the right to say that we speak on behalf of organized worker and peasant youth." He also said the League spoke for "all conscious worker and peasant youth." [46] The Komsomol Program of 1920 indicated that just as the Party claimed to represent the proletarians, who were presumably the best element of the general population, so the Komsomol claimed to represent the best elements of Soviet youth and, implicitly, to serve as the spokesman for Soviet youth in general.[47]

Helping to give substance to the League's claim that it represented all "organized" youth was the Bolshevik policy toward other youth groups. For example, soon after the founding of the Komsomol, some Jewish students attempted to form an organization of their own. Ryvkin told what happened:

A comparatively small episode in the work of the CC was that of the congress of Jewish students. But it was a characteristic episode. A congress of Jewish students was convoked in Moscow. It was a camouflaged Cadet organization, a Zionist organization. At this congress there were twenty or thirty representatives of Jewish bourgeois youth. The CC faced the question of what to do with this congress, whether to permit it to open or not, and, if to permit it, then what tactic to pursue. And the CC said that it was not necessary to disperse this congress, that this bunch of boys, numbering twenty-five or thirty, had to be shown that in Soviet Russia any non-class national organizations are unthinkable, that now there can survive only our League or Denikin's national center. The CC decided to disrupt this congress from within. We sent our representative, who did that. He managed it so that this congress of Jewish students voted in the majority against creating a league of Jewish students. This had great significance. If we had chased them away and closed the congress, then they would have boasted of themselves as heroes suffering for the Jewish people. By its tactics the CC obtained more than a simple dispersal. We showed at that congress the utter futility of those who wanted to establish that Jewish youth organization.[48]

More forceful tactics were required in order to disrupt an established rival like the Boy Scouts. At first the Bolsheviks tried to win parts of the Scout organization over to a Bolshevik-inspired auxiliary group called the "Young Communists," formed in 1918 on the model of the Scouts. Its principal defect was that, according to a statement approved by the Komsomol Congress in 1919, "The political education of the Young Communists remains only verbal. In fact the control of the Party is not being maintained owing to lack of strength." The Congress therefore voted to liquidate the "Young Communists."[49] While acknowledging the failure of that flanking attack, the Congress of 1919 launched a frontal assault. Scout organizations "in all towns" were charged with "leaning in the direction of the White Guards." [50] Scout discipline was condemned:

In the Scout organizations a strict authoritarianism was instituted, embodying on the one hand a strict rule from the top and, on the other, submission from below—rule and unquestioning obedience. Strict discipline permeated the whole organization from beginning to end. This discipline, as distinguished from class, proletarian, collective discipline, was a discipline of the cane, a militaristic discipline. One had to obey one's officer unquestioningly; the subordinates had no voting rights.

The Scouts were accused of fostering a "bourgeois outlook" and of enrolling worker youth "in order to split the proletarian youth movement." In the world-wide revolutionary struggle, the Boy Scouts were said to be allied with the YMCA and other Christian groups in a "Black International" which stood opposed to the "Red International" of proletarian youth. After reciting the sins of the Scouts the report concluded: "Therefore we say that Scout organizations cannot exist in a country where the power is in the hands of the proletariat." [51] Although the delegates apparently voted to liquidate the Scout organization,[52] it lingered on as an opposition body for several years before succumbing.[53]

As to other groups, Ryvkin in 1919 was willing to let anarchist youth organizations, composed largely of students, carry on a "struggle of ideas." But if they attempted to use violence, he warned, then naturally they must be shot.[54] On the other hand, a separate Communist student organization (not sponsored by the Komsomol) was closed down, owing apparently to a fear that it might be less than adequately controlled by the Party.[55]

The non-Komsomol groups mentioned thus far were clearly potential (if not very threatening) competitors of the Komsomol, and it is not hard to understand why the Bolsheviks sought to restrict or suppress them. But the Party's fear of possible rivals to the Komsomol extended even further, to youth groups that had been or might be set up under Komsomol sponsorship. This policy is more difficult to understand. It involves fundamental questions concerning the role and nature of the League. Was the Komsomol to be a tight organization—a sort of junior Party—or was it to be a mass organization? In other words, was it to be an instrument for controlling other mass youth organizations, or was it to be itself the mass organization of Soviet youth? Also, should the Komsomol be a purely working-class organization, or should it unite the bulk of Soviet youth? The way these questions were answered would help to determine how far the members of the Komsomol were to be permitted to use their own initiative in organizational matters.

Before the founding of the Komsomol, the Communist youth groups in the various localities had evolved their own policies. In the sessions of the First Congress it became apparent that several representatives of youth groups in the Ural region (Matveev, Khazan, Sorvin, Iurovskaia) had been working on plans for "Young Proletarian Homes." Evidently these Homes were intended to become mass clubs, which all worker youth would be expected to join. The Homes would be directed by the Komsomol-to-be.[56] One advocate of the Homes (Khazan) declared that only the "most conscious elements" would enter the Komsomol; hence, an auxiliary instrument was needed through which the Youth League could influence the broad masses of proletarian youth. He concluded with a plea (greeted with applause by the delegates) that some leeway be given to the various groups to push ahead with indoctrination as far as local conditions permitted, even if the techniques employed were not everywhere the same.[57] Another delegate (Iurovskaia, from Orenburg) stressed that the Homes would serve as clubs where the youths could spend all their leisure time and that the Homes would be especially valuable as a means for educating peasant youths who had come to town. But Tsetlin, one of those who had been instrumental in summoning the Congress,[58] dismissed the Ural delegates' proposal, and it was defeated (by an unstated majority) in the final vote of the Congress.[59] The justification subsequently given by Shatskin for that defeat was that the Komsomol should itself be a mass organization.[60] To be sure, Shatskin had told the delegates that the League should be open to "the broad masses of still uncommitted worker and peasant youth" and should not be limited to "definite and conscious Bolsheviks." [61] But at the same time he had characterized the Komsomol as, in effect, "an organization of sympathizers of the Party"; [62] he had favored excluding "rightists" (even non-Bolshevik socialists); and he (with other leaders) had insisted on using the name "Communist," despite the numerous protests that this would frighten away the mass of youth, particularly peasant youth. One explanation of these seemingly conflicting desires—to limit the League to "uncommitted" and pro-Communist youth, and yet to prevent the creation of an instrument for reaching still broader circles of youth—might be that the Bolsheviks in this early day expected that the "masses" would soon be pro-Communist. But an equally likely explanation might be that the Bolshevik leadership felt it would be wise to keep the new and untried Youth League on a short leash until its obedience to Party commands could be assured.

The defeat of the proposal for Young Proletarian Homes did not kill the idea of some sort of mass organization for proletarian youth.[63] A similar dispute came to the surface soon after the First Congress. This time the question was whether to establish, under Komsomol influence, "youth sections affiliated with the trade unions," which would unite all worker youths and give them an effective means of protecting their own economic interests. This question was considered by the Plenum or augmented session of the Central Committee on April 26–28,

1919, and then was submitted to both the regular Central Committee and the local organizations for further discussion.[64]

A prominent advocate of the "youth sections" was V. Dunaevskii.[65] An article in the May, 1919, issue of *Iunyi kommunist* (Young Communist)—then the official journal of the Komsomol—reported Dunaevskii's advocacy of "youth sections" and stated that the Presidium of the Moscow Council of Trade Unions had approved of Dunaevskii's position. In another article in the same issue, Dunaevskii proposed the establishment of "councils of worker youth." [66] This suggestion, too, was aimed at organizing the bulk of proletarian youth outside of the Komsomol but under the Komsomol's influence.[67] Taken together, Dunaevskii's proposals seemed to envision the Komsomol as a rather influential instrument for organizing and protecting working-class youth.

Such ideas were coolly received by those at the helm of the League. The enlarged Plenum of the Central Committee met again July 15–17, 1919. It rejected the idea of "youth sections affiliated with the trade unions," while at the same time reiterating that the Komsomol should be, and would be, a mass organization.[68] But Dunaevskii, instead of accepting his defeat and observing "League discipline," continued to urge his views.[69]

Then came the Second Komsomol Congress. The agenda as initially presented did not provide for any discussion of the Dunaevskii proposals. A delegate named N. Zander rose from the floor to observe that within the League there was some "difference of opinion" on those proposals, and he asked that they be added to the agenda. Ryvkin, who was presiding, denied the existence of any controversy worthy of being called by that name; he asserted that "the whole League and the Party" agreed that the "only form of the Communist movement of worker youth is the Russian Communist League of Youth." "Of course," he went on,

it would have been useful to consider this question if doubts had arisen in the minds of any of the comrades. But they would have had to say something about this earlier, to submit theses, and to indicate what they wished to say in their reports. On the other hand, it is impossible to place a question before the Congress in this way, without any warning.[70]

"This," Zander protested, "is demagogy!" He told the delegates that he had indeed discussed the matter beforehand with Ryvkin and that Ryvkin had said it would not be placed on the agenda but that Zander could bring it up at the Congress. Now, said Zander, Ryvkin was refusing to permit that very thing! Zander went on to state his conviction that the Komsomol, as the "foremost vanguard," could not expect to embrace at once all worker youth. In order to influence the broad masses of worker youth, he said, the Komsomol needed as its instrument an inclusive organization such as the proposed "youth sections affiliated with the trade unions."

Ryvkin, still speaking from the chair, denied Zander's charge of demagogy. He said Zander could express himself in one of the minor section meetings. He declared that the Komsomol membership would grow rapidly and that the Komsomol must be *the* organization of youth. Then he called for a vote. The chairman's position won, but thirty-six delegates (out of 348) still held out for Zander's view.[71]

In the meeting of the section dealing with the protection of economic rights, Dunaevskii and Zander clung to their position.[72] After some debate, a member of the Central Committee, M. Dugachev, spoke out firmly against the "youth sections," and the ensuing vote upheld his position.[73] Nevertheless, when the resolutions of the various sections were presented to the assembled Congress for approval, Dunaevskii was permitted to introduce his own resolution on "youth sections." The Komsomol, he stressed, would control them through its cells. It was again Dugachev who presented the view of the leadership, denying the need for "youth sections" and asserting that the Komsomol itself could adequately protect and organize worker youth. The great majority sustained the Central Committee's view, although there were nineteen noes and ten abstentions.[74]

Dunaevskii's views had been voted down. But when, at the close of the Congress, the new Central Committee was elected, he was on it—with the sixth highest number of votes![75] There had been a precedent at the First Congress, where three sponsors of the Young Proletarian Homes (Khazan, Iurovskaia, and Matveev) had been elected to the Central Committee, and thereafter seemed to have ceased their deviationism. But Dunaevskii did not follow the same path. Even after the Second Congress he carried on his compaign for special bodies for working youth outside of the Komsomol. The Congress's official rejection of his proposals placed him in the position of flouting Komsomol discipline, and thereby also the authority of the Party.[76]

Meanwhile, a related deviation had arisen in the shape of the "Ukrainian Opposition"—an appellation which covered various shades and types of protest, stemming from the military and economic crisis and the nationalistic sentiment in the Ukraine as well as from the heterogeneous resistance to the centralizing drive of the leaders of the Komsomol. Already before the Second Congress there had been founded in Kiev a league which considered itself to be a provincial segment of the Komsomol, but which insisted upon restricting membership to *working*-class youth of town and countryside and accordingly called itself the "Communist League of the *Worker* Youth of the Ukraine." [77] The Ukrainian group was hostile to intelligentsia youth.[78] Furthermore, the group took the position that the majority of peasant youth could not be drawn immediately into the League, and therefore the League should establish rural "non-Party collectives," or groups for peasants outside of the Komsomol. For those proletarian youths who were not embraced by the League, the Ukrainian Opposition, like Dunaevskii, advocated the founding of separate young workers' organizations. Apparently, too, the Ukrainian Opposition was guilty of a desire for some measure of autonomy for Ukrainian youth.[79] Taken together, the views clustered under the heading of the Ukrainian Opposition—with their bias against intellectuals and Great Russians and their advocacy of extra-Komsomol youth groups—represented a sharp challenge to the as yet not completely consolidated Party control of the Komsomol.

At the Second Komsomol Congress (1919) the Ukrainian dispute was not important.[80] But soon thereafter, action was taken against both the Dunaevskii and the Ukrainian types of deviationists. Early in 1920 the Ukrainian League was persuaded to change its name, striking out the word "Worker" and becoming simply the Communist League of Youth of the Ukraine.[81]

On September 15, 1920, the Party, through its Central Committee, announced that it had intervened in the Dunaevskii dispute. Dunaevskii and his fellow dissenters were charged with "non-Communist deviations." The proposals for either "councils of worker youth" or "youth sections in the trade unions" were stigmatized as pitting young proletarians against adult proletarians. The nonconformists were accused of having constituted a "secret fraction" and of having begun an "underground struggle" against the majority of the League's Central Committee. The Party revealed that in order to avoid an "internal crisis" in the Komsomol, it had "removed" Dunaevskii, Polifem, and Iakovlev (the first two being members of the Komsomol's Central Committee) "from work with youth." [82] The directive further stated that Dunaevskii had persisted in urging his views through "circular letters" to active Komsomolites in the provinces, thereby developing "a whole plan for the struggle of a non-Party RCLY [Komsomol] against the CC of the RCP [Party]." This manifestation of lack of discipline, it was disclosed, had led the Party to suspend Dunaevskii from the Party for a period of six months.[83] Dunaevskii apparently confessed his sins and did suitable penance, for when the Third Congress of the Komsomol convened a few days later (October 2–10, 1920), he appeared as a staunch defender of the Central Committee's position and a co-author (with Bukharin and Shatskin) of the new Program for the League.[84]

Other "deviationists" remained. The Party brought to the Third Congress plenty of heavy artillery: Lenin called for discipline and solidarity, and Preobrazhenskii, Lunacharskii, and Bukharin participated actively in the proceedings.[85]

The conflict with the Ukrainian Opposition was aired especially in the meeting of the Organizational Section. Shatskin, presenting the official viewpoint, acknowledged that there was an abnormally high proportion of intelligentsia in the directing bodies of the League. This situation should, he agreed, be corrected, but not by barring intellectuals generally from the League or battling with those who were already members. The Komsomol must take in "the best part of intelligentsia youth," because they could be extremely useful in the League's work. Meanwhile, through education the Komsomol must bring the "cultural level" of the worker youth up to that of the student youth.[86] Okulik, one of the deviationists, favored the virtual elimination of bourgeois and intelligentsia elements from the League.[87] For those proletarian young people who were not in the Komsomol, Okulik advocated "collectives [local groupings] of worker youth" as a "transitional form" leading to the Komsomol cell. Such "collectives," he reported, had worked well in Kiev, Ekaterinoslav, and other factory towns, as a means for drawing worker youth gradually into League activities.[88] Okulik did receive some support, but the decisive voices were on the side of the Central Committee.[89] Ryvkin assured the Ukrainians that they could get the results they desired with other, officially approved, instruments—the "delegates' assembly of youth" or the "non-Party Conference" (neither of which, apparently, would have possessed any permanent character).[90] The Organizational Section accordingly rejected the Ukrainian proposal for mass non-Party youth organizations in the factories. Following suit, the full Congress banned any "collectives of non-Party youth," even as a transitional device for forming Komsomol cells, and also upheld the Central Committee in condemning the Ukrainians' intolerance of intelligentsia youth.[91]

The discussion in the Organizational Section also checked a deviation in the opposite direction, that is, toward too broad a concept of the political spectrum to be included within the

League, or too literal an interpretation of the official line that the Komsomol was a "mass organization." In their zeal to discredit the idea of non-Party youth organizations, two delegates named Malyshev and Starostin had advocated that all peasant and intelligentsia youths who were not clearly hostile to the regime should be kept within the Komsomol so that they could be educated.[92] But Ryvkin, in his authoritative closing address, warned that this concept of Malyshev and Starostin would embrace too many.[93]

What is the significance of the many-faceted controversy related above concerning the role and nature of the League? In particular, why did the Party insist on beating back at this time all suggestions for mass youth auxiliaries run by the Komsomol? The usual official argument, as has been shown, was that to permit such groups would have imperiled the Komsomol's present and future position as a mass organization.[94] That official argument requires analysis and interpretation.

The basic problem was one of control. The Bolsheviks certainly were not (as they would later demonstrate) opposed in principle to the idea of using the Komsomol to direct other less exclusive youth groups. But before the League could be that sort of tool, it had to be not only strong in its own right but also securely controlled by the Party. The lingering dissent in the Komsomol placed the firmness of that control in doubt. The Party leaders probably reasoned that as long as such doubt existed, they should prevent the Komsomol from getting too strong and, particularly, should prevent it from acquiring influence over satellite organizations that might embrace large segments of Soviet youth. The Bolsheviks apparently feared that the groups suggested by Dunaevskii and others might mushroom too fast for both Komsomol control and Party control to keep pace; competing power centers might develop, which could challenge the Komsomol's exclusive claim to lead Soviet youth—power centers which might even question the dictatorship of the Party. Plainly, too, when the Bolsheviks said the Komsomol was to be a "mass organization," they did not mean that the Komsomol would embrace all the broad masses of politically heterogeneous youth. The categories of youth to be included—sympathizers with Communism, "conscious" workers and peasants, "uncommitted" youths—were ill defined, but it was clear that they were not to extend even to all youths who merely lacked hostility to the regime. The largest membership attained by the League during the period 1918–20—about 400,000—was probably under 2 percent of those in the eligible age group; certainly that membership was far from representing the "mass" of Soviet youth in any numerical sense. The term "mass organization," then, as applied to the Komsomol in this period, meant that the Komsomol was to have a *unique opportunity to become* a mass organization of Soviet youth. And even though, under the Party policies and the conditions of the time, the League was not and could not soon become a genuine mass organization, at least no other youth organization was to be allowed to embrace a large following, even under the supervision of the League.

RELATIONSHIPS AND PROCEDURES WITHIN THE LEAGUE

The Party's insistence on dictating the general role of the League could not fail to affect the relationships and attitudes that would be prescribed within the League. How and to what extent would the Party try to regulate intra-Komsomol behavior? What would be the approved mixture of discipline and initiative?

The organizational structure of the Komsomol was patterned after that of the Party. The Komsomol Regulations enacted in October, 1920, declared: "The RCLY is constructed on the principles of democratic centralism on a territorial basis." Although a formal definition of democratic centralism was avoided at that time,[95] its meaning can be discerned in the various provisions of the regulations. At each echelon in the League there were designated two bodies—one larger and ostensibly deliberative in nature, the other small and executive. At the top, for example, the large deliberative body was the All-Russian Congress, and the smaller executive body was the Central Committee. Similar pairs of bodies were designated for each union republic (except the RSFSR), each krai and oblast, each guberniia, each uezd, and, at the bottom, each "local organization" and "cell." In general the larger and formally more authoritative body was called the "congress," the "conference," or, at the bottom, the "general meeting," while the smaller executive and theoretically subordinate body was known as the "committee" or the "bureau."[96] In every case the executive body was to be elected by the "congress," "conference," or "general meeting" at the same echelon. The method of election was not specified in the Regulations but apparently was to follow the practice approved officially by the First Congress—that is, open voting.[97] At the top, the All-Russian Congress was to meet at least once a year; at the bottom, the cell was to meet at least once a week. The meetings of intermediate deliberative bodies were scaled between those extremes. The deliberative body at each echelon was to discuss questions suitable to that echelon, hear and confirm reports from its executive group, and elect its delegates to the "conference" at the next higher echelon. The All-Russian Congress, called "the highest guiding body of the RCLY," was to hear and confirm reports of the Central Committee and the Inspection Commission, confirm the Program and the Regulations of the League, lay down the general line of the movement, make decisions on current questions, and elect the Central Committee and the Inspection Commission. In the interval between congresses the Central Committee (elected by the Congress) was to be the "highest guiding body." [98] Since the Congress met for only a few days out of each year, the Central Committee was left to run the League most of the time.[99] The same was true of the subordinate executive bodies. Each executive body was expected to report constantly, especially through the press, to the members of the broader deliberative group which elected it and to the membership at large.[100] "Free discussion" was to be permitted on "any question of the youth movement." However, said Shatskin, "in so far as the CC has taken a definite decision on this or that question, we can only carry out the decisions of the CC." On such a matter "there can be no argument whatsoever. The lower levels must carry out the instructions of the higher bodies. This is indisputable." [101] The individual member, as well as each body of the League, was expressly obliged to obey the directives from higher bodies.[102] Although the Regulations said League bodies were to be elected, the Third Congress resolved that in oblasts where the "struggle with the survivals of oppression" required it, appointed bodies could serve instead of elected ones.[103] Democratic centralism, then, even as an abstract formula, was hardly democratic.

The Central Committee of the League early evinced a tendency to make full use of its strategic position. The Central Committee that had been elected by the Second Congress simply reversed a decision of that Congress and then reported the accomplished fact to the ensuing Congress.[104] The central leadership insisted on maintaining a close watch over local Komsomol bodies.[105] The local bodies were told to submit regular reports.[106] Komsomol officials and organizational workers were told they must be willing to go where they were needed. Apparently some Ukrainian members had objected to assignments in the north, while some others working in the center had tried to avoid assignments in the outlying regions—especially Siberia, Turkestan, and the Ukraine. The CC of the Komsomol had resorted to the "assistance" of the CC of the Party in order to transfer some members.[107] The Party stepped in on its own initiative, as noted above, to reassign members of the Komsomol CC. Shatskin revealed that the Party committees at the guberniia (provincial) echelon had the right to transfer, reassign, and otherwise dispose of all Komsomolites who occupied responsible posts, and that the Party's guberniia committees had often been taking the best Komsomol workers away for Party assignments. The Komsomol CC had persuaded the Party CC, said Shatskin, to issue instructions discouraging, but apparently not preventing, this practice.[108]

The demand for careful control was also reflected in the provisions for the admission of members. In the Regulations of the First Congress, it was left to the local organization to decide what to require in the way of recommendation. The person recommended was then considered a "candidate" until the general meeting of the local organization had approved of his entry.[109] In the summer of 1919 the Central Committee directed that students and intelligentsia youths must be "conscious Communists" in order to enter. The local organization still could decide how to regulate this—whether by requiring recommendations from members of the Komsomol or the Party, or by requiring a trial period, or by some other means.[110] That policy was reiterated at the Second Congress.[111] The new Regulations voted by the Third Congress, however, laid down a uniform procedure:

2. Worker and peasant youths are accepted into the League without any recommendations. All other youths are accepted on the recommendation of two members of the RCP and RCLY who have been in these organizations not less than three months.

3. Newly admitted members are confirmed by the general meeting [of the local Komsomol body].[112]

The Regulations of 1918 did not specify a lower age limit, but set the upper limit at twenty-three.[113] In 1920 a lower limit of fourteen was instituted. Those over twenty-three were permitted to continue as members, but without a vote unless they occupied a post on a "guiding body" of the League.[114]

As to expulsion, the first Regulations provided that a member could be expelled by the committee of his local organization for "deeds contradicting the Program and the Regulations of the League, for disobedience to its directives, and for nonpayment of membership dues." The expelled member could appeal to the CC.[115] The Regulations of 1920 placed the initial expulsion in the hands of the general meeting. The expellee could then appeal to unspecified higher bodies in the League. The causes for expulsion remained about the same except that the phrase became "for misdemeanors and breach of League discipline, and for disobedience to the directives of leading bodies," and three months of unexcused nonpayment of dues became grounds for automatic expulsion. Notice of the expulsion was to be sent to the guberniia committee and published in the press.[116]

The Komsomol took over from the Party the device of the "cleansing" or "purge," designed to maintain the ideological purity of the organization. At the Third Congress, Shatskin declared that during the past year of rapid growth some "casual elements" had "stuck on" to the League, since the Komsomol membership card did offer "means for a career" (although to a lesser extent than a Party card). He recommended, and the Congress approved, a "reregistration" of members which would eliminate the "bourgeois elements." [117]

The conduct of the congresses in such matters as the electing of officers, the expressing of criticism, and the discussing and determining of policy illuminates further the meaning of democratic centralism and the pattern of intra-Komsomol relationships desired by the Party.

For the election of officers, the style of voting was set by the First Congress, which resolved to use the show of hands.[118] Nominations for the Central Committee were made both by local organizations and by individual delegates. Those nominated were then voted on individually. The fifteen who received the highest number of votes became members of the Central Committee, while the next seven became "candidate-members" (alternates eligible to replace any members in case of need). All of the members, and all but one of the candidate-members, belonged to the Party; but the voters had a fairly wide range of choice, for the leading contestant (Tsetlin) received only 127 out of a possible 175 votes, and one man (Dugachev) was elected to the CC with only 59 votes.[119] Hence there was apparently no definite Party slate. It must be noted, however, that individuals elected to the Central Committee did not necessarily serve on that body. Ryvkin reported in 1919 that the operations of the first CC had actually been conducted, not by its full fifteen members, but by a "narrow staff" of eight, and sometimes only two or three. Some of those originally elected had been detailed to Party jobs, or taken into the Army, or sent on other assignments presumably dictated by the Party. Others had been adjudged "not suited to work in the center; therefore," Ryvkin said, "we did not call them away from their provinces." [120] This "we" was apparently the "narrow staff," which must have been subject to Party control.

At the Second Congress the nominating procedure was modified. For the eleven places on the new CC, the outgoing CC nominated seven; [121] additional nominations could now be made only by groups of delegates representing at least five guberniias. Obviously this gave greater influence to people who were already active in the central apparatus. The delegates were still allowed to vote for individual nominees. All those elected as members or candidate-members were Party people, but one of those (Loginova) nominated by the old CC was *not* elected, and the other six openly sponsored by the old CC did not uniformly receive the highest number of votes. (These six placed first, second, third, seventh, eighth, and ninth.)[122] This suggests, again, that there was no obligatory Party slate.

With the Third Congress there came a marked change in the technique for electing the Central Committee. Ryvkin said that at the previous Congress the election of the CC had been "almost casual." [123] That "mistake" was not repeated. Here is the official record:

Chairman: Now we turn to the elections to the CC. Comrade Tatarov has the floor for proposing the personnel of the CC and the number of members.

Tatarov: The Communist fraction of our Congress proposes to elect a CC composed of the following seventeen comrades: (1) Shatskin, (2) Ignat, (3) B. Tseitlin, (4) Smorodin, (5) Feigin, (6) Tatarov, (7) Iutt, (8) Podvolotskii, (9) Leont'ev, (10) Starostin, (11) Pliasunov, (12) Poltoratskii, (13) Barkhashev, (14) Zabirov, (15) Fominykh, (16) Ryvkin, (17) Kurellia.

Chairman: First we will vote on how many members will be in our CC. The Communist fraction proposes seventeen. Who is opposed? No one. Who puts forward any other list or other candidates? No one.

Tatarov: There has been a proposal that a short sketch of the candidates be given. I support this on the basis that we need to know whom we're electing to the CC.

Chairman: I'll put it to a vote. Who is for the proposal of Comrade Tatarov? Who is against? A majority. And so we proceed to vote for the list of the Communist fraction. Who is for the list? Who against? One. Who abstains? Two. And so the overwhelming majority, against one, and with two abstentions, accepts the list proposed by the Communist fraction. Now we must elect the candidate-members of the CC, from whose number there may be selected replacements for those members who for any reason leave the CC. Comrade Tatarov has the floor for reading the list.

Tatarov: The [Communist] fraction proposes that there be four candidates, in the persons of the following comrades: B. Kuznetsov, Kuznetsov [sic], Okulik, Malyshev.

Chairman: Are there any other suggestions?

Voice: Include among the candidates comrades Polifem, Dunaevskii, and Iakovlev.

Chairman: Those comrades have been removed from work in the RCLY by the CC of the RCP and the question is not subject to discussion by us, since the CC of the RCP is a higher body to which our League is subordinate. And so I put to a vote the list proposed by the Communist fraction. Who is for this list? Who is against? No one. Who abstains? Three. Now we proceed . . .[124]

Thus by the time of the Third Congress (1920), the practice of voting by list had been adopted for the elections to the Central Committee. The real process of nominating—and hence electing—had been removed from the hands of that "highest" of all Komsomol bodies, the All-Russian Congress, and placed in the hands of the "Communist fraction," which operated behind the scenes and was necessarily subject to Party orders.

"Free discussion" as exemplified at the congresses of 1918–20 was conducted by a chairman who followed no Robert's Rules of Order. It was not uncommon for him to take a definite position and to participate actively in debate.[125] When he wanted to eliminate certain items from the agenda, he combined them and called for a vote on all at once.[126] By persuading the majority to limit discussion, he effectively removed certain questions from the jurisdiction of the Congress. At the Third Congress one delegate complained:

Comrades, this is an outrageous fact in the history of the Congress when they don't give an old League member, an old Party worker, the floor to propose concrete measures for the renovation of our degenerating organization, and when they transform the Congress into an all-Russian chewing of old cud.

He then proposed a vote of censure on the Presidium "for a police-parliamentary attitude." But the chairman, who had al-

ready persuaded the majority to bar additional proposals, refused to put the delegate's request to a vote and proceeded to
the next item of business.[127] When the delegates were proposing amendments to the Regulations, the chairman rejected one
suggestion as a "trifle" and did not put it to a vote; he termed
another amendment a "purely editorial correction" and ignored it.[128] Often, when a delegate expressed an opinion but
failed to put it in the form of a motion, the chairman, rather
than call on someone else to formulate a motion, formulated it
himself.[129] But even when resolutions were precisely worded by
their originators, the chairman took the liberty of combining
those he thought were similar.[130] It must be added that Shatskin
and Ryvkin, even when they were not occupying the chair,
seemed able to arrogate to themselves the presiding function.[131]

The tone of the debate varied considerably. Sarcasm and
crude polemical tricks, including accusations of disloyalty to
Communism, often prevailed rather than serious argument.[132]
On the other hand some subjects, like that of the age limits of
the League, were deliberated calmly, perhaps because the matter was not vital.[133] And even on some vital matters, such as the
"Dunaevskii dispute" discussed above, the minority was permitted to express itself.[134]

As would be expected in any large gathering which met only
annually, many speeches were planned in advance. At the First
Congress, time limits were set for various categories of speeches,
and it was voted that "all statements are [to be] submitted to
the Presidium of the Congress in written form." [135] This rule
did not prevent many lively and evidently impromptu exchanges.[136] As noted above, the chairman at least once rebuked
a delegate for raising a disputed question "without warning." [137]

What sort of criticism was the Komsomol member supposed
to express in this early period? Although he was not to challenge fundamental policies that had already been laid down,
he could logically and legitimately criticize the *fulfillment* of
those policies. A frequent target of such criticism was the
Central Committee of the Komsomol. The CC was blamed for
inadequate contact with the lower echelons and the masses, in-

sufficient vigilance against hostile elements, and many other failures.[138] One delegate even accused the CC of lying in its report.[139] But while the criticism was often rather sharp, not everything was permissible. One delegate, who charged that the whole CC was of poor quality, was reprimanded by Bukharin, who made it clear that the Third Congress should approve the general line of the CC while criticizing its shortcomings.[140] The delegates followed that formula.[141] Even in this formative period there was no criticism of the Party as such. Similarly, none of the high leaders of the Party was really criticized, although Shatskin did disagree—gently and tactfully—with Bukharin,[142] and the delegates criticized to some extent the Program that had been drafted with Bukharin's help.[143]

The lack of criticism of the top Party leaders did not imply that they were to be glorified. The main way in which individual Party leaders were singled out was in the election of "honorary chairmen" of the Komsomol congresses (or, in the case of the Third Congress, honorary members of the Presidium). At the First Congress the honorary chairmen were Lenin and two foreign socialists, Karl Liebknecht and Friedrich Adler.[144] The Second Congress elected Lenin, Zinoviev (as head of the Comintern), Trotsky (as leader of the Red Army), and Arnoldi (a Swiss youth leader who had been arrested).[145] At the Third Congress those honored were all Russians—Lenin, Trotsky, and Lunacharskii (then Commissar of Education).[146] There were other references to individual leaders,[147] but they were not magnified as persons. Lenin, the only possible exception, was referred to as one of the few "great people" who "correctly defined the political line," [148] and as "our leader" (vozhd'—a word with military connotations), or "dear leader and comrade." [149] But such references to Lenin were few. Restraint prevailed even in the enthusiasm of the closing ceremonies. The speeches that closed the Second Congress made subdued references to the Party but did not extol any individual leader,[150] while at the First and Third congresses the concluding speeches mentioned neither the Party nor any of its leaders.[151] The implicit assumption was that the leaders possessed authority not as individuals but only as spokesmen for the Central Committee, which in turn represented the Party of the proletariat.

The voting on issues, just as in elections, was by show of hands.[152] Unanimous votes were very common; however, in a substantial minority of cases at these first three congresses, the vote was divided, sometimes rather evenly.[153] Disagreements and split votes on individual parts of a document such as the Regulations did not prevent the congress from accepting the finished product "unanimously." [154]

What happened in those rare instances when the voting on issues got out of hand? In one case (at the First Congress) where serious disagreement was developing, the matter was referred (on Ryvkin's motion, approved by the delegates) to the Presidium for decision.[155] In another incident (at the Third Congress), after a vote had gone against the position of the leadership, Shatskin "proposed" (from the floor) that the matter be turned over to the Central Committee for decision. The chairman thereupon justified and complied with this suggestion without even putting it to a vote.[156] An especially revealing incident occurred in 1919, when the Second Congress was evaluating the work of the outgoing Central Committee. Four resolutions were presented. One expressed unqualified approval. Two cited shortcomings but approved the CC's work in general. The fourth, by one Pletnev, was critical throughout. Ryvkin proposed from the floor that Pletnev's resolution be voted on first, saying that if it was defeated—as he seemed to expect—then the other three could be combined by the Presidium into one version agreeable to everyone. But when the chairman, Drebezgov, put Pletnev's resolution to a vote, it was approved, 112 to 89, with 15 abstentions. Now the excitement began. Someone declared that Drebezgov was not fit to preside and should surrender the chair to Ryvkin. But Drebezgov stayed on. Someone said the voting procedure had been technically incorrect. Ryvkin rejected that idea and went on to say that the vote signified "censure of the former personnel of the CC." This interpretation evidently worried many of the delegates, for soon, "after noise and disturbance in the delegates' seats," the session was abruptly suspended by Ryvkin, speaking not from the chair but in the name of the Central Committee. The record is silent on the events of the half-hour recess that followed. When the curtain went up again, Ryvkin had replaced Drebezgov as chairman. He offered an apology for a "little mistake," explaining that "in closing the session and declaring the recess, I was somewhat carried away and declared the recess in the name of the CC. I did not have the right to do that. I should have declared the recess in the name of the Presidium of the Congress." His confession of a "little mistake" seemed to give the signal for other self-criticism. Several supporters of the Pletnev resolution now jointly announced that they had not meant to censure, or to express lack of confidence in, the old CC; "on the contrary," they said, "we greet them as our best and most self-sacrificing comrades." A Ural delegate said the incident was a "disgrace." A Moscow delegate said that "to express lack of confidence in the CC means to admit the bankruptcy of our organization," and he castigated those who voted "light-mindedly," "transforming such an important political act into a simple mechanical raising of hands [!]." A delegate who ostensibly spoke for the Northern Oblast and Petrograd decried the "shameful occurrence" and the "flippant attitude." Finally a representative of the Central Industrial and Western Regions bemoaned the "misunderstanding" and proposed a new resolution expressing confidence in the CC. Thereupon Ryvkin as chairman called for a vote on the question of reconsidering the resolution on the CC, and this was carried with only two noes and four abstentions. He then called for a vote on a resolution expressing confidence in the CC, and this, too, was carried (with one no and four abstentions).[157]

The procedures and relationships obtaining within the League show that by 1920 the Party had already gone far in dictating the internal affairs of the Komsomol. The organizational structure, the role of the Central Committee and other high Komsomol bodies, the assignment of Komsomol posts, the admission and expulsion of members, the nomination and election of leaders, and the conditions of deliberation and criticism—all bear the heavy imprint of the Party's tendencies toward authoritarian control. However, Komsomolites were not asked to regard any of their chiefs as an object of worship, and a modicum of dissent and disagreement, including split votes, was a permitted feature of the Komsomol pattern.

THE NATURE OF THE GOOD KOMSOMOLITE

Up to this point the analysis has focused on the institutional setting within which Komsomolites were expected to think and act. It is almost time now to turn to the content of their action—the functions demanded of Komsomolites in Soviet society. But first it is important to inquire what sorts of persons these Komsomolites were expected to be.

The Communist society of the future, as the Bolsheviks envisioned it, implied and presupposed important transformations in human nature. There was to be a new Communist generation, reared in part by the Komsomol. What attitudes and qualities of individual character was the Komsomol intended to inculcate? Was there to be one pattern for members and another for nonmembers? One pattern for future leaders and another for mere followers? One pattern for the current stage—the so-called dictatorship of the proletariat—and another for the future stages of socialism and Communism? These are questions one has a right to ask, in view of the Bolsheviks' announced intention to create a New Man.[158]

The problem of the ethical basis of the New Man was faced by Lenin in his speech to the Third Congress. To counter the accusation that Communists had no ethics, he repeated the familiar argument asserting the existence of a Communist morality "derived from the interests of the class struggle of the proletariat" and "completely subordinated to" those interests. What were those interests? The class struggle, he said, had changed its form with the passing of the Revolution: now the proletariat must unify all toilers (including the peasants) against "the return of the old exploiters," as well as "against any petty private property." "At the basis of Communist morality," he declared, "lies the struggle for the strengthening and attaining of Communism." [159] The meaning of that broad, not to say elastic, ethical base was illuminated by the qualities of individual character that were deemed appropriate to it.

The quality most frequently mentioned and most insistently demanded was discipline. It was demanded in the name of the revolutionary struggle, and it was to spring from one's acknowledgment of the Communist goal. Komsomol discipline was expected to be "conscious," or self-willed and self-enforced. It was ostensibly to be free from any militaristic or authoritarian spirit, but it must nevertheless produce unity and solidarity. [160] Said Lenin:

In place of the old drill which was instituted in bourgeois society despite the will of the majority, we place the conscious discipline of workers and peasants . . . in order *to create, out of the will of the millions and hundreds of millions* [of separate individuals] . . . , *a single will: for without this single* will we shall be beaten *inevitably*. Without this solidarity, without this conscious discipline of workers and peasants, our cause is hopeless. Without this we cannot vanquish the capitalists and landlords of the whole world. We will not even secure the foundation, not to speak of building on this foundation the new Communist society. [161]

Hence, however voluntary it might be, this discipline was expected to be manifested in strict obedience to higher authority in the Party and the Komsomol. [162] Said Shatskin in 1920:

There are some comrades among us who say that there is one discipline in the Party and another in the League. They say that since our organization is an educational one, we can somewhat loosen the reins with which the leading bodies must hold their subordinate Komsomol organizations in check. This opinion must be refuted root and branch. . . . We must finally establish the most unconditional and unquestioning subordination of all active workers to the leading bodies of our organizations, and the personal responsibility of each responsible worker for each member of our League, for that work which these members are performing. [163]

As this statement suggests, the demand for discipline was especially insistent at the Third Congress. [164] In part this may have been due to concern over the numerous new members who lacked indoctrination. [165] Also, with the Civil War on the wane, the external military threat was no longer an obvious stimulus to tight control. The Third Congress made this closing appeal:

Comrades!

The Third All-Russian Congress of the RCLY, having defined the policies of the League for the immediate future, addresses itself to all members of the League with an appeal for the greatest self-control and discipline. The proletarian republic lives and struggles in conditions of unprecedented difficulty, surrounded by hordes of enemies, amid famine, cold, and destruction. In this gigantic world struggle even among the proletariat there are tired people, who have gone astray and lost confidence in the possibility of victory. Nevertheless, the thunder of the approaching revolution in the whole world is more and more audible.

In such conditions there stands before the whole proletariat and also before proletarian youth first of all the task of pre-serving, developing, and strengthening iron discipline in the ranks of their organizations! Only with such discipline, consolidating the proletariat into an impregnable granite rock, can it resist the crowd of enemies and the loose petit-bourgeois element.

The Third Congress appeals for the preservation of such an iron discipline in our ranks. May the ranks of our League be invincible battalions of young proletarians storming the old world.

Long live our militant front!

Long live the victorious proletariat!

Long live revolutionary proletarian discipline! [166]

A similarly militant outlook was expressed in many of the other traits demanded of League members. Battlefield virtues predominated. The Komsomol was to create "staunch fighters for Communism." [167] Bravery and self-sacrifice were much de-manded.[168] Preobrazhenskii spoke frankly of the ultimate choice:

Perhaps the League will consciously order you to be the very man who lays down his dead body so that the others can advance over him, and you must do this for you are a member of a great class. This great whole must conquer, but we don't know who will perish. And if this death is ordered by our Party and League, we must accept it in the interest of the common cause.[169]

Self-sacrifice required self-control.[170] Alertness and vigilance were needed to forestall attack by hostile forces.[171] Komsomo-lites were exhorted to develop strength, endurance, toughness, and dexterity, along with such traits as rapidity, precision, accuracy, industriousness, and a sense of responsibility.[172]

At the same time, Komsomolites were expected to display initiative and spontaneity,[173] along with confidence and enthusiasm.[174] Said Krupskaia: "A Communist does not have any doubt that Communism will conquer."[175] Mme Kollontai acknowledged that the situation in 1919 was difficult. "But you, comrades, must joyfully look around at life and say: 'Life is bright and colorful. We are builders, called upon to create.' " [176]

The League's roles as the organizer, teacher, guardian, representative, and foremost element of Soviet youth all suggest the idea of leadership. To what extent and in what ways was the Komsomolite urged to be a leader? Lenin said the good Komsomolite should be part of a "shock group," demonstrating "initiative," the ability to begin new things. He should serve as a model of good upbringing and discipline and show others "the true road." He must not be dogmatic or boastful and must be ever the servant of the people.[177] That dim picture was supported (but not much clarified) by other speakers.[178] Bukharin said:

We need conscious Communists who have both a fiery heart and a burning revolutionary passion, who will hurl it into the greatest contemporary battle, but who have calm heads, who know what they want, who can stop when necessary, retreat when necessary, take a step to the side when necessary, move cautiously, weighing and calculating each step.[179]

Preobrazhenskii reiterated the importance of a serious knowledge of Marxism:

If our Party has won a great many glorious victories, if at a given minute it has been able to calculate where to hit the enemy, if it knew when to hit the enemy and when to retreat, and in the final reckoning gained brilliant victories, then for these we are obligated not to some miracle, not to some intuition and not to chance, but to our mastering of the very methods which Marxism furnishes.

But while thus urging Komsomolites to prepare for leadership through acquiring knowledge, Preobrazhenskii at the same time cautioned them against being too ambitious to reach positions of leadership in a hurry. They must, he said, "wave aside" such thoughts and "remember that only by having an adequate foundation can you rise to the highest level you should reach in accordance with your ability and the interests of the cause." [180]

In evaluating these rather ambiguous references to leadership, one can infer that the Bolsheviks were, on the one hand, aware of the need to train new leaders in the younger generation. They spoke of the Komsomol as the future reserve of the Party, and they expected the Komsomol to organize and guide Soviet youth, to imbue it with the Bolshevik ideology, and to mobilize it in the service of the regime. Within the Komsomol itself some individuals (like Ryvkin and Shatskin) were already important leaders. They and other Komsomolites were called upon to acquire knowledge, develop initiative, and lead fellow Komsomolites and other youths. But on the other hand the overwhelming preponderance of demands reflects the Bolshevik preoccupation with control. To "acquire knowledge" meant to learn Marxism—as interpreted by Lenin and the Party. To "set an example" meant in effect to follow Party instructions faithfully so that others would do likewise. The warnings against dogmatism, against overconfidence, and against ambition fit into the same pattern. The demands for conscious discipline, strict obedience, self-sacrificing courage, and other soldierly virtues were directed at all youths indiscriminately, the most eminent Komsomolite as well as the least significant non-Komsomolite. The catalogue of Komsomol demands in this period seemed to make no real distinction between leaders and followers, members and nonmembers. On the basis of the proceedings of the first three Komsomol congresses, one is obliged to conclude that in regard to Komsomolites, the Bolshevik architects of the New Man were mainly concerned with producing good followers.

But what about the more distant future? Might the end be something more appealing? All the discipline and devoted service demanded of the Komsomolite were held to be for the sake of the ultimate goal, Communism. Since that goal was used as the basic justification for all Bolshevik demands, one must ask what picture of it was presented to the members of the League.

Within the period and the sources under consideration, the most authoritative and at the same time most extended remarks on this subject were made by Lenin himself at the Congress of 1920. His topic was "The Tasks of the Leagues of Youth [the Komsomol]," and he centered those tasks around the "building of Communist society." [181] He forecast that "that generation which is now fifteen years old will both see Communist society and will itself build this society." Becoming more specific, he predicted that the youths of 1920 would "live in Communist society in from ten to twenty years." [182] One might have expected, then, some description of the goal and how to reach it.

Those of his hearers who were looking for hints about the future must have pricked up their ears when Lenin, after one of his many references to "building the edifice of the Communist society," indicated he would explain the meaning of "Communist."

Communist is a Latin word. Communist is from the word "common." Communist society means all in common—land, factories, common toil. That is what Communism is.

Can toil be common if each manages his own economy on a separate plot? You will not create common toil immediately. It won't drop down from the sky. It must be earned, achieved through suffering, created; it is created in the course of the struggle. Here there is no little old book. No one would believe a mere book. Here there is only the experience of life.[183]

In that partial definition Lenin thus explicitly rejected the idea of a "little old book" containing detailed plans for the future. He said: "We can build Communism only out of that sum of knowledge, organizations, and institutions, and with that store of human strength and means which are left to us from the old society." [184] He likewise declared that Communism "should not be something learned by rote but should be something thought out by yourselves." [185] Along what lines?

Lenin's own references to the nature of Communism were largely cast in negative terms. He said that in the old society there had been exploitation of man by man, profit of some at the expense of others, and a regime of rob-or-be-robbed, be-a-slaveholder-or-be-a-slave; under Communism those evils were not to be. The sense of personal property, the tendency to look after oneself alone, would be done away with.[186] At the same time, Lenin was not promising "a land flowing with milk and honey," but rather "iron discipline and firmness in the hard struggle." [187] (Lenin did not make it clear whether he thought "iron discipline" could ever be dispensed with, even under perfect Communism.) The immediate "tasks" which Lenin assigned to youth added little to the definition. One big task was the spreading of education.[188] The other was economic development, including electrification—which, he thought, would constitute one of the biggest steps toward Communism. Economic development presupposed hard work, and members of the League must "be able to toil." [189] That toil must be organized so as to ensure that all jobs, even the most unpleasant, would be performed:

We must arrange each and every job, no matter how dirty and hard, so that each worker and peasant looks at himself and says: I am a part of the great army of free labor and can myself construct my life without landlords and capitalists, I can establish a Communist system.

The league of Communist youth must rear everyone from an early age, from twelve years of age, in conscious and disciplined labor.[190]

Everyone, he said, would "work according to one general plan on common land, in common factories and plants and according to a common system." [191] Lenin went no further toward defining the good society that was his announced goal.

While Lenin's statements on Communism were hardly clear, the other statements made during the first three congresses were even hazier. The first Program of the League spoke of Communism simply as "new forms of society" and "a world of free toil and thought." [192] Shatskin spoke of a "new order, new relations between people, new forms of human society," and a "new comradely community," [193] but got no further in specific terms than to say that under Communism there would be no military weapons.[194] Trotsky (while urging, to be sure, greater support for the Red Army!) also held out the hope of peace, maintaining that

the Soviet government exists not for war but for the creation of a new order in which there will be no struggle and no bloodshed, and there will be no army. That order is called Communism.

Communism is that greatest of all ideals, which renders attractive for us all the future development of mankind. Those many hundreds of thousands of years during which man developed and struggled would be nothing else than a mockery of us if, with this high price, we did not buy a new society where everything will be based on close concord, where each man is a brother and not an enemy.[195]

To Mme Kollontai, the chief distinguishing feature of the future good society was that "then labor will cease being for us a cross and a burden and will become a joy." [196] Balabanova referred to Communism as creating a situation in which "young persons until a certain age [will] need only to learn and to know the beautiful, bright side of life," and said that thanks to Communism "for the first time in the world, air and sunlight will not be only for a small number of children but will be the indivisible property of all youth." [197] Slightly more comprehensive was the new Program adopted by the Third Congress. Here, in its entirety, is that section of the Program that dealt most fully with the ultimate goal:

2. The working class can carry out the heroic task of saving humanity only if, under the guidance of its Communist Party, it destroys the bourgeois state and organizes its own government, its own dictatorship, with whose help it will deprive the bourgeoisie of its riches, annihilate the bourgeois opposition, and lay the foundation for the new society in which mankind will be a united and friendly great toiling workshop, without bosses and rulers, without landlords and capitalists, where it will toil for itself, where there will be no parasites, where each will be given room to develop his strength and abilities. The working class can purchase the realization of this noble and inevitable task only at the price of

the selfless struggle, the greatest heroism, the readiness to sacrifice oneself, and the suffering and the deprivation which are demanded by the great struggle against capital.[198]

Thus, although "Communist society" was, according to Lenin, only "ten to twenty years" away, its shape was unclear. Apparent references to the ultimate goal of Communism were indiscriminately jumbled together with what could have been (in the light of Engels and Marx) references to the transitional period or to socialism. The Komsomolites were being promised that the New Man would have a "new society," without war, slavery, exploitation, oppression, poverty, ignorance, idleness, selfishness, and individualism. But those who referred to Communism eschewed further descriptions and launched instead into discussions of the tasks of the moment and the current demands upon the members of the League. For the time being, at least, the Komsomolite was asked to be a good follower and to submit willingly to iron discipline, for the sake of a goal still obscured by a roseate fog.

RESPONSIBILITIES IN MILITARY AND WORLD AFFAIRS

Among the specific functions that Komsomolites were expected to perform in public life, military obligations assumed an important place, as one would expect in a time of civil war. The First Congress formally committed the League to aid in the armed defense of the Soviet regime and to encourage military training among youth.[199] In the ensuing months there were several "mobilizations" or mass appeals for Komsomol members to go into military service. Since a "general conscription of workers and peasants" had long since been decreed by the Soviet government (May 29, 1918),[200] these Komsomol mobilizations were simply one means of recruiting young people. The first "all-Russian" (i.e., nation-wide) mobilization of Komsomolites came on May 10, 1919, while Kolchak's White forces were threatening from the east. In connection with that appeal, the Central Committee of the League instructed all local Komsomol bodies to select their "responsible workers" for training

in "command courses" and for organizational and agitational
work on the Eastern Front. Komsomol bodies in regions adja-
cent to the front were ordered to mobilize 20 percent of their
members and place them at the disposal of the local Party committees. All Komsomol groups were immediately to institute
military training for all able-bodied members.[201] This first
call brought 3,000 Komsomolites into the armed forces.[202] Subsequent calls for special Army projects (for clerks and for ski
troops) brought in about 1,335 more recruits before the Second
Congress.[203] Most of the Komsomolites who were mobilized
into the Red Army joined regular units, where they served as
commissars and agitators, as well as combat soldiers. However,
there were some special units formed entirely of youths, such
as a Petrograd unit of bicyclists, a Ural youth detachment,
and a Ukrainian armored train.[204] Komsomol members were
called upon also to collect funds for the Red Army, to help
treat the wounded in hospitals, to combat desertion, and to
help soldiers' families with the harvesting.[205] In the Ukraine,
the Komsomol claimed to be conducting underground work
behind Denikin's lines.[206]

When the Second Congress met, Denikin's Volunteers were
only a little over 200 miles away from Moscow, and Iudenich
was near Petrograd. Trotsky, speaking on behalf of the Red
Army, cited the Army's dependence on the young and enumerated some of the various capacities—cavalry, ski detachments, reconnaissance, liaison—in which youth could serve.[207]
The Congress confirmed the previous decision of the Central
Committee requiring all Komsomol groups to conduct military
training [208] and announced the second all-Russian mobilization
of Komsomol members.[209] This decree called up all Komsomolites over sixteen years old in the provinces bordering on
the battle zone (Kaluga, Tula, Riazan, Orel, Tambov, and
Voronezh) and 30 percent of those over sixteen elsewhere.[210]
It brought about 10,000 Komsomolites into the Red Army.[211]
Four other mobilizations yielded almost another 10,000 Komsomol recruits in the one-year interval before the Third Congress.[212]

By that time (October, 1920) the Soviet regime was ending its war with Poland but was still struggling against Wrangel in the south. The League, in line with a decision of the Party's Ninth Congress, was to help establish a "militia army" which would "make of all the toilers 'an armed people.' " The new system was to introduce a stage of preliminary military training, both physical and ideological, for youths before their induction into the Army. The Komsomol was made particularly responsible for the ideological preparation of both Komsomol and non-Komsomol youths under this program. All Komsomolites were required to undergo the indoctrination and other training.[213]

A significant question that faced both the Second and Third congresses was whether or not there were to be Komsomol cells in Army units. In 1919 the Central Committee reported that it had been almost evenly divided on the question and was submitting it to the Second Congress for a decision.[214] In the absence of specific instructions, some organizations had already formed such cells.[215] This policy was approved by the Military Section of the Congress. But Tsetlin, one of the leading figures on the Central Committee, presented a resolution banning them. He was supported by V. Nevskii (representing the Party CC), who argued that Komsomol units in the Army would breed a spirit of separatism inimical to military unity. Party cells, he declared, were sufficient. Akhmanov, a candidate-member of the CC of the League, also decried the consequences of a "double apparatus." The vote followed immediately. By a majority of 120 to 94 (with 8 abstaining), Komsomol cells in the Army were forbidden.[216] It is noteworthy that there could be a vote so nearly evenly divided, on an issue where the Party's position had been made so clear.

By the time of the Third Congress, the Army had set up special rear-area labor detachments for transportation and production. The CC of the Komsomol, Ryvkin reported, had decided that the Second Congress's ban should apply only to combat-type units and had permitted cells to be formed in the labor detachments.[217] Some delegates proposed that Komsomol cells be established also in reserve units of the Army and in command courses. Shatskin and the chairman both opposed this resolution, but it was carried nevertheless. A voice from the floor then proposed that the matter be turned over to the Central Committee of the Komsomol for decision. Without calling for a vote on this new proposal, the chairman heeded it, adding that the Party CC and the Revolutionary Military Council would make the final decision.[218] The fact that the Congress's vote was unceremoniously set aside cannot fully erase the significance of the debate. At both congresses the Komsomol delegates had been permitted to discuss what was really a matter of Party and Army policy.

It can be seen that the military demands upon Komsomolites, both individually and collectively, were well developed during the first years of the League, even though the Party still appeared to feel that its control was not adequate to permit Komsomol cells in combat units.

Closely related to the military duties of the good Komsomol member were his obligations in the realm of world affairs; for the Soviet regime, by its revolutionary proclamations, had virtually declared war against all the governments of the world. Statements at the First Congress amply reflected the Bolshevik view that World Revolution was near and that at the proper moment the worker youth in other countries would rise, along with all proletarians, to create a world-wide Soviet Republic.[219] One of the leaders (Dugachev) declared that "with this [Red] Army we shall help the proletariat of the whole world to establish the reign of socialism." [220] When the Second Congress met, the World Revolution had not yet arrived, but its supposedly imminent approach was hailed in confident tones,[221] and Moscow was referred to as the center of the future World Communist Republic.[222] A message from the Congress appealed to foreign proletarian youths: "Arrange meetings, demonstrations, strikes; let the voice of the worker youth of the whole world sound a final and menacing warning to the bourgeoisie!" [223] At the Third Congress Bukharin justified the Red Army's recent invasion of Poland, telling the delegates that "for us, as revolutionaries . . . it was obligatory . . . to come to the aid of the rising Polish workers," who had called for "Soviet power in Poland." [224] One delegate asked Bukharin why, since the conflict with the bourgeoisie was irreconcilable, Soviet Russia should be trying to conclude peace with Poland. "Very simple," replied Bukharin. When Soviet Russia was weak, it wanted peace. "Any day we may arrive at the position where we are forced to conclude peace with the capitalists in order to gather our strength." [225] He left no doubt what the Soviet leaders intended to do when they became strong: "If we had an army of nine million men; if all of us had shoes and a full stomach, were living in clover, and all were in robust health—then, of course, we wouldn't be offering such peaceful terms, but would be thrashing all the bourgeois, right over to London and Paris." [226]

Meanwhile, for dealing with young people abroad a special instrument was created—the Communist International of Youth.[227] Komsomolites were from the start encouraged to regard their League as part of an already-established international movement of proletarian youth. Among their honored predecessors was the "League of the Young Guard," formed in Belgium in the 1880s. ("Young Guard" was to become the name of the official Komsomol publishing house.) A meeting of Russian and Polish youth representatives in 1907, at Stuttgart, was honored as the "first International Congress of proletarian youth organizations." [228] The Komsomol's First Congress announced the aim of creating a Youth International.[229]

Soon after that Congress, the Komsomol CC set up a delegation to establish contact with foreign youth groups.[230] The way was further prepared by the launching of the parent organization—the Third, or Communist, International—in March, 1919. On May 29, 1919, Zinoviev, as head of the new Comintern, declared that "the hour has come to organize the International of Youth. . . . The Communist International . . . summons all [proletarian] youth organizations to unite and to attach themselves to the Communist International." [231] A commission composed of members of the executive bodies of the Komsomol (the CC) and the Comintern (the Executive Committee) drew up the Program and the Regulations of the projected youth International. The Russians desired to have the first meeting take place in Moscow, but gave way to the wishes of the foreign youth organizations. On November 20–26, 1919, the First Congress of the Communist International of Youth assembled secretly "in a dark, cramped, and dirty room of a tavern in the suburbs of Berlin." [232] There were eighteen "delegates" present, including representatives of the Comintern, the Komsomol, and the Communist youth groups of some ten other countries.[233]

How Komsomolites were expected to think and act in regard to the CIY (Communist International of Youth) was indicated in Lazar' Shatskin's report to the Third Komsomol Congress.[234] Shatskin had been one of the Komsomol delegates present at the founding of the CIY, and he had been elected to its Executive Committee.[235] He discussed first the question of the relation of the various Communist Leagues of Youth to their respective Communist Parties, and, correspondingly, of the new CIY to the Comintern. In the beginning, the Western Communists at Berlin all insisted that their Communist youth organizations must have "absolute independence" from any party. Why was this? Shatskin explained it this way: The revolutionary youth of the West had had previous experience with adult "social patriots" who, being afraid of the "revolutionary spirit of youth," had tried to control the youth organizations. Youth had therefore developed a "hatred toward adult organizations in general." Furthermore, during the World War the Communist youth groups in Western Europe "had been obliged against their will to take upon themselves the functions of political parties," inasmuch as the adult parties had forsaken social democracy for "social patriotism" in supporting their governments in the war. But the situation now, declared Shatskin, had changed. Communist Parties had been organized in Western Europe. They "had no need to fear the revolutionary youth organizations," and therefore were not inclined to hamper their development. Moreover, these Communist Parties could now relieve the youth organizations of their "functions as political parties," which the youth groups had "fulfilled involuntarily during the war." Therefore, Shatskin explained, the old slogan of "absolute independence of the youth movement"— which had been necessary in order to break youth off from the "social patriotic parties"—was out of date.[236] The type of relationship suited to the present, he went on, was that which obtained in Russia. Here, "we can have full confidence in the Communist Party," which is "model in all respects." Therefore, he said, "we, while recognizing the necessity of youth's spontaneous activity in organizational work, at the same time recognize the necessity for the centralization of all Communist forces, including the League, under the guidance of the Party." The Russian type of relationship between Youth League and Communist Party was characterized as "the most advanced," and the relationships prevailing in all other countries were graded, from the most "backward" (as in Denmark and France) through the "intermediate" or "transitional" stage of greater "trust" and centralization (as in Germany) to the "most advanced" type as in Russia.[237]

That gradation was not merely an acknowledgment of a trend. Shatskin made it clear that the Komsomol delegates had to "bring the Western European youth organizations over to the platform that we have in Soviet Russia." At the Berlin Congress, Shatskin and his Russian colleague had found all the Western Europeans opposed to the Soviet view. But after the application of what he called "pressure (theoretical)," and "an extremely great struggle," he had managed to persuade the other youth organizations to "relinquish the functions of political parties and accept the program of the Communist Parties of their countries." By the same logic, apparently, the Western delegates were persuaded to make the CIY a part of the Third International. But dissenters remained, and only by continued effort had they been brought around to the Russian view. As of October, 1920, Shatskin exulted, "We may with complete justification announce that on this question the Russian Communist League of Youth . . . is now the victor in all respects." [238]

Thus, by October, 1920, the reins of authority in the Communist International of Youth were already securely in Bolshevik hands. Obviously facilitating this was the great prestige enjoyed by the one Communist Party that had ridden successfully through a revolution. But the Russian Communists were not relying on that prestige alone. They had obliged those youth groups that wished to call themselves "Communist" to acknowledge the authority both of the Comintern and also of the Communist Parties in their respective countries. Meanwhile, at the Second Congress of the Comintern (July 17 to August 7, 1920), the Bolsheviks had obtained the enactment of regulations which required all Communist Parties to subordinate themselves to the Executive Committee of the Comintern and which, at the same time, guaranteed that the Executive Committee of the Comintern would be controlled by the Russian Communist Party.[239] The result was that the leaders of the Russian Communist Party had created a system of multiple controls leading from the apex of the RCP down to all foreign Communist youth groups. One line of control went through the Comintern to the CP of each country concerned, and thence to the national youth league. A second line went through the Comintern to the CIY, and thence to the various national youth leagues. And still a third line went through the CC of the Komsomol to the CIY, and thence to the other youth leagues.

Not content with annulling the CIY's claim to independence, the Russian Komsomol representatives strove to achieve unity of outlook in the CIY. Some of the foreign youth groups, for example, had been clamoring for universal disarmament. The Soviet position at the moment was that "the slogan of universal disarmament is in fact counterrevolutionary, for it suggests to the workers the thought that they can seize power without using arms." The Russians had succeeded, reported Shatskin, in having the CIY reject pacifism and come out for the

Soviet position.[240] In order to insure conformity in the future, the Russian delegates had insisted that the policies to be followed by youth groups in other countries must be determined by "the experience of the Russian youth league, whose basic principles are suited to any youth organization under conditions of proletarian dictatorship." [241] The Russian leaders were alert to safeguard the CIY against the "yellow" (i.e., procapitalist) or "social patriotic" youth groups, the "socialist center" youth groups, and the "super-Lefts." Very pernicious, said Shatskin, were the "socialist center" people who had tried to join the CIY in order to "demoralize" it by urging "autonomy" for youth groups within the CIY. But the Communists, Shatskin reported with satisfaction, had turned the tables on them and in several cases had managed either to split the rival organizations or to take them over from within.[242]

Acting in response to Shatskin's report, the Third Congress ratified the entry of the Komsomol into the CIY. The delegates promised "spiritual and material help [probably meaning money] to the youth of the countries oppressed by capitalism." They declared their obligation "to serve as a model for the international youth movement and to take the most active part in all the struggle and work of the Communist International of Youth." The delegates also accepted it as their task "to rear the members of the League in the spirit of the international solidarity of the young proletarians of all countries." [243] The new League Program adopted at the Third Congress characterized the CIY as the "military staff directing the struggle of the young workers and peasants of the whole world" and the Komsomol as "the foremost detachment of the international army of proletarian youth." [244] What specific activity this might mean for the rank-and-file Komsomolite was not clear. The Central Committee hailed the establishment of "close ties" with Western youth.[245] But so far, under the conditions of the Civil War, it had not been possible either for many foreign youths to come to Russia or for many Komsomolites to go abroad. It remained to be seen how much contact would prevail later, after the return of relative peace. For the time being the demands upon Komsomolites in regard to world affairs would, for the most part, be restricted to propaganda among Soviet youth. Only a few selected Komsomolites, like Shatskin, could work directly with pro-Communist youths of other countries, persuading or obliging them to follow the Soviet leadership.

GENERAL ECONOMIC OBLIGATIONS: PROTECTION
AND PRODUCTION

Bolshevik propaganda of 1917 and before had made attractive promises to improve the living and working conditions of youth. The members of the Komsomol from the start took an interest in fulfilling those promises. At the First Congress the authoritative Shatskin declared that "the defense of the economic interests of youth is one of the most important tasks of our organization." [246] By formal enactment, one aim of the League was decreed to be "the defense of the legal and economic interests of youth." In pursuing this aim, it was declared, the Komsomol "works out and promotes the putting into practice of laws improving the situation of youth" and "takes part in various governmental and workers' organizations in the center as well as in the provinces." [247] Judging from the First Congress, this was going to be an important area of Komsomol responsibility.

In March, 1919, the Party (at its Eighth Congress) restated in its Program the Soviet provisions for the protection of juvenile workers, including a prohibition against labor for persons below the age of sixteen and a maximum workday of six hours for persons aged sixteen to eighteen. At the same time, however, the Party asserted that the destruction caused by the war made necessary certain "retreats," one of which was to "permit" those between fourteen and sixteen to work four hours a day.[248]

At the Second Congress (October, 1919), questions of youth's economic rights received attention not only in Ryvkin's report of the Central Committee but also in a special section meeting, with reports by S. Kaplun and M. Dugachev. The dominant view expressed in these discussions was that Komsomol members must not think of the protection of youth's economic interests as the business of youth itself. Such an attitude had been appropriate under capitalism; but under a proletarian state it was wrong, for it might place youth in opposition to the proletariat as a whole. There should not be any special agencies for protecting youth; the Komsomol should approach this problem through the "organs of the whole working class" such as the government and the trade unions.[249]

As to the organizational forms, Ryvkin stated that the Central Committee of the League had arranged for the Komsomol to have representatives on the "Commission for Removing Minors from Work" and (without vote) in the Departments of Labor Protection and Social Security; the Komsomol was authorized to set up "non-Party conferences of worker youth" for propaganda purposes, and also "economic rights commissions"; the CC had tried to arrange for Komsomol representatives to sit with vote on the factory committees, but that had not been possible. Some matters, reported Ryvkin, were still undecided: one was the role of the Komsomol in the "inspection of labor"; the other concerned the setting up of Komsomol cells within trade unions.[250]

One function to be performed by Komsomolites was to teach young workers to understand their own role in relation to the whole (and thus, presumably, to understand why some of their desires could not be fulfilled). Another duty was to report violations of the laws concerning the protection of labor. Said Kaplun: "This is already the business of each member of the Communist League of Youth, who must constantly be the ears of the proletariat in the realm of labor protection." Kaplun urged the Komsomol to arrange meetings at which young workers would be encouraged to report violations of the law, as well as unhygienic or harmful working conditions. Dugachev, a member of the Central Committee, endorsed that approach. He added that there would be no point in relieving underage youths from factory work until schools were ready for them. He said the Komsomol, acting through its "economic rights commissions," should collect information on the number of underage youths then working, and help to set up schools.[251] He stressed that the Komsomol was not to work independently in these matters but was to cooperate with the proper governmental agencies. As to the labor inspection, he predicted that the All-Union Central Council of Trade Unions would permit the Komsomol to elect "assistant inspectors," but they would have to be approved by the trade union and would not confine their work to youth.[252]

These authoritative speakers seemed to be relegating the Komsomol to an ineffectual role in the protection of youth's interests. So it seemed, at any rate, to Dunaevskii. He protested that the Komsomol Central Committee was neglecting the interests of working youth. He charged the trade unions with failing to provide, for minors, pay raises as generous as those given to adults. "Youth itself," he demanded, "must undertake the settling of this question." It was in this connection that he pushed the idea, discussed above, of "youth sections affiliated with the trade unions" which could make youth's influence felt.[253] But Dugachev opposed this idea firmly, declaring that young workers, like adults, had their votes as trade-union members and that the Komsomol cell in the factory could handle youth affairs adequately. In the vote in the section, Dugachev's view defeated Dunaevskii's, thirty-six to twelve, and similar action was subsequently taken by the Congress as a whole.[254]

These restrictive measures were accompanied by oratory in praise of toil. (It should be noted that a decree of the Soviet government on October 31, 1918, had established compulsory labor for all persons from sixteen to fifty, inclusive.)[255] Labor was said to have educative value for producing "a Communist world outlook, a Communist frame of mind."[256] Mme Kollontai of the Party's Central Committee told the delegates that under capitalism "forced hired labor" was an especial curse for the young. But in the Soviet Republic, she asserted, if the work a person was doing did not bring him satisfaction, he could use his spare time to train himself for the work he wanted; there was no conflict between young and old; all paths were open to youth, and youth could share fully in building the new society.

And so to work, comrades, in all walks of life, in order to tighten labor discipline, in order to develop the brotherhood of peoples so that each of you can put to use all the abilities that lie within his nature! Then work will cease being a cross or a burden for you and will become a joy. Then each of us will devote all his time, all his twenty-four hours, to the thing he likes.[257]

In harmony with the tone of Mme Kollontai's exhortations, the reduction in the minimum working age from sixteen to fourteen—described in March as a "retreat"—was now interpreted by Ryvkin in a positive light. "Productive labor," he said, was "the foundation of socialist upbringing." [258] Thus already at the Second Congress one could discern a shift in emphasis from protection to production.

By the time of the Third Congress that shift had become even more distinct. The League's new Program reiterated such aims as the protection of child labor, the improvement of working conditions, and the furnishing of medical care and better food and clothing for young workers.[259] The Congress proposed that the Komsomol construct sanatoriums for invalid youths and ask the government to build communal living quarters for unattached young workers.[260] It was reported that provision had been made for young assistants to the inspectors of labor; the Komsomol had obtained representation on the agencies for the protection of labor; the Commissariat of Health had cooperated by setting up "colonies" for sick Komsomol members.[261] But the new Program stressed that this was not a field in which the Komsomol could operate by itself, since (according to the argument) the improving of the situation of worker youth was a matter of concern to the "whole working class." Hence the proper techniques were for the League to "send representatives to government agencies," "propose new measures," "take part in deciding the main questions," and "check up on the putting into practice of published decrees." [262] League members were warned that in all such work the Komsomol cell was the only authorized organizational form (rather than the prohibited "councils of worker youth" and "youth sections attached to the trade unions").[263] In most cases, the agencies through which the League would operate would be the trade unions. And just in case any of the delegates still entertained notions of the trade unions themselves as instruments mainly for bettering the workers' condition, the delegates were reminded that under the proletarian dictatorship trade unions had been transformed into a pillar of the Soviet government.[264]

When criticism was voiced that the League was neglecting the protection of young workers, the official answer was that the Komsomol was simply seeking that protection in the correct way, through striving for a general improvement of economic conditions.[265] Accordingly, production was the keynote. Lenin told the delegates that the next big task for the League, once the war was over, would be that of economic construction. "The old has been destroyed. . . . The ground has been cleared, and on this ground the young Communist generation must build the Communist society." Modernization was needed, including "the electrification of the whole country, of all branches of industry and agriculture." A prerequisite for this great technical advance was literacy, and, beyond that, technical education.[266] Thus Lenin demanded both study and work. As will be explained more fully below, the projected educational system was intended to combine school with factory training from the age of fourteen (sometimes twelve) to eighteen and thus to turn out workers who were both technically skilled and ideologically indoctrinated.[267]

The responsibilities in production that were to rest upon the Komsomol as an organization were clarified in one of the resolutions of the Third Congress: "The RCLY, not being an economic organization of the proletariat, does however take part in the work of the government and the trade unions, helping them with the organizing of the economy and with the labor of worker youth." The resolution went on to explain more specifically that the Komsomol was to organize youth for "campaigns" for such purposes as the procurement of raw materials, fuel, and foodstuffs; the work on the railroads; and the "combating of labor desertion." Labor productivity was to be raised through improved discipline and competition. Street urchins and juvenile delinquents were to be drawn into "a healthy laboring life." [268] Already the League had been assembling young people for unpaid volunteer labor, such as cleaning up rubbish in railroad yards, cutting firewood, and collecting pine cones for fuel.[269]

Thus in the general economic sphere the pattern of demands upon Komsomolites had become fairly clear in the years 1918–20. The League's initial emphasis on helping and protecting worker youth had been quickly restricted. Although it remained one of the aims of the League, it was to be furthered only in close collaboration with regular governmental and economic agencies. There must be no pitting of young against old. All must work for greater output, whether on their individual jobs as producing citizens or on special projects for the Komsomol.

GOVERNMENTAL AND SOCIAL FUNCTIONS

The governmental and social demands made upon Komsomolites in 1918–20 had to do with such matters as the soviets, rural youth, crime, national minorities, women, the family, religion, and recreation.

One task of the League was to train "worker and peasant youth to be able to govern their state." [270] Although some Komsomolites were serving, along with other citizens, as members of the soviets at various echelons,[271] the first three congresses witnessed no specific encouragement of such service. The First Congress did, however, discuss the possibility of obtaining representation for the League on the executive committees of both central and local soviets, and the delegates voted "to empower the Central Committee to obtain the right to be present at executive committee meetings [of soviets; levels unspecified] with the right to vote in all cases." [272] Shatskin, after checking with the authorities, brought back the humiliating news that the All-Russian Central Executive Committee had denied the League the right to send representatives—even without voting powers—to the All-Russian Congress of Soviets, on the ground that "this would violate the Soviet Constitution." [273] This supposed constitutional barrier apparently was hurdled only a little over a year later, when the Komsomol Central Committee was allowed to send representatives to the Seventh Congress of Soviets (December 5–9, 1919).[274]

Meanwhile, under the disorganized conditions of the Civil War, many Komsomol bodies demonstrated youthful initiative by assuming greater governmental responsibilities than the Party apparently desired them to assume. The check was administered at the Congress of 1920. Shatskin laid down the line. During the preceding two years, he declared, "we have done very many things that the proletarian state should have done. We have merged with the proletarian state apparatus, we have very often grown into this apparatus, we have busied ourselves more and more with state affairs, and therefore we must clearly define the bases of our relationship with the proletarian state." [275] In defining these bases, he first stressed that *the decision on all questions concerning the life and labor of youth belongs to the proletarian state.* Moreover, he declared, *"the fulfillment of all the tasks relating to youth must be mainly the job of the state apparatus."* He warned that *our League never can take the place of the proletarian state and must not try to do this."* At the same time, Shatskin maintained that the Komsomol should furnish initiative in deciding questions of principle, should prepare bills and measures, should show an example to state agencies, and should exercise supervision over the fulfillment of published state directives.[276] The proper limits of Komsomol activity in government were thus left somewhat unclear.

Special problems confronted the League in the rural areas. If the Bolsheviks were to feed their cities, supply their industries with agricultural raw materials, and man their armies, they had to control the peasantry. This need was recognized by those who guided the first three congresses of the Komsomol. The First Congress resolved to develop the "class consciousness" of the rural young people and to cement their ties with urban youth.[277] At the Second Congress, V. Nevskii, speaking for the Central Committee of the Party, stressed the need for building a firm base of support for the regime among the propertyless farm laborers and the poorer peasants; for defending both poor peasants and "middle peasants" against the kulaks or village bourgeoisie; and for convincing all peasants that the state farm (sovkhoz) and the commune were the highest and necessary ultimate forms—that it was "either death, or collective life." [278] Nevskii said each rural Komsomol member "must so conduct his work that there remains not one sphere of direct practical work in the countryside which is not guided by our Party organization or the organization of the [Communist] League of Youth." [279] During the interval between the Second and Third congresses there was increased Komsomol activity in the rural areas.[280] In May, 1920, the Party issued a special letter to all its local committees emphasizing the need for working especially with peasant *youth* in view of the "backwardness and conservatism of the adult peasantry." And in June, 1920, at a joint Party-Komsomol meeting on rural problems, the Party instructed all of its members up to the age of twenty-three to enter and to work in the cells of the League.[281]

Among the specific obligations of rural Komsomolites, the collection of agricultural produce was obviously important. By 1919, if not earlier, Komsomolites were being sent among the peasants to confiscate grain, fuel, and other supplies, for the cities and the Red Army.[282] Although techniques of persuasion were said to be preferred, it was acknowledged that the proper indoctrination would take a long time.[283] Bukharin conceded (at the Congress of 1920) that there was no point in trying to persuade the peasants to give up their grain for the sake of the "international Revolution"; they weren't interested in that. He advised Komsomolites to try first to persuade the peasants on the basis of defeating Wrangel. Then if the peasants didn't yield, the Komsomolites were to take the grain forcibly. Bukharin assured his hearers that the peasants would thank them for it eventually.[284]

Another big task was to obtain soldiers from the peasantry.

It was reported in 1919 that Komsomolites were propagandizing the "poor and middle peasants" for that purpose. Nevskii stressed the crucial nature of this work.[285] A related mission was the dispatching of Komsomol "harvesting detachments" into the countryside "to help the families of Red Army men." [286]

Among the other activities suggested for Komsomolites in the rural communities, some were mainly economic, such as organizing agricultural communes,[287] setting up communal kitchen-gardens and experimental fields, erecting bathhouses and barracks, making carts, combating erosion, draining swamps, and repairing roads.[288] Other activities were recommended mainly for the purpose of "attracting peasant youth into the [Komsomol's] sphere of influence," since many young peasants were admittedly too "backward" to become members of the League. Such activities included the establishing of libraries, reading rooms, clubs, and circles for various hobbies; the arranging of discussions, reading sessions, and evening entertainments; and the staging of plays.[289] Komsomolites were especially urged to publish peasant newspapers. If these were to be effective propaganda instruments (said Nevskii), they must "smell" of the village. They must be newspapers "in which the toiling peasants themselves write in their clumsy, simple, ordinary, but genuine peasant language." [290] Komsomol cells were to be established wherever possible, the ultimate goal being one in every village. Village teachers were especially to be won over.[291] Special effort was to be made to split young people away from their elders—to induce "a psychological stratification in the rural family, drawing rural youth over to the side of the toilers' government." [292] In that spirit, a resolution of 1919 directed Komsomolites to give help particularly to young Cossacks "who are rising up against their fathers." [293] Thus in many ways were the members of the Komsomol made responsible for helping the largely urban-based Party to control the rural majority of the Soviet population.

Crime was linked with "speculation" or "profiteering" and with such jobs as that of errand-boy, messenger, and peddler.

Such enterprises, it was argued, diverted young people from productive labor and brought them into contact with prostitutes, tramps, and criminals.[294] To deal with juvenile criminals, ordinary "police measures" were said to be inferior to "agitation." The Komsomol was to penetrate the gangs of delinquent youths and attract the "more healthy elements" of them into the League.[295] When possible, the youths were to be taken off the streets and placed in productive work in factories or in special communes established for that purpose.[296] The delegates were reminded (in 1920) that youths aged sixteen to eighteen were subject to compulsory premilitary training and compulsory labor; hence the appropriate governmental agencies should be summoned in cases of "juvenile speculators" who were evading these obligations.[297]

As to national minorities, the policy to be followed within the League was not at first made clear. The First Congress (1918) included representatives of a "Vitebsk League of Hebrew Youth" and a "Latvian League of Youth." [298] The Ukrainian league was virtually independent. Between the First and the Second congresses, the Ukrainian organization was brought under closer control. So, too, was the Latvian organization (summer, 1919). All Latvian Komsomolites who could speak Russian were to enter regular local Komsomol bodies. Those who could not yet speak Russian were permitted to belong to special Latvian-speaking "sections" of the League. The various Jewish sections of the Komsomol, acting on their own initiative, tried to arrange a special meeting in Voronezh, but the Komsomol Central Committee, insisting that it alone could call such a meeting, forced them to cancel their plan.[299]

The essentials of the Komsomol policy on national minorities were laid down in October, 1919, by the Second Congress and were reaffirmed in slightly amplified form by the Third Congress. The general principle was said to be that the League must give "full possibility to the youth of various nationalities to develop in political and cultural respects" without permitting "national seclusion and isolation," since the League's aim must be "the unification within the League of the youth of various nationalities." [300] There must be no special national Communist leagues of youth. "All Communist work among youth of all nationalities" was to be conducted by the Komsomol. The "national sections," like the one permitted for the Latvians, were designated as a "transitional form" and were authorized only within local Komsomol bodies which embraced large numbers of non-Russian-speaking youths. The sections were to serve those youths only until they learned enough Russian to transfer into the regular local Komsomol body. All members of the national sections were to attend the general meetings of their regular local Komsomol cells, and could participate in Komsomol elections only through those regular cells.[301]

In addition to limiting the use of local "national sections," the Komsomol leadership prevented the growth of regional blocs. Between the Second and Third congresses, the Central Committee frustrated an attempt by the Siberian units of the Komsomol to set up a separate Komsomol committee for their region.[302] At the Third Congress the Siberian question came up again, as well as a similar question in regard to the Caucasus. Shatskin, justifying the policy of the leadership, drew a distinction between those areas that did, and those that did not, require special methods in order to deal with "survivals of former national oppression." Those that did—like the Ukraine and the Tatar areas—were organized politically in "self-standing republics" and given "broad rights, even to separation from Great Russia," in order to overcome their previous mistrust. Such areas, Shatskin explained, could have Komsomol committees which were considered to be on the same plane as the oblast committees within the RSFSR. But in the Caucasus and Siberia, Shatskin argued, such "special national conditions" did not exist. If, he declared, it was necessary for purposes of administration to set up an "oblast center" embracing all Komsomol bodies in Siberia, then it could best be done by a bureau appointed and sent out from the CC. He explained that elected committees "which have such a large territory of operations, feeling themselves strong, act against the policies of the Central Committee, and this hampers the Central Committee in guiding the guberniia committees [the next echelon below the proposed oblast center] in Siberia or the Caucasus." [303] That was frank enough.

The Komsomol member was expected to help liberate women from the supposedly "oppressed and enslaved" conditions they had suffered under the capitalistic system.[304] Mme Kollontai at the Second Congress declared that prostitution was being checked. Woman, she said, was no longer being looked upon as "only a wife or a cheap toy." Now, Mme Kollontai asserted, young men "are encountering girls everywhere—in the Army, where they work both in supply and as political commissars, and in soviet work"; consequently, woman "is becoming a comrade, conscious of her human dignity." [305] Except for such general remarks, the three Komsomol congresses of the Civil War period neglected the problem of sexual promiscuity, although it may have been a source of some anxiety at that time.[306]

The policy toward young women within the League itself was outlined in a resolution of the Second Congress. It called women "the most backward element of the working class and the peasantry" and instructed all Komsomol bodies to devote special effort to drawing them into League and Party activities. Youth meetings were to be held to explain this policy, while at Party meetings, parents' meetings, and women's meetings, mothers were to be urged to have their daughters join the Komsomol. In order to make the League more attractive to women, League bodies were to set up courses for women in reading and writing, "medico-sanitation," and "social insurance." But there were to be no special women's sections within the Komsomol, and the League's activities among young women were to be supervised by Komsomol commissions composed of both sexes.[307] Although the official Regulations treated male and female Komsomolites as equals, in practice the period 1918–20 saw the males sharply predominating. Women probably constituted less than 15 percent of the membership at that time.[308] They did not fare any better at the top. Among the twenty-two members and candidate-members of the first Central Committee, two were women; among the sixteen in the second CC, three were women; and among the twenty-one in the third CC, judging from the endings of the names, there were at most two women, and possibly none at all.[309]

The family relationships of the good Komsomolite received little attention at the congresses of 1918–20. It was noted with satisfaction that the Revolution had caused "the rapid collapse of the family and of the old system of upbringing." [310] Duna-evskii classed the family along with household industry as an unfortunate survival not yet eliminated. He regretted that "the annihilation of the family" and "the transferring of child-rearing to the organs of the state" had not yet been accomplished, and bemoaned the fact that "as long as this is so, fathers will love their own children more than their neighbor's children." [311] The Komsomol Program of 1920 called upon Komsomolites to improve the living conditions of worker youth "by means of creating a broad network of communal houses of youth, replacing the rearing of youth in the family with [rearing in] the comradely Communist community." [312] Valuing young people for their revolutionary spirit, the Bolsheviks wanted to tear them away from the conservative influence of their parents.[313] Peasant families, as has been said, were especially singled out to be sundered. The Bolsheviks posed as the true friends of youth—friends with whom, of course, there could be no conflict of interest. The old society was said to hold back and oppress the young, while the new was said to free the young from parental discipline and to give them the same opportunities as their elders.[314]

Hostility to religion was expected of all Komsomolites. Lenin depicted religion as a tool used by the former ruling classes to exploit the masses.[315] Trotsky asserted that man had progressed from polytheism through monotheism to the Bolshevik attempt to make man "the free master of his own life." [316] The League's Program, approved at the Third Congress, declared that the Komsomol "conducts an ideological struggle against the religious ulcer which is corroding the young generation of toilers and aiding the representatives of the overthrown bourgeoisie to deceive the people." [317] The first three congresses did not, however, deal at length with religion, nor did they seem especially concerned to combat it.

Leisure in the unrestricted sense was incompatible with the all-pervading purposefulness of the Komsomol ideal. Lenin was making no unusual request when he urged that Komsomolites "must use their every free hour" to advance the work at hand.[318] This did not rule out recreation altogether. But there was apparently a feeling that close limits must be drawn. A delegate who, at the First Congress, suggested dancing parties as a means of bringing peasant youth within reach of Communist propaganda was rebuked by several other delegates.[319] Two years later, one speaker criticized dancing parties as "backward," and another pointed to both dances and "flirting" as evidences of a "lack of seriousness which does great harm to our League." [320] The general principle laid down (in a "thesis" of the Second Congress) was that "reasonable diversions" must be an essential part of the educational program. Specific suggestions included going on excursions, attending the theater, seeing museums, visiting country places, inspecting experimental factories, and just plain walking.[321]

EDUCATION AND INDOCTRINATION

While indoctrination permeated all Komsomol activity, it was especially prominent in the sphere of education. Education both within and beyond the school (and connoting a large element of indoctrination) was recognized from the start as one of the most important tasks of the Komsomol.[322]

The general purpose of Communist schooling was outlined by Lenin in his keynote address to the Komsomol Congress of 1920.[323] (That Congress devoted more attention to the schools than did the congresses of 1918 or 1919.) Perhaps Lenin wanted to attract the Komsomol to a task which would demand all its energies and yet not involve it in governmental or Party affairs. In any case, his principal theme was that the tasks of the Komsomol and of youth "can be expressed in one word: The task is to learn." [324] They must "learn Communism," which, said

Lenin, meant to learn to act as a Communist should. Youth must avoid the "capitalist" evil of "a complete cleavage between books and practical life." Youth must shun knowledge that was "useless" or "distorted." Youth must learn the "fundamental facts" and approach them "critically." It was in this sense that he coined what became a Komsomol slogan: "You can be a Communist only when you enrich your memory with a knowledge of all those riches that mankind has produced." [325] At the same session Lunacharskii, the Commissar of Education, stressed the importance of inculcating "class consciousness" and "political consciousness," which he said were merely other words for education.

A good commander and soldier is a good thing, but at the same time he can prove to be very bad for us when he is a tool in the hands of forces hostile to us. He becomes good for us only when he has political consciousness. All accomplishments are turned into blessings when to them is added political consciousness, otherwise not.[326]

The Bolsheviks argued that if the school were to give ideological as well as general training and were to avoid the alleged "cleavage between books and practical life," then school and factory work should be closely associated: "productive labor" must be "the basis of socialist upbringing." [327] Lunacharskii explained to the Komsomol delegates in 1920 that machine labor was especially efficacious for inculcating a Communist "spirit of collectivism." Machine labor, he said, "does not stupefy." Rather, through its own operations, it teaches "the necessity for labor discipline, the necessity for collective, factory, or plant production. It changes your world outlook; it makes you aware that it is not 'I' alone who function, but 'we.' " [328]

How to combine school and factory work was discussed in mid-1919, when representatives of the League met with officials of the People's Commissariat of Education. On June 13, 1919, the Komsomol Central Committee declared that the Commissariat of Education must not put worker youth into the old secondary schools, where "elements of the old upbringing predominate," but rather must concentrate on establishing new "schools for worker youth." [329] At the Second Congress [330] a special subsection discussed how the schools should be organized. Although the Commissariat of Education was said to favor using the existing secondary schools, the section voted for the new separate "schools for worker youth." [331] The Third Congress devoted one whole session to these new schools and even tried to decide which department of the Soviet government would be best suited to handle them.[332] The old secondary schools were again dismissed as bourgeois and unfit for worker youth.[333] The arrangement recommended at the Congress would have combined school with factory work for youths between fourteen and eighteen [334] and would have imparted technical training and also a "Communist world-outlook," a "spirit of collectivism." [335] It seems worth noting that, in their discussions on the schools, the delegates in both 1919 and 1920 debated matters of fairly high government policy.

Besides expressing such opinions, just what was the Komsomol expected to do in regard to the schools? At the initial Congress of the League, there were authoritative-sounding but vague statements that the new League would actually share in establishing and directing the schools.[336] The Second Congress called on Komsomolites to help create schools for worker youth.[337] More specific instructions were given at the Third Congress. Shatskin told Komsomol bodies to urge the local departments of popular education to requisition the necessary buildings and teachers in order to set up schools for worker youth,[338] and a resolution of the Congress instructed Komsomolites to help find suitable sites for schools, to contribute labor to repair school buildings, to assist in the selection of teachers, to help plan the program of instruction, and to publicize the schools among young workers.[339]

The Komsomol's responsibility for organizing students was early made clear. One sign was the already-recounted suppression, before the Second Congress, of the independent league of student youth which called itself Communist. On May 11, 1919, the Party (through the Orgburo of its Central Committee) ordered that the Party's work among school children and students was to be concentrated in the hands of the Komsomol, through cells organized in each school. Admission to these cells was placed under an extra safeguard. Previously, in the Regulations approved at the First Congress, the League had been declared open to "anyone not over twenty-three who recognizes the Program and Regulations of the League, enters one of its organizations, subordinates himself to all its directives, and pays membership dues." According to those Regulations, the local organization could arrange the admission of new members as it chose.[340] But now the Party added the requirement that those *secondary-school* students who were admitted to the League must be "Communist by conviction" and must be recommended by two members of the Party or the Komsomol (in the latter case the sponsor must have been in the League for at least three months). The local body of the League was still to make the final decision. At the same time, it was provided that school cells could organize groups of registered "sympathizers" and permit them to attend cell meetings.[341] Within the schools, the Komsomol was expected to sponsor various special-interest clubs (political, literary, dramatic, musical, artistic, journalistic), set up courses in "political grammar" (elementary Marxism), lead excursions to museums, arrange lectures, organize conferences for non-Komsomol youth, stage other special events, and establish libraries and reading rooms.[342] The Komsomol cell was to establish student self-government in each school.[343]

In addition to operating within the schools, which still served only a minority of youth, the Komsomol was to conduct programs of education and indoctrination for Komsomolites and other youths who were not in school. Komsomol-sponsored clubs were approved by the First and Second congresses as a means of reaching these youths. The clubs could provide libraries and reading rooms. Within each club, several circles could be established—political, self-educational, literary, historical, scientific, and dramatic. The political circle was to be obligatory, decided the Second Congress, for all participants in the club. Lectures and courses of study could be set up within the club. Such youth clubs were authorized only under Komsomol sponsorship. The League was required to cooperate with the local Department of Education in connection with the clubs, but the Department of Education was expected to leave the internal operation of the clubs entirely in the hands of the Komsomol.[344]

The Komsomol press constituted another means of educating and indoctrinating youth beyond the confines of the school. The First Congress announced officially that the Komsomol would issue its own publications, including newspapers, magazines, and brochures.[345] Between the First and the Second congresses the League formed a Press Bureau and launched the magazine *Young Communist*, its first periodical.[346] The Komsomol did not at first have its own newspaper, but instead published "Youth Pages" in other newspapers, including *Pravda*. By October, 1919, Youth Pages were appearing in some thirty central and provincial newspapers.[347] Further progress in Komsomol publishing was demanded at the Third Congress.[348]

The realm of art was not to be neglected in the campaign of indoctrination. The Komsomol Central Committee said (October, 1919) that "into the field of art . . . must be introduced a new understanding . . . —a recognition of the social essence, a shifting of the center of gravity over to the survival of the collective."[349] Lunacharskii told the Third Congress that it was improper "simply to learn to recognize beauty." Art, he said, "must be somehow passed through the prism of our Communist consciousness; may be—must be—taken as a force uniting all people except those who do not want such unification."[350]

The indoctrination of children who were too young to become Komsomolites was at first apparently handled variously by local bodies. At the Third Congress (1920) there was some sentiment in favor of organizing "children's sections," associated with the Komsomol, for those between ten and fourteen. The children's sections were voted down after it was asserted that they would duplicate work being performed by the People's Commissariat of Education and that they would not include all children and therefore would create a privileged group.[351] Neither of those arguments sounds genuine. Duplication was conspicuous in much of the Komsomol's work, such as in the overlapping spheres of the Party and the Komsomol. As to the second objection, the children's sections could have been made broadly inclusive, as were the Pioneers later (though it is by no means sure that even there privilege was avoided). The real reason, it seems probable, was that the Party did not yet feel that it controlled the Komsomol tightly enough to entrust it with the indoctrination of younger children.

In any case, the Third Congress resolved that all work among children was to be "conducted through the agencies of popular education." The Komsomol was to aid with the political education in "children's homes" (for orphans and others), clubs and dining halls; to set up "self-government" in children's institutions, while at the same time "guiding its work"; to organize study circles, clubs, excursions, lectures, and plays; to arrange mass celebrations, such as youth days; to inculcate "discipline and community spirit by means of general meetings and conferences"; to organize *subbotniks* (unpaid "voluntary" workdays) "where they accustom the children to collective labor"; to develop the children's creative ability through children's magazines and other publications; and to encourage athletics. The work with children was called "extremely important" for both the soviet agencies and the Komsomol.[352]

Physical education for youth in general was also a responsibility of the members of the Komsomol. They were instructed to help organize gymnastic exercises, train athletic instructors, and build athletic fields and "houses of physical culture." [353] Physical education and sports were consistently justified at the first three congresses by references to the military needs of the period.[354] Military training and physical education were organizationally linked through the program of preliminary military training.[355] Non-Communist athletic groups (e.g., the Sokols) were either to be brought under Komsomol influence or, in the case of the Boy Scouts, dissolved.[356] Indoctrination was not to be forgotten: Komsomolites were to bring the "Communist spirit into physical education." During athletic events they "must set aside a certain time for speeches of an agitational sort." [357]

By the end of its two-year formative period, the League was still not large: it was only two-thirds the size of the Party [358]— and the Party, unlike the League, did not pretend to be open to the masses. But the League had been assured of a monopoly in the field of youth and had been assigned many important public responsibilities. Those responsibilities must have been a major source of the League's appeal to youths eager to build the new society.[359] However, in several fields the controlling hand of the Party had limited the League's responsibilities and activities. Some Komsomolites had wanted to establish cells in combat units of the Army; they had been prevented from doing so. Some Komsomolites had tried to protect the interests of worker youth; they had been told to labor for the general welfare, not to seek special advantage for the young, and not to take any steps in this area without the approval of the Party or the government. Some Komsomol bodies had been very active in governmental affairs; they had been warned not to try to displace the agencies of the state. In seeking to extend the League's influence over the broad masses of non-Komsomol youth, some Komsomolites had wanted to establish mass auxiliary organizations for worker and for peasant youth, under Komsomol supervision. Those proposals had been sternly rejected. At the Congress of 1920, Lenin and others told the Komsomolites to concern themselves especially with education and indoctrination. Komsomolites were urged not to be ambitious for quick promotion. In these and in many other ways that have been discussed here, the Party's insistence on discipline and control was limiting the sphere of spontaneous activity and initiative that was open to Komsomolites.

Within the League, meanwhile, some freedom for dissent

existed, but only in the face of strong authoritarian tendencies. From its Central Committee to its smallest cell, the Komsomol was expected to operate under the direct supervision of the appropriate echelons of the Communist Party. The leading individuals in the Komsomol were themselves to be Party members, subject to Party discipline and removable on Party command. The League must not dare—and must not be strong enough—to question in the slightest degree the supreme authority of the Party. The League could claim—in fact, must claim—to be "self-standing" and autonomous, but had to guard against calling itself "independent." The League must demand that its members show initiative and spontaneity, and at the same time must demand strict discipline.

The problem of discipline and initiative may be regarded as in part a problem of harmonizing the League's roles as "reserve" and as "helper." As the Party's reserve, the Komsomol was to educate and indoctrinate youth. As the Party's helper, the Komsomol was to perform various practical and immediate services (e.g., military and economic) in Soviet society. The educative role might, within limits that were still unclear, make considerable use of initiative and spontaneity, while the more utilitarian role would tend to require immediate compliance with Party commands.

It seems significant that only once in the course of the first three congresses did any speaker openly suggest that the Party's demands for centralized control were excessive and should be relaxed in the future. The speaker was Shatskin who, at the Congress of 1920, justified the new Program's emphasis on discipline by saying that the sharp revolutionary struggle required the concentration of Communist forces "in one fist" and a sacrifice of spontaneity. "But," he went on, "if the situation becomes less tense, if we gradually turn to peaceful construction, then youth will become more self-standing, for the objective conditions will ensue under which there will not be needed such tight centralization and such subordination of all organizations to the Communist Party." [360] Yet the very Program which Shatskin had been justifying omitted his rationale; that is, it made no mention of the possible conflict between discipline and spontaneity and held out no hope for any future loosening of centralized control.[361]

Shatskin's slip, if that is what it was, serves as a helpful reminder that the obvious authoritarian tendencies within the Komsomol did not necessarily reflect a uniformly authoritarian intent on the part of the Komsomol leaders themselves. On the basis of their published words, one might infer that these leaders spoke primarily as mouthpieces of the monolithic Party. But the Party was not yet the monolith that Stalin fashioned. Many of the early leaders of the Komsomol may have been more loyal to the youth movement as such than they were to the Party. From the standpoint of such men, whip-cracking decrees may have been a necessary price of survival. Rather than seeking merely to advance their own careers in the Party, some leaders must have been trying to make only such concessions to the Party as would enable the Komsomol to keep on growing under the Party's wing. Even after a fuller exploitation of relevant sources it will not be easy for the observer to pass judgment on individual Komsomol leaders like Shatskin and Ryvkin, for each of them embodied a complex and changing combination of intentions, loyalties, and motivations.

Although by 1920 the Komsomol pattern had been rather clearly defined, many of its aspects required further clarification and elaboration. First, it was uncertain just how closely the Party would control the League and its members. Even if Party control of the League was intended in the abstract to be complete, there remained in actuality an important question of degree. Secondly, although the proceedings of the Third Congress suggested that the League was to concentrate on preparing young people mentally and physically for later service in and under the Party and was to devote less energy than previously to military, economic, and other current tasks, it was not clear just what would comprise the future combination of Komsomol functions. Then, too, there was still some uncertainty concerning how inclusive the membership would be and just what powers the Party would assign to the League in connection with other youth groups. Finally, intertwined with the rest, there was this question: In what capacities would the Komsomol member be expected to function as an individual Soviet citizen, and in what capacities would he act as a member of the League? These and other problems were to be faced by the Komsomolites as their organization, building upon the foundations laid in 1918–20, proceeded to develop in the years that followed.

III. The Early Years of the New Economic Policy

THE CONGRESSES OF 1921 AND 1922

THE retreats associated with the New Economic Policy (NEP) were especially hard for youths who had supported enthusiastically the extreme measures of the era of War Communism and Civil War. The dispiriting effect of the NEP on the League was admitted only indirectly at the time of the Fourth Congress (September 21–28, 1921).[1] But by the time of the Fifth Congress (October 11–19, 1922) the situation had evidently become so serious that during the opening session P. Smorodin (a prominent member of the third and fourth Central Committees of the League), M. I Kalinin (chairman of the Central Executive Committee of the RSFSR), and A. V. Lunacharskii (Commissar for Education) all acknowledged openly a problem of low morale among Komsomolites and other youth.[2] N. I. Bukharin, theorist of the Party, said that one reason for the extraordinary demoralization among youth was the "growth of social contradictions," "the contrast between the stores brilliant with lights where there is everything including pineapples [a symbol of luxury in Russia], and on the other hand a whole row of cripples and beggars." Another reason was the contrast between the psychological atmosphere of the New Economic Policy and that of the Civil War. The NEP, said Bukharin,

has not set before youth any vigorous, colorful, sharply defined, militant, heroic task. In the period of the Civil War there stood before youth a colossal task of unprecedented beauty. It captivated them; their relations to it were unusually clear and obvious: they had to kill the common enemy—world capitalism. . . . The grandeur of the war united them, organized them, gave them . . . an aim. . . . The switch over to the rails of the New Economic Policy immediately tore out this pivot [sic]. What is heroic about fighting against concessionaires? . . . Petty humdrum work like that . . . could not attract youth. So there has come, after the period of intense heroic struggle and with the shift to the New Economic Policy, a sort of demoralization, a sort of spiritual crisis among Communist youth and among youth in general.[3]

The sagging of morale was accompanied by a decline in the size of the Komsomol.[4] At the time of the Third Congress the membership stood at about 400,000, and it was apparently as high or higher at the beginning of 1921.[5] (In accordance with what appears to be the practice in the Komsomol sources, the writer assumes that membership figures include candidate-members unless the latter are specifically excluded. When the source refers explicitly to candidate-members, the writer has consistently recorded that fact.) The first drop in membership was connected with a so-called reregistration that ran from about February 20, 1921, through most of the spring of that year. It is not clear to what extent members were expelled, and to what extent they withdrew for lack of interest in the League. In any event, after the reregistration the membership was down to around 250,000.[6] During the summer of 1921 the League enrolled many new members, particularly urban worker youths, and expanded the membership temporarily to perhaps about 400,000 or more by the time of the Fourth Congress (September).[7] But the succeeding year saw a precipitous drop. By the time of the Fifth Congress (October, 1922) the membership apparently had slid back to the vicinity of 250,000.[8]

THE CRUSADE AGAINST "BOURGEOIS" PERILS

The Komsomol response to the psychological perils of the NEP was strikingly reflected in the qualities of individual character demanded of Komsomol members. The Communist-indoctrinated leaders of the Komsomol looked upon themselves as surrounded by a resurgent bourgeois tide which threatened to undermine their ideological walls. Fearing that proletarian youth would become "scattered" and "declassed" by bourgeois influences, they appealed repeatedly for "strong inner cohesion and solidarity in the League." [9] The type of person needed was described at the Fourth Congress by Lazar' Shatskin (who, with Oskar Ryvkin, had served on the first three Central Committees):

Our Party under the new conditions needs strong, steadfast Communists who are not able merely, as during the Civil War, to agitate among the non-Party masses and fight with a rifle in their hands. Now the Party needs people who can direct the petit-bourgeois element with benefit to the proletariat, but not be penetrated by this element—who can remain Communists and clearly perceive our final goal and steadily move toward that goal. [10]

Lunacharskii said the Komsomolite must be vigilant and keep his "armor" strong against bourgeois "temptations." [11]

High standards of personal morality were now demanded, notably by Bukharin at the Congress of 1922. [12] The Bolsheviks, he said, had previously striven to destroy all bourgeois morality concerning sex and personal relations, and they had succeeded; there was now "utter chaos," "anarchy in the realm of rules of conduct, in the realm of standards of relations between one person and another"; this anarchy was extremely dangerous, since it might enable the pernicious bourgeois morality to sneak back into the new society. To combat this evil, economic improvement alone would not be enough. Warily, as though sensing that his audience was hostile to the idea, Bukharin suggested that youth needed to formulate new "rules of conduct," new "commandments." Condemning the old bourgeois code as a "fetishism" of obeying rules without knowing why, he argued that worker youth needed rules of conduct "in order to reach socialism." The Komsomolites must draw up the rules and then teach them to the basic element or "link" among youth—the link which, if grasped (to use a familiar Russian image), would pull along with it the rest of the chain of worker youth. The vital link, he said, was "that stratum of youth which is eager to learn" and which could be used to teach others. In the propagandizing process, he said frankly, the Komsomolites must ap-

peal to "the whole complex of human emotions." [13] Attractive
novels, movies, and plays should carry the message to those who
were unable to absorb the lesson in other ways.[14] The Komsomolites must also cultivate music, processions, and other
ceremonies, since they produced a deep impression on crowds
of people. "The Catholic Church understood this. Why then
should Communists not understand?" [15] Such was Bukharin's
approach.

What should the new moral code contain? In general, Bukharin declared, "We must inculcate a completely instinctive
[sic] attitude of impassioned hatred toward our class enemy."
The code should depict "the socialist ideal characterized by
extreme unity; this must be the point of departure in our
work." [16] Becoming more specific, Bukharin observed that certain League members "looked with contempt on propaganda
against alcohol and tobacco." Such contempt, he recalled, had
been popular before the Revolution, "because through such
trifles we ruined the discipline of the old order." In those days
it had been "fun to walk right by the superintendent with a
cigarette in one's mouth." But now, he insisted, things were
different: "From the physiological and educational standpoint,
the attraction to tobacco and alcohol is of direct harm." [17]
Drunkenness, he said, had "contaminated wide circles of
youth" and was "now one of the wickedest evils in our social
life." [18] He urged that "in the League there must be set up
groups that will wage a conscious struggle against alcoholism
and [the use of] tobacco." Sexual licentiousness he also attacked, saying that directives to combat it should be worked out
by the League in consultation with physicians and educators.[19]
Another virtue to be instilled in the Komsomolites, Bukharin
asserted, was a sense of honor.

For example, formerly there was the honor of the colors, the
honor of the nobleman, and so forth. This must be cultivated among
us as well. You will say that this is all very strange. . . . It is not
in the slightest degree strange. When in war they talk about the
honor of the regiment or about the honor of the colors, this is
a very useful thing which binds the forces together and organizes
them. We must take the same viewpoint with respect to each

and every group in the Komsomol, the Party, and the class, beginning with that little cell to which we belong, and ending with the mightiest organization in whose ranks we stand, that is, our class and then our Soviet state. Imagine that you find yourself abroad and that some bourgeois insults the Soviet Republic. You must immediately sock him in the snoot one way or another. You can't give in to him, you can't hold your tongue. This is not at all a feudal crossing of swords, because here the class content is different, but there is a formal resemblance just the same. We must rear a generation of youth which will guard the honor of its group, Party, class, and state, and won't let anybody spit in its face.[20]

During the discussion some delegates expressed fear that Komsomolites would become sissies;[21] they protested that smoking was not really such a terrible sin;[22] and they argued that rough worker youth would not take to such petty "rules of conduct."[23] But Bukharin countered the arguments,[24] and the Congress subsequently passed a resolution that followed his presentation rather exactly, adding an exhortation to combat graft.[25]

Bukharin in the same address also broached an idea related to the familiar demands for discipline and initiative or spontaneity. (Those demands had been reiterated at the previous Congress, where one policy was recommended on the ground that it would simultaneously be "giving more initiative and controlling each member" [!].)[26] Bukharin's proposal was to develop in youth "a spirit of competition." In athletics, he said, small teams should be set up and competition arranged among them. This would produce "a combination of the two principles, a combination of the principle of the community with the principle of free movement. . . . The competitive principle must be manifested in all games."[27] His suggestion was challenged by a delegate who thought that to stimulate that sort of small-group spirit would conflict with the development of the collective spirit which should embrace the whole League and the entire working class.[28] Bukharin replied: "I declare that between the general centralized organization and the individual person entering the League there needs to be a freely

assembled *intermediate unit,* unified completely freely through
the strength of some internal attraction." As examples he cited
the formation of groups interested in political theory, in chess,
and in soccer, as well as the practice of honoring certain regi-
ments and factories in order to stimulate them to do better.
"What is heretical in this?" he asked. Earlier, perhaps, such an
approach had not been necessary.

But in our era, when we need to seek certain stimuli for greater
mobility and flexibility of the whole apparatus, then should we
not call for competition in all areas of life between various groups
and sometimes even between individuals? Beware of the view that
says: "Don't give freedom of movement to any small cells; the
leaders are over there; everyone will follow them and they will
give all the assignments from the center." That view represents
a harmful tendency.[29]

Although Bukharin used the words "competition in all areas
of life," his examples were chosen from areas generally remote
from the sources of economic and political power.[30]

The protection of the League's prized "proletarian" essence
involved the problem of the class composition of the League
and the related question of how broad or how narrow the
League should be. These issues came to the fore at the Congress
of 1921. Oskar Ryvkin outlined them from the viewpoint of
the leadership.[31] Worker youths, threatened with unemployment and demoralization, must be helped; they must be drawn
into production, taught skills, and oriented politically. These
tasks could be facilitated by drawing more worker youths into
the League, where they could be converted into "genuine Communists." [32] That in turn would help to strengthen the "proletarian base" or "kernel" of the League. Ryvkin said the
"proletarian kernel" stood as low as 25–27 percent at that time,
which meant that the League was "very weak" and was exposed
to too many "petit-bourgeois" elements.[33] It was to meet this
danger that a special Conference of the League, called on June
1, 1921, had introduced a probationary stage for intelligentsia
elements entering the League. Ryvkin demanded that the Congress confirm this action.[34] Next, while granting that more

should be done for the older Komsomolites, he rejected a proposal to raise the minimum age for Komsomol membership from fourteen to sixteen, saying that it would mean throwing many youths into the street without an organization.[35] As to rural activities, which had become more difficult under the NEP, Ryvkin said the Komsomol would have to rely on young people of farm-laborer and poor-peasant background, and not on those from the category of the middle peasants.[36]

Ryvkin's report aroused warm dispute on two points. One was the question of the minimum age. Those who advocated raising the minimum to sixteen argued that the purging of "children" was necessary if the League were to play an influential and active role.[37] The leadership's reply, given by a prominent Party man, Preobrazhenskii, was to accuse the advocates of the sixteen-year minimum of desiring to gain greater political influence for the League. "With whom will you compete, anyway?" he asked. "With the Communist Party and the trade unions?" Voices from the audience responded, "We'll help," whereupon Preobrazhenskii assured them that they could help best by taking in young people from the age of fourteen and educating them.[38] Some dissenters persisted,[39] but they grew silent after Shatskin suggested darkly that their proposal was one manifestation of a "serious deviation" tending to create a "political youth organization." [40] Despite that threat there was a sizable opposing vote, although the majority upheld the official position leaving the age at fourteen.[41]

The second dispute, closely associated with the first, was over a proposal by some delegates that the League should purge itself of nonproletarian elements. The consequent relative increase in the size of the "proletarian kernel" would, they argued, make the League stronger and more effective in carrying out its functions.[42] Preobrazhenskii struck at this argument by emphasizing that the League, unlike the Party, was dealing with immature youths. The League, he said, was only the "first sieve for the Communist Party" and consequently "must choose as many elements as possible for screening." [43] It would be wrong, he maintained, to expel intelligentsia youths before they had been put through a considerable program of Communist indoctrination. The same principle applied to peasant youths, for, said Preobrazhenskii, the Komsomol was second only to the Red Army as a mass organization for indoctrinating them.[44] Of course the League would still need to purge those who opposed its policies, but a general purge of nonproletarians was, he said, associated with the unhealthy desire to see the League perform governmental functions and thus to compete with the Party.[45] When the vote came—apparently a voice vote —it was challenged from the floor by a delegate who questioned the chairman's accuracy in declaring that the majority had opposed the purge. At this critical juncture Shatskin intervened, displaced the chairman, and, unceremoniously assuming the presiding function, announced authoritatively that the vote had gone against the purge.[46]

In contrast to these contested points, Ryvkin's recommendation on the probationary stage for intelligentsia youth was unopposed and became a part of the revised Regulations of the League. "Worker and peasant youth," as before, could enter directly into the League without any recommendation. "Other youths" (unspecified, but including intelligentsia) now had to obtain recommendations from two persons who had belonged to either the Party or the League for at least six months, and then, before they could become full members, had to pass successfully through a six-month period of "candidacy" designed to test their "genuine loyalty to the cause of the Revolution." During that probationary stage the candidates were to perform all the duties of members but had only an advisory voice in League meetings.[47] The official position on peasant youth was likewise not seriously challenged. Shatskin implied that the advocates of a purge intended to get rid of peasant youths as well as intelligentsia youths,[48] but those who spoke on this question at the Fourth Congress did not openly advocate such a policy,[49] and the theses approved by the delegates called for special stress on work with poor-peasant and farm-laborer youth.[50]

In that debate of 1921 on the composition of the League, the disputants do not seem to have been very far apart. They agreed on the need to strengthen the proletarian core of the Komsomol. The probationary stage for intelligentsia (and "other") youths aroused no objections. The policy toward peasant youths was apparently not a real bone of contention. The need for some purging was acknowledged by all. Everyone favored having a larger proportion of older youths in the League. But where the official position called for retention of the fourteen-year minimum, the dissenters wanted to substitute sixteen, and where the official position endorsed limited purging, the dissenters wanted more—without even discussing precise measurements of permissible purging. The differences do not seem substantial, but they were treated as if they were. Why? The answer probably is that the Party-bred leaders of the Fourth Congress thought they detected an attitude which might later countenance a challenging of Party authority. Accordingly, they labeled it a "serious deviation" and they fought vigorously to stamp it out. The good Komsomolite could see the moral in so far as obedience to the Party was concerned. But that did not settle the question of the composition of the League. The very nature of the problem precluded any exact solution, especially since social classes were not susceptible to the Bolsheviks' crude and arbitrary definitions. Kindred deviations were destined to live on and to reappear.

At the next Congress (October, 1922) the question of the composition of the League turned especially around the problem of peasant youth. Smorodin, eminent spokesman of the outgoing CC, stated two reasons for the sharp drop in membership during the preceding year. First (and quite understandably), some peasant youths—classified by him as "kulak and petit-bourgeois elements"—had quit the League when it tried to use them to collect the tax-in-kind from the farmers. A second factor had been purges, which, he said, had been conducted in violation of the instructions of the Central Committee. Smorodin singled out the Komsomol organizations in the Ukraine and the Caucasus as having been particularly guilty.[51] Several dissenters, now increasingly labeled as "Ukrainians,"[52] protested that the local Komsomol bodies knew best just which members deserved to be dropped, and that anyway the CC had not provided adequate guidance respecting the proper line to follow.[53] Smorodin conceded, though foggily, that the CC had given permission for some purging.[54] The issue was elusive, for even if the class distinctions had been clear, how was one to draw the line between the removal of hostile individuals and a general purge? The matter was not fiercely pursued, and the policy changes were slight. The probationary period for those who were not "worker" or "peasant" youths was now increased from six months to one year, and the sponsors were required to have been members of either the League or the Party for two years.[55] The Congress reiterated the need for caution in admitting middle-peasant youths [56] and resolved that they must pass through the probationary stage.[57]

In the discussions of 1921 and 1922 on the composition of the League, one observes the checking of a deviation within the Komsomol. In view of the bourgeois revival under the NEP, the Party wanted the League to be somewhat protected against intelligentsia, petit-bourgeois, or middle-peasant youths who might alter the League's ideological and political tone. But the Party evidently feared that some elements within the Komsomol were going too far—were excluding too many, were forgetting the League's mission of indoctrination, and were making the League into a sort of "junior Party" that would emphasize other, especially governmental, tasks. Hence the question of the composition of the League was intertwined with that of the League's general role.

Some elements within the Komsomol had evidently persisted, despite such warnings as those at the Third Congress, in performing governmental functions. At the Fourth Congress, Ryvkin in his official report reiterated that the League should be unburdened of governmental functions, in order that it might devote its energies to its proper task of creating Communists.[58] Several speakers from the floor challenged his view.[59] Some of the dissenters argued that political indoctrination, which was an undeniable part of the League's work, could not be effective unless it were linked with political practice and active participation in governmental affairs.[60] Others maintained that unless the League were permitted to engage in political activity, the older youths would see no point in belonging to the Komsomol.[61] On this issue, too, it was Preobrazhenskii who authoritatively reprimanded the dissenters. He said there had been a time "when it was necessary to increase and strengthen the political influence of the League, when you [Komsomolites] fulfilled governmental tasks owing to the disorganization of the governmental apparatus." But that was the "yesterday" of the League, he declared; the League must now make a decisive turn away from governmental tasks. "To the extent that the CC [of the Komsomol] suggests that you turn the rudder, and in so far as it [the CC] is acting in accordance with the CC of the RCP, you must make this turn in earnest." [62] The Komsomol should not concern itself with trying to control Soviet agencies, he insisted, but should concentrate on political indoctrination.[63]

The theses approved by the Fourth Congress made the official line on this question very clear. Komsomol members *as individuals* were to be encouraged to participate in "political and economic life," including particularly work in those state agencies devoted to helping and protecting worker youth. But it was plainly indicated that for Komsomolites *as an organization* to perform "governmental functions" (as they were said to have done during the Civil War) was wrong.[64] The question of "governmental functions" seemed to have been settled for the time being and was not raised in that form at the Fifth Congress. However, that Congress did add to the Komsomol Regulations a statement which, while demanding that Komsomolites help the Soviet government, put this on the plane of an individual obligation.[65]

During the period of the Fourth and Fifth congresses, then, Komsomolites were being warned not to make their organization too exclusive and not to compete with the Party in a governmental role. At the same time they were to ward off bourgeois influence and to strengthen the League's bonds with "proletarian" youth.

Many of the public responsibilities laid upon Komsomolites in this period manifested an emphasis on worker youth. With the Kronstadt uprising freshly in mind, the Tenth Party Congress (March 8–16, 1921) directed the Komsomol to place more emphasis on helping worker youth both in the field of education and in the improvement of working and living conditions.[66] Accordingly, those questions were discussed at the Fourth Komsomol Congress.[67] One particular fear was that, under the partially free economy of the NEP, many underage workers would be thrown out of work [68] and might turn to peddling and private trade, thereby becoming "declassed." [69] Optimistically the Congress endorsed a reduction of output quotas and advocated a four-hour day for those under sixteen and a six-hour day for those between sixteen and eighteen—with the wages for both categories to be the same as for those who worked a full eight-hour day! [70] The delegates also voted that Komsomolites should help to provide communal living quarters, medical care, and adequate rations for underage workers.[71] To achieve those ambitious goals where *private* industries were concerned, Komsomolites were told that they should seek to apply, through the proper government agencies, "administrative as well as economic compulsion," including fines, legal suits, and boycotts. But no such drastic remedies were suggested in regard to *nationalized* industries. Here, Komsomolites were told, they must cooperate closely with economic (i.e., governmental) and trade-union bodies.[72] Komsomol groups must not parallel or supplant the functions of those governmental and quasi-governmental agencies. The Komsomol could call the attention of those agencies to pressing problems, but must not itself become involved in economic administration.[73] As individuals, some Komsomolites were already helping to inspect labor conditions.[74] But as a group, apparently their appropriate sphere for relatively autonomous activity was limited to such things as planting kitchen-gardens and repairing young workers' apartments.[75]

By the time of the Fifth Congress many young workers had lost their jobs. The proportion of minors in trade unions had fallen from 9.4 percent in July, 1921, to 3.6 percent in April, 1922.[76] Meanwhile, the Komsomol had been negotiating with the All-Union Central Council of Trade Unions, trying to persuade it to approve the idea (endorsed by the Fourth Congress) that minors should receive eight hours' pay for a four-hour or six-hour workday.[77] Hitherto the trade-union body had refused, but during the course of the Fifth Congress it was announced that the Commissariat of Labor had agreed to the League's suggestion in so far as it applied to those who worked a six-hour day.[78]

Evidently some youths had been involved, probably with older workers, in attempts to improve working conditions by unauthorized methods, for both Trotsky and Bukharin spoke out against using the strike weapon. Trotsky acknowledged that conditions for working youth were worse than they had been before 1914 but maintained that there was now no exploitation, for the factories belonged to the working class. He asserted that although the strikes were ostensibly for the betterment of the workers, they were in reality motivated by a desire to return to capitalism. He labeled them "organized sabotage" and said the League must fight them as such.[79] Instead of striking, Komsomolites were told to report cases of improper pay or working conditions to the appropriate governmental or trade-union bodies.[80]

The relations between the Komsomol and the trade unions at the factory level had not been entirely smooth. Shokhin, then a prominent Komsomolite, recommended that in cases where the trade-union officials rejected Komsomol suggestions concerning measures to improve the lot of working youth, the League should be permitted to carry out those measures itself, with an eye toward proving their feasibility to the trade-union organization. Critics objected that such action would constitute a direct appeal to the workers and would undermine the authority of the trade unions, which, it was recalled, were in turn controlled by the Party. The delegates, surprisingly, voted with Shokhin.[81] But the resolution as finally approved contained the necessary check: "In case of especially important disagreements between the RCLY and the trade union, the question is to be clarified by the Party organization." [82] It was enacted moreover that every wage-earning Komsomolite must be a member of the appropriate trade union.[83] Thus the Komsomol member working in a factory or plant would be subject contemporaneously to trade-union and to Komsomol discipline, while the Party presumably strove to see that the demands of both channels on the Komsomol member were compatible and reinforced each other.

Closely related to the problem of protecting worker youth was that of combating crime. Many children had been orphaned or made homeless as a result of the years of economic and social chaos. In cooperation with the appropriate government agencies, Komsomolites were to assist in rounding up the homeless waifs, sending them to special "closed colonies" when possible, or simply putting them to such tasks as harvesting fields and orchards, clearing away snow, and cutting wood. They could be formed into small-scale producers' cooperatives. In any case they were to be kept busy so that they would not engage in crime or "speculation"—that is, private trade or peddling.[84] Special schools and clubs for homeless children were also to be set up by the League. Komsomolites were to arouse "public opinion against those parents who send their own children into the streets, organizing special show-trials of parents and children and influencing the parents by a whole series of strict exemplary punishments." The same lessons would be brought home to worker youth through the Komsomol cells in the factories. Prostitution was to be combated, in collaboration with the Commissariat of Health.[85]

The problem of educating youth, especially worker youth, occupied an important place at the Fourth and Fifth congresses. The fundamental aim of this training was still that of indoctrination, of "making Communists," for in the official view there was no point in training specialists who might later succumb to bourgeois influences and turn into "saboteurs." [86] A means toward that end, and also an end in itself, continued to be the combining of labor with education.[87] This would augment the supply of skilled men needed to build Soviet industry and permit the displacement of old non-Communist specialists.[88] It would serve to keep unemployed youths usefully occupied and out of crime.[89] An additional aim of the training was to instill in worker youth the feeling that factory labor was "a privilege" conveying "the rights of political citizenship." Apparently there had been some disappointment among youths who expected to rise more rapidly under the new regime. Komsomolites must explain to them that only a few exceptionally capable youths could expect to continue "up the ladder" beyond factory labor (presumably into technical, supervisory, or governmental positions).[90]

Komsomolites were expected to further the technical training [91] and the indoctrination of worker youth both inside and outside the League.[92] Continuing their opposition to the traditional secondary schools run by the Commissariat of Education, Komsomol spokesmen and delegates at the Fourth and Fifth congresses endorsed schools of two general types: (1) schools that gave only "theoretical" training to youths who were concurrently working in factories and (2) combination factory-schools that gave both theoretical and practical training while at the same time actually producing goods.[93] The second (and preferred) type came to be known as FZU or Factory Training Schools.[94] At the time of the Fourth Congress, schools of both types were said to total 200, with 32,000 pupils enrolled.[95] By the time of the Fifth Congress, the total of both types was given as 524 schools, serving about 50,000 worker youths.[96] (Of these only 5,000 were said to be attending the favored Factory Training Schools.)[97]

As to the regular secondary schools, Shokhin, in a major report to the Fifth Congress, said they should be abolished entirely and replaced by professional-technical schools that would turn out skilled workmen.[98] Against that view, Krupskaia (Lenin's wife) insisted vigorously that despite their defects the secondary schools were useful as feeders to higher educational institutions,[99] and Lunacharskii averred that the secondary schools should be continued for a considerable time.[100] But several delegates supported Shokhin;[101] he courteously but firmly disputed both Krupskaia and Lunacharskii,[102] and a special section meeting under Shokhin recommended that the Congress vote for the "most rapid liquidation" of the secondary schools.[103] After some warm exchanges, the delegates approved the viewpoint of Shokhin and his section, rejecting both an amendment advanced by Shatskin and a proposal made by Lunacharskii.[104]

Government policy also became an issue in regard to the financing of the schools. Lunacharskii perhaps unwittingly provided an opening when he asked the Fourth Congress (which obviously had no power in the matter) to endorse his request that the Commissariat of Education be given an increased budget.[105] The delegates assented.[106] However, when Lunacharskii made a similar request at the next Congress,[107] he was outdone: Shokhin introduced a bolder resolution which declared that the Soviet government had not been allocating enough funds to education.[108] Another delegate supported him, charging that the Soviet government was allocating only 1.8 percent of its budget to education, whereas the tsarist regime had allotted 4 percent.[109] Shokhin's resolution was approved by what was apparently a rather close vote. This created a furor. It is not clear just what happened, but Shokhin's criticism does not appear in the resolution on education as it was finally published.[110]

It is interesting, of course, in regard to the above controversies, to observe that many Komsomol delegates in 1921 and 1922 felt free to discuss the budget and the structure of the school system—both of which were matters of relatively high government policy—and to vote against the views of not only their own leader, Shatskin, but also Lunacharskii and even Lenin's wife. On the other hand, these incidents do not warrant the inference that the Komsomolites were being given any high policy-making responsibilities in regard to education. The fact that both of Shokhin's aforementioned resolutions were apparently tampered with, after the vote, indicates that the leaders were not going to let their Komsomol flock get far out of hand.

Outside of those policy realms, of course, Komsomolites bore a continuing responsibility to improve the educational system. Komsomol individuals and groups were told to help establish schools for worker youth and to help provide equipment, books, students, and teachers.[111] The recruitment of teachers was especially urged. The difficulty was said to be that although most proletarian youths were unwilling to become teachers, the profession must not be predominantly bourgeois.[112] As to student self-government, the "American system," under which the schools were (it was said) run by the students themselves, was rejected, partly on the ground that bourgeois students might be too influential. The feeling seemed to be that if there were any student self-government, it should be limited to such functions as allocating student duties, distributing food, and organizing clubs; and it should be guided by the Komsomol cell.[113]

As to the League's other semieducational responsibilities, Bukharin's insistence on promoting a competitive spirit through athletics has already been mentioned. Even more controversial was a dispute (also at the Congress of 1922) over whether or not to organize a separate "Red League of Physical Culture." Those who favored such a body said it would draw in many non-Komsomolites, yet could be steered by a firm core of Komsomol members.[114] The debate was marked by a clash between Smorodin (then presiding) and Shatskin. Shatskin argued that the Komsomol was the only authorized movement for worker youth and that if such an athletic league were established, "in the summertime worker youth would not come to us but to that league which was organizing athletics." The delegates upheld Shatskin, maintaining that the proposed body would in fact be a second mass youth organization and would infringe on the Komsomol's exclusive province.[115] In that decision again was manifested, it would seem, the Party's fear that the Komsomol was too weak (or too undependable) to control a large athletic organization. At the same time, all Komsomolites were instructed to set up athletic clubs and contests locally and to get rid of the "old bourgeois athletic organizations, the Sokols and Maccabees, etc., first by means of the development of our own athletic work, then through legislative means, material isolation of them [this was not explained], boycott, barring [them] from competitions and so forth, right up to liquidation." [116]

In the publishing field, it was reported at the Fifth Congress that the principal organ of the CC, *Iunyi kommunist* (Young Communist), was appearing more regularly and that another periodical, *Molodaia gvardiia* (Young Guard), was also being published.[117] Komsomolites were urged to expand greatly the output of attractive propagandistic material for each category of youth, classified according to age group, vocational interest, language and nationality, and rural or urban environment.[118] To issue such works, the Congress approved the establishment of the publishing house Molodaia gvardiia under the Central Committee of the League.[119]

An important new task for Komsomolites was added by the same Congress (1922) when it recommended that local groups called "Young Pioneers"—"pioneers of the new society"—be organized under Komsomol supervision to conduct the indoctrination of children from ten to fourteen years of age. These groups were to inculcate class consciousness, "instincts" of group formation and of competition, a sense of social living, an esteem for creative labor, a striving for knowledge, and a willingness to subordinate personal interests to those of society.[120] The basic unit was to be a "link" (*zveno*) of ten children, who would elect their own link leader. Three or four links would form a "group," run by a "group council" (*sovet gruppy*), at the head of which would be an instructor designated by the local Komsomol organization. All Pioneer groups in any given city were to be united in an "Organization of Young Pioneers," run by a council also appointed by the local Komsomol committee.[121] In order to "clear the ground" for the new organization, it was declared that "all hostile bourgeois organizations influencing proletarian children (Scout troops, children's organizations of the 'Maccabees,' and other nationalistic leagues)" must be "moved out of the way." Their members could join the Pioneers, and even leaders of the Scouts could be taken into Pioneer work, provided they adopted "sincerely and fully" the Pioneer platform.[122] The pattern of activities recommended for the Pioneers was obviously modeled in part on that of the Boy Scouts (nature study, practical skills, outdoor living, hygiene, athletics, community service, crafts) but was designed particularly to teach loyalty to the program and the leadership of the Communist Party.[123]

Despite its concern for worker youth, the League was not to forget the young peasants. At the Congress of 1921 rural conditions were admitted to be serious, partly because of the famine.[124] Rural Komsomolites were instructed to preserve their Komsomol organizations and also to do what they could to feed starving people, especially children.[125] Conditions grew worse, and at the Congress of 1922 the rural tasks of the League were treated more prominently.[126] The ties of peasant youths to their families were regretfully said to be growing stronger, except (it was reassuringly noted) among the poorest peasant families and those stricken by the famine.[127] Religious and other non-Communist groups were persisting.[128] The Party had declined in the villages, and so had the Komsomol, its rural cells being only half as numerous as they had been in 1920.[129] However, some Komsomol cells were said to be leading village soviets and otherwise fulfilling the functions of Party cells, and the Komsomol remained an important carrier of Communist influence to the peasantry.[130]

Rural Komsomol leaders were needed. Komsomolites were

told to pick "the best" peasant youths, preferably from the most downtrodden peasant background, and send them to special schools and to urban Komsomol units for indoctrination. Most of the trainees would, it was planned, then fill Komsomol posts at the level of the volost (small rural district), taking occasional tours of duty in town to maintain contact with the proletarian core of the League.[131] Peasant youths working on the sovkhozes (state farms) were singled out as good potential Komsomolites, owing to their wage-earning proletarian status.[132] As indicated earlier in this chapter, middle-peasant (unlike poor-peasant) youths had to be especially scrutinized during a probationary stage before they could become full Komsomolites.

The Komsomol was to guide (together with the Party) the elections in the local soviets; it was to encourage agricultural cooperatives and require Komsomolites to join them; it was to set up village reading rooms; it was to arrange demonstration kitchen-gardens; it was to train rural teachers, librarians, and volost clerks; it was to help hired farm laborers to receive adequate wages from private employers; and it was to combat all non-Communist organizations, including religious ones (Baptists and Evangelists were named). Komsomol-directed circles of various sorts (dramatic, agronomic) were to be set up to supplant the blacklisted non-Communist groups. The disapproved groups were to be fought by means of persuasion "as a general rule," although they could be "dispersed" (presumably by force) if they were "counterrevolutionary." [133]

"DEFENSE" AND WORLD REVOLUTION

The general military obligations of the Komsomol member, already set forth in Chapter II, continued to receive attention at the Fourth and Fifth congresses.[134] Military training, long since a legal obligation for all worker and most peasant males between eighteen and forty, was made a formal requirement for each Komsomolite, according to the League's Regulations as revised by the Fourth Congress.[135] At the time of the Fifth Congress, young men born in 1902 were about to be drafted for military training. Trotsky said that they were entering the Army "without coercion, voluntarily, willingly, and gladly," and that the Komsomol must reinforce this attitude (!).[136] The question of Komsomol cells in the Army was raised again. One delegate proposed a compromise by which cells would be permitted in Army units in peacetime but would be dissolved in the event of war.[137] The Congress, however, upheld what appeared to be the leadership's position, prohibiting Komsomol cells in the Army on the ground that they would be "violating the harmony and wholeness of the structural scheme of our armed forces." (This suggests that the Party still felt unsure of controlling Komsomol cells in the Army.) In each Army unit, League members were to be directly under the unit's Party cell. They were to attend the cell's open meetings (with voice, but no vote) and to follow its instructions, while at the same time fulfilling their Komsomol obligation to be models "of discipline, self-control, and consciousness [i.e., political orientation] to all Red Army men." [138] In spite of the outcome of the debate on the cells, it remains noteworthy that the delegates were permitted to disagree openly on an issue so closely bound up with military and Party policy.

Premilitary training, that is, the physical and political preparation of youths before their actual military service, was being handled at this time by the agencies of Universal Military Training. Although the details of the League's work were not made clear, it appeared that its role in assisting this program was meant to be considerable, both in regard to physical education and political indoctrination.[139]

"Patronage" (*shefstvo*) or sponsorship was, in this period, the most significant innovation of the League in the military sphere. It was at the Fifth Congress that the Komsomol voted to assume "patronage" of the Red Navy (October 16, 1922).[140] Behind this action lay the regime's determination to revitalize the fleet—partly in view of the Kronstadt uprising of 1921. (Already in the spring of 1922, over 2,000 Komsomolites had been sent to naval service.) [141] Explaining what "patronage" would involve, the Congress in its announcement first told

Komsomolites who were in the Navy to "be the best fighting element in the Navy, serve as an example to all young sailors." To the other sailors, the announcement said that the Komsomol was preparing to establish close "moral and material ties" with them, "to help and support" them, and to ease their life. To all Komsomolites and all toiling youth, the appeal was "daily to help the Red Navy and its sailors: to correspond with sailors, to help their families, to take up collections and arrange allotments, and to propagate the idea of creating a mighty Red war fleet." [142] The League would help to end the "caste spirit, the spirit of isolation, of seclusion, and of group haughtiness" which still lingered "in certain nooks and crannies of our Navy as a trace of the past." [143] Trotsky, as Commissar for Naval Affairs, sought to answer the objections of some who thought this whole business sounded militaristic: "Militarism that is built with the voluntary conscious participation of worker and peasant youth is not militarism, but rather is a weapon for the liberation of the toiling masses [!]." [144]

The Fifth Congress also announced one of the early extensions of the institution of "patronage." The representatives of the Ukraine announced that their Komsomol organizations had assumed "patronage" over the corps of Red Cossacks and had already sent some 600 volunteers into its ranks.[145]

In the realm of world affairs, it was conceded at the Fourth Congress that the World Revolution had not come as rapidly as had been expected. The bourgeoisie, said Trotsky, would "only fall when the working class, organized and class-conscious, can take it by the throat, knock it down, and strangle it." [146] But Trotsky saw no immediate prospect of this. What Soviet Russia needed now, he explained, was peace, and this need was dictated by "cold state calculation." [147] Both Trotsky and Zinoviev painted a picture of a threatening capitalist enemy waiting to attack the Soviet Union.[148] Even the Western efforts of that time to aid the famine victims in Russia were depicted as part of the same diabolic bourgeois plot.[149] While the strength of the Soviet regime and the influence of the European proletariat were adduced to show that an immediate attack on Russia was not likely,[150] each Komsomolite was urged to be aware of his responsibility for the eventual success of the world-wide Revolution.[151] A year later that goal was again mentioned prominently.[152] However, Radek alone hazarded a specific prediction, asserting that within thirty years the Revolution would have triumphed "in all the centers of the industrial world." [153]

The Komsomol obligation to guide the Communist International of Youth was recalled at both congresses. At the Fourth Congress Shatskin, then the most prominent Komsomol representative in the CIY, gave a long report.[154] He told of building up Young Communist Leagues in Europe, Asia, Africa, and the Americas, while at the same time eliminating various sorts of oppositionists.[155] The total membership in the CIY, including the Russian Komsomol, now stood at about 800,000, he stated, the largest numbers being in countries (like Russia) where the youth movement was new, rather than in the countries of Western Europe which had had youth movements for some time. Competitors for the allegiance of proletarian youth had arisen in the shape of the "International of Working Youth" (affiliated with the "Amsterdam International") and the "Two-and-a-Half International of Youth" (belonging to the "Two-and-a-Half International"). Shatskin said Communists were working secretly within the "yellow" (i.e., in Bolshevik eyes, procapitalist) trade-union movement and the "yellow" youth movement, in order to prevent the "yellows" from collaborating closely with each other.[156]

Shatskin reported that the Third Congress of the Comintern (June–July, 1921), after ascertaining that the revolutionary wave had subsided in Europe for the time being, had instructed Communists everywhere to campaign for those things (such as higher wages and shorter hours) that interested the average worker, and thus to win the proletariat to the long-term Communist program.[157] As to youth, the Third Comintern Congress had decreed that the youth leagues would no longer concern themselves with political leadership but would "turn their face to the masses of worker youth," concentrate on propagandizing the masses, and become "mass organizations." [158] In accordance with this directive, the CIY at its subsequent (Second) Congress had instructed its branches to stop trying to be independent of their respective Communist Parties. The aim, said Shatskin, was "the annihilation of the remnants of the old democratic strivings among youth." [159]

Shatskin's account accentuated the role of the Russian Komsomol in controlling the CIY. The Russian representatives had beaten down the idea of Austrian youths and others who wanted to organize "youth sections in the trade unions" as a means of reaching non-Communist worker youth. The main reason for the Russian view, Shatskin frankly admitted, was that such "youth sections" could not always be controlled by Communists in trade unions where the "yellows" were strong. Where youth sections already existed, the young Communists were to work from within them.[160] A hard battle had been fought, Shatskin recounted, over moving the headquarters of the CIY from Berlin to Moscow. When European youth delegates had argued that Moscow was too far away for good contact, the Russian reply as reported by Shatskin was that if the Executive Committee of the CIY remained in Berlin, "then it would make many mistakes." Even if its directives did not reach the local organizations as well from Moscow as from Berlin, he said, "perhaps an absence of directives is better than the existence of poor directives." [161] Difficulties had also arisen over the Soviet wish that the Second Congress of the CIY be held in Moscow. The CIY Executive Committee, elected by the First (Berlin) Congress, flouted the Soviet wish and held a second Congress in Jena, Germany. But the Russian Komsomol did not take part, and when subsequently the more faithful CIY delegates assembled in Moscow, the Jena Congress was declared a "mistake," and the Moscow meeting was officially termed the Second Congress of the CIY.[162] The Fourth Congress of the Komsomol praised Shatskin and the other Komsomol representatives for increasing the influence of the Komsomol within the CIY.[163]

One year later Shatskin reported to the Fifth Congress that the CIY had progressed toward still tighter centralization and discipline.[164] Shatskin also explained that the obligation of each Young Communist League to obey the Communist Party of its own country (as well as the CIY) was in force only when the native Communist Party was obeying the Comintern [165] (which in turn had been made subservient to the Russian Communist Party). Thus the Soviet leaders sought to prevent any contradictions from arising through their use of multiple chains of command from the Politburo out through both Comintern and CIY channels to the local Young Communist Leagues.

The Fifth Congress also clarified the question whether the Komsomolite should be patriotic. Apparently there had been some misunderstandings on this point. Radek explained that nationalism, defined by him as "a striving to oppose other peoples," was taboo. But patriotism was different; it was "a sense of love toward that country which first raised its hand against the rule of capital"; it was not contrary to internationalism, he asserted, for the interests of the international proletariat required that "the first country of the victorious proletariat be strong." He told the delegates that "your internationalism demands that you be Soviet patriots." And he went on to say that

our task does not end with the defense of our country. We . . . still will have a tremendous task—the task of giving help to the working men and women of other countries when they find themselves in battle with an adversary who is learning from the experience of our Revolution and who is arming himself from head to toe against the working class. In the future, having emerged from the ruins, having healed our wounds, we must fulfill our task and obligation with respect to the world proletariat. For this is needed a strong, healthy Russia, able to defend her international frontiers.[166]

In these remarks Radek gave another clear indication that under favorable circumstances the Soviet regime intended to take the offensive, and that Komsomolites should be prepared for that eventuality.

Both the Fourth and the Fifth congresses offered the opportunity for real disagreements to be expressed and for closely contested votes to be taken.[167] Criticism of the Central Committee was plentiful at both congresses. Much of it merely took the CC to task for not doing enough of something—such as being vigilant against deviationists or maintaining contact with the lower echelons.[168] But some of the criticism was sharp. At the Fourth Congress, for example, one delegate accused the CC of lying,[169] another implied that the CC was an instrument of Muscovite domination over Ukrainians,[170] while still another was so crude and sarcastic toward the CC that the delegates became unruly (it is not clear whom they supported) and the chairman had to call for order.[171]

Some rather eminent individuals were exposed to criticism, including Lunacharskii, Preobrazhenskii, and Bukharin.[172] When Bukharin resorted to sarcasm to undercut his critics, one of them was bold enough to shout: "Shame on Bukharin for using demagogy!" [173] Even Krupskaia, Lenin's wife, was not immune from criticism, although it was expressed courteously.[174] Some excesses were checked. A severe critic of Lunacharskii was reprimanded (by both Lunacharskii and Ryvkin) for making irresponsible charges.[175] The critics of Preobrazhenskii were accused (by Shatskin) of having exhibited "a very serious deviation." [176] And at the Fifth Congress certain sharp-tongued spokesmen for the so-called Ukrainian Opposition were rebuked by both Smorodin and Shatskin for being "unbusinesslike" in their criticism.[177] On the other hand, Komsomolites could see that some sorts of "criticism"—such as the complaints that the Central Committee was not giving precise enough guidance to the lower echelons, or was not controlling the League tightly enough—were beyond reproach.[178] For cautious Komsomolites, the way to criticize safely was being marked.

The elections of officers were fairly mechanical. The Presidium and other administrative bodies of the Fourth Congress were apparently all elected by list (that is, not individually) and without discussion.[179] The same appears to have been true for the new Central Committee; at least no discussion is recorded.[180] At the Fifth Congress the Presidium was elected with similar dispatch.[181] But in the election of the new Central Committee the machine balked momentarily. The chairman, Smorodin, read the list of nominees, including two men, Leonov and Petrovskii, identified as representing the CC of the Party.[182] Then came the following demonstration of election technique:

Chairman: Are there objections to any comrade?
Voice: Why isn't Comrade Shokhin [a member of the outgoing CC] entered on the list?
Chairman: It would have been necessary to nominate him [apparently at some earlier meeting], but not to raise this question now. He wasn't entered because they [presumably the Party fraction or a nominating group] didn't consider it necessary to enter him. I shall put to a vote the acceptance of this list as a basis. Who is for this list as a basis? Adopted. Are there any changes or challenges of the candidacies?
Voice: I nominate Comrade Shokhin instead of Comrade Petrovskii. [Evidently the acceptance of the list as a basis meant that to nominate a new candidate one had to challenge another.]
Chairman: Are there any other challenges? No. Shokhin withdraws his candidacy.

The anonymous voice from the floor continued to argue for Shokhin. The chairman repeated, without any apparent consultation with Shokhin himself, that Shokhin was not a candidate. However, the chairman did then put to a vote the question of removing Petrovskii. As one would expect in view of Petrovskii's previous designation as a special nominee of the CC of the Party, he was retained. But the voice from the floor would not be stilled:

Voice: I nominate Comrade Shokhin and move that the vote be taken not by list, by person-to-person.
Chairman: The list has been adopted as a basis. I now put to a vote the list as a whole. No one is opposed. Five abstentions. Next is the election of candidate-members . . .[183]

And he proceeded to the next order of business (which witnessed similar interruptions and similar results). The reader's
initial reaction is to nod knowingly and to mutter, "Steam-
roller!" But in order to appreciate the significance of the subsequent developments in Komsomol procedure, it must be
emphasized here that (1) as of 1922 a Komsomol delegate was
able to speak from the floor without identifying himself; (2)
he could persist in nominating someone who was evidently
not wanted by the ruling circles; (3) he was not afraid to challenge the nomination of a candidate labeled as having been
presented by the CC of the *Party;* (4) five delegates were bold
enough to abstain from voting, in the face of strong pressure
from the leadership for an affirmative vote; and (5) this whole
exchange, in spite of its damaging implications for Komsomol
democracy, was published as late as 1927.

The statistics that were published concerning the delegates
at the Fourth Congress provided a fuller view than ever before
of a segment of the leadership of the League.[184] There were
471 voting delegates (plus 143 without vote, giving a total of
614). Only 3 percent (or fourteen) of these were women, indicating that the idea of bringing women into positions of leadership in the League was still not an operating principle. The
voting delegates were relatively young: only 2 percent of them
were over the upper age limit of twenty-three, and those older
ones were only twenty-four and twenty-five. Just over 76 percent were in the age group from eighteen through twenty-one,
inclusive. Nineteen-year-olds were most heavily represented.
Twenty-six percent of the delegates were "veterans" who had
joined the League in its first months, before 1919. The im-
mensity of the educational task that lay ahead was suggested
by the fact that among the delegates only about 38 percent had
received secondary-school education, including those (only 1
percent) who had attended a higher educational institution.
Eighteen percent of the delegates were listed as Jewish (about
nine times as large as the proportion of Jews in the population
as a whole), while 62 percent were either Great Russian,
Ukrainian, or Belorussian.[185]

Whatever freedom there was in debate by no means obscured the ruling principle of Party control. It was evidenced
not only in the elections of officers but also in other ways. One
was the Party's promotion of certain key figures from Komsomol work to Party work. Lazar' Shatskin, Oskar Ryvkin,
Andrei Shokhin, and Efim Tseitlin were among those whose
transfer was announced at the Fifth Congress. In celebration
of the event, they and five other prominent retiring Komsomol
leaders were voted the title of "Honorary Komsomolite." [186]
The proportion of Party members among the delegates at the
Fourth Congress was somewhere between 79 and 90 percent.[187]
Although no complete statistics were given on the delegates
at the Fifth Congress, partial indications suggest that the proportion there was roughly the same.[188] Several formal measures
taken by both congresses also emphasized the Komsomolites'
obligation to follow the Party's leadership. The Komsomol
Regulations of 1920 had provided that the units of the League
were to establish "mutual relations" with the corresponding
Party units. The new Regulations as revised by the Fourth
Congress were more specific:

61. The CC of the RCLY [Russian Communist League of Youth]
is directly subordinated to the CC of the RCP [Russian Communist
Party]. The local organizations of the RCLY work under the control of the corresponding raion, uezd, guberniia, and oblast organizations of the RCP; [this control by the Party is] effected through
[its] representation on the committees of the RCLY.[189]

The Fourth Congress also issued a new Statute on the Inter-
relations of the RCP and the RCLY. In it, the role of the
Party's representative on the committees (that is, the executive bodies) of the League at the local, district, and provincial
levels was explained more fully than before:

9. The representative of the Party in the committee of the RCLY
is present at all sessions of the latter, at all meetings, conferences,
and so forth, takes part in settling all questions, making known
the Party's viewpoint on all questions under consideration, and
issues actual instructions in the [course of the League's] work. Each
month he reports to the [corresponding] Party committee on his
work and on the condition of the League.[190]

Beyond this, two "experienced Party workers" were to be assigned to each uezd (moderately small district) Komsomol organization to supervise "political education." [191] The financial support of the League was now declared to be wholly the task of the Party committee at each level, and all the financial and economic apparatus within the League was to be abolished.[192] It was again provided that all Party members up to the age of twenty *must* be active members of the Komsomol.[193] Special administrative procedures were prescribed for handling those Komsomolites who were simultaneously members of the Party, the fundamental principle being that they were to be kept "on a special roster of the League, as attached personnel," and held at the disposition of higher agencies of the League and the Party.[194] The Fifth Congress introduced the significant requirement that secretaries of Komsomol committees for the guberniia (large unit or province) must have been members of the Party for at least one year (or two years if they were intelligentsia). At the uezd echelon, all secretaries except those of the "worker" class had to have been members of the Party for at least one year.[195]

The mildly accentuated recognition of Party control was not accompanied by any marked tendency to idolize the top leaders of the Party and the state. True, such figures as Lenin, Trotsky, and Zinoviev were not criticized. Lenin, who was not present at either Congress but sent a greeting to the Fifth, was referred to on that occasion as "the glorious leader of the international proletariat." [196] The honorary chairmen elected by the Fourth Congress were Lenin, Trotsky, and Zinoviev (listed in that order).[197] At the Fifth Congress they were Lenin, Trotsky, Zinoviev, Bukharin, and Kalinin (in that order).[198] Thus Lenin was listed first both times. But aside from what has been cited here, Lenin was not given special recognition. Leader-worship was not yet one of the traits required of the good Komsomolite.

While the fundamental character of the Komsomol pattern persisted in the early years of the New Economic Policy, the proceedings of the congresses of 1921 and 1922 reveal certain changes. After the failure of World Revolution abroad and the failure of War Communism at home, the NEP marked a real retreat, whose effects the Komsomol could not escape. The revival of private enterprise—in trade, small industry, and farming—undermined Komsomol strength on the one hand by disheartening and demoralizing those youths who were ardently pro-Communist and, on the other hand, by placing new alternatives before those who were on the fringes of the youth movement. By 1922 the Komsomol enrollment was reportedly less than two-thirds of what it had been in 1920, and in the rural areas the number of Komsomol cells was reduced by roughly half.

In the face of those difficulties, the Komsomol had emphasized and extended its demands in some respects. In the effort to foster Komsomol solidarity and a "proletarian" morality that would not succumb to "bourgeois" temptations, the League had striven to stimulate a sense of proletarian honor and had endorsed rules of conduct that frowned on the use of alcohol or tobacco, as well as on sexual looseness. In order further to prevent the League from being infected with "bourgeois" attitudes, barriers had been raised against those who were not "proletarian": whereas admission continued without special restriction for "workers" and most "peasants," in 1921 a six-month probationary stage had been introduced for "others," including "intelligentsia"; and in 1922 the probationary period had been lengthened to one year, while "middle peasants" had been added to the doubtful category. For the sake of strengthening the "proletarian kernel" of the League and reinforcing the League's bonds with young workers, Komsomolites had been told to do what they could, in collaboration with governmental and trade-union agencies, to improve the living and working conditions of worker youth. The League had also urged its members to foster the schools for worker youth, particularly by helping to furnish equipment, students, and teachers. Komsomol resources had been enlisted to meet the problem of the hordes of homeless waifs. The responsibility of

Komsomolites for organizing and indoctrinating children had been extended with the establishment of the Young Pioneers. In anticipation of future wars against capitalist powers, Komsomolites had been given the special duty of helping to build up the Red Navy. All of the foregoing elaborations and extensions of the initial Komsomol pattern, designed to meet the particular needs of the time, were evidently applied with the Party's approval or by its positive command.

But the Party's role had not been solely positive. It had also been a restraining force. Komsomolites who had tried to strengthen the League by weeding out all nonproletarian or lukewarm elements had been accused of a "serious deviation." Komsomol bodies had been emphatically told to stay out of governmental functions. The League's request for generous wages for minors had apparently been, in part at least, ignored. The efforts of Komsomolites to help worker youth had been checked by the leadership's insistence that all such activities be conducted only in full accord with other agencies of the regime, including the trade unions. The participation of some Komsomolites in strikes had been denounced as sabotage. When Komsomol delegates had attacked the government for spending too little money on education, or for favoring the old-style secondary schools, the sharpest criticisms—even when contained in resolutions formally voted by the delegates—had somehow been softened or eliminated in the official printing of the decisions. Komsomolites who wished to extend the League's influence by means of an athletic league had been forbidden to do so. Komsomolites had again been prohibited from forming cells in regular units of the Red Army. In those several ways, the members of the Komsomol had been curbed by the Party, or by Komsomol or government leaders who expressed the Party's command. In no phase of organization or activity could the good Komsomolite have failed to be aware of the controlling hand of the Party.

Yet that basic and undeniable fact is perhaps *not* the most significant characteristic of the Komsomol pattern in the early years of the NEP. More significant, especially in view of later developments, is that the vetoed attempts could be *made at all,* that criticism of policies could be *expressed* in a congress, that dissension and split votes could be *recorded* and *published,* and that the top leader could still be regarded as not much different from ordinary mortals. In those respects, the combined demands for Komsomol discipline in the early years of the NEP— the closing years of Lenin's rule—were not markedly heavier than they had been in the previous period.

IV. Adjustments during the Struggle for Power in the Party

THE CONGRESSES OF 1924 AND 1926

THE middle years of the New Economic Policy brought a growing prosperity, an expanding school system, and a general recovery from the wounds of war and revolution. Meanwhile, as Lenin faltered and died, his associates contended for power. Their contest reached beyond the Party and affected the demands upon youth in the Komsomol.

The enrollment of the League grew. From a low of perhaps 200,000 in mid-1922, and about 250,000 at the time of the Fifth Congress (October, 1922), the total climbed back to 400,000 by April, 1923.[1] (As before, all membership figures are understood to include both members and candidate-members, unless candidate-members are specifically excluded.) By the time of the Sixth Komsomol Congress (July 12–18, 1924, after the "Leninist levy" which brought in 170,000 members in honor of the departed chief) the membership rose to about 840,000.[2] A year later (June, 1925) it apparently jumped to 1,503,000;[3] by December 1, 1925, it had risen to 1,708,000,[4] and by the time of the Seventh Congress (March 11–22, 1926), to 1,750,000.[5] Using the data of the Soviet census of 1926, one may calculate that the Komsomol at this time comprised about 5.5 percent of all Soviet youths in the Komsomol age group (fourteen through twenty-two).[6] Since the proportion of men (81 percent) and women (19 percent) in the Komsomol was also given at the Congress of 1926,[7] one may calculate that the Komsomol then embraced about 9.2 percent of the males in the Komsomol age group and about 2 percent of the females.[8]

The name of the League was modified twice. The Sixth Congress, not long after Lenin's death, honored his memory by making the full designation "Russian *Leninist* Communist League of Youth," or RLCLY.[9] At the Seventh Congress it became the *"All-Union* Leninist Communist League of Youth," or ALCLY.[10] So the name remains to this day.

THE CAMPAIGN AGAINST DEVIATIONS

Nineteen twenty-three was the first year since the founding of the League in which no congress was held. Twenty-one months elapsed before the Sixth Congress.[11] That delay violated the Regulations, which ordered that a congress be held at least once a year. But no explanation or excuse was offered, even when the length of the interval was mentioned.[12] The most obvious delaying factor—the struggle within the Party—could not be openly blamed. At the opening session of the Sixth Congress, Chaplin rejoiced that the League since its last congress had recovered from its phase of decline and discouragement (1921–22) and had been growing steadily stronger.[13] It had passed successfully, he said, through the "great test" following the illness and death of Lenin and the critical days of the "Party discussion" (meaning the controversy between Trotsky and the Triumvirate—Zinoviev, Kamenev, and Stalin).[14]

The lessons that the good Komsomolite should have drawn from these experiences had to do in part with extirpating "deviations" which had appeared in the League during the fight.[15] Zinoviev, who at that time appeared to be one of Lenin's most likely heirs, warned the delegates against both the deviation that sought "to copy the Party" (especially in respect to influence) and the opposite extreme, "Komsomol syndicalism" or "chauvinism," expressed in the attitude, "the Komsomol for the Komsomolites." [16] Zinoviev also attacked the idea (which he attributed to the Opposition) that there was, between the Party and the Komsomol, a problem of an older and a younger generation, and that the Party, in accordance with intra-Party democracy, should give the younger generation the opportunity for " 'active . . . participation in the political life of the Party and the country.' " Zinoviev said the Thirteenth Party Congress (May 23–31, 1924) had denounced that view.[17]

Some Komsomolites, seeing the Party giants clash, and perhaps seeking a safe haven in the subordinate status of the League, had tried to stay out of the Party dispute. Their caution had led them into a different deviation, called "neutralism." It was assailed by both Zinoviev and Chaplin. Zinoviev admitted that the League should not take part in every Party discussion; but he maintained that in the recent Party dispute, where some Komsomolites had sided with the Opposition and had echoed its talk about the conflict between the generations, the Komsomol could not be "neutral." He said that the "mistake" (which had been made even by some members of the CC) had fortunately been corrected soon, and the League had come out "for the Party, for Leninism"—by which of course he meant the victorious faction to which he at that time belonged.[18] The correction of the "mistake" had been the work of the Plenum of the Komsomol Central Committee which was held in January, 1924.[19] But merely for the CC of the League to fall into line with the "Leninist" element in the Party had not been considered sufficient, and during the early months of 1924 a "League discussion" of the problem of "strengthening the Party's influence over the League" had been conducted throughout the Komsomol. In general, Chaplin reported, the League had successfully passed this "second test" (apparently an ideological cleansing process), despite disconcerting evidence of some "petit-bourgeois" individuals who had revealed thoughts about "the independence of the League from the Party." The worst area of "mutiny," however (in the Kuban'), had displayed an opposite exaggeration: many Komsomolites, in their zeal to condemn neutralism, had advocated "the discussion at League meetings of all the basic questions of Party work." True, conceded Chaplin, the Thirteenth Party Congress had demanded that "the Komsomol must not be neutral in the struggle against deviations in the RCP." But on the other hand, he said, "there may be moments when the Komsomol must not participate in the consideration of this or that question which the Party cannot discuss too widely." [20] Thus were the deviations—too much and too little discussion of Party issues—pointed out to the good Komsomolite. He must watch his step! When one delegate merely suggested that the "League discussion" had been unnecessarily prolonged to the detriment of other League work,[21] he was accused of opposing the Central Committee.[22] Clearly, the slightest resistance to the thought-purifying operation must have been treated as a sign of actual or potential revolt. The (unanimous) resolutions on both Chaplin's and Zinoviev's reports compliantly commended the "League discussion" for having eliminated wavering elements and having demonstrated the League's solid support for the "Bolshevik core" of the Party. Both resolutions warned against tendencies toward "independence" and toward "setting the League against the Party," and one resolution explicitly praised the increase in the "guidance" which the Party CC was giving to the League.[23]

The demand for ever closer control of the Komsomol by the Party was manifested also in certain amendments to the Komsomol Regulations approved by the Sixth Congress. Previously the Regulations had required that applicants for admission who were not workers or peasants (including some "middle peasants") must obtain the recommendation of two Komsomolites or Party members, each of at least two years' standing. Now an amendment required recommendations from two Komsomolites of three years' standing and one Party member of two years' standing, or two Party members of three years' standing. Thus two new elements were introduced: the requirement of sponsorship by at least one Party member and the equating of one Party man to two Komsomolites. In addition, the probationary period of candidate-members was lengthened from one, to one and one-half, years.[24] "Nonproletarians" would need to negotiate higher hurdles than before. Another significant group of amendments which tended to increase the Party's control were those concerning the amount of previous service in both League and Party which was required of Komsomol secretaries of guberniia committees and uezd committees. Along with a general extension of the required length of previous Party service, the most important innovation was that even persons of worker origin serving as uezd secretaries now had to have at least one year's Party membership behind them.[25]

No Komsomol congress was held in 1925, and almost twenty months passed before the Seventh Congress (March 11–22, 1926). Again, despite this flagrant violation of the official Regulations, no explanation was offered, but it seems not unreasonable to attribute the delay to the unsettled conditions within the Party, stemming from the continuing fight for leadership. Again it was Chaplin who opened the first session, dwelling on the controversy within the Party and the Komsomol's reaction thereto. He said the Komsomol had successfully passed two "political tests" during the period since the previous congress. One was the League's repulsion of Trotsky's "anti-Leninist attempts" in connection with his book *Lessons of October*. The second was "the struggle against new anti-Leninist deviations, the struggle against the New Opposition, which manifested itself at the Fourteenth Congress of the Party." [26] (It was at the Fourteenth Party Congress, December 18–31, 1925, that Stalin won acceptance of the doctrine of "socialism in one country" and used it to improve his position in the struggle for power.) [27] As the Seventh Komsomol Congress unfolded, the delegates witnessed moments of exciting drama and developments profoundly significant for the members of the Komsomol.

In his report for the Central Committee, Chaplin identified the "mistakes" of the New Opposition that had arisen in the Komsomol (as well as in the Party) since the preceding Congress. Fundamental to all the other mistakes was "lack of faith in the victory of socialist construction," said Chaplin, quoting Stalin. This lack of confidence had been expressed in demands for "leveling" (that is, reducing wage differentials) and in protests that the workers were being exploited—ideas dangerous

to the morale of young and impressionable Komsomolites.[28]
The second mistake was the "underestimation of the middle
peasant." Zinoviev, who was blamed for this error, had advocated using "delegates' meetings of middle-peasant youth"
in order to influence such youths without taking them all into
the League. Such a device, Chaplin asserted, might have led to
a split between the "middle peasants" and the "poor peasants,"
and the "middle peasants" might have allied themselves with
the "kulaks"; hence that proposal had to be combated.[29] The
third big mistake of the Komsomol Opposition, Chaplin went
on, was "pitting the Komsomol against the Party." In docu-
menting this charge, Chaplin went back to certain writings of
Leningrad Komsomolites in the spring of 1925. One writer had
said that the most revolutionary organization in the struggle
against Trotskyism was the Komsomol, while another had declared that the CIY (Communist International of Youth) had
come out against Trotsky one month earlier than the Comintern. Chaplin saw evil implications in these remarks. They recalled the outmoded "vanguard of the vanguard" concept.
They implied, he said, the inadmissible "theory of the equality
of the Komsomol and the Party." An allied mistake, made by
Tarkhanov, a prominent Komsomolite, had been to question
whether Party guidance was in itself an adequate safeguard of
the League's "proletarian" character. Chaplin stated the official
position:

You know that our line has been as follows: The League is a proletarian organization in its class composition; consequently the
leading role in the League belongs to worker youth. But worker
youth, which fulfills the leading role in the Komsomol, cannot by
itself preserve the correct proletarian policies; worker youth can
preserve the correct proletarian policies only under the guidance
of the Party, the highest form of class organization of the proletariat.[30]

Chaplin related, further, that on January 14, 1926, the bureau
of the Leningrad guberniia committee of the Komsomol had
failed to acknowledge as correct the decisions of the recently
completed Fourteenth Party Congress. Said Chaplin: *"Never
was there such a fact in the history of the Komsomol move-*

ment, when a Komsomol organization refused to recognize as correct a decision of a higher body of the Party." [31] Chaplin declared that although the Komsomol Opposition in Leningrad had claimed to speak in the name of all the young workers of Leningrad, it had really embraced only the *aktiv* or active element, the "upper layer"; the Leningrad *aktiv* had not practiced enough "democracy" in its Komsomol organization and thereby had "lost contact" with the "masses." To remedy that error, representatives of the Komsomol Central Committee had worked in Leningrad during January and February, 1926. With their "help," Chaplin related, the bulk of the Leningrad Komsomol had quickly condemned the old *aktiv,* whereupon a new, "sound" *aktiv* "came forward almost immediately." Along with that neat example of Komsomol spontaneity, Chaplin cited a fourth mistake—the attempt of Leningrad Komsomolites to call a country-wide conference in their city. This was, said Chaplin, a nefarious attempt to set up a second center of authority in the League, which "would mean the dissolution of the League." [32]

The discussion of Chaplin's report was unusually long, extending through four sessions and thirty-seven separate speeches.[33] Some members of the Komsomol Opposition wanted a chance to defend themselves. The preservation of Leninism required that they be overwhelmed.

The first few speakers praised the Central Committee for routing the Opposition.[34] Then came Tarasov, one of the members of the CC who had been accused of siding with the Opposition. Tarasov first denied that there had been any intent to exclude middle peasants from the League. He and his colleagues, he said, had merely been criticizing what they thought were manifestations (particularly on the part of Gorlov, also a member of the CC) of a tendency to undervalue the proletarian core of the League.[35] Tarasov next charged a subversion of democracy within the CC: twenty members of that body, he asserted, had been prevented from attending this Congress by having been conveniently "removed from League work." His biting humor brought forth what seemed to be a sympathetic laugh from the delegates, whereupon the chairman (Sobolev) reprimanded them with a curt "What are you laughing at?" Tarasov came to the defense of the Leningrad *aktiv,* complaining: "As a result of a disagreement in which this Leningrad *aktiv* turned out to be in the minority, they [the leaders] at once declare that it [the minority view] is anti-Party, anti-Lenin, and so on." He protested that some of the defeated minority were being taken out of Komsomol work and ousted from their jobs in factories and plants. "There is our democracy! When was there anything like that in our League? . . . Criticize on principle the position of the minority, and oppose to it your own line, but don't fall back on that kind of democracy." Tarasov's speech was interrupted at many points by shouts and challenges from Chaplin and from the audience. A good deal of tension must have been in the air. The delegates voted to let Tarasov exceed the normal time limit, and they gave him some applause at the end.[36]

A repentant Oppositionist, Fedorov, spoke next. A member of the CC, and formerly second secretary of the Leningrad *gubkom* (guberniia committee), he presented the delegates with a full confession. He said the Oppositionists, including himself, had indeed feared the influx of middle peasants into the League; they had criticized among themselves the policy of the majority of the Komsomol CC and of the Party; they had to some extent actually attempted to persuade other members of the Leningrad Komsomol to support their view (!). Now, he said, he could see what serious mistakes these had been.[37] Fedorov was followed by several others who spoke against the Opposition.[38] One of them made the point that confession was a prerequisite to pardon: "Amnesty in our League and our Party can be granted only when a comrade admits his mistake." [39]

But some were still not ready to confess. One of these, Katalynov, next defended himself in a well-reasoned speech received with applause and friendly laughter by the delegates. He, too, was given extra time to state his case.[40] The gist of Katalynov's argument was that the so-called Opposition in

Leningrad did *not* challenge the principle of Party leadership of the Komsomol, that it did *not* want to pit the young against the old, that it did *not* disagree with the policy of admitting the best elements of the middle peasantry; but granting that, there still remained the questions of *what proportion* of the middle peasantry would be taken in and *through what means* the Komsomol would influence the rest; it was in this connection that the proposal of "delegates' assemblies of middle-peasant youth" had been made. Katalynov said he personally disapproved of that particular device. But what had happened, he said, was that when the Leningrad organization was discussing this question, "rapid-fire weapons" had suddenly been turned against Leningrad and against the idea of delegates' assemblies; a big noise had been made over an idea which the Leningrad Komsomolites did not fully approve but which they were discussing as one possible solution for the difficult problem of how the League was to influence the mass of non-Komsomol peasant youth. Intra-Komsomol democracy had been violated, he charged. Naming eleven members of the Central Committee, he asked why they had been removed from their Komsomol posts and where they had been sent. He inquired about large-scale removals of Komsomol leaders in Leningrad, Moscow, and the Ukraine. Boldly he decried the attitude that was being introduced into the minds of Komsomol members:

There is being instilled in them this kind of psychology: Whom are you for? A Stalinist or a non-Stalinist? If he's not a Stalinist, push him down, suppress him, put him where he can't make a peep. *We must fight against such a psychology. This kind of thing in our League has nothing in common with Leninist upbringing, and it must be made clear that our League is not Stalinist but Leninist.*[41]

The stubborn Katalynov was followed by a penitent former Oppositionist who now confessed that "delegates' assemblies of middle-peasant youth" would have been wrong because they would have permitted middle peasants to assemble by themselves. He also conceded that the Opposition, by inviting representatives of seventeen other Komsomol bodies to a meeting in Leningrad and by trying to persuade other Komsomolites that the Opposition was right, had tried to split the League and had challenged the Party's control over it.[42]

One other nonconfessing Oppositionist (Minaev) spoke in his own defense,[43] after which Sobolev took the floor. Sobolev was apparently a Leningrad leader who had not sided with the Opposition. He claimed to give the inside story of the shocking incident in which the Bureau of the Leningrad *gubkom* had failed to endorse the decisions of the Fourteenth Party Congress. What had happened, as he told it, was that the Bureau had passed a resolution which called upon all Komsomolites under its jurisdiction to *obey* and *support* those decisions. But it had rejected Sobolev's proposal to affirm, in addition, that it *approved* the decisions of the Party. This, Sobolev maintained, constituted a "march against the Party." [44] In other words, mere obedience was not enough; active approval was required. The next speaker (Matveev) clarified this further, explaining: "The guiding role of the Party cannot be understood to mean that I have one opinion about the Party's decisions for myself but another opinion which, in compliance with Party discipline, I export to the masses." [45] Another supporter of the orthodox position, Mil'chakov, undertook to reply to Katalynov's assertion that the League was not Stalinist but Leninist.

Yes, our League is Leninist: it works under the guidance of the Party of Lenin, under the guidance of the CC of the ACP [All-Union Communist Party]. But why did Katalynov need to bring in the name of the general secretary of the Party, Stalin? Where does Katalynov's sally lead? In my opinion, this is a new and most abominable *assault* against the CC of our Party. (Applause.) [46]

Mil'chakov went on to declare ominously that since none of the other delegates would accept the Opposition view, the Oppositionists merely by speaking at the Congress were really appealing to the "masses" outside of the Congress and were thus undermining Party unity.[47] That thought was seconded by Saltanov, one of several other delegates who then took their turns at whipping the dissenters.[48]

Chaplin, in his concluding remarks, stated clearly the official position on intra-Komsomol democracy:

You think that if we proclaim intra-Komsomol democracy in the League, then this means that we will permit you to spit wherever you want and do whatever you want? No. Intra-Komsomol democracy is intended as a means for the correct Leninist rearing of youth, and so if you, Comrade Katalynov, Comrade Tarasov, and Comrade Minaev, do not promote the correct Leninist rearing of youth, then intra-Komsomol democracy in regard to you consists in throwing you out.

And if they protested, he said, they were challenging not merely the CC of the Komsomol but the CC of the Party.[49]

The last act of this drama at the Seventh Congress came during the closing session, when the resolution on the report of the CC was presented for the approval of the delegates. The resolution was devoted chiefly to condemning the "New Opposition." [50] As soon as Matveev had finished reading the resolution, Tarasov presented a statement on behalf of himself and five other members of the outgoing CC (Minaev, Katalynov, Rogov, Teremiakina, and Kolmakov). These persons declared that they recognized as binding upon them all decisions taken by the Congress of the Komsomol. They said they had *not* wanted to undermine the Party's guidance in the League and did *not* underestimate the middle peasant. However, they criticized Matveev's resolution for not giving enough attention to the problem of maintaining the proletarian nature of the League and for not treating fully enough the matter of intra-Komsomol democracy. They declared that in stating their opinion they did not think they were violating Bolshevik discipline. Matveev retorted by characterizing their statement as a lie. Then the chairman, Mil'chakov, took over. He at first proposed that the Congress refuse to consider Tarasov's statement. When Tarasov protested that no one could prevent him from placing the statement on record, Mil'chakov proposed that "the Congress brushes aside as hypocritical the statement of the Opposition." This "resolution" he then declared to have been passed "unanimously"—without even giving an opportunity for any negative votes to be cast.[51] Those misguided Komsomolites who earlier had laughed sympathetically with the Opposition could not have missed the point of the lesson.

The spirit that inspired the hunt for deviationists in the Komsomol was naturally manifested in other ways. It is not irrelevant that among the delegates at both the Sixth and Seventh congresses the proportion of Party members and candidate-members was reported to be over 97 percent,[52] which was higher than at any previous congress. (In the Komsomol membership at large, the "Party kernel" remained at about one-tenth during the years 1924–26.) [53] Meanwhile a significant change took place in the presidiums (elected by list and unanimously) that managed each congress. At the Sixth Congress the Presidium contained forty-five persons; at the Seventh, sixty-three.[54] Previous presidiums, in contrast, had ranged from seven to fifteen members; [55] that is, they had been groups of workable size which actually could have steered the proceedings. The sudden jump to forty-five and sixty-three suggests that the Presidium was to have even less actual power than before and was to be used increasingly for honoring certain delegates and for disseminating decisions made by a small group of representatives of the Party. The same kind of inflation affected the Central Committees (which were also elected by list, without discussion, and "unanimously"). The sixth CC numbered fifty-one, plus sixteen candidate-members, while the seventh included sixty-nine members and twenty-four candidate-members. These were huge compared with previous Central Committees, which had never exceeded twenty-six members and candidate-members combined.[56]

Within those big Central Committees, a small core of key people provided continuity. Although Zinoviev (at the Sixth Congress) demanded a "fairly frequent change in the leaders of the Komsomol," to move them upward into the Party "once or twice a year," [57] and although most members of the Komsomol CC served only one or two terms, a selected few trusted Party members remained on longer assignments in the League's governing body. On the third CC (elected in 1920), there had been two such holdovers—Shatskin and Ryvkin, each for the third term; on the fourth CC (elected in 1921), only one—Shatskin, for his fourth term; and on the fifth CC (elected in 1922), three—Smorodin, Zabirov, and Kurellia, each for his third term. On the sixth CC (elected in 1924), despite the vastly swollen size of the body as a whole, there were only four men held over for third terms—Mil'chakov, Fedorov, Faivilovich, and Chaplin.[58] On the seventh CC (elected in 1926), Mil'-chakov, Fedorov, and Chaplin were reelected to their fourth consecutive terms, while Shatskin was brought back (after an absence of two terms) for a fifth, and a new third termer, Sorokin, was included.[59] It seems safe to assume that the individuals named had particularly heavy responsibilities to ensure Party control over the League.

The voting on issues seemed more mechanical than in previous congresses. At the Congress of 1924, most of the resolutions were passed unanimously and without noteworthy discussion.[60] However, there were some disagreements and at least one divided vote (probably more than one, but the indication is not precise).[61] At the Congress of 1926, aside from the rejection of the Opposition statement recounted above, and one very minor matter, the votes on resolutions were either unanimous or without apparent contest.[62]

"Criticism" at the congresses of 1924 and 1926 was generally milder than before. Most of the criticism in 1924 was delivered in a restrained manner and acknowledged similarly.[63] The representatives of the Commissariats of Agriculture (Sviderskii) and Education (Pokrovskii) were assailed,[64] but Bukharin was not.[65] At the Congress of 1926, in the course of the debate with the Opposition, the belief in "socialism in one country" (and attendant formulas) became a prime test of orthodoxy. The savageness with which doubters were attacked showed that the good Komsomolite must now be more careful than before to watch the statements of the Party leaders. He must be alert to detect the sort of utterance that might become a matter of

Party dogma, and to express wholehearted approval. The battle with the Opposition exacerbated the discussions of peasant youth, assistance to worker youth, and intra-Komsomol democracy.[66] Otherwise, where orthodoxy was not at issue, the criticism was humdrum [67] and often was merely a plea for more of some obviously permissible thing, like Party guidance.[68] The only high Party official who addressed the Seventh Congress in person was Bukharin (then prospering as an ally of Stalin against Zinoviev). The delegates (as in 1924) were given no opportunity to criticize Bukharin after his report.[69] A lesser official (Kamenskii), representing the Supreme Economic Council, was attacked, but on a minor issue.[70]

The heightened restrictions on criticism were not at this stage accompanied by demands for glorification of the top Bolshevik leadership. Lenin's name was increasingly used as a term of approbation, but he was dead. Furthermore, Krupskaia argued strongly against making an "icon" out of Lenin or any other revolutionary leader. She said Lenin would rather have been *read* than glorified.[71] The Sixth Congress, in a gesture toward the top, elected as "Honorary Komsomolites" Zinoviev, Stalin, Bukharin, and Krupskaia, in that order.[72] At the Seventh Congress, aside from the remarks about Stalin made during the debate with the Opposition, apparently only one delegate pointed explicitly to Stalin as someone whose suggestions should be followed.[73] Both congresses closed ceremonially with references to the League and to the Party, but not to individual leaders of the Party.[74]

In the lower echelons of the League, the exorcising of Oppositionist spirits made it mandatory that rank-and-file Komsomolites denounce suspected deviationists promptly—without (it was said) waiting for a signal from one of the leaders.[75] (Apparently some Komsomolites were learning discipline too well!) Another principle, illustrated in the Leningrad case above, was the obligation of lower-echelon groups to remove, by the initiative of the "masses," those local leaders who fell out with the victorious faction in the Party.[76] In only two cases was it openly admitted that the Party CC had intervened to remove an Oppositionist.[77] The process of removal by the "mass" was rather transparently described by a Central Asian delegate, who said that "when we, under the guidance of the CC and with the materials of the CC, became acquainted with their [i.e., the Oppositionists'] line, then we ourselves, wholly supporting the CC, posed the question of removing these [Oppositionist] comrades." [78]

Lest such treatment of Oppositionists give some Komsomolites the wrong idea about intra-League democracy, several delegates took pains (in 1926) to insist that that democracy was being preserved intact. Democracy was not (it was said) concerned with such things as that "over there somewhere they removed another comrade who was opposing the definite Party line," but was rather a matter of assuring the "mass discussion of all current questions on the basis of a definite political Party line." [79] Attention was turned to the preservation of "democracy" in the election of Komsomol officials, the official formula being that the elections to Komsomol committees were to be "free elections," "without any kind of pressure or lists." [80] At the same time, higher Komsomol bodies were castigated for *not* participating in the elections of the bureaus and other directing bodies of lower echelons! The approved view seemed to be that "the carrying out of intra-League democracy does not at all mean a weakening of the guidance of the higher bodies of our League." [81]

The qualities of individual character demanded in 1924 and 1926 reflected that attitude toward intra-League democracy. Appropriately, since the debates in these congresses ostensibly involved theoretical differences, the principal trait demanded of Komsomolites was faithfulness to Leninist theory. Such prominent leaders as Krupskaia, Bukharin, Kalinin, and Chaplin said that theory was not to be learned as dogma but as a guide in following and applying the Party line, and as a criterion for distinguishing between things fundamental (which could not be yielded) and things secondary (on which concessions could be made in order to gain the objective).[82] While the principle of correctly interpreting Marxist-Leninist theory was thus, in a sense, placed above the principle of obeying Party directives, it is plain that since the Party leadership could enforce its claim to possess the only correct interpretation, the two ideas were mutually reinforcing. Moreover, the emphasis on interpretation made it easier to attack Komsomolites who might be considered to be carrying out the letter of a Party directive but misconstruing its spirit. Mere obedience, while necessary, was not enough: it must be accompanied by active enthusiasm for the Party line.[83]

Buttressing the new emphasis on theory were the standard demands for unity and solidarity,[84] inward and conscious discipline,[85] and militant Bolshevism.[86] Meanwhile the demand for spontaneity was preserved.[87] The persistent principle of allowing no separation between political and private life was emphatically restated (at the Sixth Congress) by Krupskaia:

We live in an era when we already understand clearly that personal life cannot be separated from life in society. In former times it was perhaps not clear that such a break between personal and public life sooner or later leads a person to betray the cause of Communism. We must now strive to tie our personal life to the cause of the struggle, the cause of the building of Communism.

This does not of course mean that we must reject personal life. The Party of Communism is not a sect, and therefore must not preach asceticism. In one factory I happened to hear how a working girl told her fellow workers: "Comrade working girls, you must remember that once you enter the Party you must refuse to have husband or children." Of course that is not the way to approach the matter. It is not a matter of giving up husband and children, but of bringing up the children to be fighters for Communism, and of making the husband into the same kind of fighter.

One must be able to merge his own life with public life. That is not asceticism. On the contrary, thanks to that fusing, thanks to the fact that the common cause of all toilers becomes a personal cause, personal life is enriched. It does not become poorer; it produces brilliant and profound experiences such as never were produced by petit-bourgeois family life. To be able to fuse your life with your work for the benefit of Communism, with the work and the struggle of the toilers for the building of Communism—that is one of the tasks which stands before you. You young people are only beginning your lives and you can build them so that there will be no separation between personal life and public life.[88]

THE FRUSTRATED TURN TOWARD THE VILLAGE

The rural activities of the League were given an important place at both the Sixth and Seventh congresses. This new emphasis did not signify neglect of worker youth, which was still regarded as the base of the League. The proportion of the League's membership that was composed of worker youth had risen from 28 percent in October, 1922, to 41.7 percent by February 1, 1924.[89] It was in July, 1924, after the strengthening of the proletarian core, that Chaplin told the assembled Komsomol leaders that "the Sixth Congress must turn the whole League toward the village." [90] Zinoviev told the Congress that the 240,000 peasant Komsomolites constituted a mere one and one-third percent of the peasant youths of Komsomol age.[91] Both Zinoviev and Chaplin urged that the League, while continuing to recruit as many worker youths as possible, now proceed more energetically to expand in the countryside, taking in especially former soldiers and sailors, poor peasants and farm laborers, and rural teachers.[92] The chief speaker on rural affairs, Shokhin,[93] said the League's main rural job was "the mobilization of our Komsomol and our peasant youth for an agricultural revolution." To that end, he said, rural Komsomolites must possess technical agronomic skills and knowledge, they must teach collective and cooperative forms of work, and they must "lead the struggle against petit-bourgeois instincts of private property." Komsomolites must establish "agricultural circles" among peasant youth; and circles which might spring up independently of the Komsomol were to be brought under Komsomol influence by persuasion rather than "iron measures." In these Komsomol-controlled agricultural circles, he explained, as well as in the regular schools, the desired training and indoctrination would take place.[94]

Between the congresses of 1924 and 1926, the "turn toward the village" brought a rise in the proportion of peasants and farm laborers in the League. The combined total of the two categories increased from 45.3 percent in 1924 to 53.7 percent of the League's membership in 1926.[95] The total number of rural Komsomolites of all classes grew from 300,000 in July, 1924, to 530,000 on January 1, 1925, and 900,000 on December 1, 1925.[96] The rural tasks of the Komsomol remained substantially the same.[97] But the sharp increase in the rural membership of the League (even though it still embraced only a very small fraction of rural youth) created problems of control. The "middle peasants" were a special problem. They had been already recognized as a suspicious element, to be admitted to the League only with caution. Moreover, it had been reported at the Congress of 1924 that in the richest farming areas the hostility of the middle peasants toward the Komsomol—as well as toward the collection of taxes in kind!—had grown intense. In Poltava guberniia, it was revealed, Komsomol bodies had been virtually militarized and were under arms in order to fight "criminal and political banditry." [98] But in spite of those warnings, between the Sixth and the Seventh congresses the proportion of Komsomolites who were middle peasants reportedly increased.[99]

Whether because of that increase, or simply because of the larger over-all total of rural Komsomolites, the Seventh Congress—while reaffirming the policies of 1924 in regard to the class composition of the League—[100] was much concerned to provide better "guidance" of the rural units of the League. One obstacle was a shortage of rural Party people.[101] In many villages there was no Party cell at all, and the Komsomol constituted the chief instrument of Party influence.[102] A delegate proposed that only Party members should serve as the secretaries of rural Komsomol cells, but this was shown to be impracticable since there were 41,000 rural Komsomol cells and only 47,000 Party members and candidate-members available in all the Party's rural assignments.[103] One remedy advocated was that of increasing the size of the cells.[104] It was also urged that the Party choose better qualified persons for attachment to Komsomol cells.[105]

On a broader scale, the problem of improving "guidance" was tackled through the efforts of strong urban units of the League. Certain city units had already assumed the responsibility of "patronage" in respect to specific rural Komsomol bodies and were sending reading materials and advice to their adoptees.[106] One difficulty encountered, however, was that city-bred Komsomolites were often unable to cope with the hostile reception they so frequently got from the villagers. Rural Komsomolites, it was said, must be taught not to regard their city brethren as hostile interlopers or "Varangians" come to rule them.[107] This meant in turn that rural Komsomol leaders should be able to answer the questions thrown at them by peasant youth, such as, "Why does worker youth have the Factory Training Schools, why does worker youth work a six-hour day, why does worker youth have such privileges?" Most lower-echelon Komsomol leaders were said to be unable to handle such questions. That called for better Komsomol leaders and organizers. But they were hard to get, partly because the pay of rural Komsomol organizers and officials was very low. While some of the delegates recommended that the pay be raised, the approved solution seemed to be to select volunteers who anticipated deprivation and economic sacrifice.[108]

The League's weakness among rural youth was also manifested in the partial failure of the propaganda against religion. True, it was announced in 1924 that a "Komsomol Christmas" and a "Komsomol Easter" had attracted some youths away from the church holidays.[109] But the same Congress heard the discouraging news that many peasant Komsomolites were not themselves sufficiently antireligious to be able to conduct such propaganda effectively. When they tried, sometimes their cell disintegrated.[110] Poorly prepared Komsomolites were worsted in religious arguments.[111] Some Komsomol enthusiasts had resorted to breaking church windows and smashing altars, but such tactics were not endorsed at the Congress.[112] Two years later, hooliganistic attacks on churches were apparently continuing, although the League was said to have prohibited such activity. At the same time, that prohibition had evidently taken much of the fun out of "atheism," for when the League's policy was announced, many "atheist circles" (apparently led by rural Komsomolites) had simply stopped functioning: their number had declined from a peak of 2,100 (the date was not given) to a mere 500 at the time of the Seventh Congress! [113]

The rural expansion of the League from 1924 to 1926 brought the League's proletarian core during the same period down from around 40 percent to around 36 percent of the League's total enrollment.[114] However, owing to the large absolute increase in proletarian members (no precise figure was given), the Komsomol in 1926 reportedly embraced about 45 percent of all "youth in production" (apparently urban and factory production), as against a mere 20 percent in 1924.[115] Meanwhile in the League's upper echelons, as exemplified by the delegations at the congresses, "proletarians" continued to predominate. At the Sixth Congress, 54 percent of the voting delegates were said to be of worker origin (although by current occupation 87 percent of all delegates were full-time League employees),[116] and at the Seventh Congress the proportion that was of worker origin was said to be 60 percent.[117]

In its policies toward worker youth the League faced obstacles in some respects as difficult as those it encountered among the peasants. The general economic situation was improving in the middle twenties under the New Economic Policy, but unemployment was said to be a problem, particularly among worker youths under the age of eighteen.[118] What could Komsomolites do? The Congress of 1924 could not conceal their impotence. Some Komsomol bodies in factories had, on their own initiative, called meetings of young workers to discuss means of improving their economic situation. The trade unions had apparently responded by trying to push the Komsomol bodies out of economic work. The Komsomol CC and the All-Union Central Council of Trade Unions had reiterated the "correct" formula, which was for the Komsomolites to carry on all their economic work "through the apparatus of the trade unions." Rebuffed, some Komsomolites had withdrawn from economic work entirely. This was of course labeled improper.[119] Other vague suggestions were made, like aiding and awaiting a general improvement in industry [120] and expanding the school system,[121] particularly the Factory Training

Schools.[122] But Komsomolites were given little hope of solving the young workers' plight soon.

Two years later, unemployment was still present, and the leaders admitted that they saw no immediate prospect of its end.[123] But there was this difference: Komsomolites had now been given (by the Fourteenth Party Congress) slogans with which to try to convince the doubters—slogans (like "socialist construction" or "building socialism") related to the principle of "socialism in one country." The task of "drawing the broad masses of worker and peasant youth into socialist construction" was frequently proclaimed during the sessions.[124] Special emphasis was placed on the need for all youths to acquire the technical skills needed for that task.[125] Apart from that emphasis, however, Komsomol responsibilities with respect to worker youth remained about the same as before, and just as restraining. The delegates did discuss whether industries should be required to reserve for minors a certain proportion of jobs; but no conclusions were reached in this matter, which, after all, involved high economic policy.[126] Although the Komsomol was still formally represented as the protector of worker youth,[127] Komsomolites were not encouraged to help worker youth directly, but rather to help the Soviet system in general.[128]

CHANGES IN OTHER PUBLIC FUNCTIONS

Aside from the training of worker youth, treated above, the congresses of 1924 and 1926 concerned themselves little with the schools.[129] The still inadequate state of formal education was suggested by the report that 4 percent of the members of the League were illiterate at the time of the Congress of 1924 and 6.7 percent were illiterate as of October 1, 1925 (the increase being due to the influx of illiterate new members).[130] Among the 750 voting delegates at the Sixth Congress, none had completed higher education, and only 15 percent had finished secondary school. Moreover, only 12 percent of the delegates were currently enrolled in any educational institution.[131] Although it was recognized at the time that the League was weak in the higher educational institutions,[132] proposals to expand the League's work in those institutions were apparently viewed with suspicion as a sign of petit-bourgeois or Oppositionist leanings.[133] Two years later it was pointed out that the League was so weak in the school world that in high schools and technical schools, student organizations were springing up spontaneously and the Komsomol was not exerting any influence in them.[134] With this failing in mind, evidently, the Seventh Congress exempted from the probationary stage for Komsomol membership those students under eighteen who were not exploiting anyone's labor and whose parents were workers, peasants, or handicraftsmen.[135] At that same Congress, Kalinin appealed to Komsomolites to show more respect for teachers and to concentrate on acquiring knowledge from teachers rather than ridiculing their idiosyncrasies.[136]

Outside of the schools the Komsomol was carrying on its indoctrination through the Komsomol press. At the time of the Congress of 1926, seventy-six newspapers with a combined weekly total of 1,000,000 copies (the nature of the count was not explained) were reportedly being published by the League. Foremost among them was *Komsomol'skaia pravda* (Komsomol Truth), which had been founded on May 24, 1925.[137]

The Young Pioneer organization, meanwhile, was growing in importance. Its task was rendered especially vital by the continued presence of roving bands of homeless waifs.[138] From its inception at the Fifth Congress (1922), the Pioneer organization had expanded rapidly. By January 1, 1924, it numbered 161,000, and by July, 1924, it numbered between 200,000 and 250,000.[139] Six months later it had already passed 1,000,000,[140] and at the time of the Seventh Congress (March, 1926) it stood at 1,586,000.[141] In spite of its growth, the Pioneer organization still embraced only a small fraction of the Soviet youth of Pioneer age (ten to fourteen), estimated in 1924 at 20,000,-000.[142]

The Komsomol delegates were informed of several problems in their work among the Pioneers. One was a lack of appealing programs suited to each age group. At the Congress of 1924 it was said that there was too much emphasis on athletics and out-door life of the Scout type.[143] But two years later it was declared that, in their effort to counteract such a tendency, Pioneer leaders had swung too heavily to purely political discussion, which was often dry and uninteresting to children.[144] It was also complained that Pioneers were being overburdened with duties and were showing marked tendencies toward nervous-ness, overexcitability, and tuberculosis.[145] There was a shortage of Pioneer leaders. Although all Pioneer leaders were formally required to be Komsomolites, too few Komsomolites were undertaking this work, with the result that former Scout lead-ers and other non-Komsomolites constituted about one-quarter of the Pioneer leaders at the time of the Congress of 1924. Thirty-nine percent of the leaders were girls.[146]

Krupskaia underlined the importance of the Pioneer or-ganization for rearing the "new man." "The Pioneer detach-ment," she declared, "must be, for the Pioneer, something like what the family used to be." Pioneer leaders must not permit the child to feel lonely, she warned, for out of loneliness could spring religious tendencies. The children should be taught to think "we" rather than "I," she urged, and to approach all questions from the standpoint of the collective.[147] Gorlov, the principal speaker on the Pioneers at the Seventh Congress, denied that the Komsomol was teaching children to spy on their parents and to inform on them, but said that the Kom-somol must try to see that children were not thrashed and were not subjected to authoritarian rule by their parents.[148] At both congresses, Komsomolites were reminded to make sure that the League controlled all Pioneer work—in line with Party instructions, of course.[149]

A significant development which received little attention at this time was the beginning, between the congresses of 1924 and 1926, of the "Little Octobrist" organization for children below Pioneer age. By the time of the latter meeting, it em-braced about 200,000 members. The exact nature of the Kom-somol's relationship with the new organization was not indicated, but Komsomolites were told it was their job to develop techniques for handling the Little Octobrists.[150]

Under the conditions prevailing during the New Economic Policy, there were still some non-Communist-sponsored organizations competing with the Komsomol for the allegiance of youth.[151] The Boy Scout organization, whose struggling survival had been noted at the congresses of 1921 and 1922,[152] was said to linger still in the Transcaucasus.[153] There was also mention (in 1926) of the existence of "leagues of Christian youth" (*Khristomol'tsy*) among peasant youth in the Urals,[154] and other non-Communist groups.[155] In dealing with all rival youth groups, the approved policy remained that Komsomolites should triumph by being culturally superior, rather than by applying "mechanical means" or "administrative pressure" alone.[156]

The demand for Komsomolites to pay more attention to drawing young women into the League received recognition in both 1924 and 1926. During the interval between the two meetings, the proportion of women rose from 15 percent to 19 percent of the total membership of the League.[157] Even so, as indicated above, the League in 1926 included only some 2 percent of all Soviet women of Komsomol age. Urban women had joined the League a little more readily than those from rural areas.[158] The proportion of women delegates increased from 3 percent at the Sixth Congress to 6.7 percent at the Seventh [159]—still well below the proportion of women in the membership at large. Komsomolites were told to give still more positions to women.[160]

The Fifth Congress had advocated increasing the proportion of older youths in the League. At the Sixth Congress, Chaplin reported with satisfaction that this had been done and that now 75 percent of the League's members were over eighteen.[161]

The customary demands for more and better work among the minority nationalities were reiterated at both the Sixth and Seventh congresses.[162] As of January 1, 1924, the League was reported to have the following national composition: Russians,

68 percent; Ukrainians, 7 percent; Jews, 4 percent; Georgians and Armenians, 2 percent each; Turks, Tatars, Kirghizes, and Uzbeks, 1 percent each; and forty other nationalities, a combined total of 10 percent.[163] It will be observed that the proportion of Ukrainians was far below their strength in the Soviet population at large (about 21.2 percent in 1926).[164] Even more striking was the report that, of the delegates at the Sixth Congress, only 4 percent were Ukrainians.[165] Corrective measures were urged,[166] and at the next Congress the proportion of delegates from the Ukraine stood at 10 percent. On the other hand, the Jews, who constituted 15 percent of the delegates at the Sixth Congress (and 18 percent at the Fourth), were down to 7 percent of the delegates at the Seventh (as compared with less than 2 percent in the population at large).[167] At that meeting Mil'chakov demanded that Komsomolites combat the anti-Semitism which he said had been present recently in some parts of the League.[168] National sections within the League, embracing those who did not yet know enough Russian to function as ordinary cell members, increased their enrollment from 34,000 to 118,000 between the two congresses.[169] Meanwhile "patronage" was put to use as a new instrument for dealing with minority nationalities. The Leningrad Komsomol, for example, was the patron of the Uzbek organization, and Tula was the patron of the Turkmen unit. The patron body was expected to send reading matter to its adopted unit, and Komsomolites of the minority nation were supposed to visit the parent city for training and indoctrination.[170]

In the realm of physical education, it was reported that the number of participants in the general athletic movement jumped from 630,000 to 2,500,000 during the interval between the congresses of 1924 and 1926. As of 1926, although almost all (97 percent) of the 2,500,000 were youths, only a little over 10 percent of them (about 263,000) were Komsomolites. Only about 15 percent of all League members were taking part in the athletic movement. Chaplin expressed concern lest many youths active in athletics escape the influence of the Komsomol, and also lest the few Komsomolite athletes become inactive politically.[171]

Virtually nothing was said at the Congress of 1924 about Komsomolites working in the soviets, but at the Congress of 1926 there was some mention of this participation. Before the elections of 1925–26, only 3.1 percent of those serving on village soviets had been Komsomolites; since then, the proportion had been increased to 4.2 percent.[172] In the town soviets the situation was even worse, for in the recent elections only 1 or 2 percent of those elected had been Komsomolites.[173] Bukharin warned that petit-bourgeois elements were gaining influence in the town and village soviets, and called for Komsomol vigilance there.[174]

The military obligations of League members were not stressed at the congresses of 1924 and 1926. The Army was reportedly being rebuilt after the demobilization of 1921–23,[175] and in 1926 was said to contain about 100,000 Komsomolites.[176] Komsomol cells were still forbidden in regular Army and Navy units, but just before the Congress of 1924 the Party CC decreed that Party cells in the Army and the Navy could organize Komsomol "assistance groups" (gruppy sodeistviia) in their units. The "assistance group" was not to have its own elected executive but was to work under an organizer assigned by the Party cell in the military unit.[177] Thus the assistance groups were a means of coordinating and controlling the Komsomolites in a military unit without giving them the rights of Komsomol cell-members. Apparently the Party did not feel sure enough of Komsomol discipline at that time to permit the establishment of cells—even though cells were normally expected to be under Party control.[178] The new groups worked well, to judge by the report at the next Congress.[179] At that time (1926) it was recommended that an elected Komsomol bureau should be permitted at the regimental level, to aid the Party-designated organizer in distributing responsibilities among the 300 or 400 Komsomolites normally found in each regiment.[180]

The Navy, having been "adopted" by the League in 1922, received some special attention at both congresses. At the Congress of 1924 it was reported that in recent recruiting drives for the Navy, almost three-quarters of those who enlisted had been Komsomolites.[181] Komsomolites were said to constitute 40 percent of the entire personnel of the Navy.[182] In naval officers' training schools, the proportion of Komsomolites was 35 percent (one must remember that many officers were Party men), and in naval specialists' schools, from 80 percent to 95 percent.[183] Improvements in literacy and discipline were noted. There had reportedly been virtually no desertions, in contrast with previous years. Komsomol work in naval units had been managed by an "organizer of Komsomol work" under each Party cell. The new "assistance groups" were welcomed as an improvement. Among the measures proposed for the Komsomol's work with the Navy were: (1) to decentralize the "patronage" so that a local Komsomol body would be the patron of a specific naval vessel or training school; (2) to stimulate more correspondence between Komsomol and naval units; (3) to send more Komsomol literature to the Navy; (4) to arrange visits of Komsomol officials to fleet units; (5) to have each Komsomol cell subscribe to some Navy newspaper or magazine; (6) to stimulate interest in naval aviation; (7) to organize propaganda campaigns about the Navy in all Komsomol bodies, especially around October 16 (anniversary of the assumption of patronage in 1922) and May 15 (the beginning of summer naval maneuvers); and (8) to recruit League members for the Navy.[184] It was proposed and voted to establish a "Society of Friends of the Navy." [185] An assessment of forty kopeks on each League member was voted to finance the construction of six naval airplanes.[186] The Congress of 1926 witnessed no significant changes in the Komsomolite's obligations to serve the Navy, but the delegates were frequently reminded of the need to do more along the lines already indicated.[187]

The primary task of Komsomolites in the Communist International of Youth (CIY), at the time of the Sixth Komsomol Congress, was to "Bolshevize" all the other youth leagues in the international organization.[188] First and foremost, this meant to ensure that each foreign youth league stood loyally on the side of the Russian Communist Party (that is, its victorious faction) and against the Opposition in Russia.[189] The report on the CIY was mostly concerned with making sure that the various youth leagues were following what was euphemistically termed the "line of the Comintern." [190] Western youth leagues were being reorganized on a factory-cell principle, which was judged to be better suited to a period of sharper, and often illegal, struggle than the old territorial style of organization (based on place of residence).[191] Strikes were being fostered.[192] The activities of youth league members in the German and Bulgarian uprisings of 1923 were praised.[193] Cells were being planted in the armies of bourgeois countries.[194] The German representatives assured the delegates that within two years the Red Flag would fly over Germany—to which the chairman replied that Russian youth stood ready to help when the time came.[195]

Two years later, plans were still being made. The spokesman of the CIY refused to give details on the Young Communist Leagues in bourgeois armies, because of "conspiratorial considerations." [196] The "united front" policy, characterized as a "retreat" necessitated by the recession of the revolutionary wave, was said to have caused some discontent among the members of foreign youth leagues—especially the "ultra-leftists" who objected to compromising for tactical purposes.[197] But the revolutionary wave was said to be once again on the rise, and so, too, was the membership of the CIY.[198] The spokesman for the CIY acknowledged that until the Communist conquest of power in capitalist countries, the CIY would not be able to embrace a majority of worker youth; bourgeois organizations— Fascist, YMCA, YWCA, Catholic, and socialist—were too strong. But the CIY could nevertheless influence the majority of worker youth, it was said, by following its united front tactic, participating in the economic demands of youth, and catering to athletic interests through the Red Sport International.[199]

Komsomolites who were working abroad required special instructions, like those given by Bukharin, who warned that Soviet representatives working in China must not talk about "Russia" doing this and that, or they would "wipe out our influence among the broad masses of the Chinese population." He emphasized that the Soviets stood in Manchuria "not as 'Russia.' . . . We stand there at our revolutionary post." All "chauvinistic feelings" must be combated.[200] For the ordinary member at home, however, the main task seemed to be to conduct better propaganda about the CIY.[201] Komsomolites should be made to feel that the other branches of the CIY looked to them for an example and for leadership.[202] The familiar demand for closer ties with foreign youth was this time (1926) joined with the recommendation that Soviet youth delegations be sent to other countries, particularly to Austria.[203]

The League had mushroomed from below 250,000 members in 1922 to 1,750,000 in 1926, yet it still embraced only about one-twentieth of the young people of Komsomol age. It was still cautious (even increasingly so, to judge from the formal requirements) about admitting "nonproletarians." It still had to contend (though probably to a lesser extent than before) with youth groups existing beyond its control. It still faced the combination of unsatisfactory conditions for worker youth, an avowed responsibility to improve those conditions, and very restricted means of fulfilling that responsibility. It was still weak in the schools and extremely weak among the peasantry.

Against that background, there had been some increase in concern to assure the loyalty of peasant youth. The "assistance groups" suggested a quickening activity in the armed forces generally, and special attention was given to helping the Navy. The growth of the Pioneers (to almost the size of the League itself) and the establishment of the Little Octobrists testified to increasing responsibilities for Komsomolites in the indoctrination of younger children.

The most striking changes in the demands upon Komsomolites were related to the struggle for power in the Party. Since that struggle was masked in ideological trappings, Komsomolites had been exhorted to improve their knowledge of Marxist-Leninist theory and to combat deviations from the correct interpretation of it. The permitted limits were narrow. A person deviated if he tried to avoid taking sides in the intra-Party quarrel and also if he presumed to discuss Party issues too extensively. The intra-Party strife made the victorious faction increasingly sensitive in interpreting what it chose to regard as attempts by Komsomolites to be independent or to set the League against the Party. Enthusiastic support of Stalin's "theory"—socialism in one country—was becoming a necessity. The good Komsomolite must join the pack in hunting down real or alleged Oppositionists. Dissenting Komsomol leaders were reproached more roughly than before and apparently were removed from their positions with even less hesitation than before. Divided votes in the congresses became increasingly rare. When the congresses were postponed, in violation of the Regulations of the Komsomol (and evidently on Party command), Komsomolites were not even shown the courtesy of an explanation, and no Komsomol delegate dared to mention the fact of the violation.

Yet despite those changes one must remember that at the congresses of 1924 and 1926, Komsomolites were still able to disagree openly on moderately consequential issues; they could still register dissenting votes; and their sharp criticisms of arbitrary rule within the League could still be spread in the published record. However heavy the demands for Komsomol discipline were by other standards, time would show that, by Bolshevik standards, they had been relatively light in the years of the NEP.

V. Adjustments
during the Emergence of Stalin and
the Renewed Drive for Socialism

THE CONGRESSES OF 1928 AND 1931

THE period represented by the Eighth Congress (May 5–16, 1928) and the Ninth (January 16–26, 1931) witnessed on the one hand the emergence of Stalin as the preeminent leader of the Communist Party, and on the other hand the drive for socialism—or what Stalin called socialism—under the First Five-Year Plan. Both of these developments left many imprints on the Komsomol pattern.

The congresses themselves were becoming less frequent: between the Sixth and the Seventh, about one year and eight months had elapsed (July 12–18, 1924, to March 11–22, 1926); between the Seventh and the Eighth the interval grew to about two years and two months; and between the Eighth and the Ninth, to two years and eight months. The official Regulations still required that congresses be held not less than once a year, but no speaker attempted any explanation of the delay.[1] The thoughtful Komsomolite would have observed again that the ostensibly inviolable Regulations could be disregarded, presumably on Party command, by the leaders of the League.

The membership of the League continued to climb. From March, 1926 (when it was 1,750,000), to May, 1928, it rose by only about one-seventh, to 1,960,000.[2] Increasing then somewhat more rapidly, it stood at 2,897,000 on July 1, 1930,[3] and, by January, 1931 (Ninth Congress), at 3,000,000.[4]

INCREASED PARTY "GUIDANCE" AND
HARRYING OF THE OPPOSITION

From 1926 to 1928, according to Chaplin's report to the Eighth Congress, "the overwhelming bulk of the strength and energy of the Komsomol had to be diverted from creative work to the struggle against the [Trotskyite] Opposition." [5] The Congress itself was full of the struggle against enemies—real or imagined, present or potential. Various types of "class enemies" were identified by Bukharin, so as to aid Komsomolites in combating them. There were the kulaks who, he said, had killed several Komsomolites recently and must receive "severe punishment and harsh retribution." There were "masked" enemies, including religious organizations—the Baptist youth (Baptomol), the Christian youth (Khristomol), and the League of Young Believers (Soiuz veruiushchikh molodykh liudei), whose combined membership, Bukharin warned, approximately equaled that of the Komsomol. These youth groups espoused worthy causes like the battle against smoking and excessive drinking, he said, and thus attracted many of the best youths including some of the working class. Another disguised class enemy was the purveyor of nationalism. Bukharin deplored especially what he characterized as a fairly widespread anti-Semitism, explaining at the same time that the battle against anti-Semitism "does not preclude but presupposes a struggle against NEP men [private traders] of all nationalities, including the Jewish." Still another category of masked enemy Bukharin termed the "enemies within ourselves," such as alcoholism, "bureaucratism," and "petit-bourgeois dissoluteness." [6]

Stalin joined others [7] in sounding the tocsin. Speaking on the last day of the Eighth Congress, he complained that a few years of peace had led people to forget the enemy. This was exceedingly dangerous, he warned, for if people then suddenly were exposed to the enemy they might be seized with panic, and panic must be avoided at any cost. Stalin said the class enemies were growing, as evidenced by the industrial sabotage allegedly committed by agents of international capitalism and by difficulties in the collection of grain from "rural capitalistic elements" during the preceding winter.[8] He called for more militancy and vigilance "as long as there are classes in our country and we have the capitalistic encirclement." At the same time, Stalin said that some Communist officials had "carried the Party's monopoly to an absurd extreme, stifled the voice of the lower echelons, got rid of intra-Party democracy, and brought in bureaucratism." Within the Komsomol, too, said Stalin, certain "corrupt elements" had been engaged in an "unprincipled group struggle." Such evils were to be combated through "organizing control . . . from below," which meant organizing "the criticisms of the million-headed masses of the working class against the bureaucratism, the deficiencies, and the mistakes of our agencies." Those who made mistakes, he said, including even those who had previously rendered distinguished service, must be subjected to *"mass criticism from below,"* and this criticism must be used by those higher up.[9] Stalin's demand for criticism gave added weight to similar demands by other speakers.[10] Mislavskii, then a leading Komsomolite, pointedly deplored the tendency among League members to exempt from their criticism those at the top, including the Central Committee of the Komsomol.[11] Others insisted that cliquishness be eradicated within the League.[12] These exhortations to combat bureaucratism, to criticize from below, and to uproot cliques may be seen as expressions of one basic aim: to facilitate control from the top, by eliminating persons who tried to build their own power centers in the Komsomol or anywhere else beneath the apex of the Party pyramid.

At that apex, meanwhile, changes were taking place. As of 1928, Stalin, having long since discredited Trotsky, Zinoviev, and Kamenev, shared the limelight with his current allies, Bukharin, Rykov, and Tomsky.[13] Stalin's name was first on the list of the Honorary Presidium elected by the Eighth Congress,[14] and he apparently received more than the usual volume of applause before and after his short speech,[15] but he was otherwise scarcely mentioned during the Congress [16] and not at all in the closing ceremony.[17] By the time of the Ninth Congress (1931) a transformation was under way. The opening remarks by Aleksandr Vasil'evich Kosarev (then the leading Komsomolite) hailed Stalin as the leader of the World Revolution.[18] The mention of Stalin's name at the head of the Honorary Presidium reportedly brought the Congress to its feet in "prolonged stormy applause, becoming an ovation." [19] With Stalin present in the hall, Kaganovich not only quoted him but went on to declare:

The Party triumphed, its line triumphed, because the CC firmly and undeviatingly stood on the Leninist path (*applause*) and because the leader of our Party is the best exponent of the ideas of Lenin— Comrade Stalin. (*Prolonged applause*. Exclamations: "Long live Comrade Stalin, the leader of world Communism—hurray!" Voice: "Long live the leader of the Communist Party, Comrade Stalin!— hurray!" *Stormy applause*. Exclamation in unison: "Glory, glory, glory!" *Applause*. Voice: "Red front!" *The Congress stands and gives an ovation to Comrade Stalin*.) [20]

In the subsequent proceedings of the Congress of 1931, Stalin was referred to as "the leader of the world proletariat," "our friend, our comrade, our leader," "the sole leader of the Komsomol," Lenin's "best pupil," the "leader and theoretician of the Party," the Komsomol's "beloved friend, leader, and teacher," and the "best guide and leader of the Party and the Komsomol." [21] By previous standards this was extravagant. Yet out of the more than two hundred speeches and resolutions of the Congress, Stalin was mentioned in only a little over a dozen.[22] Thus the limits of Komsomol "initiative" were still far from being reached.

The struggle against "deviations" in 1931, when Stalin was opposing both his former allies of the Right (Bukharin, Rykov, Tomsky) and his long-standing enemies of the Left (Trotsky and others), was labeled "a fight on two fronts." The Right Deviation was depicted as especially dangerous; by questioning the wisdom of rapid industrialization and collectivization, and overestimating the durability of the capitalistic system, it was creating "panic." [23] Through a clever juxtaposition of phrases, Kosarev linked Bukharin's Rightists with the "Leftists" or

"Trotskyists." [24] Denying that the so-called Leftists were really leftists, he stigmatized all deviationists as fundamentally "petit bourgeois" in outlook and as lacking confidence in the Soviet state and its ability to build socialism without the help of other countries.[25]

How did the hunt for deviationists affect the Komsomol? At the Congress of 1928 there was no evidence of drastic removals. Some speakers said that it was time for many old Komsomol leaders to be replaced by younger people,[26] but those leaders who were announced as transferring to Party work were accorded full honors. Nikolai Chaplin, who had served as general secretary of the League since 1924, was liberally commended (by Kosarev, who, in 1928, was just rising to prominence) and was elected an Honorary Komsomolite. Lazar' Shatskin, who had continued to serve in the Communist International of Youth after his announced withdrawal from regular League work (1922), was already an Honorary Komsomolite from the time of that earlier "retirement." Now, in 1928, he was effusively praised, both by the chairman (Mil'chakov), who called him "the most popular and famous worker in the Komsomol," and by Kosarev, who spoke warmly of his "invaluable service" to the League.[27]

By the time of the Congress of 1931, however, the League, now led by Kosarev, had tracked down big deviationist quarry, including—previous encomiums notwithstanding—Shatskin and Chaplin! [28] The deviationists were said to have contaminated virtually every sphere of Komsomol activity, and their inculpation presumably afforded many lessons to the virtuous Komsomolite. Shatskin, it was charged, had been a "Leftist" and had tried to copy Trotsky's tactic of pitting the Komsomol against the Party.[29] Moreover, Shatskin had espoused the "famous thesis about the right to doubt." One of Chaplin's sins was that, "knowing of Lominadze's [another deviationist's] tendencies," he "did not tell the Party about those tendencies, did not fight against them." He was accused of having aided what was called the "Right-'Leftist' Bloc," which was taxed with (1) denying that the last stage of the NEP was also the first period of socialism, (2) questioning the rate of industrialization, (3) questioning the capability of the cadres to handle such rapid changes (which Kosarev termed a "blow at the CC, at the leadership"), and (4) accusing the state of taking a "feudal-lord attitude toward the needs and interests of the working class and the peasantry." A mistake of the Rightists in the Komsomol had been their policy *"not to inflame the class struggle among youth,* not to cultivate anger toward the class enemy, but to soften this struggle and to cultivate the desire to live with everyone in peace." In connection with this error, Kosarev charged, the Rightists had advocated trying to "reeducate the young kulak in the Komsomol" (whereas the current policy was to "liquidate the kulaks as a class"). Charged more particularly against the Leftists were the crimes of questioning the exiling of Trotsky; arguing for the "equality of rights" between the League and the Party; advocating the "organizational separateness" of the League from the Party; and looking upon Stalin's slogan of "socialism in one country" as merely an agitational tool rather than an operational plan—thus being guilty of saying in effect "that the Party puts out some slogans for practical action and others only for agitation." [30] Another subspecies of deviation embraced the "theory of permanent lag"— that is, that the Party was continually setting up new tasks and that the League would always be justifiably a little behind in fulfilling those tasks. This argument was inadmissible, Kosarev made clear, for it was tantamount to charging that "the general line of the Party is the sort of line that sets before the Komsomol tasks that are beyond its strength." Hence, while there might be lags in specific tasks, Kosarev declared, there could be no talk about "a lag stemming from the general line of the Party." [31] Thus one more possible device for excusing nonfulfillment of Party orders was eliminated from the Komsomol tool kit.

As to the Honorary Komsomolites who were said to have strayed from the path of Leninism, Kosarev made it clear that past services could not atone for present sins. He warned all Komsomol leaders that it would be wrong for them to maintain any contact with Shatskin.[32] The Congress, acting on the proposal of its Presidium, withdrew the title of Honorary Komsomolite from Chaplin and Shatskin, on the ground that they had "not justified the trust of the ALCLY." Going further, it voted (unanimously) "to consider that those Honorary Komsomolites who placed themselves outside of the general line of the Party in so doing placed themselves also outside the ranks of Honorary Komsomolites." Yet even that was not enough. The delegates voted that "henceforth the existence of the institution of Honorary Komsomolites is considered unsuitable."[33] Although the reason for the abolition was not explained, its clear implication was that times were uncertain, the Party line was harder than ever to follow, and the trusting Komsomolite could not tell which Komsomol leader, awarded a "permanent" honor today, might fall into error tomorrow.

Komsomol spokesmen seemed to be learning, to judge from the congresses of 1928 and 1931, that it was unwise to call for spontaneity and self-standingness without adding that these could best be assured by closer Party guidance.[34] At both congresses the "request" for closer Party guidance was voiced repeatedly,[35] almost like an incantation to ward off evil spirits. At the same time the relative size of the Party core in the Komsomol was declining. In May, 1928, Komsomolites who concurrently belonged to the Party constituted 9.2 percent of the total membership of the League. By January, 1931, the absolute size of the Party core had grown, but the League as a whole had grown even more, so that the relative size of the Party core dropped to 7.9 percent.[36] A decrease was likewise recorded in the Party core among the delegations: at the Eighth Congress, 94.9 percent of the voting delegates were Party members or candidate-members,[37] while at the Ninth Congress the corresponding figure was 90.9 percent.[38] Both percentages were lower than those for the Sixth and Seventh congresses (over 97 percent). A possible reason for the decline was hinted at the Eighth Congress when Kosarev explained a new departure, which was to bring into the CC some lower-echelon Komsomolites and factory workmen "from the bench."[39] Many of those people might not have belonged to the Party. The same desire for a stronger dash of proletarian flavor may have lain behind the composition of the congresses. If so, it by no means signified a weakening of the Party's grip and may have signified that the Party felt surer than before of its control. The Komsomol was reported to be serving increasingly as a reservoir for new Party members. The League had furnished "more than 300,-000" of its members to the Party, and in "recent years" Komsomolites had constituted 37 percent of those taken into the Party.[40]

Since there had reportedly been several cases of mishandling of funds within the League, it was announced at the Eighth Congress that henceforth all League funds would be managed by the Financial Section of the CC of the Party.[41] In another administrative change heightening Party control, the Ninth Congress raised the requirements of Party service for those Komsomolites occupying the posts of secretaries of krai and oblast committees of the League: to qualify for such a post a worker or peasant now had to have three years of Party standing (instead of two), and an office worker or person from the intelligentsia had to have five years of Party standing (instead of four).[42]

A tantalizingly incomplete glimpse of the working relationships between the Party and the Komsomol was provided by an incident at the Congress of 1928. Mislavskii, on behalf of the Komsomol's Central Inspection Commission, attacked the Tambov *gubkom* (guberniia committee) of the Party for installing, through its "Party fraction" in the corresponding *gubkom* of the Komsomol, a secretary who was unacceptable to that Komsomol body.[43] The Tambov Party *gubkom* telegraphed a protest to the Congress, whereupon the Secretariat of the Congress investigated the matter. The arguments advanced against the Party *gubkom* were (1) that the Party fraction had interfered when "there was no disagreement over principles and no instance of distortion of the Party line"; (2) that the leadership that had been imposed on the Komsomol *gubkom* by the Party fraction had subsequently shown itself to be "incapable" and "weak"; and (3) that the Party fraction had acted in such a way that "not only the Komsomol *aktiv* and the delegates to the guberniia conference but almost the whole guberniia organization [of the Komsomol] knew that the leading personnel of the *gubkom* had been chosen without reference to the will of the majority of the delegates." [44] The Komsomol Secretariat, in a verdict published with the proceedings of the Congress, found that there had not been any "political disagreements among the Komsomol workers" at the Tambov guberniia conference, and that therefore Mislavskii had been right in calling attention to "this violation of the principles of Party guidance." [45]

The Tambov case is evidence, then, that under certain conditions a body of the Komsomol really could criticize a body of the Party. But what were those conditions? First, the Komsomol organ voicing the criticism was the Central Inspection Commission, near the apex of the Komsomol hierarchy, while the Tambov *gubkom* was at a lower point in the Party hierarchy. Secondly, the Komsomol Secretariat of the Eighth Congress almost certainly checked with the Party CC before reaching its verdict, and perhaps even before allowing Mislavskii to present his charge. (Bespalov, who presided over the inquiry, was elected to the Komsomol CC's in 1928 and 1931, and therefore may well have been, himself, fairly high in the Party.) And finally, one cannot fail to wonder about the relative weight given to the three charges made against the Party *gubkom*. What if the leaders chosen by the Party fraction had been capable, or what if the "election" had been conducted so smoothly as to conceal its dictatorial nature from the rank-and-file Komsomolites? Would the Komsomol body then have felt able to protest? One may only guess, keeping in mind that a limited amount of this sort of criticism could be useful to the Party CC in supervising lower-echelon Party units and preventing the growth of cliques.

The discussion at the congresses of 1928 and 1931 generally suited the Komsomol requirement of being "businesslike"—of attacking poor performance without questioning established policies. In 1928 the Komsomol CC, as usual, was fair game.[46] One delegate, more biting than the rest in his criticism of Chaplin and the CC,[47] was rebuked by both Mislavskii and Chaplin. Chaplin charged that the delegate "took the floor with interpellations of the CC, just as one interpellates the government in the English Parliament"—clearly an inadmissible procedure in the Komsomol.[48] Lunacharskii was blamed for alleged shortcomings of his Commissariat of Education, but this criticism was generally within proper bounds. The lone delegate who dared to criticize Kalinin was reprimanded unceremoniously.[49] The savage criticism of Gastev, which will be treated in a later section, was launched by Chaplin in the official report of the Central Committee. That action apparently signaled open season on Gastev. He was allowed to defend himself, and he evidently evoked some sympathetic laughter, but he was heckled several times from the floor.[50] The votes on resolutions were apparently all "unanimous," with small numbers of abstentions in some cases.[51] Yet the delegates must not vote perfunctorily: when Shatskin, in presenting one resolution, said that his committee had adopted it "in a Marxist way and unanimously," voices from the floor urged him to dispense with reading the resolution; but Shatskin in all seriousness rebuked them, saying: "Comrades, never before has an All-Union Congress adopted a resolution which it hasn't read and doesn't know." He then proceeded to read it, whereupon it was—without discussion—unanimously approved.[52] All the elections at the Eighth Congress were conducted by list and were apparently unanimous.[53]

In 1931 the discussion was more "businesslike" than ever before. Bitter denunciations of the Deviationists and the Oppositionists, who had already been defeated and who were absent from the Congress, provided a safe way for Komsomolites to show their mercilessness toward error.[54] Proper vigilance also required that the delegates find fault with their own Central Committee. One formula for this was common. The delegate would assert vigorously that the report under question had "failed to give enough attention" to such-and-such a problem—

say, the industrialization of the Urals. The critic, who would happen to be from the Urals, would then proceed to discuss the work of the League in that area.[55] The other basic ingredients of the discussion were reports of shortcomings and achievements in various fields, demands for higher production or better performance, and praise of the principle of Party guidance. The discussion of the report of the CC went off so smoothly that Kosarev upbraided the delegates for not criticizing the CC more sharply.[56] Nevertheless, subsequent reports received similarly gentle treatment.[57] The voting on resolutions and theses at the Ninth Congress apparently was unanimous except on one minor administrative issue.[58] In the elections the unanimity was complete. (As the list of nominees for the new CC was being read off, the delegates supposedly had the right to challenge any name, but no one took advantage of that opportunity.)[59] An explanation for all this harmoniousness was provided by none other than Kosarev:

> Our Congress has been extraordinarily unanimous. Unanimity on political questions always has characterized the Leninist Komsomol. However, unity on organizational questions has by no means always been adequate. But the Ninth Congress was also unanimous on organizational questions. . . .
> Speaking of organizational unity, one cannot be silent about the role of the Party in this matter. It is a fact that our Congress is as one, that our movement is as one. But he would be making a mistake who would think that this is due to certain individuals or to the guiding collective of the Komsomol. No, comrades, he who thinks that way simplifies the question. *The basic thing is that the system of Party guidance, the relationship of the Party to youth and the Komsomol—only this and precisely this is what has given us the possibility of coming to the Congress united and of conducting the Congress unanimously.*[60]

It has been shown that the demand for rejuvenating the leadership of the League was followed by the removal of some prominent leaders. What other evidence was there of turnover in the leadership of the League? At the Eighth Congress, just over half (50.8 percent) of the voting delegates were above the member's normal age limit of twenty-three.[61] This proportion was criticized as excessive. Yet at the next Congress the corresponding proportion was even higher—57.3 percent.[62] The trend was similar with respect to length of service in the Komsomol. At the Eighth Congress (1928), 8.7 percent of the delegates had entered the League in 1920 or earlier, that is, had already been in the League for at least seven years.[63] At the Ninth Congress, those who had entered in 1920 or earlier had risen to 9.1 percent of the delegates; and since this was in 1931, it meant that they had been in the League for at least ten years.[64] Thus the demand to make the leadership younger was apparently yielding to the far more insistent demand for tight Party control.

But was there another sort of turnover? Were the faces, if not younger, at least new? Going back over the rosters of the Central Committees for purposes of comparison, one finds that out of the first Central Committee (1918), comprising twenty-two members and candidate-members, six, or 27.3 percent, were held over for service on the next CC—that is, the CC that was elected at the Second Congress (1919) and served until the Third (1920). Taking members and candidate-members together in that manner, the succeeding proportions run as follows: Of the second CC, 25 percent were held over (4 out of 16). Of the third CC, 43 percent were held over (9 out of 21). Of the fourth CC, 54.2 percent were held over (18 out of 24). Of the fifth CC, 46.2 percent were held over (12 out of 26). Of the sixth CC, 38.8 percent were held over (26 out of 67). Of the seventh CC, serving from 1926 to 1928, 37.6 percent were held over (35 out of 93). Then, of the eighth CC, serving from 1928 to 1931, *only 18.3 percent* were held over (22 out of 120). This was a lower proportion held over than at any previous time in the history of the League and was less than half of the lowest proportion since 1920. (It was to be lower even than the proportion—23 percent—held over in 1936, after a *five*-year span of service!) That was evidence of a real turnover, engineered by those at the top who drew up the lists of nominees for membership in the Central Committees. The Komsomol delegates apparently understood that this subject was taboo, for they avoided it even though they might have used it as proof that they were trying to do what was being demanded of them.[65]

Just beneath the personnel of the Central Committee itself was that Committee's rarely publicized administrative staff. The Ninth Congress revealed that this staff of the CC, numbering 113 persons in May, 1928, and 80 persons in January, 1931, experienced in that period a turnover equivalent to more than two complete changes of personnel.[66] This rate of turnover was said to be far too high, but no comparable figures were given for other periods.

Among the voting delegates to the congresses, too, the turnover was considerable. Of those present in 1931, 88.9 percent had not attended any previous congress, 7.1 percent had attended one other, and only 4 percent had attended two. Yet three-quarters (74.8 percent) of the delegates had been in the League since 1925 or before and, as mentioned above, 9.1 percent had been members since 1920 or earlier.[67] Thus it appears that while the delegates in 1931 tended to be chosen from among the older members of the League, they were to a large extent persons other than those who had occupied similar positions of leadership in 1928.[68]

There were other problems related to leadership. Mislavskii (speaking for the Central Inspection Commission in 1928) revealed that many secretaries of cells were being appointed, rather than elected as they should be according to the Regulaations, because the pay for secretaries at the lower echelons was too low.[69] Many Komsomol leaders were said to lack skill in probing the thoughts and feelings of each member in the cell meeting.[70] Kaganovich in 1931 stressed the need for such skill. He recognized that when the individual Komsomolite saw "difficulties in supply, shortcomings in production," he was likely to think: "We've entered the period of socialism, but what kind of socialism is this if I don't have enough of this and that?" His trouble, Kaganovich explained, is that "he is not able to tie the prospects of the near future in with the present" (to translate: not able to subsist in part on hopes); he needs to have the whys and wherefores explained to him, "and then he'll understand and will be an excellent fighter for socialism and won't go around with repressed thoughts in his soul." Summing up his insistence on personal guidance, Kaganovich said:

One must always remember that the Komsomol cell is not a platoon, and the secretary of the cell is not a platoon commander. Some comrades do not always understand this. The Komsomol cell is a spontaneously active cell, which works on the basis of self-criticism, on the basis of the development of the creative initiative of each Komsomolite, while the secretary is the guide, the tutor, the person who leads these Komsomolites into the foremost ranks of the fighters for the Revolution.[71]

The principle of ensuring "proletarians" the leading role in the administration of the League was apparently making headway, to judge from the composition of the delegations at the congresses: at the Congress of 1926, 60 percent had reportedly been of worker and farm-laborer origin; at the Congress of 1928 the proportion was 71 percent.[72] By the time of the Congress of 1931 the composition was said to be 82.2 percent "workers" (apparently including farm laborers) by social origin.[73] By *occupation,* it should be noted, 69.5 percent of the delegates at the Eighth Congress were full-time paid employees and officials of the Komsomol, while only 20.1 percent were genuine "workers from the bench" (that is, workers by occupation), only 3 percent were farm laborers, and less than 1 percent were peasants.[74] At the Ninth Congress full-time employees and officials of the Komsomol were 61.4 percent, and workers from the bench were only 20.8 percent. But agricultural workers (including tractor drivers) were now 19 percent, and peasant collective farmers were 6.7 percent.[75] Meanwhile the proletarian core of the membership at large was on the increase: the proportion of Komsomolites who were workingmen or farm laborers rose from 44.3 percent in May, 1928, to 48.8 percent in January, 1931.[76] Komsomolites were alerted in 1928 against a "dangerous phenomenon": many students from white-collar families were reportedly going into factory work for short periods of three months or so, in order to acquire the classification of "worker" and thus to enter more readily the Komsomol and the Party.[77]

The problem of the overage Komsomolites (those over twenty-three) was becoming serious. In 1925 they had constituted 4 percent of the total membership of the League; by 1928 they were 16 or 17 percent, which was considered too high. Mil'chakov said there was too much pity shown for those (apparently many) who had not been accepted into the Party. Yet merely to release them "mechanically" from the League, he said, was not desired; they should be assigned civic tasks—in the villages, for example—where they could prove whether or not they deserved to be taken into the Party and where they could earn the necessary recommendations.[78]

The demand that women be given more representation in the League was reiterated in both 1928 and 1931.[79] It was termed "extremely abnormal" that, at the Congress of 1928, only 9.7 percent of the voting delegates were women, when women constituted 23 percent of the Komsomol's membership.[80] At the Congress of 1931 the proportion among the delegates was raised to 22.8 percent. Unfortunately, the proportion of women in the League as a whole at that time was not stated.[81]

The already familiar Bolshevik virtues, such as discipline, "organizedness," solidarity, Partyness, confidence, vigilance, atheism, and mastery of Leninism, continued to be extolled at the congresses of 1928 and 1931.[82] The two congresses contrasted interestingly in regard to strictures against such vices as alcoholism and sexual looseness. At the Eighth Congress, Bukharin led the attack on this sort of immorality, citing among other things the case of a Komsomol official in Sochi who had been acting as a procurer of Komsomol girls for his drunken comrades.[83] Chaplin, Mil'chakov, and other speakers at that Congress joined in condemning drunkenness and debauchery.[84] At the next Congress, on the other hand, such matters were not discussed, and Kaganovich even ridiculed the fallen Bukharin as having wanted to make the League's "main task" the "struggle against smoking" instead of the more important struggle for socialism.[85] Both the Eighth and the Ninth congresses seemed to hear more urging of spontaneity and initiative than had previous congresses, in part because of the demand for "shock work." [86] The increased talk of spontaneity and initiative may also have been intended to obscure the fact that the Party's grip was actually growing tighter; or it may have reflected, in some cases, real concern over a diminution in Komsomol spontaneity. Spontaneity and initiative, whatever their fate in practice, were proving to be hardy ideals!

BUILDING A SOCIALIST ECONOMY IN TOWN AND VILLAGE

The task of "socialist construction," especially in heavy industry, was set prominently before the delegates at the Eighth Congress (1928).[87] Chaplin announced that, to help Komsomol members draw the millions of worker and peasant youth into production, there had begun in the League a "new voluntary movement." At the heart of the movement were "initiative groups" or "initiating cores," to which Chaplin applied the term "shock groups"—a phrase used by Lenin in his address at the League's Third Congress in 1920.[88] Chaplin stressed that the shock-group movement, now to be vastly expanded by the Komsomol, must not set young workers apart from old but must on the contrary draw the young workers *into the general current of the constructive work of the proletariat.* It must also be tied to concrete tasks in the factory, school, or club.[89] Having taken pains to depict the shock groups as voluntary, Chaplin went on to deplore an (evidently too literal) interpretation of this voluntariness by some Komsomolites in the Leningrad and Moscow organizations:

We will assign tasks, we will demand the fulfillment of League obligations; otherwise we will crumble to pieces, otherwise we will not be a solidary, Bolshevik, Communist organization. Therefore *the Komsomolite must combine both voluntariness and obligatory tasks, placing the main stress on the development of initiative and voluntariness.*

The insistence on voluntariness, far from diminishing the role of the leadership, actually increased it, he said:

The development of the voluntary movement places an increased demand on the leadership, for there is the danger that it [i.e., the voluntary movement] may not proceed in our channel, may develop apart from our leadership, may take on an incorrect political coloration and fall under other leadership.[90]

In other words, Komsomol obligations *must* be properly performed and *must* be performed "voluntarily"!

Komsomolites were urged to increase production by encouraging inventions and improved methods ("rationalization of production"),[91] maintaining vigilance against "saboteurs,"[92] taking good care of tools and instruments, maintaining cleanliness, economizing on fuel, and working a full day without loafing on factory time.[93] Bukharin suggested that special groups of Komsomolites be formed to walk through stores, institutions, bazaars, shops, and commissariats, acting like ordinary customers or petitioners and seeing what treatment they got. Such unofficial inspection teams or "light cavalry," said Bukharin, were the only effective way to "dig out the bureaucratic adversary." Bukharin also thought the Komsomol could be useful in supplementing the regular agencies for receiving complaints and grievances.[94]

In accordance with the early spirit of the League, several delegates spoke in favor of better wages for minors working in industry, better living conditions for young workers, and more help in solving the problem of unemployed youth; but suggestions for specific action by Komsomolites were lacking.[95] In connection with the kindred topic of training skilled cadres,[96] however, the Komsomol delegates at least had an outlet for such frustrations as they may have felt. The principal victim was Gastev, the head of the Central Institute of Labor. He was accused of wanting to eliminate minors from factory work; of seeking to abolish or reduce the quotas of jobs reserved for minors in industry; of advocating a general education not directly combined with productive labor; of being overly concerned with bodily efficiency ("Fordism"); and of intending to make the worker a mere "appendage to the machine" instead of a "creator of social production."[97] Similar attacks were made on the representative of the Supreme Economic Council, M. L. Rukhimovich.[98] Much of the criticism was more than usually abstract. The following excerpt will serve as an example, while also providing an interesting insight into one minor Komsomolite's picture of socialism. How, asked this critic, does Gastev envision socialism?

> He imagines socialism in the form of a huge factory, where there will be thousands of machines and one workman will operate 96 or 120 looms instead of 4. He will go around on roller skates on, let's say, a wood-inlaid floor, and will be a duster, a weaver, or a checker. That is not socialism, but slavery. That is the role of the appendage to the machine, against which the working class came forward and triumphed in our country. It [the working class] took power, and it will combat this slavery, it will rebuild production. What will the future socialist production consist of? Socialist production will, indeed, consist of huge plants, where there will be thousands of machines, where maybe there will be a wood-inlaid floor, but where the worker will not go around to each machine but will stand in a certain place and regulate the work of this whole factory, regulate and control the process of work of thousands of mechanisms, thousands of machines.[99]

How many angels can dance on the head of a pin?

The League in its effort to encompass worker youth was evidently not keeping pace with the expanding industrial population, for of the youths working in industry, the League embraced a smaller share in 1928 than in 1926.[100] While more working youths were to be drawn into the League, material inducements were discountenanced. Chaplin said there had been cases, in Moscow and Leningrad and elsewhere, in which Komsomolite workingmen had been promoted or otherwise favored because of their League membership. He said that this must be stopped and that promotions must be made only on the basis of skill.[101]

Between the Eighth and the Ninth congresses of the Komsomol, Stalin announced (at the Sixteenth Party Congress, June 26–July 13, 1930) that since the "socialist sector" had come to dominate the national economy, the Soviet Union had entered the "period of socialism," on the way to the full "socialist society" which lay further ahead. At the Ninth Komsomol Congress (January, 1931), Kosarev quoted that pronouncement.[102] He assured the delegates that, in one or two more Five-Year Plans, "we shall live in a developed socialist society." [103] They must now hasten, he said, to achieve "the abolition of the contradiction between city and countryside," "the erasing of the distinction between mental and physical labor," "the drawing of the masses into the administration of the state," and "the drawing of women into production," thus ending their status as "kitchen slaves" and undermining the "economic foundation of the old bourgeois family." [104]

Entrance into the period of socialism was said to pose the questions of the labor and the protection of worker youth in a "new way": no longer would Komsomolites need to take special measures to protect youthful laborers, for "the successes of socialist construction have guaranteed the increase of the material and cultural well-being of the working class and the toilers, including youth as well." It was now only a question of drawing youth, including minors, into suitable forms of production and into the Factory Training Schools and other training institutions.[105] Those Komsomolites who thought this meant neglecting the true interests of the workers and peasants were placed among the villains of the "Right-'Leftist' Bloc." [106] Both Kaganovich and Kosarev tried to convince the delegates that Soviet youth was already better off economically than youth in capitalistic countries,[107] and Kaganovich took special pains to deny that there was forced labor in the Soviet Union.[108]

Among the specific instruments of the Komsomol in the economic sphere, shock work had been joined by its cousin, socialist competition. In recognition of the League's work in stimulating these movements, Kaganovich announced, the Central Executive Committee of the USSR had just voted to award the Komsomol the Order of the Red Banner of Labor.[109] Kosarev reported that, on the average, 62 percent of the Komsomolites (apparently referring to those in trade unions) were shock workers, that is, workers who consistently overfulfilled their production quotas.[110] Shock workers formed "shock brigades" which (like the shock groups already mentioned by Chaplin at the Eighth Congress) performed special production feats. The appearance of "the new man of socialism—the shock worker" was welcomed, and the self-sacrificing deeds of Komsomol shock workers and shock brigades were extolled by many speakers at the Congress.[111] Kaganovich said Komsomol shock brigades were "transferring labor into a matter of valor and honor." He told of a Komsomol "battalion" putting on a "storm night" in pouring concrete for a tractor factory in Kharkov; he told of young shock workers building a dam near Magnitogorsk; and he told of one thousand Komsomolites recruited by the Party for work in the coal mines south of Moscow.[112] Later during the proceedings, Kaganovich—apparently with a straight face—asked pardon for being absent during some of the discussions, saying that he himself belonged to several shock brigades.[113] He demanded that *all* Komsomolites be shock workers in their respective fields of endeavor,[114] and the Congress unprotestingly added this requirement to the official Regulations of the League.[115]

Socialist competition, like shock work, was asserted to be a "voluntary movement" begun by the League.[116] A resolution of the Eighth Congress had instructed Komsomolites to organize production contests between individual young workers, between groups of young workers of similar levels of skill, between shops in the same factory, and between factories, thus drawing the masses into the competition.[117] By 1931 socialist competition had been greatly expanded, reportedly through Komsomol initiative. In addition to the shock brigade there was the "light cavalry" (presumably resembling the inspection teams suggested by Bukharin), the "public tugboat" (by which advanced enterprises took more backward ones in tow), the "rationalizing brigades" (or efficiency teams), the "signal posts" (for watching the progress of certain shops), the "planning-operative groups," the "mixed brigades" (combining personnel from several shops), and other weapons in what was termed the "fight for speed." [118] The delegates were told that socialist competition differed from the savage bourgeois rivalry said to prevail under capitalism, but the precise nature of the difference was left unexplained.[119]

Just as the Komsomol had mobilized some of its members for military service during the Civil War, now, in order to complete "the Five-Year Plan in four years," [120] it mobilized some of them for work on the "industrial front," including mining and lumbering. Between the congresses of 1928 and 1931 the League reportedly "mobilized 350,000 of the best Komsomolites for various sectors of construction." [121] Doubt whether the "best" had really been sent was implied by several speakers, one of whom reported that among 15,000 Komsomolites sent from all over the USSR to work in the mines and factories of the Donets Basin, desertions had run as high as 45 or 47 percent.[122] The good Komsomolite should accept his mobilization without grumbling and should be on the alert against "wreckers," including agents of capitalism.[123]

Komsomolites needed technical knowledge, it was stressed at the Ninth Congress, if they were to guide and organize youth effectively.[124] Kosarev said the doors were open wide to youth in all fields—scientific, economic, technical, managerial, and political. "It's only a matter of desire," he said. But—and here came the limitation—the Komsomol must be "able fully to organize and direct this desire of the broad masses into suitable channels." [125] The Factory Training Schools, important in the preparing of skilled and semiskilled workmen, were reported to embrace almost 600,000 students at the time of the Congress. Only about one-third (33.6 percent) of these students were in the League, while only 3.4 percent were in the Pioneers, and Kosarev demanded that they all be brought into the one or the other.[126]

Komsomolites were assured by Kaganovich that "at the end of the Five-Year Plan, we will give the population plenty of fat, butter, and all necessary products"; "the hour is not far away when we shall overtake and surpass the foremost country—the United States of America." [127] Under capitalism, said Kosarev, work was monotonous and oppressive, and "clerks remain clerks all their lives." But under socialism it was different:

"Today you're a blacksmith, and tomorrow you're the chairman of a village soviet. Today you're a young lathe-worker or locksmith, and tomorrow you're the secretary of a Komsomol committee." [128] Such presumably were the vistas of the convinced Komsomolite in 1931.

In the rural communities the main task of the Komsomol at the time of the Eighth Congress was already that of collectivizing the farms.[129] The importance of the Komsomol in this process was stressed by Bukharin when he pointed out that there were but 18,000 rural Party cells, whereas there were 49,000 rural cells of the Komsomol.[130] In many villages, therefore, the Komsomol might be the Party's chief agency for carrying out the collectivization. Concerning the methods to be used, Bukharin strongly advised the use of example and persuasion rather than repressive "administrative measures." [131] One difficulty was poor indoctrination within the rural Komsomol units themselves. Some Komsomol cells, Chaplin reported, had failed to assist the recent grain-collection and self-taxation campaign, thanks to crafty kulaks who had persuaded Komsomolites that the government's demands were excessive. All too many cells, said Chaplin, were under kulak influence— sometimes because a Komsomol official became friendly with the daughter of a kulak or a priest or a miller! [132] Another source of difficulty reportedly was that there were too many middle peasants in the rural cells of the League: fifty-one percent of the rural membership of the League consisted of middle-peasant youth; only 29.9 percent were poor-peasant youth (evidently including farm laborers), while 16.4 percent were well-to-do peasants, and 4 percent were kulaks.[133] (The categories were, as usual, not defined. Moreover, they add up to 101.3 percent.) Improper criteria, said Chaplin, were often used for judging who were the "best" middle peasants: Komsomolites were esteeming the peasant who was a good farm manager or who built a good house. That was wrong. The best middle peasant was "he who helps the poor," "he who is for collectivization," "he who helps the Party and the Soviet government." There must be no glossing over the distinction between those who helped the Party and those who did not: "A decisive campaign is needed against the smoothing over of the class struggle in the countryside. Komsomolites who reason thus: 'all peasants, rich and poor, are equal,' and 'the kulak is also a man'—those are not Komsomolites, those are kulak-supporters." [134] All kulaks and their allies were to be expelled from the League.[135] Urban Komsomolites were to help, despite their apparently widespread disinclination to go out into the villages.[136] Antireligious propaganda was to be intensified, and Komsomolites were to "unmask" the priests as defenders of the kulaks.[137] Any Komsomolite who was the head of a rural household, the Congress resolved, must belong to a collective farm as soon as one was started in his village.[138] In paving the way for regular kolkhozes (collective farms), Komsomolites were told to use intermediate devices, such as producers' cooperatives and improvement associations. Once within a kolkhoz, Komsomolites were to push the collective toward "higher"—that is, more completely socialized—forms leading to the full "commune," in which not only production but also consumption would be on a communal basis.[139]

Between the Eighth and Ninth congresses, the Party (in its Sixteenth Congress) announced the policy of "the liquidation of the kulaks as a class," on the basis of "complete collectivization." These aims then became one of the chief concerns of the Ninth Komsomol Congress.[140] Saltanov, a leading Komsomolite and the chief speaker on rural matters, reported progress: as of May, 1928 (Eighth Congress), there had been only 36,000 League members in collective farms. By May, 1930, there were 550,000, and by January, 1931, 750,000 or 800,000.[141] This meant that as of January, 1931, when only 25.7 percent of all peasant households had been collectivized,[142] over 60 percent of all rural Komsomolites were in collective farms. In some areas (Ukraine, northern Caucasus, Siberia) the proportion was 90 percent or higher.[143] However, with 90,000 kolkhozes already established, there were only 60,000 rural Komsomol cells, and only half of those were in kolkhozes; hence there was only about one Komsomol cell for each three kolkhozes.[144]

The kulak segment in the League had been purged.[145] The decisive tests of each rural Komsomolite were said to have been whether he fought against the kulaks or not and whether he entered a collective farm or not.[146] Komsomolites were warned that even when all kulaks were gone, the "kulak bourgeois ideology" would remain,[147] and that even the poorest Komsomolite would have to be on guard against harboring kulak ideas such as the desire for private property, the acceptance of inequality, and the tendency to think more of one's own stomach than of one's commitment to deliver the assigned amount of produce to the government in order to fulfill the Plan.[148]

The Ninth Congress resolved that Komsomolites should draw the peasants "on a voluntary basis into the collectives, proving through concrete experience the advantage of the collective farms over individual farms, and being guided by the aim that [quoting Stalin] 'by the end of the Five-Year Plan the collectivization of the USSR must be substantially completed.' " [149] That official resolution was ambiguous, for the "voluntary basis" might very easily be incompatible with the demand that collectivization be "substantially completed" by the end of the Five-Year Plan. But for individual Komsomolites the resolution was clear: any members who "maliciously" refused to enter a kolkhoz must be expelled from the League as "kulak agents." [150]

The League was to admit to its ranks not all, but the "foremost," collective farm youth, without distinguishing between former poor and middle peasants.[151] (Collective farm youths were now specifically exempted from the probationary stage in becoming members.) [152] Outside of the kolkhozes, and in areas where kolkhozes did not predominate, the League was still to concentrate on poor-peasant and farm-laborer youths, plus those "best" middle peasants who worked for collectivization.[153]

More urban "help" was needed for both labor and propaganda in the countryside.[154] Certain urban Komsomol organizations continued to serve as "patrons" of rural bodies of the

League.[155] The Komsomol was especially urged to build silos [156] and to provide electricity in the villages.[157] Komsomolites were to serve on the administering bodies of the kolkhozes,[158] to learn to drive tractors, and to assist the growth of sovkhozes and machine-and-tractor stations.[159]

It was in such terms, then, that Komsomolites received their instructions for the great drive to bring the Soviet rural population under the firm control of the rulers of the state. "Collectivization on a voluntary basis," "more help from the cities to the countryside," "electrification of the villages"—such slogans sound gentle enough. Even the demand to "liquidate the kulaks as a class" did not, in its proper sense, necessarily imply the physical destruction of human beings. Yet under those slogans there proceeded the movement that brought agony and death to millions of Soviet citizens. Dimly indeed do the Komsomol congresses reflect some aspects of Soviet reality!

PROBLEMS OF TRAINING AND INDOCTRINATION

The First Five-Year Plan required skilled people, of whom Soviet Russia had relatively few.[160] The training of Bolshevik specialists was being hampered (Stalin told the Congress of 1928) by an improper tendency to honor the illiterate person simply because he was "from the workbench," and to accuse the worker who had acquired an education of having "torn himself away" from the masses and of having ceased to be a worker. Komsomolites must put an end to such a preposterous attitude, Stalin indicated. "The working class cannot become the real ruler of the country . . . unless it can create its own intelligentsia, unless it masters science and can direct the economy on the basis of science." To bravery and daring must be added knowledge.

In order to build, one must know, one must master science. But in order to know, one must learn—learn persistently and patiently, learn from everyone, both enemies and friends, especially from enemies. One must learn, clenching his teeth, not being afraid that enemies will laugh at us, at our ignorance, at our backwardness. Before us stands a fortress. This fortress is called science with its many branches. We must take this fortress at any cost. Youth must take this fortress, if youth is to be the builder of the new life, if youth is to become the real relief of the old guard.[161]

Before specialists could be trained in the large numbers that would be needed, there remained the elementary problem of teaching people to read.[162] In recognition of the gravity of the problem, a special session of the Eighth Congress was held with representatives of the Commissariat of Education and the "Down with Illiteracy" Society.[163] The Congress voted that the League should wipe out illiteracy immediately within its own ranks and that each literate Komsomolite should teach at least one illiterate person to read.[164] The problem was confronted again in 1931, and the Ninth Congress called for the mobilizing of one-quarter of a million Komsomolites to "liquidate" illiteracy.[165]

With respect to the schools, at the Congress of 1928 Krupskaia discussed Komsomol repsonsibilities in student self-government. She outspokenly (and perhaps in terms not fully approved by the Party chiefs) protested that student self-government in many schools was being improperly run; that it was being made to carry on "police surveillance" over the students and to inform on those who weren't doing what they should.[166] Lunacharskii and his Commissariat of Education were criticized repeatedly for divorcing schooling from productive labor and not spending enough money on education.[167] The Congress of 1931, however, as was pointed out by Shokhin, a former Komsomol leader now representing the Commissariat of Education, was the first one at which there had been "no disagreements in principle between the Commissariat of Education and the Komsomol." [168] The continuing need for expansion of the school system was indicated by the fact that of the voting delegates at that Congress, only 13.3 percent had finished secondary school. The Congress again urged Komsomolites to go into teaching and instructed them to "surround the teacher with attention and comradely help" and to combat improper attitudes toward teachers.[169]

The Pioneer organization occasioned some anxiety at the

Congress of 1928. The Pioneer membership had reportedly suffered a decline.[170] Blame fell on the Komsomol. Methods suited to adults had been carried over mechanically, it was said, causing excessive "politicization" of Pioneer work and thus impeding proper training.[171] Chaplin caricatured the wrong kind of Pioneer meeting: "The detachment having assembled, the leader commands 'attention'; after they've marched a little while and sung the song 'We are Pioneers,' then the leader gives a lecture on political literacy and the meeting is over." [172] Furthermore, too few Komsomolites had been undertaking the responsibilities of serving as Pioneer leaders. Of the 67,698 Komsomol cells, 20,000, or well over one-quarter, were not operating Pioneer detachments.[173] Bukharin reminded the delegates that the Pioneer organization, being at the base of the "pyramid," should be far larger than the Komsomol.[174] Krupskaia underlined the importance of the Pioneers for teaching and indoctrinating those children who were not in the Soviet school system.[175] (In this connection, the homeless waifs were declared to be still a serious problem. Children's homes and labor communes were two of the institutional remedies mentioned which needed assistance from the Komsomol in order to take care of the delinquents.) [176]

The Pioneer enrollment had approximately doubled by January, 1931, when it was in the neighborhood of 3,300,000.[177] Sever'ianova, in the main Pioneer report at the Ninth Congress, said that sharp disputes had taken place two or three years earlier, when the movement had been in difficulty. At first, in order to appeal to children, the Pioneers had developed "cultural" activities, such as parties, bookbinding workshops, and shoe repair shops. Then, with the period of "socialist construction," the children had helped in election campaigns and other political work. But in August, 1930, the first (presumably all-Union) assembly of Pioneers had inaugurated a policy of *"widespread participation in the struggle for industrialization and for the collectivization of agriculture."* Sever'ianova said this program had proved popular with the Pioneers. Tens of thousands of the older children had worked in factories as shock workers. They had publicized, on factory "blackboards," the names of workers who idled on the job. Rural Pioneers had "succeeded in exposing kulaks who were trying to hide their property against confiscation" and helped to "unmask" kulaks who had entered collective farms and were trying to sabotage them from within. About 15,000 Pioneer "brigades" had been sent out from city Pioneer organizations to aid with collectivization and had also helped with the sowing on collective farms.[178] Among the other activities approved for Pioneers were: collecting sacks and scrap metal, searching for useful minerals, campaigning against filth, combating "wreckers" (saboteurs), cleaning seed, organizing child labor on the collective farms, putting the children's summertime to better use, and organizing kindergartens and nurseries so that more mothers could work in factories.[179] The delegates resolved as follows:

The IX Congress of the ALCLY considers that the basic line of the Komsomol in the work among children must be to *place the whole matter of education on the basis of the systematic participation of all children in the productive and public life of the factories, state farms, MTS's [machine-and-tractor stations], and collective farms.*[180]

The resolution accordingly declared that Pioneer work must not be merged with the life of the school but must be based principally in the factories and on the farms, that is, the productive units.[181] Rapid expansion of the membership was demanded, to include all children of workers, farm laborers, poor peasants, and collective farmers.[182]

Leadership for the Pioneers was still a problem. Many Komsomolites shirked Pioneer duties, Sever'ianova complained; 2.9 percent of the Pioneer leaders were not even members or candidate-members of the Komsomol or the Party;[183] over half of the Pioneer leaders were eighteen and under and had been in the League less than two years.[184] Better guidance was needed, she said: "We stand for the spontaneous activity of children, but we stand for firm Komsomol guidance. Ideas of free upbringing are alien to us."[185] Komsomolites who worked with Pioneers were expected to foster the proper relationship between younger children and their parents. Sever'ianova asserted that the Soviet regime had done away with the "fetish of the family, the subordination to the parents," and that children now concluded "social contracts" with their parents. Soviet fathers and sons should be united by the class struggle. And what if they were not? She mentioned approvingly cases "where children rebel against their mothers if they [the mothers] don't want to enter the collective farm." As opposed to the interests of the family, she said, "we have taught children to proceed from higher interests—from the interests of the proletarian class." Yet Sever'ianova denied that the Bolshevik aim was to destroy the family.[186] The resolution of the Congress spoke euphemistically of the "extension of our influence in the family through the children themselves." [187]

The work of the Little Octobrists was not discussed at either the Eighth or the Ninth Congress, but at the time of the Ninth they may have numbered about 700,000.[188]

In the realm of the Komsomol press, the official daily newspaper, Komsomol'skaia pravda, expanded its circulation from 260,000 in September, 1930, to 630,000 in January, 1931. After the purge of "Leftists" a new editorial group had taken over in December, 1929.[189] The Komsomol publishing house, Molodaia gvardiia (Young Guard), was said to have published 50,000,000 books and brochures for Komsomol use during 1930, of which 20,000,000 dealt with Party policy in the rural areas.[190]

Both congresses (1928 and 1931) heard the customary phrases about literature and art aiding the work of the Soviet state and combating hostile influences.[191] The All-Union Congress of Proletarian Writers, meeting in 1928, reported that more than half of its members were Komsomolites.[192]

The participation of Komsomol members in the soviets of town and village apparently increased only slightly during the period under consideration.[193]

The Komsomol CC on the eve of the Congress of 1928 organized a Touring Bureau under the slogan, "Put touring in the service of the Komsomol." Developing as the "Society of Proletarian Touring and Excursions," it had managed tours (including hikes) for about one million persons in 1930. In January, 1931, it had 250,000 members. Through it,

hundreds of thousands of toilers on trips and excursions see the achievements of socialist construction, the concrete results of the Bolshevik Five-Year Plan. They are convinced of the successes of the construction, of the correctness of the general line of the Party; they arm themselves with still greater enthusiasm for the struggle for the Five-Year Plan and store up new creative energy, directing it to the overcoming of difficulties.

The tourists also were said to engage in election campaigns, to "explain the decisions of the Party and the Soviet government," to "carry socialist culture to the remote border regions of the Soviet Union," and to lend a hand in the villages, "creating thousands of brigades for the repairing of equipment, for siloing, and for gathering in the harvest." Workers visited other factories; civilian tourists were forged into prospective soldiers by means of camp life and outdoor marches. Thanks to the guiding influence of the Komsomol, the report declared, "opportunism" and "nonpoliticalness" in the touring society were being combated.[194]

The treatment of minority nationalities received new attention at the Congress of 1928, since many of the peasants due to be dispossessed were non-Russian. Chaplin quoted Stalin on the basic policy:

It ought to be remembered that besides the right of nations to self-determination there is also the right of the working class to strengthen its government. And to this latter right is subordinated the right to self-determination. The national question is subordinate to the worker question. National culture is not an end in itself but a means for drawing the nationalities together, for the creation of the friendly family of toilers of the whole Soviet Union. This is the road to socialist culture.[195]

Clearly, cultural and other concessions to minority nationalities were a means to the end of tighter Party control and must not interfere with that end. A resolution of the Congress directed Komsomolites to use the native poor peasants and farm laborers in expropriating the native landlords. The Moslem mullahs or priests were to be regarded as allies of the native landlords;

particularly dangerous were those mullahs who adopted Soviet slogans. Komsomolites were told to discover Moslem schools wherever they were operating secretly, so that they could be suppressed by the authorities.[196] Although the Komsomol's campaign against "chauvinism" in minority nationalities was represented as a struggle of classes within each nationality, the resolution complained that in the national-minority republics the majority of "worker youth" *did not know the language of the local nationality,* and it said the Komsomol *aktiv* or core of active personnel must study the language of the area in which it was working.[197] That was as close as the resolution came to suggesting that the campaign against a given minority depended upon outside "help" from convinced Komsomolites of other nationalities (usually the Great Russian).

At the Congress of 1931, with collectivization in full swing, the problem of minority nationalities was reported on by a prominent Komsomolite named Dzhavakhidze. He said that almost half of the Komsomol membership was now non-Great Russian. He instructed the League, in its work in the minority areas, to conquer illiteracy, set up schools to teach industrial skills, send Komsomol cadres to assist in industrializing outlying regions, prepare Komsomolites to serve in the village soviets, conduct military training for the youths, and, not least, advance the "liberation of women," particularly among the Moslem peoples. Separate Komsomol cells for Moslem women were still approved (as they had been in 1928) [198] as a means of persuading those women to discard the veil and enter public life.[199]

Deviations to either side were described, so that Komsomolites could guard against them. The deviation toward local minority nationalism was illustrated by the proposal of some Komsomolites that the League's work with non-Russian youth be handled by non-Russian Komsomolites. This proposal was stigmatized as being "anti-Party" (!). In the other direction, the deviation toward Great Russian chauvinism was illustrated by the proposal to abolish the national republics and oblasts. The desired end product, Dzhavakhidze indicated, was a "monolithic union" of all the nationalities of the USSR, characterized by an "unbounded determination to fight for it." [200]

The only spark of dispute among many colorless speeches occurred when a Ukrainian delegate, Boichenko, objected to what he interpreted as a statement that every Komsomolite must learn Russian.[201] Dzhavakhidze agreed with Boichenko that Russian was not *the* language of the October Revolution of 1917, but he asserted on the other hand that "by Russian culture we mean proletarian culture," and he said non-Russians who were active in the League ought to learn Russian. As to Komsomolites working among national minorities, Dzhavakhidze said they ought to learn the local language, but he explicitly rejected any definite requirement to that effect.[202] The resolution passed by the Congress made it clear that adherence to the Party line was the essential thing and that the use of local languages and customs was a means of ensuring that adherence.[203]

One reflection of the nationality problem could be found in the national distribution of the 767 delegates: Russians were 54.1 percent, Ukrainians were 12 percent (as against about 21 percent in the general population), and Jews were 10.3 percent (as against about 1.8 percent in the general population), the remainder being distributed among forty-one nationalities.[204] Thus, in this sample of the leadership of the League, Ukrainians were much underrepresented, while Jews were greatly overrepresented.

THE PERSISTENT AIM OF WORLD REVOLUTION

At the opening session of the Congress of 1928 a ceremonial device was used for impressing upon the delegates the military obligations of all Komsomolites. Unshlikht (Unschlicht), of the Revolutionary Military Council, read a proclamation of the Central Executive Committee of the USSR, dated that same day (May 5) and signed by Voroshilov, awarding to the Komsomol the Order of the Red Banner, in recognition of the League's services on all fronts of the Civil War of 1917–21.[205] In celebration of the occasion the delegates approved a special appeal urging all Komsomolites to prepare again for war and vowing: "We give an oath not to lay down our arms until the victorious chorus of the 'International' sounds in every place where flows today the blood and sweat of workers and peasants." [206] At the Congress of 1931 a dramatic touch was provided by proud references to Soviet victories against the Chinese in Manchuria.[207] A representative of the Far Eastern Army lauded that Army's "defense" of the USSR during the battles of 1929 along the Chinese Eastern Railway in Manchuria. Solemnly he turned over to the Komsomol the battle flag of the Far Eastern Army, "stained with the blood of our heroic fighters." It was accepted with a promise that the Komsomol would fight "in order that the Red Banner may wave over all the world." [208] There were numerous references to the threat of imperialist attack, the Soviet policy of peace, the need for preparedness, and the military and naval obligations of each Komsomol member.[209] A definite effort, evidently somewhat more concerted than that witnessed during the NEP, was being made to stimulate a belligerent spirit.

The number of Komsomolites currently serving in the armed forces was reported as 130,000 at the Congress of 1928,[210] and 200,000 at the Congress of 1931.[211] In the Komsomol's special adoptee, the Navy, 25 percent of the personnel were said to be members of the League as of the time of the Eighth Congress.[212] At the Ninth Congress, 45 percent of naval personnel were reported to belong to the Party or the Komsomol, the proportion being 54 percent among the command personnel. In the naval schools training future commanders, 64.5 percent were said to be Komsomolites.[213] A special submarine, the *Komsomolite,* ostensibly financed in part by contributions from Komsomolites and Pioneers, was the chief current stimulus to interest in the League's duty as patron of the Navy.[214]

The Congress of 1931 also marked the opening of a new sphere of military activity for the League. Voroshilov "proposed" that the League assume patronage over the Soviet Air Forces; [215] his proposal was subsequently accepted at a ceremonial session of the Congress on January 25, 1931, where the head of the Air Forces (Baranov) read a decree of the Revolutionary Military Council of the USSR granting the "unanimously expressed wish" of the Congress to assume this new responsibility. It was disclosed that Party and Komsomol members together comprised 70 percent of the Air Forces in 1930.[216] Komsomolites were exhorted to be exemplary pilots and mechanics, to produce more aircraft, to learn gliding, and to encourage the making of model planes.[217]

The official Regulations of the League as revised by the Congress of 1931 obliged each Komsomolite to study some branch of the military service. A small yearly contribution (20 kopeks) by each Komsomolite to the Navy and the Air Forces was made a formal requirement.[218] Komsomolites were urged also to participate more actively in the Osoaviakhim, or Society for the Promotion of Defense and of the Aviation and Chemical Industries, which gave some preinduction military training. Only 38 percent of all League members were reported to be then in the Osoaviakhim, and they constituted only 16 percent of its total enrollment (9,000,000).[219]

In the realm of world affairs, the duties of the Komsomolite with respect to the Communist International of Youth were discussed extensively at the Congress of 1928.[220] Shatskin reported that Trotskyites had been weeded out of the CIY fairly easily and that the over-all picture abroad was not discouraging.[221] However, the membership of Young Communist Leagues outside the USSR had declined.[222] He blamed this in part on the fact that in capitalistic countries the temptations of the cultural and recreational activities of bourgeois youth groups made it difficult for the more strictly political Young Communist Leagues to attract many youths. A change in policy was needed, said Shatskin, and it was up to the Komsomol Congress to reach decisions for the guidance of the forthcoming Fifth Congress of the Comintern of Youth. Essentially it was a question of the policy on "transmission belts from the Young Communist League to the non-Party masses of worker youth"

—that is, a question of Communist fronts. In the USSR, said Shatskin, the Komsomol "has not only state support but also a monopoly on political work among worker youth." In capitalist countries, on the other hand, it was the non-Communist groups that received state help, he asserted, and the Young Communist Leagues could not expect under those conditions to embrace the majority of worker youth. Shatskin said the Second Congress of the CIY, not understanding this, had overestimated the immediate potentialities for growth of the YCL's themselves and had mistakenly prohibited the establishing of other youth organizations on the ground that they would only compete with the YCL's. The Young Communist Leagues now must reverse this policy, he said, and must energetically develop all sorts of auxiliary groups, such as athletic organizations and youth groups in the trade unions. These front organizations could serve as legal covers for the Leagues in the countries where the Leagues were outlawed, he explained, and could aid them in reaching farm youth.[223] The other policies to be followed by Young Communist Leagues abroad, under the watchful guidance of Komsomolites working in the CIY, involved little change.[224] In countries having voluntary military service, Shatskin said the Young Communist Leagues must not boycott these armies

because the army will have colossal significance at the time of decisive political events. We must enter into the voluntary armies not only singly but by sending large groups of people into the armies to work for their demoralization, to work on the revolutionizing of the young workers who are there.[225]

Another speaker commended French Young Communists for participating in "disturbances" in seventy different units of the French armed forces during the past year.[226]

At home, the yearly contribution of each Komsomolite to the CIY was increased from five to ten kopeks, with the understanding that the collection must be primarily an occasion for effective indoctrination concerning the CIY.[227] The combined aims of stimulating interest in the CIY and of training more Komsomolites for work in it were to be served by encouraging the study of foreign languages.[228] Foreign youth delegations were to be invited to the USSR.[229] Soviet youths were to correspond with Young Communists and working youth abroad.[230] A special question arose concerning Komsomolites who were corresponding in Esperanto. The trouble was, one delegate explained, that many of the letters from abroad asked such questions as, "Is it true or not that in your country there are peasant uprisings?" or, "What's the situation in your country regarding the Opposition?" or even such diabolical questions as, "Tell me, my good fellow, how does the democracy that you have in your country tie in with such a disloyal attitude toward former leaders, such as Trotsky, for example?" The delegate went on:

You see what a mess? We must answer all this correctly. If we don't go after our young people who are studying Esperanto and have many Esperantist connections, if we don't bring these young people under control, . . . this will be very bad. But if we bring them near to us and take them under our control, we shall have extraordinarily good results.[231]

On Shatskin's recommendation, the Congress voted that Esperanto was to be discouraged in favor of conventional languages and that those who still wanted to work with Esperanto were to do so under the supervision of the committees of the League.[232]

At the Congress of 1931 the work in the CIY was again the focus of some attention. Khitarov reported that the Fifth Congress of the CIY, held not long after the Komsomol's Congress of 1928, had failed to give sufficiently specific instructions for the fight against deviations from the Party line. Consequently, difficulties had arisen. In Germany, "in September, 1929, we completely renovated the leadership" of the YCL, he candidly reported. By November of 1929, the membership of the Young Communist Leagues had melted away in several countries.[233] To the rescue came the "historic" November (1929) Plenum of the Executive Committee of the CIY. It had laid down the line of the "struggle on two fronts," against both the Rightist and the Leftist perils. This shift in the policy of the CIY, Khitarov pointed out quite frankly, had been achieved with the "direct help" of the Executive Committee of the Comintern.[234] Victory over the deviationists had enabled the Young Communist Leagues to begin enlarging their membership again.[235] But much improvement was still needed under the guidance of the Komsomol, said Khitarov.[236] The ultimate purpose of the CIY was not forgotten. Kaganovich, for example, promised the Komsomolites: "You will be the masters of the whole world!" [237] Such allusions to the world-wide aim, expressed in both 1928 and 1931, in reference not only to the Communist International of Youth but also to the military duties of Komsomolites, as indicated above, showed clearly that "socialism in one country" by no means implied the abandonment of the aim of World Revolution.

The congresses of 1928 and 1931 yield evidence of several changes in the pattern of Komsomol demands. Increased attention was given to military affairs, as symbolized in part by the League's assumption of patronage of the Air Forces. There was an expansion of the work of the Pioneers, who by 1931 had become more numerous than the Komsomolites. The League's long-standing but sharply circumscribed mission of protecting worker youth was declared to be unnecessary as a consequence of the country's alleged entrance into the period of socialism. Among the more striking changes was the emergence of Stalin and the beginning of the Stalin cult. Discipline was tightening; the hunt for "deviationists" and "saboteurs" was widening. Many Komsomol leaders, including Shatskin and Chaplin, fell as victims of the intra-Party struggle. The range of criticism and discussion at the congresses was restricted still further than before. Meanwhile, Komsomol members were confronted with a challenging economic program. Through the "voluntary" institutions of shock work and socialist competition, as well as through the even less subtle "mobilizations" for the "industrial front," many Komsomolites were being drawn into the heavy construction of the First Five-Year Plan. Other Komsomolites were assigned the mission of collectivizing the farms, first with mild pressure, and then with increasing harshness. In many spheres Komsomolites were being asked to perform tasks which, in the name of the bright promise of an approaching socialism, would bring hardship to many, not excluding Komsomolites themselves.

VI. Adjustments during
the Consolidation of Stalinist Socialism

THE CONGRESS OF 1936

THE events of the early and middle 1930s—rapid industriali-zation, forced collectivization, and the progressive consolida-tion of Stalin's dictatorship—transformed the face of the Soviet Union. By 1936 Stalin was ready to announce the attainment of what he called socialism. He was also ready to permit the holding of a new Komsomol Congress, the Tenth, which met April 11–21, 1936. Although the Regulations of the League still required a congress every year, more than five years had passed without one. Obviously that delay represented the desire of Stalin and the Party. There were plenty of possible reasons for the postponement—the collectivization, the famine in the Ukraine, the murder of Kirov, the purging of the Party—but they were not openly admitted as such, and Komsomol officials again did not dare publicly to explain why their own Regula-tions had been disregarded.[1]

Between 1931 and 1936, all was not well within the League. In January, 1931, the enrollment had been about three million, and Kosarev had predicted rapid expansion to eight or ten mil-lion within "the next few years."[2] But five years had gone by, and the membership was still below four million (3,981,777).[3] At the Tenth Congress, silence was maintained on the loss of 900,000 members in 1932,[4] as well as the impermanent rise to 4,500,000 in 1934.[5] It was revealed, however, that of those who were members in April, 1936, 73.3 percent, or almost three-quarters, had entered the Komsomol since the Ninth Congress,

and 26 percent had come in during 1934–35.[6] Partly explaining
the large turnover were the reports that the Ukraine had been
a scene of trouble in 1931–33; "hostile elements" had been trying to stir up Ukrainian youth both for Ukrainian nationalism
and against the collectivization of the farms; the situation in
the Ukrainian Komsomol had been "entirely unsatisfactory" in
1933 because the leaders had been building cliques on the basis
of personal loyalty. The delegates were told that Party leaders
Kosior and Postyshev, working with Kosarev and the Komsomol CC, had intervened to "help" the Ukrainian Komsomol
to "liquidate" its "backwardness" and to "crush the enemies,"
and that this intervention had been "unanimously supported
by the mass of Komsomolites," who participated enthusiastically in the "liberation" of the Ukrainian Komsomol from its
subversive leaders.[7] The year 1933 had also witnessed a general
turnover of Komsomol administrative personnel.[8] And the
murder of Kirov (1934) had brought in its wake a thorough
"overhauling" of the Leningrad Komsomol, carried out under
the personal supervision of Zhdanov.[9] Altogether, during 1933,
1934, and the first half of 1935, 449,571 Komsomolites were said
to have been expelled from the League.[10] Others had been
simply demoted. For example, during the year before the Tenth
Congress, over one-sixth (614 out of 3,507) of the Komsomol
propagandists in the Leningrad organization had been removed
from propaganda work. The reasons adduced for their removal
were probably generally symptomatic: fifty-four persons had
been removed for belonging to the "Zinoviev-Trotskyite Opposition," 119 because of improper social origin (presumably
their parents were of the former "ruling classes"), 50 because of
having received Party and Komsomol reprimands, 85 for
having a "direct tie" with foreign countries, 5 for "loss of class
vigilance," and 301 for "inadequate political literacy" (that is,
not being careful enough in following the Party line).[11] In view
of both the troubles within the League and the cataclysmic
events in the country at large, it is not surprising that the Congress of 1936 brought changes in the formulas for the role and
functions of the League and its members.

The changes that the Congress was expected to make in the formal Program of the League were explained by Evgenii L. Fainberg, a leading Komsomolite, in a highly significant report.[12] The Program or general statement of principles had not been changed since the Congress of 1921.[13] Fainberg said the old Program was out of date in some respects. In 1921 capitalism had not yet been fully crushed, and the Program therefore had dwelt on such problems as "the defense of the economic interests of worker youth" and the need to assure to Soviet youths the civil rights they deserved, such as voting. But as of 1936 and the triumph of socialism, he asserted, "The Soviet government attentively and solicitously cares for the younger generation and protects its labor and health. . . . Therefore we have no need to carry on a struggle to defend the interests of youth and to introduce into our Program any demands for protecting their rights and interests." [14] The old Program also contained, said Fainberg, "the profoundly erroneous, anti-Leninist statement that Russia 'can reach socialism only through world proletarian revolution' "—a blemish which reflected, he said, "the Trotskyite views and leanings" of Shatskin and others who had participated in drafting that Program and who "subsequently [eight years later!] were in opposition to the Party." [15]

The new Program, said Fainberg, was "wholly and completely based on the teachings of Lenin and Stalin," and Stalin had "proposed" that the role and character of the Komsomol be described this way:

The All-Union Leninist Communist League of Youth is a mass non-Party organization attached to [primykaiushchei k] the ACP(B) [All-Union Communist Party (of Bolsheviks)], and uniting in its ranks broad strata of the foremost politically literate youth of town and village. The ALCLY has the task of helping the Communist Party (of Bolsheviks) to rear youths and children in the spirit of Communism. Sympathizing with the Program of the ACP(B), the ALCLY helps the Party of Bolsheviks and the Soviet government to fulfill the great historic task—the building of the Communist society. The ALCLY is the assistant of the ACP(B) and its reserve.

During the preliminary discussions of the new Program, some people, said Fainberg, had thought that the phrase "sympathizing with the Program of the ACP(B)" was too weak and passive: they had favored stating that the Komsomol "shares" and "acknowledges" the Program of the Party and "fights for its realization." These comments, Fainberg declared, revealed a tendency "to identify the Komsomol with the Party, not understanding the essential difference between the Party, which is the guiding force, the vanguard of the proletariat, and the Komsomol, which is one of the mass organizations working under the guidance of the Party." [16] He observed ominously that to speak of "sharing" or "acknowledging" the Party Program suggested Trotsky's ideas that youth was the "vanguard of the vanguard" and that there should be created a "second Party." If the Komsomol was to be a mass movement it must *not* have the same standards of admission, for example, as the Party.[17] In helping the Party, Komsomolites must not claim any "leading role in the worker movement" but must serve as propagandists, for, said Fainberg, Stalin had unequivocally declared "that the Komsomol is a propagandistic organization." [18]

As to the social composition of the Komsomol, Fainberg went on, the old Program had characterized the League as a "class proletarian organization" whose "basis and leading element is worker youth," although the League had also embraced the "poorest peasant and farm-labor youth," the "best elements of middle-peasant youth," and some loyal individuals from the petite bourgeoisie. The triumph of socialism, said Fainberg, had swept away such class distinctions, leaving only "free toilers of town and countryside—workers, peasants, and intelligentsia"; hence one could now speak of the Komsomol as bringing together simply the "foremost Soviet youth of town and countryside." [19]

Although the Komsomol was a "non-Party" and "mass" organization, it remained "Communist," said Fainberg, both because its job was to rear young people in the spirit of Communism and because it was controlled by the Party. "Ensuring the guidance of the Party" was, he declared (quoting Stalin), "the main and most important thing in the whole work of the Komsomol." [20]

Apparently there was apprehension lest Komsomolites interpret the insistence on the non-Party and propagandistic nature of the Komsomol as indicating a diminution in the role of the League, for Fainberg took special pains to deny this. He asserted that, on the contrary, the Komsomol's role was being increased, since the League now was to deal with *all* classes of toiling youth instead of chiefly the proletariat.[21] The limitations of that clever bit of reasoning were soon illustrated. In showing that the "basic questions of the labor and education of youth" had already been decided in favor of Soviet youth and therefore did not need to be included in the Program any longer, Fainberg cited the claims of the Soviet regime: unemployment had been eliminated; the working day had been limited first to eight and then to seven hours, with six hours for youths aged sixteen to eighteen; child labor below the age of sixteen had been abolished, and underground and other dangerous work had been prohibited below the age of eighteen; training had been combined with productive work through the Factory Training Schools; collectivization of the farmers was erasing the former contrast between worker and peasant youth in regard to access to education and use of machines; and Soviet youth was now able to obtain not only secondary but also higher education, and freely to choose any occupation. Could the Komsomol take part of the credit for this? By no means. "Certain former leading officials of the Komsomol of the Shatskin type," said Fainberg, had tried to give the Komsomol credit for improving the working conditions for youth; but their attempt was a Trotskyite trick for pitting the League against the Soviet government, for they failed to recognize that the Soviet government and the Party provided everything that was needed by youth! [22]

Fainberg turned next to the task of technical and especially political "education." He gave Stalin's formulation of one passage in the new Program:

The ALCLY establishes schools and circles and undertakes other measures for imparting political literacy to youth [and] for the study of the basic historical events in general and particularly the history of the USSR and the All-Union Communist Party, and organizes the study, by youth, of the fundamental ideas of Marx, Engels, Lenin, and [no false modesty here] Stalin.[23]

Fainberg noted especially Stalin's interest in seeing that youth learned the history of the USSR and of the Party.[24] Such training, one may observe, would ensure that the good Komsomolite kept abreast of the successive Bolshevik revisions of history and could refute those who happened to have read an "outmoded" or "bourgeois" version, including the earlier recognized writings of Pokrovskii and Popov.

Beyond the "educational" task, there still remained the "building of Communist society." This task was seemingly brought closer by the proclamation that socialism had already been achieved, for that in turn meant that now in the USSR (as the new Program put it) "the conditions are being prepared for the transition from socialism—the first stage of Communist society—to full Communism." [25] Actually, however, the goal remained as vague as it had been in 1920.[26] Meanwhile, Komsomolites were expected to keep on doing their best in the factory or on the farm [27] and to observe Communist morality. Fainberg tried to show that Communist morality manifested a "solicitude for man"—in proof of which he adduced a remark of Stalin's that "of all the precious capital goods that there are in the world, the most precious and most decisive capital is people, cadres." [28] That was solicitude of a special sort! Fainberg denied that Communist morality embraced any definite set of rules for conduct. Stalin did not want everyone to dress alike and think alike, Fainberg asserted; on the contrary, socialism should permit the broadest development of individuality, of all one's talents. Soviet youth, he said, wants to have a "Stalinist character." And what was that? Fainberg answered by quoting the master himself: "I will continue to be prepared to give, for the cause of the worker class, the cause of the proletarian revolution and world Communism, all my strength, all my talents, and, if need be, all my blood, drop by drop." [29]

In closing, Fainberg tried to convince his hearers that the new Program he was proposing on behalf of the CC was sincere. Other political parties, he said, write programs merely for external consumption, programs in which the inner circle of leaders does not really believe.[30] Not so with Communists, he declared, recalling Stalin's reply to the question whether the phrase "worker-peasant government" was merely an agitational slogan:

The posing of such a question implies that our Party can issue inwardly false slogans, worthless in fact, in which the Party itself does not believe, but which are nevertheless used by the Party in order to deceive the masses. . . . But our Party can never under any circumstances . . . [do that], for it is a Marxist Party, a Leninist Party, a rising Party, drawing its strength from the fact that its word and its deed are inseparable, that it does not deceive the masses, that it tells the masses only the truth and builds its policies not on demagoguery but on a scientific analysis of class forces.[31]

Therefore each point of the Komsomol Program, declared Fainberg, "not only can be carried out, but will of necessity be carried out." [32] It is interesting that he thought it necessary to conclude on such a note, aimed evidently at those sharpeyed Komsomolites who, observing the contradictions between Soviet claims and Soviet reality, were becoming infected with a corrosive cynicism.

ON THE ROAD TO MONOLITHISM WITHIN THE LEAGUE

On the one hand, the Tenth Congress was reviving an emphasis on formulas reminiscent of 1920 and 1921—that the League was not a junior Party, that there was only one Party, that the League must not try to copy the Party, and that the League must not try to perform the governmental and economic directing tasks which belonged to the Party but must concentrate on the "educational" part of its mission.[33] On the other hand, the Congress was giving dramatic evidence that both the League's relations with the Party leadership and the League's internal operations had changed considerably since Lenin's day.

Stalin stood on the platform with other Bolshevik leaders as the Tenth Congress opened. There were cries of "Long live Comrade Stalin!" "A Komsomol greeting to Comrade Stalin!" and "Thank you, Comrade Stalin, for a happy, joyful life!" [34] Kosarev, in his brief introductory address, was interrupted by "stormy applause" or an "ovation" each time he mentioned Stalin's name—which was often.[35] After electing (by list and without discussion) an Honorary Presidium headed by Stalin,[36] the delegates unanimously approved a greeting which called Stalin the "teacher," "best friend," and "father" of the younger generation.[37] Whenever in the subsequent course of the Congress a speaker extolled some other prominent Bolshevik, he took pains to rank him below Stalin.[38] The achievements of industrialization, collectivization, and the liquidation of "hostile elements" were all attributed to Stalin's "genius." [39] His directives were equated with guarantees of success.[40] He was cited as a model of heroism for Komsomolites to follow in his readiness to sacrifice for Communism all his blood, "drop by drop." [41] The proper attitude for female Komsomolites was demonstrated by one of them who, after a special visit with Stalin, told the delegates with girlish enthusiasm: "Comrade Stalin was very jolly and smiled all the time. Comrade Stalin looks after us as our own father, and I feel like saying again and again how deeply we love him." [42] Similar homage was paid by speaker after speaker.[43] Kosarev's peroration is typical of the flourishes used in closing each of the main addresses at the Congress:

> Long live our glorious Stalinist generation of youth!
> Long live the invincible Leninist Party of Bolsheviks!
> Long live the one who nurtured us, who rears us, who toughened us, who readies us for the battles ahead—the great Stalin! (*Stormy applause swelling into an ovation. All stand. From each delegation come exclamations of greeting:* "Long live Comrade Stalin!" "Hurrah!" "Hurrah for Comrade Stalin!") [44]

At the closing session, in his presence once again,[45] the delegates reportedly broke into "ovations in honor of Comrade
Stalin" which lasted for fifteen minutes.[46] Clearly, the good
Komsomolite must now practice nothing less than lavish worship of The Leader.

The elections held at the Tenth Congress went like clock-
work. The Presidium and other bodies designed to administer
the Congress itself were elected at the opening session, by list,
without discussion, and apparently unanimously.[47] The elections of the new Central Committee of ninety-three (plus
thirty-five candidate-members), and of the Central Inspection
Commission of seventeen, were conducted at the closing session
with similar dispatch, all votes being unanimous.[48] Similarly,
in all other matters where a vote was taken (including the
new Program and the new Regulations), the votes were recorded as unanimous with no abstentions.[49]

The "discussion" at the Tenth Congress exhibited a solidarity that should have warmed the heart of the best Komsomolite. There was much less criticism of the report of the
CC at this Congress than at any preceding one. The typical
delegate docilely endorsed that report, praised the leadership of
Stalin and the Party, and dared not venture beyond such safe
themes as complaining about inadequate guidance from
above.[50] Kosarev was all too accurate when he observed that
the speakers participating in this discussion had indulged over-
much in generalities, in high-sounding praise of the Central
Committee, and in flattery of himself.[51]

Several delegates went through the motions of suggesting
changes in the drafts of the new Program and amended Regulations, although those apparently were meant to be enacted
in the form in which the leadership submitted them.[52] The
suggestions were generally unassailable in that they demanded
more of the Komsomolite than did the drafts as "proposed." [53]
Two delegates, somewhat bolder than the rest, mentioned the
flouting of the Regulations concerning the required frequency
of the meetings of various Komsomol bodies. One of these
delegates cited delays in the meetings of bodies from the lower

echelons right up to the Plenums of the CC, but conspicuously failed to mention the similar delay in holding the All-Union Congress, which was the direct responsibility of the Komsomol CC.[54] The complaint of the other delegate was recorded as follows:

The Regulations must be carried out steadfastly and unconditionally. Take our Far East. In the old Regulations it says that krai [large territorial unit] conferences are to be held not less than once every three years, and we haven't had a krai conference for five years and four months. (*Laughter. Exclamations:* "Oho!") The CC of the Komsomol knew about this.[55]

From the bare language of the stenographic report, one cannot tell what kind of laughter it was, or what was the intonation in the cries of "Oho!" But one may infer a reaction of mock surprise, and one may conclude that some or perhaps many of the delegates took it for granted that this particular provision of the Regulations was *not* operative—was, indeed, something for the masses but not for the inner circle of the League to worry about. The fact that this record was published seems to show that cynicism on this point was not feared, despite the aforementioned protestations of Fainberg (and Stalin) that there could be no such private language for the top leaders, and despite the seemingly unconditional demands tor strict observance of the Regulations in every respect.[56]

The delegates had a special duty and opportunity to display "Bolshevik criticism" during the discussion of educational work—this field allegedly having been neglected in the attempt of treacherous Komsomolites to "copy the Party." Vasilii A. Muskin, who presented the main report on the League's work in the schools, heavily accentuated its shortcomings.[57] Catching that cue, the delegates then pitched in with a will, flaying the Komsomol CC, the Commissariat of Education, and others connected with the schools or with other educational work.[58] Muskin gave blanket acknowledgment of all the "healthy dissatisfaction" and "sharp criticism" of the CC which the delegates had expressed. He asserted that there had been some unfounded reproaches, but declined to specify them, saying that he would "leave them on the consciences of the comrades" (which brought laughter from the delegates).[59] Then, despite all their criticism, the delegates voted unanimously to approve Muskin's recommendations.[60] Thus in general the delegates observed carefully the demand that "criticism" by the good Komsomolite "must be directed toward the better realization of the decisions of the Party and toward the still greater solidarity of the Komsomol around the Party"[61]—that is, must follow clearly the channels indicated by those who spoke for the top leadership.

The new Regulations, which were explained by Petr A. Vershkov, a member of the Komsomol CC,[62] reflected in part a policy of expanding the membership. As of 1936 the League contained only about one-tenth of the youths in the eligible age group.[63] Ever since 1924 all youths who were not unquestionably of "worker" or "peasant" origin (and many "middle peasants" could not even qualify as "peasants" for this purpose) had been obliged to meet stiff entrance requirements, including recommendations from two Party members of three years' standing (or one Party member of two years' standing and two Komsomolites of three years' standing), and a probationary period of eighteen months.[64] Now peasant, worker, and intelligentsia youths were intended to enter on an equal footing.[65] Even offspring of the "alien classes" were to be taken in, provided they were among the "most loyal to the Soviet government," for Stalin had announced (said Kosarev) that "the son is not responsible for the father."[66] The League was told not to be so "narrow," not to try to apply the standards that would be required for Party membership, but still to choose the "foremost politically literate, toiling youth of town and countryside," "the foremost tested youths loyal to the Soviet government."[67] A probationary stage of "candidacy" was retained for those of any class who needed additional "political preparation," but the period was reduced to six months. Every prospective member had to be recommended, but the recommendation of two Komsomolites of one year's standing (or one Party member, no matter how new) was enough.[68]

The age limits of the Komsomol were changed in the new Regulations. Vershkov "proposed" that the lower limit be raised from fourteen to fifteen, since the Factory Training Schools, which formerly took youths at fourteen, now were taking them at fifteen. The upper limit of twenty-three he proposed to raise to twenty-six. The reason he gave was that 30 percent of the membership of the League was now over twenty-three, and that there were many worthy youths between the ages of twenty-three and twenty-six who could not quite qualify for the Party but deserved to be allowed to continue fully active in the League.[69] The age limits, unlike almost all other topics discussed by the Congress, were something upon which the delegates felt it was safe to disagree. Proposals of twenty-eight and thirty for the upper limit were heard but were rejected on the ground that there was too much difference between people of those ages and youths of fifteen.[70] The Regulations as enacted provided that the limits would be fifteen and twenty-six and that "members of the ALCLY who have reached the age of twenty-six may remain in the organization with the right of advisory voice, and in cases where they are elected to directing bodies they may have the right to vote." [71] That this provision (which had previously applied when the limit was twenty-three) was being liberally used was indicated by the composition of the Congress itself. Of the 801 voting delegates, 13.9 percent (111) were born in 1905, while 45.4 percent (364) were born in 1906–9. Thus almost three-fifths (59.3 percent) of the delegates were twenty-six or older. As for the rest, 26.2 percent (210) were born in 1910–12, and 14.5 percent (116) were born in 1913. These figures add up to the total of 801, meaning that all the voting delegates were twenty-two or older! [72]

Democratic centralism, according to the new Regulations, comprised:

a. the election of all leading bodies of the Komsomol, from the top to the bottom;

b. the periodic reporting of Komsomol [governing] bodies to their Komsomol organizations;

c. strict Komsomol discipline and the subordination of the minority to the majority;

d. the strict obligatoriness of the decisions of higher Komsomol bodies upon all lower Komsomol bodies and all members of the Komsomol.[73]

The elective principle, Vershkov explained, gave "to any organization or any member of the Komsomol the full right to demand the replacement of unsatisfactory leadership." [74] The description of the elective system within the League remained virtually unchanged: at each echelon, the relatively large deliberative body (Congress, conference, or "primary organization" [cell]) was to elect the executive body (Central Committee, committee, bureau, or secretary) at that same echelon and also the delegates who were to be sent from that echelon to the deliberative body at the next higher echelon. Thus, above the lowest echelon, all bodies were to be elected *indirectly*—a practice which facilitated control by the Party.[75] The new Regulations, like the old, did not specify exactly how the individual in charge at each echelon (the secretary) was to be chosen but, unlike the old, did say that the secretary of the primary organization (cell) was to be elected.[76] Except for that provision, the way was apparently open for the secretary at each echelon to be either elected or appointed. However, if the Regulations were to be observed strictly, that person should have been chosen from among those already elected to the executive body at the echelon in question. In that respect, at least, the Regulations had been consistently disregarded by those at the top, for there was ample evidence that the prevailing practice had been for the Central Committee to appoint and to send down people to serve as secretaries of the subordinate Komsomol units.[77] Only one delegate had the temerity to suggest openly that there was too much appointing from above and to recommend that when certain lesser officials (not secretaries, but Komsomol organizers and political assistants) were sent down by the Central Committee, they should be only "recommended" and not officially "confirmed" by the CC until they had proved themselves and, in the case of the political assistants, until they had been "elected" by the local organization.[78] But no general change in appointive practice was even proposed. The Komsomol leadership obviously expected to continue to violate the Regulations. Again, the good Komsomolite presumably must learn to reconcile that violation with the demand for strict obedience to the Regulations and with the assertion that no directives of the Party or League could conceivably be issued for merely agitational purposes.

Komsomol officials complained bitterly of inefficiency, excessive paper work, delay in answering correspondence, carelessness in keeping records, and inadequate supervision from the center.[79] (The example was cited of a directive issued by the CC on February 23, requiring an answer from all committees at the oblast level before March 15. When March 15 arrived, not even one of the subordinate bodies had yet replied.) [80] In order to handle the increased volume of paper work, the administrative and clerical staff of the CC had been almost doubled since 1931 (from 80 to 156).[81] It was also reported that not long before the Tenth Congress, the Komsomol had been given its own "self-standing" budget, separate from that of the Party. This action was said to place greater responsibility upon Komsomol officials to exercise economy in their expenditures and to collect dues more faithfully.[82] (The latter obligation was not insisted upon very strenuously, to judge from the report that during 1935 in some oblasts only 65 percent or 70 percent of the dues had been collected.)[83] The reversion to a separate budget for the Komsomol may have been another means to persuade Komsomolites that they were being given more responsibility, at a time when they were actually subject to increasing restrictions.

The typical Komsomol leaders of the time were relatively old, judging from the delegates' ages reported above. They were characterized likewise by long service in the Komsomol: of the 801 voting delegates, well over half (449, or 56 percent) had been members since 1925 or earlier, that is, more than ten years. Only 14.2 percent (114) had joined in 1931 or later.[84] Despite the age and long service, considerable turnover in the leadership was suggested by the fact that only 15.7 percent (126) of the voting delegates of 1936 had attended the Congress of

1931.[85] That turnover, however, was less than that between 1928 and 1931 (see Chapter V). Although class distinctions were supposedly no longer to be observed in admissions to the League, the official report on the delegates at the Tenth Congress continued the practice of listing their distribution by social origin.[86] Class distinctions were also still made in the requirements of Party service for certain positions in the League: according to the new Regulations, secretaries of the Komsomol at the oblast, krai, and national republic levels needed four years of Party service if they were of worker origin (parentage), but five years if they were not; [87] at the city and okrug levels, secretaries who were of worker origin needed to have had two years in the Party, while others had to have three years; at the raion level the Party requirement was the same (two years) but nonworkers had to have more Komsomol service (four years) than workers (three years).[88] In this period when the grip of the Party on the Komsomol was being further strengthened, it is interesting to observe that the proportion of Party members and candidate-members among the delegates was permitted to drop to 78.2 percent, as compared with 90.9 percent in 1931.[89] Apparently the Party now felt secure enough in its control of the League to bring in more low-echelon people than before for propagandistic purposes.

As to the techniques of leadership desired within the Komsomol, the stress was again on guidance suited to each individual.[90] Heavy sarcasm was directed at Komsomol leaders who sought to win popularity through speeches rather than hard work.[91] At the same time, some officials of the Komsomol, including Kosarev, Muskin, Dmitrii D. Luk'ianov, and Vasilii T. Chemodanov, got special recognition.[92] By far the most honored was the thirty-three-year-old Kosarev, who had been prominent at the Congress of 1928, had led that of 1931, and was now in charge.[93] Youths were expected to write to him about their troubles. Viktor I. Kozlov (of the Central Inspection Commission) told of several cases in which youths of all sorts—"homeless waifs, thieves, and rogues, who want to get back on the straight and narrow path"—had written to Kosarev and had received careful attention from him. In one case, a group of ten young workers had been arrested for "hooliganism and fighting" and had been promptly found guilty and sentenced to as much as six years of "deprivation of freedom." The court of appeals had perfunctorily approved the sentence. The youths had then written to Kosarev. An investigation had been conducted by a representative of the Komsomol CC and a representative of the Procurator's Office of the USSR. They discovered that the charge had been based on someone's "false report." The Supreme Court had thereupon revoked the sentence. The guilty officials had received "deserved punishment." Kozlov urged other leaders in the Komsomol to follow Kosarev's example.[94] Here the leaders of the League were depicted, then, as persons who could intercede with the governmental authorities on behalf of Komsomolites and other youth, and Kosarev personally was placed on a pedestal. Of course he in turn depicted himself as only a pupil and follower of Stalin. But the future was to show that, under Stalin, Komsomol leaders should appear even more self-effacing, and that rank-and-file Komsomolites accordingly should observe most scrupulously their officials' passion for humility before The Leader.

THE PARTIAL CURB ON GOVERNMENTAL AND ECONOMIC RESPONSIBILITIES

"Our [Komsomol] organizations, instead of handling the training of youth, want to guide and direct everything. In this lies a fundamental defect of our work. We do not need to guide and direct—for this there are other organizations: the Party and the soviets." [95] That warning from Kosarev was not meant to check individual participation in the Soviet government. Komsomolites were still to help with election campaigns and to serve in the soviets.[96] Kosarev released statistics on both urban and rural soviets, showing that from 1931 to 1934 the representation of Komsomolites on these bodies had increased both absolutely and proportionately.[97] But while he suggested that Komsomolites should be more active in the soviets, he made it clear that they should participate as Soviet citizens and individual Komsomol members, rather than with any aim of directing the soviets on behalf of the Komsomol as an organization.

In economic activity the line was similar. The delegates were told that the Komsomol had been overburdening itself with tasks of economic construction.[98] The League, as an organization, must not try to control economic activity. (In this connection, the new Komsomol Regulations provided that primary organizations [cells] in important economic institutions where there was a Political Section [i.e., a section for political surveillance] must be directed by an official of that section [an assistant for Komsomol work]. That official, in turn, had to be not only selected by, and under the immediate supervision of, the Central Committee of the Komsomol but also supervised by the head of the Political Section [that is, a trusted Party man].) [99] At the same time, there was no diminution in the economic obligations of Komsomolites as productive citizens.[100] The attainment of socialism, said Kosarev, had made toil "a matter of honor, valor, glory, and heroism." [101] In 1928 and 1931, socialist competition had been urged largely as a rivalry of groups. By 1936, however, the emphasis was on individuals— Stakhanovites—who were honored for having increased production, ostensibly through evolving a more efficient technique rather than solely through harder work. Of the 801 voting delegates at the Tenth Congress, 218, or 27.3 percent, were said to be Stakhanovites working in industry, agriculture, or transportation.[102] Numerous were the speeches telling of the League's role in the Stakhanovite movement.[103] Although (according to the new Program) all occupations chosen by Soviet youth were "equally honorable and respected," [104] many youths were said to be avoiding factory work. Teacher-Komsomolites were told to use worker Stakhanovites in order to "show the students in the upper grades what they can become in [factory] production." [105]

The regime's objections to Komsomol control of economic activity did not imply that the regime was reluctant to call upon the League to recruit labor. Speakers at the Congress extolled the many special mobilizations that had again been conducted to draft Komsomolites for work on important projects. The Komsomol Central Committee alone was reported to have sent about two hundred thousand League members out to construction jobs, and many more members had been recruited by local Komsomol organizations particularly in the Urals, the Ukraine, western Siberia, Moscow, and the Northern Krai.[106] The construction of the Moscow subway was credited largely to the Moscow Komsomol organization, which had received the Order of Lenin in recognition of this achievement. Another Order of Lenin had been earned by the League for the shock work of Komsomolites in building the great dam on the Dnieper.[107] Perhaps the most spectacular achievement attributed largely to Komsomolites was the construction in the Far East of the city named after the League, Komsomol'sk-on-the-Amur.[108]

Komsomolites were reminded that all of them who were working should belong to trade unions.[109] Shvernik said that Komsomolites constituted only 5.4 percent of the personnel of the governing councils of trade unions at the oblast, krai, and republic levels and that the percentage should be increased.[110] Under the new League Regulations, a Komsomol primary organization in an institution or plant where there was a trade union was required to send a representative to that union. The Komsomol representative was to help carry out Party and Komsomol decisions and to see that the laws relating to youth were obeyed.[111] The double-edged latter provision, taken together with the elimination, in the new Program, of reference to the League as a protector of youth,[112] seems to mark the formal burial of the function, previously claimed by the Komsomol, of protecting the interests of worker youth. As previous chapters have shown, this claim had always been subject to qualification and limitation by the Party and the government. In 1931 the claim had been termed unnecessary, but it had remained in the Program. Now, with the supposed attainment of socialism, the claim itself was withdrawn.

In agriculture, collectivization had been largely completed

by 1936, said Party secretary Andrei A. Andreev.[113] Tribute was paid to Komsomolites who had aided the especially difficult collectivization in the Don and Kuban regions [114] and in the Ukraine.[115] On 74.5 percent of the collective farms in the Ukraine there were now primary organizations of the Komsomol.[116] That proportion compared favorably with the 40 percent obtaining in the country as a whole: there were only a little over 100,000 Komsomol primary organizations in kolkhozes, although there were 250,000 kolkhozes in existence.[117] Moreover, in an apparently random sample of 565 rural Komsomol units studied by the CC, over half (55 percent) were found to be on collective farms where there was no Party cell.[118] This situation entailed a heavy responsibility for which many of the Komsomol bodies were said to be unfitted. About 6 percent, or over 6,000 of the Komsomol organizations in kolkhozes, were said to consist of only one or two members— incidentally a breach of the Regulations, which prescribed a minimum of three.[119] A reflection of this weakness was that the Komsomol embraced only about 7 percent of the youths on the collective farms.[120] At the machine-and-tractor stations, however, about 14 percent of the tractor drivers and 16 percent of the combine operators were Komsomolites.[121] The Komsomol was expected to improve its work in the rural areas and to stimulate Stakhanovism in agriculture.[122]

Thus in agriculture and in industry the demands upon the individual Komsomolite for higher production had not slackened. The prohibition on directive functions may, however, be understood as signaling a change in emphasis. Abandoning its economic focus of the early thirties, the League was now expected to turn toward educating the young.

THE STRESS ON EDUCATION AND INDOCTRINATION

The "educational" task that was emphasized at the Congress of 1936 was a task of indoctrination as well as education in a stricter sense and embraced both Komsomolites and nonmembers, both inside and outside the regular school system.[123] Indoctrination beyond the schoolhouse walls had always been an important reason for the existence of the Komsomol, but in 1936 that responsibility was deemed central.[124] The regime, having decreed that socialism had been attained, evidently had to redouble its efforts to condition the minds of its subjects against an awareness of the persistent realities of poverty and arbitrary rule. To be sure, certain promises inherent in the official ideology—like the new Program's reference to the happy day when "the last traces of economic inequality among people will be eliminated"—pertained to the undefined second stage, or "full Communism," [125] and could be postponed without embarrassment. But the explicit announcement that socialism (that is, "the first stage of Communist society") had "become a reality" [126] required that many blessings which previously had been referred to the future now had to be spoken of in the present tense. It had to be asserted, for example, that the New Soviet Man was already in existence, or at least just coming onto the scene. As Muskin expressed it:

People are growing up who are eagerly taking possession of the cultural heritage accumulated by mankind.

People are growing up who love boundlessly their Soviet homeland, the fatherland of the toilers and the oppressed of the whole world, people who hate the world of exploitation and slavery.

People are growing up who are strangers to national differences, strangers to bourgeois individualism and selfishness, people in whom internationalism and comradeship are innate qualities.

People are growing up with new Bolshevik qualities—strong-willed, manly, fearless in the face of difficulties—for whom clarity of goals, persistence in attaining goals, and firmness in overcoming all and sundry obstacles are the main rules of conduct.

People are growing up who have been trained from childhood to guard socialist property as the apple of their eye.

There is growing up a generation of physically hardened, strong, and joyful Soviet children.[127]

These qualities were generally so imponderable that even the not-so-good Komsomolite might be persuaded that they were beginning to prevail. But in some other respects the Komsomolite would need broad blinders. Despite the hard conditions in the USSR, he was asked to believe that poverty had been eliminated and that Soviet youth was the best cared for and the

happiest in the world.[128] At a time when wage and salary differentials were increasing, and Stakhanovites were receiving
generous monetary rewards, the Komsomolite was asked to believe that the New Soviet Man was not striving to be rich but
was merely doing his duty to socialist society.[129] Such facts,
now that socialism had been proclaimed, obliged all good Komsomolites to build higher than before the ideological walls that
protected their belief in Soviet orthodoxy.

The leaders in this campaign of political indoctrination were
to be Komsomolites who, as concurrent members of the Party,
had undergone rigorous training in Party schools. The importance of this training was underscored by the fact that the
Tenth Congress, unlike previous congresses, gave a detailed
listing of the proportions of delegates who had attended each
type of school.[130] While all Komsomolites were expected to
be propagandists of a sort, those who specialized in that duty
and bore the professional designation of "propagandist" numbered, at the time of the Tenth Congress, about one hundred
thousand Komsomolites, including 18,000 Party members assigned to the Komsomol for this particular function.[131] Some
of the problems encountered by the indoctrinators were discussed by Kosarev. Many young people, he acknowledged,
failed to appreciate the "wonderful actuality" of Soviet life.
Why? Because "they do not know the dismal prerevolutionary
past, do not know the horrors of the Intervention and the fiery
days of the Civil War." [132] (In other words, they were expecting
too much.) In order to detect and to eradicate such discontent,
Kosarev went on, Komsomolites must work with each youth
individually; they must not penalize any youth too severely
for unorthodox questions or statements; they must not mistake
ignorance or curiosity for deviation. "We must," he said, "be
irreconcilable toward class enemies, toward their agents, and
toward those who are losing their revolutionary vigilance, but
revolutionary vigilance itself requires that we shall not permit
the groundless pinning of labels and tags, that we shall not permit education to be replaced by shouting." Undeserved reprimands, he pointed out, "embitter people" and this "breeds

enemies." [133] Kosarev did not even hint at the existence of the coercive machinery of the Soviet regime.

Belles-lettres were expected to continue to serve the ends of political indoctrination.[134] An official of the Children's Publishing House sponsored by the Komsomol CC reported that about 9,000,000 children's books had been published in 1933, over 18,000,000 in 1935, and that for the year 1936 the number was expected to total 36,000,000—four times the amount published in 1933.[135]

For the indoctrination of children below Komsomol age, the Pioneers and Octobrists [136] evidently now had the field to themselves, for the Tenth Congress made no mention of the Boy Scouts or of the religious groups which had existed, albeit with difficulty, before the Stalinist consolidation. An important shift had occurred in the Pioneers. At the time of the Ninth Congress the Pioneer organization had its main base in the factories and the collective farms, with mere "outposts" in the schools. But later in that same year (1931) the base of Pioneer work had been transferred to the schools.[137] By the time of the Tenth Congress the close connection between the Pioneers and the schools was everywhere in evidence. For example, it was the head of the Pioneer Section of the Komsomol CC (Muskin) who delivered the major report on the work of the Komsomol in the schools.[138] The Commissar of Education of the RSFSR, Andrei Sergeevich Bubnov, called for especially close cooperation between the home-room teacher and the Pioneer leader.[139] The new Program and the new Regulations both directed the Komsomol to cooperate with schools and educational agencies (as well as with trade unions) in constructing Pioneer playing fields, clubhouses, and camps.[140] The first seven grades were designated as the appropriate sphere for the Pioneers, while the eighth, ninth, and tenth grades of the recently instituted "ten-year schools" were said to be better left to the direct efforts of the Komsomol.[141] Like Komsomolites, Pioneers were expected to encourage conscientious study and other appropriate conduct.[142] Children of all social classes were to be drawn into the organization.[143]

Several benefits had accompanied the Pioneers' shift to the school. The membership had expanded from 3,447,325 in 1931 to about seven million in 1934 and 1936.[144] Pioneer leaders had reportedly been easier to recruit.[145] The grade structure of the school had facilitated the organizing of the Pioneers by age groups, thus making it easier to suit the activities to the interests of each group.[146] Still another advantage was a negative one: the use of the school had discouraged the holding of Pioneer meetings in the homes of individuals. Muskin complained that such meetings often were "without any leadership"; they turned into "dull bourgeois parties" with "bourgeois games," fox-trotting, and "very dubious tea," which "facilitated the infiltration of petit-bourgeois influences into the Pioneer milieu." [147] One may observe that the transfer of the Pioneers to the school harmonized with the Soviet policy during the thirties of returning to the more conventional concept of the school and restoring the discipline of the teacher.

The more than 40,000 regular paid Pioneer leaders [148] and their part-time or volunteer helpers (many of whom were doing that work as their Komsomol "burden") were said to be grossly inadequate in both quantity and quality.[149] Komsomol organizations were told to steer some of their best Komsomolites into the work with the Pioneers.[150] Pioneer leaders were directed to stimulate "initiative" and "spontaneous activity" in the young Pioneers, while at the same time "guiding" the Pioneers so that (seemingly of their own accord) they did the right things.[151] In order to facilitate individual attention, the Congress resolved that the Pioneer detachments, which had supposedly included fifty, but actually contained often sixty or seventy, children, should be limited to forty.[152]

In accordance with the current Soviet policy of strengthening the "new family," the Tenth Congress instructed Komsomolites to show respect for their parents.[153] Greater respect for women was also urged.[154] The increasing participation of women in public life was praised.[155] Women Stakhanovites were prominently mentioned, to show that there were equal rights for women in production.[156] Thirty-four percent of the League's

members were now women, as compared with 23 percent in
1928, but a still further increase was demanded.[157] The work
among women was particularly poor in the kolkhozes, where in
some areas only 3 percent of the League members were women,
and in some national minority areas, where the proportion of
women was only 10–15 percent. [158] Women were still not receiving a proportionate share of representation in the higher
circles of the League: only 23.5 percent (188) of the delegates
at the Tenth Congress were women,[159] and in the new Central
Committee of 128 members and candidate-members, only 19
(or 14.8 percent) were women [160]—far below their proportion
in the League as a whole.

Previous congresses had discussed the problem of crime,
partly in connection with the roving hordes of homeless waifs.
The Congress of 1936 said nothing about the waifs, and that
omission may be natural enough, since the children made
homeless in 1917–20 were, by 1936, either grown up or dead.
The same consideration cannot, however—even in view of the
undoubted improvement in police control—entirely explain
why the Tenth Congress scarcely discussed crime except in
references to "hooliganism." [161] That omission had in part an
ideological basis. The previous discussions of hooliganism and
crime (connected, as they were, with the homeless waifs and
the conditions of the NEP) had left room for the inference that
Soviet society shared the blame for the problem growing out
of the Revolution and the Civil War. But now, when socialism
had ostensibly been attained, hooliganism had to be depicted
as a phenomenon of only isolated groups of youths who had
come under the influence of "enemies of the Soviet people." [162]

In the schools the enrollment was reported to be rising
markedly.[163] Illiteracy among youth was hoped to be eliminated within two years.[164] Primary (that is, four-year) schooling
was virtually universal, said Bubnov, noting that in the RSFSR
96.7 percent of the children aged eight through eleven were
currently in schools.[165] Komsomolites were accordingly told
to turn their attention toward the wider extension of seven-
year or partial secondary education and ten-year or full sec-

ondary education. Kosarev reminded his listeners of a Komsomol slogan issued in 1932—"each Komsomolite to have secondary education."[166] Here the League had a long way to go. Ten-year schools, embracing the eighth, ninth, and tenth grades, had graduated their first class only in the preceding year (1935).[167] Among even so select a group as the voting delegates at the Tenth Congress, one-third (268) had nothing but primary schooling and another 28.6 percent (228) had partial secondary schooling, while only 29.6 percent (237) had full secondary schooling, and only 8.5 percent (67) had some amount of higher education.[168]

The shortage of qualified teachers was a special concern of the Komsomol at this time. Among primary- and secondary-school teachers (numbering 709,000 in 1934–35)[169] about half were estimated to be of Komsomol age.[170] Yet only about 20 percent of all teachers were Komsomolites.[171] Among the principals of primary schools, 17.4 percent were said to be in the League.[172] Along with increasing these percentages, Komsomolites were to see that teachers were shown more respect. A recent decree, said Bubnov, had raised the pay of teachers and had made the outstanding ones eligible for "personal titles" such as Honored Teacher.[173] Komsomol organizations were urged to avoid overloading teacher-Komsomolites with League duties and to leave the teachers time in which to improve their qualifications.[174] The desperate need for such improvement was clear: in the RSFSR in 1935 one-third of the primary-school teachers had themselves finished only a primary education, and only 1.5 percent had gone beyond the secondary school. Among the secondary-school teachers of the RSFSR, 9 percent had themselves completed only primary (!) schooling, while only 24 percent had gone beyond secondary schooling.[175] The Komsomol was to see that teachers took correspondence courses and other special work in order to complete at least secondary schooling. The League could help teachers to obtain books, magazines, newspapers, and also radios.[176] The Congress resolved that in 1936 there should be a special campaign to attract Komsomolites into teacher-training institutions.[177] The question arose whether the teacher-Komsomolites in each school should form a separate group to discuss common problems, but this proposal was greeted with cries of "incorrect" from the floor,[178] and a CC member who was especially responsible for student matters said that both teachers and students should be in the same Komsomol primary organization. He added that its secretary should usually be a teacher [179]—an emphatic demonstration of the new policy of tying in the Komsomol with the school.[180]

In a detailed and important resolution,[181] the Komsomol and Pioneer organizations were told to work with the school principal and the teachers to expand the activities of extracurricular circles for the study of literature, mathematics, physics, chemistry, geography, music, photography, and other subjects. The Komsomol was to arrange special lectures and to help build up the library in each school. Komsomol and Pioneer bodies were to help the school authorities to enforce discipline among all pupils.[182] In contrast to the earlier emphasis on group achievement, individual competition was now to be stimulated. Komsomolites and Pioneers were to set the example by making high marks. At Komsomol and Pioneer meetings, members were to be asked to report on their grades. Competitions were to be set up for the highest marks in each subject. At the same time, however, the poorer pupils were not to be neglected.[183] In harmony with the new policy on admissions, the Komsomol was to expand its membership in the schools and higher educational institutions without trying to restrict itself to students of worker origin.[184]

The development of athletic associations, athletic facilities, and physical education remained a Komsomol obligation.[185] The most conspicuous direct purpose of athletics continued to be military. Institutionalizing this was the system—which Komsomolites must support—called "Ready for Labor and Defense." It included a series of tests in various skills such as swimming, skiing, gymnastics, rifle marksmanship, and running through a military obstacle course. Satisfactory performance was rewarded by the RLD (Ready for Labor and Defense) badge first class (intermediate) and second class (advanced).[186] Since the founding of the RLD system five years before, 4,000,-000 persons had earned RLD badges.[187] The Komsomol delegates were told that by 1937 each student graduating from secondary school should have earned the RLD first-class badge, and each student graduating from a higher educational institution should have earned the second-class badge.[188]

WAR PREPARATIONS AND THE UNITED FRONT

The warnings of 1936 concerning the German and Japanese threat fitted in with the perennial talk of capitalist attack and entailed no basic change either in the general military outlook of Komsomol members [189] or in the League's responsibilities in the Army.[190] Kosarev depicted Komsomolites as eager to volunteer for military service, but he betrayed some apprehension lest in battle they should surrender too readily. The Komsomolite, he said,

will not let himself be taken prisoner, for capture is for him a dishonor, an indelible disgrace. Among our youth there cannot be deserters. Treason, betrayal of the homeland, is the most despicable and serious crime, the most infamous deed against the revolutionary people.

We, young Soviet people, do not fear death on the field of battle and will not lose our heads under the fire of the enemy.[191]

In the Navy, under the League's patronage, 67 percent of the "commanding personnel" were now either Party members or Komsomolites, as compared with 45 percent at the time of the Congress of 1931. Among the "fleet and younger command personnel" of the Navy, more than one-third were Komsomolites, while among the cadets in naval academies, 31 percent were Party members, 67 percent were Komsomolites not concurrently Party members, and only 2 percent were "non-Party people," i.e., not in either organization.[192] In the Air Forces, also under Komsomol patronage, 87 percent of the personnel now belonged to either the Party or the Komsomol. Among pilots and other flying personnel the proportion was 95 percent, while among aviation technicians it was 86 percent.[193]

The Osoaviakhim (the Society for the Promotion of Defense and of the Aviation and Chemical Industries) was said to be receiving strong support from the Komsomol.[194] Under the Osoaviakhim were the aero-clubs, developed (during the previous three years) in connection with the League's patronage over the Air Forces. These clubs were training parachute jumpers, reserve pilots, glider pilots, and aviation mechanics.[195] The Osoaviakhim was also training hundreds of thousands of youths in rifle marksmanship, map reading, and other military skills.[196] The attention of the delegates was called to a decision of the Central Committee of the Party which declared that it was "necessary" that "each Komsomolite participate actively in the work of the Osoaviakhim." [197]

An unusual feature of the Tenth Congress was the praise directed toward the NKVD Border Guards, particularly in connection with the frontier engagements against the Japanese in 1935 and 1936. Komsomolites and other heroes of these battles were paid tribute.[198] It was revealed that the Belorussian Komsomol was serving as the patron of the NKVD Border Guards along the Belorussian frontier. Several Komsomolites were saluted for their "heroic example" in catching "spies and saboteurs" in those border regions.[199]

In the report on the CIY (Communist International of Youth), Chemodanov related that after ridding itself of the harmful influence of Shatskin and other "opportunists," the CIY had gone through a lean period in which many Young Communist Leagues neglected nonpolitical means of attracting support from youth.[200] Remedial action had been taken, he said, by the Seventh Congress of the Comintern and, soon thereafter, the Sixth Congress of the CIY (September 25 to October 11, 1935).[201] The CIY Congress, under the "direct guidance of Comrade Dimitrov" (of the Comintern), had told Young Communist Leagues to follow the path of the "united front" of all non-"Fascist" youth and to create "various joint organizations [i.e., fronts] for the fight for the vital interests of the younger generation." [202] While the policy of the "united front" had brought in many new members,[203] it had also brought a characteristic difficulty: some of the YCL's had gone so far in catering to youth's desires that they had "lost all political orientation" (that is, Communist control had become too weak). The YCL's must be definitely "anticapitalist" (i.e., pro-Bolshevik), Chemodanov insisted,[204] and dedicated to the defense of the USSR.[205]

Chemodanov's report gave some indication of the work of that rare Komsomolite who was assigned to the apparatus of the CIY. But what about the rank-and-file Komsomolite? At previous congresses there had been talk of corresponding with foreign youth. This time there was no mention of it. At previous congresses there had been talk of encouraging foreign youth delegations to visit the USSR and sending Soviet delegations abroad. This time, perhaps just coincidentally, that subject was not mentioned. To be sure, reports and greetings came to the Congress from representatives of the Young Communist Leagues in other countries, assuring the Komsomolites that foreign youth loved them, admired them, and looked to them for guidance.[206] But there was no indication that the vaunted brotherly contact between proletarian youths would be realized more concretely. After all, the delegates had before them the above-mentioned example of the eighty-five Leningrad propagandists who had been removed from their positions solely for the sin of having a "direct tie" with someone beyond the borders of the USSR!

Yet the apparent isolationism was not accompanied by any renunciation of the long-term goal. Said the authoritative Kosarev: "The struggle for Communism throughout the world —that's what awaits us, comrades!" [207]

The Tenth Congress, which was said to usher the Komsomol into a new era, the era of accomplished "socialism," recorded significant innovations in the Komsomol pattern. Until that time, the League had been relatively small (in 1936 it still did not embrace more than about one-tenth of the youths in the eligible age group) and had concentrated on "proletarian" youths; the barriers against "others"—in the form of Party recommendations and probationary stages—had been high. Now those barriers were lowered. Entrance to the League was, nominally at least, open to youths regardless of social class, provided they could qualify on the basis of loyalty to the regime. The upper age limit was extended from twenty-three to twenty-six, encouraging the continued participation of older youths. Thus the League, long a "mass" organization in name, was now prepared to become one in actuality.

These preparations for expansion were accompanied by warnings. The League was told not to undertake directive responsibilities in the government or the economy (although such directive responsibilities had not been large in any case). The League was not to try to be influential like the Party. (If the League had in fact tried, certainly it had never come close to succeeding!) The League was no longer even nominally to claim the function of protecting worker youth. These injunctions by no means abolished the economic and other responsibilities of the Komsomol and its members: for instance, the Komsomol was still expected to play a big role in the collective farms. But through these injunctions, whatever their other significance, ran an important implication: that education and indoctrination, always important duties of the League, were now to be its predominant function. The League's younger auxiliary, the Pioneers, had already shifted its base to the school, and the League itself was becoming increasingly a partner of the school, at a time when the school was being strengthened as an arm of the Soviet state. Komsomolites were to labor within and outside the school to teach necessary skills and inculcate loyalty to the regime.

If the stress on the League's "mass" nature and on education and indoctrination constituted the officially recognized marks of the new era, there were others no less conspicuous to the outside observer of the Tenth Congress. The increased "solidarity" of the "discussion," the heightened "unanimity" of the "voting," the intensified public demonstrations of worship for Stalin—these were revealing signs of the consolidation of Stalinist socialism.

In what way were these changes related to each other? To some extent, they were simply a reflection of increased industrialization (which demanded increased education) and centralized power (which made expansion of the schools and the Komsomol both desirable and possible). But it seems proper also to conclude that the changes stemmed in part from the proclamation of "socialism." That proclamation, with its implication that Communism was not far off, possessed appeal for many people, indoctrinated or not, at home or abroad. But it also created problems. How could the cult of Stalin be reconciled with traditional Marxism-Leninism? How could the intense individual competition that was stimulated by Stakhanovism be reconciled with the collectivist ideal? How could a miserable living standard be reconciled with the official claim that poverty had been eliminated under socialism? How could purges and other hardships be reconciled with the assertion that Soviet youth was now the happiest in the world? How could obvious inequalities among jobs be reconciled with the claim that, under socialism, all occupations were equally honored and respected? Finally, within the League itself, how could dictatorial rule be masked as democratic centralism, and how could cynical violations of the League's own Regulations be adequately explained? For all of these problems, the obvious solution was—*indoctrination*. For, now that socialism had officially been reached, only the most firmly and rigorously indoctrinated young people would be capable of accepting Soviet claims in the face of Soviet reality.

VII. The Komsomol Pattern
under Postwar Stalinism

THE CONGRESS OF 1949

THE Congress of 1949 assumes a special importance for its portrayal of the Komsomol pattern under full-blown postwar Stalinism.

FROM THE TENTH CONGRESS TO THE ELEVENTH

Between the Tenth and the Eleventh congresses of the Komsomol lay an interval of almost thirteen years of political turmoil, economic expansion, war, and reconstruction. Those developments were mentioned so briefly at the Congress of 1949 that one must turn to the pages of *Komsomol'skaia pravda* for the years 1936–49 in order to gain even a general idea of the major shifts of emphasis in the demands upon Komsomolites.

The emphasis on indoctrination which had characterized the Congress of 1936 soon gave way to the dominant theme of 1937, 1938, and early 1939—the "unmasking" of "enemies of the people." For a time it appeared that the Komsomol might escape serious involvement. In July, 1937, however, came the announcement that several prominent Komsomolites, including Saltanov, Luk'ianov, and Fainberg, had been found to be "enemies." [1] Accordingly the Fourth Plenum of the CC of the ALCLY, meeting in August under Kosarev's direction, turned its attention particularly to the problem of detecting more "enemies of the people" within the Komsomol. The Plenum "elected" four new secretaries of the CC and eight new members of the Bureau of the CC. Three of the new people (Bogachev, Brusnikin, and Nikitin) had not been elevated to the CC by the preceding Congress, and hence were appointed in violation of the Regulations.[2]

In February and March, 1938, at about the time of the trial of Bukharin, Komsomolites were instructed to "unmask" a new sort of internal enemy—the "slanderers" and "overinsurers," or those who sought to guarantee their own reputation for vigilance by irresponsibly denouncing others.[3] (The term "overinsurer," one may note, is especially fascinating, implying as it does that people might quite properly insure themselves by denouncing others, so long as they did not carry it too far.) A campaign ensued to restore to membership those who had been unjustly expelled and to punish their self-seeking accusers.[4]

Meanwhile Kosarev, the League's general secretary, was coming into increasing prominence. He was elected to the Supreme Soviet of the USSR in December, 1937, and a month later was further distinguished by being chosen for the Presidium of that Soviet.[5] On October 29, 1938, when the League observed its twentieth anniversary,[6] Kosarev delivered a speech and stood with the Politburo of the Communist Party during the celebration.[7] After nine years at the helm of the League, he was achieving a degree of public recognition not previously accorded to any Komsomol leader. How high could this Komsomolite go?

The answer came within a month. Komsomolites suddenly learned that their hitherto honored chief had not been vigilant enough against enemies within the League—such, at least, was the opinion of the Central Committee of the Party. He had been ruling the Komsomol with an iron hand and suppressing criticism of himself, continued the charge; he had forgotten the Bolshevik virtue of modesty.[8] Acting on that condemnation, the Seventh Plenum of the CC of the League, meeting November 19–22, 1938, removed Kosarev as general secretary. Other leaders accused of sharing his lack of vigilance were also removed,[9] as well as many other lesser fry down through the Komsomol hierarchy.[10] (In 1956, it may be noted, Nikita S.

Khrushchev declared that Kosarev had been the victim of false accusations fabricated upon instructions from Stalin.) [11]

The new first secretary of the Komsomol was Nikolai Aleksandrovich Mikhailov. Three other secretaries of the CC were elected: S. E. Zakharov, O. P. Mishakova, and G. P. Gromov. Elected as the new Bureau of the CC were those four, plus N. N. Romanov, E. P. Volkova, and V. A. Aleksandrov.[12] Who were these people? Mikhailov, the new leader, had been the editor of *Komsomol'skaia pravda* during the current year, and in March had been elected by the Fifth Plenum to a post on the Bureau of the CC.[13] But in order to be legally eligible for the Bureau of the CC, he should have been elected first to the CC itself by the Congress of 1936. He had not been so elected. He had not even been a delegate at that Congress.[14] That was strange, but subsequent biographies reveal something still stranger: he had never even joined the Komsomol until the end of 1937 when, at the hardly juvenile age of thirty-one, he had been transferred by the Party from *Pravda* to become editor of *Komsomol'skaia pravda*. Before that he had served seven years in the Party, doing mostly journalistic work.[15] Thus the topmost position in the Komsomol was given to someone who had never been a rank-and-file Komsomolite, and whose total prior service in the League was only about one year!

Among the other six new officials of the League, only two (Aleksandrov and Volkova) had been among the 1,103 leading Komsomolites assembled at the Congress of 1936, and only one (Volkova) had been elected to the CC at that time and thus was genuinely eligible according to the League's allegedly inviolable Regulations.[16] Thus, only two and one-half years after the Tenth Congress had elected a Central Committee of ninety-three members and thirty-five candidate-members, the Party saw fit to use only *one* of them in staffing the new top bodies of the League! This fact, however dramatic, can of course do no more than suggest the full impact of the Great Purge as it swept through the Komsomol.[17]

The other responsibilities of Komsomolites continued meanwhile.[18] In particular, Komsomolites were called upon to help conduct much of the propaganda which accompanied the single slate elections of 1937 and 1938, under the new Stalin constitution.[19] During this time the enrollment of the League rose slowly, from a little under four million at the time of the Congress of 1936 to only 4,947,000 in January, 1938.[20] Even in October, 1938, the membership was apparently not much over five million.[21] But as the purge reached its final stages, concurrently with the removal of Kosarev and his followers during the winter of 1938–39, the gates of the League were apparently opened wide,[22] and by March, 1939, the membership was officially reported at 8,000,000.[23]

At the Eighteenth Congress of the Communist Party (March, 1939), Zakharov of the Komsomol CC reported for the League. In addition to giving the figure mentioned above, he said the Pioneers now embraced 11,000,000 children.[24] Looking back at the purge, Zakharov gave thanks to the Party and to Stalin for having helped to destroy the "foul traitorous fascist band of Kosarev." He credited Stalin himself with having convoked that Plenum of the League's CC which had deposed Kosarev in November. Now, said Zakharov, "new young cadres" had come into the leadership of the League. For example, out of 385 secretaries of oblast committees, krai committees, and central committees of union republics, 319 were newly chosen, he said —remarking significantly that "to the leadership have come comrades from Party work." [25]

The provisions for the Party's control of the League were modified. The Party Congress decreed that "members of the ALCLY who are members or candidate-members of the Party leave the Komsomol from the moment they enter the Party, unless they occupy leading posts in Komsomol organizations." [26] This definitely superseded the Party directives of earlier years, which had required all Party members who were of Komsomol age to remain active in the Komsomol. Directly associated with this change was a directive issued by the CC of the Komsomol a few weeks later:

For the purpose of training and promoting new cadres more rapidly it is deemed permissible to elect to leading Komsomol work: as secretaries of *obkoms, kraikoms,* and central committees of union republics—Komsomolites with three years of membership; as secretaries of *gorkoms* and *raikoms*—Komsomolites with two years of membership.[27]

No Party service was required. In contrast, it may be recalled, the Regulations enacted by the Congress of 1936 had required from two to five years of Party service and from three to six years of Komsomol service for persons serving at the echelons named. (Of course the Plenum of the CC had no legal right to alter the Regulations of the League, but evidently it was not felt necessary to remind Komsomolites of that fact, much less to attempt any explanation of the irregularity.) To complete this group of changes in the relationship between the Party and the Komsomol, a subsequent decree of the Party CC set August 1, 1939, as the date by which all Party members or candidate-members not serving in leading posts of the League were to have left the League. Those who actually had to leave may not have been very numerous, since the holders of "leading posts" were defined as including all members of committees of primary organizations, all group organizers and members of shop bureaus, all members of *raikoms, gorkoms, okruzhkoms, obkoms, kraikoms,* and central committees of the Komsomol in the union republics, all heads of sections and instructors of committees of the ALCLY, all Pioneer leaders, and all political assistants for Komsomol affairs. Even with that all-encompassing definition, the decree provided a legal way for the sending down of additional Party men to take charge of Komsomol units: members and candidate-members of the Party who were *not* members of the League might be "elected" to leading bodies of Komsomol organizations "with the permission of the appropriate Party organization." Such persons then had to become members of the League, but the Party exempted them from the usual requirements of the Komsomol Regulations: their admission was to be immediately confirmed by the *raikom* or *gorkom* of the Komsomol, "without discussion of the ques-

tion of admission at the meeting of the primary Komsomol
organization, and without requiring the recommendations required by the Regulations of the ALCLY." Finally the decree
stated that Party members and candidate-members who were
serving as agitators, propagandists, or lecturers in Komsomol
organizations could continue in these functions even after
having surrendered their membership in the League, if the
Party wished it.[28]

An important reason behind the changes just described
would seem to have been the Party's need to economize in the
use of those junior leaders who, in the wake of the purge, could
be classed as dependable. A large Party core in the League was
not essential; the Party could control the League well enough
through those Party members who held strategic positions in
the League. Young Party members who did not hold significant
Komsomol posts could be relieved of minor Komsomol responsibilities and given more important assignments elsewhere. The
Party provided for the rapid dispatching of Party members to
take command of any Komsomol unit in case of need, yet at the
same time enabled all but the topmost Komsomol bodies to be
staffed ordinarily by Komsomolites who were not members of
the Party. Those Komsomolites could be tested and could gain
administrative experience. The aim, apparently, was not any
less control, but rather more flexible control, with a more efficient use of Party and Komsomol personnel.

After the Eighteenth Party Congress the purging of
"enemies" faded into the background [29] and economic responsibilities came to the fore. The new Party Regulations described in these words the duties of the League:

65. The ALCLY is an active helper of the Party in all state and
economic construction. Komsomol organizations must be in fact
active conveyors of Party directives in all fields of socialist construction, especially where there are no primary Party organizations.
66. Komsomol organizations have the right of broad initiative
in discussing and in placing before the appropriate Party organizations all questions of the work of enterprises, kolkhozes, sovkhozes,
and offices, in connection with the tasks of eliminating deficiencies
in the work of those institutions, giving them the necessary help

in improving their work, organizing socialist competition and shock work, conducting mass campaigns, and so on.[30]

A subsequent leading article in *Komsomol'skaia pravda* called the provision for "broad initiative" a "decisive turning-point in the work of the Komsomol," and said the Party was now increasing the role of the Komsomol on the many collective farms where there was no Party unit. On such a farm the Komsomol primary organization was directed to concern itself with such matters as sowing, providing equipment, and apportioning farm hands among the "links" or working units. The administrators of the kolkhoz were to be informed clearly of the opinion of the Komsomol organization on kolkhoz problems. Komsomolites were instructed to see that violators of kolkhoz discipline were appropriately punished. In case of trouble with the machine-and-tractor station (for instance, if the MTS did not carry out its contract with the kolkhoz), the Komsomol body was to have recourse to the authority of the *raikom* of the Party.[31] In compliance with the Party's wish, the Eighth Plenum of the CC of the League (April 7–13, 1939) not only decreed that the rural work of the League must be expanded but also announced that the League would assume patronage of certain vital industrial projects, such as the building of a larger fleet, the construction of a hydroelectric plant at Kuibyshev, the development of the coal mines near Moscow, and the building of a new railroad from Kartaly to Akmolinsk (that is, from near Magnitogorsk in the Urals to near the Karaganda coal fields of Kazakhstan). Rural Komsomol organizations were to send not less than 1,500,000 kolkhoz youths per year to the growing industries of the towns.[32]

The League's responsibilities in education and indoctrination were mentioned in 1939 by the Eighth [33] and Ninth [34] Plenums and emphasized by the Tenth (in December, 1939, at the time of the Soviet attack on Finland). The Tenth Plenum announced that of the 35,000,000 young people then in Soviet educational institutions, 1,500,000 were Komsomolites and 13,-000,000 were Pioneers. The Komsomol was cautioned that it must not permit its economic activities to lead to a neglect of its responsibilities for the enforcing of proper discipline in the schools.[35] Mikhailov insisted especially that the authority of the teacher must be strengthened. He noted a recent decline in the influx of teachers into the League and said this situation must be corrected.[36]

The propaganda function of the League was called into play in June, 1940, to explain in "a Bolshevik way" the new law instituting the seven-day week and restricting departures from jobs.[37] In October, along with the decree on tuition for secondary schools and higher educational institutions, there was enacted the decree on the Labor Reserves and the schools of Factory-and-Plant Training (FZO). Komsomolites were urged to volunteer for the Labor Reserves and to urge other youths to do likewise.[38] Meanwhile the League had grown to 9,000,000 by October, 1939,[39] over 10,000,000 by January, 1940,[40] and 10,223,000 by June, 1940.[41]

With the outbreak of war with Germany in June, 1941, the League's military obligations—which had by no means been forgotten during 1939 and 1940 [42]—naturally became primary. A few days after the German attack, Mikhailov called upon Komsomolites to enter "the first ranks of fighters for homeland, for honor, for freedom!" [43] The League was told to shift all its work to the military side.[44] The paper soon displayed stories of Komsomol heroes in the front lines and such slogans as "Your life belongs to the homeland" and "Blood for blood, death for death!" [45] The Moscow units of the League reportedly mobilized 260,000 Komsomolites in 1941 to defend the endangered capital.[46] As the war continued, German atrocities were given prominence, especially when the victims were Komsomolites engaged in guerrilla warfare behind the German lines.[47] In 1943 guerrilla warfare was glorified and dramatized in the story of the "Young Guard" of five Komsomolites who had operated in southern Russia under the German occupation.[48] During the course of the war, 3,500,000 Komsomolites on military duty (100,000 of them young women) reportedly received medals for heroic or otherwise outstanding achievement.[49] The wartime services of the League as a whole earned it the Order of Lenin, awarded on June 14, 1945.[50]

Activities behind the front were also vital. Praise went to the "two-hundred-percenters," each of whom produced double his quota in order to compensate for a fellow worker who had gone to the front.[51] Youths who excelled in the factories were honored in much the same way as military heroes.[52] For agriculture, orders were issued in the style of military campaigns, and achievements were reported in bulletins from the "Sowing Front" in the spring and from the "Harvest Front" in the summer and fall.[53] "Komsomol control posts," allegedly started through Komsomol "initiative" in October, 1941, strove to promote efficiency in transportation and in production.[54]

The membership of the League grew considerably during the war. Very possibly the standards for admission were somewhat relaxed and semiactive members were more reluctantly dropped from the rolls. Of course, millions of youths were in the Army where they could be propagandized and persuaded to join more effectively than in civilian life.[55] Two million youths joined the League in approximately the first fifteen months of the war.[56] In November, 1942, the Central Committee of the League decreed the admission into the Komsomol of youths from the age of fourteen, instead of fifteen as specified in the Regulations (which supposedly could be changed only by a new congress). The Komsomol was called upon to expand its work among fourteen-year-olds, especially in trade schools and Factory-and-Plant Training Schools (FZO schools, connected with the Labor Reserves), and in orphanages.[57] The main reason later given for lowering the age limit was that it would enable the League to take in the younger participants in the Labor Reserve program.[58] On October 29, 1943, in connection with the twenty-fifth anniversary of the Komsomol, it was reported that since the beginning of the war, 5,351,247 youths had entered the Komsomol and 1,379,766 Komsomolites had entered the Party.[59] (In another connection, Mikhailov said that since the start of the war, 49.6 percent of those who had entered the Party had been Komsomolites. Unfortunately he gave no indication how this compared with the percentage in previous years.) [60] In 1945 the membership apparently reached 15,000,000.[61]

As the tide of war turned and victory came into view, increased attention was evidently given to the mission of the Komsomol in the schools. In 1943 separate primary organizations for teacher-Komsomolites began to operate, despite the earlier rejection of that idea by the Tenth Congress.[62] The reason which Mikhailov later adduced for the change was simply that the Central Committee of the Komsomol "considered it unsuitable that student- and teacher-Komsomolites be in the same [primary] organization." [63] That word "unsuitable" may be readily deciphered. Just as separate messes in an army underscore the distinction between officers and enlisted men, so would separate primary organizations elevate the status of the teacher.[64]

While the end of the war did not entirely silence the propaganda for military preparedness,[65] there was to be a considerable demobilization and the Komsomol was to help returning soldiers to find their place in civilian life.[66] One focus of Komsomol effort during the immediate postwar years was economic reconstruction and development. The Komsomol undertook a project in 1946 to aid in rebuilding fifteen cities destroyed by the Germans.[67] The restoration of Stalingrad was a separate and special Komsomol project.[68] Komsomolites were of course expected to bend all efforts toward fulfilling the postwar Five-Year Plan for 1946–50.[69] Demands for higher production were the most conspicuous feature of the celebration, in October, 1948, of the thirtieth anniversary of the League.[70]

A second main focus of Komsomol effort during those postwar years was indoctrination.[71] This indoctrination was evidently considered necessary not only in order to "reeducate" Soviet citizens who, during and after the war, had learned of the comparative economic and political well-being in some of the countries of Central and Western Europe, but also in order to combat the disappointment of Soviet citizens who had been led, by the wartime Soviet policies, to expect a relaxation of the Communist dictatorship after the defeat of the Nazis. A massive campaign of propaganda and agitation was conducted in 1945–46 in connection with the elections to the Supreme Soviet of the USSR. The campaign, in which Komsomolites apparently played a large role, began in October, 1945,[72] and lasted until February 10, 1946, when the single slate was "elected." [73] Stalin's election speech, and other items in the Komsomol press, warned that the threat of foreign attack was not at an end.[74] The concern with indoctrination was manifested during 1946 and 1947 in numerous reports of oblast Komsomol conferences and of Komsomol congresses in the union republics.[75] The new crop of postwar League officials was being indoctrinated also through meetings arranged by the CC for officials of *raikoms, gorkoms,* and sections for propaganda and agitation at all echelons.[76]

The postwar years apparently brought a drop in the membership of the League, but no figures have been found admitting the extent of the decline. A front-page article in July, 1946, complained that in recent months many Komsomol organizations had not grown at all, and called for remedial action.[77] One measure already facilitating expansion was the above-mentioned lowering (in 1942) of the minimum age from fifteen to fourteen.[78] Another probable aid to expansion was the virtual elimination of the probationary stage of candidate-membership in the League. Informal instructions on this must have gone out by late 1946, for of the 1,700,000-odd youths admitted in 1947, only 2,790 went through the stage of candidacy, and of the 1,900,000 admitted in 1948, only 1,617 did.[79] (At the Congress of 1949, when there were only 3,012 candidate-members in the whole League, it was argued in good Bolshevik style that since "form is inseparable from content" the Regulations must eliminate a form that had outlived its usefulness; more cogently, it was argued also that the change would aid the League's expansion. The delegates approved.) [80] Expansion was apparently furthered, too, by an absence of large-scale purging, despite the campaign against "cosmopolitanism." [81] Yet while the recruiting effort brought in over 3,600,000 youths in 1947 and 1948 alone, the total membership at the end of March, 1949 (at the time of the Eleventh Congress), was only 9,283,289.[82] If the League's peak membership had been 15,000,000 in 1945, then the officially unacknowledged postwar decline must have been a sharp one.[83]

The data available for 1949 permit an estimate, albeit a crude one, of the relationship of the Komsomol membership to the total number of Soviet youths in the eligible age group. One difficulty is that, since the distribution of the League's membership by ages was not revealed, it is uncertain how many of the 9,283,289 members were older than the nominal upper limit of twenty-six. The composition of the Congress itself, where almost half of the 1,362 voting delegates were overage,[84] does not provide a reliable basis for estimating, since Komsomol officialdom was considerably older than the mass of the membership. (For example, in the League as a whole about 68 percent [6,320,000] were in the age group up to [and presumably not including] twenty-two,[85] as compared with about 18 percent among the delegates.) [86] A second difficulty is that although members over the age of twenty-six were barred from voting in League elections, they could participate fully in all other Komsomol activities, and it is therefore somewhat unrealistic to consider the eligible age group as extending only from fourteen through twenty-five. Still another difficulty lies in the inadequacy of statistics on the general Soviet population by ages. Mindful then of these complications, one may hazard the guess that at the time of the Eleventh Komsomol Congress the Soviet Union contained about forty-three million youths aged fourteen through twenty-five,[87] and that the Komsomol at this time embraced roughly one-fifth of that age group.[88] Since both the Party and the Pioneers overlapped into this age group, the proportion of youths aged fourteen through twenty-five who, in 1949, belonged to one or more of the three—Party, Komsomol, or Pioneers—might well have exceeded one-fourth of the total.[89]

The Eleventh Congress of the Komsomol was held from

March 29 to April 8, 1949.[90] The declared purpose of the Congress was

to formulate generalizations based on thè rich experience amassed by the Komsomol; to discover, with Bolshevik keenness, the shortcomings [of the Komsomol]; and to outline a program for the further participation of the Leninist-Stalinist Komsomol in the general struggle for the building of Communist society in our country.[91]

The general concept of the role of the League at this time was outlined in a letter sent to the Congress from the Central Committee of the Communist Party.[92] This letter contained most of the key phrases which resounded repetitively through the proceedings. In harmony with the letter's reference to Komsomolites as "active builders of Communist society," the Eleventh Congress was termed the "Congress of the Young Builders of Communism," [93] and Mikhailov brought forth "stormy applause" with the assertion that "our generation will build Communism. Our generation will live under Communism." [94] In accordance with another passage of the Party's letter, the main task of the Komsomol during this transitional stage was announced as the Communist rearing of youth.[95] The letter manifested also the continuing assumption that the Komsomol properly represented all Soviet youth, including the very large majority who did not belong to the League.[96] The implicit theoretical justification for this was that the Komsomolites were the "most advanced" element of Soviet youth, its "vanguard," and that the "best" segment of Soviet youth desired to enter the Komsomol.[97] As before, the emphasis was on inclusiveness rather than exclusiveness: non-Komsomolites were to be viewed generally as potential Komsomolites, who should be readied for membership and then drawn in.[98] Thus the line between the "vanguard" and the "masses" of youth was blurred. At the same time, the letter implicitly assumed that the League was a firm monolithic unit.[99] The image apparently was one of concentric circles. In the middle was Stalin. Massed solidly around him was the Communist Party. Grouped closely around the Party was the Komsomol. While the Komsomol must reach out further and further to embrace the "best" elements of Soviet youth, the solidarity of the League must remain such as to repel all hostile elements.

THE "HERO OF OUR TIME"

At the Congress of 1949 the "overwhelming majority" of Soviet youth was said already to possess "all the elements of the character of the man of Communist society," [100] and Komsomol members, as the foremost among Soviet youth, were held to embody "these noble qualities which brilliantly characterize the striking moral countenance of the hero of our time." [101] What qualities were expected in this Komsomol hero?

Worship of Stalin was the most conspicuous requirement. Even more than in 1936, grandiloquent salutations to Stalin were the trusted mainstay of Komsomol oratory, and (according to the accounts) elicited thunderous applause. The chief elements of the ideal Komsomolite's relationship to Stalin were flamboyantly portrayed in the letter sent to him by the Eleventh Congress:

Dear Comrade Stalin:
In the name of Komsomol men and women and the whole young generation of the land of socialism, the Eleventh Congress of the All-Union Leninist Communist League of Youth sends to you, our great leader of the Soviet people, our beloved father and wise teacher, a flaming Komsomol greeting.

Accept, Comrade Stalin, our expression of great love, supreme loyalty, and heartfelt gratitude for the fatherly care and attention which you show to the Komsomol and to all Soviet youth.

. . . .

. . . the [Komsomol] delegates . . . , speaking in the name of the multimillion-strong army of Komsomol men and women and all the youth of the Soviet Union, give to you, great leader and teacher, a solemn promise always and in everything to be loyal sons and daughters of our mother, the All-Union Communist Party of Bolsheviks, to be flaming patriots of the great socialist homeland, to live, learn, work, struggle, and win after the fashion of Lenin and Stalin.

. . . .

We vow to you, dear Comrade Stalin, warmly to love our socialist homeland, mortally to hate her enemies, not to know fear in the struggle, patiently to endure hardships and misfortunes, to display determination and persistence in reaching the goal that has been set. The young generation of our country is ready to carry out all your instructions and all the instructions of the Communist Party and the Soviet government. We promise you always to be watchful, ready to deliver a crushing rebuff to the imperialist aggressors, ready to give all our strength and, if necessary, our lives in the defense of our socialist fatherland.

You teach Soviet youth perseveringly to master knowledge, culture, science, and technology.

We vow to you, Comrade Stalin, to carry out with honor these instructions of yours. We promise you . . . with great determination to master the wealth of knowledge which mankind has produced. . . .

Then followed what was apparently part of a poem or a song. It is translated here literally, without any attempt to reproduce the rhyme or rhythm.

> Our firmament transparent and crystalline,
> Our people surrounded us with care.
> And your life, your road, Comrade Stalin,
> Is taken as an example by all the youth!
> Love of you and loyalty to the fatherland
> Is the life and the spirit of the youth of our country!
> Comrade Stalin!
> With the sunlight of your life
> All the corners of the earth are illuminated!
> Stalin is the Party of Bolsheviks.
> Stalin is the banner of the great struggle.
> Stalin is the song of future centuries.
> Stalin is the sun of the people's destiny.
> Stalin is the happiness of the Soviety people;
> Stalin is the pride and glory of victories;
> Stalin is the wisdom of immortal ideas;
> Stalin is the Lenin of today.[102]

As this letter illustrates, Stalin was depicted as the leader (*vozhd'*), military commander (*polkovodets*), teacher, father, and best friend of each Komsomolite. Such adjectives as "wise," "greatest," and "beloved" were liberally employed, along with extravagant honorifics like "our sun," "our banner," and "our happiness." Stalin was the model. He was the fit recipient of vows and pledges. His "instructions" were commands.[103] He was given the credit for all Soviet achievements and the "joyful life" of each Komsomolite,[104] while the unpleasant aspects of Soviet life were to be blamed on someone else—including lesser members of the government or the Party. To the Komsomol believer, it should have seemed as though Stalin's fatherly attention extended right down to each individual. He "knows deeply and thoroughly the demands and interests of youth, its needs and expectations, and envelops our youth with great love and care." Painstakingly he "molds in our youth the new, Communist traits, the new qualities of the man of socialist society." [105] He was a source of strength and inspiration. "Comrades," averred Mikhailov, "many times in both difficult and joyous moments all of us have mentally turned to Comrade Stalin and have drawn from his words new strength, energy, and will to victory." [106] To the devout but antireligious Komsomolite, then, Stalin was to be virtually a god.

Along with the obligation to worship Stalin went the obligation to be devoted, respectful, loyal, and obedient to the Party. Stalin in theory expressed the Party's wish, and the Party in theory expressed Stalin's wish. To some extent the Party shared with Stalin the credit for the good things in Soviet life, and specifically for the achievements of the League.[107] The Komsomol was called the "devoted son" of the Party, while the Party was referred to as the "mother," "tutor," and "teacher" of the Komsomol.[108] The Party's direct control over all echelons of the Komsomol hierarchy[109] was not something to be concealed but something to be proud of.[110]

Among the more abstract and general qualities demanded in the good Komsomolite, prominence was given in 1949 to self-sacrificing patriotism.[111] Its antithesis was "cosmopolitanism." "The cosmopolite is a man without a country," said Mikhailov. "Cosmopolitanism is an ideological weapon of imperialist reaction." [112] One's love for the socialist fatherland was paired as before with that other allegedly noble trait—hatred for the fatherland's enemies.[113] Against these enemies, the Komsomolite must be ready to fight with self-sacrificing courage and daring.[114]

Another set of desired characteristics could be grouped around the idea of all-out and never-ending effort.[115] The good Komsomol member, like many of his counterparts in Western society, was expected to be oriented toward a goal of unattainable perfection. He would never be satisfied merely to maintain a standard previously set. He would say with Mikhailov: "In our country the Bolshevik rule prevails: never to stop with what has already been achieved." [116] An interesting manifestation of this tendency to demand constant improvement without retrogressions appeared in the references to the Komsomol's total enrollment. The nine-million-odd figure of 1949 was often compared with the figure of slightly less than four million for 1936 and was used by Komsomol spokesmen as the starting point for self-congratulatory words on the League's rapid growth.[117] Other sources indicate, as has been shown above, that the Komsomol membership had already reached ten million by 1940 and that during the war it had risen perhaps as high as fifteen million; but all figures for the years between 1936 and 1949 were completely ignored during the Eleventh Congress. The desire to show steady movement upward apparently caused the Komsomol leaders to neglect less favorable comparisons and to go back to 1936 in order to get a membership figure that would make the total for 1949 look impressive.

Moving onward and upward required persistence and industriousness. The good Komsomolite loved to work: "Soviet youth . . . is persistent in attaining the goals set for it, loves work, and does not see any life for itself except toil in the interests of the homeland." [118] Difficulties should be esteemed and welcomed as a wholesome challenge.[119] Komsomolites should believe that "indeed for us, for Soviet youth, the situation is this: What one plans, one can achieve, if only one has the desire, the persistence, and the will." [120] Related to that attitude were the demands for initiative—which, at the Eleventh Congress, almost always meant the increasing of production [121] —and for the customary Komsomol discipline.[122]

With a vigilant concern for principle, the Komsomol devotee was to guard his ideological purity, as Mikhailov said, "against any sort of foreign, decadent influence," and was to "struggle steadfastly for a pure Soviet ideology." "We will permit no one," he went on, ". . . to poison our youth with the venom of disbelief, pessimism, and decadence." [123] Self-interest and greed were to be condemned, along with other manifestations of a lack of personal morality.[124] "Moral steadiness is a prerequisite for political steadiness," said Mikhailov. "Communist ethics, exalting the civic honor and virtue of Soviet man as an active builder of Communist society, necessarily presupposes Soviet man's correct conduct in daily life." [125] The good Komsomolite was to serve as a model or example for Soviet youth in general, Soviet students, Young Pioneers, and the youth of the whole world.[126] At the same time, he was of course expected to model himself not after his immediate superiors but after Stalin, Lenin, and other individuals singled out for specific virtues.[127] That hardly surprising asymmetry may be viewed as one aspect of the picture of the Komsomol hierarchy discussed below.

The Eleventh Congress, in common with most previous congresses, virtually neglected the subject of the relationship of the ideal Komsomolite to his family and friends.[128] Presumably his bond with even his closest intimates was to be based on their sharing a complete loyalty to Stalin, the Party, and the Soviet Union. If his intimates wavered in that loyalty, he would reject and condemn them just as cruelly as he would reject and condemn any "enemies of the socialist fatherland."

Seemingly at variance with all the stern traits of watchfulness, discipline, constant striving, and hatred of enemies was another characteristic of the official version of the Komsomol member: cheerfulness. The contexts in which cheerfulness was mentioned suggest that while it did not preclude some satisfaction with the present, its essential basis was to be optimism regarding the future.[129] Rather than to dwell on the "ugly aspects" of Soviet life, which were said to be "not typical of our youth," [130] the Komsomolite should look on the bright side and rhapsodize with Mikhailov: "Words are lacking in which to express all our feelings about the beautiful Spring of our life—

to tell how good, how intelligent, how ideologically rich and full is the life of our youth, the young builders of Communist society." [131] Such allegedly ineffable joy was apparently based upon the proviso that "for us and for all there cannot be any greater happiness than the happiness of self-sacrificing service to the Komsomol, to the Party of Lenin and Stalin, and to the socialist fatherland." [132] The nature of the desired Komsomol cheerfulness was summed up by the large drawing which filled part of the front page of *Komsomol'skaia pravda* on the opening day of the Eleventh Congress.[133] The picture showed a procession of young people; in front, a boy held high an immense banner depicting Lenin and Stalin, and a girl clasped a copy of Stalin's *Problems of Leninism*. This was no happy-go-lucky, frivolous crowd! Their set and unsmiling faces breathed a look of firm purpose, a sober confidence that all would be right in the world of the future.

But what about this world of the future? The Bolsheviks' traditional ultimate aim—world Communism—had not been forgotten, and, as stated above, Mikhailov had assured the Congress that in the Soviet Union "our generation" would live under Communism. The traditional intermediate aims were recalled, including an increased productivity of labor, an abundance of consumers' goods, a heightened "cultural-technical level" for the working class so as to achieve the "liquidation of the contrast between mental and physical labor," improvements in agriculture so as to eliminate the contrast between town and village, and a general development of education, science, and literature.[134] But beyond these attractively painted signposts on the road toward Communism, the nature of the goal was left still undefined—left to be dimly discerned through a rosy haze, and thus to preserve its utopian appeal.

LEADERS AND FOLLOWERS WITHIN THE MONOLITHIC LEAGUE

In the years since the previous Congress, the innermost core of the ostensibly monolithic League had been transformed. According to the Regulations, any vacancies created among the ninety-three members of the CC elected by the Tenth Congress should have been filled by some of the thirty-five candidate-members elected at that time, and thus a good many of the total group of 128 should have been still serving as the Eleventh Congress opened. Yet none of the 128 was on the 45-man Presidium elected on the opening day to administer the Congress of 1949; [135] none of the 128 was among the persons who presented formal reports, or the 85 others who spoke at the Congress of 1949; [136] and none of the 128 was among the 150 members and candidate-members of the new CC.[137] The old CC was really gone! As to the rest of the 1,103 delegates who had attended the Congress of 1936, complete data are lacking,[138] but the available evidence indicates that one man—the A. A. Krivtsov who represented the Kirghiz organization of the League at the Congress of 1936, and who was sufficiently obscure not to have spoken at that meeting—had survived and risen to serve on the Presidium of the Congress of 1949 and to present the report of the Central Inspection Commission there. He was not elected to the new CC. With the lone exception of Krivtsov, none of the 1,103 leading Komsomol figures who had attended the Tenth Congress appeared in the proceedings of the Eleventh. The mere passage of time was by no means the whole story, since 195 or about one-seventh of the delegates in 1949 were over thirty, including the forty-three-year-old Mikhailov [139] and many others who, to judge by their published photographs, were of his generation.[140] Thus it is rather the purge and the war that must explain the virtually total replacement of the leadership of the League.

Women constituted 43.3 percent (590) of the delegates at the Congress,[141] as contrasted with only 23.5 percent at the Congress of 1936. This suggests that a concerted effort had been made to bring the representation at the Congress into line with the proportion in the League as a whole, which was now 42 percent, as compared with 34 percent in 1936.[142] Almost as much effort was evidently made in connection with the nominations (and consequently the elections) to the new Central Committee. Of the 150 members and candidate-members, 53 had feminine names, while the number of indeterminate names was such that the total of women may have been around 57.[143] Similarly, in the Presidium of forty-five persons which formally administered the Congress, about one-third were women. However, only three of the women were Komsomol officials at the oblast level or higher, and most were students, specialists, kolkhoz link leaders, and other minor figures. On the other hand, the positions given for the men indicated that most of them were high officials of the League.[144] Speakers at the Congress did, in fact, suggest that women were still not receiving their fair share of positions in the governing bodies of the League, and Mikhailov urged that this situation be corrected.[145]

Activities and relationships within the League continued to be governed in principle by democratic centralism.[146] The Regulations were amended to specify that the elections to the governing committees of Komsomol organizations (by the large deliberative body at each echelon) must be conducted by individual candidature rather than by list and must be voted by secret ballot.[147] The Eleventh Congress was said to be the first All-Union Congress ever elected by secret ballot.[148] In connection with this reform it was acknowledged that in the past, and especially during the war, democratic centralism had often been violated; leading bodies of the Komsomol had been coopted rather than elected. Such violations were now explicitly condemned.[149] But those pretended enlargements of the "democratic" side of democratic centralism were accompanied by a partial curtailment of it. The Regulations of 1936 had provided that extraordinary congresses and conferences at various echelons could be called upon request of one-third or more of the delegates to the last regular meeting of the body concerned.[150] At the Congress of 1949, however, Ivanov reported that the Party had so firmly guaranteed the "organizational-political unity" of the Komsomol that it was no longer necessary to provide this machinery for the discussion of "disputed questions."[151] The section was accordingly eliminated from the Regulations.[152]

In his role as a leader, as depicted at the Eleventh Congress, the Komsomolite was to be motivated by idealism. Although medals, some of which carried monetary benefits, were much in evidence (out of the 1,362 voting delegates, 1,031 had been decorated with some kind of government award, and 399 delegates had received four or more awards each),[153] in theory neither the money nor the public acclaim connected with these awards was a legitimate inspiration to virtue, but merely an incidental recognition of it. The Komsomol leader was expected, as indicated above, to set an example. He must both formulate general instructions and be able, taking into account differences in age and in interests among Komsomolites, to employ a "differentiated, concrete" approach to each unit.[154] He must not shower the lower echelons with directives but rather must visit them on the spot in order to make sure orders were being followed. He must not become bogged down in trifles but must train good subordinates and use them properly. Avoiding excessive reprimands or other negative measures lest he impair group confidence, and shunning what was said to be the all too prevalent tendency toward "commanding," he must instead control through comradely explanation and persuasion.[155] At one and the same time he must "increase the activity and initiative of the members of the ALCLY and must heighten their organizedness and discipline." [156] Finally, pervading all the instructions for Komsomol leadership was the theme of maintaining close contact between higher and lower Komsomol echelons, and between the Komsomol and the masses.[157]

In his role as a follower, the dominant principle for the ideal Komsomolite clearly was discipline. In the words of the official Regulations, "The strictest observance of Komsomol discipline is the first obligation of all members of the Komsomol and all Komsomol organizations." This obligation was especially serious for the active Komsomol official.[158] Of course all Komsomolites were followers of those above them, just as they were leaders of those below them, in the system. It is worth noting, however, the continuing absence of any emphasis on one's immediate superior as the person to be obeyed.[159]

In connection with this lack of stress on the individual links in the chain of command, it is interesting to examine the question of consciousness of rank. There were, for example, the obvious distinctions between the main steps in the Komsomol hierarchy, from the top down to the primary organizations— one expression of which were the reprimands and punishments especially provided for "members of leading bodies of the Komsomol," and in particular for the members of the Central Committee.[160] There was the granting of more authority to teacher-Komsomolites than to student-Komsomolites. There was also the important distinction between Komsomolites who were Party members and those who were not. While the total size of the Party core was not revealed,[161] the proportion of Party members in the leading positions in the League was reported rather precisely. Almost 70 percent of the 1,362 delegates at the Eleventh Congress were members or candidate-members of the Party.[162] Among the secretaries of Komsomol organizations at the oblast, krai, and union republic echelon, 99.3 percent were in the Party; of the first secretaries at the town echelon, 99 percent were in the Party; and of the first secretaries at the raion echelon, 95.2 percent were in the Party.[163] (These figures represented surprisingly slight changes from the situation in 1936, when all of the officials in such posts had been required to be in the Party, and it is of interest that the Eleventh Congress reintroduced the requirement of Party membership for the posts named above, while leaving the length of required Komsomol service the same as that established in 1939 by the action of the CC.) [164] More was expected of those Komsomolites who were also Party members than of the mass of ordinary Komsomolites. For the purpose of admission to the League, the recommendation of one Party member continued to be equivalent to the recommendations of two non-Party Komsomolites of at least one year's standing.[165]

More precise indications of a concern for rank could be seen in the proceedings of the Congress. When the Presidium of the Congress was announced, the first four names were those of members of the Central Committee of the Party; the other forty-one names followed in alphabetical order.[166] When the members of the Politburo were listed, it was in the non-alphabetical sequence popularly assumed to represent their relative rank at that time.[167] When at the opening session there were five leading bodies of the Congress to be nominated and elected, the lists of nominees for these bodies were presented, in turn, by the secretaries of the Moscow, Ukrainian, Leningrad, Belorussian, and Kazakhstan organizations—clearly not a haphazard sequence.[168] (The nominated lists were voted openly and unanimously, without discussion, even though the Congress later specified, as shown above, that nominees must be voted on individually and by secret ballot.) The responsible job of presiding at the various sessions rotated first through the five secretaries of the Central Committee (in the order Mikhailov-Ivanov-Shelepin-Kharlamov-Ershova), then through the five nominators mentioned above (only this time in the sequence Ukraine-Moscow-Belorussia-Leningrad-Kazakhstan), to the secretary of the Azerbaidzhan organization. Then Kharlamov presided again (apparently because he was the only one of the five secretaries of the Central Committee who did not make a speech), and Mikhailov, the leading secretary, piloted the last session.[169]

Closely related to distinctions of rank were the evidences of a powerful force for conformity operating throughout the Congress. In their voting, the delegates at the Congress of 1949 presented a model of perfect unanimity. The fact that all delegates were lined up on the "unanimous" side of each issue before the vote was called suggests something more than mental telepathy. In the discussion of the reports of the Central Committee and the Central Inspection Commission, which was characterized by Mikhailov as having been "on a high ideological-political level, in conditions of Bolshevik criticism and self-criticism," [170] the only targets of criticism were the always-vulnerable administrators of certain branches of the government and the Komsomol, and the criticisms centered on failure to follow the announced policies, or failure to do enough of some manifestly approved thing.[171] There were no significant disagreements visible among the fifty-six delegates who participated in the discussion of these reports, and the content of their

criticism followed closely along the lines laid down by Mikhailov and Krivtsov in their own reports. Of the whole group
of seventy-eight Komsomol speakers at the Congress (excluding
the fourteen spokesmen of foreign youth movements and the
eighteen speakers who were government officials or other adult
celebrities apparently not officials of the Komsomol), sixty-nine,
or 88 percent, were among those nominated and elected by the
Congress to some high governing body of the Komsomol. Since
only about 200 of the 1,362 delegates to the Congress were
elected to such bodies, there was a high correlation between
speaking at the Congress and being elected to one of its
offices.[172] The only delegates who spoke more than once were
the same few who presided over the sessions. The published
record of the Congress gives no suggestion of any impromptu
utterances or exchanges between delegates. All of this leaden
conformity strongly suggests some working chain of command.

A contrast could be discerned, then, between the evidences of
scrupulous regard for rank and an operating chain of command
on the one hand, and, on the other, the vagueness of the official statements on these matters—obscurity related in part to
the Communist vision of collective leadership. In this realm,
even the hypothetical ideal Komsomolite might have had
trouble reconciling theory with practice.

THE CRUCIAL IMPORTANCE OF INDOCTRINATION
AND EDUCATION

Among the public functions of the Komsomol and its members, the Eleventh Congress laid primary stress on the indoctrination and education that were needed in order to
achieve the other aims of the Soviet leadership.[173]

It was the schools, as the institutional expression of those
two virtually inseparable tasks, that now constituted apparently
the most important single field of Komsomol activity.[174] The
expansion of the Soviet school system was underscored by the
announcement that about 68 percent of the delegates had
completed secondary school, as compared with only about 38
percent at the Congress of 1936.[175] Although the Soviet school

system was claimed to be "the most advanced and progressive in the world," [176] even seven-year schooling had admittedly not yet been made universal and compulsory.[177] Much remained for Komsomolites to do, it was said, in building schools, gaining influence in schools, and improving the quality of schoolwork and discipline.[178] This did not mean that the Komsomol as an organization should dominate the schools, for "all the activity of the school Komsomol organizations must be subordinated to the educational work conducted by the directors and the teachers in the schools." [179] This deceptively simple principle was complicated in practice by the prevalence of Komsomol and Party membership among the school authorities, so that while the Komsomol as an organization was to consider itself subordinate to the school authorities in regard to all work in the schools, the Komsomol as the agent of the Party could transmit binding instructions to individuals who were serving as principals or as teachers.

The teaching profession was vigorously promoted at the Congress.[180] Komsomol members were told that they must help the teacher, must strengthen the teacher's authority, and must love, honor, and respect the teacher and his work.[181] The separate primary organizations for teachers were directed to "take an active part in all work of the school's Komsomol and Pioneer organizations." [182] These teachers' groups now reportedly numbered 25,000 and had 224,000 members,[183] which was a little under one-fifth of the reported total number of Soviet teachers (1,250,000) [184]—a high proportion in view of the many teachers who must have been too old for Komsomol membership. Mikhailov explained that "the majority of teachers' Komsomol organizations work in schools where there is no primary organization of the Party." He went on: "From this it is clear what a great responsibility rests upon them for successfully carrying out the Party's and the government's directives in the school." [185] Tamara I. Ershova, who delivered the principal report on the school, exhorted teachers' Komsomol organizations to "bring more courageously before principals, organs of popular education, and Party and Soviet organizations those questions having to do with improving the work in the school." [186]

The basic principle to be observed by students was discipline.[187] The Komsomolite would unfailingly follow the government's "Rules for Students" [188] and would "obey the instructions of the principal, the teacher, and the class leader [home-room teacher]." [189] He must not try to fence himself off from teachers, as some had incorrectly done. He must set an example by studying hard and getting good marks—without stooping to cheat, for that was a prerevolutionary vice.[190] Discipline also required that, as the Komsomolites approached graduation, they would combat the reportedly common tendency of young people to seek office jobs instead of production jobs. The disciplined youth would be ready to work wherever he was needed, and he would not object (as some did) to being sent to one of the less favored regions of the country.[191]

In order to extend its influence in the schools, the Komsomol was directed to draw more students into its ranks.[192] Already, Komsomol primary organizations were said to exist in all seven-year and secondary (that is, ten-year) schools,[193] and "over half of all the pupils in the upper grades [not defined] of the seven-year and secondary schools" were said to be members of the League.[194] Similarly, among the over two million students in higher educational and technical institutions the Komsomol was said to embrace more than half.[195]

Within the framework of the educational plan as supervised by the school authorities, Komsomol organizations were to play an important supplementary role. They must encourage the reading of newspapers. They must organize political lectures and reports, surveys of current events, "readers' conferences," discussions of books they had read, and debates. (Likely topics for these discussions, as listed by one speaker, were "I Am a Citizen of the Soviet Union," "The Moral Countenance of Soviet Man," and "All Roads Lead to Communism.") [196] They must set up circles or clubs of young naturalists and young technicians, and arrange contests between young mathematicians, physicists, chemists, and geographers. They should arrange visits to museums and exhibits, excursions to productive enterprises, and collective attendance at, and discussion of, new movies and plays.[197] Among the other Komsomol projects reported upon were to build and equip school laboratories for physics and chemistry; to build "Pioneer rooms" and kolkhoz clubs; to electrify and "radiofy" schools and the homes of collective farmers; to enlarge school libraries; to build athletic fields; to plant trees, berry-patches, and flower-beds; to protect birds; and to help build homes for students and collective farmers.[198] These activities were not to conflict with the regular school program, and Komsomol organizations were especially enjoined to stop overburdening school children with extracurricular work which would injure their health and deprive them of time needed for studying.[199] Komsomol organizations in schools, unlike those in other settings, were not to try to maintain separate "politcircles" and "politschools" for youth, since political indoctrination was an integral part of the school program.[200] Furthermore, any mass activities of the school Komsomol organizations could be conducted only with the permission of the school principal.[201]

In line with the reiterated demand that Komsomol work in the schools be suited to the age of the members, Ershova proposed that where there were more than 100 Komsomol members in one school, it be permissible to set up a primary organization for each grade.[202] The Congress amended the Regulations accordingly.[203] The Congress also called for more active Komsomol help to evening schools [204] and to Labor Reserve schools.[205]

The mission of indoctrination extended beyond the school into all the public functions of the League. Komsomol leaders, trained in Party schools, in the six-month course at the newly established Central Komsomol School, or in special seminars,[206] were expected to transmit the ideological message to Komsomolites and other Soviet youths everywhere, through lectures, seminars, "politschools," "politcircles," and other means.[207] Indoctrination was the heart of Komsomol activity in the

Pioneers, the press, literature, art, and even physical education.

The Pioneers were drawing at this time on the age group from nine to fifteen,[208] which meant approximately from the first or second grade through the seventh grade.[209] The Pioneer membership at the time of the Eleventh Congress was reported as 13,000,000.[210] This was the same as at the end of 1939, almost a decade before.

The main sphere of Pioneer activity continued to be in the school.[211] Komsomolites who bore responsibility for Pioneer work were warned that "all activity of the Pioneer organizations must be subordinated to the educational tasks of the school" [212] and must be "under the leadership of the school principals, teachers, and class leaders." [213] Those Komsomolites who were selected (by the town and raion committees of the Komsomol) to be Pioneer leaders were to be top-quality Komsomolites.[214] Many Komsomol organizations were accused of not giving enough support or respect to Pioneer leaders and were told to remedy this.[215] In particular, the League was to help Pioneer leaders to receive the necessary training in pedagogy and in leadership.[216] Teacher-Komsomolites were urged to double as Pioneer leaders, but were specifically warned not to transform Pioneer activities into another classroom affair.[217]

Outside the school, the leisure time of Pioneers was to be more effectively organized. "Pioneer houses" and "Pioneer rooms" were to be built and operated, along with houses or "stations" for young naturalists and other special-interest youth groups. Athletic facilities were to be constructed. In the summertime especially, there should be excursions to places associated with the lives of Lenin and Stalin, to battle sites of World War II, and to construction sites of the postwar Five-Year Plan, so as to fill the children with love of the fatherland. Pioneer summer camps were to inculcate discipline, to improve the health of the Pioneers, and to accustom them to the life of soldiers in the field.[218]

In the orphanages (*detskie doma*), Komsomolites were told to work with educational agencies in helping to build and equip school workshops, athletic fields, and Pioneer rooms and corners, and thus to prepare the children for productive work.[219]

The Komsomol press remained a massive means of indoctrination. The Komsomol press was now reportedly publishing thirty-seven Komsomol newspapers and nineteen Pioneer newspapers, plus eight Komsomol and fifteen children's magazines. *Pionerskaia pravda* (Pioneer Truth), a daily newspaper, was said to be published in 1,000,000 copies, and the daily paper *Komsomol'skaia pravda* was published in 700,000 copies. The Young Guard press reportedly had published 75,000,000 copies of books (probably including booklets) for children and young people during the two years preceding the Congress of 1949. It was the duty of all Komsomolites—through the schools and through village reading rooms, libraries, and all possible means—to help disseminate that literature and to encourage youth to read it.[220]

Soviet writers and artists, some of whom were Komsomolites, were urged by Mikhailov and Ershova to do a better job of depicting "our young contemporary, the hero of our time," and to write more about workers, collective farmers, Pioneer leaders, and teachers.[221] The delegates endorsed a resolution that called upon Soviet writers to create new "works of high idealism, instilling in school children high moral qualities, revealing the wisdom of the policies of the great Communist Party, glorifying our socialist homeland, and revealing the courage and heroism of Soviet people." [222]

A special problem of indoctrination, despite more than thirty years of Bolshevik rule, was the combating of religious beliefs. Mikhailov declared:

Recently in certain localities there has been observed some revival of the activities of clergymen trying to strengthen their influence on the young. There are cases where even members of the Komsomol, under the influence of a backward frame of mind, are participating in religious rites. . . . The Komsomol must not hold itself neutral with regard to religion. The Komsomol is called upon to propagate the foremost science, while religion is the direct contradiction of science. Komsomol organizations must decisively improve their natural-science propaganda, so that Komsomolites may explain to youth, daily and skillfully, the nature of religion. Participation in religious rites is incompatible with remaining in the ranks of the ALCLY.[223]

A broader development of physical education and sports was demanded by the Congress as part of "the preparation for labor and for the defense of the socialist homeland." The recent achievements of Komsomol organizations in building stadiums, athletic fields, and swimming pools were enumerated, and Komsomolites were urged to complete, within the next two or three years, a stadium in each raion and an athletic field in each school and in the majority of the kolkhozes. Komsomol organizations were to foster athletics among peasants and workers, thus checking the harmful tendency toward a "caste spirit" among athletes. Komsomol activity was to be increased in the various institutes training physical education instructors, athletic coaches, and referees.[224] Among the approved sports, hunting was particularly recommended. It was said to develop "watchfulness, endurance, and will power—traits necessary in the defenders of our homeland." [225] A pretty teen-age maiden recited some not-too-feminine lines:

> Today, we hunters are excellent marksmen.
> But tomorrow from the hunters will be formed regiments
> And, under Stalin's orders, if the homeland calls,
> We, proud and brave, will march ever forward! [226]

The RLD ("Ready for Labor and Defense") program, giving an important place to rifle marksmanship, continued to serve as a measuring-stick for athletic prowess. Mikhailov reported that during the past year a total of over 2,700,000 youths had won RLD badges, and that out of these over 1,400,000, or more than half, had been Komsomol members.[227] As to international athletic competition, Komsomolites were told that "each new athletic attainment furthers our national sports and increases their international prestige," and that it was a "duty of the Komsomol" to produce more athletes who could "successfully defend the honor of the homeland in international competitions" and who were "capable of beating world records." [228] Thus even in his outdoor recreation the ideal Komsomolite could not seek mere personal pleasure but must think of his patriotic duty.

ECONOMIC AND OTHER PUBLIC FUNCTIONS

With regard to the economic aspect of "the great program outlined by Comrade Stalin for the building of Communist society," [229] the Congress resolved as follows:

A most important obligation of the ALCLY is to rouse youth to the struggle for the furthest development of the productive forces of the country, the introduction and mastery of new techniques, the observance of a regime of economy, and the growth of the productivity of labor, as the most important and principal condition for the victory of the new social structure.[230]

The primary organizations of the Komsomol—cooperating closely with the trade unions [231]—were to transmit Party directives "in all fields of socialist construction, especially where there is no primary organization of the Party." [232] There were reported to be about 30,000 primary organizations of the Komsomol in industry and transport, and 188,000 in kolkhozes, sovkhozes, and machine-and-tractor stations, plus 4,329 in Labor Reserve institutions.[233]

The Congress showered praise on Komsomolites who had excelled in production. "These people," the press report stated, "display indeed the Communist attitude toward toil; for them, the concern for increasing the productivity of labor constitutes a law of life." [234] How were these medal-bedecked heroes —the Stakhanovites, "innovators of production," and "masters of high productivity"—expected to achieve the increase? As one of their appellations suggests, they were to introduce new methods. But the chief means was simple: hard work.[235] They should show "initiative" by doing extra work; [236] they should perfect their skills; they should engage in "socialist competition," either in collective work units or as individuals.[237]

While the delegates discussed the activities of Komsomolites in almost every type of economic enterprise,[238] they gave particular attention to agriculture. Apparently the League was still far weaker in the rural areas than in the cities. Of the 188,000 primary organizations of the Komsomol in kolkhozes, sovkhozes, and machine-and-tractor stations, a goodly proportion were of recent origin; 56,000 rural primary organizations had reportedly been established during the last three years alone. But the League had not yet achieved its long-standing goal of establishing a primary organization in every kolkhoz.[239] Kolkhozes alone evidently numbered about 250,000 at this time,[240] while sovkhozes totaled about 5,000 and machine-andtractor stations about 8,100.[241] Out of a total of over 150 oblasts, krais, and republics,[242] there were only fifty-four in which the Komsomol had a primary organization for every kolkhoz, machine-and-tractor station, and sovkhoz.[243] Rural primary organizations of the Komsomol altogether were reported to number more than 200,000 and to include 2,200,000 Komsomolites.[244] (This indicates, incidentally, that these rural primary organizations averaged about eleven members each, or about half the over-all average for the country.) The 2,200,000 members constituted only about 24 percent of the total enrollment of the Komsomol (9,283,289), at a time when the Soviet population was still about 62 or 64 percent rural.[245] This would suggest that the League was much less inclusive in the countryside than in the cities. However, judgment must be suspended on this important question, since the sources do not reveal to what extent the census categories corresponded to the Komsomol categories—do not show, in particular, to what extent Komsomolites who lived in communities that the census called rural but who were not engaged in farming were omitted from the Komsomol's rural category.

The principal demands on rural Komsomolites as exemplars for all rural youth were to increase production, to check violations of labor discipline, to ensure prompt delivery of agricultural produce to the government, and to encourage new methods, including the use of machinery and particularly electricity, for the Komsomol was still "the patron of electrification." Komsomol bodies were also told to engage in a wide variety of projects designed to improve living conditions in the village, such as building houses, roads, and bridges; sinking wells; erecting water tanks; and planting trees along the village streets.[246]

In order the better to exert their influence, Komsomolites were urged to accept individual posts of responsibility within the kolkhozes. Over 300,000 Komsomolites reportedly were serving as chairmen or members of managing boards and control commissions of kolkhozes, or as brigade and link leaders and supervisors of farms.[247] Komsomol organizations were reminded once more of their particular obligation to secure leadership in those kolkhozes where there was no Party organization.[248] In the newly acquired western parts of the USSR, the Komsomol had the special task (reminiscent of the years of the First Five-Year Plan) of helping the Party to "attract" the farmers to join collective farms.[249]

Little was said at the Eleventh Congress about the activities of Komsomol members in the soviets. As evidence that this sphere was not being forgotten, however, it was reported that out of 190,000 "youths" who were serving as members of local soviets, about 95,000 were Komsomolites.[250]

The Eleventh Congress, like the Tenth, ignored the problem of crime. It also remained silent on the whole machinery of coercion. The exhortations to firmer discipline were not accompanied by allusions to punitive action, except for reprimands, rebukes, and other punishments within the Komsomol and expulsion from the Komsomol. The general demands for political vigilance and for purging hostile elements were not accompanied by any specific references, laudatory or not, to the practice of informing on one's associates. Praise went to almost every principal vocation, but there was no mention of a good or a bad police official. Perhaps the task of making the coercive apparatus attractive to Komsomolites and other youth was considered impossible for even the Soviet propaganda system.

On the question of minority nationalities, the Eleventh Con-

gress reflected the postwar official position of the Russians (that
is, the Great Russians rather than the Ukrainians or Belorussians) as "the first among equals." True brotherhood, Soviet
style, now demanded greater emphasis on teaching everyone the
Russian language. This was particularly true, said Ershova, in
Georgia, Armenia, Uzbekistan, and in the Tatar, Bashkir, and
Mordov autonomous republics. "The Russian language helps
youth to unite itself with the high culture of the Russian
people and binds together the brotherly peoples inhabiting
our multinational socialist state." All Komsomolites should
"instill in youth a love of the Russian language, a striving to
study and to know it thoroughly." [251] In so far as the record
revealed, all speeches by delegates from within the USSR were
delivered in Russian. This was in contrast to the practice at
previous congresses, where Soviet linguistic diversity had apparently been prized. The Russians were better represented
among the delegates (64.5 percent) than in the population as
a whole (about 56.6 percent). Ukrainians were poorly represented, being only 13.1 percent of the delegates but about 18.3
percent of the population. Other peoples notably underrepresented included the Lithuanians (0.4 percent of the delegates,
as against 1.3 percent of the population) and the Tatars (1.1
percent of the delegates, as against 2.3 percent of the population). Relatively heavily represented, on the other hand, were
the Georgians (3.1 percent among the delegates, 1.2 percent in
the population) and the Azerbaidzhanians (2 percent among
the delegates, 1.2 percent in the population).[252] Three significant minorities were not listed at the Eleventh Congress: the
Jews, the Poles, and the Germans, who at the Tenth Congress
had constituted respectively 13.3 percent, 1 percent, and 0.5
percent of the delegates. Although the Volga German Republic
had been liquidated, and although many Jews had been killed
by the Nazis and repressed under the Soviets, it seems unlikely
that there were at that Congress *no* persons of Jewish, Polish,
or German ancestry—especially because the territories annexed
by the USSR since 1939 included many people of those nationalities. Evidently those Jews, Poles, and Germans who were

present thought it prudent to list themselves otherwise, probably mostly as "Russians." Unfortunately no clear indications were given of the ethnic composition of the League's membership as a whole.[253]

WAGING THE COLD WAR

"The defense of the fatherland is the sacred duty and the first obligation of each Komsomol member," said the Regulations of the Komsomol as amended by the Eleventh Congress, adding that "a member of the ALCLY must . . . study military affairs, be supremely loyal to the great socialist homeland, and be prepared to give up, for it, all his strength and, if necessary, his life." [254]

Although the armed forces still constituted one of the principal areas of Komsomol activity, at the Congress of 1949 precise data were withheld, presumably for reasons of state security. Not only did the speakers fail to mention the numbers of members currently in the armed services, but they did not even reveal how many primary organizations there were in military units. They did, however, provide the basis for a guess. The total number of all primary organizations of the Komsomol was reported by one official as 447,310 and by another as 447,600.[255] Separate totals were given for the number of primary organizations in industry and transport (about 30,000), in kolkhozes, sovkhozes, and machine-and-tractor stations (188,-000), in seven-year and secondary schools (over 47,000), in training institutions of the Labor Reserves (4,329), and in higher educational institutions and technical and specialist schools (over 3,000).[256] Adding these together, with a rough allowance for the unspecified amount of excess indicated, one obtains a total of about 273,000. That still leaves about 174,000 primary organizations unaccounted for. The only large categories not named above would appear to be those in government offices (including the Ministry of Internal Affairs) and in the armed forces. Hence it seems probable that a considerable proportion of the "missing" 174,000 primary organizations were in military units. Similar secrecy cloaked the distribution of military personnel among the delegates. The occupational categories that were listed, covering almost everything except the armed forces, added up to 1,062—just 300 short of the total of voting delegates present.[257] It seems proper to assume that a great many of the 300 were military personnel.

The nature of Komsomol activity in military units was discussed at some length but only in general terms. The chief aims were said to be instilling Soviet patriotism in the soldiers, aiding in their political education, and helping the commanders and the Party to strengthen military discipline.[258] Komsomol organizations within military units were to maintain close contact with local civilian Komsomol organizations and participate in all phases of their program, including elections.[259]

The Congress's discussion of the Komsomol's semimilitary activities outside of the military establishment was hardly more enlightening. The general mission, in addition to that of fostering Soviet patriotism, was to encourage young people to "master military knowledge" and to make them physically fit for military service.[260] A companion aim was to inspire Komsomolites to become Soviet officers.[261] The chief instruments for accomplishing these ends were the already familiar institution of Komsomol patronage and the recently reorganized paramilitary organizations.

The Komsomol's patronage or support of the Navy was now said to include training Komsomol members in swimming and other naval skills, writing patriotic letters to sailors, and sending Komsomol delegations to visit ships.[262] The Moscow organization of the ALCLY had the mission of helping the Northern Fleet, while the Ukrainian Komsomol was to serve the Black Sea Fleet, and the Leningrad Komsomol had as its ward the Baltic Fleet.[263]

The paramilitary organization called Osoaviakhim had been divided in 1948 into three "voluntary societies for cooperation" with the Army, the Air Forces, and the Navy. The Komsomol was expected to be the "soul" of these societies and to draw into them wide masses of Soviet youth.[264] The official representative (N.P. Kamanin) of the three societies avoided membership statistics but declared that "each Komsomolite must be a member of one of the societies and take an active part in the work of one of its primary organizations." Looking ahead to the first raion, town, oblast, and republic conferences of these societies, which would mark the completion of their organizing period, Kamanin urged that the Komsomol prepare carefully for the meetings and that it elect the most active Komsomolites to the governing bodies of these voluntary societies. In connection with the societies' purpose of providing training in militarily useful skills, he discussed such activities as aero-clubs, gliding stations, and "military-athletic work." [265] Through them Komsomolites were not only to learn military skills before being called up for military service but also to keep themselves prepared in later life to defend the socialist fatherland.

World affairs were not stressed at the Eleventh Congress, despite the postwar expansion of the Soviet empire. Mikhailov devoted only a small section of his report to the international situation.[266] Representatives of foreign "democratic" youth organizations did speak at the Congress, but their speeches were short, if one may judge from the exceedingly brief summaries that were published.[267] World Communism, the traditional goal of Marxism-Leninism, was implied but not discussed, and Mikhailov's reference to Stalin's "proof" that Communism could be built in the Soviet Union, even while the capitalistic encirclement persisted, suggested that the Komsomolite was not to expect world Communism to be realized very soon.[268] The international revolutionary movement, including foreign Communists and their followers in the "democratic camp," was to carry on under such slogans as "for a durable peace, against the instigators of a new war, for democracy, for freedom, and for the national independence of [all] peoples." [269] Komsomol officials spoke not of offense but of defense —the defense of the socialist fatherland and its "state interests." [270]

What about the Soviet military campaigns conducted beyond the borders of the Soviet Union in recent years? Here elastic euphemisms were employed. "All progressive humanity" was declared to be obligated to Stalin for its "deliverance from the menace of Fascist slavery." [271] The German youth representative thanked the Soviet people for liberating the Germans from Hitlerite slavery.[272] In similar fashion the delegate from North Korea expressed gratitude to the Soviet Army for making possible the establishment of "political independence" for North Korea.[273] The postwar extension of Soviet power over the small countries of Eastern Europe, and the establishment of Soviet-style "people's democracies" there, were glossed over with the statement that those countries "fell away from capitalism," [274] and the Bulgarian and Czech representatives expressed appreciation for the "help" they were receiving from the Soviet Union.[275] Violent actions of Communists abroad were heartily applauded. The military triumphs of the Chinese Communists were called "historic victories" in the "struggle for freedom and national independence." [276] The disruptive tactics of Communist youths in France were approvingly termed a "struggle against reaction." The French representative promised that "the young toilers of France will do all they can in order that the crafty schemes of the imperialists and instigators of war never will be realized." [277] Thus the well-indoctrinated Komsomolite, if he were ordered to participate in military operations beyond the borders of the Soviet Union, would have no trouble justifying that action.

Soviet youth, still allegedly "in the vanguard of the democratic youth of all countries," [278] was said to be "the most educated, the most energetic, and the most humane youth in the world," [279] as well as "the keenest, the most inquiring, the most exacting and strict, the most noble and cultured." [280] Now that the Communist International of Youth was dead, one Komsomol instrument for contact with the "democratic" youth of the world was the "Anti-Fascist Committee of Soviet Youth," founded in 1941 "upon the initiative of the Komsomol." It was said to maintain connections with two hundred youth organizations in seventy countries. Another instrument was the "World Federation of Democratic Youth," established in 1945. From a membership of 30,000,000 in that year,[281] it had reportedly risen to 52,000,000 members in sixty-three countries by the time of the Congress of 1949.[282] The representatives of foreign youth organizations who addressed the Eleventh Congress expressed admiration for the achievements of Soviet youth and said that young people the world over were looking to Soviet youth for example and guidance.[283]

But in spite of the vaunted organizational bonds between Soviet youth and millions of foreign "democratic" youth; in spite of the Congress's resolution that the Komsomol was "obliged to assist the strengthening of democratic youth"; [284] and in spite of the above-cited commendatory references to Soviet military action abroad in support of Soviet aims, there was little evidence of direct contact between foreign and Soviet youth. In part this situation undoubtedly reflected the concern of Stalin and other Soviet leaders to preserve the ideological "purity" of Soviet youth. And yet the leaders deemed it necessary to import a claque of foreign youths and to have them sing worshipful paeans to Soviet youth. One is struck by these staged demonstrations of foreign support, and one wonders whether, when the flesh-and-blood Komsomolite heard his own theme songs played back to him, he was actually convinced of the assertedly universal appeal of Stalinism.

VIII. In the Era of Collective Leadership

THE CONGRESS OF 1954

THE Twelfth Congress of the Komsomol was held March 19–26, 1954, about one year after the death of Stalin. As the first youth convention of that transitional period, it invites comparison with the last congress of the Stalin era.

According to the Komsomol Regulations, the Twelfth Congress should have been held not later than the spring of 1952. The delay of two years, for which no public explanation was offered, probably resulted at least in part from the scheduling of the long-postponed Nineteenth Party Congress for October, 1952, and then from the uncertainty that reigned during the months preceding and following Stalin's death.[1]

The League's total membership expanded rapidly between the congresses. By April, 1950, the enrollment was already over 11,000,000,[2] and by February, 1951, more than 12,000,000.[3] Indirect evidence indicates that this growth was being achieved despite a rate of departures that was high enough to have brought virtually 100 percent turnover in a mere four to six years—in sharp contrast to the twelve- to fourteen-year span separating the minimum and suggested maximum ages of membership.[4] The continuing increase brought the total to about 14,000,000 by January, 1952;[5] about 16,000,000 by June, 1952;[6] over 17,000,000 by May, 1953;[7] about 18,000,000 by November, 1953;[8] and, by March, 1954, to 18,825,327[9]—more than double the total of 1949.

With that huge enrollment, the Komsomol embraced perhaps around 35 percent of all Soviet youths in the eligible age group.[10] Taking into account the overlapping memberships at either end of the age scale, perhaps between 40 and 50 percent of the young people of Komsomol age were in either the Party, the Komsomol, or the Pioneers.[11]

Fully as striking as the size of the new membership figure was the revelation that the growth had occurred almost entirely in the towns, the military service, and other nonfarming settlements,[12] even though the Soviet population was still about three-fifths rural.[13]

THE LEAGUE AND THE PARTY, WITHOUT STALIN

The close organizational links between the League and the Party had been reaffirmed in the new Party Regulations approved by the Nineteenth Party Congress in October, 1952.[14] Mikhailov, who served as the League's first secretary until November, 1952, had been a full member of the Central Committee of the Party since 1939. In October, 1952, he became a member of the twenty-five-man Presidium of the Central Committee and one of the ten secretaries or administrative heads of the Party in the Secretariat of the Central Committee.[15] Not long after leaving his Komsomol post,[16] he replaced Khrushchev as first secretary of the Party Committee of the Moscow Oblast,[17] and, in 1954, he went on to become the Soviet ambassador to Poland.[18] It seems worth observing that Mikhailov, the only Komsomol chief thus for to attain high positions in the Party and the government, had not worked his way up through the Komsomol but had come into it at the top as a seasoned Party worker. His successor as first secretary of the League was Aleksandr Nikolaevich Shelepin, who had already risen to prominence in the Komsomol before the Congress of 1949 [19] and had been elected a full member of the Central Committee of the Party in October, 1952.[20]

The delegates at the Twelfth Congress, like those at earlier gatherings, were largely Party members and candidate-members, but the proportion—66.5 percent (886 out of 1,334) [21]— was a little lower than the 70 percent that obtained at the previous Congress. Apparently the Party leaders did not feel a higher percentage was needed in order to ensure control. A similar view was reflected in the action of the Twelfth Congress in amending that portion of the Komsomol Regulations that, since 1949, had required all secretaries of Komsomol *raikoms* and *gorkoms* to be members or candidate-members of the Party. The amendment of 1954, permitting the appointment of non-Party members in exceptional cases (as had been done before 1949), was intended to facilitate the developing of younger leaders.[22]

While the phrases that were used in 1954 to describe the Komsomol-Party relationship followed very closely the formulas of 1949,[23] there was naturally a difference in the treatment accorded the top leadership. The elaborate obeisances to Stalin which had been required at the Eleventh Congress had continued as long as he still lived. On the occasion of his seventieth birthday, December 21, 1949, "38,323,867 Komsomolites and young people" sent him extravagantly worded greetings.[24] Some sort of peak—or nadir—was reached when *Komsomol'-skaia pravda* then proceeded to print the lists of organizations and groups that had sent greetings, and kept on fairly regularly devoting part of its meager four-page space to this so-called "torrent of greetings" throughout the whole of 1950 and on until October 6 of 1951—*almost two years* after the occasion that was being celebrated! [25] After it reported Stalin's death, *Komsomol'skaia pravda* devoted virtually every inch of its space to Stalin for four consecutive issues, and for five more issues devoted most of its space to him. Although the panegyrics were then curtailed, he was not disgraced. The first anniversary of his death, for example, was observed with almost as much show as the thirtieth anniversary of Lenin's death.[26]

By the time of the Twelfth Komsomol Congress Stalin was still on a pedestal, but he was much nearer life size. The word on "collective leadership" had already gone out to all followers of the Party line,[27] and the Congress elected as honorary delegates to the Congress the whole top group of Party chiefs.[28] Stalin was the subject of a brief commemorative ceremony at the opening session.[29] In references to Communist doctrine and achievements, his name was used to complete the customary sequence Marx-Engels-Lenin-Stalin.[30] However, his name was almost never used alone, and only one delegate—significantly, a representative of Communist China—applied to his name any honorific adjective (in this case "great").[31]

Partially filling the unaccustomed void, there appeared a curious and sometimes awkward transfer, in which extravagant expressions formerly applied to Stalin were now applied to the Party and especially its Central Committee.[32] The letter sent by the Congress to the Party's Central Committee, for example, said:

> The young men and women of the land of the Soviets have boundless love and loyalty for the Communist Party. Their most cherished thoughts and hopes are bound up with the Party; they are obligated to it for all the happiness and joy of their lives. . . . In all its activities the Leninist Komsomol senses the daily, fatherly care of the Communist Party and its Central Committee. . . .
>
> The Communist Party is the wise teacher and mentor of youth. For the Komsomol, the word and deed of the Party come before all else. The Congress assures the Central Committee of the Communist Party that the Komsomol, true to the immortal ideas of Leninism, will continue to follow the Communist Party firmly and steadfastly, like its loyal son, like its dependable reserve and helper. . . .
>
> Long live the Communist Party of the Soviet Union, the great directing and guiding force of the Soviet people in the struggle for Communism!
>
> Long live the Central Committee of the Communist Party of the Soviet Union! [33]

When this letter was read at the closing session of the Congress, all delegates rose (according to the official report) "in a united transport of boundless love for their own Communist Party," giving a "tumultuous ovation" and, at the end, shouting "Glory to the Communist Party!" [34]

STRENGTHENING THE SOVIET ECONOMY

Economic matters occupied the center of attention during most of the Twelfth Congress of the Komsomol. The Stalinist policy of accelerating at all costs the growth of heavy industry had been amended to the extent that the collective regime, with Malenkov in the forefront, was insisting simultaneously on the expansion of agriculture and light industry. This policy was translated into official Komsomol language by Shelepin in his report on behalf of the Central Committee of the League:

Many Komsomol bodies, shutting themselves up in the sphere of intra-Komsomol affairs, are shunning productive life; they are conducting their activities aloof from the struggle to fulfill the production plans of industrial enterprises, kolkhozes, machine-and-tractor stations, and sovkhozes; they are failing to display the necessary initiative and fighting spirit. Instead of organizing youth to solve concrete problems of how to increase output, many Komsomol officials busy themselves frequently with general talk; they have forgotten to feel responsible for shortcomings in the work of industrial enterprises, kolkhozes, machine-and-tractor stations, and sovkhozes; they are not training youth properly in the spirit of the strict observance of state and labor discipline and the socialist attitude toward public property.[35]

Shelepin then launched into a lengthy discussion of the current duties of the League and its members in all branches of the economy, ending this portion of his report with the following summary statement:

Before the whole Soviet people the Communist Party has taken upon itself the obligation of satisfying in abundance within two or three years the increasing needs of our country's population for foodstuffs, and of assuring ample raw materials for the food-processing and other light industries. And if the Party has decided, then that is what will come to pass. (*Applause.*) Our duty, our first obligation, is to arouse all the energies of Komsomolites and other young people for the selfless struggle to realize the majestic aims set by the Communist Party for the further development of the national economy and the raising of the living standards of our country's workers.[36]

The delegates followed Shelepin's lead by giving primary attention to such matters in both their "discussion" of his report [37] and their first resolution on that report,[38] and by adding appropriate lines to the preamble of the League's official Regulations.[39] The newspaper reports of the Congress took pains to list the names of many delegates who had won honors in production, from bulldozer drivers to swineherds.[40] Some, like Nadezhda Reva, a Hero of Socialist Labor and holder of the title of "distinguished milkmaid," were permitted to address the delegates—"to share with them in detail," as the newspaper put it, "her remarkable experience." [41]

In industry, the specific prescriptions for raising output were in the conventional pattern. They included the familiar injunctions to promote socialist competition, stimulate "initiative" (in the restricted sense that has already been noted), tighten labor discipline, avoid waste, introduce new techniques, and improve quality.[42] Komsomol-run "control posts" and "raiding brigades" were to detect inefficiency and waste. The Komsomol was to take corrective action against tardiness and loafing. On the more positive side, the Komsomol was to encourage and help young workers to gain additional technical training and was to do what it could to improve their living conditions, including their cultural environment. Local Komsomol officials were told that they must take an interest in the operations of facilities serving young workers, such as dining rooms, dormitories, bathhouses, laundries, barbershops, and repair shops. Komsomol bodies were instructed to organize the young workers to fix up their dormitories, prepare and equip athletic fields, and plant greenery. Some of these measures Komsomol bodies could undertake by themselves; others could be approached through the appropriate ministry.[43]

In agriculture, to which the Congress devoted even more attention than industry, the focus was on expanding the acreage under cultivation. Such attempts were of course not new to Komsomolites. At the time of the previous Congress, for instance, the Komsomol had been sending out young people to plant a forestation belt from Kamyshin to Stalingrad and, in Central Asia, to farm the so-called Hungry Steppe.[44] These and other projects had been continued during the next several years as part of what was grandiosely termed the Great Stalin Plan for the Transformation of Nature.[45] But the so-called New Lands Campaign under way in 1954 was even more intensive and was destined to change the course of life for many Komsomolites. The ground had been prepared in the fall of 1953 by Khrushchev's unprecedented disclosures of the deficiencies of Soviet agriculture, especially Soviet livestock,[46] and by the subsequent decrees on animal husbandry, vegetables, consumers' goods, and food production.[47] The Komsomol had helped to dramatize the need.[48]

Then, early in February, 1954, an all-Russian conference of leaders in agriculture, including the heads of many Komsomol bodies, had launched the assault on the "new" or "virgin and long-unused" lands.[49] The lands covered by these loosely interchangeable phrases lay mainly in the south and east—the Volga region, the north Caucasus, the Urals, Kazakhstan, and western Siberia. They were areas of low and irregular precipitation, areas marginal for farming (like the western fringe of our own Missouri basin)—areas which had been in part never touched by the plow and in part abandoned after earlier attempts at cultivation. To these areas Komsomolites were now asked to go as volunteers. Fervid publicity recalled the Komsomol "mobilizations" of 1929 and hailed them as an honored Komsomol tradition which was now being revived.[50] On February 22, 1954, the first group of "volunteers" was given a well-advertised send-off from Moscow, with a band playing and celebrities on hand.[51] Some of the Komsomolites who had helped build the city of Komsomol'sk-on-the-Amur sent special greetings to the new generation of volunteer frontiersmen,[52] and the arrival of the successive groups in the New Lands was publicized in a way which, while emphasizing the economic challenge, also suggested that amid the frontier hardships young males would find female companionship and that sweethearts might well go to the New Lands together.[53] On March 2, 1954, the Party's Central Committee, ostensibly in response to a request from the Komsomol, decreed that the Komsomol would send 100,000 farm machine operators as "volunteers," from among Komsomolites and other young people, to work in machine-and-tractor stations and on state farms in the New Lands.[54] In view of the missionary tone of the appeal, it is noteworthy that bonuses and other material incentives were offered.[55]

By the time of the Twelfth Komsomol Congress, the campaign was in full swing. On the opening day of the Congress,

Komsomol'skaia pravda announced that in an upsurge of "tremendous joy" more than 400,000 young people had volunteered to go to the New Lands and over 60,000 "young patriots" and "young enthusiasts" had already left.[56] The tasks of the Komsomol in the New Lands were outlined in Shelepin's report of the CC. Reviewing the progress of the campaign thus far, he said that much remained to be done in order to speed the remaining young volunteers on their way. In the New Lands themselves, Komsomol bodies must help the Party and the government to prepare for the arrival of the volunteers, by assisting in the construction of housing and by meeting in other ways the physical and cultural needs of the newcomers. Shelepin proposed the issuing of a special badge for those who distinguished themselves in the New Lands Campaign.[57]

Shelepin also spoke more generally of the League's work in the countryside. He said Komsomol bodies had pledged that young people would produce more than two billion planting pots made of peat-humus, and other containers for growing vegetable seedlings. He said that Komsomolites of the Moscow area had already made about 120 million pots, and Komsomolites and young people of the Ukraine, over 250 million. Many Komsomol bodies had helped to build silos on collective farms, he said, and in Uzbekistan the Komsomol was furnishing fifteen thousand young people to help construct an irrigation canal 200 kilometers long.[58] One problem, Shelepin revealed, was inadequate knowledge of agriculture on the part of rural Komsomol leaders (many of whom, one could infer, must have been sent out from the cities). In several oblasts, he said, the Komsomol had set up special seminars—ten days long for Komsomol leaders in the *raikom* and five days long for the leaders of primary organizations—in which the fundamentals of good farming were set forth.[59] Shelepin declared that more education was needed concerning the proper use of fertilizer, the proper treatment of livestock, the recovery of flooded lands, and the best techniques for growing sugar beets, corn, potatoes, fruits, and berries.[60] Komsomol leaders at all echelons in the countryside, he stressed, must stop grinding out general directives and exhortations to higher output and must instead give concrete and direct guidance by going out into the field themselves frequently and learning enough about the technical side of farming so that they would be able to give intelligent guidance.[61]

The organizational weakness that had plagued the rural Komsomol in 1949—when, among the more than 150 major political subdivisions of the country (oblasts, krais, and republics), there were only fifty-four in which the Komsomol had a primary organization for every farming unit (see Chapter VII) —had been largely remedied by 1954, and virtually every farming unit had its Komsomol body. This improvement could hardly be credited to the Komsomol alone. Between 1949 and 1954, the Soviet regime had carried out a vast consolidation of collective farms, presumably in the interests of tighter control.[62] By the time of the Twelfth Congress, the number of state farms had remained around 5,000 and the machine-and-tractor stations had increased slightly from about 8,100 to over 9,000, but the number of collective farms had dropped precipitously from about 250,000 to about 89,000.[63] It is hardly surprising, therefore, that by that time Komsomol units were in operation not only on all state farms and in all machine-and-tractor stations [64] but also on virtually all, if not literally all, collective farms. (Shelepin did not say "all," but he said that there were Komsomol primary organizations on "more than 89,000" collective farms, which would seem to come very close to complete coverage.) [65]

But one must note immediately that this extension of administrative coverage was not accompanied by any commensurate growth in the numbers of Komsomolites in kolkhozes, sovkhozes, and machine-and-tractor stations. That total had reportedly risen to 2,702,000 (comprising 220,000 primary organizations) in June, 1950,[66] but then had declined to 2,500,-000 by May, 1951,[67] and apparently failed to change significantly during the ensuing three years.[68] In 1954 Shelepin told the Congress that there were then 2,000,000 Komsomolites on collective farms, over 200,000 on state farms, and 297,000 in machine-and-tractor stations.[69] That would mean a total of about 2,497,000. Such a small figure, compared with the 2,200,-000 reported in 1949, bespeaks a striking contrast between the rural growth and the urban growth of the League, for, as indicated above, the membership as a whole had more than doubled between 1949 and 1954 (rising from 9,283,289 to 18,825,327). In March, 1949, when about 62–64 percent of the Soviet population was rural, about 24 percent of all Komsomolites lived in farming units, whereas in March, 1954, when the Soviet population was still about 59 percent rural,[70] only about 13.3 percent of all Komsomolites were living in farming units. The uncertain comparability of the census categories and the Komsomol categories, complicated by the question of Komsomolites in school and in the armed forces, unfortunately again prevents any exact calculation of the relative inclusiveness of the League in the towns and in the countryside.

In order to strengthen the League's rural position despite this numerical lack, the Twelfth Congress made one structural change. In his report on proposed amendments to the Komsomol Regulations, V. I. Kochemasov explained that especially since the consolidation of collective farms and the enlarging of machine-and-tractor stations, groups of Komsomolites in the brigades on collective farms, the sections on state farms, and the tractor brigades in the machine-and-tractor stations often found themselves far from the administrative center of the farming unit and therefore unable to participate in all activities of their primary Komsomol organization. (One may infer that in many of the newly merged collective farms, what was formerly a separate kolkhoz village became simply the location of a brigade of the new and larger farm while the physical position of the village remained unchanged.) In order to remedy this difficulty, Kochemasov proposed (and the delegates voted) that wherever the primary Komsomol organization of a kolkhoz, sovkhoz, or machine-and-tractor station had more than fifty members (rather than one hundred, as before) it could form subordinate organizations in each brigade, livestock farm, or other appropriate section, and give them the rights of primary organizations.[71]

The exhortations and instructions to Komsomolites to participate more directly in "state and economic construction" did not imply any change in the relations of the Komsomol to the soviets and other governmental agencies. Komsomolites were still expected to criticize ministries and other government bodies with respect to the execution of Party policies.[72] Such criticism, as before, was recognized as part of the game and did not seem to disturb the ministerial spokesmen, who customarily acknowledged the criticisms in sweeping and glib phrases and vowed to take appropriate corrective measures.[73] The Komsomol continued to help in the propaganda and agitational campaigns associated with elections to the various soviets.[74] The delegates at the Twelfth Congress included sixteen deputies to the Supreme Soviet of the USSR, eighteen deputies to supreme soviets in the union republics, and 421 deputies to lesser soviets, giving evidence of the continuing overlap of the soviet and Komsomol hierarchies.[75]

IDEOLOGICAL TRAINING FOR COMMUNISM

In the League's continuing program of ideological training —criticized in 1954 for being "detached from life" or "unconcrete" or "poorly linked with the tasks of Communist construction" [76]—the delegates confronted problems both of content and of technique.

The most conspicuous change in the content of the ideological message was of course the disappearance of the Stalin cult, which has been treated above. The other changes were much less spectacular. The nationalities question received special attention in connection with the forthcoming tricentennial celebration, in May, 1954, of the "reunion of the Ukraine with Russia"—the treaty of the Dnieper Cossacks with Muscovy under Tsar Alexis—which Komsomolites of all nationalities were expected to assist in honoring.[77] A high official of the Komsomol in the Ukraine set the example by saying that "in the heart of each Ukrainian boy and girl burns an inextinguishable love for the Russian people, for Moscow, which helped the Ukrainian people to win its freedom and independence," [78] and representatives of other nationalities echoed the familiar refrains about the "great Russian people," the "elder brother" of the rest.[79] For the first time at any Komsomol congress in more than twenty-five years, there was a complete silence on the numerical representation of the various nationalities among the delegates at the Congress. The report of the Credentials Commission named twenty-seven of the nationalities represented (omitting, as in 1949, the Jews, Germans, and Poles), but released neither percentages nor absolute numbers.[80] This curious omission, hardly a simple oversight, suggests the leadership's special concern for the nationality problem in the immediate post-Stalin period.

There was somewhat more talk than usual about initiative and spontaneity [81] (without, of course, forgetting discipline) [82] and also, in keeping with the theme of production, a noticeable emphasis on industriousness or "love of work." [83] Shelepin's report of the CC bemoaned the presence among Soviet young people of some "white hands"—that is, youths who were afraid of physical work, afraid to get their hands dirty. He declared:

The schools and the Komsomol are not doing enough to imbue the pupils with work habits and to draw them into work appropriate to their strength. Rural schools are doing a poor job of arousing in their pupils an interest in farm work. It is wrong when some Pioneer leaders and Komsomol officials, and also teachers, tell the school children only: "Study hard and you're sure to be a scientist, engineer, or writer"—and fail to interest him in becoming a skilled workman, mechanic, tractor driver, or combine operator.

The Komsomol, he added, must do a great deal more to implant in young people a "love of manual labor." [84]

Antireligious propaganda—said the report of the Central Committee—had been seriously neglected of late by the Komsomol; some Komsomol personnel had underestimated the pernicious influence of the church; some young people were becoming infected with religious ideas; atheistic propaganda must be restored to full vigor.[85] Little was said at the Congress respecting family and personal relationships,[86] but a perusal of *Komsomol'skaia pravda* for the period since the Congress of 1949 suggests a continuation of earlier themes.[87] A characteristic contemporary note was the condemnation of "zoot-suiters" (*stiliagi*). They were described as "young people with Tarzan haircuts, dressed up like parrots," who molested girls and spent their nights in bars. "The Komsomol," said Shelepin, "must declare a relentless and determined war against all kinds of 'zoot-suiters,' 'aristocrats,' and other spongers and hooligans. All of them must be forced to work, to work honestly, and to behave as Soviet people should." [88]

The apparatus for ideological training had been in some respects expanded since 1949. The number of Komsomolites studying within the Party education system had risen from about 640,000 in 1949–50 to over 1,000,000 in May, 1953.[89] At the time of the Congress, the number of young people studying in Party and Komsomol political schools and circles reportedly stood at five million. However, said Shelepin, the training of Komsomol propagandists and agitators was inadequate. He called upon oblast committees of the League to organize month-long courses during the coming summer, in order to turn out not less than twenty-five or thirty thousand propagandists. Mass agitational work must be expanded too, he said, in youth brigades, factory shifts, dormitories, field camps, and farming units, with the revival of such devices as young people's agitational brigades, "living newspapers," and "campaign leaflets." [90]

The Komsomol now published ninety-three newspapers for "young people" of Komsomol age and twenty for "children." Strikingly, the number of newspapers for those of Komsomol age had grown since 1949 from thirty-seven to ninety-three, while for those of Pioneer age the increase was merely from nineteen to twenty. The total circulation of both categories in 1954 was about eight million copies per issue (frequency of appearance—daily, weekly, or at some other interval—not

being stated). The Komsomol press also published ten magazines for young people and twenty-two magazines for children,
with a total circulation of over two million (the frequency
again being unstated). The total circulation of all these newspapers and magazines was reported to be ten million, or two
and one-half times the corresponding figure in 1949.[91] The
Young Guard Publishing House was said to be producing more
than fifteen million books for young people every year, and
the Children's Publishing House was reported to have produced seventy-one million books in 1953.[92] Amidst this mass
of paper, the search for satisfactory heroes in literature—models
of the youthful versions of the New Soviet Man, who could be
imitated by children and young people—was still proceeding.
Too many of the available "heroes" were still not convincing
or lifelike, it was complained, while the villains did not demonstrate clearly enough the negative traits still lingering among
the younger generation.[93]

Among the usual reminders about cultural activities, the
only discernible new note was a musical one—a special stress
on the fostering of choral singing. Only in a few Moscow or
Leningrad schools, it was reported, was there any systematic
singing instruction. Qualified teachers were exceedingly scarce.
The Komsomol was urged to encourage teachers and would-be
teachers to seek the necessary training and to help organize
choral groups in schools, on collective farms, and in other
places.[94]

Komsomol responsibilities in the expanding school system
demanded the delegates' attention.[95] Complaints were leveled
at the Komsomol for failing to apprehend truants; for neglecting to enforce study discipline among school children; for permitting too many school children to repeat grades; for overburdening school children with Komsomol and Pioneer activities; for condoning hooliganism and disrespectful behavior
toward teachers and other adults; and for tolerating ineffective
ideological training.[96]

In response, seemingly, to these complaints, the role of the
teacher in the Komsomol was being enlarged. Nominally the

Komsomol continued to embody the functions of leading and representing the pupils (and thus to render student self-government superfluous).[97] But now Shelepin on behalf of the Central Committee proposed (that is, in effect, commanded) that primary organizations of Komsomolites in the ninth and tenth grades—the last two grades in the secondary school—should elect as their heads (secretaries) not pupils but teachers. Shelepin's justification was that pupils in those grades could not readily manage large primary organizations along with their studies.[98] To the outsider, however, it seems likely that the most important reason for the change was the need to combat breaches of discipline and to cope with the difficult ideological questions that sixteen- to eighteen-year-old students were asking in the early post-Stalin era.[99] Mere good fellowship between teacher-Komsomolites and students was not the motive, since separate primary Komsomol organizations for teachers continued to be the rule.[100] Hence the new measure can be interpreted as another in the long series of measures designed to bring the Komsomol under the control of the school authorities. In this connection it seems significant that Shelepin cautioned against duplicating the work of the teacher.[101] This warning, apparently a new one so far as Komsomol (as distinct from Pioneer) bodies were concerned, suggests the extent to which control by teachers had already progressed.

In institutions of higher education the Komsomol's ideological training was said to be weak. This theme had already been emphasized in the Komsomol press between the congresses. In September, 1952, when 82 percent of all students in higher educational institutions (*vuzy*) were reported to be members of the Komsomol, the Komsomol Central Committee demanded not increased membership but more effective attention to the students' ideological training, discipline, and material and cultural needs.[102] Shelepin told the Twelfth Congress that not only was the Komsomol still neglecting the students' needs for better dormitories and eating facilities (in the construction of which the Komsomol should cooperate with the appropriate governmental agencies), but—and his emphasis was here—the ideological and political training of these university and institute students was still poor. He referred to acts of hooliganism and of disrespectful behavior toward instructors, against which the Komsomol had failed to take appropriate disciplinary measures. He cited the tendency of some graduates of higher educational institutions to avoid going to the jobs to which they were assigned, and said the Komsomol bore direct responsibility for correcting this. These and other shortcomings, he indicated, reflected poor ideological training, in that the students were not being sufficiently impressed with their duty to do whatever work was need by the homeland.[103]

The Young Pioneer organization had apparently been experiencing difficulties in the interval since the Eleventh Congress. One indication of difficulty was the failure of the speakers at the Twelth Congress to disclose the current membership of the Pioneers.[104] This omission could hardly have been accidental, for, ever since the founding of the Pioneers in 1922, the numerical strength of the organization had been publicly announced at the time of each Komsomol congress. What had happened, apparently, was that the Pioneers had shot up from 13,000,000 in March, 1949, to "about 19,000,000" in October, 1951,[105] but then had virtually stopped growing. Several reports were issued from January to August of 1952, all describing the membership as "more than 19,000,000." [106] Then in October, 1952, it was again placed at "about 19,000,000." [107] And from that time up through the Congress in March, 1954, so far as this writer has been able to discover, secrecy was preserved. That secrecy, together with the issuance in the spring of 1953 of an appeal for increasing the Pioneer membership,[108] suggests a decline. Even if the total of 1952 had been maintained without further increase until 1954, it would probably have been mentioned, since it was higher by an impressive six million than the figure reported at the previous Congress. To the outsider appraising the probable effects of World War II on the age structure of the Soviet population, it seems reasonable to assume that the generation born in 1941–45 would be a relatively small one and that by the middle 1950s the number

of children of Pioneer age (nine to fourteen) would be temporarily diminished.[109] In that case the Pioneer membership
could hardly fail to drop, since the Pioneer organization by this
time embraced the vast majority of the children in the eligible
age group.[110]

The Congress devoted much time to the presumed weaknesses of the Pioneer organization.[111] Z. P. Tumanova, in the
principal report on the Pioneers, said that many troops, distort-
ing the principle of subordinating Pioneer work to the educational aims of the school, had foolishly devoted Pioneer meetings to regular school subjects, such as "The Noun," The Par-
ticles 'Not' and 'Neither,' " "The Soils of the USSR." Members
had had to report on their school marks at Pioneer meetings.[112]
In other cases, long and tiresome lectures had predominated.
There was too much formality. In one school, for instance, two
or three times a week the leader taught current events by lining up all Pioneers from the third to the eighth grades in front
of the school, shouting "Attention!" and reading aloud from
the newspaper.[113] Many adult leaders, said Tumanova, tended
to appoint the members of troop and patrol councils instead
of letting them be elected, to issue commands instead of really
guiding, and in other ways to regiment their Pioneer troops
and kill all spontaneity.[114] At the root of many of the weaknesses, said Tumanova, was inadequate leadership. In the current school year, she said, there were 9,000 Pioneer troops that
lacked regular leaders (that is, Komsomolites properly selected
and assigned to such positions). The turnover was high: half
of the professional senior Pioneer leaders remained less than
a year with one troop. And many of the leaders lacked training:
of the 51,000 professional senior Pioneer leaders, more than
9,000 had not had secondary education. Only 56 percent of
the leaders had graduated from pedagogical training institutions.[115] Male leaders were especially scarce.[116] Similar criticisms were echoed by other delegates,[117] two of whom declared that weak Pioneer work was causing school children to
shun the Pioneers and to organize their own unofficial groups
with their own leaders and their own secret passwords.[118]

The remedies proposed by Tumanova and others to revivify the Pioneers were numerous. Of course all Komsomol units and also the ministries of education all over the USSR were to help improve the quantity and quality of Pioneer leaders.[119] The Congress voted that the Central Committee of the Komsomol should award a special badge, "Superior Pioneer Leader," to all who successfully completed three years in that capacity.[120] Pioneer traditions that had been neglected were to be revived, such as planting trees, caring for the families of soldiers who died in the war, and holding yearly assemblies and parades, along with song festivals and campfires. Pioneers were to take more hikes and organize more summer camps, especially on collective farms.[121] They were to expand the network of groups or circles fostering such hobbies as meteorology, photography, model airplane building, radio operating, and nature study. Wherever possible, the activities of the circles were to be tied in with the needs of Soviet agriculture, so as to mix fun with useful labor and inculcate a love of farm work.[122] For both town and country children, all kinds of "socially useful labor" —like planting trees and gardens and building athletic fields— were recommended. Pioneers, said Tumanova, "must be trained from their early years to do physical labor." [123] Athletics were to be pushed—partly in connection, as before, with the Ready for Labor and Defense program and its tests in obstacle-course running and other semimilitary skills.[124] The regular Pioneer meetings were to be enlivened. Some of the topics suggested as appropriately stimulating were "our Communist Party," "the great socialist Homeland," and "the successes of the Soviet people in building Communism"(!).[125] The members could also discuss books, plays, and movies, display what technical or artistic work they had done, and learn games, songs, and dances. They should observe the proper customs, such as lining up and reporting at the beginning of each meeting and having the flag on hand at troop meetings.[126] In these and other ways, Pioneer activities must be endued with a "romanticism" that would make them long remembered.[127] Along with all the insistence on making Pioneer activity more lively, democratic, and spontaneous,[128] the demand for discipline was not forgotten.[129]

A new Pioneer Statute, growing out of the Twelfth Komsomol Congress, set forth the approved procedures, activities, structure, and aims of the organization.[130] In the official oath, where each Pioneer had formerly promised that he would "steadfastly support the cause of Lenin and Stalin, the victory of Communism," he now promised "to be true to the precepts of Lenin and to support steadfastly the cause of our Communist Party, the victory of Communism." And the Pioneer motto, which had been "For the struggle for the cause of Lenin and Stalin, be prepared!" was now altered to read "For the struggle for the cause of the Communist Party, be prepared!" [131]

In the realm of military and world affairs, the Soviet propaganda line at the time of the Twelfth Congress, as exemplified in Shelepin's report on behalf of the Central Committee, called for the prevention of war, the relaxation of world tensions, and the restoration of normal relations between states.[132] This "struggle for peace" theme had been used at other times since 1949, notably during the opening weeks of the Communist aggression in Korea, when Komsomolites had been mobilized to collect signatures to the Stockholm peace appeal.[133] In 1954, as before, protestations of peacefulness were mingled with the familiar elastic phrases which could so easily be used to justify Soviet expansion. Shelepin promised that the struggle of "our friends" in "capitalistic, colonial, and dependent countries" for "freedom" and "independence" would have the support of Soviet youth.[134] The Korean War was classified as a "heroic struggle" for "independence" on the part of Korea.[135] The ultimate victory of "Communism in our country" as well as just plain "Communism" was still proclaimed.[136] Shelepin said the Komsomol must continue to rear youth in a spirit of "hatred for the enemies of the socialist homeland," and expressed pride that the Soviet armed forces were "ready at any moment to cool off the hot heads of all kinds of warlike adventurers and provocateurs and force them to respect the socialist conquests and might of the Soviet Union." [137] The role of the Komsomol in the armed forces was described in the same general terms as before,[138] and athletics were discussed in the previous semi-military and chauvinistic way.[139]

Broadened contacts between Soviet and foreign youth were endorsed in 1954 as they had been in 1949. In the interim between the congresses, Shelepin reported, 121 delegations of Soviet young people (the number of individuals involved was not disclosed) had gone abroad. Meanwhile the years 1949 through 1953 had seen 236 youth delegations including more than 6,000 young people visit the USSR upon the invitation of the Anti-Fascist Committee of Soviet Youth, he said. In 1953 alone, he said, there had been 3,746 young visitors from fifty-five countries.[140] The World Federation of Democratic Youth, which claimed 52,000,000 members in sixty-three countries as of March, 1949, and 60,000,000 members in seventy-four countries as of April, 1950,[141] was reported as of March, 1954, to contain 83,000,000 members in ninety-three countries. (No figures were given for individual countries.) The International Union of Students was said to have a current membership of 6,000,000,[142] distributed among some seventy-two countries.[143] Representatives of thirty-three countries addressed the Twelfth Congress.[144] Amidst their unvaried chorus one voice stood out—that of the Chinese representative. With its laudatory references to Stalin and its repeated mention of Communist China's own leader, Mao Tse-tung, it was like an echo from the era before "collective leadership." [145]

LEADERSHIP AND DEMOCRACY WITHIN THE LEAGUE

The proceedings of the Twelfth Congress reveal some significant developments respecting the internal operations of the Komsomol and the related demands upon Komsomol members.

While the total membership had doubled, the number of primary organizations had dropped from 447,000 in 1949 to 431,000 in 1954.[146] The number of primary organizations in the towns had increased by about 40,000,[147] but that increase had been more than offset by the diminution in the countryside—a diminution readily explainable by the consolidation of collective farms. The net effect of the consolidation in the countryside and the swelling enrollment in the cities was to raise the size of the average primary organization from about twenty-one members in 1949 to about forty-four members in 1954. Thus the great expansion in total membership had been achieved probably without making administrative control from the center any more difficult than before.

No demand for further expansion was expressed at the Congress of 1954. One measure even paved the way for a reduction. Previously, the League had had a formal but not an effective upper age limit, for although members twenty-six or over had been disqualified to vote at Komsomol meetings (unless they held a Komsomol office), in all other respects they had enjoyed the full rights of membership. The result, according to the official report of V. I. Kochemasov, was that the League had accumulated a large number of overage members. He did not reveal any number or proportion. (One may note in this connection that N. A. Mikhailov reached the age of forty-six before he left his position at the head of the Komsomol [148] and that Shelepin, to judge from the large photographs of him published in 1949 and 1956, was probably about forty in 1954.) [149] He did say, however, that to expel from the League all those over twenty-six who did not hold office would deprive the League of too many active members. He proposed a compromise which the Congress readily enacted as part of the new Regulations. Komsomolites who reached the age of twenty-six and who were not officeholders would have a choice: if they remained silent they would be dropped; if they indicated a desire to continue, they would be kept in for two years, that is, until twenty-eight. But beyond that age only those holding Komsomol offices could continue as members.[150] Both that remedy and the problem itself are interesting. The new rule for the first time set a deadline before which the shift from the Komsomol to the Party must be made by those who wished to remain on one of the escalators leading to a favored position in Soviet society. The admitted abundance of overage members, and the choice of twenty-eight rather than twenty-six as the cutoff point, suggest that many young adults, while anxious to remain in the Party's good books, did not wish to accept the risks and responsibilities of Party membership. Perhaps the choice of twenty-eight rather than twenty-six also reflects the increasing availability of higher education which, together with military service, would in many cases prevent an ambitious young person from settling into his chosen work until he had reached his middle or late twenties. It remained to be seen how the new rule would affect the enrollment of both the League and the Party.

Improved leadership within the Komsomol reportedly constituted a serious need. The leading officials of the Komsomol, said Shelepin, should be well-trained people who have a talent for administering efficiently without imperiousness. Officials should not be transferred from one post to another so frequently. Full-time paid officials should be used as little as possible, and unpaid volunteers should receive special encouragement. More women should be brought into posts of leadership. There should be more rapid advancement for promising young Komsomolites.[151]

The composition of the Congress itself affords partial clues to the force or lack of force behind these demands. Of the 1,334 delegates, 594 listed their occupation as executives ("guiding workers") of the Komsomol. They were salaried professionals. The remaining delegates listed themselves as pursuing other occupations, although almost all of them probably held positions of leadership in the Komsomol. The other occupational groups listed were: 118 workers; 116 collective farmers; 62 farming specialists and employees of machine-and-tractor stations and state farms; 46 employees in engineering, technology, and science; 33 workers in the press, the arts, and literature; 48 teachers and leaders of Pioneer troops; 55 students in higher educational establishments; 10 students in trade and factory training schools; and 34 students in secondary schools and technical schools.[152] That left 218 delegates not accounted for. Probably most of those were "delegates from the Komsomol organizations of the armed forces of the USSR and the border guards," for whom no numbers were released.

Delegates with some higher education were slightly more prevalent at the Twelfth Congress than at the Eleventh (43.3 percent as compared with 37.7 percent), but in other respects the educational achievements of the delegates of 1954 do not seem to have been markedly better than those of 1949.[153] Women constituted 41.9 percent of the delegates, which was about the same as the proportion at the previous Congress.[154]

The delegates to the Twelfth Congress were markedly older than those at any previous congress, including even the Congress of 1949. Delegates thirty-one or older constituted 20.6 percent (271) in 1954, as against only 14.3 percent in 1949. Delegates aged twenty-nine or thirty constituted 15.6 percent (206) in 1954, as against 12.8 percent in 1949. Delegates twenty-six through twenty-eight constituted 27.6 percent (364) in 1954, as against 22 percent in 1949. In order to obscure the embarrassing nature of the comparison between 1949 and 1954, the report of 1954 not only maintained complete silence on the figures for 1949 but also gave out only absolute numbers instead of percentages, and furthermore—in contrast to all previous practice—lumped together all delegates under twenty-six, in order to make the absolute figure for that group (477) larger than the figure for any other single group. In these ways the Credentials Commission probably prevented most of those who heard or read its report from realizing that whereas in 1949 the proportion of those under twenty-six had been 51.1 percent, in 1954 it was down to only 36.2 percent.[155]

The figures released on the delegates' length of service in the Komsomol showed a similar trend. The proportion with fourteen or more years of service had risen from 23.1 percent in 1949 to 27.8 percent in 1954. A new category was established within this oldest group. At previous congresses there had never been statistics covering persons admitted to have served more than eighteen years, but now a category of those with service of nineteen years or more was established. This category embraced 3.5 percent of the delegates.[156] From the statistics on the delegates, one would conclude that the announced policy of rapidly promoting younger Komsomolites had of late been neglected.

At a higher echelon—that of the Central Committee—the policies of promotion and replacement can be examined in greater detail. The Central Committee elected at the Congress of 1949 had consisted of 103 members and 47 candidate-members, or a total of 150 persons. According to the Regulations, their term of office was still continuing as the Twelfth Congress opened in 1954. But very few of them were in evidence. The bodies elected at the start of the Congress—the forty-one-man Presidium, the nine-man Secretariat, the eleven-man Editorial Commission, and the nineteen-man Credentials Commission—included only twelve members of the old Central Committee.[157] Only nine old members—all of them from the same group of twelve mentioned above—were among the approximately seventy-one Komsomol speakers during the proceedings.[158] And only twelve old members (very largely the same individuals) were found on the new CC elected at the end of the Twelfth Congress—a CC that contained, just as in 1949, 103 members and 47 candidate-members, or a total of 150.[159] If those members who had fallen ill or had been otherwise incapacitated had been replaced according to rule, one would expect some of the forty-seven candidate-members elected in 1949 to have been full members in 1954. Yet not one of those forty-seven appeared either among the eighty members of the bodies running the Congress itself (Presidium, Secretariat, Editorial Commission, and Credentials Commission), or among the 150 new members and candidate-members of the Central Committee.[160] Taking into account members and candidate-members in both cases, the proportion of the former CC that was retained in 1954 was only 8 percent. This was lower than at any previous congress except that in 1949 (zero percent), which followed an abnormally long gap of thirteen years including the Great Purge and the war. The other nearest approaches to such high mortality had been at the congresses of 1931 (when 18.3 percent were held over) and 1936 (when 23 percent were held over)—

and those congresses followed intervals of intense struggle within the Party. The period 1949–54 had witnessed intra-Party struggles, too, but it would be rash to guess how many of the dismissed 92 percent were political casualties and how many were simply promoted by the Party to other assignments.

The almost total turnover among the Central Committee as a whole contrasted sharply with the stability among the topmost handful of leaders. Of the seven persons who, as the Congress opened, were serving as secretaries of the CC, six had been on the CC since 1949,[161] and four had even been on the eleven-man Bureau of the CC since that time.[162] The same seven were reelected as secretaries of the CC following the end of the Congress, and the new thirteen-man Bureau elected at that same time included nine persons whose tenure on the CC dated at least from 1949.[163] Thus on the basis of the available evidence one would conclude that during the period 1949–54 the explicit double-barreled demand to promote new leaders without causing excessively rapid turnover had been translated into remarkable permanence for those at the very top and remarkable impermanence for the rest of the leading element.

The pronouncements at the Twelfth Congress might have seemed to herald a post-Stalin democratization of the internal operations of the Komsomol. Shelepin castigated some parts of the League for "violation of the principle of collectivity" in leadership. Right within the Central Committee itself, he said, this principle had been violated by the Secretariat when it "decided many important questions" without convening the Bureau of the Central Committee, let alone the Central Committee in its entirety. Such violations of the collective principle must stop, he said, so that "the broad masses of Komsomolites may be able continually to control the activity of Komsomol committees and their bureaus and secretaries." There must be, he declared, a revival of "criticism from below," since criticism was the best way to combat shortcomings.[164] The Congress added special demands for criticism to several sections of the amended Regulations and made it each Komsomolite's solemn obligation to carry his criticism fearlessly right up to the top, no matter how high the position of the person at fault.[165] There was a strong attack on "crude violations of the voluntary principle" on the part of Komsomol leaders.[166] In those and in more general terms, wider democracy was demanded all through the operations of the League.[167] An observer looking for hopeful signs could point also to the new Regulations, which omitted (without explanation) the former demand that hostile elements be purged.[168]

Of course, collective and democratic leadership had always been one element of the explicit Komsomol ideal. Dictatorial methods among Komsomolites had been periodically denounced, even during Stalin's most arbitrary period,[169] and the content of this sort of editorial appeal did not change noticeably between the time of Stalin's death in March, 1953, and the Twelfth Komsomol Congress one year later.[170] Therefore the Twelfth Congress's insistence on intra-Komsomol democracy and collective leadership was merely a matter of a new emphasis. As such, it might nevertheless have been expected to influence the actual conduct of the Congress. But did it?

The "discussion" of the major reports seemed every bit as thoroughly planned as before, and just as devoid of controversy. The style of "criticism and self-criticism"—for which the delegates were formally commended [171]—observed the same strict limitations as it had at the Eleventh Congress. Once again, government ministries and the Central Committee of the Komsomol were excoriated, but only for failing to meet the standards of performance laid down by the Party leaders and only along lines suggested by Shelepin's keynote speech. And once again, a very common criticism of lower-echelon spokesmen was that the higher bodies had not given enough "guidance." [172] Of the approximately seventy-one strictly Komsomol speakers, all but fifteen were nominated (and consequently elected) as members or candidate-members of the new Central Committee.[173] Since both the speakers and the nominees for the Central Committee were selected from a total pool of 1,334 delegates, a very high correlation is indicated between speakers and Central Committee members, and this suggests close control of the proceedings. The usual concern for rank was evidenced in the use of the same nonalphabetical sequence each time the highest leaders of the Party were named.[174] So far as the published record showed, all votes concerning the approval of the agenda, the approval of reports and resolutions, and the election of the Presidium which ostensibly governed the Congress were unanimous.[175] The new Central Committee and Central Inspection Commission were reportedly elected by secret ballot, in accordance with the Regulations.[176] But since it was subsequently announced that "all those nominated were elected," [177] it can be assumed that there was only one candidate for each position, and hence no real contest.[178] One is forced to conclude, on the basis of the proceedings, that the Twelfth Congress in its own conduct offered no concrete evidence of a broadened democracy at the end of the first year of the post-Stalin era. Subtler changes were possibly taking place at the lower echelons or behind the scenes, but the example set by the Congress was certainly not designed to inspire any very radical notions.

As one looks back over the two congresses of 1949 and 1954 —the one representing the apogee of Stalinism and the other the uncertain early months of "collective leadership"—one is struck first by their similarity. Many aspects of the Komsomol pattern did not appear to have changed at all. Some changes— like the enlarged role of the teacher in the League, the advancing age of the leadership, and the swelling network of Komsomol newspapers—were merely extensions of previous trends. Other changes—like those associated with the New Lands Campaign, the "struggle for peace," and the lagging Pioneers—appeared to be ephemeral variations on ancient themes. One may, however, perhaps distinguish a third category of changes discernible in 1954—those developments which, while in themselves slight, nevertheless could portend significant transformations in the future. First among these was the cutting back of the Stalin cult, which was bound to promote irreverent questioning on the part of youth. Along with this went the intensified protestations of intra-Komsomol democracy, which might serve to sharpen the contrast between practice and preaching, and thus also to encourage youthful queries. Similarly, the broadened intercourse with foreign youth, even though still confined almost entirely within the Soviet bloc, could arouse intellectual unrest among Soviet youth. The indications in 1954 of an unusually high turnover in the Komsomol CC, and of growing concern over the ideological state of university students, suggest that some stirrings had already begun. However, the evidence of the Twelfth Congress provides no basis for predicting that such challenges would proceed very far or would materially alter the pattern of Komsomol demands.

IX. Conclusion

THROUGH all the years from 1918 to 1954 the Komsomol pattern retained many of the same elements. The general role of the League in its formative era—to help the Party and to supply it with fresh reserves—remained characteristic of the League later on. Throughout the period studied, Komsomolites were called upon to assist the regime in political indoctrination, general education, industry, agriculture, social relations, military activity, and world affairs. Certain qualities of individual character—such as loyalty to the Party chiefs, iron discipline, self-sacrificing bravery, ideological purity, unshakable conviction, incessant vigilance, uncompromising militancy, and hatred toward enemies—were generally esteemed throughout. These and other consistent elements in the Komsomol pattern reflected the fundamental continuity of the Soviet regime; the totalitarian and authoritarian nature of the Communist Party; the atmosphere of crisis, partly internally generated, which helped to sustain Communist militancy; the solicitude of Communists to maintain doctrinal orthodoxy; and the persistent need of the Soviet regime to win support from each fresh crop of impressionable and not yet disillusioned youth.

Against that background of constant general purposes, there were many significant changes. The size of the League increased —notwithstanding the contractions associated with the beginning of the NEP and the years after World War II—from about twenty thousand in 1918 to almost nineteen million in 1954. For most of that thirty-six-year period, however, the League by no means deserved to be called a "mass" organization. Not until 1926 did it embrace even 5 percent of Soviet youth of Komsomol age. The 10 percent mark was not reached until the mid-

1930s, and as late as 1949 the proportion was only about 20 percent. The doubling of the membership by 1954 left the League still in a minority position, except among urban youth.

Meanwhile there were changes in the composition of the membership. In the mid-1920s the proportion of rural Komsomolites had been rather large (about 36 percent of the members in 1924 and about 51 percent of the members in 1926), but by 1954, although the general population was still heavily rural, the rural segment of the League's membership had sunk to a tiny minority.[1] In the early years the membership was overwhelmingly male. Not until 1924, apparently, did the proportion of females reach even 15 percent. From then on the proportion rose (1926—19 percent; 1927—21.3 percent; 1928—23 percent; 1936—34 percent) until, in 1949, young women constituted 42 percent of the membership of the League. The age of the membership increased: in 1925 only 4 percent of the members were over twenty-three years old. By 1928 about 16 or 17 percent were over twenty-three, and by 1936 about 30 percent were over twenty-three. Roughly that same distribution obtained in 1949, but by 1954 there may have been a further growth in the proportion of older members, to judge from the discussions surrounding the raising of the age limit for full membership from twenty-six to twenty-eight.

The changes in the general membership were accompanied by changes in the composition of the leading personnel of the Komsomol. One dramatic displacement occurred in 1928–30. At that time several key figures of the first decade of the League, including Shatskin and Chaplin, were discredited because of alleged Trotskyite or other subversive tendencies, and the turnover in the Central Committee of the Komsomol was more complete than at any other time between 1918 and 1936. The second large-scale discarding of prominent Komsomol officials came in 1937–38. Here Kosarev, who had come to the top with the fall of Shatskin and Chaplin, in his turn fell victim to the purge, and the 128 members of the Central Committee of 1936 passed, in one way or another, into oblivion. The third big transfer, whose details are still unclarified, occurred in the period preceding the Congress of 1954 and left only a hardy handful of officials to provide continuity in the League's top leadership during the transition from the Stalinist era to the era of collective rule.

Apart from those changes of personnel, there were changes also in the general character of the leading element. The clearest evidence of these changes is found in the composition of the congresses themselves. The more recent congresses afford somewhat less reliable indices of the leadership than do the congresses of the 1920s, for the progressive consolidation of the regime brought an enlargement of the ceremonial and propagandistic functions of the congresses, which meant the inclusion of some lower-echelon Komsomolites and a reduction in the proportion of Party members and full-time Komsomol officials among the delegates (see Appendix C). But even when all of that is taken into account, the other changes in the composition of the delegates retain enough magnitude to be significant.

For one thing, the proportion of women among the delegates rose from a mere 3 percent in 1921 and 1924 to over 40 percent in 1949 and 1954. The Komsomol was still run chiefly by men, especially at the highest echelons, but the increase in the women's role was nevertheless striking.

The incomplete data on the class composition of the congresses (see Appendix C) indicate that the peak period for those who either were, or posed as being, of worker parentage was in 1928 and 1931. The percentage of "workers" had fallen sharply by 1936 and thereafter was not even reported, as one might expect in view of the rise of the new Soviet bureaucracy and intelligentsia and the inclusion of nonmanual workers in the esteemed category of "toilers."

The median age of the assembled leaders rose markedly with the passage of time (see Appendix D). In 1921 the median age of the delegates was twenty, and there were none reported over twenty-six. By 1931 the median age was twenty-three, and about 10.6 percent of the delegates were twenty-six or older. In 1936 there were no delegates under twenty-two, and 59.3 percent were twenty-six or older. In 1949, despite the well-publicized importation of younger Komsomolites, the median delegate's age was on the upper edge of twenty-five, and 14.3 percent were about thirty-one or older. By 1954 the median had risen to about twenty-seven, and over one-fifth were thirty-one or older. The job of running the Soviet youth organization was increasingly being entrusted to those who were "mature."

Along with increased age went, quite naturally, increased length of service in the Komsomol (see Appendix E): among the delegates in 1926, the median length of service was six years; in 1936 the median was about eleven years. Despite the aforementioned leavening of junior Komsomolites at the Congress of 1949, the median service was about nine or ten years, and 23.1 percent of the delegates had served about fourteen or more years in the League. In 1954, 27.8 percent fell into that senior category, including 3.5 percent with nineteen years' service or more. For many people the work in the League must have constituted an important part of a bureaucratic career.

Formal education, at first relatively slight among the leaders of the League, became widespread (see Appendix F). In 1924 about two-thirds of the delegates had only primary (four-year) education or less, and not even 1 percent had gone beyond secondary school. By 1949 two-thirds of the delegates had completed secondary school and 37.7 percent had gone on to obtain some higher education, while in 1954 the last-named category had risen to 43.3 percent.

As to ethnic composition, the available statistics (see Appendix G) indicate that Ukrainians were consistently less numerous among the delegates than their proportion in the general population would have warranted and that Belorussians also suffered from underrepresentation. On the other hand, Georgians and Jews were overrepresented, the Jews most heavily—until 1949 when they were pointedly no longer listed as a category.

Paralleling the changes in the composition of the League, and similarly reflecting the major stages in the life of the Soviet regime, were shifts in emphasis within the basic pattern of Komsomol demands. In the early period of the League, the Civil War naturally dictated a stress on military duties. Political indoctrination, the education of worker youth, and campaigns against deviationists marked the period of the struggle for power under the NEP. Economic tasks came to the fore during the First Five-Year Plan, to be partially eclipsed in the middle and late thirties by the tasks of indoctrination and the liquidation of "enemies of the people." Meanwhile, the lavish worship of Stalin had become a requirement for all Komsomolites. World War II of course brought military demands again into prominence, while postwar Stalinism meant a combination of demands for "defense," hard work, idolization of Stalin, education and indoctrination, and the extirpation of "cosmopolitanism" and other heresies. In 1954 the needs of the economy were once again in the forefront. While the congresses have yielded fresh material respecting the nature of the demands at each stage, they have not uncovered any startling anomalies.

The same may be said respecting the changes observed through time in each of the topical elements in the Komsomol pattern. In the field of agriculture and rural life, for example, the foregoing chapters have depicted the demands on Komsomolites to confiscate grain, to draw peasant youths away from their parents, and to recruit soldiers during the Civil War; to propagandize the peasants during the NEP; to collectivize the farms and wipe out the "kulaks" under the initial Five-Year Plans; to ensure maximum deliveries to the state in 1949; and to support the New Lands Campaign in 1954.

The congresses portrayed the League's early aim of protecting worker youth; the channeling and progressive restriction of that aim; and, by 1936, its virtual elimination in the face of the leaders' insistence that the interests of youth were already fully protected by the Soviet government. That protective purpose was undermined, too, by the intensified glorification of work as such: in 1921 Komsomol delegates advocated reduced output quotas and a full eight hours' pay for minors working a four-hour or six-hour day; in 1928 the demand for increased production could still be accompanied by the suggestion that minors ought to receive higher pay; but under the early Five-Year Plans, socialist competition and Stakhanovism became watchwords and hundreds of thousands of Komsomolites were "mobilized" to expand Soviet industry, while under both Stalinist and post-Stalinist "socialism" all youths were expected to love work, for all work had ostensibly become a matter of "honor, glory, valor, and heroism."

In regard to world affairs, the congresses mirrored the bright revolutionary hopes of the early years; the steady encouragement to foreign Communist youth to conduct subversive activity; the recurrent purges of opposition in the ranks of Young Communist Leagues abroad; the fading of the Communist International of Youth; the Stalinist era of extreme xenophobia and isolation of Soviet youth from foreign youth even while the world revolutionary goal was being preserved; and, in the recent period, some signs of slightly broader contacts.

Although the military obligations of Komsomolites remained important throughout the period 1918–54, the nature of the demands changed somewhat. In the days of the Civil War, Komsomolites were hastily mobilized for the Red Army and rushed to the front. After the fighting was over, some sort of military training remained a formal requirement for all Komsomolites. Through the institution of "patronage," Komsomolites were given special responsibilities toward the Navy (from 1922) and toward the Air Forces (from 1931). In the thirties, Komsomolites were expected to help teach military specialties to civilians outside the armed services. The all-out military effort of World War II was followed by an era of "peace" in which, nevertheless, preparations for military "defense" remained a prime obligation of each Komsomolite.

The mission of education (with its accompanying indoctrination) was important also throughout the period under consideration. Until the mid-twenties, the attention of the congresses was directed toward education outside of the conventional schools, and especially education combined with factory work. The Pioneer organization, formed in 1922 as the Komsomol's instrument for indoctrinating children of pre-Komsomol age, had its main base, throughout the twenties, in the living and producing units, rather than in the schools. The League in its admission policies favored youths who were unquestionably "proletarian," and tended to shun those who sought an education. With rapid industrialization and the urgent need for Soviet specialists, however, it became the duty of Komsomolites to work increasingly in the expanding system of conventional-type Soviet schools. In 1931 the Pioneer organization, which had just surpassed its parent body in size (see Appendix H), shifted its base to the schools. The Komsomol, both directly and through the Pioneers, was expected to improve scholastic performance. In 1936 the League was told to disregard distinctions of social class in admitting students to its ranks. Thereafter the League remained committed to the closest possible support of both indoctrination and traditional education within the regular school system.

The survey of the topical elements could also cover the League's part in such developments as the growing physical education program and the subjection of the many nationalities of the Soviet Union to strong central control. The pictures unfolding in each field follow, again, the familiar lines of Soviet history. Although many of the details are new, their combined message is not; for they demonstrate that the Komsomol was an integral part of Soviet society and that Komsomolites were called upon to fulfill obligations in virtually every area of Soviet life.

If one is to distinguish in the whole of the Komsomol pattern a dominant theme, it is surely that of control—an obsession of the Party leaders and a source of extreme pressure on the members of the Komsomol. Beneath all the demands, including the frequent exhortations to spontaneity and initiative, lay this principle: nothing, no matter how conducive it was to the enthusiasm, vigor, size, or influence of the Komsomol, could be tolerated if it appeared to present the slightest impediment to control by the Party chiefs. Few pages of the present study are free of some sign of that obsession. The very establishment of a youth auxiliary was delayed until control was assured. Then, when the fledgling League tried to spread its wings, the Party clipped them: the proposals for the Young Proletarian Homes and the Youth Sections Affiliated with the Trade Unions were quashed. Why? Because behind those proposals lurked the possibility that the League might assume an intermediate directing function, might become a "Young Communist Party," guiding broader mass organizations which would embrace the bulk of youth. The Party avoided delegating this authority to the Komsomol, even though the leaders of the League were Party members and the League was avowedly Communist in allegiance, and even though such a role would have enhanced the League's prestige among youth. The Party insisted that the Komsomol must itself be a "mass" organization—"mass" in the sense that it must have no rivals in the field of youth; "mass" in the sense that it must be as large as possible, consistent with the maintenance of Party control; and "mass" in the sense that it must be too large and too loose to develop a cohesiveness and a mind of its own.

The obsession with control manifested itself early in the use of a certain terminology. At the founding congress of the League, when some delegates urged that the new group not be called a *Communist* League since that name would scare away the masses of politically undecided young people, the Party-dominated leaders insisted on the "Communist" tag, even though it retarded the League's expansion. A significant terminological distinction, too, was made in the next year (1919), when Komsomolites were given to understand that they could refer to their organization as "autonomous" and "self-standing," but could not call it "independent."

The evolution of elections within the League further illustrates the theme. In 1918 and 1919 Komsomolites elected the members of their Central Committee by voting for the nominees individually. An element of real competition was present, for there were more nominees than positions. In 1918 all of the members so elected, and all but one of the candidate-members, were concurrently members of the Party. In 1919 all of those elected were Party members. To the outside observer that might seem to have ensured adequate control, while still preserving a modicum of autonomy within the League. But the Party leadership was not satisfied. In 1920 the Party intervened to remove Dunaevskii from the Central Committee of the Komsomol. In the elections to the new Central Committee in that year, the element of choice was eliminated. The delegates were presented with a single list of nominees, drawn up in advance by the Party fraction that directed the Congress. There was only one nominee for each vacancy. The delegates were required to vote on the list as a whole. From that time onward, the principle of election, while still ostensibly sacred, was inoperative. And even that did not suffice: in the 1920s the Party increasingly resorted to arbitrary removals of Komsomol officials, and subsequent decades brought more than one wholesale turnover in the Komsomol leadership, in utter contempt of the Regulations respecting election.

The desire for control caused a flouting of the Regulations also in regard to the scheduling of the congresses. The Regulations originally required that congresses, being the supreme authority in the League, must be held at least once each year. After 1922 the leadership ignored that rule, and the interval between congresses became longer and longer (see Appendix A). At the Congress of 1936 (held after an interval of five years), the Regulations were amended to provide for a three-year interval—whereupon the next two congresses were called after intervals of not three years, but thirteen years and five years, respectively.

The conduct of the deliberations at the congresses gave other vivid evidence of the concern for control. "Democratic centralism" was from the beginning far more centralized than democratic. Nevertheless, the early congresses made room for some expressions of dissent, and there were many divided votes on issues. In the mid-1920s, however, it became increasingly hazardous to differ—witness the harsh treatment of the Opposition at the Congress of 1926. By 1936, unanimity was outwardly complete; not even any abstentions from voting were recorded. The congresses of 1949 and 1954—in the latter case despite special protestations of democracy—demonstrated conclusively that the never very broad autonomy of the League as an organization had been practically abolished and that the individual Komsomolite's scope for spontaneity and initiative had been narrowly restricted.

The recurrent demands for spontaneity and initiative were always placed in a context of discipline. Even in such formal materials as the proceedings of the Komsomol congresses, the demand for discipline and control—whether couched in terms of "Partyness," "knowledge of Marxism-Leninism," or "Soviet patriotism"—was fundamental and all-engulfing. Small wonder that Soviet authors were criticized, at more than one congress, for failing to portray characters who embodied the traits of the New Soviet Man—and who were at the same time lifelike! The ideal Komsomolite—if such an abstration could have been incarnated—would have been so completely at the beck of the Party chiefs, and so devoid of ordinary human sentiments, as to be a mere robot. So pervasive was the implicit demand for control that it might be imagined to have provided a subconscious key—a very necessary key—for the Komsomolite in interpreting other, and especially explicit, demands: if a demand facilitated Party control, it must be obeyed without question; but if a demand in its openly expressed form might conceivably reduce or hinder Party control, then the Komsomolite must go beneath the surface to ascertain the true wish of the Party leaders.

A realization of the importance of the theme of control may assist the outsider to understand the fate of the "helper" functions—the operational or public functions—of the League. The congresses do not provide in themselves an adequate basis for appraising accurately the extent of the changes in these functions, but some tentative conclusions may be drawn. During the disordered conditions of the Civil War, the League evidently exerted considerable influence in the new economic and governmental institutions. Ambitious Komsomolites wished to continue to assist the Party in that way. Shatskin in 1920 tried to harness their ambition when he implied that if the League were sufficiently disciplined, it would be given appropriate responsibilities by the Party. At the Congress of 1921, however, the Party's spokesmen made it clear that the Komsomol as an organization was not to perform "governmental functions." Komsomol ambitions were not immediately quenched, to judge from ensuing congresses, including that of 1936. One of the most significant areas was that of the schools, where the hope of preserving the influence of the League as an organization lasted relatively long. In the deliberations of 1918, 1919, and 1920, it appeared that the Komsomol might have an important role in building up a new school system: the delegates discussed the organizing of "schools of worker youth" and debated which department of the government would be best suited to run them. At the congresses of 1921 and 1922 the organizational form of the schools was again discussed and the size of budget allocations to the schools was even questioned. The delegates opposed the viewpoint of the Commissariat of Education in regard to the fate of the traditional secondary schools. The same sort of disagreement was in evidence, though less so, in the congresses of 1924 and 1928. But by 1936 it would have been unthinkable for such questions to be raised; by 1949 the Komsomol organizations in the schools appeared to be on their way toward becoming largely an instrument of the school authorities, and the evidence of 1954 confirmed that tendency. In the confused and overlapping networks of command extending downward from the Politburo, the Komsomol channel always had been subordinate, of course, to the main channels of the Party, the Police, and the Army; but while its relationship to the lesser channels of the soviets, the trade unions, and the ministries had long been unclear, by 1949 and 1954 the Komsomol channel appeared to be inferior to them all, including particularly the school channel. Hardly anywhere except in the kolkhozes—and there only in the absence of a primary organization of the Party—did the Komsomol apparently retain a "junior Party" status as an organization. Elsewhere, membership in the Komsomol might bring preferential treatment; the individual Komsomolite might be influential in school or factory or other administration, and his membership in the League might well enhance his authority; but apparently the Komsomolite simply as a Komsomolite had little power. That diminution of the operational or "helper" role of the League was accompanied, however, by emphasis on the educative or "reserve" role—that of providing well-indoctrinated recruits for the Party and obedient citizens for the state. The stress on indoctrination rather than current operation or administration did not necessarily reduce the over-all importance of the Komsomol. The reverse could well be true. For one would expect many Soviet citizens, as they matured, to awake to the contradictions between Soviet claims and Soviet reality. The process of maturation may well have been accelerated after World War II, and even more so after the death of Stalin, making it increasingly necessary for the Soviet rulers to win the loyalty of the oncoming young people who were and are such a large part of the Soviet population. As an instrument of indoctrination not only for Komsomolites but also for millions of Pioneers and other young people, the Komsomol may have been increasingly important in the Soviet system.

In the minds of most outsiders, perhaps, the cumulative impression of the Komsomol pattern arouses neither admiration nor respect. The suppression of autonomy and spontaneity, the restriction of the League to a subordinate status, and the sternness of the demands would seem to have limited severely the appeal of the Komsomol for Soviet youth, while the manifest contradictions between claims and reality would seem bound to have bred cynicism. And yet the Komsomol pattern was being applied to millions of Soviet youths during the period under study, and obviously it was not entirely ineffectual. How effective was its application? what part was played by compulsion? how important was careerism in accounting for the growth of the League? how much genuine appeal did the various Komsomol demands possess for Soviet youth? what were the attitudes of flesh-and-blood Komsomolites toward the demands made upon them?—in short, to what extent did the Komsomol pattern seen in the congresses correspond to the reality of Soviet youth? The answers lie in large part beyond the scope of the present work. But it is to be hoped that, by analyzing the proceedings of the congresses, and in particular the demands expressed there, this study has laid a foundation that will assist the further exploration of the development of the Komsomol and its true role in Soviet life.

Notes

ABBREVIATIONS

BSE—Bol'shaia sovetskaia entsiklopediia (Large Soviet Encyclopedia)
CDSP—Current Digest of the Soviet Press
KP—Komsomol'skaia pravda (Komsomol Truth)
MSE—Malaia sovetskaia entsiklopediia (Small Soviet Encyclopedia)
S"ezd—Congress; used here to designate the variously-titled bound volumes of proceedings of the congresses from the First through the Tenth; see Section I of the Bibliography
VLKSM—ALCLY; the initial letters of the full name of the Komsomol; alphabetized in Soviet reference works sometimes by those initials and sometimes by the spelled-out words Vsesoiuznyi leninskii kommunisticheskii soiuz molodezhi (All-Union Leninist Communist League of Youth)

Notes

CHAPTER I: PREREVOLUTIONARY ORIGINS OF THE KOMSOMOL PATTERN

1. Lenin, *Sochineniia*, X, 188 (Dec. 20 [7], 1906). (It is explained in the notes [*ibid.*, p. 492] that the editors searched in the work of Engels which Lenin cited as the source of this quotation but found no such passage.) Unless otherwise noted, citations of Lenin's *Sochineniia* (Works) refer to the second edition.

2. Some might ask whether Marxist determinism should not logically preclude exhortations to Party members to follow any ideal. Lenin said not. "Determinism," he insisted, did not mean "fatalism" but rather supplied the basis for rational action (Lenin, *Sochineniia*, I, 292 [1895]). More specifically, in discussing the conflict between determinism and personal morality, Lenin explained his position as follows: "In fact, there is no conflict here. It has been imagined by Mr. Mikhailovskii, who fears (and not without foundation) that determinism will cut the ground from under that middle-class morality he loves so well. The idea of determinism, which establishes the necessity of human actions and rejects the silly tale about freedom of will, does not in the least abolish either reason, or man's conscience, or the evaluation of his acts. Wholly on the contrary, only through the deterministic view is it possible to have a strict and correct evaluation, rather than a shifting of whatever one wishes over to the sphere of free will. Likewise, the idea of historical necessity does not detract one whit from the role of the individual in history. . . . The real question . . . is, under what conditions is this activity ensured success? What is the guarantee that this activity will not remain a solitary act, drowning in a sea of opposing acts? This then is the question . . . : How must activity, which is directed toward realizing a socialist system, draw in the masses in order to bring serious results? It is obvious that the solution to this question directly depends upon one's idea about the grouping of social forces in Russia, about the struggle of classes, of which Russian reality is made" (Lenin, *Sochineniia*, I, 77 [1894]).

That was one of Lenin's attempted answers to the problem of freedom and necessity; to many, his answers to this problem seem self-contradictory, but Lenin never appeared to feel that this was so. His revolutionary fervor impelled him to try to have the best of both positions. When, on the one hand, he needed to reinforce his hopes of success, he could refer to the inexorable laws of dialectical materialism; on the other hand, when he needed to choose a course of action and to argue for it, he could think of those same laws as mere guiding principles which left him considerable scope for his own initiative in the shaping of history.

3. Lenin, *Sochineniia*, I, 94, 261–62, 292; II, 541–42; IV, 58–59, 383, 391–92,

401, 423, 452–55, 462–63; VI, 120–23, 354; VII, 149; VIII, 302, 386–90, 400–1; IX, 390; X, 230–31; XV, 202; XVII, 25–26; XX, 419. For fuller details respecting this and other sections of Chapter I, the interested reader may consult Appendixes IX, X, and XI of the author's doctoral dissertation, listed in the Bibliography.

4. Lenin, *Sochineniia*, IV, 69–73, 105–6, 299; V, 13–14, 52–55, 79, 347, 353–64; VII, 105; VIII, 278–79, 294, 311–16, 325–26, 347; X, 51; XII, 336–41; XX, 299, 303, 305, 306; XXI, 319–20. See also *Lenin i Stalin o molodezhi,* pp. 90–104, 132, 206–17, and *Leninskii sbornik,* V, 412.

5. Concerning the organizational roots, there are several Komsomol histories from which to choose. Written at different times, under the changing demands of Communist orthodoxy, they are not alike. But by collating them, one may attempt to reconstruct an account which, if not wholly accurate in detail, is at least a composite of the Communist traditions surrounding this development. The accounts consulted by the author include (listed in chronological order from 1925 to 1951; for full citations see the Bibliography): Kirov and Dalin, *Iunosheskoe dvizhenie,* 325 pp.; Shokhin, *Kratkii ocherk,* 123 pp.; Barkhina, "VLKSM," *MSE* (1st ed.), Vol. II, cols. 190–94; Shatskin, "VLKSM," *BSE* (1st. ed.), Vol. XI, cols. 618–58; Afonin, *Komsomol,* 86 pp.; Panteleev, "VLKSM," *MSE* (2d ed.), Vol. II, cols. 536–57; Ostriakov, *20 let VLKSM,* 126 pp.; "VLKSM," *Politicheskii slovar',* pp. 90–92; Tiurin, "VLKSM," *BSE* (suppl.), cols. 1712–40; "VLKSM," *BSE* (2 ed.), IX, 330–47. A fairly detailed account of the origins of the Komsomol is currently being prepared by Sidney I. Ploss in a dissertation for the University of London.

6. See, for example, Lenin, *Sochineniia,* IV, 69–73 (Feb., 1901), and IV, 345–47 (Dec., 1901). Concerning working-class youths, see Kirov and Dalin, *Iunosheskoe dvizhenie,* pp. 21–24, 31–32; Shatskin, "VLKSM," *BSE* (1st ed.), Vol. XI, cols. 633–34; Ostriakov, *20 let VLKSM,* p. 6. On peasant youths, see Shatskin, "VLKSM," *BSE* (1st ed.), Vol. XI, col. 635.

7. Lenin drafted the resolution, and it was voted as he drafted it except for the elimination of one section warning against "false friends of youth." That section is stressed in the histories of 1934 (Panteleev) and 1938 (Ostriakov) as the first point of conflict between Bolsheviks and Mensheviks (or "opportunists") in the realm of youth movements.

8. *S"ezdy RKP o molodezhi,* pp. 7–8, containing the resolution as presented by Lenin, the discussion on it, and the resolution as voted.

9. Shatskin, "VLKSM," *BSE* (1st ed.), Vol. XI, cols. 635–36. The groups mentioned here are said to be under liberal or Socialist Revolutionary influence. In the 1938 history it was apparently thought unwise to mention this (Ostriakov, *20 let VLKSM,* pp. 6–8).

10. Barkhina, "VLKSM," *MSE* (1st ed.), Vol. II, col. 192, gives the starting date of this organization as 1901, but the other accounts use 1902. For a brief summary, see Shatskin, "VLKSM," *BSE* (1st. ed.), Vol. XI, col. 636. For further details, see Kirov and Dalin, *Iunosheskoe dvizhenie,* pp. 40–52, 59.

11. Kirov and Dalin, *Iunosheskoe dvizhenie,* p. 59 (a reprint of the *Iskra* article).

12. *Ibid.,* p. 48.

13. It is interesting to note that while the South Russian Group is mentioned in the Komsomol histories of 1925 (Kirov and Dalin), 1929 (Barkhina), and

1930 (Shatskin), it is left out of the post-1930 histories of Panteleev (1934), Afonin (1934), Ostriakov (1938), and Tiurin (1948). Perhaps this is for lack of space. Perhaps it is because neither Lenin nor Stalin figured in it, and even the Party's role was not all-important (although this "defect" could have been "corrected").

14. In the 1938 history (Ostriakov, *20 let VLKSM*, pp. 8–11), this phenomenon is attributed largely to the activity of the Bolsheviks "headed by Lenin and Stalin," but earlier accounts are more modest in their claims. In exaggerating the role of Lenin and Stalin, and also of the Party, Soviet historians seem to risk minimizing the supposedly "spontaneous" nature of their movement.

15. Shatskin, "VLKSM," *BSE* (1st ed.), Vol. XI, col. 634. An exception here was the Jewish Jugendbund, which lasted from 1905 to 1906 (Barkhina, "VLKSM," *MSE* [1st ed.], Vol. II, col. 192).

16. Shatskin, "VLKSM," *BSE* (1st ed.), Vol. XI, cols. 636–37.

17. Lenin, *Sochineniia*, VII, 102–3, 149; VIII, 325–26, 343–44, 412–18. See also Shatskin, "VLKSM," *BSE* (1st ed.), Vol. XI, col. 634.

18. Among young proletarians, these included a Polish group which lasted from 1909 till 1914 (Barkhina, "VLKSM," *MSE* [1st ed.], Vol. II, col. 192; Shatskin, "VLKSM," *BSE* [1st ed.], Vol. XI, col. 634). This Polish group was named first Pravda, then Budushchnost'. In 1911 it shook itself loose from direct Party control. See *S"ezd I*, p. 67.

19. Shatskin, "VLKSM," *BSE* (1st ed.), Vol. XI, col. 636.

20. Shatskin places the blame for this sudden end on the assertedly reactionary temper of the times, plus the involvement of the organization's leaders in Party work. Concerning this and short-lived organizations of Social Democratic students in other cities, see Shatskin, "VLKSM," *BSE* (1st ed.), Vol. XI, cols. 636–37. See also Ostriakov, *20 let VLKSM*, pp. 10–11. In the face of this discouraging trend, Lenin's views on youth organizations remained about the same as in 1905. For example, see Lenin, *Sochineniia*, XII, 336–41 (Oct. 16 [3], 1908), and XII, 382 (Nov. 14 [1], 1908).

21. Lenin, *Sochineniia*, XIX, 294–95 (Dec., 1916). An example of Leninist persuasion in that period appears in a piece written for the eyes of young workers in the fall of 1916: "You will soon grow up. They'll give you a gun. Take it and learn military science well. This science is essential for the proletarian—not in order to shoot against your brothers, the workers of other countries . . . —but in order to fight against the bourgeoisie of your own country" (Lenin, *Sochineniia*, XIX, 328).

22. For three versions, see Barkhina, "VLKSM," *MSE* (1st ed.), Vol. II, col. 192; Ostriakov, *20 let VLKSM*, p. 16; and "VLKSM," *BSE* (2d ed.), IX, 332.

23. Ostriakov, *20 let VLKSM*, pp. 14–15; Shatskin, "VLKSM," *BSE* (1st ed.), Vol. XI, col. 637.

24. The 1938 history by Ostriakov avoids giving "Labor and Light" (*Trud i svet*) the prestige of being first. Instead, Ostriakov finds a "Socialist League of Working Youth" of the Peterhof-Narva District, formed at the end of April on the initiative of young workers of the Putilov factory. Vasilii Alekseev is said to have led this League, which worked "under the direct guidance of the district committee of the RSDLP(B)." Alekseev's organization is alleged to have had a membership of about two thousand and is thus credited with being

"the first mass organization of working youth bearing a clearly expressed class revolutionary character" (Ostriakov, *20 let VLKSM*, pp. 17–18). Ostriakov's version becomes suspect when it is compared with the earlier accounts (e.g., Shatskin), in which *Trud i svet* is clearly given first place. From the summary prepared in 1926 by O. Ryvkin, one of the early leaders of the Komsomol, it appears that the Bolsheviks tried to control *Trud i svet* from the start, but that non-Bolshevik influences were too strong for them. See Ryvkin's prefatory remarks in *S"ezd II*, pp. 5–6.

25. Shevtsov is referred to in not too unfriendly fashion in Shatskin's version of 1930 as one who "later became a Communist." In Ostriakov's account of 1938, however, he has become a collaborator of the Black Hundreds and "an ardent enemy of the working class."

26. Shatskin, "VLKSM," *BSE* (1st ed.), Vol. XI, col. 638; Ostriakov, *20 let VLKSM*, p. 18; Panteleev, "VLKSM," *MSE* (2d ed.), Vol. II, col. 541.

27. Shatskin, "VLKSM," *BSE* (1st ed.), Vol. XI, col. 638; *S"ezd II*, p. 6; and Ostriakov, *20 let VLKSM*, p. 19. In Ostriakov's interpretation, this is represented as an expansion of Alekseev's original district organization into an interdistrict body. The Russian name is Sotsialisticheskii soiuz rabochei molodezhi.

28. *S"ezd I*, p. 43; *S"ezd II*, p. 6; Barkhina, "VLKSM," *MSE* (1st ed.), Vol. II, cols. 192–93; Shatskin, "VLKSM," *BSE* (1st ed.), Vol. XI, col. 638; Panteleev, "VLKSM," *MSE* (2d ed.), Vol. II, col. 541; Ostriakov, *20 let VLKSM*, p. 23. The Russian name was Sotsialisticheskii soiuz rabochei molodezhi Petrograda.

29. *S"ezd I*, pp. 43–44 (Ryvkin's report). Shatskin, "VLKSM," *BSE* (1st ed.), Vol. XI, col. 638, gives 15,000 for December. Ostriakov (*20 let VLKSM*, p. 24) gives 50,000 for October, but this is so far out of line with the figures cited for November and December that it would seem to be an error.

30. *S"ezd I*, p. 45; *S"ezd II*, p. 6. The Russian name was Soiuz molodezhi pri MK RS-DRP(b).

31. Shatskin, "VLKSM," *BSE* (1st ed.), Vol. XI, cols. 638–39; *S"ezd I*, p. 45. A slightly different account appears in Ryvkin's summary of 1926 (*S"ezd II*, p. 6). Here the Youth League of the MC of the RSDLP(B) is pictured as transforming itself into the League of Working Youth of the Third International (Soiuz rabochei molodezhi III internatsionala) in accordance with instructions formulated by the Sixth Congress (in August) of the Bolsheviks.

32. Ostriakov, *20 let VLKSM*, pp. 23–25; *S"ezd I*, pp. 45, 50; Shatskin, "VLKSM," *BSE* (1st ed.), Vol. XI, col. 639. Those accounts indicate that when Bolshevik control had been achieved, the Youth League of the MC of the RSDLP was finally dissolved, leaving the Third International to be run by the Bolsheviks but with no open Party affiliation.

Elsewhere in the country under the Provisional Government the Bolsheviks apparently had some success among the youth, especially in the cities. For more on this, and for various descriptions of the role of youth in the November coup, see the accounts of Barkhina, Shatskin, Panteleev, Ostriakov, and Tiurin, and "VLKSM," *BSE* (2d ed.), IX, 332.

33. *S"ezdy RKP o molodezhi*, pp. 9–12 (p. 10 for the quotation).

34. *Ibid.*, pp. 13–23. See also the summary in *S"ezd II*, pp 177–78.

35. *S"ezdy RKP o molodezhi*, pp. 22–23.

36. *VKP (b) o komsomole*, p. 77.

CHAPTER II: THE ESTABLISHMENT OF THE KOMSOMOL

1. *S"ezd I*, p. 40.

2. For details, see Bunyan and Fisher, *The Bolshevik Revolution*, pp. 304–8; Afonin, *Komsomol*, p. 28; Ostriakov, *20 let VLKSM*, p. 30; Panteleev, "VLKSM," *MSE* (2d ed.), Vol. II, col. 542.

3. *S"ezd III*, pp. 82–83; Panteleev, "VLKSM," *MSE* (2d ed.), Vol. II, col. 542. In the Socialist League of Working Youth of Petrograd, the membership fell from about 15,000 in November, 1917 (*S"ezd I*, p. 44), and 16,000 in January, 1918 (*S"ezd II*, p. 7), to about one-tenth of that, or 1,500, in October, 1918 (*S"ezd I*, p. 44). In the Third International in Moscow, there was a drop from about 4,000 in October, 1917, to about 2,500 a year later (*S"ezd I*, p. 46). For similar indications in other areas (although there were some exceptions), see the "reports from the provinces" at the First Congress (*S"ezd I*, pp. 43–57).

4. For a region-by-region survey of this activity, see *S"ezd I*, pp. 43–57. In the Socialist League of Working Youth of Petrograd, a challenge to Bolshevik policy arose early in 1918. A group (led by Leske) demanded that the Petrograd league be abolished as a "mass" organization and that there be created instead a smaller, tighter body suited to the revolutionary struggle. This proposal was defeated (Ostriakov, *20 let VLKSM*, p. 31; Afonin, *Komsomol*, pp. 28–29).

5. *S"ezd I*, pp. 33–35; Ostriakov, *20 let VLKSM*, p. 31; Afonin, *Komsomol*, pp. 30–31.

6. *S"ezd I*, p. 89. The itemized figures total 176. It is not stated whether they include nonvoting delegates or not. Districts most generously represented were those of Moscow, Petrograd, the Central Industrial Region, and the Urals. Some representation was claimed from all provinces under Red control, plus the Ukraine. Nine of the delegates were women (Afonin, *Komsomol*, p. 34). For a photograph of the delegates, see "VLKSM," *BSE* (2d ed.), IX, between pp. 330 and 331. See also Shatskin, "VLKSM," *BSE* (1st ed.), Vol. XI, col. 640; and *S"ezd II*, p. 181.

7. *S"ezd I*, pp. 38–46.

8. The chairmen referred to are Efim Tsetlin (later spelled Tseitlin) and Lazar' Shatskin (both representing Moscow), Oskar Ryvkin and Gerr (both representing Petrograd), Aleksandr Bezymenskii (Central Industrial Region), and Dugachev (Northern Oblast). See *S"ezd I*, pp. 38, 46, 67, 75, 84, 90–92.

9. The votes on these "theses" were unanimous, with only two and three abstentions, respectively (*S"ezd I*, pp. 75, 97). For Shatskin's ambiguous formulation of the Party-Komsomol relationship, see *ibid.*, p. 68. The official Program of the Komsomol, as issued subsequently by the Central Committee, was no more definite: "The League, being—for the purpose of demonstrating the self-standingness [*samostoiatel'nost'*] of youth—a fully independent [*nezavisimyi*] organization, is, in its revolutionary work, solidary with the Russian Communist Party (of Bolsheviks)" (*ibid.*, p. 98).

10. "For us to admit into our organization, our fortress, the enemies of the working class and, consequently, our own enemies, would be, to say the least, unwise" (*S"ezd I*, p. 69).

11. *S"ezd I*, p. 70. "Uncommitted" is a translation of *neopredelivsheisia*.

12. *Ibid.*, pp. 70–74. Some addresses are omitted from the record (*ibid.*, p. 74).

13. *Ibid.*, p. 74. "Spontaneous activity" is a translation of *samodeiatel'nost'*.

14. Rossiiskii kommunisticheskii soiuz molodezhi. *S"ezd I*, p. 75, gives the vote as a "majority, with 60 against and 17 abstentions." But in Shatskin, "VLKSM," *BSE* (1st ed.), Vol. XI, col. 641, quoting from the record of the Congress, it is given as "majority, with 6 against and 17 abstentions." Either the 6 or the 60 is apparently a misprint, but the writer at present does not know which. Other accounts, such as Afonin, Panteleev, and Ostriakov, do not clear up this matter.

The Central Committee subsequently required that all local organizations forming part of the RCLY change their names accordingly by January 1, 1919 (*S"ezd II*, p. 40).

15. *S"ezd I*, p. 99.

16. *Ibid.*, p. 91. For further details see later in this chapter.

17. *Ibid.*, pp. 36–37; Afonin, *Komsomol*, pp. 33–34; Ostriakov, *20 let VLKSM*, p. 34. At the First Congress the delegates realized that membership dues could not finance the League's program. They thereupon resolved that the League "requires a subsidy to the organizations of the League from the Commissariat of Education." Each local Komsomol organization was to work out its own estimate and submit it to the local section of the Commissariat of Education. In case of any disagreement the estimate was to be sent up to the Komsomol Central Committee (*S"ezd I*, pp. 89, 100). It was indicated in the report of the Central Committee at the Second Congress (October, 1919) that the League was indeed being partially subsidized in this way (*S"ezd II*, pp. 42–43, 55). (At the same time, some local bodies were being financed by the local Party organization; see *S"ezd II*, pp. 80–89, especially pp. 83 and 89.) On December 15, 1919, the system was changed, and apparently the Komsomol was henceforth subsidized directly by the Party, except for dues and other contributions from Komsomol members (*S"ezd II*, p. 182). The latter note was written *ca.* 1926. For the pertinent (but vague) section in the subsequent Regulations, see *S"ezd III*, p. 321. For later arrangements, see subsequent chapters.

18. *S"ezd I*, pp. 80–83, 97–99.

19. *VKP(b) o komsomole*, pp. 8–9; *S"ezd II*, p. 183.

20. *S"ezd II*, pp. 183–84; Shatskin, "VLKSM," *BSE* (1st ed.), Vol. XI, cols. 645–46.

21. *S"ezd II*, pp. 45–46, 183–84.

22. The formation of fractions was recommended "only in case the latter [the Komsomol units] are following a non-Communist line, or conducting political work weakly, or if petit-bourgeois kulak elements have entered the organization, or if there are no Party members in the governing body [of the local Komsomol unit]." See *VKP(b) o komsomole*, pp. 77–78; *S"ezd II*, pp. 183–84. For Ryvkin's explanation on "fractions," see *S"ezd II*, p. 72.

23. *VKP(b) o komsomole*, p. 78. "Spontaneity" is a translation of *samodeiatel'nost'*, which means literally "self-activity." "Control" is a translation of *kontrol'*. "Autonomous," a translation of *avtonomnyi*.

24. *S"ezd II*, pp. 183–84.

25. *S"ezd I*, p. 98. Later histories pretend the word "independent" was never used; see, for example, "VLKSM," *BSE* (2d ed.), IX, 333.

26. The itemized figures for delegates total 447 rather than 429. No explanation of the discrepancy is given (*S"ezd II*, pp. 7, 45, 113). As to the membership total, the chairman maintained that the figure really was higher (*ibid.*, p. 113). A comparison of the totals by localities given in *ibid.*, pp. 80–88, with those in the table in *ibid.*, p. 174, suggests an extreme inaccuracy of membership data at that time.

27. *S"ezd II*, pp. 46–47. See also *ibid.*, p. 91, expressing the familiar idea that "our Communist Party is the sole party that correctly expresses the strivings of the broad toiling masses." On the level of local "control," the Congress resolved that the Komsomol "in all its activities and undertakings works in full contact with the RCP" (*ibid.*, p. 168).

28. *Ibid.*, p. 57. The two were Akhmanov and Arsh.

29. *Ibid.*, pp. 111–12, 117–18. See later in this chapter for further details.

30. *Ibid.*, p. 112.   31. *Ibid.*, pp. 89, 121.   32. *S"ezd III*, p. 86.

33. *Ibid.*, p. 204.

34. *Ibid.*, p. 20. The figure of 400,000 at the time of the Third Congress is accepted by Panteleev, Shatskin, Ostriakov, and Tiurin. Mehnert (*Youth in Soviet Russia*, p. 59) says 480,000, without apparent reason. It is necessary to note, however, Shatskin's statement that the statistics at this time were extremely inaccurate (*S"ezd III*, pp. 254–55). Misleading, too, is a reference to "half a million," apparently meant very loosely (*S"ezd III*, p. 236).

35. *S"ezd III*, pp. 84–85. This is related to the dispute over the "mass" nature of the League, discussed later in this chapter. See also *ibid.*, pp. 103–32 *passim* and 255–76 *passim*.

36. *VKP(b) o komsomole*, pp. 80–82. For Bukharin's reference to this intervention by the Party, see *S"ezd III*, pp. 34ff. It might be noted that in July of that year (1920) the manner by which the Party would control the Komsomol at the guberniia echelon had been further defined. The practice in some Party *gubkoms* (guberniia committees) of setting up their own youth sections, working parallel with the Komsomol, was condemned. The Party *gubkom* was instructed to designate one of its responsible Party men as its representative on the *gubkom* of the Komsomol (*S"ezd II*, p. 184). For the text of the circular, see *Pravda*, July 27, 1920, as quoted in *VKP(b) o komsomole*, pp. 78–80.

37. *S"ezd I*, pp. 97–98.

38. *S"ezd III*, pp. 188, 193. Shatskin's report justifying the new Program occupies pp. 186–98 in *ibid.*

39. *Ibid.*, p. 101.

40. *Ibid.*, p. 308. See also *S"ezd II*, pp. 184–85. Curiously, a sentence emphasizing self-standingness, which had been contained in the preliminary version proposed by the Komsomol CC, was omitted in the Program as approved at the Congress. The omitted sentence declared: "At the same time the RCLY is a self-standing organization—that is, has its own centralized organization, and self-standingly [*samostoiatel'no*] determines the form of its participation in socialist construction and the methods of [its] organizational education, and agitational-propagandistic work" (*S"ezd III*, p. 323).

The new Regulations required Komsomol bodies at all echelons to receive representatives from, and to send representatives to, the corresponding Party bodies (*S"ezd III*, p. 321). Incidentally, one of the speakers (Preobrazhenskii) mentioned that the Komsomol Central Committee had its offices in the same building with, and one floor beneath, the offices of the Central Committee of the Party (*ibid.*, p. 28).

41. *VKP(b) o komsomole*, pp. 8–9.

42. *S"ezd II*, p. 13 (Trotsky); *S"ezd III*, pp. 28–29 (Preobrazhenskii).

43. *S"ezd I*, p. 98.

44. *Ibid.*, p. 40; *S"ezd II*, pp. 21 (Trotsky), 103; *S"ezd III*, pp. 40 (Bukharin), 86–87 (Ryvkin).

45. Panteleev, "VLKSM," *MSE* (2d ed.), Vol. II, col. 543.

46. *S"ezd II*, pp. 124–25. See also *S"ezd I*, pp. 98–99.

47. *S"ezd III*, pp. 306–14.   48. *S"ezd II*, pp. 52–53.

49. *Ibid.*, pp. 172–73, 192–93, also pp. 9, 105. The group's name in Russian was Iunye kommunisty.

50. *Ibid.*, p. 39.   51. *Ibid.*, pp. 103–5, also p. 39.

52. *Ibid.*, p. 193; see also pp. 106 and 172–73, and observe that the session of the military section—where the Scout issue was to be voted on—is not reported in pp. 129–52.

53. See subsequent chapters. See also *S"ezd III*, pp. 114, 117.

54. *S"ezd II*, p. 72.

55. This unofficial Communist league of student youth emerged as a problem between the First and Second Komsomol congresses. There was an All-Russian Congress of Student Communists, at which representatives of the Komsomol Central Committee apparently tried unsuccessfully to bring the student organizations into the Komsomol. But, subsequently, joint conferences with Party representatives and the Central Bureau of Student Communists resulted in the dissolution of the latter. The local groups of student Communists were put through "a preparatory purge," and then the "best elements" were admitted to the Komsomol, which set up cells in the schools. In this way, it was claimed, students of intelligentsia and "petit-bourgeois" background were brought under the leadership of worker and peasant youth (*S"ezd II*, pp. 47–49). No dates are mentioned in this account by Ryvkin. The writer assumes, in the absence of contrary information, that these events preceded the Party decree of May 11, 1919, concerning which see a later section in this chapter.

56. *S"ezd I*, pp. 48–49. "Young Proletarian Homes" is a translation of Doma iunogo proletariia.

57. *Ibid.*, pp. 77–78.   58. *Ibid.*, p. 90.

59. *Ibid.*, pp. 94–95. Tsetlin supported his position with the statement that "this question was decided by us at earlier sessions." The published record of the Congress does not include anything which would deserve to be called a real discussion of this issue. It may be either that the published record omits a discussion which actually took place, or that Tsetlin was using a questionable debating technique to brush off an opponent. The remarks of Gerr (*ibid.*, pp. 77–78), an influential Petrograd delegate, suggest that the leaders had decided earlier against the Young Proletarian Homes.

60. Shatskin, "VLKSM," *BSE* (1st ed.), Vol. XI, col. 641.

61. *S"ezd I*, p. 70. "Uncommitted" is a translation of *neopredelivsheisia*.

62. *Ibid.*, p. 75.

63. A sign of this was visible in the Congress's elections to the Central Committee of the League. In those elections the delegates were allowed to vote for individuals, so that to some extent the results served as an indication of the personal following of those elected. Of the four delegates who had spoken in favor of the Young Proletarian Homes, three (Khazan, Iurovskaia, and Matveev) were elected members or candidate-members of the Central Committee. And Khazan, the most persistent advocate, received the second highest number of votes, exceeded only by those for Tsetlin (*S"ezd I*, pp. 90–91).

64. *S"ezd II*, p. 180. The "youth sections" in Russian were *sektsii molodezhi pri profsoiuzakh.*

65. Ostriakov, *20 let VLKSM*, p. 46, says Dunaevskii was at this time a member of the Central Committee of the Komsomol. He is not listed as having been so elected by the First Congress (see *S"ezd I*, pp. 90–91), but perhaps he was subsequently appointed. Ostriakov may be in error.

66. In Russian, *sovety rabochei molodezhi* (*Iunyi kommunist*, No. 5, May, 1919, as quoted and summarized in *S"ezd II*, pp. 179–80).

67. At about the same time, Dunaevskii advanced still another suggestion: that a special "youth inspection of labor" be set up, presumably to enforce the laws covering the employment of minors (*S"ezd II*, p. 74). See Chapter III.

68. *S"ezd II*, pp. 74, 180–81. The Plenum also turned down the idea of a youth inspection of labor (*ibid.*, p. 74). The attack on Dunaevskii's proposals was continued by Shatskin, a leading member of the Central Committee, in the August and September (1919) numbers of *Iunyi kommunist*. In an attempt to counter both of Dunaevskii's arguments for the "councils of worker youth," Shatskin declared first that, as mass organizations, the councils would constitute only a needless duplication of the Komsomol, which, if not yet a mass organization, would soon be one. Secondly, Shatskin maintained that the councils were not needed for the special purpose of protecting the interests of worker youth, inasmuch as that was the concern of the whole proletarian state (*Iunyi kommunist*, No. 6–7, August, 1919, and No. 8–9, September, 1919, as quoted and summarized in *S"ezd II*, p. 180).

69. *S"ezd II*, p. 74. Dunaevskii was aided by Tolmachev.

70. *Ibid.*, pp. 34–35.   71. *Ibid.*, pp. 35–38.

72. Before this section meeting, Dunaevskii apparently stated his views to the whole Congress during the discussion on the report of the Central Committee. Dunaevskii's speech (along with others) does not appear in the official report of the Congress. A footnote says that no stenographic record of his speech was available (*S"ezd II*, p. 60).

The arguments of Dunaevskii and Zander in favor of the "youth sections" revealed very clearly that they envisioned them as organizations through which the younger workers could protect their *own* interests rather than to rely on the solicitude of the Soviet state. Dunaevskii charged the Komsomol's Central Committee with neglecting the interests of the majority of worker youth (*ibid.*, pp. 141–42). Zander, too, was quite outspoken. "We must defend the interests of youth," he declared, "and who, pray, can defend them better than youth itself?" (*ibid.*, pp. 143–44).

73. *S"ezd II*, pp. 144–47. The vote was thirty-six to twelve.

74. *Ibid.*, pp. 108–10.   75. *Ibid.*, p. 118.

76. *VKP(b) o komsomole*, pp. 80–82; Panteleev, "VLKSM," *MSE* (2d ed.), Vol. II, col. 545; Shatskin, "VLKSM," *BSE* (1st ed.), Vol. XI, cols. 646–47.

77. *S"ezd II*, p. 188.

78. The reason was said to be the prevalence of nationalistic and counter-revolutionary convictions among the Ukrainian students in general (*ibid.*, p. 56).

79. *Ibid.*, pp. 181, 195; Shatskin, "VLKSM," *BSE* (1st ed.), Vol. XI, cols. 647–48; Panteleev, "VLKSM," *MSE* (2d ed.), Vol. II, col. 545; Ostriakov, *20 let VLKSM*, pp. 46–47; Afonin, *Komsomol*, p. 47. In these materials the terms "Ukrainian Opposition" and *Klassoviki* ("class-ists") seem to be used synonymously. The writer has not ascertained whether there was in fact any distinction between them. They seem to be analogous in part to the Workers' Opposition in the Party.

80. In fact, the Ukrainian policy of barring student youths was even justified by Ryvkin (speaking for the Central Committee) on the basis of the local conditions peculiar to the Ukraine (*S"ezd II*, p. 56).

81. Kommunisticheskii soiuz molodezhi Ukrainy. See *S"ezd II*, p. 188; *S"ezd III*, p. 98.

82. *VKP(b) o komsomole*, pp. 80–82. Afonin (*Komsomol*, p. 47) incorrectly attributes this action to the CC of the Komsomol.

83. *VKP(b) o komsomole*, pp. 80–82. The effective date of the suspension was not given, so it remains unclear whether, at the time of his participation in the Third Congress, Dunaevskii had been reinstated. For various accounts, see Shatskin, "VLKSM," *BSE* (1st ed.), Vol. XI, col. 648; Panteleev, "VLKSM," *MSE* (2d ed.), Vol. II, col. 545; Ostriakov, *20 let VLKSM*, pp. 46–47; Afonin, *Komsomol*, p. 47; and *S"ezd II*, p. 195.

84. *S"ezd III*, pp. 186, 195. Dunaevskii also helped to prepare the "theses" on the role of the Komsomol in the trade-union movement (*ibid.*, pp. 297–98). However, he was not entirely forgiven. When, toward the close of the Third Congress, someone nominated him from the floor as a candidate-member of the Central Committee, the chairman said Dunaevskii was not eligible because the Party's Central Committee had removed him from work in the Komsomol (*ibid.*, p. 235). Polifem and Iakovlev were similarly nominated from the floor and similarly rejected by the chair.

85. For a quick view, see *S"ezd III*, table of contents on p. 327. Bukharin said the existing policy conflicts must be resolved (*ibid.*, pp. 33–34). In answering one proponent of a selective, narrow League (Okulik), Bukharin explained that the Komsomol did *not* need to be so strict in regard to intelligentsia as was the Party. The Komsomol was working with more malleable youths, he said, and should be prepared to "communize" them (*ibid.*, pp. 123–25). For Okulik's speech, see *ibid.*, pp. 110–12. The attack against the "narrows" was continued in the discussion of the new Program. Shatskin accused another deviationist (Kh. Garber) of wishing to pare down the membership to "an insignificant handful of conscious Communists." On the contrary, Shatskin asserted, the Komsomol's true task lay in attracting the *masses* of youth into the League (*ibid.*, pp. 197–98). For further debate on this issue, see *ibid.*, pp. 198–212.

86. *S"ezd III*, pp. 247–48.

87. *Ibid.,* pp. 257–61. He favored using the coming "reregistration" for that purpose.

88. *Ibid.,* pp. 271–73.

89. *Ibid.,* pp. 257–76 *passim,* also pp. 198–200. For Dunaevskii, in his new role as defender of the orthodoxy, see *ibid.,* pp. 269–70.

90. *Ibid.,* pp. 273–76.

91. See especially *ibid.,* pp. 300, 302 (for the resolutions), and 212–40 (for the voting).

92. *Ibid.,* pp. 262–66. Starostin favored a probationary stage for peasant and other nonproletarian youth. On the elements to be excluded, see also *S"ezd II,* pp. 47–48, and *S"ezd III,* pp. 197–98.

93. *S"ezd III,* pp. 273–76.

94. For the arguments given in Soviet secondary accounts (including the argument against creating a "second youth party"), see Panteleev, "VLKSM," *MSE* (2d ed.), Vol. II, col. 543; Afonin, *Komsomol,* pp. 41–42; Ostriakov, *20 let VLKSM,* p. 46. In Ostriakov, the Dunaevskii proposals are further stigmatized as "Trotskyite."

95. *S"ezd III,* p. 180.   96. *Ibid.,* p. 316.   97. *S"ezd I,* p. 43.

98. *S"ezd III,* pp. 316–21.

99. Furthermore, it was provided that the CC "makes the preparations for the All-Russian Congress, defines the norms of representation, and outlines the agenda of the Congress" (*S"ezd III,* p. 321). Once every four months the CC was supposed to call an "All-Russian Conference" which brought together the CC with the representatives of the guberniia committees. This "All-Russian Conference" replaced what had been called, before the Third Congress, the "enlarged plenum of the CC" (*S"ezd III,* p. 321, and *S"ezd II,* p. 191). The advisory nature of the "All-Russian Conference" was brought out during the discussion. Someone proposed that the decisions of the Conference be made binding on the CC, and this was rejected by the chairman as "ridiculous." He used the amusing argument that the CC was elected by the Congress, whereas the Conference was not (*S"ezd III,* pp. 233–35).

100. *S"ezd III,* pp. 252, 301.   101. *Ibid.,* pp. 243–44; see also p. 299.

102. *Ibid.,* pp. 315–20. See below for further details.

103. *Ibid.,* p. 301. This resolution contains interesting examples of the simultaneous demands for freedom and control (*ibid.,* pp. 299–301).

The organizational structure of the Komsomol cannot be treated fully within the scope of the present study. Readers interested in further details on organizational developments are referred to *S"ezd I,* pp. 84–89, 99–100; *S"ezd II,* pp. 34–38, 40–45, 56, 74, 111–12, 174, 182, 188, 194–96; *S"ezd III,* pp. 87–88, 98–99, 250–51, 253–54, 315–21.

104. *S"ezd III,* p. 91. (The question was related to the Army. See Chapter III.)

105. For example, *S"ezd II,* pp. 43–44, 157; *S"ezd III,* pp. 34–35, 251, 269. The rapid swelling of the Komsomol bureaucracy was decried on the ground that it would hamper contact with the masses (*S"ezd III,* pp. 251–53, 301). For Bukharin's ideas on "bureaucratism" in the Komsomol, see *ibid.,* pp. 125–28.

106. *S"ezd II,* pp. 44–45, 55; *S"ezd III,* p. 100.

107. *S"ezd II,* p. 56; *S"ezd III,* pp. 99–100 (some were said to consider an assignment to Siberia as "political exile"). It was said that "very often" League

members failed to obey instructions from the CC respecting such changes of assignments (*S"ezd III*, p. 243).

108. *S"ezd III*, p. 246.   109. *S"ezd I*, p. 99; see also p. 83.

110. *S"ezd II*, p. 182.

111. *Ibid.*, pp. 45, 47–48 (Ryvkin in the report of the CC).

112. *S"ezd III*, p. 315. For an interpretation, see *ibid.*, p. 257.

113. *S"ezd I*, p. 99. For the discussion, see *ibid.*, pp. 80 ff.

114. *S"ezd III*, p. 315. The reasoning behind the age limits was explained as follows: The age of fourteen was desired in order that youths could be drawn via the Komsomol into the premilitary training program before the age of sixteen, since after that time they were liable to be called for service at the front. The upper limit of twenty-three was designed to give the League time to bring in peasant youths who were not entering the Party (*ibid.*, pp. 173–76, 256–57).

115. *S"ezd I*, p. 99; see also p. 83, on the rejected proposal of "comradely courts" to judge disputes concerning expulsion. For a slightly different sort of "comradely court" proposal, see *S"ezd III*, pp. 176–77.

116. *S"ezd III*, pp. 315–16. That dues were mainly symbolic in purpose was indicated by their amount—one-half of 1 percent of the monthly wage (*ibid.*, p. 321). Lenin had explained in 1918 that if Party dues proved any barrier to the admission of young people into the Party, the dues would be abolished (Lenin, *Sochineniia*, XXIII, 175). For further information on the subject of dues at the start of the League, see *S"ezd I*, pp. 83, 99.

117. *S"ezd III*, pp. 255–56. For further discussion, see *ibid.*, pp. 256–76. For the vote, see *ibid.*, p. 302. Shatskin proposed the period December 1, 1920, to January 1, 1921, but the resolution merely said the CC would decide the time and send out instructions. This may have been the first League-wide reregistration or purge, although purging had apparently been done locally even before the Second Congress (*S"ezd II*, p. 86). The Party in March, 1919 (Eighth Congress) had ordered a similar reregistration or purge. See *History of the CPSU(B)*, p. 236.

118. *S"ezd I*, p. 43.   119. *Ibid.*, pp. 89–91.   120. *Ibid.*, pp. 56–57.

121. *S"ezd II*, p. 112.   122. *Ibid.*, pp. 117–18.

123. *S"ezd III*, p. 102. "Casual" is a translation of *sluchainyi*, which could also be rendered as "accidental."

124. *Ibid.*, p. 235.

125. For some examples, see *S"ezd I*, p. 79; *S"ezd II*, pp. 35–38; *S"ezd III*, pp. 216–19, 221, 232–33.

126. *S"ezd II*, p. 38 (Ryvkin).   127. *S"ezd III*, pp. 177–79.

128. *Ibid.*, p. 180.

129. For examples, see *S"ezd III*, pp. 212–37. In some other cases the exact phrasing was left up to a commission which was to meet after the Congress was closed (*ibid.*, pp. 216–19).

130. *S"ezd II*, pp. 76–80.   131. *Ibid.*, pp. 76–80; *S"ezd III*, p. 225.

132. For illustrative sessions, see *S"ezd I*, pp. 67–75; *S"ezd III*, pp. 212–37.

133. *S"ezd I*, pp. 80–83.   134. *S"ezd II*, pp. 108–10.

135. *S"ezd I*, p. 43. Those giving formal reports could have forty minutes, plus twenty minutes for "concluding remarks" after the discussion of the report.

Those discussing from the floor could have fifteen minutes the first time and three minutes the second.

136. Some of these have been referred to in other connections, such as the "Dunaevskii dispute." For a few other indications of the absence of total planning, see *S"ezd III*, pp. 103–32 (especially 112, 130–32), and 213.

137. *S"ezd II*, p. 35.   138. *Ibid.*, pp. 60–71; *S"ezd III*, pp. 103–23.

139. *S"ezd III*, p. 98.   140. *Ibid.*, pp. 121–30.

141. *Ibid.*, pp. 278–79 (resolution).   142. *Ibid.*, p. 251; see also pp. 207–9.

143. *Ibid.*, pp. 186–211.

144. *S"ezd I*, pp. 38–39. Karl Liebknecht (1871–1919), German socialist, leader of the Spartacist uprising, was shot in January, 1919. Friedrich Adler (1879–), then secretary of the Austrian Social Democratic Party, later became an outspoken opponent of Bolshevism. He was still living in Brussels as of 1948.

145. *S"ezd II*, p. 33.   146. *S"ezd III*, p. 26.

147. For example, *S"ezd I*, p. 62 (Lenin and Zinoviev); *S"ezd II*, pp. 154–55 (Lenin, Trotsky, Kollontai, Zinoviev).

148. *S"ezd I*, p. 62.

149. *S"ezd II*, pp. 67, 154. The delegates voted to send him "our oath that all worker and peasant youth will carry out the precepts of the leader."

150. *Ibid.*, pp. 121–25.   151. *S"ezd I*, p. 95; *S"ezd III*, pp. 236–37.

152. Voted at the First Congress, *S"ezd I*, p. 43.

153. Unanimous votes may be found almost anywhere in the accounts of resolutions being voted. For some examples of split votes, see *S"ezd I*, pp. 75, 82, 87, 90–91; *S"ezd II*, pp. 38, 63, 107–10, 112, 114, 116, 147; *S"ezd III*, pp. 179–85, 211.

154. *S"ezd I*, p. 83.   155. *Ibid.*, p. 82.   156. *S"ezd III*, pp. 219–23.

157. *S"ezd II*, pp. 76–80. It is interesting that the stalwarts who had participated in this little session of self-criticism were elevated to the CC either at the close of that Congress or at the next. The men were Iutt, Dunaevskii, Kankin, and Feigin. For the CC's, see *S"ezd II*, pp. 117–18, and *S"ezd III*, pp. 235–305.

158. See Lenin's speech to the Third Congress, later in this section. For Kollontai on this subject, see *S"ezd II*, p. 27. Trotsky told the delegates that they were "that generation which is destined to transform, change, reeducate the very character of the Russian people." He went on to describe this process of transformation: "We live in the tremendous forge of history. Bright flame is blazing, sparks are showering, tens and hundreds of hammers are beating. Of course this forge of history is cruel, and individual sparks and flashes of flame will injure us, scorch, and snatch many from our midst. But this flame and the blows of the hammer will harden the national character. From your midst there must emerge new thousands, tens and hundreds of thousands, of conscious, courageous people, forged out of one piece of steel" (*S"ezd II*, pp. 16–17).

Lunacharskii explained clearly that "making Communists" was not simply a matter of molding the intellect: "Pedagogues teach us with complete definiteness that man is in the final analysis ruled not by knowledge but by feelings. This means that we need to educate all the senses emotionally in the new generation. In what spirit? In the spirit of collectivism, of course. One must strive for the school to represent a brotherhood, a concord not of the narrow cell, not of the little monastery where people are used to each other and live according to their Communist ideals, but a union in which the windows and doors are open, [a union] which feels itself a cell of the world economy and the world proletariat. This all-embracing humaneness, this broad openheartedness toward each toiling individual must be instilled in people . . . [we must inculcate] a prodigious kindness toward one's own, and a flaming wrath toward the enemy who stands athwart the road to our ideal attainments, and a readiness, if necessary, to sacrifice oneself for this great cause" (S"ezd III, pp. 146–47).

159. S"ezd III, pp. 14–18.

160. For example, S"ezd I, p. 64; S"ezd II, pp. 123, 125, 171–73; S"ezd III, pp. 31–37, 242, 243, 305.

161. S"ezd III, p. 11. Preobrazhenskii and Bukharin echoed the same thoughts (ibid., pp. 31, 37).

162. The first Regulations of the Komsomol defined a member in part as one who "obeys all its [the League's] instructions" (S"ezd I, p. 99). As noted above, the failure of League members to obey instructions was one of the themes of criticism at the congresses. See, for example, S"ezd II, pp. 55–56; S"ezd III, pp. 100, 242–43.

163. S"ezd III, pp. 242–43.

164. Compare the citations to each of the three congresses in the foregoing passages. For some additional citations, see S"ezd III, pp. 279, 299, 315, 317.

165. S"ezd III, pp. 86–87.   166. Ibid., p. 305.   167. S"ezd I, p. 68.

168. For a few of the many references to bravery and self-sacrifice, see S"ezd I, p. 62; S"ezd II, pp. 16, 19 (an especially colorful passage by Trotsky), 20–21, 30–31, 66; S"ezd III, pp. 29, 31.

169. S"ezd III, p. 31.   170. S"ezd II, p. 13.

171. S"ezd I, pp. 40, 62; S"ezd III, pp. 18, 277, 306–7.

172. S"ezd II, pp. 12–13, 103, 146, 171; S"ezd III, pp. 6–22, 139, 141. See also Chapter III.

173. S"ezd III, pp. 193–96; also see the section on the establishment of the League, earlier in this chapter.

174. S"ezd I, pp. 39–40, 97; S"ezd II, p. 14; see also the Party decree in VKP(b) o komsomole, p. 9.

175. S"ezd II, pp. 65–67. For a similar statement by Bukharin, decrying pessimism and demanding confidence in the victory of Communism, see S"ezd III, pp. 61–63.

176. S"ezd II, p. 28.   177. S"ezd III, pp. 7, 18–20.

178. S"ezd II, p. 157; S"ezd III, pp. 36–37, 244–45, 300.

179. S"ezd III, p. 37.   180. Ibid., pp. 29–30.

181. Ibid., p. 18; see also pp. 6, 12–13.

182. Ibid., pp. 21–22.   183. Ibid., pp. 18–19.

184. Ibid., pp. 6–7. The present writer has omitted the italics (wide spacing in the Russian) found in certain passages of this edition, since there is some indication this was not in the original version of the address. See, for example, the 1947 edition of Lenin's Zadachi soiuzov molodezhi (pp. 4–5), which is stated (ibid., p. 28) to have been based on the brochure of 1920, "collated with the text of the newspaper"—i.e., Pravda for October 5, 6, and 7 (Nos. 221, 222, and 223), 1920.

185. *S"ezd III*, p. 12.   186. *Ibid.*, pp. 6, 16–17, 21.   187. *Ibid.*, p. 19.
188. *Ibid.*, pp. 7–13, 19.

189. *Ibid.*, pp. 12, 20–21. Specifically Lenin mentioned such activities as culti-
vating kitchen-gardens, contributing labor on one's free days (*subbotniks*), and
preserving cleanliness or distributing food in one's city block or one's village.

190. *Ibid.*, pp. 21–22. Lenin here and elsewhere (*ibid.*, p. 18) mixes the word
order, saying "league of Communist youth" instead of "Communist league of
youth." All lesser speakers, so far as the writer has observed, were careful never
to make this mistake, since it smacked of the "narrow" deviation.

191. *Ibid.*, p. 15.   192. *S"ezd I*, p. 97.   193. *S"ezd III*, p. 189.
194. *Ibid.*, p. 74.   195. *S"ezd II*, pp. 12–13; see also pp. 14, 17.
196. *Ibid.*, pp. 27–28.   197. *Ibid.*, p. 29.
198. *S"ezd III*, p. 307; see also p. 313.

199. *S"ezd I*, pp. 96–97, 99. The reports of several regional youth bodies (including those of Moscow, Kiev, the Urals, and Vladimir) revealed that the com-
ponent parts of the new League had already been taking an active part in recruiting youth for the Red armies (*ibid.*, pp. 41, 46–52, 54, 56; Afonin, *Komsomol*,
pp. 35–37).

200. Bunyan, *Intervention, Civil War, and Communism*, pp. 267–68.

201. No restrictions as to age or sex were given in the available materials. See
Iunyi kommunist (organ of the Central Committee of the RCLY), No. 5, May 10,
1919, as cited in Afonin, *Komsomol*, pp. 37–38; also *S"ezd II*, p. 188, and Ostriakov, *20 let VLKSM*, p. 36.

202. Tiurin, "VLKSM," *BSE* (suppl.), col. 1719; Shatskin, "VLKSM," *BSE* (1st
ed.), Vol. XI, col. 641; Afonin, *Komsomol*, p. 43.

203. Shatskin, "VLKSM," *BSE* (1st ed.), Vol. XI, col. 641, apparently citing
Beliakov, *Komsomol na frontakh* (Moscow, 1928); also Afonin, *Komsomol*, p. 43
(apparently from some earlier source than Beliakov, but presenting the same
statistics on mobilization). Beliakov's work was not available to the present
writer. For Ryvkin's references to these mobilizations in his report to the Second
Congress, see *S"ezd II*, pp. 51–52.

204. Shatskin, "VLKSM," *BSE* (1st ed.), Vol. XI, cols. 641–42. Ostriakov, *20 let
VLKSM*, p. 36, also mentions the work of girl Komsomolites as nurses and
cultural-political workers.

205. *S"ezd II*, pp. 51–52.   206. *Ibid.*, p. 55.

207. Presumably, adult Komsomolites served in any military capacity. Trotsky
did not define "youth" (*ibid.*, pp. 16–18).

208. *Ibid.*, pp. 158, 160.

209. This mobilization was specifically requested by V. Nevskii, representing
the CC of the Party, and was voted immediately and unanimously by the delegates (*S"ezd II*, pp. 119–21). For an indication that the Komsomol CC did not
have advance knowledge of this demand, see *S"ezd III*, p. 90. The Congress
thereupon held its closing ceremony (*S"ezd II*, pp. 121–28).

210. Because of the danger to Petrograd from Iudenich's army, that province
was wholly exempted from the mobilization. In each local organization, at least
three active members were to remain in order to carry on the work of the League
(*S"ezd II*, pp. 155–56). A subsequent Party directive provided that those Komsomolites who were taken into the Party cell in their military units would be

given suitable assignments such as commissars and agitators (*VKP*[*b*] *o komso-mole*, p. 246). Presumably many received combat posts, too.

211. Shatskin, "VLKSM," *BSE* (1st ed.), Vol. XI, col. 641; Tiurin, "VLKSM," *BSE* (suppl.), col. 1719; *S"ezd II*, pp. 196–97. The mobilization was apparently carried through so rapidly that a subsequent Party decision to reduce the percentage called could not be complied with (*S"ezd III*, p. 90; *S"ezd II*, pp. 196–97; and Afonin, *Komsomol*, p. 43). The Party instruction apparently referred to is in *VKP*(*b*) *o komsomole*, pp. 246–47. It speaks not of an outright reduction but of a step-by-step mobilization rather than an attempt to call everyone at once.

212. A special mobilization for the defense of Petrograd (October, 1919) netted 1,500 Komsomolites. The other three mobilizations (which netted about 8,000 recruits) were (1) the third all-Russian mobilization for the Western Front (March, 1920), and (2) the mobilization of Ukrainian Komsomolites against Wrangel (August, 1920), and (3) the mobilization of Komsomolites for command courses (summer, 1920). There was also a partial mobilization in May, 1920, after the start of the Polish war (Shatskin, "VLKSM," *BSE* [1st ed.], Vol. XI, col. 641; Ostriakov, *20 let VLKSM*, p. 37; Tiurin, "VLKSM," *BSE* [suppl.], col. 1719 [says May for the "third all-Russian mobilization"]; *S"ezd III*, pp. 88–92).

213. *S"ezd III*, pp. 286–89, also pp. 26–28, 91–92, 314, 324. The Third Congress also directed League members to render help to the Red Army itself, both at the front and in the rear areas. Activities specifically referred to include fighting, nursing, assisting in mobilizations, combating desertion, conducting educational work in the rear areas in infirmaries and other detachments, helping with special "weeks" and "days," and in general explaining to Soviet youth the struggle of the Red Army (*ibid.*, pp. 277, 311).

For a discussion of the controversy over the militia system, see Fedotoff White, *The Growth of the Red Army*, pp. 183–98.

214. *S"ezd II*, p. 73.   215. *Ibid.*, pp. 80–88.

216. *Ibid.*, pp. 114–16. Akhmanov was apparently expected to defend the majority view of the section, but instead swung around to support Nevskii.

Komsomolites in the Army were instructed to set up civilian Komsomol cells in the localities occupied by the Red Forces. All civilian Komsomol bodies were directed to aid in the political education of young soldiers, to help with the wounded, and to send girl members to nurses' training (*S"ezd II*, pp. 157–58).

217. *S"ezd III*, pp. 90–91.

218. *Ibid.*, pp. 219–23. For the resolution, see *ibid.*, p. 302.

219. *S"ezd I*, pp. 39, 57–62, 92–94, 96, 97.

220. *Ibid.*, pp. 61–62. "Reign" is a translation of *tsarstvo*.

221. *S"ezd II*, pp. 13–14, 19–20, 124, 155.   222. *Ibid.*, p. 125.

223. *Ibid.*, pp. 153–54.

224. *S"ezd III*, pp. 43–44. That part of Bukharin's address that has been printed covers *ibid.*, pp. 38–52. The editor explains that part of the address was lost.

225. *Ibid.*, p. 58.   226. *Ibid.*, p. 57.

227. In Russian, Kommunisticheskii internatsional molodezhi, or KIM.

228. *S"ezd I*, pp. 64–67. See also *S"ezd II*, pp. 178–79, reciting Karl Liebknecht's contributions to the organizing of German radical youth.

229. *S"ezd I*, pp. 95, 98, 99.

230. Panteleev, "VLKSM," *MSE* (2d ed.), Vol. II, col. 544.

231. *S"ezd II*, p. 190.

232. *Ibid.*, pp. 58–59, 189; Panteleev, "VLKSM," *MSE* (2d ed.), Vol. II, col. 544; Ostriakov, *20 let VLKSM*, p. 48.

233. The total membership claimed was 247,300. In addition to Russia (80,000 members—this may represent the August estimate) and the Volga Germans (1,800), the following countries were said to be represented: Germany (35,000); Austria (1,000); Switzerland (2,000); Rumania (6,500); Sweden (30,000); Norway (12,000); Denmark (12,000); Italy (30,000); Spain (5,000); and Czechoslovakia (9,000). See *S"ezd II*, p. 189.

Communications with foreign youth, as well as with Komsomol representatives abroad, were poor. This was illustrated at the Congress of October, 1919, when Ryvkin, reporting for the CC, stated that although the CIY was to have been founded late in August in a certain European city, he had not yet received word of the event, more than a month later (*S"ezd II*, pp. 57–59). Ryvkin went on to assume that the CIY had been founded anyway (*ibid.*, pp. 59, 125)—an expectation that was not fulfilled until six weeks after he spoke (*ibid.*, pp. 188–89). (This edition of the Second Congress contains supplementary notes telling of events after the time of the Congress itself.)

After beginning as a completely European affair, the CIY expanded to Asia. On September 9 and 10, 1920 (immediately after the Congress of the Peoples of the East), in Baku, there was held a "Congress of the Youth of the East." Through this meeting ties were reportedly established with the revolutionary youth of Persia, Turkey, and other areas of the Caucasus and Central Asia (*S"ezd III*, p. 79; also p. 32).

234. *S"ezd III*, pp. 64–81.   235. *S"ezd II*, p. 189.   236. *S"ezd III*, pp. 65–66.

237. *Ibid.*, pp. 66–68. "Spontaneous activity" is a translation of *samodeiatel'-nost'*.

238. *Ibid.*, pp. 65, 68–69.

239. The Statutes of the Communist International, approved at the Second World Congress, are given in English in Chamberlin, *Blueprint for World Conquest*, pp. 35–40. Those provisions that are most pertinent include paragraph eight, which obliquely ensures Soviet Russian control over the Executive Committee of the Comintern, and paragraph nine, which provides for the dictatorial control by the Executive Committee over the member Communist Parties (*ibid.*, pp. 37–38).

240. *S"ezd III*, p. 74. On economic tactics, see *ibid.*, pp. 75–76.

241. *Ibid.*, pp. 70–73 (including discussion of various questions in which this principle is invoked).

242. *Ibid.*, pp. 76–78.

243. *Ibid.*, p. 278. See also Ostriakov, *20 let VLKSM*, p. 49. For reference to the CIY in the report of the CC, see *S"ezd III*, p. 86. See also *S"ezd II*, p. 189.

244. *S"ezd III*, p. 309.   245. *Ibid.*, p. 98.   246. *S"ezd I*, pp. 68–69.

247. *Ibid.*, pp. 98–99.   248. *VKP(b) o komsomole*, pp. 134–36.

249. *S"ezd II*, pp. 134–35 (Kaplun) and 49 (Ryvkin).

250. *Ibid.*, pp. 49–51. The language is unclear concerning the trade unions.

251. *Ibid.*, pp. 135–36 (Kaplun), 137–40 (Dugachev). The "economic rights commissions" were described as being composed of representatives of the factory cells

and of the cells in the trade unions (*ibid.*, p. 138). For a fuller description of their work, see *ibid.*, p. 166.

252. *Ibid.*, pp. 139–40. In 1920 the Council of People's Commissars did issue a decree on assistant inspectors of labor. They were to concentrate their attention on putting into practice the laws on child labor. The scope of their work was strictly defined (*ibid.*, p. 194). See *S"ezd III*, p. 95, for an indication that this matter had not been entirely settled by the time of the Third Congress.

253. *S"ezd II*, pp. 141–42.

254. *Ibid.*, pp. 146–47, 108–10. See earlier section in this chapter for fuller treatment in connection with the "Dunaevskii dispute." For Dugachev's "theses," see *ibid.*, pp. 165–66. See *ibid.*, p. 194, for an explanation of the absence of the resolution itself.

255. Meisel and Kozera, *Materials*, p. 96.   256. *S"ezd II*, p. 146.

257. *Ibid.*, pp. 25–28.

258. *Ibid.*, p. 163. Marx was quoted: "Child factory labor must be transformed from a curse into a source of healthy and complete knowledge" (*ibid.*). See also *ibid.*, p. 167. At the same time, it was apparently still intended to enforce eventually the law forbidding work by children under sixteen (*ibid.*, pp. 50, 129–33).

259. *S"ezd III*, pp. 313–14. As to the continuing intent to enforce the laws relating to the protection of juvenile labor, see *ibid.*, p. 293.

260. *Ibid.*, p. 294. The communal living quarters were, according to the new Program, to "take the place of upbringing in the family" (*ibid.*, p. 313).

261. *Ibid.*, p. 94.

262. *Ibid.*, p. 309. The Komsomol was to work with "agencies of the productive unions, offices of the people's commissariats (labor, social security, public health, food, etc.)." Through the institution of "assistant labor inspectors," it would aid in checking up on the protection of child labor (*ibid.*, p. 314).

263. *Ibid.*, p. 294. For the pertinent provision in the new Regulations of the Komsomol, passed at the Third Congress, see *ibid.*, p. 317. On the "youth sections," see also *ibid.*, p. 94.

264. *Ibid.*, p. 297.   265. *Ibid.*, pp. 227–30.   266. *Ibid.*, pp. 12–13.

267. In the resolution on the "school of worker youth," it was admitted that the desperate need for production would undoubtedly hinder the progress of professional training (*ibid.*, p. 282).

268. *Ibid.*, pp. 293–94. The economic tasks were restated in the new Program of the League, passed at the Third Congress (*ibid.*, pp. 311–14). For references to the aim of equal pay in this period, coupled with a recognition of its impracticability at the time, see *S"ezd II*, p. 164, and *S"ezd III*, pp. 128–29, 285–86.

269. *S"ezd III*, p. 91; Shatskin, "VLKSM," *BSE* (1st ed.), Vol. XI, col. 643; Ostriakov, *20 let VLKSM*, p. 43. In the closely related field of public health, League members had been combating epidemics by creating "cleanliness committees" and by helping to organize special bath and sanitary "weeks" (*S"ezd III*, p. 90).

270. *S"ezd II*, p. 168 (in the "theses" approved by the CC). "Govern" is a translation of *upravliat'*.

271. Shatskin, "VLKSM," *BSE* (1st ed.), Vol. XI, col. 643. Shatskin said the enthusiastic Komsomolites had contributed especially by detecting cases of "sabo-

tage" on the part of older officials carried over from the previous regime. In other Komsomol histories, Komsomolites were given credit for aiding the Cheka in uncovering subversives (Afonin, *Komsomol*, p. 37; Ostriakov, *20 let VLKSM*, pp. 36, 43).

272. *S"ezd I*, pp. 85, 88. The First Congress also voted to send delegates to other special bodies, including the Proletkult and the Committees of the Poor.

273. *Ibid.*, p. 91.

274. *S"ezd II*, p. 197. This reference, which is in a footnote in the third edition (1926) of the Second Congress, gives the source as the Report of the CC to the Third Congress. The present writer has not been able to locate, in *S"ezd III*, pp. 82–102 (Report of the CC), the sentence quoted. It may come from an earlier edition.

275. *S"ezd III*, p. 195.   276. *Ibid.*, pp. 195–96.

277. The resolution announced these tasks: "(a) the unifying of the youthful forces of the village poor and the developing of their class consciousness; (b) the creation of an indissoluble bond between the young proletariat of the town and of the countryside; (c) propaganda for the idea of Communist agriculture [undefined] and the organization of labor communes" (*S"ezd I*, p. 99). On the need for controlling the peasantry, see also *ibid.*, pp. 69, 80.

278. Nevskii identified the various categories of peasants. The elements most congenial to the Bolshevik regime were, he said, the propertyless farm laborers, who were to be organized into trade unions, and those—usually poor—peasants who had entered either communes (in which equipment and capital were pooled) or state farms. These categories were to be won over first, in order to build a base for support in the countryside. The next (and wavering) group consisted of those—often "middle peasants"—who had gone into "artels," in which the work was cooperative but the individual retained title to some animals and equipment. Finally there were the (sometimes relatively wealthy) "individualists" who thought they could get along independently (*S"ezd II*, pp. 89–102; see also *ibid.*, p. 8).

279. *Ibid.*, p. 99.

280. *Ibid.*, pp. 193–94, contains a summary of this. From the Central Committee on down, a special Department for Work in the Countryside (Otdel po rabote v derevne) was set up at the various levels, as directed by the Second Congress (*ibid.*, p. 159). This Department was abolished by the Third Congress (*S"ezd III*, p. 295).

281. *S"ezd II*, pp. 193–94. Whether this applied only to rural members was not specified. See also *S"ezd III*, p. 97. At the Third Congress, most of what was said on rural matters merely reiterated the promises and exhortations of the previous assembly (see, for example, *ibid.*, pp. 19, 29, 91, 97, 295–97, 312, 325).

282. Afonin, *Komsomol*, p. 37; Tiurin, "VLKSM," *BSE* (suppl.), col. 1720; Ostriakov, *20 let VLKSM*, pp. 36, 43; *S"ezd III*, pp. 278, 296. Komsomolites were reminded at the Congress of 1920 that in these activities they were to work in conjunction with the regular agencies of the People's Commissariat of Agriculture (*S"ezd III*, p. 296).

283. *S"ezd III*, pp. 154–56 (Lunacharskii).

284. *Ibid.*, pp. 50–52. In the same vein there was a circular issued by the Central Committee jointly with the People's Commissariat of Food in 1920. It

told the local food agencies to make full use of Komsomolites in ferreting out hidden stores of grain, collecting the grain, and carting it away. Of course, in these "assessments," the "class principle" was to be carefully observed. The circular is displayed in Shatskin, "VLKSM," *BSE* (1st ed.), Vol. XI, cols. 642–43.

285. *S"ezd II*, pp. 22–23. The Eighth Congress of the Party, in March, 1919, had approved the formula of cooperating with the "middle peasants" (*ibid.*, p. 192). See later in this chapter. That the work in the villages was still poorly organized is suggested by the report of the Central Committee of the Komsomol (*ibid.*, p. 53).

286. *Ibid.*, pp. 52, 158–59.   287. *Ibid.*, pp. 158–59.

288. *S"ezd III*, pp. 296, 312. For a few words by Shatskin on the need for being practical in the approach to the peasants, see *ibid.*, pp. 187–88.

289. *S"ezd II*, pp. 158–59. See also pp. 147–49.   290. *Ibid.*, p. 101.

291. *Ibid.*, pp. 52, 158–59.   292. *Ibid.*, p. 168.   293. *Ibid.*, pp. 159–60.

294. *Ibid.*, p. 108; see also pp. 50, 109, 141–43.

295. *Ibid.*, pp. 50, 142–43. It was reported in October, 1919, that in the Moscow courts, out of 7,000 cases in the preceding year, 9 percent had involved juveniles (undefined) (*ibid.*, p. 142).

296. *Ibid.*, p. 109. At the Third Congress, similar ideas were expressed (*S"ezd III*, pp. 95, 293–94, 314, 324).

297. *S"ezd III*, pp. 293–94.   298. *S"ezd I*, pp. 55, 82.   299. *Ibid.*, pp. 41–42.

300. *S"ezd III*, pp. 303–5.

301. The national sections could not have their own clubs but could have "circles" within the general clubs sponsored by the League (*S"ezd II*, pp. 9, 108, 161; *S"ezd III*, pp. 303–5, 308, 310).

During the Third Congress (1920), a "leftist deviation" which would have prohibited all special language sections was beaten down, as was a "rightist deviation" which favored permitting separate national minority organizations (*S"ezd III*, pp. 223–27). (Concerning the Ukrainians in particular, see earlier in this chapter, and also *ibid.*, pp. 115–16.) For evidence that, in dealing with minorities, the Komsomol consciously used convinced Communists of the minority nationalities, see *ibid.*, pp. 98–99, 101–2. (Apparently the conference mentioned there for September 10, 1920, was in connection with that held at Baku, mentioned in the section on world affairs earlier in this chapter.

302. *S"ezd III*, pp. 98–99.   303. *Ibid.*, pp. 250–51.

304. *Ibid.*, p. 21 (Lenin).

305. *S"ezd II*, p. 26. See also Balabanova's remarks, *ibid.*, pp. 29–30, demanding "that there be no distinction made as to whether a fighter for socialism belongs to the male or female sex." See also the resolution of the Third Congress mentioning, as military duties suited to women, "rear-area work, liaison, and so forth" (*S"ezd III*, p. 289).

306. For a discussion of this subject by an early student of Soviet youth, see Mehnert, *Youth in Soviet Russia*, pp. 203–23.

307. *S"ezd II*, p. 161.

308. The distribution of the sexes in the membership was not reported statistically until 1924, so far as the writer has been able to determine. In that year the proportion of women was given as 15 percent. Presumably up to that time it had been below that figure. The League often declared the aim of drawing

more women into active participation. From 1924 on, the proportion of women rose. In 1926 it stood at 19 percent; in 1936, at 34 percent; and in 1949, at 42 percent (see later chapters).

309. *S"ezd I*, pp. 90–91; *S"ezd II*, pp. 117–18; *S"ezd III*, pp. 235, 305. These tallies are based on the form of the last name. In the third CC the names Kurellia and Fominykh could be either male or female.

310. *S"ezd III*, p. 302.   311. *S"ezd II*, p. 141.   312. *S"ezd III*, p. 313.

313. *Ibid.*, p. 147 (Lunacharskii).   314. *S"ezd II*, p. 26 (Kollontai).

315. *S"ezd III*, p. 14.   316. *S"ezd II*, p. 13.   317. *S"ezd III*, p. 310.

318. *Ibid.*, p. 20. In this case his interests were that "members of the League must use their every free hour in order to improve the kitchen-garden or to organize the training of youth at some factory or plant, and so forth."

319. *S"ezd I*, pp. 71–74. Another delegate recommended that the League not prevent dancing, but try to divert it into wholesome channels (*ibid.*, pp. 79–80).

320. *S"ezd III*, pp. 259, 263.   321. *S"ezd II*, p. 170.

322. *S"ezd I*, p. 97, also pp. 75–76, 98–99. Shatskin expressed one view of this purpose of the League when he said in 1920: "Our basic task is educational, and we undertake practical work not because this practical work is important in itself, but in the main only in order, in the practice of work itself, to rear the members of the League in the Communist spirit" (*S"ezd III*, p. 254; see also p. 248).

323. *S"ezd III*, pp. 6–22 (also Lenin, *Sochineniia*, XXX, 403–17; Lenin, *Zadachi soiuzov molodezhi* [Moscow, 1947], 38 pp., and many other editions).

324. *S"ezd III*, p. 6. The verb here translated as "to learn" is *uchit'sia*, which may be translated also as "to study."

325. *Ibid.*, pp. 6–11.

326. *Ibid.*, pp. 22–24. Concerning educational matters see also *ibid.*, pp. 92–93, 95–97, 101, 144–57, 248, 312–13.

327. *S"ezd II*, p. 163. The Second Congress was probably taking its cue from the Party's Eighth Congress. See *VKP(b) o komsomole*, p. 202. See also the economic section earlier in the present chapter, and see *S"ezd III*, p. 147 (Lunacharskii, saying that Marx espoused this view).

328. *S"ezd III*, pp. 148–49, also pp. 144–47. (See also Shatskin, in *ibid.*, p. 170.) On making Communists, see earlier in this chapter.

329. *S"ezd II*, pp. 186–87; see also pp. 50–51. These theses were adopted by the Second Enlarged Plenum of the CC of the RCLY on July 15–17, 1919 (*ibid.*, p. 187).

330. The abrupt curtailment of the Congress caused the topic to be treated only in one of the sections, rather than before the full assemblage (*S"ezd II*, p. 187). For the brief mention in the Report of the Central Committee, see *ibid.*, pp. 50–51. For the meeting of the section, see *ibid.*, pp. 149–52. See also the remarks of Angelica Balabanova, *ibid.*, p. 29.

331. *Ibid.*, pp. 149–52, 162–64.

332. *S"ezd III*, pp. 133–72. The departments in question were Narkompros (People's Commissariat of Education) and Glavprofobr (Main Committee for Professional-Technical Education)—the latter a subsidiary of the former (see *ibid.*, pp. 143–44).

333. *Ibid.,* pp. 133–38. (According to Shatskin, the original decree on schools for worker youth was issued in February, 1919. *Ibid.,* p. 171.)

334. *Ibid.,* pp. 140–42. Adolescents down to the age of twelve could be admitted with permission of the local authorities (*ibid.,* p. 143). One speaker recommended that pupils regularly be admitted from the age of twelve (*ibid.,* pp. 157–59). It was urged that the Komsomol cell in each factory take the lead in setting up a "school for worker youth" in connection with its factory—of course working in conjunction with the educational authorities (*ibid.,* pp. 143–44).

335. *Ibid.,* pp. 144–47.   336. *S"ezd I,* pp. 76, 78, 97–99.

337. *S"ezd II,* p. 164.   338. *S"ezd III,* pp. 171–72.   339. *Ibid.,* pp. 285–86.

340. *S"ezd I,* p. 99.

341. *VKP(b) o komsomole,* pp. 9–10, citing *Pravda,* May 17, 1919.

342. *S"ezd III,* pp. 309–11; see also pp. 290–92, including special instructions for tactics to be pursued in clubs. For the pertinent section in the Regulations of the League approved at the Third Congress, see *ibid.,* p. 317. For the pertinent section in the pre-Third Congress draft Program, see *ibid.,* pp. 323–24. For a brief historical account of the developments concerning school clubs and their administration, see *S"ezd II,* p. 187. For one recognition of the overlapping responsibilities of the Komsomol and the Narkompros in the matter of "circles," see *S"ezd III,* pp. 200–5. For an early mention of Komsomol-sponsored circles of students, see *S"ezd I,* pp. 75–76 (Tsetlin).

343. *S"ezd III,* pp. 171–72 (Shatskin). See also *ibid.,* pp. 279–86 (including much on other Komsomol functions in the school).

344. *S"ezd II,* pp. 167–70; *S"ezd I,* pp. 97–99. See also *S"ezd I,* p. 79 (proposing evening entertainments). The "Young Proletarian Homes" were advocated to accomplish the same purpose as the clubs, but, as explained earlier in this chapter, they were prohibited (*S"ezd I,* pp. 94–95).

Sometime between October, 1919, and April, 1920, the CC of the Komsomol apparently proposed the establishing of a special collegium within the Commissariat of Education to direct both schools and clubs (*S"ezd II,* p. 187). The writer encountered no record of the fate of that proposal.

The Third Congress spoke of Komsomol "collectives" operating in the factories for the prospective students of the schools for worker youth. The function of these "collectives" seems to have been the same as that of the clubs described above (*S"ezd III,* pp. 285–86).

345. *S"ezd I,* p. 98.

346. The Russian title was *Iunyi kommunist* (*S"ezd II,* pp. 53, 55). Sixteen issues, at varying intervals, had appeared by the time of the Second Congress. By the time of the Third Congress the magazine was apparently appearing regularly (*S"ezd III,* pp. 97, 249–50).

347. The Press Bureau had also published various brochures and reports (*S"ezd II,* pp. 53–55).

348. *S"ezd III,* pp. 97, 249–50, 309–11.

349. *S"ezd II,* pp. 169–70.   350. *S"ezd III,* p. 147.   351. *Ibid.,* pp. 214–18.

352. *Ibid.,* pp. 302–3.   353. *S"ezd II,* pp. 105, 160, 171–73.

354. *S"ezd I,* p. 99; *S"ezd II,* pp. 103, 105, 160, 171, 173; *S"ezd III,* pp. 286–89, 314, 324.

355. *S"ezd III*, p. 314; see also p. 324. At the Third Congress the Komsomol was even directed *not* to conduct "self-standing" work (*samostoiatel'naia rabota*) in the field of physical education, in order instead to concentrate all its strength on strictly premilitary training (*ibid.*, p. 288).

356. *S"ezd II*, p. 160. On the Scouts, see earlier in this chapter.

357. *Ibid.*, p. 106.

358. The Party's membership at the time of the Third Komsomol Congress was 600,000, according to Preobrazhenskii (*S"ezd III*, p. 28). The League at this time had about 400,000 (see earlier in this chapter).

359. See, for example, *S"ezd III*, pp. 86–87.

360. *Ibid.*, pp. 192–95, especially 194–95.

361. *Ibid.*, p. 308. The whole Program occupies *ibid.*, pp. 306–14. For the projected Program before the Third Congress—apparently *before* Bukharin went to work on it—see *ibid.*, pp. 322–25.

CHAPTER III: THE EARLY YEARS OF THE NEW ECONOMIC POLICY

1. See, for example, *S"ezd IV*, pp. 10–19, 23–24, 26–27, 29. Concerning the date, both Panteleev and Tiurin, in their histories, give October as the time of the Fourth Congress. The September dates given above appear, however, on the title page of the stenographic report of the Fourth Congress and at the beginning of each session. Perhaps neither Panteleev nor Tiurin had access to the politically explosive sources.

2. *S"ezd V*, pp. 13–14, 18–20, 22.

3. *Ibid.*, pp. 113–14. "Spiritual" is a translation of *ideinyi*, which could also be rendered as "of ideas," "of principles," "of morals."

4. Another reason for the losses in membership may have been the firing of many underage factory workers, when the factories went over to some degree of autonomous operation (Panteleev, "VLKSM," *MSE* [2d ed.], Vol. II, col. 546; Ostriakov, *20 let VLKSM*, p. 52). (Minors were expected to receive the same pay as adults. Hence the factories found it unprofitable to employ immature youths.)

5. Ostriakov (*20 let VLKSM*, p. 44) gives 400,000, while Tseitlin, one of the leaders of the League, estimated that it had reached 500,000 (*S"ezd IV*, p. 110).

6. *S"ezd IV*, pp. 107–10. Tseitlin estimated that, of those eliminated, 100,000 were intelligentsia youths, another 100,000 were rural youths, and only 50,000 were worker youths and others. Tseitlin conceded that the discontent manifested in the Kronstadt uprising had caused some individuals, and even whole cells, to quit the League on their own initiative, but he maintained that the total of such persons was small and implied that most of those eliminated were undesirable "paper members" (*ibid.*).

7. Chaplin gives 400,000 (*S"ezd VI*, p. 122). Panteleev ("VLKSM," *MSE* [2d ed.], Vol. II, col. 546) gives 415,000, as does "VLKSM," *BSE* (2d ed.), IX, 335. At the Fourth Congress a figure of 470,000 was mentioned as being too inflated, but a figure of 415,000 was also rejected as being based purely on guesswork (*S"ezd IV*, pp. 270–71, 325–31). That the increase was largely made up of worker

youth was attributed in part to the fact that a Komsomol Conference which assembled on June 1, 1921, had introduced a probationary stage for the admission of youths of intelligentsia origin (*S"ezd IV*, pp. 94, 111).

8. At the Fifth Congress a figure of 325,000 was given, along with a plea that statistics were grossly inadequate to permit an accurate estimate (*S"ezd V*, pp. 373–74, also pp. 77–78). But at the next Congress the official report of the Central Committee placed the figure at either 235,930 or 248,000 (*S"ezd VI*, pp. 135, 122). (No explanation of the discrepancy was given. Possibly one includes candidate-members and the other not.) The writer takes the figures of the Sixth Congress to be more nearly correct than those of the Fifth, since by the Sixth Congress there had been time for the collection of the available statistics, and probably embarrassment at admitting a low figure would have subsided. Ostriakov (*20 let VLKSM*, p. 62) gives a figure of 260,000, but does not indicate his source.

9. *S"ezd IV*, p. 11 (Shatskin). For similar demands by others at both congresses see *ibid.*, pp. 12–19 (Zinoviev), 23–29 (Lunacharskii), 58 (Trotsky), 268 (Ryvkin); *S"ezd V*, pp. 121–23 (Bukharin), 145–46, 315–17. Zinoviev mentioned that there was at that time (September, 1921) a purge going on in the Party, which would reduce greatly the Party's pre-purge strength of 700,000 but would have the desired result of bringing complete solidarity (*S"ezd IV*, pp. 15–16). Lunacharskii warned that the Party purge would extend into the ranks of the Komsomol and would be a necessary measure "against the petit-bourgeois devil" (*S"ezd IV*, pp. 26–27, also 23–24).

10. *S"ezd IV*, p. 10.   11. *Ibid.*, p. 29.

12. *S"ezd V*, pp. 22 (Lunacharskii), 113–58 (Bukharin and others).

13. *Ibid.*, pp. 114–23. In regard to the subject of a new moral code, see Richard Kramer, "Practical Morality Taught to Soviet Children, as Illustrated in Four Official Soviet Periodicals, 1937–1951" (Unpublished doctoral dissertation, Columbia University, 1953).

14. *S"ezd V*, p. 127. He called for novels about the Cheka among other things. This was one of the rare references to the secret police in the congresses.

15. *Ibid.*, p. 128.   16. *Ibid.*, p. 123.   17. *Ibid.*, pp. 124–25.

18. *Ibid.*, pp 113–14.   19. *Ibid.*, pp. 124–25.   20. *Ibid.*, pp. 125–26.

21. *Ibid.*, pp. 133–35.   22. *Ibid.*, p. 150.   23. *Ibid.*, p. 153.

24. *Ibid.*, p. 158.

25. *Ibid.*, pp. 315–17. The idea of Komsomol honor was emphasized in a section which the Fifth Congress added to the Regulations of the League. In this section, under the title "Tasks and Obligations of Members of the RCLY," appeared these provisions:

"7. Komsomolite is a lofty title. . . . Each member of the RCLY must, through his conduct and work outside and in the League, merit this title, hold high and guard sacredly the honor of his organization and the red Communist banner.

"All Komsomolites must understand that they are future members of the . . . Russian Communist Party and must prepare themselves to fulfill this great and difficult duty.

"8. Everywhere . . . the Komsomolite must be the first of the first, the most capable, energetic, honest, and daring—an example for all the rest of youth and all toilers" (*ibid.*, p. 376).

26. *S"ezd IV*, p. 283. For other examples concerning initiative and spontaneity, see *ibid.*, pp. 10–11, 106, 167; on discipline, see *ibid.*, pp. 10–12, 58.

27. *S"ezd V*, pp. 129–30.   28. *Ibid.*, pp. 132–33. See also pp. 145–46.

29. *Ibid.*, pp. 154–55.

30. For sharpening the mind, Bukharin endorsed chess, asserting that "chess-playing provides great mental training" and that "great military commanders and public figures have almost all played chess very well" (*S"ezd V*, p. 129). The other remarks of 1921 and 1922 bearing on qualities of individual character introduced nothing really new. For example, Komsomolites were to be optimistic and enthusiastic (*S"ezd IV*, p. 12; *S"ezd V*, pp. 23–24, 132).

31. His report, which was on the next tasks of the League, occupies *S"ezd IV*, pp. 253–68. The topic had originally been "The Next Tasks of League Construction," but was broadened at the last minute, apparently on instructions from the Party (*ibid.*, pp. 253, 268).

32. *S"ezd IV*, pp. 256–60.

33. *Ibid.*, p. 264. Another speaker estimated that worker youth constituted not over 20 percent of the League and, if farm-laborer youth were included, about 35 percent (*ibid.*, p. 282).

34. *Ibid.*, p. 265. It had been explained earlier in the Congress that there was an added motivation for this measure: it was felt that at the time of the Kronstadt crisis of March, 1921, the League had been "out of touch with the mass of non-Party youth" and therefore needed to concentrate on bringing more workers under its influence (*ibid.*, pp. 111–12).

35. *Ibid.*, p. 265.   36. *Ibid.*, pp. 266–67.

37. *Ibid.*, pp. 278, 280, 297–301. One speaker declared that those under sixteen approached 40 percent of the League's membership, but he seemed to be making a debating point rather than stating the result of any precise survey. He did assert positively that such was the case in the Bashkir Republic (*ibid.*, p. 280).

38. *Ibid.*, p. 288.   39. *Ibid.*, pp. 297–301.

40. *Ibid.*, pp. 302–3. The dissenters on the age issue were further stigmatized as "Ukrainians" and as proponents of a purely "mechanical" solution—the proper one being to attract more older youths into the League (*ibid.*, pp. 306–10).

41. *Ibid.*, pp. 314–17 (Shatskin himself conducted the vote, after the incident related later in this chapter).

42. *Ibid.*, pp. 270–71, 273–74, 279–80, 283, 297–301.

43. *Ibid.*, p. 285, also pp. 290–91.   44. *Ibid.*, pp. 285–87.

45. *Ibid.*, pp. 288–89. The persistent advocates of the purge (*ibid.*, pp. 297–301) were criticized along the lines indicated earlier by Shatskin and Ryvkin, who saw this as another aspect of the same "serious deviation" (*ibid.*, pp. 304–5, 310–14).

46. *Ibid.*, pp. 314–17.

47. *Ibid.*, p. 332. Compare *S"ezd III*, p. 315. (See Chapter II.)

48. *S"ezd IV*, p. 301. Preobrazhenskii suggested a similar suspicion (*ibid.*, pp. 286–87).

49. *Ibid.*, pp. 270–71, gives probably the closest approach to an anti-peasant position expressed in the proceedings, and it is merely an attitude of not wanting to expend too much energy on peasant youths at the present time.

50. *Ibid.*, pp. 321–22.

51. *S"ezd V*, pp. 75–76. In connection with these purges it should be noted that the Fourth Congress had abolished the provision that persons expelled had the right to appeal to a higher body of the Komsomol (*S"ezd IV*, p. 332). The Fifth Congress restored this right (*S"ezd V*, p. 376).

52. Already at the Fourth Congress the deviationists were called "Ukrainian" (*S"ezd IV*, pp. 142–45, 306–14), although apparently only a few of them actually were representing areas in the Ukraine (*ibid.*, pp. 268–310). Of those participating, only Polonskii (*ibid.*, p. 268) and Erskii (*ibid.*, p. 279) are identified as Ukrainians. (See *ibid.*, pp. 127–29, for the identification of Polonskii.) As to the other dissenters, some are not identified by locality, but Feigel'son (*ibid.*, p. 276), Mitrofanov (*ibid.*, p. 281), Tuzhilkin (*ibid.*, p. 292), and Okulik (*ibid.*, p. 298) are identified as coming from other parts of the Soviet Union.

At the Fifth Congress the appellation "Ukrainian" was used still more (*S"ezd V*, pp. 86–87, 92–94, 103–4), although Shatskin deplored the tendency (*ibid.*, pp. 97–100).

53. *S"ezd V*, pp. 81–86, 89–92, 96–97.   54. *Ibid.*, p. 76.

55. *Ibid.*, p. 375. Sponsors were warned that they were responsible for those they recommended.

56. *Ibid.*, p. 326.

57. *Ibid.*, pp. 258–60. See also *ibid.*, pp. 185–87, 326 (refers to a Komsomol Conference of May, 1922, dealing with rural youth).

58. *S"ezd IV*, pp. 261–62.

59. *Ibid.*, pp. 269–70, 275–76, 280, 292–95, 297–98; see also pp. 127–29.

60. *Ibid.*, pp. 269–70, 292–93.   61. *Ibid.*, pp. 275–76, 298–301.

62. *Ibid.*, p. 288.

63. *Ibid.*, pp. 290–91. That did not end the matter. Some of the delegates persisted in expressing contrary views, challenging Preobrazhenskii openly and not always with proper respect for his dignity (*ibid.*, pp. 292–301). Then Shatskin entered the fray, ominously declaring that in the remarks of previous speakers he had detected manifestations of a perhaps unrecognized desire to create a "young Communist party"—a "very serious deviation" which must be vigorously combated (*ibid.*, pp. 302–4). Shatskin was supported by Tseitlin and Ryvkin (*ibid.*, pp. 306–14 *passim*), after which the Congress gave its vote to their (i.e., the official) position (*ibid.*, pp. 314–17).

64. *Ibid.*, pp. 317–21.   65. *S"ezd V*, p. 376.

66. *S"ezd IV*, pp. 108–9. Following the Party Congress, a Komsomol Conference of June 1, 1921, dealt with questions of the economic rights of young workers (*ibid.*, p. 109).

67. *Ibid.*, pp. 114–17 (Tseitlin in the report of the CC). For other reports bearing on the subject, see *ibid.*, pp. 153–250. For shorter references to it, see *ibid.*, pp. 132–35, 138–42.

68. *Ibid.*, pp. 170–71, 176–78, 187–88.   69. *Ibid.*, p. 191.

70. *Ibid.*, pp. 200–2. On more general aims, see *ibid.*, pp. 198–200.

71. *Ibid.*, pp. 204–7, 211–12.   72. *Ibid.*, pp. 198–202, 204–7.

73. Presumably in order to ensure compliance with this policy, it was ordered that Komsomolites working in government agencies must be under the supervision of their local Komsomol committee (in most cases that would be the city or town committee) (*S"ezd IV*, pp. 212–14, also pp. 317–21).

74. *S"ezd IV*, pp. 179–80; see also Chapter II. The Fourth Congress required that "assistant inspectors" must have been members of the League for at least six months and must have attained a certain standard of "political knowledge" set by the Central Committee (*ibid.*, pp. 202–4).

75. *Ibid.*, pp. 204–7.   76. *S"ezd V*, p. 353.   77. *Ibid.*, pp. 70–72.

78. *Ibid.*, p. 284; see also pp. 24–25, 70–72, 105.

79. *Ibid.*, pp. 34–37; see also pp. 115–16 (Bukharin).

80. *Ibid.*, pp. 353–60.

81. *Ibid.*, pp. 286–87. Details were not given concerning the ameliorative measures Shokhin had in mind.

82. *Ibid.*, p. 363.   83. *Ibid.*, p. 376.   84. *S"ezd IV*, pp. 208–10.

85. *Ibid.*, pp. 210–11. The over-all directing agency through which the League was to coordinate its efforts in the battle against crime was a unit of the Commissariat of Education called the "Department of the Rightful Defense of Children" (*ibid.*). Also mentioned was a "Commission on Minors' Affairs," but its ministerial affiliation was not made clear (*ibid.*, p. 208). The extent to which the League might operate autonomously in these matters was not made clear.

86. *S"ezd IV*, pp. 160–64, 167, 232–35, 259, 260, 317–21, 331–32; *S"ezd V*, pp. 111–12, 128–29, 315–17.

87. *S"ezd IV*, pp. 157, 165, 188–90, 260.   88. *Ibid.*, pp. 155–57, 160–64, 198–200.

89. *Ibid.*, pp. 176–78, 187–88, 191, 198–200, 256–58; *S"ezd V*, p. 113.

90. *S"ezd IV*, pp. 169–70.   91. *S"ezd V*, pp. 128–29 (Bukharin).

92. This was set forth in a section which the Fourth Congress added to the Regulations of the League: "Each member of the RCLY is obliged to master the fundamentals of Communist doctrine, to carry on agitation and propaganda among worker and peasant youth for Communist ideas and their realization" (*S"ezd IV*, pp. 331–32). (Compare *S"ezd III*, p. 315.) At the Fifth Congress it was voted to organize groups of propagandists to further the teaching of Marxism within the League (*S"ezd V*, pp. 339–41).

93. *S"ezd IV*, pp. 157–59; see also pp. 177–78. The former were called "schools associated with production" (*shkoly pri proizvodstve*), and the latter, "schools of industrial labor training" (*shkoly promyshlenno-trudovogo uchenichestva*).

94. *S"ezd IV*, pp. 157–59, 250. FZU stands for *Fabrichno-zavodskoe uchenichestvo*, literally "factory-plant training."

95. *Ibid.*, pp. 157–59. Inaccuracy in the figure is suggested by the fact that at the next Congress it was said that at the time of the Fourth Congress there had been only 50 educational institutions serving worker youth (*S"ezd V*, pp. 195–96).

96. *S"ezd V*, pp. 195–96.   97. *Ibid.*, p. 73.

98. *Ibid.*, pp. 205–7. His idea was that certain students could go on to higher educational institutions, but only after they had worked a while.

99. *Ibid.*, pp. 208–13.   100. *Ibid.*, pp. 219–26.   101. *Ibid.*, pp. 213–16.

102. *Ibid.*, pp. 228–32.   103. *Ibid.*, pp. 260–61, also p. 217.

104. *Ibid.*, p. 261. It is not directly stated how the vote turned out on the section's phrasing versus Lunacharskii's, but the fact that they proceeded to vote on Shatskin's amendment indicates that Shokhin's view received a majority. If it had not, then there would have been no point in Shatskin's amendment. However, in the final version as published, the phrase "most rapid liquidation"

is *not* used. Instead there is the less urgent phrase "must be abolished." This suggests that the wording was tampered with after the vote (*ibid.*, p. 317).

105. *S"ezd IV*, pp. 215–16, 227.

106. They also endorsed a new tax which the government had just decreed to provide funds for schools (*S"ezd IV*, pp. 217–19, 228, 250).

107. *S"ezd V*, p. 142.

108. *Ibid.*, p. 263. The text of the proposed resolution is not given, but it can be surmised from the ensuing debate.

109. *Ibid.*, p. 263.

110. *Ibid.*, pp. 264–67, and, for the resolution on education, pp. 317–21. Mentioned at both the Fourth and Fifth congresses was the idea that too much attention and money was being spent on the regular secondary schools, to the detriment of the schools for worker youth (*S"ezd IV*, pp. 238–40; *S"ezd V*, pp. 215–16).

111. *S"ezd IV*, pp. 174–78; *S"ezd V*, pp. 317–21.

112. *S"ezd IV*, pp. 157–59, 235–38 (Krupskaia); *S"ezd V*, pp. 135, 139–41 (Lunacharskii), 317–21.

113. *S"ezd IV*, pp. 166–67, 221–22, 230–31, 240–42. For an indication at the Fifth Congress that some sort of self-government in the schools was being organized and controlled by the League, see *S"ezd V*, pp. 317–21.

At the Fourth Congress it was voted that Komsomol cells could *not* be established in the regular secondary schools, since worker youths were in too small a minority there, and consequently the Komsomol cells might come under bourgeois influence. To the extent that the League found it possible to operate in the regular secondary schools, it was permitted to establish Komsomol "collectives," but these units, unlike cells, did not have the right to admit members or to elect delegates (*S"ezd IV*, pp. 333, 335, 350–51). Each member of a collective was required to belong concurrently to some regular cell of the League (*ibid.*, p. 335). Cells were authorized to be formed in factories, plants, villages, hamlets, and state institutions (*ibid.*, p. 333). At the same time, all interschool student organizations outside the League were expressly forbidden, ostensibly on the ground that the students did not have any special professional interests in common (*ibid.*, pp. 350–51). At the Fifth Congress the prohibition on Komsomol cells in schools was lifted (*S"ezd V*, pp. 275–76, 334, 377).

114. *S"ezd V*, pp. 276–79.   115. *Ibid.*, pp. 279–81, 365–66.

116. *Ibid.*, pp. 365–66. For a statement of the same sort of program before the controversy arose, see the decision of the Fourth Congress, *S"ezd IV*, pp. 353–56.

117. *S"ezd V*, p. 77. The Fourth Congress virtually neglected this field.

118. *Ibid.*, pp. 128, 146–47, 150–51, and especially pp. 348–51.

119. *Ibid.*, pp. 348–51.   120. *Ibid.*, pp. 344–45, also pp. 346–48.

121. *Ibid.*, p. 346. Apparently the organizing process had already begun, to the extent that it embraced 4,000 children (*S"ezd VI*, pp. 133, 333).

122. *S"ezd V*, p. 346. That platform was set forth in part in the Laws of the Young Pioneers:

"1. A Pioneer is true to the working class and to Communism. 2. A Pioneer is a friend and brother to each other Pioneer and Komsomolite. 3. A Pioneer is honest and upright. His word is like granite. 4. A Pioneer is disciplined. 5. A

Pioneer daily helps his fellow toilers in building the Communist society. 6. A Pioneer loves to work and esteems useful labor. 7. A Pioneer is clean in thought, word, and deed." In addition there was a Solemn Oath of the Young Pioneers which declared: "I solemnly promise that I will be true to the working class and daily will help my fellow toilers, and will know and obey the Pioneer Laws." And, finally, there was given an Iron Law of the Young Pioneers: "I will strive *always*, wherever possible, to gain knowledge in order to use it for the benefit of the toilers" (*S"ezd V*, p. 348).

123. *S"ezd V*, pp. 346–48.   124. *S"ezd IV*, pp. 40–41, 48, 56–57, 119–20.

125. *Ibid.*, pp. 119–20.

126. *S"ezd V*, pp. 163–77 (report by Chaplin), 177–92 (discussion by delegates), 258–60, 321–27 (approval of resolution and the resolution itself).

127. *Ibid.*, pp. 163–67, 321–22.

128. *Ibid.*, pp. 163–67, 177–92, 322, 324–25, 327.   129. *Ibid.*, pp. 165, 167, 323.

130. *Ibid.*, pp. 167–68, 323.   131. *Ibid.*, pp. 168–77, 323, 327.

132. *Ibid.*, pp. 326–28. The slogan for the winter of 1922–23 in rural Komsomol units was to be "attention to the youth of the sovkhozes."

133. *Ibid.*, pp. 168–77, 324–27.

134. *S"ezd IV*, pp. 56, 57–58; *S"ezd V*, pp. 43, 237–42, 245–46.

135. *S"ezd IV*, pp. 331–32. A law of April 22, 1918, made military training compulsory for "workers and those peasants who do not exploit the labor of others." Women could volunteer. A law of May 29, 1918, announced the shift to conscription for the Army. See Meisel and Kozera, *Materials*, pp. 72–73.

136. *S"ezd V*, p. 43.   137. *Ibid.*, pp. 272–74.

138. *Ibid.*, pp. 331–33, and also pp. 272–74. Komsomol cells were permitted in military schools.

139. *S"ezd IV*, pp. 117–18, 152, 351–63; *S"ezd V*, pp. 67–68, 377–78.

140. *S"ezd V*, pp. 235–37, and also pp. 26, 237–45, 249–51, 254.

141. *Ibid.*, pp. 235–37, 308–9, and also pp. 25–26, 68–70.

142. *Ibid.*, pp. 308–9; see also pp. 243–45 (Radek).

143. *Ibid.*, pp. 242–43 (Trotsky).   144. *Ibid.*, pp. 237–42 (quotation on p. 242).

145. *Ibid.*, p. 26.   146. *S"ezd IV*, pp. 38–39.   147. *Ibid.*, p. 46.

148. *Ibid.*, pp. 14–15 (Zinoviev), 33–34, 43–47 (Trotsky).

149. *Ibid.*, pp. 49, 56.

150. *Ibid.*, pp. 33–34, 39, 42–43, 50–51, 53, 55 (Trotsky).

151. *Ibid.*, p. 28 (Lunacharskii).

152. *S"ezd V*, pp. 15 (written message from Lenin), 27–47 (Trotsky, especially p. 41), 247 (Radek), 250–51 (Lunacharskii).

153. *Ibid.*, p. 247.

154. *S"ezd IV*, pp. 59–95; see also pp. 12–13 (Zinoviev), 19–20 (Unger, secretary of the Executive Committee of the CIY).

155. *Ibid.*, pp. 62–67.   156. *Ibid.*, pp. 68–77.

157. *Ibid.*, pp. 77–79.   158. *Ibid.*, pp. 82–83.

159. *Ibid.*, p. 87 (quotation), and pp. 82–87, 101–2.

160. *Ibid.*, pp. 88–89.   161. *Ibid.*, pp. 90–91.

162. *Ibid.*, pp. 92–93.   163. *Ibid.*, pp. 101–2.

164. *S"ezd V*, p. 61. See also pp. 51–67 (whole report), 313–14 (resolution).

165. *Ibid.*, pp. 62–63.   166. *Ibid.*, pp. 245–46.

167. For particularly stormy sessions, see *S"ezd IV*, pp. 268–317, and *S"ezd V*, pp. 255–88.

168. *S"ezd IV*, pp. 122–52.   169. *Ibid.*, p. 125.

170. *Ibid.*, pp. 127–29. It may be a reflection of the Ukrainian conflict that when the nationality of the delegates at the Fourth Congress was reported, Ukrainians and Belorussians were lumped with Great Russians (*ibid.*, p. 326). For further references to the issue of the "Ukrainian Opposition," see an earlier section of this chapter and also *S"ezd IV*, pp. 142–45; *S"ezd V*, pp. 86–87, 92–94, 97–104. Other nationality items include a report that the League was making satisfactory progress in its work with Jewish, Turkish, and other minorities (*S"ezd IV*, pp. 118–19). A delegate from the Caucasus boldly criticized the CC for not permitting the Caucasian units of the League to hold a congress of their own. He also protested that for seven months the Baku Komsomol organization had requested in vain that the CC designate a secretary for the Baku body (*S"ezd IV*, pp. 135–37).

171. *S"ezd IV*, pp. 137–38. Interestingly, this brash critic (Tseitlin of Petrograd) was later elected a candidate-member of the new CC (*ibid.*, p. 364).

172. Concerning Lunacharskii, see *S"ezd IV*, pp. 232–35, 238–42; *S"ezd V*, pp. 135, 148–49, 215–16, 228–32. Concerning Preobrazhenskii, see *S"ezd IV*, pp. 292–301. Concerning Bukharin, see *S"ezd V*, pp. 132–35, 153.

173. *S"ezd V*, p. 155.

174. *Ibid.*, pp. 213–16, 228–32. Lunacharskii explained that one of the points advocated by Krupskaia was not shared by a majority of the CC of the Party at present (*ibid.*, pp. 219–26). This remark must have encouraged criticism of her.

175. *S"ezd IV*, pp. 240–42, 246.   176. *Ibid.*, pp. 302–3.

177. *S"ezd V*, pp. 97, 103–4 (also 97–100).

178. *S"ezd IV*, pp. 123–27, 132–35, 152, 273–74; *S"ezd V*, pp. 81–86, 96–97.

179. *S"ezd IV*, p. 32.   180. *Ibid.*, p. 364, lists the new CC.

181. *S"ezd V*, pp. 14–15. No women were among the fifteen.

182. *Ibid.*, pp. 291, 328.   183. *Ibid.*, pp. 291–92.

184. The Fifth Congress did not produce any statistics: the credentials (Mandates) Commission simply reported that there appeared to be roughly 450 or 460 delegates (*S"ezd V*, pp. 373–74).

185. *S"ezd IV*, pp. 325–31. For further details see Appendixes C, D, E, F, and G.

186. *S"ezd V*, pp. 295–99, 370. The others so honored were Fedor Pliasunov, Ignat, Okulik, Vladimir Feigin, and Iastrzhemskii. It is interesting to note that Okulik's errors in participating in the Ukrainian Opposition were mentioned, but he was forgiven because those erroneous ideas "were dictated by love of the League" and because he had outgrown them (*ibid.*, p. 298). It should be noted that with the transfer of Shatskin—lone veteran of the first four Central Committees—and the others, the new (fifth) CC contained only three (out of twenty-one) who had served on more than one previous CC. They were Smorodin, Zabirov, and Kurellia, all of whom had been on the third and the fourth CC's.

187. *S"ezd IV*, p. 327. The statistics given were just under 80 percent for the Party members, almost 10 percent for non-Party members, and almost 11 percent not accounted for.

188. *S"ezd V*, pp. 373–74. Information as to Party affiliation had been gathered on 68 of the 450 or 460 delegates, and only 7 of those were not members or candidate-members of the Party.

189. *S"ezd IV*, p. 340. Compare *S"ezd III*, p. 321.

190. *S"ezd IV*, pp. 342–43 (pp. 341–49 for the whole Statute).

191. *Ibid.*, p. 347.

192. *Ibid.*, p. 349. For details on earlier arrangements, see Chapter II.

193. *Ibid.*, p. 343. This and some other provisions of the new Statute had been ordered by the Tenth Party Congress. See *Vsesoiuznaia kommunisticheskaia partiia v rezoliutsiiakh ee s"ezdov i konferentsii (1898–1926 gg.)*, p. 300. Those who entered the Party at age twenty or younger were required to have served in the Komsomol for one year, or, in the case of worker youth, for six months (*S"ezd IV*, p. 344).

194. *S"ezd IV*, pp. 345–47. Special safeguards were outlined for preventing such personnel from passing inconspicuously out of League work and into Party work. Evidently that was what many of these young Party members wanted to do.

195. *S"ezd V*, p. 379. To be secretaries at the guberniia level, intelligentsia had to have served in the League three years and in the Party two years; peasants two years in each, and workers two years in the League and one in the Party. Uezd secretaries had to meet these requirements: intelligentsia, two years in the League and one in the Party; peasants, one in each; and workers, only one year in the League (no Party membership required).

The Fifth Congress also decreed that every Komsomolite would wear a distinctive badge. (There was no such badge for the Party.) The pertinent provision in the new Regulations was as follows: "Every Komsomolite wears the insigne of the Communist International of Youth, keeping in mind that he is a member of the great international army of young proletarians" (*S"ezd V*, p. 376; also p. 137).

196. *S"ezd V*, pp. 15, 307 (the latter for the quotation).   197. *S"ezd IV*, p. 32.
198. *S"ezd V*, p. 16.

CHAPTER IV: ADJUSTMENTS DURING THE STRUGGLE FOR POWER IN THE PARTY

1. Stalin at the Twelfth Party Congress, April 17, 1923, as quoted in *Lenin i Stalin o molodezhi*, p. 269.

2. Including 700,000 full members and 140,000 candidate-members (who were apparently always included in the totals). At the start of the Congress, the figures stated were 630,000 members and 110,000 candidate-members, for a total of 740,000 (*S"ezd VI*, p. 38). But later during the Congress, apparently after reports from all the localities had been checked, the number of full members was given as 700,000 (*ibid.*, p. 299) and the total as 840,000 (*ibid.*, p. 135, also p. 356 for a loosely corroborating figure). The discrepancy in the figures given in subsequent secondary accounts seems to stem from the above situation. See Ostriakov, *20 let VLKSM*, pp. 62 (630,000), 65 (700,000); Panteleev, "VLKSM," *MSE* (2d ed.), Vol. II, col. 549 (700,000); and a note in *S"ezd VI*, p. 28 (702,000). Incidentally, the

version of 1951 says the Leninist levy brought in 240,000 members ("VLKSM," *BSE* [2d ed.], IX, 336).

3. Ostriakov, *20 let VLKSM*, p. 65.   4. *S"ezd VII*, pp. 169–70.

5. *Ibid.*, pp. 7, 28. Whether this included candidate-members was not definitely stated, but the fact that there were only 1,175 voting delegates on a basis supposedly of one per thousand seems to indicate that it did (*ibid.*, p. 7). Chaplin stated that between the Sixth and the Seventh congresses 210,000 persons had left the League, of which 30 percent had left "voluntarily and mechanically" (*ibid.*, pp. 28–29). (See also *ibid.*, p. 170.)

6. The census data for 1926 by age and sex are contained in a table in Lorimer, *Population of the Soviet Union*, pp. 231–32. According to that table there were 29,337,358 youths aged fourteen through twenty-two. The Komsomol membership was about 6 percent of that. But some Komsomolites were beyond the age limit. According to a report of 1928 (see Chapter V), the proportion of overage Komsomolites was 4 percent in 1925 and 16 or 17 percent in 1928. If one assumes a fairly steady increase, the proportion as of 1926 may be estimated at 8 percent. If that were accurate, then the Komsomol would have embraced, instead of 6 percent, about 5.5 percent of all youths of Komsomol age. One must keep in mind, however, both the roughness of this calculation and the fact that the figure of 1,750,000 looks like an estimate in round numbers.

7. *S"ezd VII*, pp. 203–4.

8. According to Lorimer, *Population of the Soviet Union*, pp. 231–32, the males totaled 14,210,365, and the females, 15,126,993, in the ages fourteen through twenty-two. The Komsomol membership, after a deduction of 8 percent for those aged twenty-three and over, would have included about 1,304,000 males and 305,900 females.

9. *S"ezd VI*, p. 12. For some sample references to this commemoration see also *ibid.*, pp. 13–14, 23, 53, 63.

10. *S"ezd VII*, p. 500.

11. July 12–18, 1924. Tiurin, "VLKSM," *BSE* (suppl.), col. 1723, erroneously gives the month as October.

12. See, for example, *S"ezd VI*, pp. 6, 24. There was likewise no proposal to alter the Regulations (*ibid.*, pp. 361–64).

13. *Ibid.*, pp. 5–6. See also pp. 54, 121, and *S"ezd VII*, pp. 29–30.

14. *S"ezd VI*, p. 6, also pp. 7–8. For a remark definitely linking this controversy with Trotsky, see *S"ezd VII*, pp. 29–30. The story of the Party controversy of 1922–24 was not systematically related in its entirety at the Sixth Congress. For one now disapproved Communist version, see Popov, *Outline History*, II, 167–222.

15. For sample exhortations against deviations, see *S"ezd VI*, pp. 8 (Chaplin), 18 (Bukharin), 148–49 (Chaplin).

16. *Ibid.*, pp. 47–48. Zinoviev's major address on "The Fundamental Tasks of the Leninist Komsomol" is in *ibid.*, pp. 23–65.

17. *Ibid.*, pp. 49–50 (quotation said to be from *Stenograficheskii otchet XIII s"ezda RKP[b]*, Izd. "Krasnaia nov'," pp. 157–59).

18. *S"ezd VI*, pp. 52–53 (Zinoviev), 143–44 (Chaplin).

19. The Komsomol CC had also rejected neutralism at the Party Conference in January, 1924, and at the Thirteenth Party Congress in May (*ibid.*, pp.

143–44). This and most of the information given by Chaplin was contained in the report of the Central Committee, which he gave (*ibid.*, pp. 121–50).

20. *Ibid.*, pp. 144–48 (he recounts the defeat of the Opposition).

21. *Ibid.*, pp. 175–77.   22. *Ibid.*, pp. 189–90.   23. *Ibid.*, pp. 349–53.

24. *Ibid.*, p. 360.

25. For persons of other classes this had been required already at the uezd level, and for all classes including workers at the guberniia level. The precise requirements were as follows: (1) For secretaries of guberniia committees: intelligentsia—four years in the League and three in the Party; workers (including "poorest peasants" and farm laborers)—three in the League and one in the Party. (2) For secretaries of uezd committees: intelligentsia—three in the League and two in the Party; workers—one in the League and one in the Party; peasants —two in the League and one in the Party (*S"ezd VI*, p. 362). Exceptions could be made by the CC (*ibid.*, p. 363).

26. *S"ezd VII*, p. 4, also pp. 5–6.

27. For a convenient account of this period in the struggle for power, see Deutscher, *Stalin*, pp. 267–312.

28. *S"ezd VII*, pp. 49–50.

29. *Ibid.*, pp. 50–51. On this question, see also *ibid.*, pp. 68–72, 76–81, 104–6, 109–10, 502–3. Also see the sections later in this chapter on the composition of the League and on rural work.

30. *Ibid.*, pp. 52–53. Chaplin said the "vanguard of the vanguard" theory had been correct when, during World War I, certain youth groups had clung to the Bolshevik line. See Chapter II, in the section on the general role of the Komsomol.

31. *Ibid.*, p. 54.   32. *Ibid.*, pp. 55–56.   33. *Ibid.*, pp. 59–167.

34. *Ibid.*, pp. 59–68.

35. *Ibid.*, pp. 68–74. The controversy referred to here had taken place in April and subsequent months of 1925. Those members of the CC mentioned as being linked with Tarasov's view were Rumiantsev, Fedorov, Sobol', Seredokin, Grigor'ev, Rubina, Minaev, Kolmakov, Glazkov, Katalynov, Trofimov, Teremiakina, and Rogov, plus candidate-members Panov and Likhov. Tarkhanov, who had been named an Honorary Komsomolite at the Sixth Congress, was also mentioned. (Perhaps he had been reassigned to Komsomol work by the Party.)

36. *S"ezd VII*, pp. 74–76, also pp. 68–74.   37. *Ibid.*, pp. 76–81.

38. *Ibid.*, pp. 81–101.   39. *Ibid.*, p. 96 (Ovchinnikov).   40. *Ibid.*, pp. 104–8.

41. *Ibid.*, p. 108.

42. *Ibid.*, pp. 108–11 (Grigor'ev). He said a secret decision concerning the middle peasants had been made in the summer of 1925 by the Opposition.

43. *Ibid.*, pp. 112–14.   44. *Ibid.*, pp. 114–18 (resolution quoted on p. 118).

45. *Ibid.*, p. 122. Matveev also justified the removal of various former officials from the Komsomol CC, saying they had been ousted with good reason. Although the Oppositionists had carefully refrained from blaming the Party explicitly for those removals, Matveev admitted as much in one of the two cases he mentioned by name (*ibid.*, p. 123).

46. *Ibid.*, p. 127.   47. *Ibid.*

48. The speeches by the Opposition, said Saltanov, amounted to their saying, "We're still alive, boys. All of those who are dissatisfied with the policies of the

CC are uniting around us" (S"ezd VII, p. 141). For other anti-Opposition speeches, see ibid., pp. 127–56.

49. Ibid., p. 167.

50. It restated the charges that the Komsomol Opposition had been "entirely solidary with the Party Opposition"; that it had sought to "undermine the Party's guidance in the Komsomol" and to "destroy Bolshevik discipline and centralism in the Komsomol movement"; that it had tried to "use the Komsomol in its struggle against the Leninist unity of the Party"; that it had tried "to pit the younger Communist generation against the old Bolshevik guard"; and that it had committed an "unprecedented" and "impermissible" act in refusing to "recognize as correct the decisions of the Fourteenth Congress of the ACP." Among the "mistakes" of the Opposition it gave prominence to that of "not believing in the possibility of constructing socialism in our country" and "under-estimating the middle peasant" (S"ezd VII, p. 502).

51. S"ezd VII, pp. 506–7.

52. At both congresses, 88 percent were reportedly Party members. At the Sixth Congress over 9 percent, and at the Seventh, 9.1 percent, were reportedly candidate-members (S"ezd VI, p. 301; S"ezd VII, p. 489). At the Sixth Congress only 18 percent of the delegates had attended any previous congress (S"ezd VI, p. 301). No information on this item was given at the Seventh Congress.

53. As of January 1, 1924, it was reported as 9.8 percent; as of May 1, 1924, it was reported as 10.9 percent (S"ezd VI, p. 143; for slightly conflicting reports see also pp. 38, 159). Although Chaplin said the Party kernel should be raised to 25 percent (S"ezd VI, p. 149), the proportion as of March, 1926, was reportedly only 9 percent (S"ezd VII, p. 215). The proportion of Party members and candidate-members in the rural segment of the League was reported to have stood at 4.3 percent on January 1, 1925, and 5.4 percent on December 1, 1925 (S"ezd VII, p. 395).

54. S"ezd VI, p. 9; S"ezd VII, p. 8. A sidelight on the automatic nature of this process was evident in the Sixth Congress, when it was first proposed and duly voted to elect a presidium of forty-three persons. Then, without explana-tion, a list of not forty-three, but forty-five, names was read off and unanimously approved.

55. First Congress—seven (S"ezd I, p. 38); Second Congress—eleven (S"ezd II, p. 12); Third Congress—twelve (S"ezd III, p. 5); Fourth Congress—thirteen (S"ezd IV, p. 32); Fifth Congress—fifteen (S"ezd V, pp. 14–15, 371).

56. At the Sixth Congress there were six abstainers, but they later switched to make the vote unanimous (S"ezd VI, pp. 368–69; S"ezd VII, pp. 510–11). Both congresses continued the practice of electing as "Honorary Komsomolites" certain outstanding leaders who were being transferred to Party work. Honored at the Sixth Congress were Petr Smorodin and Tarkhanov (S"ezd VI, pp. 369–72). Hon-ored at the Seventh Congress was the poet Bezymenskii (S"ezd VII, p. 512).

57. S"ezd VI, pp. 64–65. Zinoviev suggested that some of the deviations present in the Komsomol resulted from a failure to follow that principle (ibid.).

58. Ibid., pp. 368–69.   59. S"ezd VII, pp. 510–11.

60. S"ezd VI, pp. 347–54, 364–68.   61. Ibid., pp. 359–64.

62. S"ezd VII, pp. 499–516 (pp. 499–500 for the divided vote).

63. For one minor exception, see S"ezd VI, pp. 189–90 (rebuke of Belorussian

delegate). There was some fairly substantial criticism on the subject of working youth (*ibid.*, pp. 206–16) and on the League's work in the rural areas (*ibid.*, pp. 234–74), but in neither case did the discussion get very heated.

64. See especially *S"ezd VI*, pp. 269–71.

65. The delegates were not even given an opportunity to discuss his report on "The Political Upbringing of Youth and Leninism." See *S"ezd VI*, pp. 274–98.

66. On peasant youth, see *S"ezd VII*, pp. 48, 68–76, 104–6, 110, 410–31; on worker youth, pp. 87–90, 356–91; on intra-Komsomol democracy, pp. 68–76, 112–14, 127, 135, 506–7.

67. For example, see the discussion on the Pioneers, *S"ezd VII*, pp. 469, 489. See also part of the discussion on peasant youth, *ibid.*, pp. 410–31.

68. On Party guidance, see *S"ezd VII*, pp. 149–51, 186, 188–90, 207–10, 215. (The instrument for this at the lower levels was a Party man "attached" to the cell of the League [*ibid.*, p. 186].) Other examples included guidance from higher Komsomol bodies (*ibid.*, p. 213), attention to minority nationalities (*ibid.*, pp. 146, 148–49, 154–56), and propaganda about the CIY (*ibid.*, pp. 307–19).

69. *S"ezd VII*, pp. 230–58 (on "The Present Moment and the Policy of the Party").

70. *Ibid.*, pp. 373–74, 377, 382–85. Moreover, it appears that some statements of Kamenskii's (about the jurisdiction over the Factory Training Schools) could be interpreted as expressing doubt concerning a decision of the Party.

71. *S"ezd VI*, pp. 13–14. For some examples of the references to Lenin, see *ibid.*, pp. 12, 14–16, 23, 53, 63.

72. *Ibid.*, p. 354.

73. *S"ezd VII*, p. 428. Stalin sent a short greeting to the Congress (*ibid.*, p. 497).

74. *S"ezd VI*, p. 376; *S"ezd VII*, p. 516.   75. *S"ezd VII*, p. 97.

76. *Ibid.*, pp. 111, 130, 143–44, 145, 166–67. It was claimed that others had been removed simply for routine reasons (*ibid.*, pp. 124, 166–67) or had requested it themselves (*ibid.*, pp. 117, 166–67).

77. *Ibid.*, pp. 123, 166–67.

78. *Ibid.*, p. 145. Other cases were passed off with a popular Russian saying: "When they chop wood, the chips fly"—that is, individuals did not matter; the organization did (*ibid.*, p. 130).

79. *Ibid.*, p. 123; see also pp. 188–90 (responsibilities of democracy).

80. *Ibid.*, p. 135; see also p. 178 (on encouraging spontaneity).

81. *Ibid.*, p. 213. An additional indication of this was found in the remarks of one of the leading figures at the Seventh Congress (Mitrofanov), who complained that in some cases the local committee of the Party had appointed poorly qualified people to Komsomol positions of leadership, but did not criticize at all the fact that those people were appointed rather than elected (*ibid.*, p. 399).

82. *S"ezd VI*, pp. 13–16 (Krupskaia), 274–93 (Bukharin); *S"ezd VII*, pp. 17 (Kalinin), 41–43 (Chaplin), 174–75 (Mil'chakov).

83. See *S"ezd VI*, pp. 7–8, 18, 148–49, 151; *S"ezd VII*, pp. 4, 48–50, 97, 118, 122, 502–3, 508–9. Condemning those who sat by tolerantly or indifferently while Marxist and Leninist theory was criticized, Zinoviev declared: "We could not have built the Bolshevik Party with such a spirit of equal rights, with such a mood of justice, with such patience" (*S"ezd VI*, p. 61).

84. *S"ezd VI*, pp. 7–8, 19, 373–76; *S"ezd VII*, pp. 12, 55–56, 62–64, 66–68, 497, 509–10.

85. For a few examples, see *S"ezd VI*, p. 60; *S"ezd VII*, pp. 11, 177, 496, 504.

86. *S"ezd VI*, pp. 58–59, 148–49, 373–76.

87. For some examples, see *S"ezd VI*, pp. 224–25, 286–87; *S"ezd VII*, pp. 178, 258.

88. *S"ezd VI*, pp. 13–14. In line with this principle, there were at the Seventh Congress several admonitions against smoking, drunkenness, hooliganism, and sexual looseness. See *S"ezd VII*, pp. 6, 16–17, 26–29, 40 (also against indiscriminate spitting), 43–45, 177, 214–15, 223, 406–7, 465–66 (swearing, too). Also at the Seventh Congress, neatness, punctuality, and precision were demanded, in keeping with the needs of socialist construction. For two examples, see *S"ezd VII*, pp. 40, 466.

89. *S"ezd VI*, p. 136. Those percentages were given by Chaplin. From a set of percentages given by Zinoviev, and said to apply to July, 1924, it would appear that Chaplin was considering state farm (sovkhoz) workers as "workers." Zinoviev gave the following *occupational* distribution: factory workers, 36.2 percent; state farm workers, 4.8 percent; peasants, 32.7 percent; and others (presumably largely students and office workers), 26.3 percent. The proportions by class of *origin* were: workers, 44.2 percent; peasants, 39.3 percent; office workers (*sluzhashchie*), 9.5 percent; and others, 7 percent (*ibid.*, p. 38).

90. *S"ezd VI*, pp. 7–8.

91. He was considering youths between the ages of fourteen and twenty-four, and he estimated, referring to a census of 1924, that there were 18,000,000 of them (*S"ezd VI*, pp. 38–41). Chaplin later gave the same figure of 240,000 for peasant Komsomolites, adding that they averaged only fourteen Komsomolites per volost (*ibid.*, p. 138; see also p. 223).

92. *S"ezd VI*, pp. 38–42 (Zinoviev); pp. 138–39, 147–48, 186–87 (Chaplin). For other remarks on the theme of more work in the rural areas, see also *ibid.*, pp. 155–57, 161–63, 171–72, 175–77, 179, 234–69.

93. For his report, see *S"ezd VI*, pp. 220–33. Shokhin was merely reviewing, he indicated, material which had been the subject of a preparatory campaign discussed, during the previous half year, at almost all uezd and guberniia conferences (*ibid.*, p. 220).

94. *S"ezd VI*, pp. 221–27. Shokhin warned that there was a widespread tendency for the "best elements of our rural cells" to gravitate toward the cities. The Komsomol must stop this, he said, but not by purely mechanical means.

95. The proportions at the time of the Sixth and Seventh congresses as reported at the latter were as follows: "industrial workers"—from 40.1 percent declined to 36 percent; peasants—from 39.4 percent rose to 46 percent; farm laborers—from 5.9 percent rose to 7.7 percent; "others"—from 14.6 percent declined to 10.3 percent (*S"ezd VII*, pp. 46–47). The discrepancy between the percentages given in *S"ezd VI* and *S"ezd VII* for the time of the Sixth Congress (see note 89) is not explained. As to the percentages given at the Seventh Congress, it is not stated whether they apply to occupation or to class of origin.

96. *S"ezd VII*, p. 395.

97. The approved activities included setting up demonstration farms and agri-

cultural cooperatives (*S"ezd VII*, pp. 255, 401, 403–4), bringing electricity to villages (*ibid.*, p. 401), draining swamps (*ibid.*, pp. 403–4), and drawing more rural youths into the schools that were being established for them (*ibid.*, pp. 40–41).

98. *S"ezd VI*, pp. 240–41.

99. The data presented to the delegates were for January 1, 1925, and December 1, 1925. Within the rural segment of the League, the proportion of middle peasants rose from 24 percent to 28.9 percent during that period. At the same time the proportion of poor peasants dropped from 57.8 percent to 48.7 percent (*S"ezd VII*, p. 395). This question is of course related to the dispute over the "delegates' assemblies of middle-peasant youth," discussed in the first part of this chapter.

100. To take in *all* worker youth; to take in farm-laborer, poor-peasant, and the best middle-peasant youth; and to take in representatives of the intelligentsia with utmost care on an individual basis (*S"ezd VII*, p. 45 [Chaplin], and see also pp. 3, 170–71 [Mil'chakov], 397–98). The Seventh Congress exempted from the probationary stage those students under eighteen who were of worker, peasant, or handicraftsman parentage, and who were not exploiting anyone's labor (*ibid.*, pp. 499–500). Chaplin explained that "the best middle peasant is the one . . . who strives to help the Party, the League, and the Soviet government in all . . . measures" (*ibid.*, p. 47).

101. The proportion of Party members or candidate-members in the rural segment of the League had been increased during the first eleven months of 1925 from 4.3 percent to 5.4 percent, but that was still considered much too low (*S"ezd VII*, pp. 395, 398–99).

102. *S"ezd VII*, pp. 398–99.

103. *Ibid.*, pp. 430–31. While it was not definitely so stated, this figure seemed quite clearly to relate to concurrent members of the League and the Party, since 47,000 is a little over 5 percent of 900,000.

104. This had already been done to some extent, the average size having been increased from sixteen or seventeen members to twenty-one or twenty-two members during the interval between the congresses (*S"ezd VII*, pp. 407–8). While a still further increase was urged, it was pointed out that administrative difficulties would impose some sort of limit. For instance, 100 members was thought to be too many in one cell (*ibid.*, p. 430).

105. *S"ezd VII*, pp. 399–400. Mitrofanov here cited an instance in which the Party volost (small district) committee had appointed a fifty-five-year-old Party man as secretary of the Komsomol volost committee.

106. *Ibid.*, p. 397.   107. *Ibid.*, pp. 184–85, 425.

108. *Ibid.*, pp. 184–85, 198, 221–22, 415.

109. *S"ezd VI*, pp. 141–42 (referring not only to peasant youths but youths in general).

110. *Ibid.*, p. 236.   111. *Ibid.*, p. 261.   112. *Ibid.*, p. 263.

113. Their proper function remained that of conducting what was termed serious and scientifically based antireligious propaganda (*S"ezd VII*, pp. 406–7). On religion, see also *ibid.*, p. 211.

114. In one place the percentages given are 40.1 percent (Sixth Congress) and 36

percent (Seventh Congress) (*S"ezd VII*, pp. 46–47). That was Chaplin reporting. Later Mil'chakov gave figures of 39 percent (Sixth Congress) and 36.5 percent (Seventh Congress) (*ibid.*, pp. 169–70).

115. *S"ezd VII*, p. 46; see also p. 4. Chaplin presented figures indicating that the Komsomol embraced a larger proportion of those youths working in small enterprises than those in large ones (*ibid.*, p. 46). He urged more emphasis on the latter.

116. *S"ezd VI*, p. 300.

117. *S"ezd VII*, p. 489. For further details see Appendix C. Also see earlier in this chapter for the warning that proletarian guidance in the League required firm Party guidance (*ibid.*, p. 172).

118. *S"ezd VI*, pp. 20, 125–27, 191–96; *S"ezd VII*, pp. 26–29, 32–35, 328–31, 341–45. Concerning such attendant troubles as hooliganism, drunkenness, despair, and "apolitical" attitudes, see *S"ezd VII*, pp. 6, 26–29, 254.

119. *S"ezd VI*, pp. 127–28.

120. *Ibid.*, pp. 191–93, 197–200 (also developing adequate laws).

121. *Ibid.*, pp. 128–29, 193–94, 205–6.

122. Their current enrollment was 65,000 as compared with 48,000 at the time of the Fifth Congress (1922) (*S"ezd VI*, p. 128). Of the 65,000, about 70 percent were said to be Komsomol members, compared with only 30 percent of the total at the time of the Fifth Congress (*ibid.*, p. 130). Somewhat different figures, but of the same order of magnitude, were given later on the Factory Training Schools: January 1, 1921—43 schools with 2,000 pupils; August 1, 1922—657 schools with 44,933 pupils; January 1, 1924—924 schools with 68,819 pupils (*ibid.*, pp. 193–94). The League was said to be making a special effort to prepare Communist teachers for those schools (*ibid.*, p. 129). Between the congresses of 1924 and 1926, there evidently was a controversy over whether the Factory Training Schools should continue to be run by the Commissariat of Education or whether they should be turned over to the Supreme Economic Council. The Komsomol was said to have favored retaining the status quo—which was the position decided upon by the CC of the Party (*S"ezd VII*, pp. 348–49, 369–72). In 1926, incidentally, Factory Training Schools were said to be approaching their fifth anniversary, which would appear to place their start in the late spring or the summer of 1921 (*ibid.*, pp. 348–49).

123. *S"ezd VII*, pp. 32–35, 345.

124. *Ibid.*, pp. 5, 10, 27–28, 30–31, 504, 512–16 (for some examples).

125. *Ibid.*, pp. 11, 29, 30–31, 87–90, 331, 332–34, 336–37, 512–16. The delegates discussed ways of teaching skills less complicated than those taught in the Factory Training Schools. The means included "brigade apprenticeship," individual apprenticeship, and evening schools. Only the last means was fully endorsed, the others being considered stopgaps. The League was said to be resisting the idea of unpaid or poorly paid apprenticeships (*ibid.*, pp. 339–41, 351–53).

126. *S"ezd VII*, pp. 341–45, 365–66, 390. See also *S"ezd VI*, pp. 208–9.

127. *S"ezd VII*, p. 212; see also p. 30.

128. *Ibid.*, pp. 32–35, 345, 353–55 (industry, schools, trade unions). They must combat demands for "leveling," or reducing wage differentials (*ibid.*, pp. 49–50, 94–96). They must counteract the impression, held by some citizens, that the workers were being exploited (*ibid.*, pp. 28–29, 49–50).

129. The familiar argument over whether or not to abolish the regular secondary schools was resumed on a small scale at the Sixth Congress (1924), this time with special reference to the rural schools, but no action was taken. Shokhin advocated special schools for peasant youth, combining regular school instruction with productive work in the fields (*S"ezd VI*, pp. 229–32). Pokrovskii, of the Commissariat of Education, backed those who supported the regular secondary schools. For the contributions to the debate, see *ibid.*, pp. 229, 258–60, 265–71.

130. *S"ezd VII*, p. 38.   131. *S"ezd VI*, p. 300.   132. *Ibid.*, pp. 131–32.

133. *Ibid.*, p. 146.   134. *S"ezd VII*, p. 205.   135. *Ibid.*, pp. 499–500.

136. *Ibid.*, p. 18.

137. *Ibid.*, pp. 38–39; Ostriakov, *20 let VLKSM*, p. 63. See also the articles published in connection with the fifteenth anniversary of the paper, in *KP*, May 24, 1940. *Komsomol'skaia pravda* was a daily as of 1928 (the date of the earliest copies in the U.S.), and the writer believes it was a daily from its start.

138. *S"ezd VI*, p. 22; *S"ezd VII*, pp. 26–29, 463–64 (gives a figure of 300,000 waifs [*besprizornye*] as of 1926).

139. *S"ezd VI*, pp. 38 (200,000 on May 1, 1924), 133 (200,000 as of July), 333 (250,000 as of July); *S"ezd VII*, pp. 43–45, 455 (both saying 200,000 for July, 1924).

140. *S"ezd VII*, p. 455.

141. *Ibid.*, pp. 4, 43–45, 455. Some shift in the Pioneers' composition apparently had occurred in the meantime. At the time of the Congress of 1924, over four-fifths of the Pioneers were in urban centers (*S"ezd VI*, p. 338). This was apparently the result of a desire to ensure the organization a proletarian flavor (*ibid.*, p. 134). The ensuing expansion, however, penetrated rural areas as well, so that by 1926 almost two-thirds (63.6 percent) of the Pioneer detachments were in rural communities (*S"ezd VII*, p. 456). Rural detachments, however, were probably smaller than urban ones, so it would not be safe to infer that the rural membership was anywhere near two-thirds of the total.

142. *S"ezd VI*, p. 338. Of these, 3,000,000 were thought to be urban.

143. *Ibid.*, p. 341.

144. *S"ezd VII*, pp. 457–62. During the last six months of 1925 the Pioneers had lost almost one-third (31 percent) as many as they had taken in (*ibid.*, pp. 456–57). In the absence of attractive Pioneer activities, it was said, children were organizing into small gangs for such purposes as pigeon-collecting, petty thievery, and sexual experimentation (*ibid.*, p. 460).

145. *S"ezd VII*, pp. 466–67; also *S"ezd VI*, pp. 336–37. An unconscious demonstration of one of the reasons was to be found in the official report on the children's movement at the Sixth Congress. The report complained that in tsarist times, children had wasted 33 percent of their time in "absolute idleness." The report went on to lay out a time chart for Pioneers, beginning with 35 percent for sleep, 22 percent for social-political work, 15 percent in the Pioneer detachment, and 18 percent in school. That left 10 percent unaccounted for, which presumably would be devoted to the other things mentioned as desirable in the future: physical development, "sensible games," labor education, and schoolwork (*S"ezd VI*, pp. 334–35).

146. *S"ezd VI*, pp. 135, 164–65, 339 (the last two citations give figures on Pioneer leaders). In 1926 the problem of inadequate personnel apparently re-

mained, and there was special concern over poor health and overwork among Pioneer leaders (*S"ezd VII*, pp. 469–89 *passim*).

147. *S"ezd VII*, pp. 469–72.   148. *Ibid.*, p. 463.

149. *S"ezd VI*, p. 135; *S"ezd VII*, p. 486. The official formula given in the latter citation is that the Pioneer organization is *"a mass Communist organization, belonging to the Party and the Komsomol, and under the direct guidance of the Party and the Komsomol."*

There was a proposal to call the members Young Leninists instead of Young Pioneers. At first glance the outsider would be puzzled to conceive of any safe way in which a Komsomol delegate could argue against using the name of the departed leader. One delegate did, however, on the basis that much study was required before one could really become a Leninist. That point of view was carried, although by a divided vote (*S"ezd VI*, pp. 361–62).

150. *S"ezd VII*, pp. 43–45, 455, 468. (Panteleev, "VLKSM," *MSE* [2d ed.], Vol. II, col. 550, says the Octobrists already numbered 100,325 in 1925.)

151. At the Congress of 1924 it was noted with satisfaction that organizations of young Mensheviks in Georgia and the Far East, and young Socialist Revolutionaries in the Far East, had finally "liquidated themselves" (*S"ezd VI*, pp. 122–23).

152. *S"ezd IV*, pp. 353–54; *S"ezd V*, p. 346.   153. *S"ezd VI*, p. 165.

154. *S"ezd VII*, p. 193.

155. One was a Zionist organization for children, which was in direct competition with the Komsomol-led Pioneers. There were also said to be various petit-bourgeois children's groups formed on the basis of social position (*S"ezd VII*, p. 461). Then, too, there were nature-study and other special-interest groups or clubs (*ibid.*, pp. 176, 461, 479).

156. *S"ezd VI*, pp. 36–37 (Zinoviev). When gaining control in local youth clubs, Komsomolites were instructed to refrain from a domineering manner which would only drive people away (*S"ezd VII*, p. 176). They were also cautioned in general against being rude to those who were not members of the Party or the Komsomol (*S"ezd VII*, pp. 256–57).

157. *S"ezd VI*, p. 137; *S"ezd VII*, pp. 180–81, 203–4. Panteleev states that by 1927 the percent had risen to 21.3 (Panteleev, "VLKSM," *MSE* [2d ed.], Vol. II, col. 548).

158. *S"ezd VII*, p. 395. In the rural segment of the League's membership, women were reported to have constituted only 12.3 percent as of January 1, 1925, and only 15.3 percent as of December 1, 1925. These proportions are somewhat lower than those given for women in the League as a whole, for which see earlier in this chapter.

159. *S"ezd VI*, p. 299; *S"ezd VII*, p. 489.

160. *S"ezd VII*, pp. 180–81, 203–4, 400. One young female delegate—the only one on the Presidium of sixty-three persons elected in 1926—complained that she had not been given any real work and had only been elected as a representative of the women (*ibid.*, pp. 203–4).

161. *S"ezd VI*, p. 136. At the same time, however, the Congress rejected once more the idea of raising the minimum age limit to sixteen (*ibid.*, pp. 359–60).

162. *Ibid.*, pp. 55–56, 140; *S"ezd VII*, pp. 146, 148–49, 154–56, 200, 409, 427.

163. *S"ezd VI*, p. 139.

164. For the main groups named above, the proportions in the population at large as of 1926 were as follows: Russians, 52.91 percent; Ukrainians, 21.22 percent; Jews, 1.82 percent; Georgians, 1.24 percent; Armenians, 1.07 percent (Lorimer, *Population of the Soviet Union*, p. 51).

165. *S"ezd VII* [*sic*], p. 490.   166. *S"ezd VI*, pp. 137–40, 144.

167. *S"ezd VII*, p. 490. For further details see Appendix G.

168. *Ibid.*, pp. 183–84.   169. *Ibid.*

170. *Ibid.*, pp. 146, 152–54. An indication of the need for better indoctrination was seen in the fact that in recent elections for rural soviets there had been cases in which the local Komsomolites had campaigned against candidates nominated by the Party (*ibid.*, p. 427). Another complaint was that in Uzbekistan, Komsomol membership cards had been sold to all comers at whatever price the market would bear (*ibid.*, pp. 409, 430, 431).

171. *Ibid.*, p. 39. Two other speakers briefly seconded Chaplin's appeal for more Komsomol activity in this field (*ibid.*, pp. 182, 217–19).

172. *Ibid.*, pp. 36–37. Roughly comparable figures are given by Mitrofanov (*ibid.*, pp. 402, 413). It was stated that in the Ukraine one-third (33 percent) of those under twenty-three years of age serving on village soviets did not belong to either the Komsomol or the Party (*ibid.*, p. 191).

173. In the Ukraine this was only 43 percent of the youths under twenty-three serving in town soviets (*ibid.*, pp. 36, 191).

174. *Ibid.*, p. 254.   175. *S"ezd VI*, p. 306.

176. *S"ezd VII*, pp. 151–52, 496–97. At the Sixth Congress it was reported that there were 29,731 Komsomolites serving in both the Army and the Navy, but the number in each was not given (*S"ezd VI*, p. 38). Despite the youth of the Komsomol delegates to the Sixth Congress, and the fact that twenty-one or twenty-two was the normal draft age at that time (*ibid.*, pp. 305, 307), fully 45 percent of the delegates had already served in the Red Army (*ibid.*, p. 302).

The general tasks of Komsomolites in the Army remained about the same: Komsomolites were to promote iron discipline (*S"ezd VI*, p. 55; *S"ezd VII*, p. 496). They were to provide political directors (*politruki*) to indoctrinate the peasant recruits, who, it was said, were illiterate, religious, and politically ignorant (*S"ezd VI*, pp. 315–18). In connection with preparing youths before they got into the Army, the Komsomol was urged to give preparatory training in discipline (*S"ezd VII*, p. 444), to teach all Komsomolites some concrete skill such as marksmanship (*S"ezd VII*, pp. 157–58), and otherwise to stimulate their interest and get them ready (*S"ezd VI*, pp. 263–64, 319; *S"ezd VII*, pp. 182–83).

The continuing intent to use the Army aggressively was indicated (in 1926) by Baranov, of the Revolutionary War Council: "The Worker-Peasant Red Army is the armed element of the vanguard of world revolution. . . . We need the Red Army, of course, first of all and mainly in order to defend and safeguard the borders of our Soviet Union from hostile attack. But we also need the Red Army in order that the working class of Western Europe, the working class and the toilers of the whole world, will know that there is on this globe an armed force upon which all oppressed toilers can rely" (*S"ezd VII*, p. 443). See also Voroshilov's speech on the need for strong armed forces (*ibid.*, pp. 493–95).

177. *S"ezd VI*, p. 55 (see also pp. 317–18, 324). The functions of the groups were not described, except in general terms of assisting the Party.

178. One reason for this apprehension might be seen in the report, given at the Congress of 1924, that, in the Army, Komsomolites outnumbered Party members by a ratio of seventy to thirty (S"ezd VI, p. 316).

179. S"ezd VII, pp. 182–83.   180. Ibid., pp. 151–52, 182–83, 220–21.

181. S"ezd VI, pp. 320–22.   182. Ibid., p. 21.   183. Ibid., pp. 21, 322.

184. Ibid., pp. 322–27.

185. Ibid., pp. 328–29, 367–68 (Obshchestvo druzei morskogo flota).

186. Ibid., p. 329.

187. S"ezd VII, pp. 182–83, 217–19, 433–38, 441, 445–50 (more funds for naval aircraft), 496. Outside of the air arm of the Navy, aviation as such was barely mentioned (ibid., pp. 332–33, 439).

It was also noted in 1926 that the Military Scientific Societies (Voenno-nauchnye obshchestva or VNO), which had already functioned within the armed forces for five years, were expanding their operations so as to conduct military propaganda in Komsomol clubs and other groups (ibid., pp. 23–24).

188. S"ezd VI, p. 76, and also pp. 8, 347–48 (resolution on the CIY). On the growth in membership, see ibid., pp. 89–91.

189. Ibid., p. 86. For the dutiful speeches of foreign representatives of the CIY, see ibid., pp. 66–69.

190. Ibid., pp. 76–102, and especially pp. 77–78, 85–88, 94–97.

191. Ibid., pp. 77–78, 87–88, 91 (operating illegally in seventeen countries), 99, 102.

192. Ibid., pp. 77–78, 88–89.

193. Ibid., pp. 78–85. In 1923 there had reportedly been in the Red Navy "a desire to go to the help of the German workers" (ibid., p. 324).

194. Ibid., p. 102.   195. Ibid., p. 70.   196. S"ezd VII, p. 324.

197. There were said to be others who found the period of "partial demands" too humdrum (ibid., pp. 246–47, 263–69 [German YCL, up to 70,000 or 80,000 in 1923, now down to 20,000]).

198. Ibid., pp. 270–71. From a low of 102,000, it was now up to 110,000. A distribution is given by countries.

199. Ibid., pp. 271–93.

200. Ibid., p. 242.   201. Ibid., pp. 305–19.   202. Ibid., pp. 13–15, 19–22.

203. Ibid., pp. 57, 504–6, 508. However, there were two protests against the showing of so many foreign moving pictures in the USSR (ibid., pp. 421, 459).

CHAPTER V: ADJUSTMENTS DURING THE EMERGENCE OF STALIN AND THE RENEWED DRIVE FOR SOCIALISM

1. S"ezd VIII, pp. 1–2; S"ezd IX, pp. 3, 32. At one point during the Eighth Congress, Kosarev referred to a "two-year period" between then and the expected date of the following congress. That appears to be the first admission at a congress that they were not to be held yearly (even though they had not been since 1922). Kosarev did not refer to the violation of the Regulations (S"ezd VIII, p. 219).

2. S"ezd VIII, p. 546. Speakers referred to it casually as two million (ibid., pp. 1, 456–58).

3. S"ezd IX, p. 405.

4. *Ibid.*, pp. 20, 22–23, 49–51. The number of cells was not reported at the Ninth Congress, but at the time of the Eighth, it was given as 67,698 (*S"ezd VIII*, p. 519; see also pp. 456–58 for a roughly corroborating figure of 50,000 in a casual reference). This would have meant an average size of about twenty-nine members per cell.

5. *S"ezd VIII*, p. 2.   6. *Ibid.*, pp. 21–26.

7. *Ibid.*, pp. 2–3 (Chaplin), 152 (Krupskaia), 216–18 (Kosarev), 247–49, 280 (Chaplin), 416.

8. *Ibid.*, pp. 535–36. Stalin, like other speakers before him, referred to the Shakhtinskii affair of March, 1928, which involved alleged sabotage by specialists in the coal mines of the Donets Basin.

9. *Ibid.*, pp. 535–38.

10. *Ibid.*, pp. 3 (Chaplin), 15 (Bukharin), 80–81 (Mislavskii), 443–46 (Kalinin).

11. *Ibid.*, p. 81.

12. *Ibid.*, pp. 197–98 (Mil'chakov), 218–19 (Kosarev), 537–38 (Stalin).

13. For a convenient account of the political maneuvers of this period, see Deutscher, *Stalin*, pp. 294–344.

14. *S"ezd VIII*, p. 6. The others, in sequence, were Bukharin, Molotov, Rykov, Tomsky, Kuibyshev, Kalinin, Voroshilov, Rudzutak, Ordzhonikidze, and Krupskaia. In the last similar list (at the Congress of 1924), Stalin's name had followed Zinoviev's (*S"ezd VI*, p. 354).

15. *S"ezd VIII*, pp. 535, 540.

16. For what appear to be virtually the only examples, see *ibid.*, pp. 6, 71–72, 514, and his speech, pp. 535–40.

17. *Ibid.*, p. 554.   18. *S"ezd IX*, p. 4.

19. *Ibid.* The others in the Honorary Presidium were the whole Politburo, plus Thälmann (a German Communist), Menzhinskii, and the secretary of the Chinese YCL.

20. *Ibid.*, pp. 21–22. For the rest of Kaganovich's report "On the International and Domestic Situation and the Tasks of the Komsomol," see *ibid.*, pp. 5–23. Kaganovich recalled Stalin's declaration at the Sixteenth Party Congress (June 26–July 13, 1930) that they were entering the period of socialism (*ibid.*, p. 6).

21. *Ibid.*, pp. 25–26, 87–88, 132, 409–11.

22. The writer does not pretend his count is absolutely complete but believes it is substantially accurate. The number of speeches and resolutions was at least 220. (A higher figure could be obtained by counting some of the shorter statements.) Those in which the writer recorded noteworthy references to Stalin are as follows: *S"ezd IX*, pp. 4, 5–23, 25, 26–31, 32–61 (especially 35, 37–38, 41), 62–70 (especially 63, 66, 68–69), 87–88, 112–13, 132, 169–70, 200–2, 208–11, 409–11, 422. It seems also noteworthy that in some of those perorations where later his name would have figured prominently, at this time it did not (for example, *ibid.*, pp. 61–62, 407–8).

23. *S"ezd IX*, p. 36 (Kosarev). The Rightists were also accused of favoring conciliation of the bourgeoisie, as opposed to the Bolshevik principle of "either they'll get us, or we'll get them" (*ibid.*, p. 37).

24. *Ibid.*, pp. 36–37. As further "proof" of the errors of Trotsky, Kosarev said Trotsky doubted that the current depression would bring the downfall of capitalism (*ibid.*, pp. 37–38).

25. *Ibid.*, pp. 39–40. See also *ibid.*, p. 22, for Kaganovich on "Leftists." Follow-

ing the example set by Kosarev, Kaganovich, and others, the Ninth Congress frequently gave the deviationists the lash. See *ibid.*, pp. 3 (Kosarev), 20–22 (Kaganovich), 36–42 and 49–50 (Kosarev), 65–70 (Dzhavakhidze), 78–81, 112–13, 131–32, 139–40, 147, 167–68, 198, 222–37, 293–95, 411–14.

26. *S"ezd VIII*, pp. 15 (Bukharin), 70 (Chaplin), 79 (Mislavskii), 196–97 (Mil'chakov), and 304.

27. *Ibid.*, pp. 549–53 (also honoring Sergei Sobolev).

28. Others named prominently are listed as follows: *S"ezd IX*, pp. 22 (Shatskin, Lominadze, Sten, Syrtsov), 38 (Shatskin, Chaplin, Lominadze, Syrtsov), 40 (Minaev, Butyrkin, Tovstukha, Kostrov), 41–42 (Dubrovin, Shatskin, Sten), 49 (Ostriakov), 79 (Shatskin, Sten), 132 (Sten, Shatskin, Lominadze), 139–40 ([Efim] Tseitlin, Shatskin), 147 (Syrtsov, Lominadze, Chaplin, Shatskin), 403 (Shatskin, Chaplin, Efim Tseitlin).

29. *S"ezd IX*, pp. 22 (Kaganovich), 132. Named with Shatskin in this connection were Lominadze, Sten, and Syrtsov. Mil'chakov, who had up to this time the longest record of continuous service on the Komsomol CC (having been elected to the CC's of 1921, 1922, 1924, 1926, and 1928), was *not* mentioned in this or any other connection at the Congress of 1931 or later. The writer has learned from a refugee friend, however, that in 1940 Mil'chakov was a prisoner in a concentration camp at Noril'sk.

30. *S"ezd IX*, pp. 38–42 (Kosarev).

31. *Ibid.*, pp. 49–50. Concerning other deviations, see later in this chapter.

32. *Ibid.*, p. 38.

33. *Ibid.*, p. 403 (Efim Tseitlin, an Honorary Komsomolite since 1922, was also specifically demoted).

34. *S"ezd VIII*, pp. 39–40, 73–74, 166–67, 249–51. For instance, one member of the Central Committee (Kurnikov), while pleading for more "self-standingness" in Komsomol work, said that the Party must point out youth's mistakes promptly. As a horrible example of what could happen without proper Party guidance, he cited a case in which, at an enterprise in the Urals, the Party cell had secretly decided on a policy to be put through at the next general meeting of the workers. The trouble was that the Party cell did not notify the Komsomolites before the meeting, with the result that at the meeting the Komsomolites argued for the wrong side of the question! (*ibid.*, pp. 250–51).

35. *Ibid.*, pp. 15 and 39–40 (Bukharin), 73–74 (Chaplin), and, for other speakers, 108–11, 131, 166–67, 169–72, 250–51; *S"ezd IX*, pp. 3–4, 32, 49–50, 54, 81, 112–13, 295, 407–11.

36. *S"ezd IX*, p. 50. The absolute figures for Komsomolites concurrently in the Party were 183,000 and 237,000 for 1928 and 1931, respectively. Kosarev spoke in absolute terms and did not give percentages, perhaps because he wished to avoid commenting on the decline.

37. *S"ezd VIII*, p. 547.   38. *S"ezd IX*, p. 405.

39. *S"ezd VIII*, pp. 548–49, 554–55. Out of the ninety-one members of the new CC, seventy were said to be workers by origin (including nine "from the bench" —that is, presumably, workers by *occupation* as distinct from birth), while one was a farm laborer, five were peasants, and fifteen were office workers by origin. Of the twenty-nine candidate-members, nineteen were workers (including three "from the bench"), five were farm laborers, one was a peasant, and four were office workers (*ibid.*, pp. 548–49).

40. *Ibid.*, p. 42.

41. *Ibid.*, pp. 75–76. The funds named included the fund for patronage of the Navy, the contribution to the CIY, the support to children's homes, especially that of the GPU, and the organizing of the All-Union *Subbotnik* or unpaid workday.

42. *S"ezd IX*, pp. 401–2. The new Regulations were not given in full in the stenographic report.

43. *S"ezd VIII*, p. 82.   44. *Ibid.*, p. 599.   45. *Ibid.*, p. 600.

46. See, for example, *ibid.*, pp. 83–268, discussion of the reports of Bukharin, Chaplin, and Mislavskii. For examples of generally "businesslike" discussion, see that on the CIY (*ibid.*, pp. 302–43) and that on the work with younger children (*ibid.*, pp. 501–33). For examples of irreverent interruptions of Chaplin from the floor, see *ibid.*, pp. 271–80.

47. *Ibid.*, pp. 222–25.   48. *Ibid.*, pp. 269–72 (quotation on p. 271).

49. By Khodorovskii, representing the Commissariat of Education (*ibid.*, pp. 430–31). Egorov, the critic and a member of the outgoing CC, was not elected to the new CC (*ibid.*, pp. 554–55).

50. See especially *ibid.*, pp. 225–31, 470–74, for Gastev's own speeches. For some other interesting examples of heckling, see *ibid.*, pp. 172, 183–85, 274–75.

51. *Ibid.*, pp. 541–45.   52. *Ibid.*, pp. 541–42 (concerning the CIY).

53. *Ibid.*, pp. 4–6 (for the Presidium and other bodies to run the Congress), 548–49, 555 (for the new Central Committee and Inspection Commission). The Presidium was again large (seventy persons) but the other managerial bodies of the Congress (Secretariat, Editorial Commission, and Credentials [Mandates] Commission) were of a size suited to actual operation (thirteen, twelve, and twelve, respectively). The new CC had ninety-one members and twenty-nine candidate-members, while the Inspection Commission had nine members.

54. See the discussion of the report of the CC, *S"ezd IX*, pp. 78–220, especially, for example, pp. 78–86, 89–90, 93, 110–12, 135–38, 144–45, 147, 155–56, 161–63, 167, 171, 173–75, 185–86, 194–95.

55. *Ibid.*, pp. 100–2. For examples of similar cases, see *ibid.*, pp. 83–84 (oil in Transcaucasus), 90–92 (Kuznetsk Basin), 123–24 (gold, etc., in eastern Siberia).

56. *Ibid.*, p. 208.

57. *Ibid.*, pp. 238–81 (on the CIY), 303–46 (rural work), and 370–87 (work with children).

58. *Ibid.*, pp. 401–5 (how to select "conflict commissions").

59. *Ibid.*, pp. 4–5, 406, and for the lists, pp. 439–40.

60. *Ibid.*, pp. 407–8 (in his closing address). Here, as elsewhere, the italics (or their equivalent) are in the original unless otherwise stated.

61. Including nonvoting delegates, the proportion over twenty-three stood at 53.7 percent (*S"ezd VIII*, p. 547).

62. *S"ezd IX*, p. 405.   63. *S"ezd VIII*, p. 547.

64. *S"ezd IX*, p. 405. In a description of the administrative staff of the Central Committee given at the Ninth Congress, it was disclosed that about two-thirds of the eighty people on the staff were twenty-five or older. The age distribution was given as follows: thirty to fifty years, 6.7 percent; twenty-five to thirty years, 59.5 percent; under twenty-five, 33.8 per cent. This composition was criticized as being too old (*ibid.*, p. 76).

65. For the various lists of Central Committees, see *S"ezd I*, pp. 90–91; *S"ezd*

II, pp. 117–18; *S"ezd III*, pp. 235, 305; *S"ezd IV*, p. 364; *S"ezd V*, p. 328; *S"ezd VI*, pp. 368–69; *S"ezd VII*, p. 511; *S"ezd VIII*, pp. 554–55; *S"ezd IX*, pp. 439–40; *S"ezd X*, Vol. II, pp. 449–51. (In references to *S"ezd X*, to avoid confusion, the abbreviations "Vol." and "p." will be used.)

66. *S"ezd IX*, p. 76. The turnover was 126 percent from the Eighth Congress (May, 1928) to January 1, 1930, and 80 percent from January 1, 1930 to January 1, 1931. Other data given indicate the social origin of the CC staff: As of the Eighth Congress, 17 percent workmen, 81.2 percent office workers, and 1.8 percent peasants; as of January 1, 1930, the workmen stood at 43.4 percent; and as of January 1, 1931, the workmen were 38 per cent, the office workers 9 percent, and the peasants 39 percent. As to Party status at the time of the Eighth Congress and the Ninth Congress, respectively, the situation was: Party members and candidates, 76.1 per cent and 76.5 percent; Komsomol members, 12.4 percent and 10 percent; non-Party, 11.5 percent and 13 percent (mostly messengers, typists, and technicians). As to type of work: "responsible workers," 74.3 percent and 63.5 percent; "technical workers," 25.7 percent and 36.5 percent. The turnover was higher among the "responsible workers," it was reported, than among the technical personnel. In addition to the 80 workers on the paid staff as of January 1, 1931, there were reported to be between 300 and 350 persons in an unpaid *aktiv*, composed largely of students and office workers (*ibid.*, pp. 74–77).

67. *Ibid.*, p. 405. Attendance at three or more congresses was not given.

68. The Eighth and the Ninth congresses may be slightly less reliable as such a criterion than any previous congresses because of the desire, mentioned earlier, to bring in more "workers from the bench."

69. *S"ezd VIII*, pp. 81–82. The secretary of a volost committee of the Komsomol, he said, was paid, on the average, only 32 rubles (the pay period was not stated), while the corresponding Party official (i.e., *volkom* secretary) averaged 60 rubles. In a factory cell of the Komsomol, the secretary was paid, on the average, 47 rubles, while the secretary of the Party cell got 97 rubles. Mislavskii did not argue that the pay of the Komsomol officials should be brought up to that of the Party officials, but that it should be raised somewhat. The women's Party organizer in the volost was paid 45 rubles, he said, and he argued that the volost secretary of the Komsomol was entitled to that much.

70. *S"ezd VIII*, pp. 72–73 (Chaplin). Another approach by the Eighth Congress to the problem of leadership was a resolution which, in order to improve the connections between higher and lower echelons, required all Komsomol officials (*rukovodiashchie rabotniki* or "guiding workers") to spend at least half of their time working in cells or other lower-echelon bodies and checking up on the fulfillment of instructions (*ibid.*, p. 562). The writer has no evidence indicating to what extent this seemingly extreme demand was enforced, if at all.

71. *S"ezd IX*, pp. 215–16.

72. *S"ezd VIII*, pp. 546–47 (other figures of 1928: peasants, 11 percent; "others," 18 percent).

73. *S"ezd IX*, p. 405. At this time another figure of 75.5 percent was given as the proportion of "workers" among the delegates to the previous (Eighth) Congress. The difference was not explained. Comparative figures on social origin given for the Eighth and Ninth congresses at the Ninth Congress follow:

workers—75.5 percent (Eighth Congress), 82.2 percent (Ninth Congress); peasants —12.5 percent (Eighth) and 3.3 percent (Ninth); collective farmers—none (Eighth) and 8.3 percent (Ninth); office workers—12 percent (Eighth), 6 percent (Ninth).

74. *S"ezd VIII*, pp. 546–47. The absolute numbers involved here are 656 for the total, and 456, 132, 20, and 5, for the groups named. In regard to a similar concern to bring "workers from the bench" into the CC, see earlier in this chapter.

75. Military personnel were 6.6 percent, students in technical and higher education institutions were 1 percent, and village librarians, rural teachers, and trade-union and cooperative workers were each represented in lesser numbers (*S"ezd IX*, p. 405).

76. *S"ezd IX*, pp. 50, 146 (absolute numbers in 1931: workingmen, 1,010,000; farm laborers, 395,000). These percentages are not necessarily comparable directly with the 36 percent given for 1926, since the precise categories included may not be the same.

77. *S"ezd VIII*, pp. 83–84.   78. *Ibid.*, pp. 70 (Chaplin), 197 (Mil'chakov).

79. *Ibid.*, pp. 84–86, 90–91, 180–83, 200–2, 447–48, 451–52, 546, and also the case of the supposedly neglected woman delegate, Stepanova, pp. 231–34, 548; *S"ezd IX*, pp. 54, 405.

80. The number was 64 out of 656 (*S"ezd VIII*, p. 546).   81. *S"ezd IX*, p. 405.

82. For some examples, see *S"ezd VIII*, pp. 3, 18–20, 24–26, 37, 71, 443–44, 496–98; *S"ezd IX*, pp. 20–21, 41–42, 49, 54, 70, 81, 147–48, 210–11 (intensify the struggle against religion), 217, 297–99, 356, 397, 407–8.

83. *S"ezd VIII*, pp. 24–26.

84. *Ibid.*, pp. 72 (Chaplin), 172, 197 (Mil'chakov), 451–52, also p. 561 (resolution).

85. *S"ezd IX*, p. 20; see also pp. 87–88 and 168 for echoes of this from delegates. Entrance into the "period of socialism" called for references to the goals, socialism and communism, but these were mentioned just as vaguely as before. For some examples, see *S"ezd VIII*, pp. 29–31 (Bukharin); *S"ezd IX*, pp. 53–54 (Kosarev), 61 (Kosarev), 356 (Sever'ianova). The comment of Kaplun, mentioned later in this chapter, cannot be considered authoritative (*S"ezd VIII*, pp. 478–79).

86. For some examples, see *S"ezd VIII*, pp. 45–47, 73–74, 111–17, 166–67, 249–51, 537; *S"ezd IX*, pp. 51–52, 54, 215–17, 364, 421–23.

87. *S"ezd VIII*, pp. 2–3 (Chaplin), 18–20 (Bukharin), 43 (Chaplin), 347, 535 (Stalin), 561, 567.

88. *Ibid.*, p. 43. As an example of what could be achieved by shock groups, Chaplin cited an "All-Union Communist *Subbotnik*," or extra unpaid workday, arranged by the Komsomol in 1927 on the eve of the tenth anniversary of the October Revolution. The special purpose of that event had been to help the homeless waifs, and it had embraced hundreds of thousands of volunteers, he reported. Such activities must be tied to some concrete task in a factory, school, or club, he insisted (*ibid.*; see also pp. 575–76). In the Komsomol history of 1951, the first "young people's shock brigade" is said to have been formed in September, 1926, at the Red Triangle factory in Leningrad ("VLKSM," *BSE* [2d ed.], IX, 336).

89. *S"ezd VIII*, pp. 44–45.   90. *Ibid.*, pp. 46–47; see also pp. 561–62.

91. *Ibid.*, pp. 360–62, 369, 568–69, 575–76.

92. *Ibid.*, pp. 416, 536–37; see also p. 576.   93. *Ibid.*, pp. 438–39, 575–76.

94. *Ibid.*, pp. 34–35.

95. *Ibid.*, pp. 59–60, 164–66, 244, 375–82, 397–400, 422–25 (representative of the Commissariat of Labor), 440–41, 480. The resolution ultimately approved by the delegates was long but vague on the disputed points (*ibid.*, pp. 567–76).

96. On this subject, see *ibid.*, pp. 51–60, 145–48, 225–31, 255–58, 276–78, 344–441, 459–84, 567–76 (resolution).

97. *Ibid.*, pp. 53–58, 145–48, 255–58, 275–78, 367, 370–71, 384–85, 394–96, 417, 426–28, 465–67, 477–79, 481–82. Gastev defended himself in a mild and matter-of-fact way, maintaining in general that the charges against him were grossly exaggerated (*ibid.*, pp. 225–31, 470–74). Ginzburg, of the All-Union Central Council of Trade Unions, defended Gastev in part on the issues of wages and job quotas (*ibid.*, pp. 474–77). For other partial defenses of Gastev, see *ibid.*, pp. 367, 405.

98. He and the Supreme Economic Council (VSNKh) were accused of some of the same things that were said of Gastev (*S"ezd VIII*, pp. 370–72, 386–88, 394–96, 407–9 [Lunacharskii], 422, 459–61). For Rukhimovich's statements, see *ibid.*, pp. 344–69, 482–84.

99. *S"ezd VIII*, p. 428 (Kaplun).

100. Of "youths" working in *tsenzovaia* industry (i.e., enterprises employing sixteen or more workers with motor power, or thirty or more without motor power), on January 1, 1926, 45.7 percent were in the Komsomol. On January 1, 1927, the proportion had declined to 44.2 percent. As of the time of the Eighth Congress, the proportion was still under half but was not given precisely (*S"ezd VIII*, p. 49). Another speaker stated that in 1928 the proportion of Komsomolites among youths working in heavy industry was lower than in 1926 (*ibid.*, pp. 104–6). Still another speaker gave the proportions of Komsomolites among highly skilled working youths as 27 percent, among semiskilled youths as 46 percent, and among unskilled youths as 26 percent (*ibid.*, p. 163). (Definition of *tsenzovaia* from *Slovar'-spravochnik po sotsial'no-ekonomicheskoi statistike*.)

101. *S"ezd VIII*, p. 51.

102. *S"ezd IX*, p. 35 (quoting from Stalin's concluding remarks at the Sixteenth Party Congress). For other references see *ibid.*, pp. 6, 26–31 (Bezymenskii's poem celebrating the new stage), 38–39, 53–54, 61, 215–16, 355, 413.

103. *Ibid.*, p. 61.   104. *Ibid.*, pp. 53–54.

105. *Ibid.*, pp. 47, 413. (Kosarev said the Sixth All-Union Conference of the Komsomol [apparently in or shortly before December, 1929] had especially marked the shift to the new outlook [*ibid.*, p. 47].)

106. *Ibid.*, pp. 38–39.   107. *Ibid.*, pp. 9–12, 42–44.   108. *Ibid.*, p. 13.

109. *Ibid.*, p. 217.   110. *Ibid.*, p. 48.

111. For some samples, see *ibid.*, pp. 3, 15–17, 34, 47, 51–52, 87, 297–98. The term "shock brigade" had been used in one of the resolutions of the Congress of 1928, but it was not given prominence at that time. The same resolution also mentioned some other types of groups for shock work (*S"ezd VIII*, pp. 561–62).

112. *S"ezd IX*, pp. 15–17.   113. *Ibid.*, p. 211.

114. *Ibid.*, p. 215. Kosarev demanded it of all Komsomolites in trade unions (*ibid.*, p. 48).

115. *Ibid.*, pp. 401–2. Also in an appeal issued on the occasion of the seventh anniversary of Lenin's death (January 21, 1924), which anniversary fell during the Congress, the delegates called upon all factory Komsomolites to be shock workers, and all rural Komsomolites to be collective farmers (*ibid.*, pp. 218–20).

116. *Ibid.*, p. 48.   117. *S"ezd VIII*, p. 576.

118. *S"ezd IX*, pp. 47–48. (Some explanations obtained orally from T. N. Sosnovy.) According to Panteleev, socialist competition as such was endorsed by the CC of the League in *KP*, March 7, 1929. Then on April 23–29, 1929, the Sixteenth Conference of the Party approved the "initiative" of the Komsomol in this regard and called upon all workers to engage in socialist competition and shock work (Panteleev, "VLKSM," *MSE* [2d ed.], Vol. II, col. 552). The Central Committee of the League was reported to have sent out thirty special "CC brigades" involving ninety people to perform especially important shock work in the industrial sphere—Dneprostroi, Turksib railroad, etc. (*S"ezd IX*, p. 73). For additional references to socialist competition, see *S"ezd IX*, pp. 51–52, 357–58, 411–14.

119. *S"ezd IX*, p. 355.

120. Recalled for the delegates by Kaganovich (*ibid.*, p. 8). For some other samples of demands for higher production, see *ibid.*, pp. 212, 402–3, 407. Serving the same purpose were the "greetings" presented to the Congress from many shops and factories, and usually calling for more output (see *ibid.*, pp. 111, 114–17, 132–34, 150–51, 242–43, 306–7).

121. *Ibid.*, p. 49. Panteleev accounts for part of these: to the Donbas mines went 44,000 Komsomolites; to lumbering, 20,000; to the Urals and the Kuznetsk Basin, 66,000 (Panteleev, "VLKSM," *MSE* [2d ed.], Vol. II, col. 552). Panteleev gives a total of only 150,000 but does not define the period clearly enough to indicate whether it covers as much as the report at the Ninth Congress. For a corroboration of the total of 350,000, and a list of enterprises involved, see "VLKSM," *BSE* (2d ed.), IX, 338. Many of the jobs were of course in the Urals or further east. Of all the Komsomolites in the Far Eastern Krai, 35 percent had been mobilized (*S"ezd IX*, pp. 144–45). Kosarev also spoke of the need to settle the Angara River basin in Siberia, in connection with hydroelectric development, and said it was the responsibility of youth to move there and to assist in this new region (*ibid.*, p. 56).

122. *S"ezd IX*, pp. 111–12, and, for another complaint, pp. 186–87. Another delegate complained that among the Komsomolites sent from the northern Caucasus to work on the island of Sakhalin in the Far East there had been found "unhealthy . . . declassed elements" (*ibid.*, pp. 144–55).

123. *Ibid.*, pp. 13–14, 59–60, 173–75. The League was given credit for having helped to oust Tomsky and the "old opportunistic leadership" from the All-Union Central Council of Trade Unions (*ibid.*, pp. 131–32; see also pp. 151, 185–86). On the other hand, the Komsomol was said to be not active enough in its work in the trade unions. Statistics were cited on the membership of elected factory committees, showing that in Leningrad only 5.2 percent, in the Urals only 9.6 percent, and in the Ukraine only 9.8 percent, of those elected were Komsomolites. And in all three cases there had recently been a drop, amounting in the Ukraine to three percentage points (*ibid.*, pp. 131–32).

124. For some sample statements, see *S"ezd IX*, pp. 17 and 19 (Kaganovich),

46, 51–52 (Kosarev), 124–26, 179–81, 381–83. Stalin had said something similar at the Eighth Congress (S"ezd VIII, pp. 538–39).

125. S"ezd IX, p. 46.

126. Ibid., p. 51. Also 0.5 percent of the students were Party members. Later during the Congress the enrollment in the Factory Training Schools was given as 163,300 in 1929 and 589,400 in 1930, with plans for expansion to 1,204,100 in 1931 (ibid., p. 351).

127. Ibid., p. 22.   128. Ibid., pp. 57–58.

129. It was underlined in several speeches. See S"ezd VIII, pp. 2–3 (Chaplin); 18–21, 31–33 (Bukharin); 42, 65–70, 73, 280 (Chaplin); 538–39 (Stalin). It was announced that the session of the Congress which would have dealt with the work in the rural areas would not be held owing to the illness of Kudriavtsev, the reporter. Instead, a smaller group of 168 persons was appointed to discuss the topic (ibid., p. 534). This group produced a lengthy resolution which was subsequently approved by the delegates (ibid., pp. 576–85; see also pp. 544, 562–63).

130. Ibid., p. 31.

131. Bukharin argued that once the more "proletarian" elements were organized in collective farms, thereby depriving the kulaks of hired labor, the superiority of the collective system would be shown. He said it would be extremely easy to destroy by force the various religious and other organizations through which the kulaks were operating. But that easy way, he said, would not be most effective from the standpoint of winning over those "toilers" who were presently also members of those organizations; hence economic means, though slower, must be employed (S"ezd VIII, pp. 31–33).

132. S"ezd VIII, p. 66.   133. Ibid., p. 252.   134. Ibid., p. 67.

135. For some examples, see ibid., pp. 21, 66–68, 183–84, 192–96, 274, 536, 578, 581–84. The League's formal admission policy in the rural areas continued about the same: to bring in all farm-laborer youth, large numbers of poor-peasant youth, and the "best" middle-peasant youth, defined as those who had "proved their loyalty to the interests of the Party and the League" (ibid., p. 584 [resolution]).

136. Ibid., pp. 31–33, 70, 583.

137. Ibid., p. 581. For a similar, more general, demand at the next Congress, see S"ezd IX, pp. 210–11 (Kosarev).

138. S"ezd VIII, pp. 544, 578.   139. Ibid., pp. 578–79.

140. See, for example, S"ezd IX, pp. 7, 18, 21, 40, 50–51, 177–79, 218–20, 286–346, 421–26.

141. These are the figures given by Saltanov (ibid., p. 295). Kosarev earlier in the Congress referred to 30,000 at the time of the Eighth Congress and 600,000 as of the Ninth (ibid., p. 50). Panteleev gives a figure of 859,000 for January 1, 1931, but cites no source (Panteleev, "VLKSM," MSE [2d ed.], Vol. II, col. 552). Saltanov observed that with the increase in Komsomolites in kolkhozes, workers in the "socialist sector" (i.e., workingmen, farm laborers, and collective farmers) had become a majority in the League, rising from 46 percent in 1928 to 58 percent as of June 1, 1930 (S"ezd IX, p. 295; see also ibid., p. 421).

142. Saltanov said that as of June 1, 1928, 1.8 percent of peasant households

had been collectivized; by January 1, 1931, 25.7 percent had, and in the key grain-producing areas (Ukraine, northern Caucasus, Lower and Middle Volga, and Transvolga), 52.2 percent had (S"ezd IX, pp. 287, 292).

143. S"ezd IX, pp. 295–96. A delegate from the Central Black Soil Oblast said that in his area over 70 percent of those Komsomolites who worked in agriculture were already in kolkhozes (ibid., pp. 177–78). In a later account (1951), it is said that in June, 1929, 93 percent of the rural Komsomolites were already in kolkhozes ("VLKSM," BSE [2d ed.], IX, 338). This seems doubtful.

144. S"ezd IX, pp. 301–2. In the Moscow Oblast, there were 4,000 kolkhozes and 1,300 Komsomol cells among them (ibid., pp. 181–83). Panteleev, with his larger figure of 859,000 Komsomolites in kolkhozes, says they formed 41,075 cells (Panteleev, "VLKSM," MSE [2d ed.], Vol. II, col. 552).

145. The size of that segment at the time of the Congress of 1928 was variously referred to as 4 percent of the *rural* membership of the League (S"ezd VIII, p. 252), and as 3.5 percent of the whole membership of the League (ibid., p. 40). Both of these percentages cannot have been correct simultaneously. It should be recalled, however, that "kulak" is an exceptionally elusive term.

146. S"ezd IX, p. 51 (Kosarev). 147. Ibid., p. 21 (Kaganovich).

148. Ibid., p. 297 (Saltanov).

149. Ibid., p. 422 ("substantially completed"—v osnovnom zakoncheno).

150. Ibid. Saltanov suggested one test of what "maliciously" might mean when he advocated that any Komsomolite who failed to join a kolkhoz when his parents joined should be expelled (ibid., pp. 298–99). Komsomolites were also to persuade their parents to join kolkhozes (ibid., pp. 50, 218–20).

151. Ibid., pp. 300–1, 344–46, 425.

152. Ibid., pp. 401–2. Also exempted were rural teachers and engineers and technicians who were directly engaged in production and who came from a proletarian or semiproletarian background.

153. Ibid., pp. 300–1, 425.

154. For example, see ibid., pp. 73 (shock brigades already sent out by the CC), 300–3, 310–12, 333–34, 359–60, 396, 425–26 (500 urban Komsomolites to be mobilized for rural propaganda).

155. Ibid., p. 396 (also apparently pp. 310–12). 156. Ibid., p. 291.

157. Kosarev referred to the League as the "patron of electrification," and as introducing "the lamp of Il'ich" (Lenin) into the rural home (ibid., p. 56).

158. Ibid., pp. 300, 340–41. As of the spring of 1930, only 2 or 3 percent of the personnel of the administering bodies of kolkhozes were Komosomolites, it was reported (ibid., pp. 340–41). In fifty-seven raions of the Ukraine, at the time of the Congress, the corresponding proportion was given as 5.7 percent (ibid., p. 300).

159. Ibid., pp. 181–83, 212–13, 288–92, 336–38.

160. The need was illustrated by the statement, at the Eighth Congress, that among students admitted to Factory Training Schools in 1926–27, only 9.7 percent had finished the desired minimum of seven years of preliminary schooling. Eleven percent had finished six, 35.2 percent had finished five, 36.4 percent had finished four, and 7.7 percent had less than four years of schooling (S"ezd VIII, pp. 373–74).

161. S"ezd VIII, p. 539, also pp. 535, 538–40 (all in Stalin's speech).

162. Of those between the ages of sixteen and thirty-five, it was reported that as of 1926–27 there were still eleven million who did not know how to read. That was compared with an estimated seventeen million illiterates in the same age group in 1920 (*S"ezd VIII*, pp. 364–65). In the age group from eight to eleven, Krupskaia estimated that half of the children were still illiterate (*ibid.*, p. 493).

163. *S"ezd VIII*, p. 442. The Russian name of the Society was Obshchestvo "Doloi negramotnost' " or ODN. This meeting, which is reported in *ibid.*, pp. 442–58 (with Kalinin, Lunacharskii, and others), was apparently in accordance with a decision of the Fifteenth Party Congress (*ibid.*, p. 449). The campaign against illiteracy was called here the "cultural revolution."

164. *Ibid.*, pp. 458, 592. Kosarev urged that the former task be accomplished within the next two years (*ibid.*, p. 219). The resolution on these matters provided also, among other things, for a campaign to draw Komsomolites into primary-school teaching (*ibid.*, p. 592).

165. *S"ezd IX*, pp. 404–5.

166. Krupskaia also deplored individual competition among school children— the rewarding of some and the punishing of others. A collective spirit must be inculcated, she thought (*S"ezd VIII*, pp. 494–95). The main ideas expressed by Krupskaia and the others were set forth in one of the resolutions approved by the Congress (*ibid.*, pp. 585–91, especially pp. 586, 588–89).

167. *S"ezd VIII*, pp. 60–63, 187, 205–8, 217–18, 278–80, 388–94, 429–30. Lunacharskii defended himself (*ibid.*, pp. 404–11), with assistance from a colleague (*ibid.*, pp. 431–36). For Lunacharskii's formal report, see *ibid.*, pp. 120–31. An interesting item of incidental intelligence was that two groups of students had been admitted to the First Moscow University in that academic year—one group of 1,100, of which 70 percent were Party members or Komsomolites, and one group of 320, of which 21 percent were Party members or Komsomolites (*ibid.*, pp. 207–8).

168. *S"ezd IX*, pp. 385–86.   169. *Ibid.*, pp. 404–5.

170. *S"ezd VIII*, pp. 524, 586. The former citation gives the loss as 178,000. But neither citation indicates clearly to what period the loss refers. Apparently it does *not* refer to the whole period between the congresses of 1926 and 1928, for the total in 1926 was given as 1,586,000, and a report made public at the Congress of 1931 gives a figure for January 1, 1928, of 1,682,000, and for January 1, 1929, of 1,792,000 (*S"ezd IX*, p. 362). Thus it seems unlikely that in May of 1928 (the time of the Eighth Congress) the enrollment would have dropped below the figure for 1926. Panteleev ("VLKSM," *MSE* [2d ed.], Vol. II, col. 550) gives a figure of 1,681,566 for the Pioneers in 1928, but does not say what month he is talking about. It looks like the January figure.

171. *S"ezd VIII*, p. 586.   172. *Ibid.*, p. 64.

173. *Ibid.*, pp. 64, 502–3, 519–22, 532 (last three references contain discussion on whether or not Pioneer leaders should receive pay), 587. The number of Pioneer detachments then in existence was given as 47,693 (*ibid.*, p. 519).

174. *Ibid.*, p. 40.

175. *Ibid.*, pp. 496–97. Other problems and weaknesses of the Komsomol's work with the Pioneers were brought out in discussion (*ibid.*, pp. 500–33) and a resolution (*ibid.*, pp. 585–91).

176. *Ibid.*, pp. 585, 589–90.

177. Sever'ianova in her report gives these figures on the growth of the Pioneers: January 1, 1928—24,500 detachments with 1,682,000 members; January 1, 1929—47,180 detachments with 1,792,000 members; January 1, 1930—63,900 detachments with 2,476,000 members; July 1, 1930—82,700 detachments with 3,223,000 members. She said that at present (January, 1931) they had four million including the Octobrists. From other data given by her, it is possible to see that she was calculating about 85,300 as the number of Pioneer detachments as of January, 1931. If their size had remained the same as it had been in July of 1930 (average 38.9 persons per detachment), then the number of Pioneers in January of 1931 would have been about 3,318,170 (*S"ezd IX*, p. 362). The figure of four million was commonly used at the Congress, without the explanation that it also included the Octobrists (*ibid.*, pp. 20, 25, 354, 426).

The sexes were evenly represented, boys constituting 50.3 percent of the total. Just under half (48.9 percent) of the Pioneers lived in towns or cities, as opposed to rural settlements. In the cities, the detachments attached to factories were somewhat more numerous (14,475, or 17 percent) than those attached to schools (12,820, or 15 percent). In the countryside, the cells in kolkhozes and sovkhozes were far fewer (7,279) than those with other rural affiliations (29,000). But apparently the kolkhoz detachments tended to be much larger than the others, for it was reported that 22.1 percent of the Pioneers had parents in kolkhozes, while 26.8 percent had parents still farming independently. As for the parents of the rest, 32.4 percent were workers, 0.8 percent were farm laborers, 12.6 percent were office workers, and 5.3 percent were "others" (*S"ezd IX*, p. 362).

The age distribution was quite wide: under ten years—5.6 percent; ten and eleven—27.8 percent; twelve and thirteen—37.3 percent; fourteen, fifteen, and sixteen—24 percent; over sixteen—5.3 percent. The last group, which would be expected to be in the Komsomol, cannot be accounted for entirely on the basis of overlapping membership, since the "Komsomol core" was said to be only 3.4 percent of the total (having dropped from 8 percent at the time of the Eighth Congress). About one-third (33.7 percent) of the Pioneers had enrolled within the previous year (1930), and another 30.1 percent in 1929, while 25.3 percent had entered in 1927–28, and 10.9 percent had entered in 1926 or earlier (*ibid.*).

178. *S"ezd IX*, pp. 357–60; also p. 25. Sever'ianova maintained (as Krupskaia had done in 1928) that the Pioneers had rejected "Scout methods of individual competition" in favor of collective competition (*ibid.*, p. 360).

179. *Ibid.*, pp. 356, 361–62, 365–68.   180. *Ibid.*, p. 427.   181. *Ibid.*, p. 429.

182. *Ibid.*, p. 427. Sever'ianova had reiterated that there were no other recognized children's organizations as opposed to the Pioneers (*ibid.*, p. 354), and called for a membership of ten million in the near future (*ibid.*, p. 362). The survival of some Boy Scout troops had been noted at the Congress of 1928 (*S"ezd VIII*, p. 500), but references to the Scouts at the Congress of 1931 did not indicate whether they still were functioning (*S"ezd IX*, pp. 352–53, 360).

183. *S"ezd IX*, p. 364. Members and candidate-members of the Party comprised 6.4 percent of the Pioneer leaders; members of the Komsomol, 88.4 percent; and candidate-members of the Komsomol, 2.3 percent. As to social origin, the Pioneer leaders were distributed as follows: workers and farm laborers—38 percent; peasants—49 percent; office workers—10 percent; others—12 percent.

184. *Ibid.*, p. 364. The distribution with respect to the time of entering the Komsomol was as follows: 1925 and before—9.2 percent; 1926–27—15.5 percent; 1928—20.4 percent; 1929—32.2 percent; 1930—22.6 percent. This is the distribution on age: sixteen and under—22.9 percent; seventeen and eighteen—31 percent; nineteen and twenty—26.3 percent; twenty-one and twenty-two—12.8 percent; twenty-three and over—7 percent.

185. *Ibid.*, p. 364.   186. *Ibid.*, p. 355.   187. *Ibid.*, p. 428.

188. Obtained by calculating the number of Pioneers as of January 1, 1931 (see note 177), and then subtracting that from 4,000,000, which was the total for Pioneers and Octobrists together (*S"ezd IX*, p. 362). Panteleev ("VLKSM," *MSE* [2d ed.], Vol. II, col. 550) gives a figure of 264,114 Octobrists as of 1928.

189. The former editors were accused of having tried to put out "an organ parallel to the all-Party central newspapers," forgetting their special obligation to serve youth (*S"ezd IX*, p. 167). For some criticism of *Komsomol'skaia pravda* at the preceding Congress, see *S"ezd VIII*, pp. 156–58, 192, 263–65, 444–46.

190. *S"ezd IX*, pp. 341–43 (no further topical distribution is given).

191. *S"ezd VIII*, pp. 217–18, 221, 453–55, 467–69; *S"ezd IX*, pp. 164–65, 341–43, 351–52 (some examples only).

192. *S"ezd VIII*, p. 221 (Kirshon reporting). Author-Komsomolites were to depict examples of the "new man" of socialism (*ibid.*, pp. 467–69).

193. At the Congress of 1928 it was reported that during the preceding two years the number of Komsomolites serving in soviets had risen to about 6,000 in the city and town soviets and to about 69,000 in the rural, or village, soviets (*S"ezd VIII*, p. 42). No directly comparable figures were given at the Congress of 1931, but it was disclosed that the proportion of those serving in local soviets who were members or candidate-members of the Komsomol had grown from 5.2 percent in 1927 to 6.4 percent in 1929 (*S"ezd IX*, p. 46). Such an increase, however, could be accounted for simply on the basis of the increased size of the Komsomol and does not suggest that there was any marked change in the pressure being exerted for such participation. At the Congress of 1931 Kaganovich demanded that the members of the League help to elect Party and Komsomol members to local soviets in the approaching elections (*ibid.*, p. 20). Another item: In the Moscow Oblast as of January, 1931, among 6,000 village soviets there were only 1,313 Komsomol cells (*ibid.*, pp. 181–83).

194. *S"ezd IX*, pp. 153–54. The Society's name in Russian was Obshchestvo proletarskogo turizma i ekskursii, or OPTE.

195. *S"ezd VIII*, pp. 71–72 (quoting from Stalin's concluding remarks on the nationality question at the Twelfth Party Congress).

196. *Ibid.*, pp. 592–97; see also pp. 544–46.

197. *Ibid.*, p. 597. At the same time the Eighth Congress heard the usual strictures against Great Russian chauvinism, with special warnings against anti-Semitism (*ibid.*, pp. 22–24, 88–90, 451–52). The proportion of Russians among the delegates to the Eighth Congress was said to be lower than that at the Seventh, but no figures were given (*ibid.*, p. 547).

198. *Ibid.*, p. 595.

199. *S"ezd IX*, pp. 63–68. The slogan current in 1931, and used by Dzhava-khidze, was that of creating, in the USSR, a culture that was "national in form, proletarian in content"—that is, which permitted cultural and other concessions

to minorities in order to ensure tighter control by the "proletariat," as represented by the Party. For reports of some delegates on the work with national minorities in their regions, see *ibid.*, pp. 99–100, 119–20 (Komsomolites among Chuvash youth had risen from 10,000 to 20,000 between the Eighth and Ninth congresses), 135–36, 138–39, 144–45, 155–57, 161–64, 194–95.

200. *Ibid.*, pp. 69–70.   201. *Ibid.*, p. 201.   202. *Ibid.*, pp. 206–7.

203. *Ibid.*, pp. 414–17 (for passage of resolution, see pp. 397–98).

204. *Ibid.*, p. 405. The figures for the general population are from Lorimer, *Population of the Soviet Union*, p. 51. They are for 1926, but by 1931 would not have changed enough to invalidate the point made here.

205. *S"ezd VIII*, pp. 8–9.

206. *Ibid.*, pp. 11, 559–60. For other comments at the Congress of 1928 respecting the League's military work, see *ibid.*, pp. 7–8, 17, 42, 45, 93, 96–98, 176–77, 235–36, 258–60, 273, 535. In the Red Army (to which the boys born in 1905 had just been called), one problem to be solved was reportedly that of widespread friction between worker and peasant elements, based on the fact that, for the workers, army living conditions were worse than those of civilian life, while for the peasants the conditions were much better than those they had known in the village (*ibid.*, p. 260).

207. *S"ezd IX*, p. 23 (Soviet vessels defeat Chinese on Sungari River).

208. *Ibid.*, pp. 25–26.

209. *Ibid.*, pp. 13–14, 23–26, 58–59, 77–78, 103–8, 121–22, 142–44, 149–53, 164–65, 184–85, 189–91, 209–10, 387–94, 400–2.

210. *S"ezd VIII*, p. 42.   211. *S"ezd IX*, p. 108.

212. *S"ezd VIII*, p. 7. Eighteen percent were said to be members or candidate-members of the Party. Whether or not this overlapped the Komsomol figure was not stated.

Chaplin observed that among the youths entering naval academies in 1927 there had been too few workers and peasants (48.3 percent and 10.7 percent) and too many "others" (41 percent). He called on the League to correct this (*ibid.*).

213. *S"ezd IX*, p. 23 ("command personnel"—*komandnyi sostav*).

214. Only 100,000 rubles had been collected so far, although the keel had been laid February 23, 1930. Special Komsomol shock brigades were said to have pushed the construction. All Komsomolites were urged to intensify the drive for funds for the submarine, so as to complete the collection by February 5, 1931 (the birthday of Voroshilov). It was suggested that the League's next special naval project be a division of torpedo boats for the Black Sea Fleet (*S"ezd IX*, pp. 23, 77–78, 142–44).

215. *S"ezd IX*, p. 106. For remarks by other speakers bringing out the needs of the Air Forces, see *ibid.*, pp. 149–50, 264, 387–94, 400–2.

216. This compared with 37 percent in 1925 (*ibid.*, pp. 388–89). The ceremonial session occupies *ibid.*, pp. 387–94.

217. *Ibid.*, pp. 388–89, also pp. 400–1.

218. *Ibid.*, pp. 401–2. Komsomolites were reminded of their obligation to learn how to handle basic weapons (including the rifle and the machine gun) and to know some military speciality (*ibid.*, pp. 58–59, 209–10). Kosarev, bringing a special weapon into play, said that female Komsomolites "must ignore, not get acquainted with, and have nothing in common with, those Komsomol activitists

who cannot shoot and who are not undergoing military training." When some laughter greeted this remark, Kosarev said: "This is a very serious question, comrades." He reminded his listeners that "we are the future army in the future conflict with capitalism" (*ibid.*, pp. 209–10). Kosarev referred briefly here to the need for physical education, along with training in marksmanship, etc. Physical education was not a matter of much concern at either the Eighth or the Ninth Congress, but there were a few references to it. They add nothing significant to the picture previously given (*S"ezd VIII*, pp. 544, 597–98; *S"ezd IX*, pp. 148–49).

219. *S"ezd IX*, pp. 121–22, 189–91. The translation of Osoaviakhim is adapted from that given in Smirnitskii, *Russko-angliiskii slovar'*, p. 482.

220. *S"ezd VIII*, pp. 281–99 (report by Shatskin), 300–43 (discussion), 564–67 (resolution).

221. *Ibid.*, pp. 281–85.

222. In March, 1925, it stood at 94,000; in June, 1927, at 117,000; while at the end of 1927 it had dropped to 93,000 (*ibid.*, p. 285).

223. *Ibid.*, pp. 285–94; also p. 565 (resolution).

224. It was explained that while the Komsomol in the USSR was fighting to make production more efficient, the YCL's in capitalistic countries must continue to do just the opposite (*S"ezd VIII*, p. 13 [Barbe, representing the Executive Committee of the CIY]). Strikes must be encouraged (*ibid.*, pp. 282–83, 564). Special attention must be given to China and other colonial and semicolonial countries (*ibid.*, pp. 294–97, 330–32, 566). Bourgeois athletic and other youth groups must be infiltrated and propagandized (*ibid.*, pp. 320–23, 564).

225. *S"ezd VIII*, p. 284. Countries mentioned here as having armies which must be especially infiltrated were France, England, Germany, and the United States.

226. *Ibid.*, pp. 334–35 ("disturbances"—*volneniia*).

227. *Ibid.*, pp. 307, 342, 567; see also pp. 75–76.

228. *Ibid.*, pp. 40–41, 297–99, 302–4, 308–12, 316–18, 325–29, 566–67. One delegate suggested that in each Komsomol cell every member could be designated an "ambassador" to a different country, and asked to report periodically on it (*ibid.*, pp. 326–29).

229. *Ibid.*, pp. 309–12, 566.   230. *Ibid.*, pp. 40–41, 307, 326–29.

231. *Ibid.*, p. 329. Another delegate cited the case of one of his Komsomolites from Orel who had been invited to attend a world congress of Esperantists—only to be refused a visa for the trip. If Esperanto was to be discouraged, said this delegate, the policy should be quickly decided and arguments should be formulated in order that the reasons could be explained to Komsomolites (*ibid.*, pp. 332–34).

232. *Ibid.*, pp. 342–43, 541–42, 567; see also pp. 297–99.

233. *S"ezd IX*, pp. 221–22. From the time of the Fifth CIY Congress to November, 1929, the following drops were recorded: in Czechoslovakia, from 12,290 to 3,100; in England, from 1,400 to 200; in France, from 14,500 to 7,347; in Norway, from 3,000 to 2,200; in Austria, from 1,300 to 617.

234. *Ibid.*, pp. 222–23.

235. The total membership of the CIY, excluding the USSR and the "Soviet regions of China," was given here as 89,750 in November, 1929, and 115,030 in

January, 1931 (*ibid.*, pp. 224–26). Other figures were given later by Marchik, of the Executive Committee of the CIY. His figures were said to cover the CIY outside of the USSR, Tannu Tuva, Mongolia, and the "Soviet regions of China." They were: as of the Fifth Congress of the CIY—103,248; November, 1929—72,254; December, 1930—93,752 (*ibid.*, p. 251).

236. *Ibid.*, pp. 226–37. The discussion of Khitarov's report covered many aspects of the work of the CIY (*ibid.*, pp. 238–83). For references to some of these aspects elsewhere in the proceedings, see *ibid.*, pp. 13–14, 24–25, 44–45, 113–14, 374, 404, 418–20 (resolution).

237. *Ibid.*, pp. 22–23. For other expressions of the same thought, see *ibid.*, pp. 21, 26, 368, 403. (See also *S"ezd VIII*, pp. 11, 14.) The military side of this task was made a bit more specific through a demand of the Fifth CIY Congress to the effect that each YCL member in a capitalistic country must make friends with one soldier in his country's army (*S"ezd IX*, p. 238).

CHAPTER VI: ADJUSTMENTS DURING THE CONSOLIDATION OF STALINIST SOCIALISM

1. The interval was simply acknowledged (*S"ezd X*, Vol. I, p. 3). In the new Regulations of the League, the required interval between congresses was changed to three years (*ibid.*, II, 434).

2. *S"ezd IX*, p. 51 (italics removed—RTF).

3. The figure given for January 1, 1936, was 3,623,000 (*S"ezd X*, Vol. I, p. 415), while that given for the time of the Congress was 3,981,777 (*ibid.*, II, 400). The comparison with the Ninth Congress was apparently considered unfavorable, for the 1931 figure was not mentioned at the 1936 Congress, in contrast to the practice at former meetings. Instead, the comparison was made in terms of numbers of "primary organizations," as the cells were now being called. At the Ninth Congress, it was said, there had been only 84,394 cells in the League. Now there were 201,704 (*ibid.*, II, 64). Thus the primary organizations of 1936 averaged about twenty members each, whereas those of 1931 had averaged over thirty-five —a marked difference. (In 1949 Ivanov said there had been 3,800,000 members and 200,000 primary organizations as of the time of the Tenth Congress. Ivanov, *Izmeneniia*, p. 5.)

4. Explained by Panteleev in 1934 as the result of voluntary departures and the elimination of "hostile elements" (Panteleev, "VLKSM," *MSE* [2d ed.], Vol. II, col. 554).

5. *KP*, March 14, 1939, p. 4 (reporting on the Eighteenth Party Congress and referring to the time of the Seventeenth Party Congress).

6. *S"ezd X*, Vol. II, p. 67.   7. *Ibid.*, I, 95, 298–99, 306–10.

8. *Ibid.*, II, 60. This was mentioned in connection with a demand for more careful selection of Komsomol officials. The writer accepts this version despite the ambiguous statement by Kozlov concerning the staff's soundness at the time of the Party purge of 1933 (*ibid.*, I, 77).

9. *Ibid.*, I, 89.

10. *Ibid.*, II, 125. One official estimated that in the Ukraine, and probably in the country as a whole, only 10 or 15 percent of those expelled ever appealed

their cases; yet of those who did, about 70 percent were reinstated. This was presented as an indication that many Komsomolites had been unjustly expelled and that more care must be used in expulsions in the future (*ibid.*, II, 125–26). A similar lesson was drawn from 782 cases investigated by the CC in 1935, in which it was found that 324 had been unjustly expelled and had been reinstated (*ibid.*, II, 60). For other references to unjust expulsions, see *ibid.*, II, 121–28, 408.

11. *Ibid.*, II, 81.

12. *Ibid.*, II, 1–41. Full name: Evgenii L'vovich Fainberg (*ibid.*, p. 412).

13. *Ibid.*, II, 2. Ever since the Congress of 1924 it had been recognized that the Program needed to be revised, but little progress had been made, despite resolutions by successive congresses calling for action (*S"ezd VIII*, p. 16; *S"ezd IX*, p. 402). Clearly a matter so basic as this had to await decisions at the highest level of the Party.

14. *S"ezd X*, Vol. II, p. 5, also pp. 1–4.   15. *Ibid.*, II, 5–6.

16. *Ibid.*, II, 6–8. The proposed Program had been published in *KP*, on March 27, 1936 (pp. 1–2), and had been discussed in other issues between that time and the opening of the Congress. Presumably Komsomol primary organizations discussed it at the same time, using the materials in *Komsomol'skaia pravda* as their guide.

17. *S"ezd X*, Vol. II, pp. 9–10.

18. *Ibid.*, II, 10–11; see also pp. 47–48 (Vershkov).

19. *Ibid.*, II, 11–13. The formula "free toilers . . ." was quoted from Stalin's interview with Roy Howard.

20. *Ibid.*, II, 13–14.   21. *Ibid.*, II, 15–16.

22. *Ibid.*, II, 16–19; see also pp. 13–14.   23. *Ibid.*, II, 20–21.

24. *Ibid.*, II, 21–22.   25. *Ibid.*, II, 425.

26. The new Program of the League included the following formula in referring to Communism: "The ACP(B) and the Soviet government are organizing a Communist system—a system in which not only is private ownership of the means of production abolished and classes and the exploitation of man by man done away with, but in which also the last traces of economic inequality among people will be eliminated; in which toil, having been a means toward subsistence, will become the first necessity of life, the joyful manifestation of the creative capacities of man; in which as a result of the development of science, technology, and the productivtiy of labor, there will be attained such abundance, such social wealth, that the principle of socialist distribution 'from each according to his abilities, to each according to his work' will be replaced by the principle of full Communism 'from each according to his abilities, to each according to his needs' " (*S"ezd X*, Vol. II, p. 425).

One of the very rare approaches to the same subject in the congresses between 1920 and 1936 was a statement by Bukharin at the Seventh Congress (1926). He spoke of "drawing everyone decisively into the business of administration, the abolition of classes, the abolition of the separation into the governed and the governing, the realization of the slogan for which we have fought, are fighting, and will fight—the slogan of genuine Communist equality!" (*S"ezd VII*, p. 258).

27. *S"ezd X*, Vol. II, pp. 24–26. They must remember the need to care for "socialist" property, the need for labor discipline, the idea of loving one's work

and respecting the jobs of others, the inculcation of a hatred for laziness and idleness, and the obligation to place the interests of society ahead of one's own interests (*ibid.*, II, 26–29). The new Soviet policy of strengthening the family was reflected in Fainberg's excoriation of an "incorrect, flippant attitude toward woman, the family, and the rearing of children." As to religion, Fainberg reported that Stalin had rejected a proposal that the Komsomol combat religion "decisively, mercilessly," and had said instead that Komsomolites must "explain patiently" the harm of religious prejudices (*ibid.*, II, 29–30).

28. *Ibid.*, II, 31–32. In his further effort to justify Communist morality, Fainberg fell back on the usual quotations from Lenin, defining Communist morality as being "entirely subordinated to the interests of the class struggle of the proletariat" (*ibid.*, II, 32–33).

29. *Ibid.*, II, 33–34. In accordance with the doctrine of Soviet patriotism, Fainberg explained that the Komsomol's "obligation before the international proletariat" was to "strengthen our socialist fatherland" (*ibid.*, II, 34–37).

The important qualities expected in the Komsomolite's character again included discipline, self-sacrifice, Soviet patriotism, and initiative-with-guidance (see *ibid.*, I, 60–61, 316–19; II, 203–6, 429, 439).

30. *Ibid.*, II, 37–39.

31. *Ibid.*, II, 39–40 (said to be quoted from Stalin, "K voprosu o rabochekrest'ianskom pravitel'stve," *Voprosy leninizma*, 9th ed., p. 239).

32. *S"ezd X*, Vol. II, p. 40.

33. For the most noteworthy other expressions (besides Fainberg's) on this general subject, see *ibid.*, I, 38, 60–61, 63–64 (all Kosarev), 410–12 (Andreev); II, 44–54 (Vershkov on the new Regulations), 425–30 (pertinent sections of the new Program), 431–40 (the new Regulations). The delegates' collective reference to the Communist Party as "our mother" (*ibid.*, I, 8) was later to become standard practice.

34. *Ibid.*, I, 1. Listed after Stalin were Molotov, Kaganovich, Voroshilov, Kalinin, Andreev, Dimitrov, Mikoian, Zhdanov, Chubar', and Kosarev, in that order. (Kosior and Ordzhonikidze of the Politburo were not present.)

35. *Ibid.*, I, 2–3. Full name: Aleksandr Vasil'evich Kosarev (*ibid.*, II, 410).

36. *Ibid.*, I, 6–7. The others were Molotov, Kaganovich, Voroshilov, Kalinin, Ordzhonikidze, Andreev, Kosior, Mikoian, Chubar', Postyshev, Zhdanov, Petrovskii, Rudzutak, Eikhe, Ezhov, Khrushchev, Dimitrov, Gor'kii, and Thälmann, in that sequence.

37. *Ibid.*, I, 8–9 (all in capital letters in the original).

38. For some samples see *ibid.*, I, 89 (praise of Zhdanov), 95 (of Kosior and Postyshev), 101 (of Kaganovich and Khrushchev), 108 (of Voroshilov), 111 (of Beriia), 128–29 (of Molotov and Kalinin), 178–84 (of Beriia), 184–89 (of Khrushchev), 202–3 (of several), 213–17 (of Kaganovich), 230–31 (of Yagoda, in connection with the NKVD border guards), 431–41 (of Voroshilov and other military heroes).

39. *Ibid.*, I, 15, also pp. 14, 16, 33.   40. *Ibid.*, I, 15 (Kosarev).

41. *Ibid.*, I, 484.

42. *Ibid.*, I, 255, and pp. 254–59 (Maria Demchenko, a Stakhanovite in sugarbeet production).

43. For samples of the various forms of homage, see *ibid.*, I, 70, 85–88, 110–18, 128–42, 155–57, 178–89, 196–98, 213–17, 224–31, 255, 258–59, 375–81, 384–89, 411, 431–41, 444–45, 484–85; II, 6, 33, 44, 141–44, 174, 415–17.

44. *Ibid.*, I, 68.

45. *Ibid.*, II, 399. Also present were Molotov, Voroshilov, Kaganovich, Andreev, Zhdanov, Chubar', and Khrushchev, listed in that order.

46. *Ibid.*, II, 415; also pp. 416–17.

47. *Ibid.*, I, 4–7. The bodies included a Presidium of twenty-five, a Secretariat of seventeen, a Credentials Committee of seventeen, and an Editorial Committee of seventeen. Kosarev did not provide any opportunity for a negative vote in the case of the last.

48. The Congress in each case went through the motions of voting unanimously that the CC (or other group) should consist of the proposed number of persons. Then the names were read off one by one, in accordance with lists which had already been handed out to the delegates. Any objections were supposed to be made when the name was read. There were none. In the unanimous votes not even any abstentions were recorded (*ibid.*, II, 408–15). The names are given with first name and patronymic, thus making a valuable list of Komsomol officials.

49. *Ibid.*, I, 450, 542; II, 167–68, 397–98, 406, 407, 408.

50. *Ibid.*, I, 85–430; for some interesting samples, see pp. 85–88, 173–76, 235–40, 250–53, 293–97. For one of the few impromptu rejoinders (on criticism of Leningrad for poor patronage of Komsomol'sk) see *ibid.*, I, 123. For the interruption of another speaker, see *ibid.*, II, 99–104 (challenging a physical education spokesman on seemingly minor points). For another instance, see *ibid.*, II, 254.

51. *Ibid.*, I, 447–49. Although Kosarev called for sharper criticism, the succeeding discussion (on the CIY) also went very smoothly (*ibid.*, I, 487–542).

52. *Ibid.*, II, 75. The discussion covers pp. 75–168.

53. For some examples, see *ibid.*, II, 75–80, 91–96, 131–34, 149–51, 156–58.

54. *Ibid.*, II, 114–16.

55. *Ibid.*, II, 112 (Demchuk of the Far Eastern Krai).

56. *Ibid.*, II, 431–32.

57. *Ibid.*, II, 169–223, especially pp. 174–84, 192–93, 197–202. The speaker's full name was Vasilii Antonovich Muskin (*ibid.*, II, 411).

58. *Ibid.*, II, 223–345, 385–92.

59. *Ibid.*, II, 394, and also pp. 394–96, for the rest of his closing address.

60. They approved his "theses" in principle, and they unanimously elected him co-chairman of a committee to prepare the final version for formal passage (*ibid.*, II, 397–98). To that final version was added the self-castigating phrase that "the Tenth Congress acknowledges the work of the Komsomol in the school to be unsatisfactory, from the CC of the ALCLY, the CC's of the LCLY's of the national republics, the *kraikoms* and the *obkoms* on down" (see *ibid.*, II, 407–8, listing also other minor changes). For some of the criticisms contained in the completed resolution, see *ibid.*, II, 441–46, especially pp. 442–43.

61. *Ibid.*, II, 439 (from the Regulations).

62. *Ibid.*, II, 42–68 (Vershkov's report), 431–40 (the Regulations). The speaker's full name was Petr Afanas'evich Vershkov (*ibid.*, II, 409).

63. *Ibid.*, I, 414 (Andreev). The membership was said to be 3,623,000 out of an

estimated total of 37,500,000 youths of Komsomol age as of January 1, 1936. (Apparently the new age limits of fifteen and twenty-six were used in this calculation.)

64. See Chapter IV; also *S"ezd VI*, p. 360.

65. *S"ezd X*, Vol. II, pp. 43, 51–53. For Fainberg's references to this see *ibid.*, II, 10–16.

66. *Ibid.*, I, 51–52.   67. *Ibid.*, I, 411–12 (Andreev).

68. The Regulations provided for a testing of each candidate-member at the end of his six-month probationary period. If he was still not deemed worthy of being a full-fledged Komsomolite, his candidacy would be prolonged, or he could be dropped. Candidate-members were to obey the same orders and fulfill the same obligations as full members, including the payment of dues, but they did not have the right to vote or to hold office in the League. Recommendations for admission to either membership or candidate-membership had to come from one member of the Party, or from two Komsomolites who had been in the League at least one year. The recommendation had to go first through the local committee of the League for its approval. Then the general meeting of the primary organization could vote on it. This decision went into force when ratified by the bureau of the *raikom* or *gorkom* of the League (*ibid.*, II, 432–33, also p. 54).

69. *Ibid.*, II, 44, 54–55.

70. *Ibid.*, I, 217; II, 54–55, 117, 131, 139, 140 (proposing that there be no limit at all for active participants, twenty-six for others), 163–64 (essentially the same).

71. *Ibid.*, II, 432.

72. *Ibid.*, II, 403. The percentages here, as in numerous other cases cited earlier, have had to be recalculated from the absolute figures given in the same source, because the two sets of data did not quite coincide.

73. *Ibid.*, II, 433; also pp. 62–63.   74. *Ibid.*, II, 62.

75. At the top, the Congress elected the Central Committee and the Central Inspection Commission (*ibid.*, II, 435). (This was the same as the Regulations of 1922, except that the latter did not mention the Central Inspection Commission [*S"ezd V*, p. 379]. The Regulations had been slightly amended in 1926, but not in this respect [*S"ezd VI*, pp. 499–500].) The oblast and krai conference, or the congress of the Komsomol in the national republic, said the new Regulations, "elects the oblast or krai committee, or the CC of the LCLY [of the national republic], the inspection commission, and the delegates to the All-Union Congress of the Komsomol" (*S"ezd X*, Vol. II, p. 436). (This was substantially the same as the Regulations of 1922, except that guberniias and uezds were then the units [*S"ezd V*, pp. 378–79]. The Regulations had been amended slightly in 1926, but apparently not in this respect [*S"ezd VI*, pp. 499–500].) The oblast, krai, or national republic committee in turn "chooses a bureau for [carrying on] day-to-day work." At the next lower level, the Regulations provided that the city, okrug, or raion conference "elects the city, okrug, or raion committee, the inspection commission, and the delegates to the krai or oblast conferences, or to the congresses of the Komsomol of the national republics" (*S"ezd X*, Vol. II, pp. 436–37). (The principle was unchanged from the Regulations of 1922, but the political units were differently arranged [*S"ezd V*, p. 378].) That city, okrug, or raion committee, too, elected a bureau. At the lowest level, the primary organiza-

tion "elects a Komsomol committee . . . for a term of one year." Smaller organizations, in shops, elected a bureau or a Komsomol organizer (*Komsorg*) for a term of six months. If there were less than ten members in the primary organization, they did not elect a committee, but simply a secretary (*S"ezd X*, Vol. II, pp. 437–38). (The Regulations of 1922 had provided for a bureau, elected for a three-month term [*S"ezd V*, p. 377].)

76. *S"ezd X*, Vol. II, pp. 437–38.

77. See *ibid.*, I, 54 (Kosarev citing delays in appointments of raion committee secretaries), 173–76 (a group of secretaries sent down to raion committees in Kazakhstan), 293–97 (incompetent secretary sent down to raion and town committees in Bashkiria); II, 115–16 (criticism of the Komsomol-wide breakdown of elective procedures, by another delegate from Kazakhstan).

78. *Ibid.*, II, 115–16.

79. For the principal remarks concerning this sphere, see *ibid.*, I, 51–68 (Kosarev), 69–84 (Kozlov), 410–16 (Andreev); II, 55–61 (Vershkov).

80. *Ibid.*, I, 70. In connection with the expansion of paper work, it was revealed that for the four months from November, 1935, to February, 1936, the CC had received and sent 56,858 pieces of correspondence (*ibid.*, I, 72).

81. Kosarev did not give absolute figures, but these could be calculated by using his percentages together with the absolute figures given at the Ninth Congress. Kosarev said, among other things, that three new sections—of young women, the press, and art—had been added. He said the proportion of Party members in the staff had declined from 76 percent at the time of the Ninth Congress to 61 percent at the time of the Tenth, while the proportion of Komsomolites (here, those not concurrently in the Party) had risen from 10.5 percent to 18 percent, and the "non-Party" group had increased from 13.5 percent to 21 percent. The last was accounted for largely by the addition of technical personnel, including economists. He said the working-class segment had increased from 38 percent to 41 percent, and the peasant segment from 39 percent to 39.7 percent, while those of office-worker origin had declined from 9.5 percent to 8.4 percent and "others" from 13.5 percent to 10.9 percent (*S"ezd X*, Vol. I, p. 76). Note that the percentages given here for the Ninth Congress differ somewhat from those given at that Congress itself.

82. *S"ezd X*, Vol. I, pp. 78–82. Kozlov gave percentages on the income from dues in 1930–35 and various categories of expenditures during that period. He gave no absolute figures, nor did he refer to the inflation in connection with the huge percentage increases which he cited.

83. *Ibid.*, I, 78. In one factory organization, half of the members were reported to be more than three months behind in their dues. According to the Regulations, such a delay would have raised the question of expulsion, but would not require it.

84. *Ibid.*, II, 402. The figures total 797 instead of 801, and the percentages total only 99.4 percent. According to the percentages recalculated on the basis of the absolute numbers given, 11.6 percent (93) had been members since 1918–21; 44.4 percent (356) had joined in 1922–25; 29.2 percent (234) had joined in 1926–30; and 14.2 percent (114) had joined in 1931 or later.

85. *Ibid.*, II, 404. This percentage, too, has had to be recalculated. No figures were given for attendance at the Eighth or previous congresses, in contrast to

the practice at earlier congresses. The turnover particularly among the secretaries of lower-echelon Komsomol organizations was termed excessive (*ibid.*, I, 53–54; II, 60).

86. *Ibid.*, II, 403. The statistics, after recalculation of two of the four percentages on the basis of the absolute figures given (which do add up to 801), are: workers, 55.1 percent (441); peasants, 31.3 percent (251); office workers, 10.7 percent (86); "others," 2.9 percent (23). As to current occupation, 64.5 percent (517) of the voting delegates were full-time Komsomol officials or employees, compared with 61.4 percent said to have been in that category at the Ninth Congress. A further analysis indicated that there were 28 officials of the CC of the ALCLY and the CIY, 126 secretaries of *obkoms, kraikoms,* and central committees at the national republic level, 53 directors of sections at that same level, 17 secretaries of okrug committees, 93 secretaries of *gorkoms,* 128 secretaries of rural *raikoms,* and 39 secretaries of primary organizations of the Komsomol. Other categories listed were as follows: 24 assistant chiefs of political departments in state farms and transportation enterprises, 10 Pioneer leaders and Komsomol organizers in schools, 18 newspaper editors, 8 teachers, 4 writers, 14 students, 22 engineers, technicians, and scientific (research) workers, 12 locomotive engineers, 58 factory workers, 2 employees of soviets, 22 tractor drivers and combine drivers, 26 farm brigade-leaders, 3 agronomists and kolkhoz chairmen, 15 collective farmers, 16 aviators, 20 military unit commanders, 32 political workers of the Red Army, and 10 soldiers and sailors.

87. *Ibid.*, II, 437. In the above cases the requirement for service in the League was five and six years, respectively. In certain cases, the requirements were one year lower, but the distinction between workers and nonworkers was preserved.

88. *Ibid.*, II, 437. At the city and okrug level the requirements for previous Komsomol service were four and five years, respectively.

89. *Ibid.*, II, 402. The percentages given have again had to be recalculated in part on the basis of the absolute figures given (which do add up to the proper total of 801). There were 579 members and 47 candidate-members of the Party. Of the full members, 259 had been in the Party since 1928 or earlier, 154 entered in 1929 or 1930, and 166 joined in 1931–32.

90. *Ibid.*, I, 56–63 (Kosarev); II, 63–65 (Kozlov).

91. *Ibid.*, I, 56–58.

92. For example, when the list of the new CC was read, applause was recorded only for these Komsomolites (*ibid.*, II, 408–12). Full names: Dmitrii Dmitrievich Luk'ianov and Vasilii Tarasovich Chemodanov (*ibid.*).

93. For some examples of the references to Aleksandr Vasil'evich Kosarev, see *ibid.*, I, 73–75, 88, 100 ("militant, talented pupil of Comrade Stalin"), 124–28, 178–84, 202–3, 231–33 ("honorary border guard"), 288–99, 308–10, 371–75 (trip to Far East in 1932), 384–85; II, 410.

94. *Ibid.*, I, 73–75. Full name: Viktor Il'ich Kozlov (*ibid.*, II, 415).

95. *Ibid.*, I, 38.

96. *Ibid.*, II, 428. The Regulations required Komsomol primary organizations to send representatives for liaison with appropriate soviet institutions, just as with trade unions (*ibid.*, II, 439).

97. The statistics given for 1934 were as follows: Among the 64,762 chairmen of village soviets, 7.9 percent were Komsomolites, who constituted more than half

of those chairmen who were under twenty-five years of age. Among the 1,328,630 members of village soviets, 11.3 percent were Komsomolites—a little less than half of those so serving who were under twenty-five years of age. Among the 202,304 members of town (and city) soviets, 10.5 percent were Komsomolites—well over half of those so serving who were under twenty-five. Finally, among the 95,217 members of raion executive committees, 6.8 percent were Komsomolites and this, again, was over half of those so serving who were under twenty-five. The corresponding percentages for 1931 were: 5.4 percent, 6.4 percent, 7 percent, and 5.1 percent, respectively. The absolute numbers in each category were fewer in 1931 than in 1934 (except that there were no figures given for town soviets in 1931). In the village soviets among the national minorities the Komsomol was represented especially well. In the village soviets of Turkmenistan, for example, 14.9 percent were Komsomolites and this was just a shade under half of those who were under the age of twenty-five on those bodies (S"ezd X, Vol. I, p. 25).

98. For some of the expressions of this thought, see S"ezd X, Vol. II, pp. 42–43, 45, 59, 199.

99. Enterprises specifically listed were state farms, railways, water transport, and the Northern Sea Route (ibid., II, 435).

100. For a general statement, see ibid., II, 428–29 (part of the new Program).

101. Ibid., I, 12; see also II, 26–29.

102. Ibid., II, 403. Some of the Stakhanovites (twenty-four in industry and forty-eight in agriculture) had received higher awards, such as the Red Banner of Labor (ibid., II, 400–2).

103. Ibid., I, 14, 18, 45, 112–18, 120–23, 124–28, 142–47, 184–89, 196–98, 290–93, 299–302, 324–28, 369–71, 408–10. The foregoing citations do not include many of those having to do with Stakhanovites in agriculture; see later in this chapter. Kosarev complained that there was a problem of excessive rewards and flattery being heaped upon some Stakhanovites, to the extent that they no longer worked at their benches, but became traveling showpieces (ibid., I, 64–67).

The over-all importance of youth in industry was brought out in the report that in many important plants, workers under the age of twenty-three constituted well over 40 percent of the labor force. As of July 1, 1935, of all the "workers" in the USSR, 34 percent were under twenty-three years of age (ibid., II, 17–18). Another roughly corroborative report, given by Shvernik, said that out of 23,700,000 workers, 7,000,000 were youths under twenty-three, and that in heavy industry the proportion of youth was over 34 percent (ibid., II, 272). (He gave no specific date for the statistics.) It will be remembered that the population of the Soviet Union is very young compared to populations of Western Europe. As of January 1, 1936, said Kosarev, 43 percent of the population of the USSR had been born since the Revolution, that is, was under eighteen years of age (ibid., I, 16).

104. Ibid., II, 425; see also II, 26–29.   105. Ibid., II, 192–93 (Muskin).

106. Ibid., I, 16. The span of time in question was not indicated. Among the more important mobilizations of Komsomolites, Kosarev listed 1,000 mobilized in eastern Siberia "for work in the gold industry"; 1,200 sent to Dal'promstroi (Far Eastern Construction); 1,500 for the "conquest" of the Arctic; 2,000 to work on

Sakhalin; 5,000 to work as "greasers" on the railroads; 6,000 for strengthening the system of communications; 7,000 for building the Stalingrad Tractor Plant; 20,000 to work in the lumbering industry; and 36,000 to the mines of the Donets Basin (*ibid.*, p. 17). (On Komsomolites in railroad work, see also *ibid.*, pp. 328–34.)

107. The contribution of Komsomolites was said to have been large in the building of Magnitogorsk, of the Kuznetsk Basin, and of many important industrial plants (*S"ezd X*, Vol. I, pp. 17, 101; see also pp. 283–86 [Kuznetsk Basin]).

108. In 1932, according to the official account, Kosarev had visited the Far East, and the building of the city began. Those Komsomolites who arrived in 1932 were greeted by dense forests and swamps; they had lived in tents through the severe winter, plagued by scurvy and other diseases, but had worked tirelessly. Their labors had borne fruit. At the time of the Congress of 1936, Komsomol'sk boasted about sixty thousand inhabitants, with factories, schools, and other facilities. While no exact figure was given, it was said that "tens of thousands of Komsomolites from all corners of the Soviet Union were sent to the Far East in order to transform it into an industrial region" (*S"ezd X*, Vol. I, pp. 119–20, also p. 17). Another speaker revealed that 20,000 Komsomolites had been sent to the Far Eastern Krai during the past year alone (*ibid.*, I, 190). The Leningrad Komsomol organization was said to have assumed "patronage" over Komsomol'sk (*ibid.*, I, 123). Apparently June 12 was considered the official birthday of Komsomol'sk. See articles celebrating its seventh and fifteenth birthdays in *KP*, June 12, 1939, p. 3, and June 12, 1947, p. 3.

For a little information about Komsomol work in the Arctic, see *S"ezd X*, Vol. II, pp. 348–52 (report of Otto Iul'evich Shmidt), 383–85 (on Igarka).

109. *S"ezd X*, Vol. II, p. 272. Only 76.1 percent of the younger workers were in unions at that time, as compared with 81.2 percent of workers of all ages.

110. *Ibid.*, II, 280. In keeping with the Komsomol's new emphasis on education, said Shvernik, the trade unions were now placing their main effort on satisfying the cultural needs of the workers (*ibid.*, II, 272–73, 275–80). The trade unions, like the Komsomol, were teaching the workers to observe labor discipline and to be clean, neat, and careful of "socialist [i.e., government] property" (*ibid.*, II, 273–75; see also II, 26–29).

111. *Ibid.*, II, 439.

112. See also *ibid.*, II, 2–6, 16–19, 423–24 (Program).

113. Andreev said that the kolkhozes and sovkhozes together had accounted for 93.6 percent of agricultural production in 1935 (*ibid.*, I, 399).

114. Reportedly not successful until 1935 (*ibid.*, I, 150).

115. There the Party had been obliged to intervene to crush the "nationalists" and "Fascists" who had been obstructing the collectivization. (The famine of 1933 had of course helped to break peasant resistance, but that could not be mentioned.) Thereafter the Ukrainian Komsomol was said to have been in good condition (*ibid.*, I, 95, 306–10).

116. *Ibid.*, I, 312–13.

117. Andreev said 102,000 (*ibid.*, I, 413–14). Snetkov said 108,000 (*ibid.*, II, 159). This was out of a grand total of 201,704 Komsomol primary organizations of all kinds in existence at the time of the Tenth Congress (*ibid.*, II, 64).

118. *Ibid.*, II, 65–66.

119. *Ibid.*, II, 159. The Regulations of 1922 (slightly amended in 1926, but not in this respect) were still nominally in force (*S"ezd V*, p. 377).

120. *S"ezd X*, Vol. I, p. 414. When giving this percentage, Andreev gave no precise definition of "youth." A few sentences later, however, he said that there were 28,000,000 kolkhoz youths between the ages of fifteen and twenty-six. A somewhat different picture was indicated by Kosarev, who reported that there were, at that time, 1,200,000 Komsomolites in kolkhozes (*ibid.*, I, 20). This would be only about 4.3 percent of the 28,000,000 cited by Andreev. It may be mentioned in this connection that one of the Komsomol histories says that as of January 1, 1934, there were 2,000,000 Komsomolites working in kolkhoz brigades (Panteleev, "VLKSM," *MSE* [2d ed.], Vol. II, col. 552).

121. *S"ezd X*, Vol. I, p. 20.

122. See *ibid.*, II, 400–3. Two women received special mention in this connection: one was Pasha Angelina, a tractor driver and organizer of women's tractor brigades in the Donets Basin (*ibid.*, I, 21, 96–97, 200–1 [her speech]). She complained that ever since she had won the Order of Lenin, she had been so in demand for speeches that she was able to work with her tractor only three days a month! The other was Mariia Demchenko, a harvester of sugar beets in the Ukraine (*ibid.*, I, 21, 96–97, 170–73, 254–59 [her speech]). For a list of some of the other prominent Komsomol Stakhanovites, see *ibid.*, I, 21.

123. For an illustration of the grouping of these functions, see *ibid.*, I, 37–48. For other references to the "educational" task, see *ibid.*, I, 51, 403–8, 446–47; II, 6–40, 42–45, 48, 59, 180–82, 199, 223–398 (discussion of the report on education), 442–43 (resolution).

124. See, for example, *ibid.*, I, 8, 38, 155–61, 194–96, 213–17, 268–72, and some parts of the discussion in Vol. II, pp. 223–398. Both the new Regulations and the new Program reflected this emphasis. The new Regulations obliged each member "to study the works of Marx, Engels, Lenin, and Stalin, and to interpret Marxist-Leninist teachings to the broad masses of youth" (*ibid.*, II, 431–32). As already explained, it was specifically to ensure "political literacy" that the six-month probationary stage for candidate-members was instituted.

The pertinent passage of the Program follows:

"1. In accordance with the dictates of Lenin to the effect that the development of a Communist world-outlook—a mastery of the scientific revolutionary theory of the proletariat—is the basic condition for rearing youth in the spirit of Communism, the ALCLY considers it obligatory for each Komsomolite to receive political education. For this purpose the ALCLY establishes schools and circles and arranges other means so that youth may acquire elementary political knowledge and may study the basic features of history in general, especially the history of the USSR and the All-Union Communist Party. It [the ALCLY] organizes the study by youth of the fundamental ideas of Marx, Engels, Lenin, and Stalin.

"2. The ALCLY conducts the political education of all worker, peasant, office-worker, and student youth and the young intelligentsia; familiarizes youth, through meetings, discussions, and lectures, with current events and the measures of the Soviet government and the All-Union Communist Party (of Bolsheviks); familiarizes youth with the living conditions of workers and peasants in the past and in capitalistic countries, and with the history of the Civil War in the USSR; and rears youth in the pattern of the heroic struggle of the working class and the toiling peasantry against the capitalists and the landlords.

"The ALCLY publishes its own newspapers, magazines, political literature, and belles-lettres, organizes youth clubs, and leads the activities of worker and kolkhoz clubs, libraries, and reading rooms.

"3. The ALCLY patiently explains to youth the harm of superstition and religious prejudices, organizing for this purpose special circles and lectures for antireligious propaganda.

"4. The ALCLY conducts educational work against remnants of the national inequality of the past and against any manifestations of chauvinism and nationalism, and rears youth in the spirit of proletarian internationalism.

"The organizations of the ALCLY conduct political education among youth in the native languages of the peoples of the USSR, in accordance with the conditions and the particularities of each of them.

"5. The ALCLY organizes various courses and schools to prepare and to retrain propagandists and organizers of the various branches of the work of the Komsomol" (S"ezd X, Vol. II, pp. 426–27).

125. S"ezd X, Vol. II, p. 425.   126. Ibid.   127. Ibid., II, 172.

128. Ibid., I, 12–13, 16, 19, 258–59, 401; II, 424.

129. Ibid., I, 26–27.

130. Among the voting delegates to the Tenth Congress, 5.4 percent (43 persons) had graduated from Institutes of the Red Professorate, from courses in Marxism-Leninism, or from military-political schools and academies, while 13.5 percent (108 persons) had finished special "Communist institutions of higher education" (komvuzy)—advanced schools for Party members. Soviet-Party schools (sovpartshkoly), which gave special secondary education to Party members, had graduated 19.8 percent (158) of the voting delegates. In addition, 16.4 percent (131 persons) had studied in various circles for political education, 30.3 percent (242) had taken political self-study programs, and 8.6 percent (70) had taken various other political courses. Only 6 percent (48 persons) were listed as not having had special political training (S"ezd X, Vol. II, p. 404). The percentages add up to 100 percent; hence apparently the categories are not overlapping (presumably each individual was classified according to his highest achievement). Concerning komvuzy and sovpartshkoly see DeWitt, Soviet Professional Manpower, pp. 15, 17, 93.

131. S"ezd X, Vol. I, p. 46 (Kosarev); see also pp. 47–48 for additional information from Kosarev on the status of political education. In Moscow alone, there were reported to be 4,500 Komsomol propagandists (ibid., I, 391).

132. Ibid., I, 60–61.

133. Ibid., I, 63–64. In addition to the remarks of Kosarev, the speeches of numerous lesser figures testified to the current importance of political education and gave information on its progress and problems. For example, see ibid., I, 101–10, 112–18, 120–23, 161–66, 218–23, 406–8; II, 20–22.

134. Ibid., I, 43–45 (Kosarev), 223–24 (greeting to Gor'kii), 334–51 (report by Bubekin of Komsomol'skaia pravda), 422–27 (Pavlenko of Union of Soviet Writers); II, 287–95 (Chukovskii on children's literature), 310–15 (Tsypin of the Children's Publishing House of the CC of the ALCLY), 316–23 (Aleksei Tolstoi).

135. *Ibid.*, II, 310.

136. Not much was said at the Congress about the Little Octobrists, except that all school children of the very early ages should be members and that both Komsomolites and older Pioneers could serve as leaders (*ibid.*, II, 215–16).

137. *Ibid.*, II, 195.

138. *Ibid.*, II, 169–223; on Pioneers especially pp. 182–85, 190–91, 195–221; for Muskin's title, see p. 239. During the discussion that followed, the criticisms of the work with the Pioneers (citing lack of guidance, of Pioneer leaders, of literature, and of funds) were intermingled with similar criticism directed at the general work in the schools (*ibid.*, II, 223–398, especially pp. 227–41, 252–56, 307, 323–26, 332–35, 371–72, 377–83 [Stroev, editor of *Pionerskaia pravda*], 383–85). For other interesting references to the Pioneers, see *ibid.*, I, 104–5, 130–34, and II, 441–46 (resolution on the work in the schools, containing frequent mention of the Pioneers).

139. *Ibid.*, II, 372, and pp. 354–77 for the whole address. "Home-room teacher" is a translation of *klassnyi rukovoditel'*, which is literally "class leader" or "class guide."

140. *Ibid.*, II, 428, 434.   141. *Ibid.*, II, 190–91.

142. *Ibid.*, II, 185, 199–202, 443. Pavlik Morozov, the boy who denounced his father, was cited as a model for Pioneers (*ibid.*, II, 195). Pioneers were to set up circles to cater to special activities which could lead to useful adult occupations (*ibid.*, II, 211–12). Suitable activities for Pioneer meetings were outlined, giving expression to the idea that the meetings must not be too formal or too boring, lest they lose the attention of the young (*ibid.*, II, 214–15, 446).

143. *Ibid.*, I, 52; II, 212–13.

144. At the time of the Tenth Congress the enrollment was reported at 6,839,030 (*ibid.*, II, 196). In 1939, at the Eighteenth Party Congress, it was reported that the Pioneers had already reached a membership of about seven million by 1934, at the time of the Seventeenth Party Congress (*KP*, March 14, 1939, p. 4). This report would indicate rapid growth in the years 1931–34 and none in 1934–36.

145. *S"ezd X*, Vol. II, p. 195.

146. *Ibid.*, II, 396. A counterargument, used in favor of organizing on the basis of living units or neighborhoods, was that this would permit more effective functioning during the summer vacation (*ibid.*, II, 267–68). This argument was rejected by Muskin. But Pioneer "outposts" were now declared to be the suitable organizational device for living units, just as they had previously been for schools when the Pioneers were based on the factories and kolkhozes (*ibid.*, II, 434).

147. *Ibid.*, II, 197–98 (see also p. 446). As an example of the type of pernicious game that might be played in such surroundings, Muskin cited one game of "voting," in which the leader called out choices such as "Who's for Communism? Who's for Fascism?" and tried to trick the players into voting wrong.

148. Bubnov was reporting. He said that in 1935, 67.4 percent of all Pioneer leaders were nineteen or over; 69.8 percent of them had been in the Komsomol longer than three years; and 49.4 percent of them had eight years or more of schooling (*ibid.*, II, 371). "Paid Pioneer leaders" is a translation of *osvobozhdennye pionervozhatye*, which is, literally, "liberated Pioneer leaders," and signi-

fies that they were relieved from their regular job obligations on account of their Pioneer work.

149. *Ibid.*, I, 132–33, 416–17; II, 182–83, 217–21, 235–37, 443. "Burden" is a translation of *nagruzka.*

150. *Ibid.*, II, 434, 446.

151. *Ibid.*, II, 203–6 (also pp. 206–10 for more on leadership techniques). One example: "The more spontaneous activity, self-regulation, and initiative the Pioneers display, the greater, more responsible, and more serious does the guiding role of the Komsomolite Pioneer leader become" (*ibid.*, p. 205).

152. *Ibid.*, II, 210–11, 225 (a contrary view), 395–96 (the answer), 408 (the vote), 446 (the resolution).

153. *Ibid.*, I, 50; II, 29–30, 202, 424, 429. For the only noteworthy mention of religious policy at the Congress of 1936, see note 27, earlier in this chapter.

154. *Ibid.*, I, 50; II, 29–30, 429 (Program), 432 (Regulations).

155. *Ibid.*, II, 424 (general statement); see also p. 84 (26 percent of members of rural soviets were women in 1934, as against only 9 percent in 1926; 71 percent of medical students were women).

156. See note 122, earlier in this chapter, and also *ibid.*, I, 196–98 (textile workers).

157. *Ibid.*, II, 86; also I, 416. See also Chapter V.

158. *Ibid.*, I, 416. For further discussion on the League's work among the women of minority nationalities, see *ibid.*, I, 142–47 (Uzbekistan), 155–57 (Turkmenistan), 173–76 (Kazakhstan); see also pp. 151–54 (Don and Kuban Cossacks).

The policy on minority nationalities remained unchanged, to judge from the proceedings of the Congress of 1936 (*ibid.*, II, 172, 426). There were indications of some trouble with nationalism in Belorussia (*ibid.*, I, 210–13) and, as mentioned above, in the Ukraine (*ibid.*, I, 95, 298–99, 306–12, 487–90). A delegate from that republic assured the Congress that the Volga Germans were united in their readiness to defend the USSR against Hitler and the Fascists (*ibid.*, I, 273–74).

In the leadership of the League, as represented by the national composition of the 801 voting delegates to the Tenth Congress, the only conspicuous disproportion was the continued very high number of Jews: they constituted 13.3 percent of the delegates although they were hardly 2 percent of the population at large. The distribution was as follows: Russians, 397 (49.6 percent); Ukrainians, 113 (14.1 percent); Jews, 106 (13.3 percent); Georgians, 19 (2.3 percent); Armenians, 18; Belorussians, 16; Uzbeks, 16; Turks and Tatars, 13 each; Kazakhs, 12; Poles, 8; Bashkirs, 6; Kirghizes, Buriats, and Germans, 5 each; Mordvinians and Turkmenians, 4 each; Kabardinians, Chuvashes, Latvians, and Estonians, 3 each; Tadzhiks, Ossetians, Avars, Lezgins, Moldavians, and Greeks, 2 each; Karachais, Kalmyks, Abkhazians, Cherkessians, Udmurts, Maris, Czechs, Altais, Chechens, Adzhars, Komis, Uls, Uigurs, Nentsy, and Kara-Kalpaks, 1 each (*ibid.*, II, 404).

159. *S"ezd X*, Vol. II, p. 402. The percentages given (23.2 percent for women and 76.8 percent for men) do not match the absolute numbers given (188 and 613); hence the writer has recalculated the percentage from the absolute numbers.

160. *Ibid.*, II, 409–14. In this valuable list, the full names with patronymics are given.

161. For example, *ibid.*, I, 50, 276; II, 222.   162. *Ibid.*, II, 222.

163. Pupils in the primary and secondary schools had reportedly increased from 25,600,000 in 1935 to 27,935,000 in 1936 (*ibid.*, I, 403–4 [1936], II, 441 [1935]). (Muskin speaks incidentally of 26,000,000 children being in school. *Ibid.*, II, 183.)

The number enrolled in technical schools (*tekhnikumy*) was given as 705,200 in 1935 and 740,000 in 1936 (*ibid.*, I, 24 [1935], 404 [1936]). No prominence was given to the Factory Training Schools at the Tenth Congress. Kosarev said that the question would be raised whether to reorganize them into technical schools embodying Stakhanovite methods (*ibid.*, I, 45).

In the higher educational institutions (*vuzy*) and higher technical educational institutions (*vtuzy*), the number of students was said to have grown from 191,100 on January 1, 1930, to over 500,000 in 1935 and 1936. Kosarev gave a figure of 522,400 for October 1, 1935 (*ibid.*, I, 24), while Andreev gave a figure of 509,000 for 1936 (*ibid.*, I, 404). For the higher educational institutions, figures were given which showed that on a per head basis Georgians and Armenians were far better represented than Russians and others. Following are the figures given for 1931: Russians, 16.8 students per 10,000 inhabitants; Armenians, 36.6; and Georgians, 60.1. And for 1935: Russians, 28.7; Armenians, 58.4; and Georgians, 81.5 students in *vuzy* per 10,000 inhabitants. Proportions were given for other nationalities as follows: Belorussians, 13.6 (1931) and 26.2 (1935); Tatars, 7.5 and 18.1; Germans, 12.5 and 24.4; Chuvashes, 8.3 and 17.4; Turks, 19.5 and 30.2. Note that the Turks were slightly better represented than the Russians (*ibid.*, I, 25).

164. *S"ezd X*, Vol. I, pp. 404–5 (Andreev). Andreev said only 8 or 10 percent were now illiterate of those aged eight to fifty. Among the youths working in four branches of industry surveyed as of January 1, 1936, only 1 percent had been found completely illiterate (*ibid.*, II, 24; contains other statistics on the educational distribution of the group studied).

165. Bubnov added that in 1930 the primary schools had graduated 1,362,000 children, while in 1935 they had graduated 3,200,000. Over the period 1926–36, he said, 21,400,000 children had finished the four-year primary school. Bubnov also said that among those of ages twelve through fourteen in the RSFSR, 86.4 percent were currently in school (*ibid.*, II, 354, 357; see also p. 424).

166. Proclaimed, he said, by the Seventh All-Union Conference of the Komsomol (*ibid.*, I, 40), which had taken place in 1932 (Panteleev, "VLKSM," *MSE* [2d ed.], Vol. II, col. 554).

167. *S"ezd X*, Vol. II, p. 190.   168. *Ibid.*, II, 404.   169. *Ibid.*, II, 441.

170. *Ibid.*, I, 405 (presumably within the new limit of twenty-six).

171. Saltanov said 20.2 percent (*ibid.*, II, 387), Muskin gave an absolute figure of 150,000 Komsomolites who were teachers (*ibid.*, II, 180–81). These figures check roughly with the total given above, assuming some increase in the number of teachers during the current year.

It seems significant to note that in Moscow Oblast, out of 35,000 teachers, only 10,500 were young people (presumably meaning of Komsomol age) and only 4,000 or about 11 percent were Komsomolites (*ibid.*, I, 391–92). In Armenia, on the other hand, over half of all teachers were Komsomolites (*ibid.*, I, 326), and in the Kara-Kalpak Republic three-quarters of the teachers (600 out of 800) were Komsomolites (*ibid.*, I, 251).

172. *Ibid.*, II, 387. In Armenia, it was reported, 61 percent of the principals of primary schools were Komsomolites, and the proportions of Komsomolites were also high in the junior high schools (*nepolnye srednie shkoly*)—56.5 percent —and in the high schools (*srednie shkoly*)—40.7 percent (*ibid.*, I, 326).

173. *Ibid.*, II, 367 (Bubnov). "Honored teacher" is a translation of *zasluzhennyi uchitel'*.

174. *Ibid.*, II, 186–87, 444.

175. The percentages follow: Elementary-school teachers—34.8 percent with elementary education, 63.7 percent with secondary education, and 1.5 percent with higher pedagogical education; secondary-school teachers (junior high and high schools)—9 percent with elementary education, 66 percent with secondary education, and 24 percent with higher education (*ibid.*, I, 404).

176. *Ibid.*, I, 404–5; II, 186–87, 444.   177. *Ibid.*, II, 444.   178. *Ibid.*, II, 254.

179. *Ibid.*, II, 301 (Leshchiner).

180. In keeping with that policy, the Komsomol delegates were given instructions concerning the school curriculum. The main point was that pupils must be given a good grounding in fundamentals such as reading and writing, mathematics, physics, chemistry, history, and geography, which would equip them for further study. See *ibid.*, II, 174 (Party directive of Sept. 5, 1931), 184, 359–67 (Bubnov), 442–45 (resolution). The need for scientists was also stressed (*ibid.*, II, 242–52).

181. *Ibid.*, II, 441–46.   182. *Ibid.*, II, 445, also pp. 427–28 (Program).

183. *Ibid.*, II, 443–44, also p. 185.   184. *Ibid.*, II, 443, also pp. 193–94.

185. *Ibid.*, II, 428 (the new Program). For some of the references to this phase of Komsomol activity during the proceedings, see *ibid.*, I, 33–34, 48–50, 202–10, 241–45; II, 69–75, 99–104.

The chairman (Mantsev) of the All-Union Athletic League (Vsesoiuznyi sovet fizkul'tury) said that as of January 1, 1936, the organized physical education movement embraced nearly nine million persons, mostly youths. Two million were women (*ibid.*, I, 204; rest of report on pp. 202–10).

While Soviet athletes were exhorted to exceed world records (*ibid.*, I, 50, 206; II, 69–75), they were warned by Kosarev that concern for individual excellence must not overshadow the need for large numbers of athletes. Kosarev cautioned also against the tendency of athletes to "withdraw from active participation in socialist construction and become apolitical people, engaging in athletics for the sake of athletics" (*ibid.*, I, 49).

186. For a description of the RLD or GTO program, see *Vsesoiuznyi fizkul'-turnyi kompleks,* especially the tables on pp. 18–43. This booklet also covers the BGTO, or lowest schedule of tests.

187. *S"ezd X,* Vol. I, p. 48. During 1935, 1,126,205 had earned the first-class RLD badge (*ibid.*, I, 205).

188. *Ibid.*, I, 49. "Higher educational institutions" is a translation of *vuzy* and *vtuzy.*

189. *Ibid.*, I, 28–30, 457–63. For the individual military man, ambition was now more conspicuously recognized: military titles had been introduced in the

Soviet armed forces, and the Commissar of Defense, Voroshilov, was quoted as telling a group of lieutenants (November, 1935): "Each of you is potentially a marshal of the Soviet Union" (ibid., I, 36, said to be quoted from K. Voroshilov and M. Frunze, O molodezhi [Partizdat, 1936], p. 103). The military personnel among the voting delegates at the Congress included sixteen airplane pilots, twenty unit commanders (komandir), ten soldiers and sailors, and thirty-two "political workers of the Red Army" (S"ezd X, Vol. II, p. 403). Sixteen of the Red Army delegates were holders of Soviet medals, including one Evdokimov who was said to hold the world record for parachutists—200 jumps (ibid., II, 401–2).

190. According to the League's new Regulations, Komsomol bodies were to function "under the direct guidance of the political organs, military commissars, and Party organizations of units of the Red Army." The Regulations added that "the rights, obligations, and work of Komsomol organizations in the Red Army are defined in a special directive of the CC of the ALCLY and the Political Administration of the WPRA [Workers' and Peasants' Red Army]" (S"ezd X, Vol. II, p. 438). For other references to the Army, see ibid., I, 30–33, 36, 165–66, 431–33, 441–43, 444–45 (Komsomol called "mighty reserve of the Red Army"); II, 429–30 (Program), 432, 438 (Regulations).

191. S"ezd X, Vol. I, p. 33.

192. Ibid., I, 434–35. For other references to the Navy, see ibid., I, 161–65, 224–29, 434–36, 439–41; II, 407.

193. Ibid., I, 436–37. For other references to the Air Forces, see ibid., I, 241–45, 436–39; II, 407.

194. Ibid., I, 33.

195. In these clubs, which numbered over 140 by the time of the Congress, 10,000 youths were being trained without interference with their regular jobs. During 1935, 3,500 youths—of whom 80 percent were Komsomolites—had qualified as military reserve pilots. Parachute jumping was apparently the most widespread activity, with 400 jumping towers in operation. One thousand new parachute instructors had been trained during the past year alone. If the Moscow proportion of 125 instructors to 2,000 parachutists was typical, then the number of parachutists trained in aero-clubs during the previous year would have been about 16,000 (ibid., I, 33–35, 241–45, 260, 278–83, 355–65 [especially p. 357]; II, 428).

196. There were now about 1,000,000 Voroshilov Marksmen First Class, it was reported, as well as about 20,000 Voroshilov Marksmen Second Class, about 1,000 snipers, 125 instructors for sniping, and over 2,000 experts in rifle marksmanship. Relatively new were the Voroshilov Cavalrymen, of which there were over 40,000, organized in about 300 clubs mostly in the Cossack regions. In addition, the Osoaviakhim was training youths in antiaircraft and chemical defense (tests passed by 1,000,000 persons), topography (tests passed by 1,000,000), horse care (passed by 1,500,000), motors (passed by 1,600,000), and hygiene (passed by 1,000,000, apparently largely girls). Also trained were 25,000 chemical instructors and 35,000 drivers (presumably for trucks) (ibid., I, 35, 259–64, 272–73, 278–83, 355–65).

197. Ibid., I, 363.   198. Ibid., I, 36–37, 134, 230–35.

199. Ibid., I, 212–13. For more on the Komsomol and the Border Guards, see KP, Feb. 15, 1936, celebrating the 15th anniversary of the Border Guards.

200. Chemodanov said that the Young Communist Leagues had been under-

going persecution, particularly in Germany, Italy, Poland, Yugoslavia, Bulgaria, China, and Japan. In many other countries, however, the Young Communist Leagues had "tried in a sectarian way to copy and even to replace the Communist Party" with their own organization. They had overemphasized political matters, "ignoring the economic, cultural, and other healthy demands of youth." (To translate: They had not masked their political aims behind a sufficient façade of other activities calculated to appeal to youths who were not already pro-Communist.) Moreover, they had failed to discriminate between the "reactionary leaders of Social Democracy and the trade unions" and the bulk of the members of those non-Communist groups. They had been treating all these "broad masses of deceived youth" as "opponents," thereby cutting off the YCL from the mass of youth (S"ezd X, Vol. I, pp. 464–65; for the whole report, see pp. 451–87).

201. Ibid., I, 465, 469, 473. See also KP, Sept. 26–Oct. 12, 1935.

202. In "Fascist" countries the Young Communists were "to work wherever there were youths, bravely infiltrating the Fascist mass organizations of youth" (S"ezd X, Vol. I, pp. 465–66).

203. Ibid., I, 470. A subsequent speaker, Prokof'ev, also an official of the CIY, gave some figures. In the six months since the Sixth Congress (i.e., from October, 1935, to April, 1936), the YCL's had grown as follows: France, from 18,000 to 32,000; Czechoslovakia, from 14,000 to 24,000; Greece, from 3,000 to 5,000; Yugoslavia, from 1,500 to 3,300; Spain, from 9,000 to 34,000; and Bulgaria, from 3,000 to 5,500 (ibid., I, 524). In contrast, there were other countries where the YCL's were still very feeble: Belgium, 800; England, 2,000; Switzerland, 350; and Holland, 1,300 (ibid., I, 521). No figures were given for the U.S.

204. Ibid., I, 470–71.

205. Ibid., I, 474–78 (especially pp. 475 and 477), 533. On the general theme of defending the USSR, see also ibid., I, 8–9, 32.

206. Ibid., I, 490–94 (China), 507–17 (France), 527–38 (Germany), 539–42 (Bulgaria), 544–46 (Spain).

207. Ibid., I, 32 (see also p. 68). The battles of the Chinese Communists against the Japanese and against the Chinese government were euphemized as being for the "full national and social liberation" of Chinese youth (ibid., I, 490–94).

CHAPTER VII: THE KOMSOMOL PATTERN UNDER POSTWAR STALINISM

1. KP, July 24, 1937, p. 1. These three and Il'inskii were designated as being from the Moscow organization, while Andreev and Klinkov were mentioned as "former leaders" of the Ukrainian Komsomol.

2. Ibid., Aug. 29, 1937, p. 1. Elected as additional secretaries of the CC were Bogachev, Utkin, Beloborodov, and Timirgalin. Gorshenin was relieved as a secretary, owing to his transfer to Osoaviakhim. Elected members of the Bureau of the CC were Bogachev, Utkin, Beloborodov, Volkov, Sorokin, Mgeladze, Brusnikin, and Nikitin. All of those elected had been delegates at the Tenth Congress. For the lists of the CC and the delegates at the Tenth Congress, see S"ezd X, Vol. II, pp. 449–81.

In September, 1937, more alleged traitors were discovered in both the Moscow and Leningrad organizations of the League. Those named in Moscow included Luk'ianov, Il'inskii, Shashirin, Lemberskaia, Khorev, Poliakov, Davidovich, and Leshchinskii; in Leningrad, Averbukh, Tumchenok, Marinushkin, Kuleshov, Shiperov, Lakhtenpen', and Sundugei (*KP*, Sept. 11, 1937, p. 2).

3. *KP*, Feb. 10; March 9 (on the Fifth Plenum of the CC), 21, and later, 1938. "Overinsurer" is a translation of *perestrakhovshchik*.

4. *Ibid.*, March 21–April 8, 1938. The Sixth Plenum of the CC, in September, 1938, provided among other things for a replacement of Komsomol membership cards (*ibid.*, Sept. 22, 1938, pp. 1–3; the Plenum was said to have ended Sept. 15). Both this process and the concurrent new election in the Komsomol were supposed to aid in eliminating enemies, including slanderers and overinsurers (*ibid.*, Oct. 2, 4, 6, 18, 1938).

5. *Ibid.*, Jan. 18, 1938. In June, 1938, he was elected also to the Supreme Soviet of the RSFSR, representing the Gor'kii Oblast (*ibid.*, May 29, p. 1, and June 25, p. 2, both in 1938).

6. For preliminary publicity, see especially the series entitled "Slavnyi put' komsomola," by M. I. Kalinin, *ibid.*, Oct. 14–18, 20–22, 1938. Among the highlights of the big day (October 29) was a special article by Kosarev on "The Young Man of the Country of Socialism" (*ibid.*, Oct. 29, 1938, p. 4).

7. *Ibid.*, Oct. 30, 1938, p. 1 (picture with Politburo); Nov. 4, 1938, p. 2.

8. *Ibid.*, Nov. 20, 1938, p. 1. Mishakova is mentioned here as one whom Kosarev improperly ignored and even removed when she, as an agent of the CC, was unmasking certain enemies in the Chuvash Komsomol.

9. They included S. Ia. Bogachev, V. F. Pikina (both secretaries of the CC), P. S. Vershkov, and I. N. Belosludtsev (members of the CC). (Bogachev and Belosludtsev had not been elected to the CC in 1936.) See *KP*, Nov. 23, 1938, p. 1, and *S"ezd X*, Vol. II, pp. 449–81.

10. For indications of the purging process, see *KP*, Nov. 23, 1938–Feb. 27, 1939.

11. New York *Times*, June 5, 1956, pp. 14–15, reporting Khrushchev's secret speech of Feb. 24, 1956, at the Twentieth Party Congress.

12. *KP*, Nov. 23, 1938, p. 1.

13. *Ibid.*, March 9, 1938, p. 1. Elected at the same time to the Bureau were V. A. Aleksandrov, A. I. Liubin, and S. E. Usenko.

14. *S"ezd X*, Vol. II, pp. 449–81.

15. Three biographies of Mikhailov have been found: *KP*, Nov. 26, 1939, p. 1; *ibid.*, Feb. 7, 1950, p. 3; and (under his name) in *BSE* (2d ed.), XXVII (1954), 609. All are brief. Although they vary somewhat, they present this outline: Nikolai Aleksandrovich Mikhailov was born in 1906 in Moscow. (Could he be a son of the astronomer Aleksandr A. Mikhailov?) Beginning in 1922 he worked in the Moscow factory "Sickle and Hammer," rising from unskilled labor to qualify as a roller. In 1930 he entered the Party. At some stage he did military service. During the thirties he was mostly occupied with Party and journalistic work, becoming a Party official in his factory (1932), a Party official in the *raikom* (Proletarskii raion of Moscow city), and the editor successively of two factory newspapers. In 1937 he joined the staff of *Pravda*. At the end of 1937 the CC of the Party named him editor of *Komsomol'skaia pravda*. He served as first secretary of the Komsomol from 1938 to 1952, becoming a member of the CC of the Party in 1939, a member of the Orgburo in the 1940s, and a secretary

of the CC of the Party in 1952. In March, 1953, he became the first secretary of the Moscow Oblast Committee of the Party, and in March, 1954, Soviet ambassador to Poland. He is now Minister of Culture.

16. S"ezd X, Vol. II, pp. 449–81.

17. One of the most valuable sources for a more complete picture, it should be said, is the Smolensk archive of the Communist Party, which is now being readied for publication by Professor Merle Fainsod.

18. In April, 1937, the Order of the Red Banner of Labor was awarded to the Komsomol in recognition of its contributions in stimulating socialist competition and shock work (KP, April 18, 1937, p. 1). Concerning the departure of more League members to help construct Komsomol'sk, see ibid., April 28 and 29, 1937, p. 1. In the succeeding months considerable attention was directed at elections within the League. See ibid., May–July, 1937.

19. Concerning the elections to the Supreme Soviet of the USSR in December, 1937, see ibid., March 6, 11; May 9, 22; June 16; July 2, 8, 10; Oct. 11, 12, 21; Nov. 1 and following through most of the month; Dec. 1–12, 1937. Concerning the elections to the Supreme Soviet of the RSFSR, see ibid., April 22; May 14; and most issues in June, 1938, up to June 26, the date of the voting.

Meanwhile, in February, 1938, a Komsomolite named Ivanov provided the opportunity for Stalin's pronouncement that the socialist state would not wither away but must strengthen itself because the final victory of socialism could not come as long as the capitalist danger still existed (ibid., Feb. 14, 1938, p. 3).

20. KP, July 12, 1940, p. 1.

21. During the celebration of the League's twentieth anniversary on October 29, Zhdanov referred to the membership as being "over five million members" (ibid., Nov. 4, 1938, p. 3). If that phrase was not used too loosely, this suggests that during the first nine months of 1938, not only was the over-all growth slow, but also the turnover was considerable, since about one million new members were reported to have joined the League during approximately the first half of 1938 (ibid., July 10, 1938, p. 1).

22. The total of new members admitted during 1938 attained the surprisingly large figure of 3,345,000 (ibid., Oct. 6, 1948, p. 2, in an article written in connection with the thirtieth anniversary of the League, coming Oct. 29, 1948).

23. Ibid., March 14, 1939, p. 4.

24. Ibid. (there were said to be 350,402 detachments at present, as compared with 154,414 detachments in 1934 [Seventeenth Party Congress] when the membership was about 7,000,000). Tiurin states that the Pioneers totaled over 10,-000,000 in 1938 (Tiurin, "VLKSM," BSE [suppl.], col. 1730).

25. KP, March 14, 1939, p. 4.

26. Ibid., March 27, 1939, p. 2 (in the new Party Regulations).

27. Ibid., April 21, 1931, p. 1 (directive of the Eighth Plenum of the CC of the Komsomol).

28. Ibid., July 10, 1939, p. 2.

29. In April, 1939, the Eighth Plenum of the CC added four persons to the Bureau of the CC. Again in flagrant disregard of the supposedly sacrosanct Regulations of the League, none of the four had been elected to the Central Committee, either as members or as candidate-members, by the Tenth Congress, and none had been among the 1,103 Komsomol delegates at that meeting

a scant three years before. The four were I. T. Grishin, N. N. Katkov, A. M. Pegov, and A. A. Poletaev (*ibid.*, April 21, 1939, p. 1). (For the list of personnel at the Tenth Congress, see *S"ezd X*, Vol. II, pp. 449–81.) Below the top echelon, the strong cathartic used in purging Kosarev and his followers apparently needed a partial antidote. The Eighth Plenum warned that the practice of expelling members for trivial reasons (including late payment of dues and tardiness or absence from meetings) must cease. Furthermore, the expelling of members because of the social origin of their parents was termed incorrect. All cases were to be investigated individually. The explanatory article published with the directive said that the member should be judged by his deeds and by whether or not he was loyal to the USSR (*KP*, April 21, 1939, p. 1).

30. *KP*, March 27, 1939, p. 2.   31. *Ibid.*, March 30, 1939, p. 1.

32. The Eighth Plenum directed all governing bodies of the Komsomol to make sure that a primary organization of the League was set up on every collective farm and that those primary organizations that were small were reinforced (*ibid.*, April 21, 1939, p. 1). In September, 1939, it was reported at the Ninth Plenum of the CC that the twenty largest League organizations alone had already sent about fifty thousand Komsomolites out on new construction projects (*ibid.*, Sept. 10, 1939, p. 1, and subsequent issues). A later account (1951) states that during the Third Five-Year Plan 120,000 Komsomolites were sent to new construction work in the Soviet Far East ("VLKSM," *BSE* [2d ed.], IX, 339).

33. The Eighth Plenum told Komsomolites to strengthen their work in institutions of higher learning, to help the teachers at all levels, and to aid youth in mastering Marxist-Leninist theory. There was created in the CC and in corresponding lower bodies the post of "secretary for work among school youth and the Pioneers."

The decree of the Plenum listed the sections of the CC and lower organs. Since such listings were not usually set forth so systematically, it will be worth while to reproduce them here. Abolished were the Section for Work among Working Youth, the Section for Work among Youth of Soviet Trading Institutions, and the Commission on Admissions and Expulsions. Under the new organizational structure, the sections (*otdely*) within the CC of the ALCLY were as follows: (1) Section of Cadres of Komsomol Organizations; (2) Organizational-instructoral Section; (3) Section of Propaganda and Agitation; (4) Section of School Youth; (5) Section of Pioneers; (6) Section of Military and Physical Education; (7) Section of Peasant Youth; (8) Section of Student Youth. ("Student" in Russian refers to one in an institution of higher learning.)

In the *obkoms, kraikoms*, and central committees of union republic Komsomol organizations, the divisions were the same. At the okrug level, numbers 1 and 2 were combined and numbers 7 and 8 were omitted. At the *gorkom* and *raikom* level, numbers 1 and 2 were combined, numbers 4 and 5 were combined, and numbers 7 and 8 were omitted. The decree of the Plenum also provided that full-time paid Komsomol secretaries could be assigned only to primary organizations having 500 members or more (*KP*, April 21, 1939, p. 1).

34. *KP*, Sept. 10, 1939, p. 1, and subsequent issues.

35. See the leading article on the Tenth Plenum, *ibid.*, Dec. 20, 1939, p. 1, and Mikhailov's speech on pp. 3–4. For more extensive information on the Tenth Plenum, see *ibid.*, Dec. 20–24, 26–30, 1939; Jan. 10, 17; Feb. 24; March

29, 1940. The 1,500,000 Komsomolites in schools were distributed among 42,140 primary organizations. This was contrasted to the situation on January 1, 1936, when there were only 234,919 Komsomolites in schools, in 18,833 primary organizations. As for the Pioneers, Mikhailov said there were 400,000 leaders of Pioneer detachments and 25,000 senior Pioneer leaders. Senior Pioneer leaders, Mikhailov declared, should be teachers who were at the same time Komsomolites (*ibid.*, Dec. 20, 1939, p. 3).

36. In the first quarter of 1939, 10,061 teachers had entered the League; in the second, 8,378; and in the third, only 4,093. Mikhailov also warned of too many expulsions of teachers without adequate cause, saying that among 278 cases of teachers expelled in 1939 who had appealed their cases to the Central Committee, only 51, or less than one-fifth, had been found to have been genuinely deserving of expulsion, and the rest had been reinstated. In demonstrating the importance attached to the work in the schools, Mikhailov incidentally revealed that the Tenth Plenum had been called at the order of the Party and that the preparations for the Plenum had been conducted by none other than the Bolshevik leaders Andreev, Zhdanov, and Malenkov (*KP*, Dec. 20, 1939, p. 3).

37. *KP*, June 27, 1940, p. 1. During July, August, and September, 1940, elections were held within the League, reportedly by secret ballot (*ibid.*, July 12, 28; Aug. 14; Sept. 5, 1940). These were followed in September by raion and oblast conferences of the Komsomol and congresses in the union republics (*ibid.*, Sept. 11, 25, 28, 29, 1940). It looked as though these might be leading up to the next All-Union congress, now more than a year overdue. But that did not come.

38. *Ibid.*, Oct. 3, 1940, and subsequent issues in October.

39. *Politicheskii slovar'*, p. 92. In September, 1939, at the Ninth Plenum of the Komsomol CC, it was stated that during the past five months, 834,000 youths had entered the Komsomol and 200,000 Komsomolites had entered the Party (*KP*, Sept. 10, 1939, p. 1).

40. *KP*, July 12, 1940, p. 1.

41. *Ibid.*, June 8, 1940, p. 1 (Eleventh Plenum). There were said at that time to be 328,000 secretaries of primary organizations (*ibid.*, p. 3). That number cannot be taken as the number of primary organizations, since the larger primary organizations were permitted several secretaries. For details on the number of paid secretaries permitted for organizations of various sizes, see the decree of the Eighth Plenum in *ibid.*, April 21, 1949, p. 1. For more on the Eleventh Plenum, see *ibid.*, June 8–12; July 4, 1940.

42. For example, see *ibid.*, April 21, 1939, p. 1 (Eighth Plenum of CC); Sept. 10, 1939, p. 1, and subsequent issues (Ninth Plenum of CC). The winter of 1940–41 witnessed cross-country ski races, frankly designed as one aspect of military preparedness (*ibid.*, Dec. 7, 1940, to March 6, 1941). The same sort of campaign can be found in the winter issues of *Komsomol'skaia pravda* during the war years and after.

43. *Ibid.*, June 28, 1941, p. 2.   44. *Ibid.*, July 2, 1941, p. 1.

45. See *ibid.*, July 11, 15; Aug. 2, 24, 1941, or virtually any other issues of this period.

46. *Ibid.*, June 15, 1945, p. 1; also Oct. 10, 1948, p. 2.

47. For samples, see *ibid.*, Sept. 6, 1941; Jan. 7, Feb. 1, April 21, 28, 1942. A

special heroine was Zoia Kosmodem'ianskaia, a girl who was killed by the Germans for partisan activity (*ibid.*, Feb. 17, 18, 1942).

48. *Ibid.*, Sept. 14, 1943, pp. 1–3; more in subsequent issues. The five were Ul'iana Gromova, Ivan Zemnukhov, Oleg Koshevoi, Sergei Tiulenin, and Liubov' Shevtsova. Made heroes from the moment of this initial telling of their martyrdom, they were subsequently further glorified in Fadeev's novel, *The Young Guard*, which ran serially (with interruptions) in *Komsomol'skaia pravda* from April 8, 1945, to March 1, 1946.

49. *KP*, Sept. 23, 1948, p. 2.

50. *Ibid.*, June 15, 1945, p. 1 (awarded by the Presidium of the Supreme Soviet of the USSR).

51. *Ibid.*, Aug. 6, 1941, p. 1, and following issues.

52. *Ibid.*, Jan. 15, 1942, p. 1, for an example. Other examples are easily located, being usually in boxes.

53. For illustrations in the year 1942, see *ibid.*, March 3, 13; May 10, 13; June 30; July 8, 10, 24; Aug. 2; Oct. 14, 1942 (all p. 1). Similar seasonal items may be found in the other war years. As indicated by the July 10 item, school children were used for harvesting during their summer vacations.

54. *Ibid.*, April 9, 1942, p. 1. The continuing variety of Komsomol efforts throughout the war may be illustrated by front-page headlines of 1943, especially: *ibid.*, Feb. 19, 28; March 14, 19; April 1, 15; May 7; June 3, 4; July 18; Nov. 18, 20; Dec. 10, 18, 1943.

55. For directives ordering the Komsomol to enlarge its ranks, especially among soldiers, see *ibid.*, Dec. 9, 28, 1941, both p. 1; Jan. 8, 10, 1942, pp. 3 and 1; and March 18, 1942, p. 1. The procedure for admitting new members in factories was slightly simplified. They could be approved by the meeting of the Komsomolites of the applicant's own shop and own shift, rather than waiting for the meeting of the primary organization of the whole factory (*ibid.*, Aug. 1, 1941, p. 1).

56. *Pravda*, Oct. 20, 1942. Julian Towster in his *Political Power in the USSR*, pp. 139–40, says the Komsomol had 12,000,000 members in October, 1942. His footnote cites the issue of *Pravda* given above. The present writer could find no such total stated in that issue, but believes the figure may be substantially accurate.

57. *KP*, Dec. 13, 1942, p. 1. The date of the decree is given in Ivanov, *Izmeneniia*, p. 10.

58. Ivanov, *Izmeneniia*, p. 10.

59. *KP*, Oct. 28, 1943, p. 1. No total for the League was given. Dallin (*Real Soviet Russia*, p. 290) reports a membership of 17,500,000 in 1943, but this figure evidently resulted from misinterpretation of a figure meant to refer to Komsomolites *and* certain other youths.

60. *KP*, Oct. 30, 1943, p. 3. During 1942 alone, 1,340,000 persons entered the Party, Fainsod, "Postwar Role of the Communist Party," *Soviet Union since World War II* (*Annals* . . . , Vol. 263, May, 1949), p. 22.

61. *Daily Worker* (New York), Oct. 5, 1945, p. 9, cols. 1–2. This figure is accepted by Towster (*Political Power in the USSR*, p. 140). The writer has so far been unable to locate a basis for this statement in the Soviet press, but that is presumably its origin.

62. Ershova, *O shkole,* p. 24; *S"ezd X,* Vol. II, p. 254.

63. *KP,* March 30, 1949, p. 3, col. 4.

64. In this connection, reinforcing the authority of the teacher was the principal concern of the Twelfth Plenum of the CC, held in March, 1944. The work in the schools was discussed by first secretary N. A. Mikhailov (see *ibid.,* April 9, 10, 11, and 12, 1944, and later issues, especially April 13, 15; May 25, 1944). The Twelfth Plenum also dealt with work in the rural areas (reported on by secretary N. N. Romanov). The time of the meeting is indicated as March in Ershova, *O shkole,* p. 23. See also *KP,* April 9, 1944, p. 1.

65. For example, see *KP,* Sept. 14, 1945, p. 1.

66. *Ibid.,* Sept. 27, 1945, p. 1, and articles in other issues during September and October.

67. *Ibid.,* March 10, 1946, p. 1. The cities were Smolensk, Viazma, Rostov-on-Don, Krasnodar, Novorossiisk, Sevastopol', Pskov, Novgorod, Voronezh, Velikie Luki, Kalinin, Briansk, Orel, Kursk, and Murmansk.

68. *Ibid.,* May 9, 1946, p. 1 (instructions of the Komsomol CC).

69. *Ibid.,* April 12, 27, and subsequent issues, 1946. In April, the Fifteenth Plenum of the CC of the League centered its attention on the Five-Year Plan (*ibid.,* April 27, pp. 1–2, April 28, pp. 1–2, and later issues, 1946). For additional information on Komsomolites in the Fourth Five-Year Plan, see "VLKSM," *BSE* (2d ed.), IX, 341–42.

70. *KP,* Aug. 31, and most issues in September and October, 1948. Beginning in the issue of October 29, and continuing in most issues to November 18, 1948, are lists of awards to Komsomol officials. These lists are valuable in that they give the full names and positions of over two thousand Komsomol officials. See also the issue of Nov. 21, 1948, p. 1.

71. For an extended treatment of this subject see Ploss, "Political Education in the Postwar Komsomol," *Amer. Slavic and E. Eur. Review,* XV (Dec., 1956), 489–505.

72. *KP,* Oct. 12, 18, and later, 1945. The Fourteenth Plenum of the CC of the League, held November 27–29, 1945, discussed the role of the Komsomol in preparing for the elections. V. N. Ivanov (one of those not elected to the CC by the Tenth Congress and not a delegate there) was elected second secretary of the CC, becoming second in command to Mikhailov. Kalinin presented the Order of Lenin to the League (*ibid.,* Dec. 1, 1945, p. 1; see also subsequent pages in this issue, and subsequent issues in December, especially Dec. 21, 1945, p. 2).

The Thirteenth Plenum had been held in February, 1945. It dealt mainly with political education (on which Mikhailov reported) and with the League's work in the trade, railroad, and FZO schools connected with the Labor Reserve program (reported on by secretary A. E. Kharlamov). See *ibid.,* Feb. 11, 14, 20; March 20, 1945.

73. For news on the Soviet-style campaign, see *ibid.,* between Jan. 1 and Feb. 10, especially Jan. 3, Feb. 2, 7, 8, and 10, 1946.

74. *Ibid.,* Feb. 10 (Stalin's speech), 23 (anniversary of the Red Army), 27; March 14, 1946; all items on p. 1.

75. See, for example, *ibid.,* Nov. 20, 1946 (Kirghizia); Dec. 8–14, 1946 (Ukraine); Jan. 19, Feb. 4 and later, 1947 (Uzbekistan); March 2 and later, 1947 (Belorussia); March 23, 28, 1947 (Leningrad); April 9 and later, 1947 (Karelo-Finnish SSR);

May 28 and later, 1947 (Turkmenistan); July 6–11, 1947 (Moscow); Dec. 3 and later, 1947 (Armenia); Dec. 17 and later, 1947 (Azerbaidzhan).

76. *Ibid.*, June 20, Aug. 12, and Sept. 13, respectively, 1947. Beginning Nov. 18, 1947, the Sixteenth Plenum of the CC dealt, among other things, with the work of the League in higher educational institutions (*ibid.*, Nov. 19–22, 25, 30, 1947). Another concern of the League during 1947 was the work in the rural areas (*ibid.*, Jan. 31; Feb. 13; March 23; April 4 and other April issues; May 11 and other May issues; and most issues through the weeding and harvesting months of 1947).

77. *Ibid.*, July 6, 1946, p. 1.

78. Although this action had been illegal, it was reported without apology at the Eleventh Congress, and the delegates compliantly amended the Regulations to make it legal (*Rez. i dok. XI s"ezda*, pp. 55–56). The number of fourteen-year-olds in the ALCLY in 1949 was placed at 315,387 (Ivanov, *Izmeneniia*, p. 10).

79. Ivanov, *Izmeneniia*, pp. 11–12; *KP*, May 22, 1948, p. 1 (both giving 1,700,000 for 1947), and March 19, 1948, p. 1 (giving 1,734,000 for 1947). There seems to be no disagreement on the figure for 1948. In the first half of that year, 900,000 entered (*KP*, Aug. 24, 1948, p. 1).

80. Ivanov, *Izmeneniia*, pp. 11–12.

81. In principle the purge remained an esteemed weapon (*Rez. i dok. XI s"ezda*, p. 53). The familiar complaint was heard in 1949 that people had been purged without sufficient investigation. But the numbers complained of (for example, ten were expelled in Leningrad in 1948; Mikhailov received 300 complaints in 1948; see *KP*, March 31, 1949, pp. 3–4), while certainly incomplete, do not suggest mass purging. In connection with expulsions, there was added to the Regulations in 1949 an explicit provision for a "thorough examination into the basis of the accusations" and a specific warning against expulsion "for insignificant misdeeds." The expelled Komsomolite was said to have the right to appeal to higher echelons of the League. The appeal was to be examined by the higher echelon within two weeks after it was received (*Rez. i dok. XI s"ezda*, pp. 53–54). See also Ivanov, *Izmeneniia*, p. 15.

82. *KP*, April 1, 1949, p. 2, col. 1.

83. A short history of the Komsomol published in 1948 (Tiurin, "VLKSM," *BSE* [suppl.], col. 1739) refers to the "ten-million-strong Komsomol," but this could have been meant very loosely. No more precise information on the slump has been found.

Another development of the postwar years which is obscure is the extent to which the composition of the League changed. Undoubtedly the proportion of the Komsomol in military service declined and the proportion in various civilian categories rose, but the statistics found by the present writer have been far from complete. For example, it was reported that on January 1, 1944, there were 565,405 Komsomolites in schools, while on January 1, 1948, the comparable figure was 1,038,548 (*KP*, Aug. 27, 1948, p. 2; the school primary organizations numbered 29,155 and 45,123 on the two dates given). From the stated enrollments it may be estimated that in 1948 between one-eighth and one-tenth of all Komsomolites were in school, while in the war year of 1944 the fraction was probably between one-twentieth and one-twenty-fifth.

Related to both the problem of growth and the problem of the changing composition of the League is the report given at the Eleventh Congress that of the 447,000-odd primary organizations, about 33 percent (147,000) had been established within the past three years. (On the number of primary organizations, see Mikhailov in *KP*, March 31, 1949, p. 3, col. 1 [giving 447,310], and Ivanov, *Izmeneniia*, p. 5 [giving 447,600] and p. 17 [147,000]. The Mikhailov citation also gives the figure for the past three years.) It will be observed that 447,000-odd primary organizations for 9,283,289 members means about twenty-one members per group, on the average. The mere fact that one-third of the primary organizations had been established during the past three years cannot be taken as proof that the growth in the membership had been proportionate. For one thing, the primary organizations vary widely in size. In the second place, some primary organizations must have gone out of existence during that period, particularly in military units.

84. It was reported that 669 were aged twenty-six or older. Within this group of 669 persons, the majority (369) were twenty-nine or older (*KP*, April 1, 1949, p. 2, col. 4). For the age limits as stated in the amended Regulations (including the change from fifteen to fourteen), see *Rez. i dok. XI s"ezda*, p. 51.

85. Ivanov, *Izmeneniia*, p. 5. In Russian: *v vozraste do 22 let*.

86. No accurate calculation is possible. The above percentage for delegates up to and not including the age of twenty-two was calculated from the following distribution as given at the Congress: aged under eighteen—75; nineteen through twenty—102; twenty-one through twenty-five—516 (of whom 75 are assumed by the present writer to be aged twenty-one); twenty-six through twenty-eight—300; twenty-nine through thirty—174; older than thirty—195 persons. (Total, 1,362.) See *KP*, April 1, 1949, p. 2, col. 4.

87. This guess was obtained as follows: The age distributions projected for 1950 (on the basis of pre-1939 boundaries, but taking into account hypothetical war losses) by Lorimer, *Population of the Soviet Union*, p. 256, were used in order to estimate the proportion of the total population which fell within the age group fourteen through twenty-five. That proportion was then applied to a population total of 186 million. That total was arrived at by taking the figure for April, 1956 (200.2 million) published in *Narodnoe khoziaistvo SSSR*, p. 18, and deducting roughly two million per year for seven years (to get back to March, 1949), or fourteen million. The two million per year is suggested by Lorimer in the same table (p. 256).

88. This guess assumes that of the 9,283,289 Komsomolites, approximately eight and one-half to eight and three-quarters million were twenty-five or younger—an assumption that does not seem unreasonable in the light of the above-mentioned report that 68 percent were under twenty-two.

89. At the end of World War II, 18.3 percent of the Party members were under the age of twenty-five (Fainsod, "Postwar Role of the Communist Party," *Soviet Union since World War II* [*Annals . . .* , Vol. 263, May, 1949], pp. 29–30). It does not seem rash to assume that about one-fifth, then, were under twenty-six. In September, 1947, the Party had 6,300,000 members; in October, 1952, it had 6,882,145 members, including candidates (Fainsod, *How Russia Is Ruled*, p. 323). In 1949 perhaps it had, then, about 6,500,000, and, if the age composition was not too different from what it had been just after the war, perhaps well over a million Party members were within the age limits of the

Komsomol. Among the Pioneers, with thirteen million members spanning the ages from nine through fourteen, the number aged fourteen and over cannot be estimated accurately, but might be between one and four million. Hence it may be surmised that between eleven and fourteen million youths in the age group fourteen through twenty-five belonged to either the Party, the Komsomol, or the Pioneers in 1949. That would be from one-fourth to almost one-third of the total.

90. In October, 1948, the Seventeenth Plenum of the CC made plans for the Eleventh Congress of the League. Elections were scheduled in all Komsomol organizations during December and January, and the Congress was originally set for February 24, 1949 (*KP*, Oct. 16, 1948, pp. 1–2, and subsequent issues), and then later postponed till March 29. The paper in the weeks before the Congress is interesting for the short biographies (with pictures) which it gives of some of the delegates.

91. *KP*, March 30, 1949, p. 1 (Mikhailov's introductory speech). Sixteen sessions were distributed over the eleven days of the Congress. All sessions were held in the Kremlin. The first long reports to the Congress were given by N. A. Mikhailov, for the Central Committee, and A. A. Krivtsov, for the Central Inspection Commission. These were then discussed by fifty-six speakers. The next matter on the agenda was T. I. Ershova's report "On the Work of the Komsomol in the School." Thirty-three delegates participated in the discussion of this report. The third main topic of the Congress was V. N. Ivanov's shorter report "On the Changes in the Regulations of the ALCLY," which was followed by remarks from thirteen commentators. (Mikhailov, Krivtsov, Ershova, and Ivanov were all secretaries of the Central Committee.) The Congress also passed resolutions on each of these reports, unanimously elected the proposed single slates of officers, heard numerous greetings from representatives of foreign youth, received its second Order of Lenin, and sent a letter to Stalin.

92. Sent March 31, 1949, and published in *KP*, April 1, 1949, p. 1, cols. 1–3, as well as in *Rez. i dok. XI s"ezda*, pp. 3–4.

93. It was carried under this caption, for example, in *Izvestiia*, March 30, 31, and April 1–6, 1949, all p. 1.

94. *KP*, March 30, 1949, p. 2, col. 4. For another optimistic view of the imminence of Communism, see Ratanov in *ibid.*, April 2, 1949, p. 3, col. 3.

95. *Rez. i dok. XI s"ezda*, p. 9. Also see *KP*, March 31, 1949, p. 2, col. 1, and April 5, 1949, p. 1, col. 1.

96. For some of the many other examples, see *KP*, March 30, 1949, pp. 2–3 *passim*.

97. For example, *ibid.*, April 3, 1949, p. 1, col. 5; *Rez. i dok. XI s"ezda*, p. 50.

98. *Rez. i dok. XI s"ezda*, pp. 20, 51.

99. For illustrations of typical characterizations, see *KP*, March 30, 1949, p. 2, col. 4; March 31, p. 4, col. 3; April 1, p. 3, col. 1; April 2, p. 1, col. 1; and April 3, 1949, p. 1, col. 6.

100. *Ibid.*, April 2, 1949, p. 2, col. 6.   101. *Ibid.*, March 30, 1949, p. 2, col. 6.

102. *Ibid.*, April 10, 1949, p. 1, cols. 1–4.

103. Good examples of these and related points may be found almost anywhere in the published texts of the speeches at the Congress. For example, see Mikhailov in *ibid.*, March 30, and 31, 1949, *passim*. For some interesting spec-

ulations on the psychological significance of the Stalin cult, see Gorer and Rickman, *The People of Great Russia*, p. 169.

104. *KP*, March 30, 1949, p. 1 ("Vchera"); April 3, 1949, p. 1, col. 6; p. 2, col. 6; April 7, p. 3, cols. 1–3.

105. *Ibid.*, March 31, 1949, p. 3, col. 3, also col. 2.

106. *Ibid.*, March 30, 1949, p. 1 (Mikhailov's opening speech). See also *Rez. i dok. XI s"ezda*, p. 8.

107. *KP*, March 30, 1949, p. 1 ("Vchera"); p. 2, col. 4; March 31, p. 3, cols. 1, 3; April 1, p. 2, col. 4; April 9, p. 3, col. 2; Ershova, *O shkole*, p. 31; *Rez. i dok. XI s"ezda*, p. 51.

While the Party was always referred to respectfully, there seemed to be no specific talk of "inculcating respect for the Party." This was in contrast to the explicit demand that Komsomolites show more respect for teachers (see the section on education later in this chapter) or the assertion that all types of work were respected (see the section on production later in this chapter).

108. *KP*, March 31, 1949, p. 3, col. 3; p. 4, col. 3; April 1, p. 2, col. 4; April 10, p. 1; *Rez. i dok. XI s"ezda*, pp. 50, 55.

109. To quote the Regulations: "All work of the Leninist Komsomol is carried on under the direct guidance of the ACP(B). The CC of the ALCLY, being the governing body of the Komsomol, is directly subordinated to the CC of the ACP(B). The work of local Komsomol organizations is directed and controlled by the corresponding oblast, krai, republic, town, and raion Party organizations" (*Rez. i dok. XI s"ezda*, p. 51).

110. For example, see *KP*, March 31, 1949, p. 3, cols. 2–3.

111. See, for example, *ibid.*, March 30, 1949, p. 2, col. 1; p. 3, col. 5; March 31, p. 2, col. 6; April 1, p. 2, col. 2; Ershova, *O shkole*, pp. 7, 11, 13, 23–25, 31; *Rez. i dok. XI s"ezda*, pp. 9, 24, 26, 28–29.

112. *KP*, March 31, 1949, p. 2, col. 4.

113. *Ibid.*, April 1, 1949, p. 2, col. 2; April 10, p. 1, col. 4; *Rez. i dok. XI s"ezda*, pp. 5–7.

114. *KP*, March 30, 1949, p. 2, cols. 1–2; March 31, p. 1, col. 2; p. 3, col. 4; April 1, p. 2, col. 2. The partisan heroes of Fadeev's *Molodaia gvardiia* were cited as examples of heroism by Sofronov in *KP*, April 6, 1949, p. 2, col. 5. See also the melodramatic tale of the doomed band of non-Komsomol partisans, whose dying wish was that they be posthumously enrolled as Komsomol members (*KP*, April 13, 1949, p. 2, col. 4).

115. *KP*, March 30, 1949, p. 2, cols. 4–5; p. 3, cols. 1–2; Ivanov, *Izmeneniia*, p. 19.

116. *KP*, March 30, 1949, p. 3, col. 5. For a typical pledge of better performance, see Mikhailov in *ibid.*, April 3, 1949, pp. 1–2.

117. For one example, see *ibid.*, March 31, 1949, p. 3, col. 2.

118. *Ibid.*, April 1, 1949, p. 2, col. 2. For other references to love of work, see Ershova, *O shkole*, p. 13; *Rez. i dok. XI s"ezda*, pp. 7, 27–28; *KP*, April 5, 1949, p. 1, col. 4 (Mikhalkov speaking). A particularly popular phrase appeared in the Congress's letter to Stalin: "For millions of young people and Komsomolites, labor has become a matter of honor, glory, valor, and heroism" (*KP*, April 10, 1949, p. 1).

119. *KP*, March 30, 1949, p. 2, col. 2, and March 31, p. 2, col. 1; Ivanov, *Izmeneniia*, pp. 7–8.

120. *KP*, March 31, 1949, p. 4, col. 3.

121. For example, see *Rez. i dok. XI s"ezda*, p. 7; *KP*, March 30, 1949, p. 2, cols. 2, 5, and March 31, p. 4, col. 3.

122. As before, this discipline must be "conscious," must include a sense of individual "organizedness" and conscientiousness, coupled with "comradeliness" and a "deep respect for the collective" (*Rez. i dok. XI s"ezda*, pp. 27–28, 31; *KP*, March 30, 1949, p. 2, col. 5; p. 3, col. 3; March 31, p. 3, cols. 2, 4; Ershova, *O shkole*, p. 8). See also the section on the schools later in this chapter.

123. *KP*, March 31, 1949, p. 2, col. 4.   124. *Ibid.*, April 2, 1949, p. 2, col. 6.

125. *Ibid.*, March 31, 1949, p. 2, col. 4.

126. *Rez. i dok. XI s"ezda*, pp. 13, 28, 50–52; *KP*, March 31, 1949, p. 2, col. 5; April 3, p. 2, col. 3.

127. *KP*, March 30, 1949, p. 2, col. 2; March 31, p. 3, col. 3; April 2, p. 2, col. 3; April 5, p. 1, col. 5; April 10, p. 1.

128. One speaker inveighed against a flippant attitude toward questions of marriage and family (*ibid.*, April 2, 1949, p. 2, col. 6), but aside from that, the problem of the family was left untouched. As to friends, a clause in the Regulations obliged the Komsomol member to "restrain [his] comrades from wrong deeds, to respect the rules of socialist intercourse, to struggle against drunkenness, hooliganism, and against remnants of religious prejudice, and against an uncomradely attitude toward women" (*Rez. i dok. XI s"ezda*, p. 52). One article on the Congress spoke in passing of "reunions of old friends" (*KP*, March 30, 1949, p. 1 ["Vchera"]), but one reads no more about friends except in abstract usages (e.g., Stalin is the "best friend of Soviet youth," the teacher gives "friendly help" to the student, etc.).

129. See *Rez. i dok. XI s"ezda*, p. 8. See also *KP*, April 8, 1949, p. 4, cols. 3, 6.

130. *KP*, April 2, 1949, p. 2, col. 6.   131. *Ibid.*, April 3, 1949, p. 2, col. 1.

132. Ivanov, *Izmeneniia*, p. 19.   133. *KP*, March 30, 1949, p. 1.

134. *Ibid.*, p. 2, col. 3.   135. *Ibid.*, p. 1; *S"ezd X*, Vol. II, pp. 449–51.

136. *KP*, April 1–13, 1949; *S"ezd X*, Vol. II, pp. 449–51.

137. The members numbered 103, the candidate-members, 47 (*KP*, April 9, 1949, p. 3; *S"ezd X*, Vol. II, pp. 449–51.

138. The complete list of delegates of the Tenth Congress was published (*S"ezd X*, Vol. II, pp. 452–81), giving last names and initials. But there was no comparable list published for the Eleventh Congress. Moreover, the Eleventh Congress did not disclose the number of its delegates who had attended any previous congress, whereas such a figure had been given at preceding assemblies. There was given a distribution according to the time of entrance into the League, showing that 315, or not quite one-quarter, of the delegates had become members in 1935 or before, but there is no way of knowing how many of them were at the Congress of 1936. The rest of the distribution follows: entered between 1936 and 1940—510 delegates; between 1941 and 1944—302 delegates; between 1945 and 1947—199 delegates; and in 1948—36 (*KP*, April 1, 1949, p. 2).

139. See note 15 earlier in this chapter, and also *KP*, April 1, 1949, p. 2.

140. *Ibid.*, April 1–13, 1949, *passim.*   141. *Ibid.*, April 1, 1949, p. 2.

142. Ivanov, *Izmeneniia*, p. 5. In the Moscow organization of the League, 59.6 percent were reported to be women (*KP*, April 1, 1949, p. 3).

143. *KP*, April 9, 1949, p. 3 (103 members, 47 candidate-members).

144. *Ibid.*, March 30, 1949, p. 1.

145. *Ibid.*, March 31, 1949, p. 3, col. 1. See also *ibid.*, April 1, 1949, p. 3, col. 3; April 6, p. 4, cols. 1–3; April 7, p. 3, col. 6; p. 4, col. 3.

146. The amended Regulations defined this as "(a) the election of all Komsomol governing bodies from the bottom upward [instead of 'from the top downward,' as in the 1936 version]; (b) periodic accounting by Komsomol governing bodies to their Komsomol organizations; (c) strict Komsomol discipline and the subordination of the minority to the majority; (d) the unconditionally binding nature of the decisions of higher Komsomol bodies for all lower bodies, and for all members of the Komsomol" (*Rez. i dok. XI s"ezda*, p. 54. Cf. *S"ezd X*, Vol. II, p. 433). The significance of the change in "(a)" would seem to be purely propagandistic.

147. *Rez. i dok. XI s"ezda*, p. 62. For Mikhailov's discussion of this, see *KP*, March 31, 1949, p. 3, col. 1. See also Ivanov, *Izmeneniia*, pp. 13–15.

148. *KP*, April 1, 1949, p. 2, col. 1.   149. Ivanov, *Izmeneniia*, p. 13.

150. *S"ezd X*, Vol. II, pp. 434, 436, 437.

151. Ivanov, *Izmeneniia*, p. 9; *Rez. i dok. XI s"ezda*, p. 43.

152. *Rez. i dok. XI s"ezda*, pp. 55 ff.

153. *KP*, April 1, 1949, p. 2.

154. *Ibid.*, March 31, 1949, p. 3, cols. 1–3; April 3, p. 1, col. 5. For other references to concrete and differentiated help, see Ershova, *O shkole*, p. 14; *Rez. i dok. XI s"ezda*, pp. 19–20. There was not at this Congress (or at the others) any discussion of different approaches to different types of personality. There was no mention of mental or physical abnormality or illness. The problem of the wounded survivors of the recent war was not discussed, even though there must have been a great many such persons still within the Komsomol age group.

155. *KP*, March 31, 1949, p. 2, col. 2; p. 3, cols. 1–2; April 1, p. 3, col. 3; Ivanov, *Izmeneniia*, p. 14; *Rez. i dok. XI s"ezda*, p. 61. The categories of punishments ranged from censure through reprimand and temporary separation from posts of leadership to the extreme measure—expulsion from the Komsomol (*Rez. i dok. XI s"ezda*, pp. 62–63).

156. *Rez. i dok. XI s"ezda*, p. 20.

157. *KP*, March 31, 1949, p. 3, cols. 1–2, 6; p. 4, cols. 1–2; April 3, p. 1, col. 4; *Rez. i dok. XI s"ezda*, p. 60.

158. *Rez. i dok. XI s"ezda*, p. 62, also p. 50.

159. For sample references having to do with obedience, see *Rez. i dok. XI s"ezda*, pp. 20, 50–52. In addition to the foregoing precepts for the leader and follower there were the many obligations, cited in other connections, that were applicable to both. For one general list, see *Rez. i dok. XI s"ezda*, pp. 51–53. The question of dues received some attention at the Congress, and several organizations were censured for a poor record in dues payment (*KP*, March 31, 1949, p. 3, cols. 2, 4–5). Krivtsov reported that membership dues were one of the main revenue sources in the Komsomol budget, along with admission dues, contributions for patronage (of the Navy and the Air Forces), and income from publishing activities (*KP*, March 31, 1949, p. 3, col. 4).

There were also certain "rights" reserved to each Komsomolite, concerning which the Congress added a new section to the Regulations. "3. The member of the ALCLY has the right (a) to take part in the discussion of all questions of the work of the Komsomol at Komsomol meetings and in the Komsomol press; (b) to elect and be elected to Komsomol bodies; (c) to criticize at Komsomol meetings any Komsomol worker and also any Komsomol body; (d) to demand personal participation in all cases when a decision is taken concerning his activity or conduct; (e) to address any questions, complaints, or declarations to any Komsomol committee, up to the Central Committee of the ALCLY" (*Rez. i dok. XI s"ezda*, p. 52).

160. *Rez. i dok. XI s"ezda*, p. 62.

161. Of the more than two hundred thousand "propagandists" (not defined) in the League, over 45 percent were said to be Party members (*KP*, March 31, 1949, p. 2, col. 2; 80 percent of this select group were reported to have either higher or secondary education). Ivanov declared that "over 99 percent" of the "active Komsomol workers" (*aktivnykh komsomol'skikh rabotnikov*) were in the ranks of the Party. In his next paragraph, he said there were one and one-half million Komsomol "activists," but it seems unlikely that he was using this as equivalent to "active Komsomol workers." Perhaps the "active Komsomol workers" were the full-time paid officials, whereas the "activists" were those who held any sort of Komsomol post (Ivanov, *Izmeneniia*, p. 15). Of little help is Mikhailov's statement that during the period 1936–49 almost four million Komsomol members entered the Party, for he did not indicate how many of these had retained their membership in the League (*KP*, March 31, 1949, p. 3, col. 1).

162. *KP*, April 1, 1949, p. 2, col. 4.   163. *Ibid.*, March 31, 1949, p. 3, col. 1.

164. The amended Regulations provided that secretaries at the oblast, krai, and union republic levels must have been in the Komsomol for at least three years and must be members of the Party. Secretaries at the raion, town, and okrug levels must have been in the Komsomol for at least two years and must be either members or candidate-members of the Party (*Rez. i dok. XI s"ezda*, pp. 58–59). In neither case was there a stated time of required service in the Party, as there had been in the Regulations of 1936 and earlier. It is curious that in discussing and recommending the change, Ivanov ignored the illegal changes which the CC had made in 1939. He treated the amendment as a reduction from the long Party service which had been required in the Regulations of 1936 and argued that this change would favor the rapid development of new cadres (Ivanov, *Izmeneniia*, p. 16). Ivanov prefaced his recommendation of all the changes in the Regulations with the explanation that whenever the Party changed its Regulations, the League always had to follow suit (Ivanov, *Izmeneniia*, pp. 6–7).

165. *Rez. i dok. XI s"ezda*, p. 53. For the same provision in the Regulations of 1936, see *S"ezd X*, Vol. II, p. 432.

166. *KP*, March 30, 1949, p. 1.

167. After Stalin, the order was: Molotov, Malenkov, Beriia, Voroshilov, Mikoian, Andreev, Kaganovich, Khrushchev, Shvernik, Bulganin, and Kosygin (*ibid.*, April 1, 1949, p. 2. col. 1). (They were elected honorary delegates to the Congress.)

168. *Ibid.*, March 30, 1949, p. 1.

169. *Ibid.*, March 30 to April 9, 1949, *passim.*

170. *Ibid.*, April 3, 1949, p. 1, col. 4. The Regulations declared that criticism

was to be expressed "without regard to the persons it involves, in order that members of the Komsomol may criticize the work of their elective bodies and their leaders, banishing from leadership posts those who are chatterboxes and who disdain rough, practical labor." Discussion, although it was to be "free," must also be "businesslike" and "must be directed toward the better fulfillment of the decisions of the Party and toward the still greater solidarity of the Komsomol with the Party." Also, it was "free only until the organization has taken a decision on the matter in question" (*Rez. i dok. XI s"ezda*, pp. 61–62; also p. 52).

171. Mikhailov, for example, criticized Voznesenskii, RSFSR Minister of Education, for not putting out enough good textbooks (*KP*, March 30, 1949, p. 3, col. 5). See also *ibid.*, March 31, 1949, p. 2, cols. 1, 5; April 2, p. 2.

172. The nine speakers not so elected fell into these categories: two "toilers" (a Stakhanovite and a kolkhoz "link" or small work-crew leader); two trade-school students; three officials of national minority organizations of the Komsomol (two Uzbeks, one Belorussian); one secretary of a raion committee; and a representative from Ulianovsk. Over sixty of the seventy-eight strictly Komsomol speakers were upper-echelon officials (secretaries of oblast, krai, and union republic organizations). See *KP*, March 30 to April 9, 1949, *passim*.

173. The chief points concerning political indoctrination and education were covered by Mikhailov in his Report of the Central Committee on the opening day (March 29) of the Congress (*KP*, March 30–31, 1949, *passim*, and especially March 31, p. 2, cols. 1–3). During the discussion of the Central Committee's report, most speakers touched on the same points. Then they were summarized conveniently in Section III of the Resolution on the Report of the Central Committee (*Rez. i dok. XI s"ezda*, pp. 13–15), which was passed unanimously by the Congress (*KP*, April 3, 1949, p. 2, col. 1).

174. *KP*, March 30, 1949, p. 3, cols. 1 and 6; Ershova, *O shkole*, pp. 14–15, 30. Ershova's report was the longest after Mikhailov's. See also Ivanov, *Izmeneniia*, p. 19.

175. The distribution was given as follows: 513 persons (38 percent) had completed and partially completed higher education; 416 persons (30.5 percent) had completed secondary school; 299 persons (22 percent) had not completed secondary shool. These add up to 1,228, leaving 134 voting delegates unaccounted for (total, 1,362) (*KP*, April 1, 1949, p. 2, col. 3). More than half of the secretaries of oblast committees, krai committees, and central committees of union republic Komsomol organizations had now had at least some schooling beyond the secondary level. Among secretaries of raion and town committees, almost two-thirds reportedly had at least completed secondary schooling (Ivanov, *Izmeneniia*, p. 15).

176. *Rez. i dok. XI s"ezda*, p. 23.

177. This goal was said to require the building of more schools (Ershova, *O shkole*, pp. 3–4; Krasavchenko in *KP*, April 1, 1949, p. 3, col. 2). Krasavchenko, secretary of the Moscow *gorkom* and *obkom*, restated also the next aim in the cities, that of universal ten-year schooling (*ibid.*).

178. *KP*, March 30, 1949, p. 3, cols. 1 and 6; Ershova, *O shkole*, pp. 14–15; *Rez. i dok. XI s"ezda*, pp. 16, 26–27.

179. *Rez. i dok. XI s"ezda*, p. 16; *KP*, March 30, 1949, p. 3, col. 3; Ershova, *O shkole*, p. 5.

180. It was alleged that Soviet teachers had risen to a height they never could

reach in bourgeois society (Ershova, *O shkole*, p. 23). Teachers were called "the foremost detachment of our people's intelligentsia" (*KP*, March 30, 1949, p. 3, col. 3). Medals were being distributed liberally in order to bolster the prestige of the profession; it was reported that over 100,000 had already been issued (Ershova, *O shkole*, p. 4).

181. Ershova, *O shkole*, pp. 5, 23–25; *Rez. i dok. XI s"ezda*, pp. 16, 24, 26–38.

182. *Rez. i dok. XI s"ezda*, p. 37. See also Ershova, *O shkole*, p. 24; *KP*, March 30, 1949, p. 3, col. 3; April 9, p. 4, col. 1.

183. *KP*, March 30, 1949, p. 3, col. 4; Ershova, *O shkole*, p. 24. Note that this would mean about nine teachers to each.

184. Ershova, *O shkole*, p. 23.   185. *KP*, March 30, 1949, p. 3, cols. 4–5.

186. Ershova, *O shkole*, p. 24. Mikhailov's and Ershova's instructions to teachers' Komsomol organizations were reiterated in the Congress's resolution "O . . . shkole" in *Rez. i dok. XI s"ezda*, pp. 36–38. Among other things, the Congress instructed all teachers to reduce the number of pupils who were held over to repeat a grade (Ershova, *O shkole*, pp. 6–7; *KP*, March 30, 1949, p. 3, col. 5). For other remarks directed at teachers, see *ibid.*, col. 6; *Rez. i dok. XI s"ezda*, pp. 16–17; Ershova, *O shkole*, pp. 9–11, 23–25, 30, 39.

187. *KP*, March 30, 1949, p. 3, col. 3; also Ershova, *O shkole*, p. 8; *Rez. i dok. XI s"ezda*, pp. 24, 28.

188. Ershova, *O shkole*, p. 8. These were not itemized at the Eleventh Congress, but presumably are the same rules as those published in Ashby, *Scientist in Russia*, p. 216.

189. *Rez. i dok. XI s"ezda*, p. 27; Ershova, *O shkole*, p. 8.

190. *KP*, March 30, 1949, p. 3, cols. 1, 3, 6; Ershova, *O shkole*, pp. 5–6, 8, 23; *Rez. i dok. XI s"ezda*, pp. 24, 25, 27–29, 39.

191. *KP*, March 31, 1949, p. 2, col. 1; see also *Rez. i dok. XI s"ezda*, p. 30.

192. *KP*, March 30, 1949, p. 2, col. 6; *Rez. i dok. XI s"ezda*, pp. 31–32; Ershova, *O shkole*, p. 14.

193. *KP*, March 31, 1949, p. 3, col. 1.

194. *Rez. i dok. XI s"ezda*, p. 24. In absolute terms, this was said to mean 1,300,000 Komsomolites—a figure which seems low, and probably indicates that few pupils in seven-year schools were included in the total from which the "over half" was computed. The number 1,300,000 was stated to be five and one-half times the number of Komsomolites in schools in 1936. The 1,300,000 pupils were said to be in 49,000 primary organizations, which indicates that the average size of these school primary organizations was about twenty-six persons, as compared with an over-all average of about twenty-one (*KP*, March 30, 1949, p. 3, cols. 1–2). Ivanov spoke of "over 47,000" primary organizations in seven-year and secondary schools. He also gave other statistics for which there is not space here (Ivanov, *Izmeneniia*, p. 10).

195. *KP*, March 30, 1949, p. 3, col. 6; Kaftanov in *ibid.*, April 8, 1949, p. 2, cols. 1–2 (for the figure of over two million for the total). There were said to be 3,500 *tekhnikums* (classed as "secondary special educations") and 800 *vuzes* (institutions of higher learning) (*ibid.*). In the *vuzes*, there were said to be 730,000 regular students (plus 270,000 correspondence course students) (Kaftanov in *Izvestiia*, March 29, 1949, p. 2, col. 1). Of all students in *vuzes*, almost half were said to be Komsomolites (Kaftanov in *KP*, April 8, 1949, p. 2, col. 2). This can

be compared with reports in September and October, 1948, that the universities and institutes contained about 700,000 students, of whom about 330,000 were Komsomolites (*KP*, Sept. 23, 1948, p. 2; Oct. 13, 1948, p. 3). At this higher level the number of Party members was probably considerable.

As to the primary organizations, Ivanov reported that there were "over 3,000" primary organizations in higher educational institutions, technical, and specialist schools (Ivanov, *Izmeneniia*, p. 17). Apparently he was referring to both *vuzes* and *tekhnikums*, in which case those primary organizations were large—in the neighborhood of 333 members in each, on the average.

196. *KP*, April 12, 1949, p. 4, col. 1; Ershova, *O shkole*, p. 12.

197. Ershova, *O shkole*, p. 6; *Rez. i dok. XI s"ezda*, p. 7.

198. *Rez. i dok. XI s"ezda*, pp. 30–31; Ershova, *O shkole*, pp. 10–11, 13, 25; *KP*, April 5, 1949, p. 1, col. 6; April 6, p. 2, col. 2; April 12, p. 3, cols. 4–6.

199. *KP*, March 30, 1949, p. 3, cols. 2–3; Ershova, *O shkole*, pp. 6–7; *Rez. i dok. XI s"ezda*, pp. 25, 28.

200. *KP*, March 30, 1949, p. 3, cols. 3–4; April 8, p. 4, col. 3.

201. *Rez. i dok. XI s"ezda*, p. 28; see also pp. 26, 32.

202. Ershova, *O shkole*, p. 14. A woman named Pomerantseva, who was the principal of a girls' school in Moscow, reported that, under instructions from the CC, she had tried the new system and had found that it facilitated the adapting of the Komsomol program to each age group (*KP*, April 12, 1949, p. 4, cols. 1–3). See also *KP*, April 6, 1949, p. 1, col. 4.

203. Komsomol organizations in separate school grades, under this amendment, could be granted the rights of primary organizations of the Komsomol (*Rez. i dok. XI s"ezda*, p. 60). The Regulations already allowed for the setting up of such sub-organizations in factories, schools, etc., wherever the primary organization had more than 100 members, but did not grant these sub-organizations the rights of primary organizations.

204. *KP*, March 30, 1949, p. 3, cols. 5–6; *Rez. i dok. XI s"ezda*, p. 17.

205. The Labor Reserve schools ("trade and railroad schools of FZO") were said to have provided over 4,500,000 qualified workers since they began in 1940. During the same period, 1,200,000 students of Labor Reserve schools had entered the Komsomol. The current Komsomol membership in Labor Reserve schools was given as almost 250,000. Komsomol responsibilities there resembled those in the regular schools (*KP*, March 30, 1949, p. 2, col. 6; *Rez. i dok. XI s"ezda*, pp. 7, 12).

206. *KP*, March 31, 1949, p. 2, col. 1; April 7, p. 3, col. 4.

207. *Rez. i dok. XI s"ezda*, pp. 13–15.

208. In Russian, *do 15 let*, which presumably means to the fifteenth birthday but not beyond. For general information on the Pioneer organization, see *BSE*, supplementary volume on the USSR (1948), cols. 1739–42, and Towster, *Political Power in the USSR*, pp. 142–44. The full name of the organization remained "Children's Communist Organization of Young Pioneers Named after Comrade Lenin." The Little Octobrists, described also by Towster, were not mentioned at the Congress of 1949, so far as the present writer could discover.

209. *Rez. i dok. XI s"ezda*, p. 25.

210. *KP*, March 30, 1949, p. 3, col. 4; April 3, p. 2, col. 2; Ershova, *O shkole*, p. 15; Ivanov, *Izmeneniia*, p. 17.

211. Significantly, the discussion of the Pioneers at the Congress came as a sub-division of the discussion of the work of the League in the schools (*KP*, March 30, 1949, p. 3, col. 4; Ershova, *O shkole*, pp. 15 ff). The qualities to be inculcated in Pioneers were the same as those desired in all school children. It continued to be the responsibility of the Komsomol to establish in each school a Pioneer troop (*druzhina*) which worked under the direct guidance of the local Komsomol organization. Each higher echelon of the Komsomol had the duty of supervising Pioneer activity within its area. At the all-Union, union republic, oblast, and krai levels, Komsomol committees published newspapers, magazines, and children's literature for the Pioneers (*Rez. i dok. XI s"ezda*, pp. 63–64).

212. *KP*, March 30, 1949, p. 3, col. 4.

213. *Rez. i dok. XI s"ezda*, p. 32. The Pioneer leader was termed "the right arm of the principal of the school" (*KP*, April 8, 1949, p. 3, col. 6).

214. The committees were to select as leaders of each troop (*druzhina*) and detachment (*otriad*) those members of the Komsomol who were "best prepared for this work" (*Rez. i dok. XI s"ezda*, p. 63). As before, each detachment was divided into "links," which were the smallest Pioneer unit. Since 1947, the link leaders were said to have been elected by the Pioneers rather than appointed. Apparently on this lowest level they did not need to be Komsomol members. Also elected were the members of the detachment and troop councils (Ershova, *O shkole*, p. 15). Concerning other attributes desired in the Pioneer leader, in accordance with the Komsomol pattern, see *KP*, April 3, 1949, p. 2, col. 3, and Ershova, *O shkole*, p. 19.

215. *KP*, March 30, 1949, p. 3, col. 4. Ershova pointed out that the Soviet government had indicated its high esteem for the work of Pioneer leaders by awarding medals and orders to many of them (Ershova, *O shkole*, p. 19). See also *KP*, April 8, 1949, p. 3, col. 4.

216. The problem was attacked on three fronts: (1) more teacher-Komsomolites must be attracted into the work of Pioneer leaders; (2) pedagogical institutes must give more training, both theoretical and practical, in the techniques of directing Pioneer units; and (3) special schools and seminars must give additional instruction to Pioneer leaders. The Komsomol was asked to cooperate with educational authorities to accomplish these ends. See Ershova, *O shkole*, pp. 19–21; *Rez. i dok. XI s"ezda*, pp. 35–36; *KP*, March 30, 1949, p. 3, col. 4.

217. *KP*, March 30, 1949, p. 3, col. 4; *Rez. i dok. XI s"ezda*, p. 33.

218. *KP*, March 30, 1949, p. 3, col. 4; *Rez. i dok. XI s"ezda*, pp. 24–25, 33–35, 63; Ershova, *O shkole*, pp. 16, 18.

219. *Rez. i dok. XI s"ezda*, pp. 33–34; Ershova, *O shkole*, pp. 26–28.

220. *KP*, March 31, 1949, p. 2, col. 3; Ershova, *O shkole*, p. 29; *Rez. i dok. XI s"ezda*, pp. 17–18. The frequency of the appearance of the other newspapers and magazines was not indicated. For the titles of many of them, see "VLKSM," *BSE* (2d ed.), IX, 346. As to books, there were apparently various ways of counting, for Mikhailov in the above citation also said that the Young Guard Press had published 13,960,000 books in 1948—which was, he added, one and one-half times the number published in 1940. The principal study materials mentioned in connection with indoctrination included the Constitution of the USSR, the "classics of Marxism-Leninism" (mainly consisting of the works of Lenin and Stalin), the officially approved biographies of Lenin and Stalin, and such docu-

ments as the Regulations of the Komsomol (Ershova, *O shkole*, p. 11; *Rez. i dok. XI s"ezda*, pp. 13–15; also *KP*, April 3, 1949, p. 3, col. 5). The Komsomol was to help in the preparation of bibliographies for study (*Rez. i dok. XI s"ezda*, p. 29).

221. *KP*, March 31, 1949, p. 2, cols. 3–4; April 6, p. 2, col. 6; Ershova, *O shkole*, pp. 28–30. See also the poet Sergei V. Mikhalkov in *KP*, April 9, 1949, p. 3, col. 4.

222. *Rez. i dok. XI s"ezda*, pp. 38–39.

223. *KP*, March 31, 1949, p. 2, col. 3. On religion, see also Ershova, *O shkole*, p. 12; *Rez. i dok. XI s"ezda*, pp. 13–15, 52.

224. *Rez. i dok. XI s"ezda*, pp. 18–19; *KP*, March 31, 1949, p. 2, cols. 4–5; A. N. Apollonov (Chairman of the All-Union Committee on Physical Culture and Sport of the Council of Ministers of the USSR) in *KP*, April 6, 1949, pp. 3–4; Zimin in *KP*, April 6, 1949, p. 3, col. 6. In the regular schools, Komsomolites were to strengthen the "physculture collectives," to improve and extend physical education, and to help build playing fields and other athletic facilities (Ershova, *O shkole*, pp. 13–14; *Rez. i dok. XI s"ezda*, pp. 30–31).

225. Ul'iana Babina in *KP*, April 1, 1949, p. 4, col. 3; also *ibid.*, March 31, 1949, p. 2, cols. 5–6.

226. Babina in *ibid.*, April 6, 1949, p. 3, col. 3. There were pictures of most of the speakers, including this one. On recreation see also *ibid.*, April 3, 1949, pp. 3–4.

227. In 1949 there were three stages of qualification, beginning with the BRLD ("Be Ready for Labor and Defense") and advancing through the RLD first and second class (see Chapter VI). A long-term desideratum was that each student finishing the seven-year school should have earned the badge of the RLD first class (*KP*, March 31, 1949, p. 2, col. 4; April 6, p. 3, cols. 4–5; N. N. Romanov in *ibid.*, April 12, 1949, p. 3, col. 2). N. N. Romanov was an official of the Physical Culture Committee and a member of the CC of the Komsomol.

228. Apollonov in *KP*, April 6, 1949, pp. 3–4. Mikhailov lent his authority to the drive for new world records, saying in part: "The setting of all-Union and world records requires immense work, patience, persistence, and time. With regard to the latter, i.e., time: In athletic literature and among some athletes one finds the assertion that several years are necessary in the preparation for new records. This view cannot be considered correct. From time to time such a 'theory' is used in order to justify negligence and indolence. . . . The practice of the best athletes shows that if one works conscientiously, persistently, and doggedly, one can significantly shorten the period required in the preparation for new records. We must rear athletes in such a way that they have confidence in their strength and patriotically strive always to improve their athletic attainments. The Soviet athlete is obliged worthily and successfully to defend the honor of the homeland in all international competitions" (*KP*, March 31, 1949, p. 2, cols. 4–5).

229. *Rez. i dok. XI s"ezda*, p. 7.

230. *Ibid.*, p. 11. See also Shvernik's statement to the Congress, *KP*, April 9, 1949, p. 3, col. 3.

231. According to V. V. Kuznetsov, Chairman of the All-Union Central Council of Trade Unions, the friendly cooperation of the trade unions and the Komsomol was described as covering such activities as production, factory social

programs, rest homes, athletics, and the efficient use of the graduates of Labor Reserve schools (*KP*, April 8, 1949, p. 2, cols. 4–6). Contact between the trade unions and the Komsomol was said to be so good that it was no longer necessary to provide any special machinery for it, and the appropriate section was stricken from the Regulations (Ivanov, *Izmeneniia*, p. 17; *S"ezd X*, Vol. II, p. 439; *Rez. i dok. XI s"ezda*, pp. 63–64).

232. *Rez. i dok. XI s"ezda*, p. 61. It must also "show wide initiative in discussing and placing before the Party and Soviet organizations all questions directed toward improving the work of enterprises, kolkhozes, sovkhozes, offices, and educational institutions" (*ibid.*, pp. 60–61). Where there was a "political department," the Komsomol organization was led by persons who were chosen by and directly subordinate to the Central Committee of the Komsomol (*ibid.*, p. 57).

233. Ivanov, *Izmeneniia*, p. 17.

234. *KP*, March 30, 1949, p. 1 ("Vchera"). See also *ibid.*, April 1, 1949, p. 2, cols. 2–3; p. 3, cols. 1–2; April 3, p. 4, cols. 1–2.

235. *Ibid.*, March 30, 1949, p. 2, cols. 4–5. See also *ibid.*, April 3, 1949, p. 4, cols. 1–2; April 7, p. 4, col. 2; April 8, p. 2, col. 4.

236. *Ibid.*, March 30, 1949, p. 1 ("Vchera"). See also the section on the "Hero of Our Time," earlier in this chapter. In honor of the Eleventh Congress there was a campaign for "overfulfillment of the Plan." See *ibid.*, March 30, 1949, pp. 1, 4; April 3, p. 1, cols. 4–5.

237. *Rez. i dok. XI s"ezda*, pp. 10–11; *KP*, April 8, 1949, p. 2, col. 3; and, for an amusing illustration, the story of Faina Ognetova in *KP*, April 30, 1949, p. 2, cols. 3–5.

238. The over-all immediate objective was pre-term fulfillment of the current Stalin Five-Year Plan, under the revived slogan, "The Five-Year Plan in Four Years" (*Rez. i dok. XI s"ezda*, pp. 10–11; *KP*, March 30, 1949, p. 2, col. 4). A long-term project for youth was the "Stalin Plan for the Transformation of Nature," involving the planting of shelter belts of trees and the irrigation of arid steppe regions (*ibid.*, p. 3, col. 2; also *ibid.*, April 2, 1949, p. 2, col. 3; *Rez. i dok. XI s"ezda*, p. 13). Other special projects for Komsomolites included rebuilding Stalingrad and restoring Ashkhabad after its severe earthquake of October, 1948 (*KP*, April 6, 1949, p. 2, cols. 4–6; April 7, p. 3, cols. 4–6). Denisov said that among the Komsomolites helping to rebuild Stalingrad there were 25,000 from Leningrad alone, along with many more from other places. All Komsomol bodies in the RSFSR, Belorussia, and the Ukraine were asked to send more workers, including Komsomolites, to the Karelo-Finnish Republic to work as lumberjacks (*KP*, April 3, 1949, p. 3, col. 6; April 8, p. 2, col. 6).

239. *KP*, March 31, 1949, p. 3, col. 1. See also *ibid.*, Jan. 8, 1949, p. 1.

240. *Pravda*, March 11, 1950, cited in Schwartz, *Russia's Soviet Economy*, p. 266, gives a figure of 254,000 collective farms.

241. Schwartz, *Russia's Soviet Economy*, pp. 287, 281, respectively (figures for 1949 and early 1950, respectively).

242. *Narodnoe khoziaistvo SSSR*, p. 21.   243. *KP*, March 30, 1949, p. 3, col. 1.

244. *Ibid.*

245. According to Soviet figures published in 1956, the population was 68.4 percent rural in 1940 and 56.6 percent rural in April, 1956 (*Narodnoe khoziaistvo*

SSSR, p. 17). In August, 1953, Malenkov indicated 60 percent was rural (New York *Times*, Aug. 9, 1953, p. 28). World War II complicates the problem of inter-polation and makes it necessary to use an approximate designation. The com-parison is complicated by the fact that a significant proportion of the Komsomol membership was in the armed forces.

246. *KP*, March 30, 1949, p. 3, cols. 1–2; April 3, p. 2, cols. 4–6; *Rez. i dok. XI s"ezda*, pp. 12–13.

247. *KP*, March 30, 1949, p. 3. Brigades and links are work crews, the link being smaller than the brigade.

248. *KP*, April 2, 1949, p. 2, col. 1.

249. *Ibid.*, April 3, 1949, p. 3, col. 2; April 7, p. 3, cols. 1–3.

250. *Ibid.*, March 31, 1949, p. 2, col. 6. Among the 1,362 voting delegates at the Congress, there were said to be 472 holding offices in soviets, including 390 at the village, raion, okrug, uezd, town, krai, and oblast levels, 36 deputies to the supreme soviets of union republics, and 46 deputies to the Supreme Soviet of the USSR (*ibid.*, April 1, 1949, p. 2). The special provisions for ensuring contact between the Komsomol and the soviets were said to be no longer necessary and were eliminated from the Regulations. See Ivanov, *Izmeneniia*, p. 17, and *Rez. i dok. XI s"ezda*, pp. 63–64.

251. Ershova, *O shkole*, pp. 8–9. Representatives of minority nationalities seconded these points. For example, one referred to the Russian people as "the elder brother in the family of Soviet peoples" and called the Russian language "the language of our great leaders Lenin and Stalin [!]" (Kerimov [secretary of the Komsomol CC in Azerbaidzhan] in *KP*, April 5, 1949, p. 3, col. 6; see also April 9, p. 4, cols. 1, 3).

252. The figures given for the delegates were as follows: Russians—850; Ukrainians—174; Belorussians—51; Georgians—41; Uzbeks—35; Kazakhs—34; Azerbaidzhanians—27; Armenians—22; Tadzhiks—12; Kirghizes—11; Turk-menians—9; Latvians—7; Moldavians—7; Lithuanians—6; Estonians—3; Tatars—15; Bashkirs—6; Chuvashes—5; Mordvinians—4; Buriats—4; Ossetians—4. These total 1,327, leaving only 35 unaccounted for (*KP*, April 1, 1949, p. 2).

The percentages in the population have been calculated from a table in Lamont, "National and Racial Minorities," *USSR: A Concise Handbook*, pp. 6–7. The figures given by Lamont are estimates of 1941. (His figures give the Jews 2.6 percent, the Poles 2 percent, and the Germans 0.7 percent of the population.) Those estimates of 1941 are used here in the absence of accurate information for 1949, even though they do not take into account losses resulting from the war or from the forcible "resettlement" of several nationalities. Also, it is im-possible to know how many non-Russian delegates were calling themselves "Rus-sian" in 1949. It may be recalled in this connection that in the census of 1939 "nationality" was a subjective matter, that is, the individual was asked with which national group he felt that he and his children were most closely identified (Lorimer, *Population of the Soviet Union*, p. 137).

253. The membership was given for some political divisions, but of course in each of them the ethnic composition was more or less mixed. Following are the political units for which Komsomol membership was given: Ukraine, 1,300,000 (*KP*, March 31, 1949, p. 1, col. 3; Ivanov, *Izmeneniia*, p. 12); Belorussia, 325,000 (*KP*, April 3, 1949, p. 3); Uzbekistan, about 300,000 (*KP*, April 13, 1949,

p. 2); Moldavia, 65,000 (*KP*, April 7, 1949, p. 3); Leningrad city and oblast, 300,000 (*KP*, April 13, 1949, p. 3); Moscow, presumably including both city and oblast, 483,000 (Ivanov, *Izmeneniia*, p. 12).

An approximate idea of the size of the membership in other political units was provided by the report on the numbers of delegates from some of them. (See Shelepin, "Doklad," in *KP*, April 1, 1949, p. 2.) The delegates were said to have been elected on a basis of one for each 7,000 members as of January 1, 1949, with one additional allowed for a remainder of 3,500 or over (*ibid.* and also issue of Oct. 16, 1948, p. 1). But a comparison of cases in which both figures were available shows that, owing presumably to the allocation of fractional remainders, the numbers of delegates give only a very rough notion of the membership in the political unit. (For instance, from Belorussia, 60 delegates would give a presumed membership of 420,000 instead of the 325,000 actually reported.)

The size of the Kazakhstan membership was not mentioned at the Congress, but in May, 1948, it was reported at 290,000 (*KP*, May 27, 1948, p. 1).

254. *Rez. i dok. XI s"ezda*, pp. 51–52.

255. Respectively in *KP*, March 31, 1949, p. 3, col. 1, and Ivanov, *Izmeneniia*, p. 5.

256. Ivanov, *Izmeneniia*, p. 17.

257. *KP*, April 1, 1949, p. 2 (Shelepin). It may be noted that at this Congress an effort was apparently made to get a wide distribution from the standpoint of occupation. However, the largest single category, by far, remained that of the full-time Komsomol officials—544 out of 1,362. Probably many of those listed under other occupations also devoted virtually full time to Komsomol work, for Shelepin reported that 832 of the delegates were members of the governing committees at the oblast, krai, and union republic levels, and 235 held similar positions of authority at the volost, raion, town, uezd, and okrug levels. Only 58 of the delegates were listed merely as holding office in the committees of primary organizations. Assuming no overlap in the categories, this would leave 237 delegates who were not Komsomol officials of some sort.

258. *Ibid.*, March 31, 1949, p. 2, col. 6; Marinov in *ibid.*, April 2, 1949, p. 3, cols. 1–2. Marinov held the title "Chief of the Department for Komsomol Work of the Main Political Administration of the Armed Forces of the USSR." He made the obvious point that soldier-Komsomolites were to increase their qualifications in military specialties.

259. *Rez. i dok. XI s"ezda*, p. 64.   260. *Ibid.*, p. 19.

261. Marinov in *KP*, April 2, 1949, p. 3, col. 3.

262. Mikats in *ibid.*, April 13, 1949, pp. 2–3.

263. *Ibid.*, p. 3, col. 1; Marinov in *ibid.*, April 2, 1949, p. 3, col. 3.

264. In Russian, the abbreviations are DOSARM, DOSAV, and DOSFLOT (*ibid.*, March 31, 1949, p. 2, col. 6).

265. *Ibid.*, April 6, 1949, p. 3, cols. 1–3. See also Mikats in *ibid.*, April 13, 1949, p. 3, col. 2. Pokryshkin, speaking on behalf of the Air Forces, also mentioned as parts of DOSAV's program parachute schools and model airplane shops and circles (*ibid.*, April 8, 1949, p. 2, col. 6).

266. *Ibid.*, March 31, 1949, p. 2 (section V of the report).

267. The countries nominally represented were Albania, Austria, Bulgaria, China, Czechoslovakia, England, France, Germany, Hungary, Italy, Mongolia, North

Korea, Norway, Poland, Rumania, and Spain (*ibid.*, March 31, 1949, pp. 1, 4; April 1, pp. 1, 4; April 2, pp. 1, 4; April 3, pp. 1, 2; April 5, pp. 1, 4). The French Communist newspaper *Humanité*, whose reports on the Congress were extremely scanty, did no better even for the speech of the French representative (*Humanité*, April 1, 1949, p. 3, cols. 4–5).

268. *KP*, March 30, 1949, p. 2, cols. 2–3.

269. *Ibid.*, March 31, 1949, p. 2, cols. 5–6.

270. *Ibid.*, col. 6; Marinov in *ibid.*, April 2, 1949, p. 3, col. 1; see also *ibid.*, March 30, 1949, p. 2, cols. 1–4, containing numerous allusions to the wartime bravery of Komsomolites in defending the USSR.

271. *Ibid.*, March 30, 1949, p. 2, col. 2.

272. *Ibid.*, April 5, 1949, p. 4, col. 1.   273. *Ibid.*, April 3, 1949, p. 1, col. 5.

274. *Ibid.*, March 31, 1949, p. 2, col. 6.   275. *Ibid.*, p. 4, cols. 1–2.

276. *Ibid.*, p. 2, col. 6.   277. *Ibid.*, p. 4, col. 3.

278. *Rez. i dok. XI s"ezda*, p. 8.   279. *KP*, April 3, 1949, p. 3, col. 1.

280. Blatin (editor of *KP*) in *ibid.*, April 6, 1949, p. 4, col. 3.

281. *Ibid.*, March 24, 1954, p. 5, col. 5.

282. *Ibid.*, March 31, 1949, p. 2, cols. 5–6.

283. *Ibid.*, pp. 1, 4; April 1, pp. 1, 4; April 2, pp. 1, 4; April 3, pp. 1, 2; April 5, pp. 1, 4.

284. *Rez. i dok. XI s"ezda*, p. 10.

CHAPTER VIII: IN THE ERA OF COLLECTIVE LEADERSHIP

1. One indication of the troubles that probably affected many parts of the Komsomol was a shake-up in the leadership of the Georgian branch of the League in April, 1953 (*Zaria vostoka*, April 29, 1953, p. 1, in *CDSP*, Vol. V, No. 18, p. 3).

The Thirteenth Plenum of the CC of the Komsomol, meeting in October, 1953, announced that the Twelfth Congress would be held in February, 1954 (*KP*, Oct. 18, 1953, p. 1, cols. 1–2), but apparently the preliminary arrangements took longer than expected, and on February 7 it was announced that the Congress would convene on March 19 (*ibid.*, Feb. 7, 1954, p. 1, cols. 1–2).

2. *KP*, April 11, 1950, p. 1, col. 1. This article, which (like many others) urges increased expansion, also says that in the preceding December, January, and February over 992,000 persons entered the Komsomol (414,000 of them in December alone) and over 16,000 new primary organizations were established (*ibid.*). The Second Plenum of the CC was largely devoted to criticism of units that lagged in expanding (*ibid.*, Dec. 8 and 9, 1949, pp. 1–2).

3. *Ibid.*, Feb. 10, 1951, p. 1, col. 1.

4. Between the Eleventh Congress (March–April, 1949) and February, 1951, "about five million" entered the League (*ibid.*, Feb. 10, 1951, p. 1, col. 1; also Mikhailov, "O roste riadov VLKSM," *Molodoi bol'shevik*, IX, No. 3 [Feb., 1951], 3). If that increment brought the total up from its earlier 9,283,289 to only a little over 12,000,000, then about two and one-quarter million youths must have left the League during this period of barely two years. Such a rate of departure, if continued, would have meant 100 percent turnover in between four and five

and one-half years (assuming a total membership between nine and twelve million).

5. *Pravda*, Jan. 4, 1952, p. 1, col. 2. As of June 1, 1951, there were 13,380,648 members ("VLKSM," *BSE* [2d ed.], IX, 330). During the year 1951, more than three and one-half million youths entered the League (*KP*, March 19, 1952, p. 1, col. 1).

6. *KP*, June 19, 1952, p. 1, col. 1 (including an editorial appeal to continue the rapid growth). That same figure was reported in October, at the Nineteenth Party Congress (*ibid.*, Oct. 8, 1952, p. 4, col. 2). Mikhailov added that since the previous Congress (that is, from 1939 to 1952) "over four million" Komsomolites had entered the Party (*ibid.*). Unfortunately, neither Mikhailov nor Malenkov (who reported on net Party growth) revealed how many had entered the Party during the same interval; hence one can only speculate concerning the possible rate of turnover and the possible proportion of Komsomolites among those entering the Party.

7. *Ibid.*, March 28, 1953, p. 1, col. 2.

8. *Kommunist*, XXX, No. 16 (Nov., 1953), 12.

9. *KP*, March 20, 1954, p. 4, col. 3. This is the figure given by Shelepin in the Report of the Central Committee. Semichastnyi, in the Report of the Credentials Commission, said that since the Eleventh Congress there had been an increase of 9,396,185 (*ibid.*, March 23, 1954, p. 2, col. 1). That would produce a total for 1954 of 18,679,474. (As has been observed before, Komsomol officials do not seem greatly concerned about ensuring accuracy in their statistics.) No distribution by sex was given, and no comprehensive figures were given on the distribution of Komsomolites by political or territorial units. There were said to be more than one million in the Moscow Oblast (*ibid.*, March 15, 1954, p. 3, col. 4; March 21, p. 6, col. 1). Krasnodar Krai reported over 250,000 (*ibid.*, March 21, 1954, p. 6, col. 3). The Ukraine reported over three million (*ibid.*, March 23, 1954, p. 3, col. 1). The Uzbek SSR reported 610,000 (*ibid.*, March 23, 1954, p. 3, col. 5).

10. The "eligible age group" is interpreted as including those from fourteen through twenty-seven, in accordance with the new provisions on the maximum limit (see later in this chapter). The number of youths aged fourteen through twenty-seven cannot be accurately known on the basis of available statistics. A guess would be 52,000,000. This guess is based, first, on the hypothetical age distribution given in Lorimer, *Population of the Soviet Union*, p. 256 (taking into account hypothetical war losses and projecting to 1954 on the basis of pre-1939 boundaries). From this, one obtains a rough estimate of the proportion which the Komsomol age group may have constituted in relation to the population as a whole. That proportion may then be applied to the estimated population of 1954. The total population as of March, 1954, may be roughly estimated at 196 million, by crude interpolation from the figures published in *Narodnoe khoziaistvo SSSR*, p. 18. The number aged fourteen through twenty-seven (using Lorimer's proportions) would be about 52,000,000. The Komsomol membership of 18,825,327 would constitute a little over 36 percent of a total of 52,000,000. But the number of Komsomolites aged twenty-eight and over is not known. If there were one million, that would pull the percentage in the "eligible age

group" down to about 34.2. The predominance of guesswork in these calculations hardly needs to be emphasized.

11. In this exceedingly rough estimate, the number of Komsomolites aged fourteen through twenty-seven is assumed to be about 17.8 million (see the preceding footnote). The number of Party members aged eighteen through twenty-seven who were not concurrently Komsomol members is assumed to be between one and one and one-half million. (The Party numbered 6,882,145 members and candidate members as of October 1, 1952. See Gruliow, *Current Soviet Policies*, p. 93. By March, 1954, this total probably had not yet exceeded 7,000,000.) If the Pioneer total was about eighteen million (see the section on ideological training later in this chapter), the number of Pioneers aged fourteen may have been about four million. In round numbers, the three categories total about twenty-three million, which would be about 44 percent of fifty-two million. Since the unknowns are compounded in this calculation, it seems less misleading to speak of a proportion between 40 and 50 percent.

12. See the section on the economy later in this chapter.

13. In August, 1953, the rural proportion was reported by Malenkov to be about 60 percent (New York *Times*, Aug. 9, 1953, p. 28). In the Soviet publication *Narodnoe khoziaistvo SSSR*, p. 17, a rural proportion of 56.6 percent is given for April, 1956. Assuming that both of these figures are accurate, the proportion in March, 1954, may have been about 59 percent.

14. *KP*, Oct. 14, 1952, pp. 1–2.   15. *Ibid.*, Oct. 17, 1952, p. 1, cols. 3–6.

16. *Ibid.*, Nov. 6, 1952, p. 1, cols. 1–3.

17. *Ibid.*, March 11, 1953, p. 1, cols. 1–2.

18. New York *Times*, March 29, 1954, p. 3.

19. Although not a delegate to the Congress of 1936, he was already a member of the Central Committee and one of the secretaries of the Komsomol before the Congress of 1949. There he presided over one session, presented the report of the Credentials Commission, and was elected to the Presidium of the Congress and to the new Central Committee elected by the Eleventh Congress (see the preceding chapter).

20. *KP*, Oct. 15, 1952, p. 1, col. 5. Z. P. Tumanova, another prominent Komsomol administrator, was elected a candidate-member of the Party's Central Committee at the same Party Congress (*ibid.*, p. 2, col. 3). In March, 1954, Shelepin was elected as a delegate to the Soviet of Nationalities of the USSR from the Northern Electoral Okrug of the RSFSR (*ibid.*, March 18, 1954, p. 3, col. 1). Although short biographies of many candidates appeared before the election, none appeared on Shelepin.

21. *Ibid.*, March 23, 1954, p. 2, cols. 1, 3.

22. *Ibid.*, March 26, 1954, p. 2, cols. 3 and 4. For the relevant portion of the new Regulations, see *ibid.*, March 30, 1954, p. 2, col. 3.

23. They stressed such themes as the loving care and guidance afforded by the Party as the "mother," and the affection, respect, assistance, support, and obedience which the Party expected from Komsomolites and all Soviet young people (see, for example, *ibid.*, March 19, 1954, p. 1, cols. 1–3; March 20, p. 2, col. 2, and p. 3, col. 3; March 24, p. 1, cols. 3–4, 6; March 26, p. 2, cols. 1–2; and March 27, p. 2, cols. 1–3). The language used in the Party's greeting to the

Congress was to a large extent identical with that used in the corresponding greeting in 1949 (see Chapter VII and *ibid.*, March 20, 1954, p. 1, cols. 1 and 2).

24. *Ibid.*, Dec. 23, 1949, p. 2, cols. 1–3.

25. The list that ended the series on Oct. 6, 1951, closed with the usual promise that more lists would appear in subsequent issues. However, this writer found none. Each list usually occupied two or three columns and included scores of groups.

26. *KP*, March 5, 1954, pp. 1–2; Jan. 21, 1954, p. 1; Jan. 22, pp. 1–3. (A. Bezymenskii was recalled to duty to retell the story of the visit of the representatives of the First Komsomol Congress to Lenin on Oct. 29, 1918. *Ibid.*, Jan. 22, 1954, p. 3, cols. 1–6.)

27. See the article by G. Shitarov in the authoritative Party journal *Kommunist*, Dec., 1953, pp. 51–66, as translated in *CDSP*, Vol. VI, No. 8, pp. 3–7, 19, 25, 42, 47.

28. The sequence of the listing was: Malenkov, Molotov, Khrushchev, Voroshilov, Bulganin, Kaganovich, Mikoian, Saburov, Pervukhin, Shvernik, Ponomarenko, Kirichenko, Suslov, Pospelov, Shatalin (*KP*, March 23, 1954, p. 1, col. 3; see also March 20, p. 1, cols. 4, 5, and March 23, p. 1, col. 5, for other lists, less complete but observing the same sequence).

29. *Ibid.*, March 20, 1954, p. 1, col. 4.

30. *Ibid.*, p. 1, col. 1; p. 2, col. 1; March 26, p. 3, col. 3; p. 6, col. 3; March 27, p. 1, col. 1; p. 4, col. 4; p. 5, col. 6. His name was coupled in other ways with Lenin's, but notably by foreign delegates (*ibid.*, March 27, 1954, p. 5, col. 1 [Brazilian]; March 28, p. 4, col. 3 [Israeli]; March 30, p. 3, col. 4 [Spanish].

31. *Ibid.*, March 24, 1954, p. 5, cols. 4–6. The French delegate used Stalin's name alone, but without any honorific (*ibid.*, March 25, 1954, p. 5, col. 6).

32. For example, see *ibid.*, March 20, 1954, p. 2, col. 2; p. 4, cols. 5 and 6; p. 5, cols. 4, 5, and 6; March 23, p. 1, col. 1; p. 2, col. 6; March 24, p. 1, col. 1; March 26, p. 2, col. 1; p. 4, col. 1; and March 27, p. 1, cols. 1 and 2. Earlier samples of some of the same expressions may be seen in the Komsomol newspaper at the time of Beriia's removal (*ibid.*, July 10–15, 1953); of the fiftieth anniversary of the Party (*ibid.*, July 30, 1953, pp. 1–3, and preceding and subsequent issues); of the trial and execution of Beriia and his accomplices (*ibid.*, Dec. 20–26, 1953).

33. *Ibid.*, March 27, 1954, p. 1, cols. 1 and 2.   34. *Ibid.*, p. 2, cols. 1 and 2.

35. *Ibid.*, March 20, 1954, p. 2, col. 1. See also the Party's letter to the Congress, in *ibid.*, p. 1, cols. 1–2.

36. *Ibid.*, p. 3, cols. 1 and 2.

37. *Ibid.*, March 21, 1954, p. 5, cols. 4–6; March 23, p. 1, cols. 3–6; March 24, p. 1, col. 5.

38. *Ibid.*, March 24, 1954, p. 1, cols. 1–2.

39. *Ibid.*, March 30, 1954, p. 2, col. 1, and, for related changes in subsequent sections, col. 3; see also March 26, p. 2, cols. 1 and 2 (report on proposed changes in the Regulations). Similar phrases had been previously included elsewhere in the Komsomol Regulations (Meisel and Kozera, *Materials*, pp. 434–35), but this does not nullify the political or propagandistic importance of the amendment.

40. *KP*, March 23, 1954, p. 2, col. 2; see also *ibid.*, March 20, 1954, p. 2, col. 1.

41. *Ibid.*, March 23, 1954, p. 1, col. 3; p. 2, col. 2. It was announced that among

the delegates there were twenty-four Heroes of Socialist Labor and that a total of 556 of the 1,334 delegates held some sort of government decoration (*ibid.*, p. 2, col. 3).

42. For example, see *ibid.*, March 24, 1954, p. 1, cols. 1–2 (resolution on the report of the CC); March 20, 1954, p. 2, cols. 1–3 (report on the work of the CC); March 24, p. 4, cols. 5–6 (Zaluzhnyi). Zaluzhnyi, a secretary of the CC, said that the number of Komsomolites in industry, transportation, and construction had increased by more than two million in the previous five years. He added that in coal mining the number of Komsomolites had doubled, while in the oil industry and in the light and food-processing industries it had tripled (*ibid.*, March 23, 1954, p. 1, col. 3).

43. *Ibid.*, March 20, 1954, p. 2, cols. 2–3. The speeches of individual delegates gave further illustrations of what Komsomolites had done and could do in various branches of industry and transport. Just as in 1949, one of the favorite devices was a special production spurt "in honor of the Komsomol Congress."

44. *Ibid.*, March 29, 1949, p. 1, col. 2.

45. For key items relating to this, see *ibid.*, April 21, 1950, pp. 1–2 (resolution on shelter belts, etc.); feature articles on the Tsymlianskoe Reservoir in the fall of 1951; March 13, 1952, p. 3 (a survey of progress during the more than three years since Stalin's initial decree on the Transformation of Nature); July 11, 1952, p. 1, and subsequent issues in July (on the opening of the Volga-Don Canal, which was related to irrigation plans); Oct. 19, 1952, p. 2, cols. 1–3 (on continuing the Great Stalin Plan for the Transformation of Nature, by A. I. Bobin of the Lumber Ministry of the USSR).

46. *Pravda*, Sept. 15, 1953, pp. 1–6 (speech of Sept. 3).

47. *Ibid.*, Sept. 26, 1953, pp. 1–4 (animal husbandry); Sept. 29, pp. 1–3 (vegetables); Oct. 28, pp. 1–3 (consumers' goods); and Oct. 30, pp. 1–3 (food production).

48. *KP*, Sept. 18, 1953, p. 1, cols. 1–2 (editorial), and, for some of the similar editorials that ensued, Sept. 23, 24, 25, 26, and 29, Oct. 2, 6, 8, 9, 15, and 17, all on page one. The Komsomol's Central Committee, at its (Thirteenth) Plenum in October, told all Komsomol executive bodies in appropriate areas to select certain Komsomolites for work in animal husbandry (*ibid.*, Oct. 18, 1953, pp. 2–3; see also subsequent issues).

49. *Ibid.*, Feb. 12, 1954, p. 1, cols. 3–6; also Feb. 14, p. 2, cols. 1–3; Feb. 16, p. 1, cols. 3–6.

50. *Ibid.*, Feb. 16, 1954, p. 1, cols. 1–2 (editorial), and other stories in the issues of Feb. 19–23 and after.

51. *Ibid.*, Feb. 23, 1954, pp. 1–2.   52. *Ibid.*, Feb. 27, 1954, p. 1, cols. 5–6.

53. *Ibid.*, Feb. 28, 1954, p. 1, cols. 3–5, and subsequent issues, including the song in the issue of April 18, p. 4, cols. 5–6.

54. *Ibid.*, March 6, 1954, p. 1, col. 1; see also March 20, 1954, p. 2, col. 4. See also *Pravda*, March 28, 1954, pp. 1–2.

55. Many categories of technicians were to be given bonuses (called grants-in-aid) amounting to three months' wages, in addition to the expenses of their transfer. All those working on state farms in the virgin and long-unused lands were to receive 15 percent above the normal salary rate for their respective positions during 1954 and 1955. On the kolkhozes in the New Lands, up to 30

percent of any grain harvested in addition to the planned grain yield could be issued in bonuses to workers of field and tractor brigades (*KP*, March 6, 1954, p. 2, col. 2).

56. *Ibid.*, March 19, 1954, p. 1, cols. 1–3; March 20, p. 2, col. 4.

57. *Ibid.*, March 20, 1954, p. 2, col. 4.   58. *Ibid.*   59. *Ibid.*

60. *Ibid.*, col. 5.

61. *Ibid.*, cols. 3–6. See also the summary of the League's duties in the resolution on the Report of the CC, *ibid.*, March 24, 1954, p. 1, col. 2. In the delegates' discussion of Shelepin's report, agriculture—including the New Lands Campaign —was given much more prominence than either industry or transportation. Many of the speeches contained rather sharp criticism of high officials of the Komsomol, including Shelepin, Semichastnyi, and Kochemasov, and also the Ministry of Agriculture, for neglecting the Komsomol's work in agriculture (*ibid.*, March 20–25, 1954). The delegates were provided with an example of the kind of response desired from Komsomolites when, upon a challenge from an Altai representative, a socialist competition was arranged between tractor brigades in the Altai region and in Kazakhstan, to see which could do the most in the New Lands Campaign (*ibid.*, March 20, 1954, p. 5, col. 5; March 21, p. 5, cols. 5, 6; March 27, p. 1, col. 6; p. 2, col. 1; March 30, p. 1, cols. 4–6). For the Party directive before the Congress, calling upon Komsomolites to develop socialist competition in agriculture, see *Pravda*, March 6, 1954, pp. 1–4, especially p. 4, col. 2.

62. For some items on the Komsomol's role in this process, see *KP*, Aug. 4, 1950, p. 2, cols. 1–3, and other issues around this date; see also the issue of April 19, 1951, p. 1, cols. 1–2, and subsequent issues.

63. *Narodnoe khoziaistvo SSSR*, p. 100. See also *KP*, Feb 3, 1954, p. 1, cols. 1–2, reporting that there were more than 9,000 MTS's.

64. *Kommunist*, XXX, No. 16 (Nov., 1953), 15.

65. *KP*, March 20, 1954, p. 2, col. 4. Complete coverage of all kolkhozes was reported to have been attained in eighty-four oblasts, krais, and republics by July, 1949 (*ibid.*, July 6, 1949, p. 1, col. 1). By June, 1950, complete coverage of all three types of farming units reportedly had been extended to ninety-eight oblasts, krais, and republics (*Molodoi bol'shevik*, VIII, No. 12 [June, 1950], 46). By May, 1951, there was said to be a Komsomol primary organization in "almost every" kolkhoz, but no figures were given (*Molodoi bol'shevik*, IX, No. 10 [May, 1951], 36). By November, 1953, Komsomol units had reportedly been established in all MTS's and on all sovkhozes, but still the coverage on kolkhozes was stated merely as "almost all," without supporting figures (*Kommunist*, XXX, No. 16 [Nov., 1953], 15).

66. V. Voropaev, "Komsomol v derevne—bol'shaia sila," *Molodoi bol'shevik*, VIII, No. 12 (June, 1950), 46. The figures were reported to include all Komsomolites in kolkhozes, sovkhozes, and MTS's.

67. *Molodoi bol'shevik*, IX, No. 10 (May, 1951), 36. The figure is simply given, without any admission that it represents a decline.

68. A total of "over 2,500,000" Komsomolites in kolkhozes, sovkhozes, and MTS's was reported in November, 1953 (*Kommunist*, XXX, No. 16 [Nov., 1953], 15). No reports have been found for other dates.

69. *KP*, March 20, 1954, p. 2, col. 4.

70. See note 13, earlier in the present chapter, and see Chapter VII.

71. *KP*, March 26, 1954, p. 2, col. 4. Kochemasov said about 10,000 rural primary organizations now had over fifty members. (It may be noted that already in 1951 there were reported to be on collective farms about 5,500 Komsomol primary organizations of fifty or more members each [*ibid.*, March 29, 1951, p. 1, col. 1].) For the pertinent section of the Regulations of 1949, see *Rez. i dok. XI s"ezda*, p. 60. For the Regulations as amended by the Twelfth Congress, see *KP*, March 30, 1954, p. 2, col. 4.

72. *KP*, March 20, 1954, p. 2, cols. 3, 6; p. 3, col. 2; March 21, p. 5, col. 4; March 23, p. 1, cols. 3–5; March 24, p. 5, cols. 1, 2.

73. See, for example, the response of the head of the Labor Reserves, G. I. Zelenko, in *ibid.*, March 25, 1954, p. 4, cols. 1–3.

74. *Ibid.*, March 20, 1954, p. 3, col. 5. For Komsomol activity in the elections to the Supreme Soviet in 1950, see *KP* between Jan. 10 and March 15, 1950. Mikhailov served during those elections as the Komsomol representative on the Central Electoral Commission and was vice-chairman of that body (*ibid.*, Jan. 17, 1950, p. 2; Jan. 20, 1950, p. 1). Among the prominent Komsomol officials nominated (and of course elected) as deputies to the Supreme Soviet were Mikhailov (*ibid.*, Feb. 7, 1950, p. 3, cols. 3–4) and Petr Mironovich Masherov, the first secretary of the Komsomol Central Committee in Belorussia (*ibid.*, Feb. 9, 1950, p. 3, cols. 1–2). Among the deputies nominated and elected to the Soviet of Nationalities were Tamara Ivanovna Ershova, secretary of the Komsomol Central Committee (*ibid.*, Feb. 15, 1950, p. 3, cols. 3–4, and Feb. 22, 1950, p. 2, cols. 1–2) and, again, Mikhailov (*ibid.*, Feb. 21, 1950, p. 2, cols. 5–6). Concerning Komsomol activity in the elections to krai, oblast, raion, city, and village soviets later that year, see *KP* between Oct. 3 and Dec. 24, 1950. In regard to the elections to the supreme soviets of union and autonomous republics, see *KP* between Jan. 5 and Feb. 18, 1951. Another cycle began again in 1954 with the elections to the Supreme Soviet and the Soviet of Nationalities (*KP*, Jan. 12, 1954, to mid-March, when the elections came). Shelepin served on the electoral commission for the elections to the Supreme Soviet (*ibid.*, Jan. 20, 1954, p. 1, col. 4), and Aleksei Arkhipovich Rapokhin, a secretary of the Komsomol Central Committee, served on the electoral commission for the elections to the Soviet of Nationalities (*ibid.*, Jan. 21, 1950, p. 1, col. 4). Shelepin was elected to the Soviet of Nationalities as a representative of the Northern Electoral Okrug of the RSFSR (*ibid.*, Feb. 9, 1954, p. 1, cols. 4–6; March 18, p. 3, col. 1).

75. *KP*, March 23, 1954, p. 2, col. 3 (Report of the Credentials Commission).

76. *Ibid.*, March 20, 1954, p. 3, col. 4; March 24, p. 1, col. 3.

77. *Ibid.*, March 20, 1954, p. 3, cols. 3–4.

78. *Ibid.*, March 21, 1954, p. 5, col. 4 (G. G. Shevel', secretary of the CC of the Komsomol of the Ukraine). Another representative from a Ukrainian-speaking region praised the "great Russian language" (*ibid.*, March 25, 1956, p. 1, col. 6).

79. *Ibid.*, March 23, 1954, p. 3, cols. 1–2 (Uzbek); p. 4, col. 6 (Azerbaidzhanian); March 26, p. 4, col. 1 (Bashkir); col. 4 (Estonian).

80. *Ibid.*, March 23, 1954, p. 2, col. 3. Partial figures were given on the distribution of the delegates by political units. Although these cannot be used as the equivalent of national origin, they have some interest in themselves. Among the delegates from the RSFSR, the largest group—82—was from the

Moscow Oblast. Then came the following oblasts, krais, and autonomous republics: Leningrad—38; Sverdlovsk—23; Krasnodar—18; Bashkir—17; Cheliabinsk—17; Tatar—16; Khabarovsk—15; Maritime (Primorskii Krai)—15; Altai—14; Molotov—14; Kemerovo—13; Kuibyshev—13. The union republics for which figures were given were these: Ukraine—231 (including Stalino Oblast—21; Kharkov Oblast—19; and Dnepropetrovsk Oblast—15); Belorussia—57; Uzbekistan —44; Kazakhstan—43; Azerbaidzhan—30.

81. *Ibid.*, March 19, 1954, p. 1, col. 2; March 20, 1954, p. 3, col. 2; March 24, p. 1, col. 3; p. 2, cols. 3–4; March 26, p. 1, cols. 3–4; p. 2, cols. 2–4; March 30, p. 2, col. 4 (sentences on initiative added to the Regulations).

82. *Ibid.*, March 24, 1954, p. 1, col. 1; March 26, p. 1, col. 2; p. 2, col. 2; March 27, p. 2, col. 4.

83. *Ibid.*, March 20, 1954, p. 2, col. 3; March 24, p. 1, cols. 2, 3; March 26, p. 1, col. 2; p. 2, col. 2; March 27, p. 1, col. 1.

84. *Ibid.*, March 20, 1954, p. 3, cols. 1–2.

85. *Ibid.*, p. 4, col. 1. For a full bibliography see Vladimir V. Almendinger, Jr., "A Bibliography of Antireligious Comment in Recent Soviet Press," mimeographed at U.C.L.A., April, 1956, 40 pp. Almendinger observes that a new antireligious propaganda drive ensued in the latter half of 1954.

One item not cited in Almendinger, but especially interesting in showing the limits of official toleration of contact with religion on the part of Komsomolites, concerned a Komsomolite whose fiancée wanted a church wedding. The Komsomolite wrote to the editors of *KP* to ask if he, as a Komsomolite, could go through that ceremony simply as a matter of form. The editors said he could not; that if he did, he would directly violate Komsomol Regulations; that he must convince his fiancée not to insist on a church ceremony (*KP*, March 21, 1950, p. 3, cols. 2–3). It seems worth observing that the editors did *not* suggest that the young man should reject his fiancée because of her religious tendencies.

86. For example, *KP*, March 24, 1954, p. 2, cols. 1–2; March 26, p. 1, col. 1.

87. For illustrations covering typical points, see *ibid.*, Feb. 6, 1953, p. 1, cols. 1–2 (on the inseparability of personal and private life); Dec. 8, 1953, p. 2, cols. 3–6 (on chastity); July 1, 1949, p. 3, cols. 2–6, March 21, 1951, p. 2, cols. 2–6, (April 20, 1952, p. 3, cols. 1–5 (on marriage and parent-child relationships); Sept. 6, 1949, p. 2, cols. 5–6 (on smoking); Nov. 19, 1953, p. 3, cols. 1–6, and Feb. 12, 1954, p. 3, cols. 1–6 (attacking drunkenness among Komsomolites).

88. *Ibid.*, March 20, 1954, p. 3, col. 6; p. 4, col. 1.

89. *Pravda*, Aug. 23, 1950, p. 2, col. 1 (this article adds that of the more than 230,000 propagandists engaged at this time in the ideological training of youth, more than half were Party members), and *KP*, May 28, 1953, p. 1, col. 2 (this article adds that as of May, 1953, about 4,000,000 Komsomolites were studying in the League's own network of political circles and schools). For further information consult Ploss, "Political Education in the Postwar Komsomol," *Amer. Slavic and E. Eur. Review*, XV (Dec., 1956), 489–505.

90. *KP*, March 20, 1954, p. 3, cols. 4–5.

91. *Ibid.*, p. 3, col. 5. Concerning 1949, see Chapter VII and also *ibid.*, May 5, 1949, p. 1, col. 1, giving a grand total of four million. It was reported in May, 1950, that the number of youth newspapers had risen from thirty-eight to sixty-

one during the preceding year, and the number of Pioneer newspapers from nineteen to twenty (*ibid.*, May 5, 1950, p. 2, cols. 2–3).

The full names of several score staff members of *Komsomol'skaia pravda* are given in the issue of June 10, 1950, p. 1, cols. 3–6. A shorter list for the staff of *Pionerskaia pravda* appears in *KP*, June 15, 1950, p. 4, cols. 5–6.

The criticisms made of the Komsomol press by Shelepin and others at the Twelfth Congress contained nothing out of the ordinary. For examples, see *KP*, March 20, 1954, p. 3, col. 5; March 21, p. 5, col. 5; March 23, p. 1, cols. 4, 6; March 24, p. 1, col. 3, p. 2, cols. 4–6 (Goriunov, editor of *KP*); March 26, p. 1, col. 5; March 27, p. 2, cols. 5, 6.

92. *KP*, March 20, 1954, p. 3, col. 6.

93. *Ibid.;* also March 24, p. 2, col. 3; March 25, p. 3, cols. 1–6; March 26, p. 4, col. 3.

94. *Ibid.*, March 20, 1954, p. 3, col. 5; March 24, p. 2, cols. 3–4; March 26, p. 1, col. 5; March 27, p. 2, cols. 4–6. The forming of choral groups had been urged earlier but apparently not pressed consistently (*ibid.*, March 16, 1951, p. 1, cols. 1–2; *Molodoi bol'shevik*, IX, No. 18 [Sept., 1951], 52–54).

95. More than fifty-seven million persons, or eight million more than in 1940, were reported to be studying. There was no comprehensive indication of the proportion of Komsomolites in the educational system (*KP*, March 20, 1954, p. 3, col. 1). In the special category of "schools for worker and rural youth"— offering seven-year and ten-year (secondary) training in the evenings—the number enrolled was placed at 1,600,000, of which about one million were said to be Komsomolites (*ibid.*, March 20, 1954, p. 3, col. 4). Shelepin said that "about 60 percent of the pupils in training institutions and schools [*ucha-shchikhsia uchilishch i shkol*] are now members of the Komsomol," but it was not clear how much of the educational system he was taking into account (*ibid.*, March 20, 1954, p. 2, col. 6). For the report of Mikhailov at the Nineteenth Party Congress, giving prominence to the role of the League in connection with the schools and ideological training, see Gruliow, *Current Soviet Policies*, pp. 147–48.

96. *KP*, March 20, 1954, p. 3, cols. 1–4; March 24, p. 1, cols. 1–4; p. 2, cols. 1–3; March 25, p. 4, cols. 1, 2, 6, and, concerning especially the Labor Reserve schools, cols. 1–3.

97. There was no mention of student self-government in the proceedings of the Twelfth Congress, but a report made between the two congresses indicated that the Party still disapproved of any "improvised forms" (such as councils, boards of monitors, and student government) that might usurp the student-leading and student-representing functions that belonged properly to the Komsomol (*ibid.*, Oct. 25, 1951, p. 3, cols. 1–6).

98. *Ibid.*, March 20, 1954, p. 3, col. 2. For an endorsement from S. M. Veselov, secretary of the Moscow *obkom*, see *ibid.*, March 27, p. 3, col. 2.

99. Other exhortations to close cooperation between teachers and the leaders of Komsomol and Pioneer bodies bespeak the same motive (*ibid.*, March 20, 1954, p. 3, cols. 2–3; March 26, p. 1, col. 4; March 27, p. 2, col. 2).

100. There was no mention of any change at the Twelfth Congress. In 1952 there were reported to be 23,020 teachers' primary organizations in the schools of the RSFSR alone (*ibid.*, Aug. 19, 1952, p. 2, col. 1).

101. *Ibid.,* March 20, 1954, p. 3, col. 1.

102. *Ibid.,* Sept. 7, 1952, p. 1, cols. 1–2, and subsequent issues. The occasion was the Ninth Plenum of the CC of the Komsomol. At about this same time, Shelepin said that in Moscow institutions of higher education, 93.4 percent of the students were Komsomolites (*Pravda,* Sept. 13, 1952, p. 2, col. 6). It was also revealed that the higher educational institutions (*vuzy*) of Moscow contained at that time a total of 130,000 students (*KP,* Sept. 14, 1952, p. 2, col. 5). No statistics were given for individual institutions at that time. It had been reported in 1949 that the Komsomol organization of the Moscow State University contained 7,500 members (*KP,* Nov. 25, 1949, p. 2, col. 2). In March, 1952, it was report that 88 percent of the students of that University were Komsomolites (*Pravda,* March 24, 1952, p. 2, col. 6).

103. *KP,* March 20, 1954, p. 3, cols. 3–4.

104. L. K. Baliasna, secretary of the Komsomol in the Ukraine, said the membership there was about four million, in 29,254 troops (*ibid.,* March 25, 1954, p. 4, col. 4). But no comprehensive figure for the USSR was given.

105. *Ibid.,* Oct. 17, 1951, p. 2, col. 1.

106. *Pravda,* Jan. 4, 1952, p. 1, col. 2; *KP,* May 10, 1952, p. 2, col. 3; *Pravda,* May 20, 1952, p. 2, col. 5; *KP,* Aug. 19, 1952, p. 2, col. 1.

107. *KP,* Oct. 8, 1952, p. 4, col. 2 (Nineteenth Party Congress).

108. *Ibid.,* March 4, 1953, p. 1, cols. 1–3 (editorial).

109. Lorimer, *Population of the Soviet Union,* p. 189.

110. The available data permit only a rough estimate. Using the table in *ibid.,* p. 256, and taking into account on the plus side the territories added to the USSR since January, 1939, and on the minus side the Soviet figures released in 1956 (*Narodnoe khoziaistvo SSSR,* p. 18), one may guess that in 1952 the number of children aged nine through fourteen was between twenty-one and twenty-five million. The Pioneer membership of 19,000,000 in 1952 would have embraced between three-quarters and nine-tenths of that total. Although many of the fourteen-year-olds would have already joined the Komsomol, there is thus no reason to doubt the claim made at the Congress in 1954 that the "overwhelming majority" of school children within the Pioneer age group were Pioneers (*KP,* March 26, 1954, p. 1, col. 1).

111. Between the congresses, the Seventh Plenum of the CC of the Komsomol (October, 1951) had devoted special attention to the Pioneers and had called for closer cooperation between teachers and Pioneer leaders (*KP,* Oct. 17, 1951, p. 1, cols. 1–2, p. 2, cols. 1–6, and more in subsequent issues).

112. *Ibid.,* March 24, 1954, p. 2, col. 1; also March 20, p. 3, col. 2; March 25, p. 1, col. 4; March 26, p. 1, cols. 1, 3. One delegate was bold enough to criticize Shelepin and Tumanova for failing to recall, in their criticisms of Pioneer meetings devoted to schoolwork (*predmetnye sbory*), that the Komsomol Central Committee itself had previously urged such meetings (*ibid.,* March 25, 1954, p. 3, col. 1).

113. *Ibid.,* March 24, 1954, p. 2, col. 2 (Tumanova).

114. *Ibid.,* p. 2, cols. 3–5; see also March 20, p. 3, col. 2; March 25, p. 4, cols. 4–6.

115. *Ibid.,* March 24, 1954, p. 2, col. 5; March 25, p. 1, cols. 2, 4.

116. *Ibid.*, March 20, 1954, p. 3, col. 2 (Shelepin).

117. *Ibid.*, March 25, 1954, pp. 4, 5; March 26, pp. 3–5.

118. *Ibid.*, March 25, 1954, p. 5, col. 1 (G. P. Sarafannikova, secretary of the Leningrad *obkom*); March 26, p. 3, cols. 4–5 (V. P. Busygin, secretary of the Primorsk *kraikom*).

119. *Ibid.*, March 24, 1954, p. 2, col. 5; March 26, p. 1, cols. 3–4. For the rules covering the various categories of leaders, see *ibid.*, April 10, 1954, p. 2, cols. 1–2 (the new Statute of the Pioneers).

120. *Ibid.*, March 26, 1954, p. 1, col. 4.

121. *Ibid.*, March 24, 1954, p. 2, col. 6; also March 20, p. 3, col. 2. It was reported that more than four million Pioneers and school children attended camps in the summer of 1953 (*ibid.*, March 24, 1954, p. 2, col. 1). This was much higher than the 2,500,000 announced in 1949 (*ibid.*, May 17, 1949, p. 1, col. 1).

122. *Ibid.*, March 24, 1954, p. 2, cols. 2–4; March 26, p. 1, cols. 2–3.

123. *Ibid.*, March 24, 1954, p. 2, col. 3; see also March 26, p. 1, cols. 1–3.

124. *Ibid.*, March 20, 1954, p. 3, col. 1; March 24, 1954, p. 2, col. 3; March 26, p. 1, cols. 3–4.

125. *Ibid.*, March 24, 1954, p. 2, col. 2.   126. *Ibid.*, p. 2, col. 5.

127. *Ibid.*, p. 2, col. 6; March 26, p. 1, col. 4.

128. *Ibid.*, March 20, 1954, p. 3, col. 2; March 24, p. 2, cols. 3–4; p. 5, col. 1; March 26, p. 1, col. 3; March 30, p. 2, col. 4; April 10, p. 2, cols. 1–2.

129. *Ibid.*, March 24, 1954, p. 2, cols. 2, 6; p. 5, col. 1; March 26, p. 1, cols. 1, 3; March 27, p. 2, cols. 4–6; April 10, p. 2, cols. 1–2.

130. The Statute (*Polozhenie*) stressed that the Party had made the Komsomol responsible for the running of the Pioneer organization. While there was to be a Pioneer headquarters at the city and raion echelon, for purposes of directing the work of the Pioneer troops within those political units, no higher Pioneer headquarters was provided for, other than the regular committees of the Komsomol (*ibid.*, April 10, 1954, p. 2, cols. 1–2).

131. *Ibid.*, April 10, 1954, p. 2, col. 1; *Pionerskaia organizatsiia*, p. 41.

132. *KP*, March 20, 1954, p. 2, col. 1. Concerning the "struggle for peace," see also *ibid.*, March 20, 1954, p. 1, col. 2; p. 4, col. 4; March 24, p. 5, col. 2; March 27, p. 1, col. 2; p. 2, col. 2.

133. *Ibid.*, June 30, 1950, p. 1, cols. 1–2, and other issues in July and August, 1950. Mikhailov had served on the Soviet Committee for the Defense of Peace (*ibid.*, June 30, 1950, p. 1, col. 3), which gathered "115,275,940" signatures in only about one month (*ibid.*, Aug. 4, 1950, p. 1, cols. 3–6). About one year later, Komsomolites had helped to obtain "117,669,320" signatures to a new peace appeal (*ibid.*, Nov. 28, 1951, p. 1, cols. 1–6, telling about the Third All-Union Conference of Supporters of Peace).

134. *Ibid.*, March 27, 1954, p. 2, cols. 2–3.

135. *Ibid.*, March 24, 1954, p. 1, col. 6; see also March 25, p. 5, cols. 4–6.

136. *Ibid.*, March 20, 1954, p. 1, col. 1; p. 2, col. 2; March 21, p. 6, col. 2; March 23, p. 2, col. 6; March 24, p. 1, col. 3; March 27, p. 1, col. 1; p. 2, col. 2; March 30, p. 1, col. 3.

137. *Ibid.*, March 20, 1954, p. 4, col. 2. Ivan Kozhedub, the much publicized major general of the Air Forces and Thrice Hero of the Soviet Union, told the

delegates that the armed forces were ready to spare neither blood nor life itself in order to achieve "full victory" over the enemies of the USSR (*ibid.*, March 26, 1954, p. 2, cols. 5–6).

138. *Ibid.*, March 20, 1954, p. 1, col. 4; p. 4, col. 2; March 23, p. 2, cols. 2–3; March 24, p. 1, col. 4; March 26, p. 2, cols. 5–6; March 30, p. 2, col. 4. It may be noted that in the interval since the Eleventh Congress the DOSARM, DOSAV, and DOSFLOT had been combined into one mass organization, the DOSAAF, or All-Union Voluntary Society for Cooperation with the Army, Aviation, and Navy. Komsomolites were responsible for participating in this work (*ibid.*, March 20, 1954, p. 4, col. 2). Concerning the DOSAAF, see also *ibid.*, March 25, 1952, p. 2, cols. 3–6. In the Army and Navy, three-fourths of those who excelled in military and political training (*otlichniki boevoi i politicheskoi podgotovki*) were reported to be Komsomolites (G. P. Shatunov in *ibid.*, March 23, 1954, p. 5, col. 4; his title is given here as Assistant in Charge of Komsomol Work in the Office of the Main Political Administration in the Ministry of Defense of the USSR). No comprehensive statistics were released on Komsomol membership in the armed forces.

139. The demands for more mass athletic activities were combined, as before, with the demand that all Komsomolites pass the Ready for Labor and Defense series of tests in militarily useful skills (*KP*, March 20, 1954, p. 4, cols. 1–2; March 23, p. 1, col. 4; March 24, p. 1, col. 4; p. 2, col. 3; March 26, p. 1, cols. 3–4). The attitude toward international athletic competition remained deadly serious. Shelepin listed the sports and events in which Soviet athletes had done poorly and called on Komsomolites to remedy these weak spots. He ridiculed "theories of overtraining" and "burning out the nervous system," and insisted that constant, arduous training was the best preparation for breaking world records (*ibid.*, March 20, 1954, p. 4, cols. 1–2). Between the two congresses, the Eighth Plenum of the CC of the Komsomol had devoted special attention to the Komsomol's work in athletics (as well as the League's work in the World Federation of Democratic Youth and the machine-building industry). See *ibid.*, April 12, 1952, p. 1, cols. 1–2, p. 2, cols. 1–6, and subsequent issues.

140. *KP*, March 20, 1954, p. 4, cols. 2–3. Soviet delegations visited France, Hungary, and Germany in May and June, 1949 (*ibid.*, May 28, 1949, p. 4; May 31, p. 4; June 2, p. 4). In August, 1949, a Soviet delegation numbering about 600 attended the World Festival of Youth and Students in Budapest (*ibid.*, Aug. 13 to Sept. 2, 1949, mostly on page one. That Festival was sponsored jointly by the familiar international front organizations, the WFDY (World Federation of Democratic Youth), of which Mikhailov was then vice-president (for this identification see *ibid.*, May 26, 1951, p. 4, cols. 5–6), and the IUS (International Union of Students), of which Shelepin was then vice-president (*ibid.*, Aug. 17, 1950, p. 4, cols. 2–3). A Soviet delegation headed by Mikhailov attended the Second World Congress of Youth in Budapest in September, 1949 (*ibid.*, Sept. 6, 1949, p. 3, cols. 1–6; Sept. 7, p. 4, cols. 3–5; Sept. 11, p. 3, cols. 1–6; Oct. 14, p. 2, cols. 1–4). In August, 1950, Shelepin headed a Soviet delegation at the Second World Congress of Students in Prague, sponsored by the IUS (*ibid.*, Aug. 17, 1950, p. 4, cols. 1–3; see also other issues before and after this date). In August, 1951, another Soviet delegation went to the Third World Festival of Youth and Students, held in East Berlin under the joint sponsorship of the

WFDY and the IUS (*ibid.*, Aug. 5, 1951, p. 3, and subsequent issues). In 1953 delegations went to both Bucharest and Warsaw. The Third World Congress of Youth and the Fourth World Festival of Youth and Students met in Bucharest in July and August (*ibid.*, July 28, 1953, p. 3, cols. 1–6, and subsequent issues up through August 20). The Festival, which closed on August 16, was said to have been attended by 30,000 young people from 111 countries (*ibid.*, Aug. 18, 1953, p. 3, cols. 1–6). Meanwhile the Third World Congress of Students (sponsored by the IUS) met in Warsaw in August (*ibid.*, Aug. 27, 1953, p. 1, cols. 1–2, and subsequent issues).

141. *KP*, April 14, 1950, p. 1, col. 6.

142. *Ibid.*, March 20, 1954, p. 4, col. 2; March 24, p. 5, col. 5; March 28, p. 3, col. 1; see also Nov. 10, 1953, p. 4, cols. 1–3.

143. *Ibid.*, Nov. 17, 1953, p. 1, cols. 1–2 (International Students' Day), and March 28, p. 3, col. 1.

144. *Ibid.*, March 23, 1954, p. 1; March 24, pp. 1, 5; March 25, pp. 1, 4; March 26, pp. 1–2; March 27, p. 1. The list of countries (*ibid.*, March 20, 1954, p. 1, col. 4) said to have sent representatives to Moscow for the Congress included the U.S., but there is no record of an American having spoken.

145. *Ibid.*, March 23, 1954, p. 1, cols. 4–6; March 24, p. 5, cols. 4–6 (respectively a report and a text of the speech by Liu Tao-shen, secretary of the CC of the New Democratic Youth League of China). In general, such themes as following the example of the Soviet youth League and considering Soviet youth as the "elder brother" were in evidence, as before. For most of the texts of the addresses of foreign youth representatives, see *ibid.*, March 24, 1954, p. 5; March 25, p. 5; March 26, p. 6; March 27, pp. 4–5; March 28, p. 3; March 30, p. 3.

146. *Ibid.*, March 20, 1954, p. 4, col. 3.

147. Primary organizations in "industry, railway transport, construction projects, and educational institutions" had reportedly increased by 44,641 between the Eleventh and Twelfth congresses (*ibid.*, March 23, 1954, p. 2, col. 1). However, one cannot be sure that all of these were urban; hence the use of "about 40,000."

148. For Mikhailov's birth year (1906) and further biographical information, see Chapter VII and also *ibid.*, Feb. 7, 1950, p. 3, cols. 3–4; Feb. 21, 1950, p. 2, cols. 5–6; and *BSE* (2d ed.), XXVII (1954), 609.

149. *KP*, April 1, 1949, p. 2, col. 2, and *Pravda*, Feb. 22, 1956, p. 8, col. 2. The only other recent member of the Central Committee for whom the writer has found a birth date is Tamara Ivanovna Ershova. She was born in 1920 (*KP*, Feb. 22, 1950, p. 2, cols. 1–2), and thus was about twenty-nine at the time of the Eleventh Congress. She was still a secretary of the Central Committee in February, 1950 (*KP*, Feb. 15, 1950, p. 3, cols. 3–4; Feb. 22, p. 2, cols. 1–2), but was removed sometime before the Twelfth Congress. To judge from the photographs published during the Eleventh Congress, she was among the younger of the high officials of the League. A Komsomol official from Uzbekistan declared that in some of the primary organizations in that republic 80 to 85 percent of the members were over twenty-six (*KP*, March 27, 1954, p. 3, cols. 4–5).

150. *KP*, March 26, 1954, p. 2, col. 1; March 30, p. 2, col. 1.

It may be noted parenthetically, apropos of membership provisions, that the never very burdensome dues had been reduced in 1951 and 1953 to the point where they were even more purely than before a device upon which to hook one strand of propaganda. The reductions were described by V. I. Kharazov, who reported on behalf of the Central Inspection Commission, as cutting the dues to from one-third to one-fourth of their former size (*ibid.*, March 20, 1954, p. 5, col. 1). The scale in force in 1954 was evidently that introduced on January 1, 1953. According to that scale, members earning up to 500 rubles per month were to pay 0.5 percent of their monthly wages in dues; those earning more than 500 but not more than 1,500 rubles were to pay 1 percent; those earning more than 1,500 rubles were to pay 1.5 percent (*ibid.*, Jan. 6, 1953, p. 2, col. 4).

151. *Ibid.*, March 20, 1954, p. 4, cols. 4–6.

152. *Ibid.*, March 23, 1954, p. 2, col. 2.

153. *Ibid.* The reporting was incomplete. For further details, see Appendix F.

154. *Ibid.*, p. 2, col. 3. The report (by V. E. Semichastnyi for the Credentials Commission of the Congress) says "559 women, or 42.4 percent." But 559 is only 41.9 percent of 1,334. On the basis of past experience with carelessness in the calculation of percentages by Komsomol officials, this writer prefers to use the percentage recalculated from the absolute numbers given. The proportion at the previous Congress was 43.3 percent. See Appendix C for the record at earlier congresses.

155. *Ibid.* See Appendix D for further comparisons. The percentages above have been calculated on the basis that 1,318 equals 100 percent, since age statistics were given on only 1,318 of the 1,334 delegates.

156. *Ibid.* See Appendix E for further comparisons. Since service statistics were given on only 1,318 out of the 1,334 delegates, the former figure has been counted as 100 percent in calculating the percentages. The basis for translating years of entry into years of service is explained in Appendix E.

157. Those old members on the Presidium were V. I. Kochemasov, P. M. Masherov, N. A. Mikhailov, I. Rakhimova, A. A. Rapokhin, V. E. Semichastnyi, G. P. Shatunov, A. N. Shelepin, G. G. Shevel', Z. P. Tumanova, and V. I. Zaluzhnyi. The Credentials (Mandates) Commission included Semichastnyi and V. L. Novikova. The Secretariat and the Editorial Commission did not include any members of the old CC (*KP*, April 9, 1949, p. 3; March 20, 1954, p. 5).

158. This count excludes the approximately thirty-five foreign speakers and the nine speakers who represented governmental and other organizations in the Soviet Union.

159. *KP*, April 9, 1949, p. 3; March 27, 1954, p. 2. Those who were full members of the Central Committees of both 1949 and 1954 were V. I. Kochemasov, P. M. Masherov, V. L. Novikova, I. Rakhimova, A. A. Rapokhin, V. E. Semichastnyi, G. P. Shatunov, A. N. Shelepin, G. G. Shevel', Z. P. Tumanova, V. N. Zaichikov, and V. I. Zaluzhnyi. It is possible that the P. G. Makeeva listed in 1954 was the same person as the A. G. Makeeva listed in 1949, and that the V. A. Orlov listed in 1954 was the same as the V. I. Orlov listed in 1949 (*ibid.*).

160. *Ibid.*, April 9, 1949, p. 3; March 20, 1954, p. 5; March 27, 1954, p. 2. It should be noted that the new Central Committee did include two members of the old Central Inspection Commission elected in 1949 (N. V. Dykhnov and M. I. Elizavetin) and one member of the Credentials Commission of the Eleventh Congress (A. A. Zhikhor).

161. The seven persons who were identified as secretaries of the CC on the first day of the Congress were A. N. Shelepin (First Secretary), R. T. Ablova,

V. I. Kochemasov, A. A. Rapokhin, V. E. Semichastnyi, Z. P. Tumanova, and V. I. Zaluzhnyi (*KP*, March 20, 1954, p. 5). All of these except Ablova had been elected to the Central Committee in 1949 and thus had qualified legally for subsequent promotion to secretary (*ibid.*, April 9, 1949, p. 3). There was at least one other instance of "illegal" appointment as secretary of the CC: in June, 1953, two persons (Z. T. Fedorova and V. M. Iurkovskii) were relieved from their posts as secretaries of the Central Committee in connection with their transfer to other work (*ibid.*, June 9, 1953, p. 1, cols. 1–2). Fedorova had been properly elected in 1949 (*ibid.*, April 9, 1949, p. 3; April 16, 1949, p. 2), but Iurkovskii had not been elected either a member or candidate-member of the Central Committee in 1949.

162. Shelepin and Kochemasov had been secretaries of the CC and Semichastnyi and Tumanova had been simply Bureau members, ever since the first Plenum of the CC after the Congress of 1949 (*KP*, April 16, 1949, p. 2, cols. 3–4). The secretaries elected then were N. A. Mikhailov (First Secretary), A. N. Shelepin, T. I. Ershova, Z. T. Fedorova, and V. I. Kochemasov. The Bureau consisted of those five and N. P. Krasavchenko, M. N. Kolmakova, V. E. Semichastnyi, Z. P. Tumanova, V. I. Chernetsov, and P. M. Masherov.

163. The First Plenum of the new Central Committee, meeting immediately after the Congress, elected the following secretaries: A. N. Shelepin (First Secretary), R. T. Ablova, V. I. Kochemasov, A. A. Rapokhin, V. E. Semichastnyi, Z. P. Tumanova, and V. I. Zaluzhnyi (all listed in alphabetical order). The Bureau, also listed alphabetically, consisted of those seven and D. P. Goriunov, M. I. Khaldeev, P. M. Masherov, S. K. Romanovskii, G. P. Shatunov, and G. G. Shevel'. Candidate-members of the Bureau were V. T. Shumilov and V. M. Striganov. The new chairman of the Central Inspection Commission was S. M. Veselov (*KP*, March 28, p. 2, cols. 1–3). V. I. Kharazov, who was elected chairman of the Central Inspection Committee immediately after the Congress of 1949 (*ibid.*, April 16, 1949, p. 2), was still in office as the Congress of 1954 opened, and he presented the report of his Committee (*ibid.*, March 20, 1954, p. 5, cols. 1–3). He was not elected to the new Central Committee, or even to the new Central Inspection Committee (*ibid.*, March 27, 1954, p. 2). Yet there is no sign he was purged; rather, it seems probable that he was simply assigned by the Party to a higher post, or transferred in order to make room for new blood.

164. *KP*, March 20, 1954, p. 4, col. 3; see also March 24, p. 1, col. 4. Some of the resultant criticism was rather revealing. K. Murtazaev, secretary of the Uzbek branch of the Komsomol, complained that during 1953 alone the All-Union Central Committee of the League had sent the Uzbek Central Committee 240 decrees, 264 directives, and 56 telegrams. During the same period the Uzbek Central Committee itself had issued 193 decrees, he said (*ibid.*, March 23, 1954, p. 3, cols. 5–6). The Udmurt Oblast representative criticized the Central Committee for hampering the initiative of lower Komsomol bodies, and at the same time complained that no secretary of the All-Union Central Committee had visited his oblast during the past ten years (*ibid.*, March 27, 1954, p. 4, col. 1).

165. *KP*, March 30, 1954, p. 2, cols. 1, 3, 4; March 26, p. 2, cols. 2–4.

166. *Ibid.*, March 24, 1954, p. 1, col. 3; also March 20, p. 3, col. 4.

167. *Ibid.*, March 20, 1954, p. 4, col. 3; March 26, p. 2, cols. 2–4; March 27, p. 3, col. 5; March 30, p. 2, col. 2.

168. *Ibid.*, March 26, 1954, p. 2, cols. 1–4; March 30, 1954, p. 2. For an English translation of the pertinent section in the Regulations of 1949, see Meisel and Kozera, *Materials*, p. 429.

169. For example, an editorial published more than a year before his death, when he ruled as absolutely as ever, told Komsomol executive bodies that they must act as a group. The first secretary must consult the others and must not dictate. The *aktiv* and all Komsomolites must be given opportunities to express their opinions. "The Party teaches the strict observance of the group principle [*printsip kollegial'nosti*, or "collegiate principle"] in the work of leading bodies. One-man [*edinolichnye*, also "individual"] decisions, Comrade Stalin teaches [!], are always or almost always one-sided decisions. Only by comparing various points of view can one work out the correct decision for this or that problem. . . . The leader who does not take into account the opinion of the Komsomolites who have been elected to the executive body, who does not develop their initiative, who dictates, who thrusts his will upon the collective—that leader harms the cause of the rearing of youth" (*KP*, Feb. 6, 1952, p. 1, cols. 1–2). Not long before the Nineteenth Party Congress, which was one of the more extreme demonstrations of Stalin's absolutism, an editorial told Komsomol officials at all echelons that they must be sure to practice Komsomol democracy and "collective leadership" (*kollektivnoe rukovodstvo*) (*ibid.*, Aug. 1, 1952, p. 1, cols. 1–2). And another editorial demanding—in the name of Stalin—more democracy within the Komsomol appeared a few weeks after the Nineteenth Party Congress (*ibid.*, Nov. 30, 1952, p. 1, cols. 1–2).

170. See, for example, *KP*, April 11, 1953, p. 1, cols. 1–2 (editorial on the need for more democracy within the Komsomol), and July 21, 1953, p. 1, cols. 1–2 (editorial on strict observance of the principle of collective leadership in the Komsomol).

171. *Ibid.*, March 24, 1954, p. 1, cols. 5–6; March 27, p. 1, col. 2; p. 2, col. 2; March 30, p. 1, col. 1.

172. For illustrative passages, see *ibid.*, March 20, p. 2, col. 5; p. 5, cols. 4–6; March 21, p. 4, cols. 4–5; March 23, p. 1, cols. 3–5; p. 2, cols. 4–6; p. 3, cols. 2, 4–5; p. 5, cols. 3–4, 6; March 24, p. 3, cols. 5–6. Some of the bitterest criticisms referred to agriculture, which was only natural in view of the emphasis the Congress was placing on increasing farm output (see, for example, *ibid.*, March 21, 1954, p. 6, cols. 2–4; March 23, p. 3, col. 3; March 24, p. 3, cols. 5–6; p. 4, cols. 1–2; March 25, p. 2, col. 3).

173. This statement is based on a comparison of the list in *ibid.*, March 27, 1954, p. 2, with the entire record of the Congress published in *KP*. Of the fifteen who spoke but were not elected to the CC, five were secretaries of important republic or oblast organizations of the League, three were lesser Komsomol officials, three were supervisors of Pioneer work in the schools, and two were employed in industry and two in agriculture.

174. *Ibid.*, March 20, 1954, p. 1, cols. 4, 5; March 23, p. 1, cols. 3, 5. Malenkov was being listed first at this time. He was followed by Molotov, Khrushchev, Voroshilov, Bulganin, Kaganovich, Mikoian, Saburov, and Pervukhin.

175. *Ibid.*, March 20, 1954, p. 1, col. 6; March 23, p. 1, col. 3; March 24, p. 1, col. 6; March 26, p. 1, col. 5; p. 2, col. 5; March 27, p. 2, col. 2.

176. *Ibid.*, March 27, p. 1, col. 3. The Credentials Committee reported that

the delegates had been selected by secret ballot in their respective local units, also in accordance with the Regulations (*ibid.*, March 23, 1954, p. 2, col. 1).

177. *Ibid.*, March 27, 1954, p. 2, col. 1.

178. The rubber-stamp character of the Congress was indirectly recognized by V. I. Kochemasov in his report on changes in the Regulations: the Central Committee, he said, considered it "expedient" to lengthen the prescribed maximum interval between congresses from three to four years and to lengthen also the intervals for the nominal ruling bodies at lower echelons of the Komsomol, so as to diminish the amount of time that Komsomol officials were spending in the preparation of reports, resolutions, and speeches (*KP*, March 26, 1954, p. 2, cols. 3–4). For the amendments as they were enacted, see *ibid.*, March 30, 1954, p. 2. The following are the changes that were made: The maximum permissible interval between All-Union congresses became four years instead of three; between plenums of the Central Committee, six months instead of four; between oblast and krai committees, and plenums of central committees of union republic Komsomol organizations, four months instead of three; between raion, town, and okrug conferences, one year instead of one and one-half (note that this interval, unlike the rest, was shortened, presumably for purposes of symmetry); plenums of raion, town, and okrug committees, four months instead of three.

CHAPTER IX: CONCLUSION

1. For the various indications of the rural proportion of the League, see the appropriate sections of the previous chapters, and also *S"ezd VI*, pp. 38, 136, 138, 223; *S"ezd VII*, pp. 46–47, 169–70, 395; *S"ezd VIII*, p. 252; *S"ezd IX*, pp. 50, 146. The data are unfortunately incomplete and not directly comparable.

Appendixes

Appendix A

DATES OF THE CONGRESSES OF THE KOMSOMOL, 1918–1954

I.	October 29–November 4, 1918	VII.	March 11–22, 1926
II.	October 5–8, 1919	VIII.	May 5–16, 1928
III.	October 2–10, 1920	IX.	January 16–26, 1931
IV.	September 21–28, 1921	X.	April 10–21, 1936
V.	October 11–19, 1922	XI.	March 29–April 8, 1949
VI.	July 12–18, 1924	XII.	March 19–26, 1954

Appendix B

SIZE OF THE MEMBERSHIP OF THE KOMSOMOL, 1918–1954

Date	Reported Membership	Date	Reported Membership
October, 1918	22,100	April, 1936	3,981,777
October, 1919	96,096	January, 1938	4,947,000
December, 1919	101,000	October, 1938	over 5,000,000
May, 1920	319,000	March, 1939	8,000,000
October, 1920	400,000	October, 1939	9,000,000
ca. June, 1921	250,000	January, 1940	10,000,000
September, 1921	400,000	June, 1940	10,223,000
June, 1922	200,000	1945	(?) 15,000,000
October, 1922	250,000	March, 1949	9,283,289
April, 1923	400,000	April, 1950	over 11,000,000
July, 1924	840,000	February, 1951	over 12,000,000
June, 1925	1,503,000	June 1, 1951	13,380,648
December 1, 1925	1,708,000	January, 1952	14,000,000
March, 1926	1,750,000	June, 1952	16,000,000
May, 1928	1,960,000	October, 1952	16,000,000
July 1, 1930	2,897,000	May, 1953	over 17,000,000
January, 1931	3,000,000	November, 1953	18,000,000
1934	4,500,000	March, 1954	18,825,327
January 1, 1936	3,623,000		

Note: The above figures include both members and candidate-members, in all cases where the two categories of members were reported separately. For sources, see *S"ezd VII*, pp. 169–70 (figure for December 1, 1925), and the early portion of each chapter from II through VIII.

Appendix C

Congress	Total Number of Voting Delegates	Percentage of Party Members and Candidate-Members	Percentage of Full-Time Komsomol Officials	Percentage of Women	Percentage Claiming "Worker" Parentage
I (1918)	175	50.0	(other statistics not reported)		
II (1919)	348	66.6	(other statistics not reported)		
III (1920)	(no statistics reported respecting the composition)				
IV (1921)	471	89.0		3.0	43.3
V (1922)	450?	89.7?	(other statistics not reported)		
VI (1924)	730	97.8	87.0	3.0	54.0
VII (1926)	1,177	97.1		6.7	60.0
VIII (1928)	656	94.9	69.5	9.8	71.0 (or 75.5)
IX (1931)	767	90.9	61.4	22.8	82.2
X (1936)	801	78.2	64.5	23.5	55.1
XI (1949)	1,362	70.0	40.0 plus?	43.3	(not given)
XII (1954)	1,334	66.5	44.5 plus?	41.9	(not given)

Note: The statistics given above are either taken directly from, or are calculated by the writer from, the reports given at the congresses (usually in the Report of the Credentials Commission). See *S"ezd I*, p. 89; *S"ezd II*, p. 7; *S"ezd IV*, pp. 325–31; *S"ezd V*, pp. 373–74; *S"ezd VI*, pp. 299–302; *S"ezd VII*, pp. 489–91; *S"ezd VIII*, pp. 546–47; *S"ezd IX*, pp. 405–6; *S"ezd X*, Vol. II, pp. 399–404; *KP*, April 1, 1949, p. 2; March 23, 1954, p. 2.

As to the proportion of Party members and candidate-members, the percentages for the Fourth, Fifth, and Sixth congresses are calculated not in relation to the total of voting delegates but in relation to the number of voting delegates concerning which the fact of Party membership or nonmembership was reported. At the Fourth Congress, the report covered 420 out of the 471 voting delegates; at the Fifth, 68 out of about 450; and at the Sixth, 729 out of 730. Thus the percentage for the Fifth Congress is based on too small a sample to be considered more than approximate.

As to the proportion of full-time Komsomol officials at the Eleventh and Twelfth congresses, the percentages given represent those delegates whose regular *occupation* was given as Komsomol official (544 in 1949 and 594 in 1954). But it should be noted that the leadership was trying in both cases to keep that proportion low for propagandistic purposes. Some full-time Komsomol officials may have been among the delegates who were omitted from the occupational distribution (300 in 1949 and 218 in 1954—probably mostly military and security personnel). The sort of distortion that might have been practiced was suggested by the report of 1949 (there were no comparable statistics released in 1954) that 61.1 percent (832 out of 1,362) of the delegates were serving on relatively high Komsomol bodies (Komsomol committees of oblasts and krais, and central committees of union republics) and 17.3 percent (235 out of 1,362) on intermediate Komsomol bodies (committees of volosts, raions, towns, uezds, and okrugs). Thus it seems likely that a good many delegates who actually were occupied mainly with Komsomol work were listed under other occupations, for the sake of appearances.

The percentage of women at the Ninth Congress is slightly imprecise, being based on the sex reported for 758 of the 767 voting delegates. The percentage of women at the Twelfth Congress was declared to be 42.4, but the absolute figures given (559 out of 1,334) indicate 41.9 percent.

Appendix D

VOTING DELEGATES AT THE CONGRESSES OF THE KOMSOMOL: DISTRIBUTION BY APPROXIMATE AGES

Approximate Age in Years, with Percentage of Delegates in Each Category

Congress	15	16	17	18	19	20	21	22	23	24	25	26	27	28	29	30	31	32	33	34
IV		0.6	4.1	15.6	27.4	17.1	16.7	10.3	6.4	1.5	0.4									
VI			0.1	0.8	5.2	16.3	30.8	24.5	9.5	7.6		5.2	?							
VII	?	1.8			30		48				21			?						
VIII					14.6							50.8			?					
IX						14.4	14.8	13.5	19.9		26.8			10.6		?				
X								14.5		26.2			45.4				13.9		?	
XI	?		5.5			7.5			38.3				22.0			12.8		14.3		?
XII	?					36.2			27.6							15.6		20.6		?

Note: The data on the ages of the delegates were expressed sometimes directly in ages (Seventh, Eighth, and Eleventh congresses) and sometimes in years of birth. Where years of birth were given, these have been translated into approximate ages by counting the year in which the Congress in question was held, *if* the Congress fell in the *second* part of that year. Otherwise the year of the Congress was not counted. For example, the age of twenty coincides with these years of birth: for the Fourth Congress, 1901; for the Sixth, 1904; for the Ninth, 1910; and for the Tenth, 1915.

The data were reported directly in percentages at the Seventh, Eighth, and Ninth congresses. Those for the Eighth were incomplete. The percentages for the other congresses have been calculated from the absolute numbers as they were reported. For the Fourth Congress, the data covered 468 out of 471 delegates; for the Sixth, 728 out of 730; for the Tenth and Eleventh, all the voting delegates; for the Twelfth, 1,318 out of 1,334. See *S"ezd IV*, p. 326; *S"ezd VI*, p. 299; *S"ezd VII*, p. 490; *S"ezd VIII*, p. 547; *S"ezd IX*, p. 405; *S"ezd X*, Vol. II, p. 493; *KP*, April 1, 1949, p. 2; March 23, 1954, p. 2. No figures were reported for the First, Second, Third, and Fifth congresses.

Appendix E

VOTING DELEGATES AT THE CONGRESSES OF THE KOMSOMOL: LENGTH OF SERVICE IN THE KOMSOMOL

Approximate Years of Service, with Percentage of Delegates in Each Category

Congress	0	1	2	3	4	5	6	7	8	9	10	11	12	13	14	15	16	17	18	19	20	21
IV	2.6	36.6	34.7	15.8	10.3																	
VI	0.6	2.3	5.5	8.5	33.0	31.8	11.7	6.6														
VII		1.6	6	11	15	11	26	19	4.8	1.8	0.1											
VIII										8.7												
IX		12.6		12.6		37.2			28.5	9.1												
X			14.3						29.4				44.7				11.7					
XI		2.6		14.6				22.2				37.4						23.1			?	
XII			15.2					23.7				33.3					24.3			3.5		?

Note: The data on length of service were customarily expressed in terms of the year of entrance into the Komsomol. For this table, that year has been converted into approximate years of service. The year in which the Congress was held has been considered the year of "zero" service, except in the case of the Ninth Congress (where 1930 has been taken as the "zero" year, since the Congress came in January, 1931). For example, with respect to the Eleventh Congress, 2.6 percent entered the League in 1948, 14.6 percent in 1945-47, etc. In the early congresses, membership in certain predecessors of the Komsomol organization was evidently included, for the dates of entrance go back to 1917 and even 1916.

The reports for the Seventh, Eighth, and Ninth congresses were stated directly in percentages. Those for the Seventh do not add up to 100 percent. The report on the Eighth was incomplete. The percentages for the other congresses have been calculated from the absolute figures reported. In the case of the Fourth Congress, those figures cover 467 out of 471 delegates; of the Sixth, 727 out of 730; of the Tenth, 797 out of 801; of the Eleventh, all of 1,362; of the Twelfth, 1,318 out of 1,334. See *S"ezd IV*, p. 327; *S"ezd VI*, pp. 300-1; *S"ezd VII*, p. 490; *S"ezd VIII*, p. 547; *S"ezd IX*, p. 405; *S"ezd X*, Vol. II, p. 402; *KP*, April 1, 1949. p. 2; March 23, 1954. p. 2. No figures were reported for the First, Second, Third, and Fifth congresses.

Appendix F

VOTING DELEGATES AT THE CONGRESSES OF THE KOMSOMOL: AMOUNT OF FORMAL EDUCATION

(In Percentages)

Congress and Year	Completed Higher Education	Some Higher Education	Completed Secondary School	Some Secondary School	Completed Elementary School	Some Elementary School	No Formal Education
IV (1921)	1.1		35.5		52.3		11.1
VI (1924)	0.0	0.5	14.0	18.7	60.8		6.0
VII (1926)	0.4	11		87			0.3
IX (1931)	1.0		12.3	24.3	62.4		[0.0]
X (1936)	8.4		29.6	28.5	33.5		[0.0]
XI (1949)	37.7		30.5	22.0	[9.8 unspecified]		
XII (1954)	43.3		22.4	20.0	[14.3 unspecified]		

Note: The columns indicate the highest educational level attained by each group. The percentages for the Seventh and Ninth congresses were reported directly, without absolute numbers. (The percentages for the Seventh do not total 100.) The other percentages have been calculated from the absolute numbers reported, which covered 470 out of 471 voting delegates at the Fourth Congress, 729 out of 730 at the Sixth, and 800 out of 801 at the Tenth. At the Eleventh Congress, both absolute numbers and percentages were reported. Since the percentages were calculated on the basis of 1,362 (the total number of voting delegates), it appears that data on the remaining 9.8 percent (134 persons) were available but were not mentioned because those 134 persons had not attained one of the desired levels (i.e., had not gone beyond elementary school). At the Twelfth Congress, the first figure was accompanied by a percentage (with apparently a slight error of 0.5 percent in the calculation), but for the other categories only absolute numbers were given. It seems quite likely that in this case some of the unspecified ones belonged in one of the higher categories. See *S"ezd IV*, p. 327; *S"ezd VI*, p. 300; *S"ezd VII*, p. 489; *S"ezd IX*, p. 405; *S"ezd X*, Vol. II, p. 404; *KP*, April 1, 1949, p. 2; March 23, 1954, p. 2. No figures were reported for the First, Second, Third, Fifth, and Eighth congresses.

Appendix G

DISTRIBUTION OF SELECTED NATIONALITIES AMONG THE
DELEGATES TO THE CONGRESSES OF THE KOMSOMOL AND IN THE
GENERAL POPULATION OF THE USSR

(In Percentages)

Congress	Great Russian	Ukrainian	Belo-russian	Jewish	Armenian	Georgian	Uzbek
IV (1921)		62.4		18.3	0.6	2.1	(1.1)
VI (1924)	65.6	4.5	1.6	13.8	2.5	1.8	1.8
VII (1926)	63.0	10.0	2.5	7.0	(statistics incomplete)		
IX (1931)	54.1	12.0		10.3	(statistics incomplete)		
X (1936)	49.7	14.1	2.0	13.3	2.3	2.4	2.0
XI (1949)	64.5	13.1	3.8	(omitted)	1.7	3.1	2.6
Proportion in Population, 1926	52.9	21.2	3.2	1.8	1.1	1.2	2.7
Proportion in Population, 1941	56.6	18.3	4.3	2.6	1.1	1.2	2.5

Note: In 1921, 1.1 percent of the delegates were said to be from "Turkestan," and Uzbeks were not separately listed.

The percentages for the Seventh and Ninth congresses were reported directly, without absolute numbers (S"ezd VII, p. 490; S"ezd IX, p. 405). The other percentages have been calculated from the absolute numbers reported, which covered all voting delegates at the Fourth and Sixth congresses (S"ezd IV, p. 326; S"ezd VI, p. 300), 799 out of 801 at the Tenth (S"ezd X, Vol. II, p. 401), and 1,327 out of 1,362 voting delegates at the Eleventh Congress (KP, April 1, 1949, p. 2).

The proportions of the selected nationalities in the general population of the USSR are shown for the purpose of rough comparison. The percentages for 1926 are from Lorimer, Population of the Soviet Union, p. 51 (and a calculation based on ibid., p. 59). The percentages for 1941 are calculated from the table in Lamont, "National and Racial Minorities," USSR, pp. 6–7. The two sets of percentages, for 1926 and 1941, are not directly comparable, because the census of 1926 was based on distinctions of ancestry, while the census of 1939 (which Lamont presumably used to some extent, along with that of 1926) was based on psychological distinctions (i.e., the individual was asked with which national group he felt that he and his children were most closely identified) (Lorimer, Population of the Soviet Union, p. 137).

No statistics on nationalities were released at the First, Second, Third, Fifth, Eighth, and Twelfth congresses.

Appendix H

SIZE OF THE YOUNG PIONEER ORGANIZATION, 1922–1952

Date	Enrollment	Date	Enrollment
October, 1922	4,000	January, 1931	about 3,300,000
January 1, 1924	161,000	1931 (month?)	3,447,325
May 1, 1924	200,000	1934	about 7,000,000
July, 1924	200,000 or 250,000	April, 1936	6,839,030
January 1, 1925	over 1,000,000	March, 1939	11,000,000
January 1, 1926	over 1,500,000	December, 1939	13,000,000
March, 1926	1,586,000	March, 1949	13,000,000
January 1, 1928	1,682,000	October, 1951	about 19,000,000
January 1, 1929	1,792,000	January, May,	
January 1, 1930	2,476,000	August, 1952	over 19,000,000
July 1, 1930	3,223,000	October, 1952	about 19,000,000

Note: This table does not pretend to be complete. It merely assembles the data on Pioneer enrollment that have been encountered in the course of the present study. For further details, see, in each chapter from II through VIII, the section that deals with the Pioneers.

Glossary

Glossary

Note: In doubtful cases, the dictionaries of A. I. Smirnitskii (*Russko-angliiskii slovar'* [Moscow: Ogiz, 1949], 987 pp.) and D. N. Ushakov (*Tolkovyi slovar' russkogo iazyka* [Moscow: Ogiz, 1935], 4 vols.) have been considered authoritative.

ACP(B)—All-Union Communist Party (of Bolsheviks)

aktiv—the most active element of the Komsomol (or other organization)

ALCLY—All-Union Leninist Communist League of Youth, the full designation of the Komsomol since 1926

CC—Central Committee; in the present study, the Central Committee of the Komsomol, unless otherwise indicated

CIY—Communist International of Youth, before World War II the nominal coordinator of the activities of Young Communist Leagues in all countries, and young brother to the Comintern

Comintern—Communist International

CP—Communist Party

CPSU(B)—Communist Party of the Soviet Union (of Bolsheviks)

druzhina—the Pioneer unit corresponding to the "troop" in the Boy Scouts

FZO—initials of *fabrichno-zavodskoe obuchenie*, or "factory-and-plant training," as applied to the schools connected with the Labor Reserve Program in existence since 1940

FZU—initials of *fabrichno-zavodskoe uchenichestvo*, or factory-and-plant training, as developed in the 1920s

gorkom—abbreviation of *gorodskoi komitet*, meaning "town committee" or "city committee" (of the Komsomol or Party)

GTO—initials of *Gotov k trudu i oborone*. See RLD.

guberniia—a large territorial unit or province before the Revolution and during the early years of the Soviet regime

gubkom—abbreviation of "guberniia committee" (of the Komsomol or the Party)

KIM—initials of *Kommunisticheskii internatsional molodezhi*. See CIY.

kolkhoz—collective farm

Komsomol—abbreviation formed from the first syllables of the words *Kommunisticheskii soiuz molodezhi*, or Communist League of Youth

komsorg—Komsomol organizer

krai—a large territorial unit similar to the oblast

kraikom—abbreviation of "krai committee" (of the Komsomol or the Party)

kulak—in Soviet usage, a term of opprobrium directed against peasants, allegedly the well-to-do who exploit others

LCLY—Leninist Communist League of Youth. The abbreviation is used in various combinations, such as the Ukrainian LCLY and the LCLY's of other lesser units.

MTS—machine-and-tractor station, a unit which operates agricultural machinery and equipment and exercises control over the kolkhozes in its area

Narkompros—People's Commissariat of Education

obkom—abbreviation of "oblast' committee" (of the Komsomol or the Party)

oblast' or *oblast* (Anglicizing the word by leaving off the soft sign)—a large territorial unit superseding the guberniia

okrug—a territorial unit sometimes found intermediate between the raion and the oblast

okruzhkom—abbreviation of "okrug committee" (of the Komsomol or Party)

Osoaviakhim—abbreviation of *Obshchestvo sodeistviia oborone i aviatsionnomu i khimicheskomu stroitel'stvu SSSR*, which may be translated as "Society for the Promotion of Defense and of the Aviation and Chemical Industries of the USSR"

raion—a territorial unit within the oblast, krai, or national republic. Some writers translate raion as "district" or "county," but the present writer believes it is clearer to use the Russian word.

raikom—abbreviation of "raion committee" (of the Komsomol or the Party)

RCLY—Russian Communist League of Youth, the full name of the Komsomol from 1918 to 1924

RCP—Russian Communist Party

RCP(B)—Russian Communist Party (of Bolsheviks)

RLCLY—Russian Leninist Communist League of Youth, the Komsomol's full name during the years 1924–26

RLD—"Ready for Labor and Defense," a physical training program

s"ezd—Russian word for "congress" or "convention." In the notes of this study, it applies to the nation-wide conventions of the Komsomol.

sovet or *soviet* (the latter is the Anglicized spelling)—"council" in Russian

sovkhoz—state farm

Stakhanovite—a worker especially rewarded for furthering high production

subbotnik—related to our word "sabbath" and to the Russian word for Saturday; a Soviet term for labor contributed by people during their time off, whether on Saturday or not. Such labor is not paid, and in theory is given voluntarily.

tekhnikum—a technical educational institution of intermediate level, classed as "secondary professional" education (Ushakov), although sometimes treated with higher educational institutions rather than with ordinary secondary schools

uezd—a territorial unit within the guberniia in tsarist Russia and in the USSR until the institution of raions

volkom—abbreviation of "volost' committee" (of the Komsomol or Party)

volost' or *volost* (Anglicized)—a small rural district

vtuz—abbreviation of *vysshee tekhnicheskoe uchebnoe zavedenie*, or higher technical educational institution. The Russian plural is *vtuzy;* the Anglicized, *vtuzes.*

vuz—abbreviation of *vysshee uchebnoe zavedenie,* or higher educational institution. The Russian plural is *vuzy;* the Anglicized, *vuzes.*

YCL—Young Communist League, as used in this study to designate the counterparts of the Komsomol in countries other than the Soviet Union

Bibliography

Bibliography

As is explained in the Preface, the literature on the Komsomol is vast. However, in view of the nature of the present study as defined in the Preface, this bibliography has been kept relatively brief. The first section deals with the proceedings of the congresses; the second, with all other materials used.

I. THE PROCEEDINGS OF THE CONGRESSES OF THE KOMSOMOL

The proceedings of the congresses, which are the foundation of the present work, were published in book form for the congresses from 1918 to 1936. The largest collections of the proceedings are in the New York Public Library and the Hoover Library. From them (and through the generosity of the Yale Library) the writer obtained a complete set on microfilm. The group author is usually designated by the post-1926 name of the League: Vsesoiuznyi leninskii kommunisticheskii soiuz molodezhi. In the footnotes, these volumes have been designated *S"ezd I, S"ezd II,* etc. The publication data follow:

FIRST CONGRESS

Pervyi vserossiiskii s"ezd RKSM, 29 oktiabria–4 noiabria 1918 g. (The First All-Russian Congress of the RCLY, October 29–November 4, 1918). 3d ed. Moscow-Leningrad, Molodaia gvardiia, 1926. 104 pp. (Abbreviated *S"ezd I.*) On the title page appears also the name Istmol TsK RLKSM. Komissiia po izucheniiu istorii iunosheskogo dvizheniia v Rossii (Histyouth CC RLCLY. Commission for the Study of the History of the Youth Movement in Russia). An explanatory note (on behalf of the Istmol) following the title page refers to the contents as a *stenogramma* or stenographic version of the First Congress but says that it has undergone "slight corrections of a stylistic character." Also, "The greetings which were presented at almost every session have been grouped together." The editorial work was done by Comrade Kirov. Several introductory articles on the youth movement have been added. They occupy pages 5–37 of this edition. The edition was published in 3,000 copies.

SECOND CONGRESS

Vtoroi vserossiiskii s"ezd RKSM, 5–8 oktiabria 1919 goda. Stenograficheskii otchet (The Second All-Russian Congress of the RCLY, October 5–8, 1919. Stenographic Account). 3d ed. Moscow-Leningrad, Molodaia gvardiia, 1926. 199 pp. (Abbreviated *S"ezd II.*) The full Istmol designation as given above also appears on the title page of the proceedings of the Second Congress. A publisher's note (pp. 3–4) explains that the proceedings of the Second Congress were published in 1920 but have become a "bibliographical rarity." This "stenogram" is described as "reedited, since the previous editing was hasty and manifestly unsatisfactory." The new edition is also said to have been condensed: "All those places have been shortened which do not have any interest: 'Comrade so-and-so has the floor,' and so on." The resolutions passed by the Congress have been placed at the end. Explanatory notes have been added. All the above changes are said to have been made by G. Iartsev in the second edition. The third edition, comprising 5,000 copies, is said not to incorporate any big changes but merely stylistic corrections.

THIRD CONGRESS

Tretii vserossiiskii s"ezd rossiiskogo kommunisticheskogo soiuza molodezhi, 2–10 oktiabria 1920 goda. Stenograficheskii otchet (The Third All-Russian Congress of the Russian Communist League of Youth, October 2–10, 1920. Stenographic Account). Moscow-Leningrad, Molodaia gvardiia, 1926. 328 pp. (Abbreviated *S"ezd III.*) This edition (3,000 copies) is also the work of the Istmol and Comrade G. Iartsev. The prefatory statement (pp. 3–4) from the Istmol says that the "stenogram" of the Third Congress was not immediately edited but lay in the archives of the CC until mid-1923. Some sheets of the stenographic notes were missing, while the writing on others was so obliterated that it had to be studied with a magnifying glass. Where the meaning was not clear, the text has been condensed, it is explained. Some reports and also some written statements were entirely missing. The Istmol asks all participants in the Third Congress to send in any corrections and additional material they possess, so that the future second edition may be well annotated and as complete as possible.

FOURTH CONGRESS

IV s"ezd RKSM. Stenograficheskii otchet, 21–28 sentiabria 1921 g. (The IV Congress of the RCLY. Stenographic Account, September 21–28, 1921). Moscow-Leningrad, Molodaia gvardiia, 1925. 366 pp. (Abbreviated *S"ezd IV.*) This edition (evidently the first, and consisting of 7,000 copies) was also prepared by the Istmol of the CC of the League.

FIFTH CONGRESS

Piatyi vserossiiskii s"ezd RKSM, 11–19 oktiabria 1922 goda. Stenograficheskii otchet (The Fifth All-Russian Congress of the RCLY, October 11–19, 1922. Stenographic Account). Moscow-Leningrad, Molodaia gvardiia, 1927. 383 pp. (Abbreviated *S"ezd V.*) A prefatory note from the Istmol indicates that this edition (of 2,000 copies) was the first full publication of the materials of the Fifth Congress, although smaller "bulletins" had appeared in 1922. This edition is described as containing the "stenogram" of the Congress, the resolutions of the Congress and its sections, plus the new Regulations and other related documents. The editing was done by Comrade P. Beliakov.

SIXTH CONGRESS

Shestoi s"ezd Rossiiskogo leninskogo kommunisticheskogo soiuza molodezhi. Stenograficheskii otchet, 12–18 iiulia 1924 g. (The Sixth Congress of the Russian Leninist Communist League of Youth. Stenographic Account, July 12–18, 1924). Moscow-Leningrad, Molodaia gvardiia, 1924, 377 pp. (Abbreviated *S"ezd VI.*) This edition, evidently the first, was published in 15,000 copies. It is simply a "stenographic account," without supplementary documents. Its date of publication is earlier than that of any of the editions of the first five congresses listed above. It bears no mark of the Istmol.

SEVENTH CONGRESS

VII s"ezd vsesoiuznogo leninskogo kommunisticheskogo soiuza molodezhi, 11–22 marta 1926 goda. Stenograficheskii otchet (The VII Congress of the All-Union Leninist Communist League of Youth, March 11–22, 1926. Stenographic Account). Moscow-Leningrad, Molodaia gvardiia, 1926. 320 pp. (Abbreviated *S"ezd VII.*) Published in 5,000 copies, and apparently the first edition. It does not bear the mark of the Istmol, perhaps because it is a current publication not involving any research in the Komsomol archives. Like the preceding one, this book contains a mere "stenographic account" without supplementary materials.

EIGHTH CONGRESS

VIII vsesoiuznyi s"ezd VLKSM, 5–16 maia 1928 goda. Stenograficheskii otchet (The VIII All-Union Congress of the ALCLY, May 5–16, 1928. Stenographic Account). Moscow, Molodaia gvardiia, 1928. 602 pp. (Abbreviated *S"ezd VIII.*) This is evidently the first edition. It was published in 20,000 copies. It bears no mark of the Istmol. In addition to the stenographic account of the proceedings, this volume contains a supplement including resolutions, special reports, and greetings connected with the Congress.

NINTH CONGRESS

IX vsesoiuznyi s"ezd VLKSM. Stenograficheskii otchet (The IX All-Union Congress of the ALCLY. Stenographic Account). Moscow, Molodaia gvardiia, 1931. 440 pp. (Abbreviated *S"ezd IX.*) Again evidently the first edition. Published in 55,000 copies. No mark of the Istmol. In addition to the stenographic account, this volume contains some supplementary materials.

TENTH CONGRESS

Desiatyi s"ezd vsesoiuznogo leninskogo kommunisticheskogo soiuza molodezhi, 11–21 aprelia 1936 g. Stenograficheskii otchet (The Tenth Congress of the All-Union Leninist Communist League of Youth, April 11–21, 1936. Stenographic Account). 2 vols. Moscow, Partizdat TsK VKP(b), 1936. 488 pp. and 552 pp. (Abbreviated *S"ezd X.*) Evidently the first edition; published in 50,000 copies. In addition to the lengthy stenographic account, the volumes include photographs of the main speakers and an appendix containing resolutions, the Regulations, and other materials.

ELEVENTH CONGRESS

The fullest account of the Eleventh Congress is to be found in *Komsomol'skaia pravda* from March 29 to April 20, 1949. From March 30 to April 9, *Komsomol'skaia pravda* carried each day a report of the previous day's session. In addition, at various times up to April 20, 1949, it published allegedly full texts of the main speeches, abbreviated "stenograms" of most of the minor speeches (excluding those of representatives of foreign youth and a few other lesser figures), and texts of resolutions and other useful documents connected with the Congress. Some of these were subsequently published in pamphlet form. Spot checks indicated that the pamphlets were accurate republications of the original articles. The writer also checked the daily articles on the Congress in *Pravda* and *Izvestiia*, scanned several other Soviet publications of the period of the Congress, and read the articles on the Congress in the French Communist newspaper *Humanité*. All of these contained considerably less detail than *Komsomol'skaia pravda*. *Humanité* stressed the foreign representations at the Congress and gave exceedingly scanty coverage to the rest of the proceedings. The version in *Komsomol'skaia pravda*, then (with its pamphlet republications), became the basis for this study. The newspaper contained close-up photographs of almost all speakers. Listed below are the principal sources used for the Eleventh Congress:

Ershova, T. I. O rabote komsomola v shkole: doklad na XI s"ezde VLKSM, 2 aprelia 1949 g. (On the Work of the Komsomol in the School: Report to the XI Congress of the ALCLY, April 2, 1949). Moscow, Molodaia gvardiia, 1949. 31 pp. First published in *Komsomol'skaia pravda*, April 5, 1949, pp. 2–3.

Humanité (Paris), March 29 to April 15, 1949.

Ivanov, V. N. Izmeneniia v ustave VLKSM: doklad na XI s"ezde VLKSM, 5 aprelia 1949 g. (Changes in the Rules of the ALCLY: Report to the XI Congress of the ALCLY, April 5, 1949). Moscow, Molodaia gvardiia, 1949. 20 pp. First published in *Komsomol'skaia pravda*, April 7, 1949, p. 2.

Izvestiia (Moscow), March 26 to April 16, 1949.

Komsomol'skaia pravda (Moscow), March 30 to April 26, 1949.

Mikhailov, N. A. "S"ezd molodykh stroitelei kommunizma" (The Congress of Young Builders of Communism), *Bol'shevik*, XXVI, No. 8 (April 30, 1949), 22–36.

Pravda (Moscow), March 26 to April 16, 1949.

Rezoliutsii i dokumenty XI s"ezda VLKSM (Resolutions and Documents of the XI Congress of the ALCLY). Moscow, Molodaia gvardiia, 1949. 64 pp. (Contains the greeting from the Central Committee of the Party to the Eleventh Congress; the Congress's resolutions on (1) the report of the Central Committee of the ALCLY, (2) the report of the Central Inspection Commission, (3) the work in the schools, and (4) the changes in the Regulations; and, finally, the new version of the Regulations of the Komsomol.)

TWELFTH CONGRESS

The proceedings of the Twelfth Congress were published in *Komsomol'skaia pravda* beginning March 19, 1954, and continuing with scattered items until April 23. Included were the daily accounts of the sessions, the allegedly full texts of the major speeches, the abbreviated texts of the minor speeches, and the texts of resolutions and other documents pertaining to the Congress. There were very few pictures of the speakers and almost no close-ups.

II. OTHER MATERIALS

Listed below are the other materials, both primary and secondary, that have been cited in the present study. The volumes by Fainsod and Towster deserve special attention for their excellent brief introductions to the subject of the Komsomol. Mehnert is useful for firsthand impressions.

Afonin, A. Komsomol; kurzer Abriss der Geschichte des Kommunistischen Jugend-verbandes der UdSSR. Moscow, Verlagsgenossenschaft ausländischer Arbeiter in der UdSSR, 1934. 86 pp.

Ashby, Eric. Scientist in Russia. New York, Penguin, 1947. 252 pp.

Barkhina, V. "VLKSM," Malaia sovetskaia entsiklopediia (Small Soviet Encyclopedia). 1st ed. Vol. II, cols. 190–94. Moscow, Sovetskaia entsiklopediia, 1929.

Baykov, Alexander. Development of the Soviet Economic System: An Essay on the Experience of Planning in the U.S.S.R. New York, Macmillan Co., 1947. 514 pp.

Bol'shevik (Bolshevik). Moscow. 1949–52 (when it was renamed Kommunist).

Bunyan, James. Intervention, Civil War, and Communism in Russia, April-December 1918: Documents and Materials. Baltimore, Johns Hopkins Press, 1936. 594 pp.

Bunyan, James, and Harold H. Fisher, eds. The Bolshevik Revolution, 1917–1918: Documents and Materials. Palo Alto, Stanford University Press, 1934. 735 pp.

Chamberlin, William Henry, ed. Blueprint for World Conquest. Washington, D.C., Human Events, 1946. 263 pp.

—— The Russian Revolution, 1917–1921. 2 vols. New York, Macmillan Co., 1935. 511 and 556 pp.

Current Digest of the Soviet Press. New York, 1949–54.

Daily Worker (New York), October 5, 1945.

Dallin, David J. The Real Soviet Russia. Translated by Joseph Shaplen. Rev. ed. New Haven, Yale University Press, 1947. 325 pp.

DeWitt, Nicholas. Soviet Professional Manpower: Its Education, Training, and Supply. Washington, D.C., National Science Foundation, 1955. 400 pp.

Fainsod, Merle. How Russia Is Ruled. Cambridge, Harvard University Press, 1953. 575 pp.

—— "The Komsomols—a Study of Youth under Dictatorship," American Political Science Review, XLV (March, 1951), 18–40.

—— "Postwar Role of the Communist Party," The Soviet Union Since World War II (The Annals of the American Academy of Political and Social Science, Vol. 263, May, 1949), pp. 20–32.

Fisher, Ralph T., Jr. "The Soviet Pattern for Youth as Revealed in the Proceedings of the Congresses of the Komsomol, 1918–1949." (Ph.D. dissertation, Columbia University, 1955.) Microfilm publication: Ann Arbor, Mich., University Microfilms, 1955. 536 pp.

Gorer, Geoffrey, and John Rickman. The People of Great Russia: A Psychological Study. London, Cresset Press, 1949. 236 pp.

Gruliow, Leo, ed. Current Soviet Policies: The Documentary Record of the Nineteenth Party Congress and the Reorganization after Stalin's Death. New York, Praeger, 1953. 268 pp.

History of the Communist Party of the Soviet Union (Bolsheviks): Short Course. New York, International Publishers, 1939. 364 pp.

Kirov, A. and V. Dalin, eds. Iunosheskoe dvizhenie v Rossii (The Youth Movement in Russia). Moscow, Molodaia gvardiia, 1925. 325 pp.

Kommunist (Communist). Moscow, 1952–54 (continuing the journal Bol'shevik).

Komsomol'skaia pravda (Komsomol Truth). Moscow, 1935–54.

Lamont, Corliss. "National and Racial Minorities," in USSR: A Concise Handbook. Ithaca, N.Y., Cornell University Press, 1947, pp. 3–15.

Lenin, Vladimir Il'ich. Sochineniia (Works). 2d ed. 30 vols. Moscow-Leningrad, Gosizdat, 1927–32. Explored with the valuable aid of the *Spravochnik* (*q.v.*). All footnote references are to the second edition unless otherwise stated.

—— Spravochnik k II i III izdaniiam sochinenii V. I. Lenin (Reference Book for the Second and Third Editions of the Works of V. I. Lenin). Moscow, Partizdat, 1935. 559 pp.

—— Zadachi soiuzov molodezhi (The Tasks of the Youth Leagues). [Moscow], Molodaia Gvardiia, 1947. 38 pp.

Lenin i Stalin o molodezhi (Lenin and Stalin on Youth). Moscow, Molodaia gvardiia, 1938. 358 pp.

Leninskii sbornik (Leninist Compilation). 32 vols. Moscow, Institut Lenina pri TsK VKP(b), 1924–38. Vol. V (1926).

Lorimer, Frank. The Population of the Soviet Union: History and Prospects. Geneva, League of Nations, 1946. 289 pp.

Mehnert, Klaus. Youth in Soviet Russia. Translated by Michael Davidson. New York, Harcourt, Brace and Co., 1933. 270 pp.

Meisel, James H., and Edward S. Kozera, eds. Materials for the Study of the Soviet System: State and Party Constitutions, Laws, Decrees, Decisions, and Official Statements of the Leaders, in Translation. Ann Arbor, Mich., George Wahr Publishing Co., 1950. 495 pp.

"Mikhailov, Nikolai Aleksandrovich," Bol'shaia sovetskaia entsiklopediia (Large Soviet Encyclopedia). 2d ed. Vol. XXVII, p. 609. Moscow, 1954.

Molodoi bol'shevik (Young Bolshevik). Moscow, 1947–52 (in October, 1952, changed name; see next item).

Molodoi kommunist (Young Communist). Moscow, 1952–54 (continuation of the preceding periodical from October, 1952).

Narodnoe khoziaistvo SSSR. Statisticheskii sbornik (The National Economy of the USSR. A Statistical Compilation). Moscow, Gosudarstvennoe statisticheskoe izdatel'stvo, 1956. 263 pp.

Ostriakov, S. 20 let VLKSM (Twenty Years of the ALCLY). Moscow, Molodaia gvardiia, 1938. 126 pp.

Panteleev, Iu. "VLKSM," Malaia sovetskaia entsiklopediia (Small Soviet Encyclopedia). 2d ed. Vol. II, cols. 536–57. Moscow, Sovetskaia entsiklopediia, 1934.

Pionerskaia organizatsiia imeni V. I. Lenina. Posobie dlia pedagogicheskikh uchilishch (The Pioneer Organization Named after V. I. Lenin. Manual for Teachers' Training Schools). Moscow, Uchpedgiz, 1950. 318 pp.

Ploss, Sidney I. "Political Education in the Postwar Komsomol," *American Slavic and East European Review*, XV (1956), 489–505.

Popov, Nikolai N. Outline History of the Communist Party of the Soviet Union. 2 vols. New York, International Publishers, 1934.

Pravda (Truth). Moscow, 1949–54.

"Rules of the All-Union Communist Party (Bolsheviks)," *American Quarterly on the Soviet Union*, II, No. 1 (April, 1939), 59–73.

Schwartz, Harry. Russia's Soviet Economy. New York, Prentice-Hall, 1950. 592 pp.

S"ezdy RKP o molodezhi (stenogrammy i rezoliutsii) (The Congresses of the RCP as They Pertain to Youth [Stenograms and Resolutions]). 2d, enlarged ed. Moscow-Leningrad, Molodaia gvardiia, 1924. 158 pp. Compiled and edited by the Istomol TsK RLKSM: Komissiia po izucheniiu istorii iunosheskogo dvizheniia v Rossii (Histyouth CC RLCLY: Commission for the Study of the History of the Youth Movement in Russia), and particularly by Comrade A. Kirov.

Shatskin, L. "VLKSM," Bol'shaia sovetskaia entsiklopediia (Large Soviet Encyclopedia). Vol. XI, cols. 618–48. Moscow, 1930.

Shokhin, A. Kratkii ocherk istorii komsomola (Short Sketch of the History of the Komsomol). Moscow, Molodaia gvardiia, 1926. 123 pp.

Slovar'-spravochnik po sotsial'no-ekonomicheskoi statistike (Dictionary-Reference Book on Socioeconomic Statistics). 2d ed. Moscow, 1948.

Smirnitskii, A. I. Russko-angliiskii slovar' (Russian-English Dictionary). Moscow, Ogiz, 1949. 987 pp.

Tiurin, M. "Vsesoiuznyi leninskii kommunisticheskii soiuz molodezhi" (All-Union Leninist Communist League of Youth), Bol'shaia sovetskaia entsiklopediia (Large Soviet Encyclopedia), supplementary volume, Soiuz sovetskikh sotsialisticheskikh respublik (Union of Soviet Socialist Republics), cols. 1712–40. Moscow, Ogiz, 1948.

Towster, Julian. Political Power in the USSR, 1917–1947. New York, Oxford University Press, 1948. 443 pp.

VKP(b) o komsomole i molodezhi; sbornik reshenii i postanovlenii partii o molodezhi (1903–1938) (The ACP[B] on the Komsomol and Youth; Collection of Party Decisions and Decrees on Youth, 1903–1938). Moscow, Molodaia gvardiia, 1938. 338 pp.

"VLKSM," Politicheskii slovar' (Political Dictionary), pp. 90–92. Moscow, Gosizdat. politicheskoi literatury, 1940.

VLKSM v tsifrakh i faktakh: v pomoshch' komsomol'skomu propagandistu i agitatoru (The ALCLY in Figures and Facts: Aid to the Komsomol Propagandist and Agitator). Moscow, Molodaia gvardiia, 1949. 143 pp.

Vsesoiuznaia kommunisticheskaia partiia v rezoliutsiiakh ee s"ezdov i konferentsii (1898–1926 gg.) (The All-Union Communist Party in the Resolutions of Its Congresses and Conferences, 1898–1926). 3d ed., corrected and enlarged. Moscow-Leningrad, Gosizdat, 1927. 704 pp.

Vsesoiuznyi fizkul'turnyi kompleks "Gotov k trudu i oborone SSSR" (All-Union Physical Culture Complex "Ready for Labor and Defense of the USSR"). Moscow, Gosizdat. fizkul'tura i sport, 1940. 177 pp.

"Vsesoiuznyi leninskii kommunisticheskii soiuz molodezhi" (All-Union Leninist Communist League of Youth), Bol'shaia sovetskaia entsiklopediia (Large Soviet Encyclopedia). 2d ed. Vol. IX, pp. 330–47. Moscow, 1951.

White, D. Fedotoff. The Growth of the Red Army. Princeton, Princeton University Press, 1944. 486 pp.

Wolfe, Bertram D. Three Who Made a Revolution: A Biographical History. New York, Dial Press, 1948. 661 pp.

Index

Index